Clinical Applications
of the Adult Attachment Interview

Clinical Applications of the Adult Attachment Interview

Edited by

HOWARD STEELE
MIRIAM STEELE

Foreword by JUNE SROUFE

Afterword by DEBORAH JACOBVITZ

THE GUILFORD PRESS
New York   London

In memory of our fathers,
in honor of our mothers,
and in dedication to our children—
Gabi, Joe, and Miki

© 2008 The Guilford Press
A Division of Guilford Publications, Inc.
72 Spring Street, New York, NY 10012
www.guilford.com

Printed in the United States of America

This book is printed on acid-free paper.

Last digit is print number: 9   8   7   6   5   4   3   2   1

Library of Congress Cataloging-in-Publication Data

Clinical applications of the adult attachment interview / edited by Howard Steele,
Miriam Steele.
    p. ; cm.
    Includes bibliographical references and index.
    ISBN 978-1-59385-696-0 (hardcover : alk paper)
    1. Attachment behavior—Testing. 2. Attachment disorder—Testing. I. Steele, Howard,
1959– II. Steele, Miriam.
    [DNLM: 1. Interview, Psychological—methods. 2. Mental Disorders—diagnosis.
3. Mental Disorders—therapy. 4. Object Attachment. 5. Psychotherapy—methods.
WM 141 C6408 2008]
    RC455.4.A84C65 2008
    616.85'88—dc22

                                                            2008000791

About the Editors

Howard Steele, PhD, is Associate Professor and Director of Graduate Studies in Psychology at the New School for Social Research, where he is Codirector (with Miriam Steele) of the Center for Attachment Research. He is senior and founding editor of the journal *Attachment and Human Development* and is the author of more than 60 journal articles and book chapters on the impact of attachment, loss, trauma, and emotion understanding across the lifespan and across generations.

Miriam Steele, PhD, is Associate Professor and Assistant Director of the Doctoral Program in Clinical Psychology at the New School for Social Research, where she is Codirector (with Howard Steele) of the Center for Attachment Research. Dr. Steele trained as a psychoanalyst at the Anna Freud Centre. She initiated the London Parent–Child Project, a major longitudinal study of intergenerational patterns of attachment, and has also carried out longitudinal attachment research in the context of child maltreatment and adoption, about which she publishes and lectures widely.

Contributors

Massimo Ammaniti, MD, Department of Dynamic and Clinical Psychology, University of Rome, Rome, Italy

Kay Asquith, MSc, Anna Freud Centre, London, United Kingdom

Heidi Neufeld Bailey, PhD, Department of Psychology, University of Guelph, Guelph, Ontario, Canada

Marian J. Bakermans-Kranenburg, PhD, Center for Child and Family Studies, Leiden University, Leiden, The Netherlands

Tessa Baradon, MA, Anna Freud Centre, London, United Kingdom

Johanna Bick, BA, Department of Psychology, University of Delaware, Newark, Delaware

Margo Candelaria, PhD, Department of Pediatrics, Growth and Nutrition Division, University of Maryland School of Medicine, Baltimore, Maryland

Dante Cicchetti, PhD, Mt. Hope Family Center, University of Rochester, Rochester, New York; Institute of Child Development and Department of Psychiatry, University of Minnesota, Minneapolis, Minnesota

John F. Clarkin, PhD, Personality Disorders Institute, Department of Psychiatry, New York–Presbyterian Hospital, Weill Cornell Medical College, New York, New York; Weill Cornell Graduate School of Medical Sciences, New York, New York

Marylene Cloitre, PhD, Child Study Center, Institute for Trauma and Stress, New York University School of Medicine, New York, New York

Judith A. Crowell, MD, Division of Child and Adolescent Psychiatry, Department of Psychiatry and Behavioral Sciences, Stony Brook University Medical Center, Stony Brook, New York

Nino Dazzi, PhD, Department of Dynamic and Clinical Psychology, University of Rome, Rome, Italy

Carey Anne DeOliveira, PhD, Child and Parent Resource Institute, London, Ontario, Canada

Diana Diamond, PhD, Department of Psychology, The City College and Graduate Center, City University of New York, New York, New York; Personality Disorders Institute, Department of Psychiatry, New York–Presbyterian Hospital, Weill Cornell Medical College, New York, New York; Postdoctoral Program in Psychotherapy and Psychoanalysis, New York University, New York, New York

Mary Dozier, PhD, Department of Psychology, University of Delaware, Newark, Delaware

Brent Finger, BA, Department of Comparative Human Development, University of Chicago, Chicago, Illinois

Karin Gleason, PhD, Riverside Educational Services, London, Ontario, Canada

Sonja Gojman de Millán, PhD, International Federation of Psychoanalytic Societies and Seminario de Sociopsicóanálisis A.C., Mexico City, Mexico

Ruth Goldwyn, PhD, Academic Department of Child and Adolescent Psychiatry, University of Manchester, Manchester, United Kingdom

Sydney Hans, PhD, School of Social Service Administration, University of Chicago, Chicago, Illinois

Stuart T. Hauser, MD, PhD, Judge Baker Children's Center and Department of Psychiatry, Harvard Medical School, Cambridge, Massachusetts

Christoph M. Heinicke, PhD, Department of Psychiatry and Biobehavioral Sciences, University of California, Los Angeles, Los Angeles, California

Christine Reiner Hess, PhD, Center for Autism and Related Disorders, Kennedy Krieger Institute, Baltimore, Maryland

Erik Hesse, PhD, Department of Psychology, University of California, Berkeley, Berkeley, California; Center for Child and Family Studies, Leiden University, Leiden, The Netherlands

Saul Hillman, MSc, Anna Freud Centre, London, United Kingdom

Jill Hodges, PhD, Brain and Behavioral Sciences Unit, Institute for Child Health, London, United Kingdom; Anna Freud Centre, London, United Kingdom; Department of Child and Adolescent Mental Health, Great Ormond Street Hospital, London, United Kingdom

Tord Ivarsson, MD, PhD, Department of Child and Adolescent Psychiatry, Queen Silvia Children's Hospital, Göteborg University, Göteborg, Sweden; Centre for Child and Adolescent Mental Health, Oslo, Norway

Deborah Jacobvitz, PhD, Department of Human Ecology, College of Natural Sciences, University of Texas at Austin, Austin, Texas

Amanda Jones, DSysPsych, NHS Parent–Infant Mental Health Service, North East London Mental Health Trust, London, United Kingdom

Jeanne Kaniuk, BA, Coram Family, London, United Kingdom

Otto F. Kernberg, MD, Personality Disorders Institute, Borderline Personality Disorder Resource Center, Department of Psychiatry, New York–Presbyterian Hospital, Weill Cornell Medical College, New York, New York; Center for Psychoanalytic Training and Research, Columbia University, New York, New York

Lauren A. Killeen, MS, Department of Psychology, Pennsylvania State University, University Park, Pennsylvania

Mónica Susana Levine, LCSW, Department of Psychiatry and Biobehavioral Sciences, University of California, Los Angeles, Los Angeles, California

Kenneth N. Levy, PhD, Department of Psychology, Pennsylvania State University, University Park, Pennsylvania; Personality Disorders Institute, Department of Psychiatry, New York–Presbyterian Hospital, Weill Cornell Medical College, New York, New York

Karlen Lyons-Ruth, PhD, Department of Psychiatry, Harvard Medical School, Cambridge, Massachusetts

Mary Main, PhD, Department of Psychology, University of California, Berkeley, Berkeley, California

Joel F. McClough, PhD, Child Study Center, Institute for Trauma and Stress, New York University School of Medicine, New York, New York

Sharon Melnick, PhD, Department of Psychiatry, Harvard Medical School, Cambridge, Massachusetts

Salvador Millán, MD, Seminario de Sociopsicóanálisis A.C., Mexico City, Mexico

Wendy Miller, PhD, Department of Pediatrics, Growth and Nutrition Division, University of Maryland School of Medicine, Baltimore, Maryland

Greg Moran, PhD, Department of Psychology, University of Western Ontario, London, Ontario, Canada

Sergio Muscetta, MD, Department of Dynamic and Clinical Psychology, University of Rome, Rome, Italy

Melissa O'Connell, PhD, Child Development Program, Children's National Medical Center, Washington, DC

Matthew Patrick, MD, Tavistock Clinic, London, United Kingdom

David R. Pederson, PhD, Department of Psychology, University of Western Ontario, London, Ontario, Canada

Fred A. Rogosch, PhD, Mt. Hope Family Center, University of Rochester, Rochester, New York

June Sroufe, PhD, private practice, Minneapolis, Minnesota

Howard Steele, PhD, Department of Psychology, New School for Social Research, New York, New York

Miriam Steele, PhD, Department of Psychology, New School for Social Research, New York, New York

K. Chase Stovall-McClough, PhD, Child Study Center, Institute for Trauma and Stress, New York University School of Medicine, New York, New York

Douglas M. Teti, PhD, Human Development and Family Studies, Pennsylvania State University, University Park, Pennsylvania

Sheree L. Toth, PhD, Mt. Hope Family Center, University of Rochester, Rochester, New York

Marinus H. van IJzendoorn, PhD, Center for Child and Family Studies, Leiden University, Leiden, The Netherlands

Frank E. Yeomans, MD, Personality Disorders Institute, Department of Psychiatry, New York–Presbyterian Hospital, Weill Cornell Medical College, New York, New York

Foreword

JUNE SROUFE

This is an extremely important and useful volume. As a clinically oriented reader, I was very pleased to find answers to three vital questions I always have when approaching a book concerning clinical applications of a research-based instrument. First and foremost, in my role as practitioner I hope to learn something that will enhance and expand my work. In this regard, the collection excels. In our modern world, with its great variety of therapeutic options and theoretic orientations, it is no small achievement to provide such a wide range of clinical considerations that are of interest to so many persons from so many different orientations. Whether one's interest is in infant development, family functioning, or psychodynamically oriented adult therapy; whether one works in a structured clinic or alone, these inspiring reports of creative uses of the Adult Attachment Interview (AAI) include ample background information on the implementation of the instrument, as well as illustrative case material.

Second, I am always curious about how well researched an instrument is, and what that research reveals about its clinical use. Again, I was very impressed to discover how much interesting and varied clinical research has been conducted using the AAI. Most of the centers represented in these chapters serve the dual function of collecting data and providing therapy, and include both in their discussions. For example, one of the many questions explored here is what intervention is best suited to a mother–infant pair when the mother is unresolved with respect to loss or trauma in her own history. A clinically experienced practitioner might have an intuitive response to this question. Here, there are also research findings.

And third, for readers, myself included, who are intrigued by theory, there is stimulating food for thought among these chapters in areas that include development across the lifespan, intrapsychic functioning, relationship process, and the important dynamics of change. How these diverse topics are brought together under the umbrella of the AAI is quite thought provoking.

Another gratifying aspect is that in spite of the impressive breadth of the material covered, this book also presents a strong and unifying coherence. Much of the credit for this high level of coherence goes to editors Howard and Miriam Steele. In this book—as in "Howard's journal," *Attachment and Human Development*—one finds scientific reports from diverse and international sources that enrich us beyond our usual expectations. And in addition to seeking out a broad range of perspectives, the editors also attend to the need for integration among the given set of chapters. They have adhered to that tradition in excellent form. The chapters chosen for this book cover a broad spectrum of unique work that reveals well how the AAI can be used in various contexts. At the same time, a unifying tone of care and commitment evident across the chapters makes the book inspiring. The credit for putting this together goes to the Steeles, and we are grateful.

Often for clinically oriented scientists there is a strong pull toward both practice and research, and increasingly we are impressed with the daunting task of doing both. So, in the face of that reality, the editors have given us an additional gift by pulling together chapters from laboratories and clinics that remind us how high-quality research and clinical work can be carried out together.

My final observation is about the AAI itself. Reading this book was for me a stunning reminder of how truly rich this instrument is. Deeply embedded in the work of John Bowlby and Mary Ainsworth, the AAI brings with it an impressive provenance. Nonetheless, the contributions made on its own merit are considerable. A major strength of the AAI (and the attachment field) is that it was developed within a normative developmental context, providing us at the outset an extensive body of research on the range of normal development. Then, in the next phase, its successful translation into the clinical realm has exhibited a powerful impact on research and practice within a relatively short time. It is no small contribution to make to the clinical field. But perhaps most important, the AAI and the attachment field in general remind us that we are a social species, that our humanness develops within a relational context, and, for the clinician, that psychological change proceeds best within that relational context.

This book provides discussion of (1) the use of the AAI in diagnosis, treatment, and evaluation of child adaptation and therapeutic outcome; (2) programmatic intervention techniques based on the AAI and attachment theory with a diverse range of populations, from adoptive and foster home placements to individual treatment of patients with borderline personality disorder; and (3) psychological and developmental considerations, such as mental representation and reflective functioning, the dynamics of dissociation as a response to trauma, and the intergenerational transmission of disturbance. Any one of these is an important contribution. It is remarkable to gain insights regarding each in the same volume.

Preface

This book arises out of what is arguably the single most important development in attachment research over the last 25 years, the Adult Attachment Interview (AAI). The AAI was developed in the mid-1980s by Mary Main and her colleagues at the University of California, Berkeley. The protocol (of questions) was devised by Carol George, Nancy Kaplan, and Main (1984, 1985, 1996). The accompanying system of text analysis—initially designed by Mary Main and Ruth Goldwyn in 1984—gradually reached its present formulation across the ensuing years through refinements and elaborations by Main and Hesse (e.g., Main & Goldwyn, 1984; Main, Goldwyn, & Hesse, 2003; Main, Hesse, & Goldwyn, Chapter 2, this volume). By the late 1980s, attachment theory and research became enormously appealing to clinicians working with adults and children. This was because the AAI was seen to tap into the kind of information often sought after in many clinical consultations, including what probably happened during an adult's childhood with mother, father, and other caregivers; how attachment-relevant developmental milestones (such as separations and illnesses) were negotiated; whether or not there were incidents of trauma (such as loss or abuse) in childhood or adulthood; and how the challenges met with in development had been coped with by the adult speaker. The AAI is increasingly appreciated for the reliable estimate it can provide regarding adults' "states of mind" with respect to attachment, and the extent to which the adult seems unresolved with respect to any past loss or trauma. In a certain sense, the AAI has brought into focus the original intention of John Bowlby, that is, to better understand and help emotionally disturbed children and adults.

The ideas foreshadowing the development of the AAI can be detected in Bowlby's writing from almost 60 years ago, in what is widely regarded as *the* paper initiating family therapy. Bowlby (1949) celebrated the enormous value to clinical work with children of also interviewing parents about their family history. He claimed that a direct route to understanding and supporting a child in the present could be obtained by taking into account parents' thoughts and feelings about their own childhood history. Bowlby argued that individual differences in parents' histories may

> lead [their] children growing up to be individually either more anxious and difficult and likely to increase tension and friction at their work and in their homes, or else friendly and cooperative, and thus able to adopt friendly give-and-take relations in their working and domestic lives. Such repercussions of early experience are obvious and one day have to be taken into account quantitatively when we assess the value of our therapeutic techniques. (p. 128)

This "one day" that Bowlby imagined in the late 1940s has been most fully realized through developments in research and theory linked to the emergence of the AAI, and the demonstrated associations across generations between parental responses to the AAI and infant responses to the Ainsworth Strange Situation procedure. These intergenerational patterns receive attention throughout this book because they point to avenues for intervention aimed at helping adults resolve emotional, cognitive, and social difficulties stemming from their attachment history. These cross-generational patterns also highlight avenues for preventive work with parents so that their children will be better able to assume, as Bowlby suggested in 1949, "friendly give-and-take relations in their working and domestic lives."

Organization of This Book

This book is organized so that its 18 chapters fall into five sections: (1) the AAI in clinical context; (2) intervention research with mothers, infants, and toddlers; (3) parent–infant relationships, adolescents, and adults in psychotherapy; (4) the AAI and trauma; and (5) the AAI, foster care, and adoptive placements.

Part I, The AAI in Clinical Context, begins with a chapter by the editors, Howard Steele and Miriam Steele. This chapter draws attention to 10 distinct but related clinical applications of the AAI, highlighting the remarkable overlap between concerns that occupy therapists in the consulting room and the material arising in response to AAI questions and follow-up probes. In particular, we alert readers to how the AAI coding system can inform and support decisions to be made with respect to diagnoses, therapeutic processes, and measurement of therapeutic outcomes. We comment as well on the historical circumstances in which the AAI was developed, noting that it was a time when the interpersonal nature of human development was being empirically identified and celebrated, but also a time when—following a most influential monograph paper concerning the "move to the level of representation," which comprehensively introduced the AAI and related narrative task for children (Main,

Cassidy, & Kaplan, 1985)—developmental attachment researchers turned their attention to the clinically relevant topics of how children and adults form mental representations of their attachment experiences, as reflected in speech, concerning emotional upset, physical hurt and illness, separation, loss, and trauma.

Chapter 2, by Mary Main, Erik Hesse, and Ruth Goldwyn, is a unique compilation outlining the main tenets of the AAI rating scales and classification system. It is the first time that the system has been presented in this much detail in the public domain. Verbatim illustrations of the AAI rating scales and classifications are provided, as well as an account of how the trained judge approaches the task of rating and classification, relying on both bottom-up reasoning (starting with individual experience and state-of-mind scales), as well as top-down reasoning (studying the fit of the narrative with features of each of the classification groups). This chapter is not meant in any way to substitute for the intensive 2-week training and access to the entire manual, necessary to coding the AAI, but it does educate the reader as to the rudiments of the system and therefore serves as an important segue to all the chapters that follow.

Chapter 3 provides an empirical summary of more than 60 AAI research studies with clinical samples and is based on interviews collected from over 4,000 participants. The authors, Marinus H. van IJzendoorn and Marian J. Bakermans-Kranenburg, well known for their original attachment work and meta-analytic publications, provide the most up-to-date synthesis concerning the use of the AAI in clinical samples, serving to examine the strength of associations between AAI classifications and a full range of clinical diagnostic categories. The organizing feature of this chapter is provided by the theoretical framework of minimizing or maximizing emotion-regulation tendencies that may underlie specific forms of psychopathology as first suggested by Mary Dozier (e.g., Dozier, Stovall, & Albus, 1999). Overall, van IJzendoorn and Bakermans-Kranenburg find insecure–dismissing (minimizing) AAI strategies to be linked to aggressive behavior problems, and insecure–preoccupied (maximizing) AAI strategies to be linked to depressive and emotional behavioral problems. Additionally, unresolved mental states regarding past loss or trauma is shown to be significantly elevated in clinical samples. This chapter helps enormously to set the scene for all chapters to follow, in which AAI insecurity and unresolved mental states tend to predominate.

Part II, Intervention Research with Mothers, Infants, and Toddlers, begins with a chapter by Christoph M. Heinicke and Mónica Susana Levine, based on their work with the UCLA Family Development Project in California. This long-running project has aimed to help mothers (and fathers) and their young children achieve positive changes against the background of deprivation, loss, and trauma. In this work, involving a home-visit intervention, they found prebirth AAIs to be uniquely valuable among a wide range of methods used to assess and support parent–child adaptation and functioning.

This is demonstrated via the presentation of empirical results in the early part of the chapter, followed by a compelling case study. The overwhelming finding from this chapter is the way that security as assessed by rating of an individual's AAI, even when present alongside unresolved mental states concerning past loss or trauma, consistently anticipated a parent's investment in, and responsiveness to, the therapeutic process. Follow-up positive effects for the children are striking, and the influence of the AAI status is evident more than 2 years after the AAI was administered.

This theme of enhanced effectiveness of therapy being linked to a secure (as opposed to dismissing) response to the AAI is amplified in Chapter 5, by Douglas M. Teti, Lauren A. Killeen, Margo Candelaria, Wendy Miller, Christine Reiner Hess, and Melissa O'Connell. Teti and colleagues report on their study of premature babies born to a mainly urban-dwelling, impoverished sample of African American mothers receiving a 20-week intervention from early in the first year, when the AAI was collected. The intervention included systematic instruction in how to "talk" (relate in a sensitive and responsive way) to one's premature baby, and training in infant massage. Investment in the intervention and 24-month infant–mother attachment was significantly linked to maternal AAIs. Those mothers whose AAIs were secure invested more fully in the intervention, and were more likely to have securely attached infants at 24 months. This finding of an empirically driven marker for likelihood of therapeutic engagement and action is of obvious clinical relevance. Interestingly, mothers with unresolved loss or trauma were *not* any less invested in the intervention program than "resolved" mothers. This speaks to the universality of the adult wish to be, and willingness to work at becoming, a good-enough parent.

Chapter 6 concerns the use of the AAI in the context of a randomized control trial of toddler–parent psychotherapy provided to children and their depressed mothers in Rochester, New York. Sheree L. Toth, Fred A. Rogosch, and Dante Cicchetti provide this impressive account of a pre–posttreatment design enabling them to examine changes in children's attachment status and changes in maternal AAI status as a function of treatment, in a depressed intervention group, a depressed control group, and a never-depressed control group. Significant positive change is reported in this chapter with respect to both the therapy improving children's attachment security and mothers' AAI status in terms of a scoring dimension highly relevant to the clinical context: reflective functioning, or RF (Fonagy, Target, Steele, & Steele, 1998; Steele & Steele, 2008). Curiously, while RF improved in the treatment group, and their children became more secure, RF did not appear to mediate this improvement in the children's profiles. This leads to an interesting discussion of the benefits that adults obtain from therapy, and the extent to which these transmit to the next generation.

Part III, Parent–Infant Relationships, Adolescents, and Adults in Psychotherapy, presents five chapters with an intense clinical focus, including detailed case studies revealing how the AAI informed and helped advance clinical work. In Chapter 7, Amanda Jones reports on psychoanalytically informed parent–infant psychotherapy as she practices it in a National Health Service project devoted to improving the lives of vulnerable children and their parents in North London. The case she presents concerns a father at risk of losing all contact with his partner and children because of a history of violence and a criminal record. Jones, with the help of the AAI she administered, identifies and recaptures (to the benefit of the father and his current family) long-neglected emotional resources. This chapter includes verbatim examples of how this father responded to his AAI, including many harsh and highly defensive/dismissing remarks, stemming from his history of being neglected and abused. Yet, also, the father's AAI reveals the brief but positive influence his paternal grandmother had upon him as a child, his understanding of the harm he has perpetrated, and an ultimate valuing of attachment. The theme of alternate caregiving from someone such as a grandparent provides an important feature of the therapeutic action as administered by Jones, which was strengthened through her innovative form of parent–infant psychotherapy, utilizing video-based feedback to good effect.

Chapter 8, by Tessa Baradon and Miriam Steele, takes the reader inside the process of parent–infant work as it is conducted at the Anna Freud Centre in London. The chapter provides a detailed account of the clinician's observations of the mother (with a traumatic history) and infant in therapy alongside the meaning inferred by the clinician. At the same time, Baradon and Steele provide verbatim excerpts of the mother's AAI-based speech, while also indicating the meaning reliably inferred by the AAI coder. The therapist (Baradon) administered the AAI, while the AAI coder (Steele) provided the rating and classification of the interview. Together, a reliable portrait is assembled of the disturbances in the mother's background, her troubled representational world, and the disorganizing influence this has on her baby. The account of the clinical work provided in Chapter 8 may stand as a model of how the AAI research perspective can inform and support clinical work to the benefit of vulnerable parents and their young children.

In Chapter 9, Tord Ivarsson moves the focus of attention to the school-age years and adolescence, exploring the extent to which obsessive–compulsive disorder (OCD) and depression can be understood from an attachment perspective. Ivarsson provides an account of his unique clinical research study based in Sweden, involving 100 adolescents comprising four subgroups: one group with OCD, another with depression, another with OCD and depression, and a "normal" control group. While the latter group is found to have AAIs that are 60% secure, insecure–dismissing (Ds) interviews are observed to be highly characteristic of the groups with OCD, whereas depression is specifically linked to high rates of unresolved mental states. Ivarsson also reports on a type of AAI response commonly found in highly disturbed clinical groups (discussed in many chapters), the "cannot classify" interview found in the responses of some young people with OCD or depression.

Chapter 10, by Massimo Ammaniti, Nino Dazzi, and Sergio Muscetta, includes three vivid case studies where repeat administrations of the AAI revealed measurable progress achieved in therapy. It provides a compelling picture of how the AAI may complement and extend therapeutic work. In one case, coherence is shown to increase as a result of progress in therapy, while in two other cases, shifts in AAI classifications are observed to link up with changes that are achieved and maintained in the therapeutic process. In particular, initially unresolved/disorganized and cannot classify AAIs are shown to become organized. The inherent similarities between psychodynamic formulations and ways of listening on the one hand, with the AAI questions and AAI rating and classification scheme on the other, come into clear view in this chapter.

Chapter 11, by Diana Diamond, Frank E.Yeomans, John F. Clarkin, Kenneth N. Levy, and Otto F. Kernberg, concerns the mutual influences of Kernberg's transference-focused psychotherapy (TFP) and attachment among adults with borderline personality disorder (BPD). Before presenting a moving case study, Diamond and colleagues summarize the positive results they have observed in a series of three empirical investigations into the effectiveness of TFP, including their most compelling randomized clinical trial of 100 patients with BPD who received treatment informed by TFP, dialectical behavior therapy, or a generic form of supportive therapy. The work of this team illuminates both transference and countertransference processes, highlighting the benefits that follow for therapists and their most troubled clients, from integrating clinical with empirical work based on the AAI. The chapter also highlights the added value that may be obtained from relying on derivatives of the AAI, such as an interview aimed at tapping into the patient's thoughts and feelings about the therapist, and the application of dimensional scoring criteria aimed at assessing the extent of reflective functioning (see Steele & Steele, in press, for an elaboration) evident in narrative material where the self and relations to others are the focus of discussion. The work of the team behind Chapter 11 has shown that for adults with BPD, AAI coherence and reflective functioning is likely to increase, and the proportion of individuals with secure AAIs is likely to triple, through TFP (Levy et al., 2006).

Part IV concerns how the AAI may specifically inform and support clinical work with traumatized populations. Chapter 12, by Sonia Gojman de Millán and Salvador Millán, takes us into the world inhabited by tens of millions of homeless children worldwide, and an estimated 30,000 in Mexico City, whose earliest experiences are of neglect, rejection, and overwhelming fear. We learn about a voluntary day program reaching out to these teenagers and their babies. Via presentation of case studies, we hear how the AAI revealed both their deeply troubling experiences and fearful states of mind while also uncovering elements of coherence and a yearning for secure attachments. A vital humanistic social service is shown to have enhanced effectiveness on account of integrating the attachment perspectives available from use of the AAI and Strange Situation procedure. In this chapter, an amazing avenue becomes visible via which traumatic pasts are being transmuted into organized and hopeful beginnings.

Chapter 13, by K. Chase Stovall-McClough, Marylene Cloitre, and Joel F. McClough, includes verbatim examples of each AAI pattern, with detailed portraits of "unresolved speech." These authors present and discuss their original work showing that a history of child sexual abuse, with accompanying unresolved mental states as identified via the AAI, may make one especially vulnerable to posttraumatic stress disorder (PTSD)–avoidant (as opposed to intrusive or arousal) symptoms. They also report on their randomized control study comparing prolonged exposure techniques with emotion regulation skills training for women with PTSD. Results confirm the differential effectiveness of prolonged exposure techniques, which involve exposure to traumatic memories through repeated narrative storytelling, which significantly ameliorated *both* PTSD symptoms and unresolved mourning in AAI terms. We are left with the useful suggestion that exposure techniques carried out in a supportive treatment environment may be a promising intervention for those with unresolved trauma.

In Chapter 14, Judith A. Crowell and Stuart T. Hauser take us into the details of a 25-year longitudinal study, including multiple administrations of the AAI, that tracks the fate of a group who were initially recruited during midadolescence when all were psychiatric inpatients. Stability and change in AAI status was followed up at three points, at ages 26, 34, and 39. Alongside the AAI, this team also collected a wide range of other measures, tapping ego development, symptoms, drug and alcohol use, and relationship satisfaction. Attachment insecurity predominates and is shown to be remarkably stable for this overall highly troubled group, but a resilient subgroup is also identified. Crowell and Hauser not only report on the AAI five-way classifications (dismissing, secure, preoccupied, unresolved, and cannot classify) but also provide details on the full range of dimensional AAI scales. Here the authors show much higher stability for the probable past experience scales than the state-of-mind scales, revealing fluctuations over time in how one thinks and feels with respect to the unchangeable past. At the same time, Crowell and Hauser show that some mental states tend not to change over time (e.g., those linked to the two main insecure AAI classifications), including anger (characteristic of insecure–preoccupation) and derogation (characteristic of insecure–dismissal).

Chapter 15, by Greg Moran, Heidi Neufeld Bailey, Karin Gleason, Carey Anne DeOliveira, and David R. Pederson, describes an intervention study with adolescent mothers from traumatic backgrounds and their babies, where a sizable minority of the mothers provided AAIs that were judged unresolved with respect to past loss, abuse, or trauma—some of whom (according to prediction) had babies who showed disorganized attachments. A brief behavioral intervention aimed at enhancing maternal sensitivity was shown to be effective, but not for the mothers with unresolved AAIs. This leads the authors into an informative search for correlates of unresolved mourning in the mothers that includes specific deficits in reading emotion accurately in their children, elevated trauma symptoms in PTSD terms, and (when their babies were disorganized) significantly elevated levels of identity disturbance on a scale indexing symptoms typical of BPD. The discussion addresses interventions to help this most troubled group of young mothers.

Chapter 16, by Sharon Melnick, Brent Finger, Sydney Hans, Matthew Patrick, and Karlen Lyons-Ruth, provides a thorough overview of the problems commonly encountered by trained judges when reading AAIs from troubled clinical samples, regardless of whether a history of loss or trauma is identified in the narrative. The criteria for rating unresolved mourning, and deciding if an interview is in the cannot classify group, are reviewed and then an additional set of rating considerations are suggested. These are applied to the full AAI narrative in order to establish whether the speaker's state of mind meets criteria for being called hostile–helpless (HH). The chapter provides a summary of three independent empirical studies where the HH coding criteria were applied, with the suggestion that when HH states of mind are evident in an AAI, this may indicate BPD in the speaker and the probability of a disorganized attachment in the speaker's child.

The final part of the book includes two chapters in which the AAI was applied in the context of studying and supporting children who were adopted or placed in foster care. In some ways, these final chapters provide some of the strongest evidence available that the AAI is a powerful tool for assessing competence in the parenting role. This is because most reports of overlap between parents' AAIs and their children's social–emotional outcomes come from families where biological/genetic ties could be considered to account for a considerable amount of the overlap between generations. But should similar levels of overlap be observed in children linked to their parents by adoption or foster care, as Chapters 17 and 18 reveal, we have added unique confirmation of the social transmission of attachment across generations. As well, we have—with the AAI—a tool to enhance interventions aimed at supporting adoptive and foster parents in the formidable challenges they take on.

Chapter 17, by Miriam Steele, Jill Hodges, Jeanne Kaniuk, Howard Steele, Saul Hillman, and Kay Asquith, reports on an ongoing longitudinal study that began with the goal of following (initially with the AAI) a group of adults (men and women) who had been approved to adopt school-age children with a history of maltreatment. This permitted the investigation of the contribution each parent's AAI status made to the adaptation of the adopted child. Children's outcomes are considered in terms of their responses to an attachment story-completion task in the first 3 months of placement and then again 2 years later. Results reveal that secure themes increased over time for all children. The AAI responses of the parents provided added value in terms of forecasting children's outcomes, with most favorable adaptation (a decline in insecure and disorganized emotional themes) being linked to having one or both parents with a secure–autonomous AAI profile.

Chapter 18, by Johanna Bick and Mary Dozier, is an account of their ongoing work testing the efficacy of a clinical effort underway with foster parents, the Attachment and Biobehavioral Catch-up intervention. The control or comparison group received a modified version of a previously tested program, the Developmental Education for Families intervention. Prior to participation in one of these interventions, all foster parents (more than 200 to date) are interviewed with the AAI. Preliminary results support the efficacy of the Attachment and Biobehavioral Catch-up intervention. Children whose foster parents received this attachment-based intervention showed fewer behavior problems, and lower cortisol levels across the day, compared with children whose foster parents were in the control group. The chapter details how the positive effects of an intervention can be maximized by taking into account the specific needs of both the children and the foster parents (as indicated by their AAI responses).

Finally, the Afterword, by Deborah Jacobvitz, provides an integrated summary of the book chapters, and includes original work from Jacobvitz's own program of longitudinal research across generations, directly informed by the AAI. The wide-ranging clinical applications of the interview are revisited, and important directions for further work are indicated.

As editors and contributors, it only remains for us to acknowledge the debts we owe to others who helped assemble this volume. First, we are grateful to our main contacts at The Guilford Press, Rochelle Serwator and Seymour Weingarten, who responded positively to the idea for this book and provided vigorous support, including the dedicated efforts of Laura Specht Patchkofsky, to help ensure its timely appearance. Second, we are thankful to our colleagues who contributed excellent chapters reflecting theoretical, empirical, and clinical advances. At The New School, where chapter manuscripts were initially received and edited, Allison Keisler provided valuable editorial assistance. Ultimately, we owe the greatest debt of gratitude to John Bowlby who, back in the summer of 1987, made sure there were places at the table for each of us at one of the first Adult Attachment Interview Institutes, led by Mary Main, and convened at The Tavistock Clinic, London.

The contributions of the AAI to research and clinical work are immense. They not only take us back to some of John Bowlby's initial formulations of the clinical relevance of attachment theory, as we indicated at the outset of this Preface, but also pave the way for new and sophisticated ways of thinking about and assessing the nature of attachment representations. We hope that the chapters in this volume serve to inspire many further contributions that will help consolidate the bridge linking empirical research and clinical practice.

HOWARD STEELE, PhD
MIRIAM STEELE, PhD

References

Bowlby, J. (1949). The study and reduction of group tensions in the family. *Human Relations, 2*, 123–128.

Dozier, M., Stovall, K. C., & Albus, K. E. (1999). Attachment and psychopathology in adulthood. In J. Cassidy & P. R. Shaver (Eds.), *Handbook of attachment: Theory, research, and clinical applications* (pp. 497–519). New York: Guilford Press.

Fonagy, P., Target, M., Steele, H., & Steele, M. (1998). *Reflective functioning manual, version 5.0, for application to Adult Attachment Interviews.* London: University College London.

George, C., Kaplan, N., & Main, M. (1984). *Adult Attachment Interview protocol.* Unpublished manuscript, University of California, Berkeley.

George, C., Kaplan, N., & Main, M. (1985). *Adult Attachment Interview protocol* (2nd ed.). Unpublished manuscript, University of California, Berkeley.

George, C., Kaplan, N., & Main, M. (1996). *Adult Attachment Interview protocol* (3rd ed.). Unpublished manuscript, University of California, Berkeley.

Levy, K. N., Kelly, K. M., Meehan, K. B., Reynoso, J. S., Clarkin, J. F., Lenzenweger, M. F., et al. (2006). Change in attachment and reflective function in the treatment of borderline personality disorder with transference focused psychotherapy. *Journal of Consulting and Clinical Psychology, 74*, 1027–1040.

Main, M., Cassidy, J., & Kaplan, N. (1985). Security in infancy, childhood and adulthood: A move to the level of representation. *Monographs of the Society for Research in Child Development, 50*(1–2, Serial No. 209), 66–104.

Main, M., & Goldwyn R. (1984). *Adult attachment scoring and classification system.* Unpublished manuscript, University of California, Berkeley.

Main, M., Goldwyn, R., & Hesse, E. (2003). *Adult Attachment Classification system Version 7.2.* Unpublished manuscript, University of California, Berkeley.

Steele, H., & Steele, M. (2008). On the origins of reflective functioning. In F. Busch (Ed.), *Mentalization: Theoretical considerations, research findings, and clinical implications* (pp. 133–156). New York: Analytic Press.

Contents

I. The AAI in Clinical Context

II. Intervention Research with Mothers, Infants, and Toddlers

III. Parent–Infant Relationships, Adolescents, and Adults in Psychotherapy

IV. The AAI and Trauma

V. The AAI, Foster Care, and Adoptive Placements

I

The AAI in Clinical Context

1

Ten Clinical Uses
of the Adult Attachment Interview

HOWARD STEELE and MIRIAM STEELE

The Adult Attachment Interview (AAI) is both a mainstay of attachment research and a uniquely valuable clinical tool. This chapter begins with an account of the emergence of AAI methodology, pointing to how it transformed attachment research and built new bridges between attachment theory and the domain of clinical work, which is where attachment theory began (see Bowlby, 1949, 1988). Each adult pattern of response to the AAI is briefly described, following an account of intergenerational patterns of attachment (Main, Kaplan, & Cassidy, 1985; van IJzendoorn, 1995), but we first review infant–parent patterns of attachment (Ainsworth, Blehar, Waters, & Wall, 1978), the initial empirical base of attachment theory. The chapter then concentrates on 10 suggestions we identify as valuable to clinical work, drawn from our reading and interpretation of the AAI protocol, coding system, and associated literature. We draw attention to the ways the AAI can help establish a therapeutic alliance, facilitate shared goals for therapeutic work, and serve as a source of understanding and motivation that facilitate the therapeutic process, measurement of progress and outcome.

Origins of the AAI Methodology

The AAI emerged in the developmental literature just as Bowlby (1988) was compiling his penultimate book, *A Secure Base: Clinical Applications of Attachment Theory*. A chapter in that book concerned the role of attachment

3

in personality development. In it, Bowlby showed his familiarity with the work of Mary Main and colleagues, who were documenting individuals' reported influences of childhood experiences on adult personality via administration and coding of an interview that probes *how* adolescents and adults think and feel about their childhood attachment experiences. That interview, the AAI (George, Kaplan, & Main, 1985), accompanied by a technical manual for rating and classifying adults' interview responses (Main, Goldwyn, & Hesse, 2003), has attracted widespread interest from clinical psychologists, psychiatrists, social workers, case workers, nurses, and other mental health professionals. This may be so because the AAI captures something at the core and central to emotional and social well-being, namely, the ability, or lack thereof, to show an organized, credible, and consistent valuing of attachment relationships. In study after study, when this capacity is inhibited or lacking, adverse mental health outcomes are likely to be found (see van IJzendoorn & Bakermans-Kranenburg, Chapter 3, this volume). In our view, this confirms the basic assumption of attachment theory; that is, if mental health is to be achieved and maintained, then one must have had either the benefit throughout childhood of being genuinely and consistently supported or have reached a level of understanding concerning self, others, and the importance of close relationships by participating in supportive partnerships or therapeutic contexts in the adolescent or adulthood years.

Indeed the AAI literature suggests that if an individual was not fortunate enough to have experienced sensitive parenting during childhood, then various compensatory pathways can be charted so that mental health comes to be achieved by way of the human capacity to seek out care, accept it, and in turn provide care in ways that were not previously familiar to the individual. These "ways" seem to involve interactions with a new relationship partner (e.g., a spouse) or a caregiving figure (e.g., a therapist) who helps one arrive at new understandings of old troubles, so that they are much less troubling (see Jacobvitz, Afterword, this volume). The language the respondent "chooses" to use in response to the AAI questions, and the ensuing rating and classification system assigned to the transcript, provides new understanding of these transformations (Main et al., 2003).

The first comprehensive report of the AAI was "Security in Infancy, Childhood, and Adulthood: A Move to the Level of Representation" (Main et al., 1985)—a publication whose influence is difficult to overstate. It has been cited well over 1,000[1] times in the published literature, which makes it, by any measure of the term, a citation classic. This publication not only caused a seismic shift in developmental attachment research but also served suddenly to make attachment theory and research of great interest to clinicians working with adults. In a short period of time following 1985, developmental attachment research was lifted beyond the level of individual differences in nonverbal behavior observed among infants in the Strange Situation (Ainsworth et al., 1978), into the representational world. Thus, moving attachment studies for the first time into the study of narrative discourse analysis, the AAI gave attachment theory a radical fresh claim to being a lifespan phenomenon and—of the highest importance—opened the field to clinical work with adults. Thus, the fact that subjects of interest were no longer only infants or young children but adult parents is critical to understanding the burgeoning interest in the AAI among clinicians treating children, adults, and families.

This great shift occasioned by the AAI was foreshadowed and followed by a growing interest across diverse fields in the nature and influence of narratives, autobiographical memory, and meaning making. In psychoanalysis, a radical and fresh interpersonal perspective on the emergence of the self was being introduced (Stern, 1985). In developmental and cultural studies, reality itself, or rather what we take to be real, had come to be widely appreciated as a set of shared assumptions encoded, stored, and communicated via narrative processes (Berger & Luckmann, 1966; Bruner, 1991). And, in cognitive psychology, the self was discovered, or rediscovered, in conjunction with observations of memory in terms of narrative processes linked to the self memory system and autobiographical memory (e.g., Conway & Pleydell-Pearce, 2000). This interpersonal and social constructionist approach to the self was being celebrated in the psychotherapy literature in ways that reflected emergent findings from AAI research insofar as there was increased attention to the task of "meaning making" with regard to one's personal history. One inspired contributor to this cross-fertilization between developmental research and psychotherapy suggested that the AAI is a measure of "autobiographical competence" (Holmes, 1992, 1993).

Infant Patterns of Attachment

Mary Ainsworth, John Bowlby's partner in science for more than 40 years, established the initial empirical evidence base for attachment theory to which she also made conceptual contributions, most famously by highlighting the role of the parent as a "secure base" in the young child's life. Ainsworth's work included field studies, detailed observations of mothers and babies, first in Uganda (Ainsworth, 1967) and later in thousands of hours of home observations over the first year of life in a Baltimore (Maryland, United States) community sample (Ainsworth et al., 1978). In the process, Ainsworth trained a generation of attachment researchers who have gone on to make landmark contributions in their own right, perhaps the most notable of which being the "move to the level of representation" achieved with the development of the AAI (Main et al., 1985).

To appreciate the clinical significance of the AAI, it is necessary first to note the intergenerational patterns of attachment observed with this instrument (Main et al., 1985; van IJzendoorn, 1995), the individual differences in parental sensitivity that underpin infant–parent patterns of attachment (Bakermans-Kranenburg, van IJzendoorn, & Juffer, 2003), and the infant behaviors that give rise to these patterns (Ainsworth et al., 1978; Main & Solomon, 1990). Ainsworth conceived of the lab-based observation sequence known as the Strange Situation, aiming to extend her home-based observational study of attachment in the first year of life with a set of tasks that would activate the attachment system in an unfamiliar, out-of-home, "strange" setting (Ainsworth & Marvin, 1995). This attempt to see whether observing mother and baby in a stressful situation involving two brief separations and reunions across 20 minutes, *outside the home*, would relate to maternal behavior in the home proved to be a resounding success, leading to many hundreds of developmental research studies (from the 1970s through the present day) across the globe (van IJzendoorn & Sagi, 1999). These studies have documented the probable consequences of individual differences in infant attachment patterns on adult psychosocial development and personality functioning that typically followed with lawful (comprehensible) variations (Sroufe, Egeland, Carlson, & Collins, 2005).

Ainsworth and colleagues (1978) built on Bowlby's (1969/1982, 1973) premises about the biological basis of attachment and the importance of actual experiences with caregivers, highlighting the need to "stress" or activate the attachment system to study and measure it. By introducing the 1-year-old and his or her mother into a brightly decorated, toy-laden playroom, she aimed to activate the child's exploratory (or play/work) system. By engineering two separations of mother from child minutes later, she aimed to activate the attachment (love) system. With one system called into action, she anticipated, the other would (normally) recede. And so it was that the normal or securely attached child who played joyfully in the presence of the mother showed a diminishment of play and joy upon separation and then bounced back upon reunion. For such children (approximately 55–60% of children in community samples), home observations confirmed a history of sensitive responsiveness from the mother. But for other less than joyful children, avoidant behavior on reunion and often ineffective exploratory play behaviors predominated, and appeared to be used defensively to mask inner distress upon reunion (approximately 20–25% of community samples fit into this insecure–avoidant pattern). For these children, home observations confirmed a history of interfering or rejecting maternal behavior. For still other children who showed resistant/ambivalent behavior upon reunion, exploration was ineffective, and distress prevailed across the 20-minute sequence, peaking on reunion, when the child would not settle with the parent. The home observations confirmed an ineffective style of maternal behavior despite (as is always the case) good intentions (approximately 10–15% of community samples fit into this insecure–resistant pattern).

As Ainsworth and her colleagues (1978) observed, mothers of infants who would later be judged secure in the Strange Situation were able to manage feedings in a manner that responded to infant signals (e.g., adjusting the provision of bottled and solid foods in step with the infant's capacity to ingest). Feeding was in response to the infant's initiative by the mothers of secure infants (Ainsworth & Bell, 1969). In face-to-face interactions, some

mothers were able to regulate pacing skillfully to establish smooth turn taking and coordination with the children's initiatives (Blehar, Lieberman, &
Ainsworth, 1977). Physical contact between secure infants and their mothers
was marked by a gentle and tender style that made the contact pleasurable for
both mothers and infants. By the end of infancy, infants who had experienced
open communication marked by sensitive care were more effective in communicating with their mothers.

   Against this background of Ainsworth's initial evidence, replicated many
times (De Wolff & van IJzendoorn, 1997), it is easy to see how security of
attachment in infancy represents a protective factor as children approach subsequent developmental challenges; similarly, a history of insensitive care over
the first year is a risk factor, in terms of not only insecure attachment at 1 year,
but also with respect to later development. In some, though obviously not all
cases, continuity of attachment persists into adulthood, such that we speak of
some adults who appear "continuously secure" in their AAIs, and others
whose security seems "earned," such that their early attachment to both parents appears insecure but their current adult profile in the AAI is secure.

   In a pioneering research development, roughly coincident with the inven-
tion of the AAI, Mary Main and colleagues discovered an important fourth
category of response to the Strange Situation, that of *disorganization* (Main &
Solomon, 1990). This term was applied to infants who did not fit easily into
any of the three organized patterns identified by Mary Ainsworth. These
babies showed a mix of strikingly divergent behaviors (avoidance and resistance) or an odd collapse into helpless or angry distress, and an overall disor-
ganized/disoriented response in which "fright without a solution" seemed best
to capture the child's circumstance (Main & Hesse, 1990). In clinical samples
of infants whose mothers had chronic mental health troubles, drug addiction,
or histories of abuse that remain unresolved, the disorganized/disoriented
response was observed in 50–80% of cases (for a comprehensive review, see
Lyons-Ruth & Jacobvitz, 1999). It seems most likely that infants who show
this pronounced fear in the presence of the parent, as Bowlby would have predicted, have had the routine experience of being cared for by a parent who is
frightening or *frightened* (Hesse & Main, 2000, 2006).

Intergenerational Patterns of Attachment Discovered via Development and Use of the AAI

The AAI correlates of infant patterns of attachment are well established (Main
et al., 1985; van IJzendoorn, 1995) and increasingly well known: AAI coherence and security links with infant security; AAI incoherence involving dismissal links with infant insecurity of the avoidant kind; AAI incoherence
involving preoccupation links with infant insecurity of the resistant kind; and,
finally, unresolved mental states regarding experiences of loss or abuse link

with infant disorganization. The cumulative size of parent–child pairs studied as of some 13 years ago was 18 samples and 854[2] pairs (van IJzendoorn, 1995). The reported magnitude of statistically significant effects predicting insecure versus secure infant status was Cohen's $d = 1.06$. This large effect by conventional standards (Cohen, 1992) merits much attention, because very many psychopharmacological interventions to prevent adverse health outcomes are advanced on much weaker evidence. Importantly, with respect to primary prevention work, the statistical significance of this cross-generational association is as powerful when the AAI is administered to the pregnant mother prior to the birth of the child whose infant–parent attachment status is being compared to the AAI (Benoit & Parker, 1994; Fonagy, Steele, & Steele, 1991; Steele, Steele, & Fonagy, 1996; Ward & Carlson, 1995).

Understanding these impressive correlations across generations requires a leap across domains from preverbal behavior in the infant to the organization of language and discourse in the adult when responding to systematic questioning concerning one's attachment history and generally what happened during one's childhood and how one thinks and feels about it in the present. The AAI questions include asking the individual to provide five adjectives to describe one's childhood relationship with both the mother and the father, and to elaborate upon these adjectives with specific memories; and to describe separations, illnesses, what happened when one was upset as a child, any loss or trauma, why one thinks the parents behaved as they did; and so on. (See Main, Hesse, & Goldwyn, Chapter 2, this volume, for a detailed rationale of the content and sequence of questions.) It is helpful to appreciate that the AAI questions serve as an activation of the attachment system in the adolescent or adult respondent (see Dozier & Kobak, 1992) by taking the adult back, in his or her mind, to childhood and earlier life circumstances, when the attachment system was *previously* activated. Thus, the AAI can be seen in this light as a test of the extent to which one can remain balanced and coherent when thinking about previously occurring attachment-related events or circumstances that were emotionally upsetting, while showing understanding and/or valuing of the persons and relationships concerned.

One of the aims of the AAI is to "surprise the unconscious" (George et al., 1985) by posing in a calm but persistent way a series of questions that serve invariably to take the interviewee back to highly emotional events in early childhood that he or she will not ordinarily have discussed or reflected upon, and to which, in some cases, he or she may not even have conscious access. In our view, Main and colleagues (1985) had taken what we would call a cognitive-developmental approach to the unconscious, thinking of it as the part of the mind that stores early memories and associated emotions not typically available to awareness, yet exerting an influence on mind and behavior. They drew on what was then a widely accepted model of memory, and one utilized by Bowlby, that posited the now well-known and extensively researched distinction between semantic and episodic memory (Tulving, 1972, 1983).

The Secure–Autonomous AAI Pattern of Response

The assumption of Main and colleagues (1985) was that security of attachment in adulthood would be evident in the adult speaker whose semantic (evaluative) memories of childhood with mother or father (e.g., it was "good," "caring," "difficult," "challenging," "unpredictable") would fit credibly with episodic (sensory) memories of events in childhood. In other words, from a psychodynamic perspective, security of attachment in adulthood should be reflected in a coherent integration of preconscious and conscious layers of mind.

Perhaps Freud (1923) was overstating the value of our integrative functions, but he appears to have alluded to this goal of integration and coherence when he wrote about the goal of therapeutic work in terms of "where id was, there ego shall be" (Freud, 1923). From this Freudian perspective, AAI questions can be seen as designed to test the ego's flexibility and strength. From the attachment perspective of the Berkeley group who formulated the AAI questions, and their well-validated approach to scoring AAIs, the goal of the interview is *to estimate as well as possible* (noting Hesse's [1999] emphasis on how these estimates may well be in error) *the probable attachment-related experiences* (e.g., loving vs. several kinds of unloving experiences with the mother, with the father) that appear to have characterized the adult's childhood *and*, most importantly, *to identify* the adult's current state of mind regarding attachment, viewed as a strategy for organizing thoughts, feelings, and behavior.

Adults who have an organized and secure–autonomous state of mind concerning attachment, have childhood memories (whether favorable or unfavorable) that are readily accessible and contained, and they are capable of discussing them in a coherent, cooperative manner. Such a speaker is an individual who appears autonomous with respect to (i.e., relatively able to deal effectively with) invasive feelings concerning the past or unreasonable worries about the future. Interestingly, "living in the present" in this way is also consistently linked to a clear valuing of attachment (see Main et al., Chapter 2, this volume; Main et al., 2003) Speech and related appraisal processes in the present reflect an integration of, or a conceivably *undefended* border between, more and less conscious aspects of memory and mind. There are two broad types of adults with a less organized or insecure state of mind concerning attachment: (1) one that *defends against* conscious awareness of childhood attachment difficulties (the minimizing or dismissing stance) and (2) another that gives sustained and compulsive attention to, or *does not defend well against*, childhood attachment difficulties (the maximizing or preoccupied stance).

The considerable number of AAI security subgroups[3] designated F for secure–autonomous represent the range of positions a speaker can take *between* the insecure poles of dismissal and preoccupation. For example, on the border with insecure–dismissing, some secure speakers have set aside some attachment concerns regarding a harsh background (F1a) or one that provided limited opportunity (e.g., hard work, poverty) for attention to attachment (F1b), or they humorously indicate some dismissal or restriction, all the while showing that they value attachment (F2). The mainstream, obviously "continuously secure" subtype (F3a) is distinguished from the "earned secure" subtype (F3b). Approaching the border with insecure–preoccupied attachment, some secure speakers show a mild preoccupation with attachment against a largely supportive background (F4a) or an unfortunate (loss) or traumatic background (F4b). Finally, there is the secure speaker who is nonetheless resentful and conflicted in some ways but accepting of continuing involvement with attachment (F5). All these secure subgroups share a relative lack of defensiveness, moderate to high coherence, and a clear valuing of attachment.

The Insecure–Dismissing AAI Pattern of Response

Insecure–dismissing interviews (designated Ds) suggest a speaker with firm or even rigid defenses aimed at keeping actual childhood attachment experiences of rejection or neglect out of conscious awareness or, at least, out of the AAI conversation with the interviewer, in both cases—we presume—to prevent the speaker from becoming upset and potentially disorganized. This latter group of interviewees refrain from disclosing information about their attachment history, so that it is hard to tell whether they can remember but choose not to, or they simply have no conscious access to their past. Commonly, dismissing interviews are evident from verbal insistence on difficulty with recall (e.g., "I just don't remember") or a normalizing of experience (e.g., "It was ok" or "They were loving. Don't all parents love their children?"), with little or no specific personal memories to support the suggestion of a normally loving experience. In addition, there is evident in some speakers' dismissing AAIs a marked claim of personal strength that presents the self as invulnerable to any adverse consequences of past attachment experiences.

Dismissing interviews typically take one of three forms being primarily idealizing (Ds1), usually accompanied by claims to lack of memory; derogating (Ds2), often accompanied by claims to personal strength; or restricted (Ds3), often involving a reasonably clear cognitive retelling of childhood difficulties in a way that is disconnected from the probable feelings linked to these difficulties. Note that in each form, attachment concerns are pushed aside, often accompanied by the speaker's insistence on lack of memory (e.g., "All is well" and "I don't remember," as well as "It was normal, just normal"), most typical of the idealizing (Ds1) subclassification. Other dismissing interviews (e.g., the Ds2 subclassification) include descriptions that deride or mock significant attachment relationships, such as an interview in which a sibling is described as having "looked silly" when she cried at their father's funeral. Some dismissing interviews, the emotionally restricted (Ds3) ones, are not notable for high indices of idealization or derogation, but are striking for the way limited difficulties are described, sometimes with limited anger but without indices of sadness, hurt, or vulnerability.

The Insecure–Preoccupied Pattern of AAI Response

In contrast to the dismissing pattern, in preoccupied interviews, designated E for enmeshed, the speaker at times appears to be flooded by emotion and unfavorable memories of childhood attachment experiences that seem to have led to, and may still leave the speaker with apparent feelings of being unloved, misunderstood, and hurt. Often, the interviewer feels a pronounced pull in preoccupied interviews to agree with or, in some cases, to help or assist the speaker's negative appraisal of attachment figures. Preoccupied interviews take one of three forms: passive (E1), angry (E2), or fearful (E3). In angrily preoccupied interviews, the speaker overwhelms the interviewer with incidents and details of parental offenses and cannot seem to get off of the topic and address the questions. In passively preoccupied interviews, the speaker may say little that is negative about the parents but seems to get lost in vague discourse usages (e.g., "dadadada" or "and this and that") and cannot stay on topic, perhaps moving into lengthy discussions of the past. In fearfully preoccupied interviews, frightening events are suddenly brought into the interview when they are not the topic, for example, when probed on how the mother was (as described) loving, the speaker may suddenly describe how a stepfather sprang out at her in the dark one night. Preoccupation is shown here—and indeed in the passive and angry subgroups—in that the speaker is too overwhelmed or focused on past events or past relationships to address the interview questions.

Unresolved with Respect to Past Loss or Trauma: Additional Responses to the AAI

Independent of the organized patterns of response to the AAI (dismissing, secure, preoccupied) and Strange Situation (avoidant, secure, resistant) that map on to one another so reliably, there is a remarkable link across generations in terms of attachment disorganization/disorientation (Hesse & Main, 2000; Lyons-Ruth & Jacobvitz, 1999; Main & Hesse, 1990; Main & Solomon, 1990). Parents whose speech about a past loss or trauma is markedly unresolved[4] in their AAI are likely to have infants who show pronounced albeit often subtle or inferred indices of fear with these unresolved parents in the Strange Situation. The various anomalous forms of infant behavior conveying this fear are well-specified in the reliable and well-known criteria for judging disorganization/disorientation (Main & Solomon, 1990), including simultaneous displays of contradictory behavior, anomalous posture or movements, trance-like stilling, and direct indices of fear, such as putting a hand to the mouth upon the parent's entrance. Among the possibly persistent long-term consequences of disorganized/disoriented attachments in infancy are severe disturbances in affect regulation, proneness to dissociation, and a propensity toward abuse and violence in intimate adult relationships (Carlson, 1998; Hesse & Main, 2000; van IJzendoorn, Schuengel, & Bakermans-Kranenburg, 1999; West & George, 1999).

Ten Clinical Uses of the AAI

Here we turn to the presentation of 10 distinct but related lessons for clinical work that follow from becoming familiar with the AAI questions and the scoring system we have provided, but for a fuller picture, see Hesse (1999; Main et al., Chapter 2, this volume).

1. Helping to Set the Agenda

The AAI carries many lessons for clinicians who approach their work in the belief that current symptoms, as Bowlby long ago suggested, derive from prior patterns of thought, feeling, and behavior acquired and reinforced in one's family of origin, and through later important relationships. The AAI questions (see Main et al., Chapter 2, this volume) serve as an alert to the patient that current troubles may possibly be based on childhood experiences, and ways of thinking, feeling, and behaving as a consequence of childhood experiences. This is most evident when an interviewee warms up slowly but steadily in the course of a 1-hour AAI experience, as is common in secure interviews that appear to serve as a welcome excuse to begin to examine the childhood roots of current adaptations and difficulties. These speakers show their competence in providing a coherent account of their childhood attachment history. In interviews that are more likely to be classified insecure, the AAI questions appear to be challenges with which speakers are often visibly ill at ease. Nonetheless, they will have been alerted to the relevance of these questions and topics to the interviewer or therapist. And for the clinician, the responses provide a thorough account of how the individual constructs his or her attachment story.

The set of 20 AAI questions resonates with some of the basic premises of John Bowlby's attachment theory, particularly his concern with separation and loss experiences. Just the experience of being asked the set of 20 questions communicates a message about the importance in the mind of the therapist or interviewer of what happened during childhood at times of upset, physical hurt, illness, separation, or rejection that *usually happen to everyone in childhood at one time or another.* Furthermore, the plain questions and follow-up queries around any possible experience of loss or abuse signal to the speaker that this interview cuts to the core of personal family experiences.

Asking the protocol questions can help to usher in the patient's belief that becoming involved in the therapeutic experience is about being with someone who is able to hear, believe, and understand a great range of difficult stories about family experience. For clients whose previous experience with the mental health profession has comprised being told that they qualify for one or more diagnostic labels with a presumed biological or genetic origin (that have been or are still being treated with medication), the AAI will be a surprising relief. "Here is someone," the client is likely to surmise, "willing to consider the possibility that some of the origins of my difficulties derive from my relationship history."

We have so far assumed that the interviewer will be a helping professional, in line with the suggestion from George and colleagues (1985) about ethical considerations involving the AAI with vulnerable populations. In our experience, this is both desirable and efficacious insofar as it helps to establish a shared agenda, and it often saves time that might otherwise have been spent unearthing slowly, if at all, vital secrets to understanding the adult's inner world and behavioral adaptations. In the context of parent–infant work, saving this time is all the more valuable (Steele & Baradon, 2004). With the AAI being conducted by the therapist, then, an agenda for therapeutic work can be established early and accurately, there is no "division of labor" (e.g., when a second person conducts the AAI), and the tasks of therapy may be tackled more quickly.

However, there are at least two reasons that a therapist may not desire to be the interviewer. First, when the AAI is to be used as a measure of outcome in a test–retest design, it is desirable for the therapist *not* to be influenced by the initial AAI, or knowledge of it, because he or she may be seen to "coach" the client toward a more secure response. Second, some clinicians may prefer to wait for personal details or "secrets" of the client's life to present themselves in the natural course of the therapeutic process, *not* in response to the demand characteristics of the AAI experience.

Thus, there are interesting considerations for the therapist contemplating inclusion of the AAI in clinical work, including if he or she, or a second clinically skilled person, will conduct the interview with a patient. In either case, going into the process with both eyes open and a familiarity with the AAI literature is vital. Relevant here is the requirement specified in the AAI protocol that before administering an interview, one should first of all *be* interviewed and obtain the practical experience of interviewing someone else. This affords the opportunity to experience firsthand the sense in which the AAI may "surprise the unconscious" or possibly activate the attachment system (see Dozier & Kobak, 1992). In addition, devoting some time to transcribing an interview[5] is highly instructive.

To sum up, if the AAI is to be used as a measure of outcome, the therapist should not administer the follow-up interview, and possibly should not be the one administering the initial interview. However, if the AAI is being used strictly as an adjunct to therapy, there is much to recommend that a therapist begin work as the AAI interviewer. Whether asked by the therapist or someone else in the clinical/research team, the AAI questions signal to the client that relationships are important—those in one's family of origin, those that comprise one's current life experience, and those that one imagines in the future. Thus, an AAI conducted at the beginning of a therapeutic relationship may help establish an agenda for meaningful clinical work.

2. Facilitating the Therapeutic Alliance and Responsiveness to Therapy

When the AAI is administered at the outset of therapy, it may be, for the patient, the first time anyone has taken the time to ask for and listen to a sustained account of his or her family experience, and *current thoughts and feelings* about self and relationships. The experience of being interviewed is always powerful, and it can be a positive experience that mobilizes the interest and commitment of the patient to the therapeutic process. Although in some instances (e.g., a fragile mother displaying psychotic features) due caution should be heeded, the administration of an AAI is in almost all cases unlikely to compromise the therapeutic process. In our view, the AAI is to be administered early in treatment, perhaps most usefully at the second meeting, as it will do much to help establish the therapeutic alliance and launch a productive therapeutic exchange based on a background of trust and a shared agenda.

The aim when administering the interview is to adopt a neutral listening stance, which for some interviewers may mean toning down one's wish to be entirely empathic and helpful. This apparently neutral listening position is often helpful in establishing a therapeutic alliance. Within the psychoanalytic tradition is a long history of musing about the role of the other in the therapeutic context; however, suffice it to say, that an interested but reserved role on the part of the interviewer allows interviewees to have their attachment story unfold exactly as they choose (consciously and unconsciously) to construct it, without undue influence from the interviewer. The interview is a demanding venture for every participant, leading to a palpable level of anxiety in some respondents, yet the skilled interviewer's role is to ask questions and pose follow-up probes in a respectful manner.

This is an absolute necessity, even in the face of the clinician's understandable temptations to (1) "rescue" the interviewee (e.g., when long and sometimes uncomfortable silences ensue) or (2) make "connections" for the client in the middle of the interview, linking up disjointed elements of the narrative. The lesson of the need for assuming a neutral, quiet, listening stance, introduced in training interviewers in the AAI, can have positive, concomitant benefits for those training to become therapists in most clinical modalities. The vital point is to resist the temptation, natural to many clinicians, to weave together the pieces of a patient's narrative, to pose questions (all variants of "I wonder what comes to mind when you say that"), and to propose possible modes of integration ("This links up with what you said before"). All of these interventions are to be cast aside by the interviewer, who must stick faithfully to the AAI protocol, asking for further elaboration only at the specified infrequent turns (e.g., late in the interview, asking "Why did your parents behave the way they did during your childhood?").[6]

Adhering to this professional interviewing stance reaps rewards in terms of the investment or commitment of many clients in the ensuing therapeutic process. A number of studies have documented this effect of enhanced responsiveness to therapy, primarily for more coherent interviewees whose narratives are likely to be judged secure (see Heinicke & Levine, Chapter 4, this volume; Jacobvitz, Afterword, this volume; Korfmacher, Adam, Ogawa, & Egeland, 1997; Teti et al., Chapter 5, this volume).

It is important to emphasize that we see the AAI as an adjunct to clinical work, and not a therapeutic modality in its own right. As this book attests, the AAI may be deployed in the context of cognitive-behavioral exposure therapy (e.g., Stovall-McClough, Cloitre, & McClough, Chapter 13, this volume), just as it can be applied in psychoanalytic parent–infant therapy (Jones, Chapter 7, this volume; Baradon & Steele, Chapter 8, this volume), toddler–parent therapy (Toth, Rogosch, & Cicchetti, Chapter 6, this volume), or a home visit program (Heinicke & Levine and Teti et al., Chapters 4 and 5, respectively, this volume).

3. Uncovering Traumatic Experiences and Important Losses

Attention to how traumatic experiences, including losses, are discussed in an AAI, or in a therapy context, can be highly revealing as to the progress the client can achieve. Often, when loss or trauma experiences remain hidden, a patient's progress may be compromised. For example, there are instances when the AAI questions lead the speaker to reveal thoughts and feelings about a particular loss experience that sometimes surprise both the interviewer and the interviewee. In one interview conducted early in the context of parent–infant work, a client who was asked how she felt about her father's death was surprised by her own response. She confessed that no one had ever really asked her how she felt. In the moment of describing the traumatic loss, she realized that having been 13 years old at the time her father was murdered meant that she deeply had felt that everyone else's reaction within her family mattered much more than her own. Having to "bury" her feelings about this important loss had a tremendous hidden impact, much more than she or the rest of her family would ever have believed. The subject's response to the question ultimately played a crucial role in addressing the trauma and the way she came to acknowledge that her feelings about her father's death had contributed to her ongoing troubled relationship with her young son. Had the AAI not taken place, many therapeutic hours might have passed without this critical feature ever arising spontaneously. Looking back at people who have benefited most from therapy, and those who have failed to improve, suggests that lack of resolution of loss experiences likely impedes or prevents progress in therapy, whereas others without this confounding emotional burden may much more readily show marked improvement (e.g., Routh, Hill, Steele, Elliott, & Dewey, 1995).

Of paramount interest for the coder of the narrative responses to the AAI questions, especially with clinical participants, is to judge whether the subject discusses the loss or trauma in a way that leads a trained judge to classify the interview as unresolved. The complex criteria for making this decision are only possible to rate (on a 9-point scale, in which a score of 5 or higher leads to a U, or unresolved, classification) after very careful study of the written transcript. However, knowledge of the unique features of interviews that are ultimately classified as U are of clinical interest, especially because the unresolved classification has been shown to have a significant association (if not a causal link) to a range of types of psychopathology (see van IJzendoorn & Bakermans-Kranenburg, Chapter 3, this volume). And in the expansive epidemiological literature, early parental loss and prolonged separation experiences have been linked repeatedly to depression in the work initiated by Brown and Harris (1978) and, more recently, early parental loss has been implicated in the background of people with schizophrenia (Agid et al., 1999). Thus, even without an intimate familiarity with the criteria that identify lack of resolution of mourning, the AAI responses provide for the therapist valuable basic background information about the *occurrence* of loss and separation experiences that may figure prominently in a client's mind, and possibly trigger heritable dispositions toward mental illness.

The criteria for identifying and scoring unresolved mourning in an AAI (Hesse, 1999; Main et al., 2003; Main et al., Chapter 2, this volume), include subtle and discrete markers of how language conveys reliable clues to the ways that loss and trauma experiences may lead to clients' persistent irrational beliefs, deep fears, and pronounced disturbances of behavior. Becoming familiar with these criteria may prompt astute clinicians to listen to their clients' descriptions of loss and/or trauma in a different way. For example, the coder is required to monitor the extent to which the speaker shows clear signs of absorption—a phenomenon linked to normative forms of dissociation that is characteristic of unresolved mourning and linked to independent measures of this construct (see Hesse & van IJzendoorn, 1999). Another important indicator of unresolved trauma is seen when the subject shows lapses in speech (confusing statements about when a loss occurred that the client does not monitor or correct) or reasoning (referring to a dead person as having animate, live qualities). (Further description and examples are provided by Main et al., Chapter 2, this volume.)

With regard to rating lack of resolution of experiences of physical or sexual abuse, the trained coder looks for speech evidence indicating a client's unreasonable sense of having been culpable, such that the victim (self) is blamed for the actions of the victimizer; or that the abusive actions are denied or normalized in an interview that also includes clear acknowledgment of the abuse. Accordingly, the coder looks for signs that the speaker several times alternately affirms and denies being abused, or that he or she clearly does not consider the experience abusive (e.g., the unresolved speaker questions whether beatings that left welts were actually abuse, or having called an incident abusive then immediately denies that it was abusive, then a few minutes later calls it abusive again).

When unresolved mental states with respect to mourning or other trauma are evident in a AAI, there is good reason for the therapist to keep such problems in the zone of concern and find ways to help patients reorganize their thoughts and feelings around this experience, so that its pernicious grip is lessened. The therapist will be helped by the patient's probable awareness regarding any significant loss or trauma discussed at length (not just mentioned occasionally, as in a slip) in the AAI. The nature of attachment is such that, once activated by AAI questions, memories and affects to do with loss and traumatic abuse experiences command attention and call upon emotional resources; here the therapeutic situation can easily be seen to provide an opportunity to advance the process of reorganization and resolution. In the most extreme cases of chronic abuse by attachment figures throughout a subject's entire childhood, a lack of resolution around abuse is all but inevitable in the context of a dissociative identity order (see Steele, 2003). Treatment in these cases can be supported by repeated administrations of the AAI at timely intervals to appraise the extent to which a subject moves toward integration. Such AAIs typically do not fit into any single classification but instead qualify for multiple classifications and also the "cannot classify" group (Hesse, 1996, 1999)—a topic that is discussed by Main and colleagues in Chapter 2, this volume.

Here, under the heading of "loss considerations," it is worthwhile to compare the fairly restrictive definition of loss in the AAI system to that applied widely in the clinical literature. In the AAI context, we are concerned exclusively with loss of a loved one, typically an attachment figure, close family member, or friend in contrast to the way attention to loss experiences pervades clinical work, including attention to loss of job, loss of house, loss of opportunity, loss of the idealized parents one imagined oneself to have as a young child, loss of meaning, and so on. There are theoretical reasons, and sound research advantages, to focusing on the loss of attachment figures or dependents (children). According to Bowlby (1973, 1979), these losses that represent the greatest threats to our survival and reproductive success are the hardest to come to terms with, and research has documented this to be so; even DSM-IV Axis IV, concerning the extent of stress in people's lives, notes that there is nothing more stressful for a child than the loss of parent, and for a parent, nothing is more stressful than the loss of a child. Correspondingly, when unresolved loss is noted in an AAI, it typically concerns a parent or other attachment figure. And, for clinicians, AAI criteria for judging whether a speaker's loss or trauma is unresolved may be usefully extended to how a patient speaks about other loss events in his or her life. In other words, listening to what the patient says about a wide range of threats and losses, using AAI criteria to determine unresolved mourning, may reveal much about what most troubles the patient.

4. Identifying the Range and Extent of a Patient's Reliance on Defensive Processes

Though the notion of defense mechanisms belongs to a psychoanalytic ego psychology perspective (after A. Freud, 1936) linked to Freud's theory of instinctual drives, and Bowlby unquestionably postulated an alternative and contrasting theory of human motivation, he did not throw out the baby with the bathwater. The "baby" for Bowlby was the notion of *defensive exclusion*, understood in terms of the fervent work we do to keep from awareness any perceptions, feelings, and thoughts that would otherwise cause unbearable anxiety and psychological suffering.[7] For Bowlby, the vital cause of defensive exclusion in the child's mind includes all things a child "has been told, . . . has overheard, . . . and what he has observed but is not supposed to know" (Bowlby, 1979, p. 23) such as when a parent (whether maliciously or unwittingly) seeks to limit what a child remembers about a painful experience so that his or her construction will be (falsely) positive. At an unconscious level (Bowlby, 1988), outside of awareness, the "true" negative experiences and associated thoughts and feelings are nonetheless stored. Evidence of this process can be detected in AAI narratives, when a speaker claims that a relationship to the mother or father was "normal" or "loving," yet, when asked to think of memories that support this image, recalls events that strongly contradict the positive image. The trained AAI coder makes notes on the "state-of-mind" scale indexing "idealization of mother or father" (Main et al., 2003; Main et al., Chapter 2, this volume). This phenomenon is linked to "insistence on difficulties with recall," and both scales *lead one to think* of the overall insecure (and defensive) AAI pattern termed *dismissing of attachment*.

The rating of idealization is another example of the way the AAI rating and classification system can alert the clinician to aspects of individuals' descriptions of their attachment history that can otherwise, quite simply, be deceiving. In most cases (except those in which the speaker may be deliberately hiding his or her past and/or feelings from the interviewer), the patient him- or herself is deceived, driven by the defensive need to exclude awareness of painful events and feelings, as are others (occasionally clinicians) as well, into accepting the positive "cover" story as true enough. Here we draw on the data from our attachment representations and adoption outcome study, in which social workers, working without knowledge of applicants' AAIs, excluded from their list of potential adoptive parents those adults in the insecure–preoccupied group. We assume this to have been the case as our sample of adoptive parents included none with AAIs judged *preoccupied*. This compared to nearly 20% of adopters who were independently classified as insecure–dismissing (see Steele et al., Chapter 17, this volume). This, we argue, is likely because the obvious demonstration of insecurity in terms of high levels of anger or passive speech spilled over into the "normal," non-AAI screening process involving detailed meetings and observations. It would seem that adults who present their history through rose-colored lenses or idealizing terms, and put forward an upbeat and/or glowing description, albeit devoid of specific intimate relationship incidents, are harder to discern as belonging to the insecure group.

Another common state of mind in dismissing interviews concerns the devaluation of others via derogation (e.g., "Who needs him/father or her/mother—they don't matter!"). Interestingly, this pattern of AAI response is linked in clinical studies to problems with aggression and externalizing disorders (see van IJzendoorn & Bakermans-Kranenburg, Chapter 3, this volume).

We suggest that this is because the border in the mind—between an idealized and ultimately false view of self as positive, and the rival (unconscious but more accurate rendering of experience)—is zealously defended. Threats to it, even minor criticisms of the dismissing stance assumed by the self, are likely to be fought off vigorously. In Anna Freud's ego psychological terms, this dismissing AAI pattern would most likely be described in terms of *isolation of affect* and *identification with the aggressor*.

For the clinician who detects this defensive AAI profile at the beginning of therapy, it may be very useful to know about the potentially explosive rage that may be shown by patients in response to any attempts to breach the internal wall and reveal patients' hidden vulnerabilities. In social-cognitive terms, a dismissing/derogating AAI is likely to be a forewarning of overreliance on hostile attributional biases in social judgments. Whatever the therapeutic plan of action, great firmness and care are needed to promote a more balanced understanding of self and others. This message is most successfully delivered in the context of demonstrating an understanding that patients have good reasons (rooted in childhood experiences) to have held to their firm (idealizing or derogating) but ultimately restrictive and unhelpful beliefs.

In addition to these "cool" distancing strategies aimed at exclusion of implicit "hot" emotions are the opposing goals evident in some AAIs, in which strategies that seem to involve, as opposed to avoid, the interviewer are evident, as in AAIs judged insecure–preoccupied. Transcripts judged to be insecure–preoccupied typically take an *angry* or *passive* form, and there is in both groups a strong pull on the interviewer to agree with the angry speaker or help finish the sentences for the passive speaker. The passive form of preoccupation readily invites *comparison with* (but is by no means identical to) what clinicians may mean by a passive–aggressive defensive pattern. The angry form of preoccupation may be seen as pointing toward defensive operations of displacement, projection, and projective identification. We make these suggestions in an attempt to make clear how readily AAI material can be rendered (albeit by no means in a one-to-one fashion) into a psychodynamic framework that relies on the identification of defense mechanisms.

In some interviews rated as preoccupied, the actual childhood experiences of these speakers seem to coders to include pronounced levels of *role reversal*, in which the child was called upon by the parent to provide care (typically because the parent was physically unwell or psychologically distressed *and* lacked the resources to cope as a parent). According to Bowlby, such a child was forced to defensively exclude the natural belief "I am a child and I need help, care, and love," so that a burdensome contrary belief could be consciously endorsed (i.e., "I am a big boy/girl who must help, care for, and love my parent who needs me"). For adults with this kind of history, especially if it has been established early in childhood and persisted through the adult years, there is likely to be either an absence of a strong sense of self and a marked passivity in speech (reflecting an ongoing dependence on parents) or—as we just discussed—a sense of self linked to a high degree of anger toward the offending parent. Here we are, of course, discussing the two main forms of insecure–preoccupied interviews presented earlier: passively preoccupied (E1) and angrily preoccupied (E2).

A third subtype of preoccupied interview, most notable among adult survivors of serious abuse during childhood, as mentioned earlier, is termed *fearfully preoccupied* (E3). In these interviews, the operative theme appears to be failure of defensive exclusion insofar as memories of past trauma frequently intrude into the narrative. To be coded as fearfully preoccupied, these intrusions must, of course, be inappropriate, such as when the subject is not being queried about abusive or otherwise frightening events, but about some more benign topic not obviously linked to trauma. These intrusions are frequent in these interviews. Such interviews often also qualify for high ratings on the scale indexing unresolved mourning to do with past trauma. Freezing, absorption, and dissociation—among the most primitive of defensive processes—appear to be at work in the minds of individuals who present with this type of AAI, and are linked to similar phenomena in their infants (Hesse & Main, 2000, 2006).

A therapist who provides an atmosphere of respect, belief in the seriousness of trauma suffered, safety, and containment is called for in such cases. A focus on the management of current, here-and-now demands (transportation, housing, child care issues, job/work demands) is likely to be necessary before ending a session in which a subject's AAI has taken this direction. Follow-up to establish that there have been no deeply unsettling thoughts, feelings, or behavior—always a relevant consideration—is particularly appropriate with speakers whose interviews qualify as fearfully preoccupied and, very likely, additionally "unresolved."

5. Identifying the Gravitational Pull from Early Relationship Patterns on an Adult's Mind and Behavior

The *move to the level of representation* in attachment research ushered in by Main and colleagues (1985) has become so central in part because it has concentrated the focus of attention back on one of the main tenets of Bowlby's theory, namely, the construct of the internal working model, which includes the apparatus of perception, memory, and affect guiding how we interpret the behaviors of others, the shaping of our sense of self, and as we presented earlier, the decisions we make defensively to exclude (from awareness) appraisals of the self or others. The *internal working model of attachment*, of course, was Bowlby's rendering of psychoanalytic ideas about the critical importance of mental representations of self and others that form the landscape of the internal world—considerations that have remained central to psychoanalytic theory and technique for many decades (e.g., Sandler & Sandler, 1998).

In this sense, the AAI provides a window upon the inner world of the adult, as well as what clinicians often term his or her *internal objects* (representations of self in relation to the mother, father, and others), enhancing the diagnostic profile that can be built up. Specifically, a closer knowledge of the internal representations of self, other, and the relationships between them (i.e., the "objects" in the mind of the patient) as is afforded by the AAI is vital, because "a source of severe resistance . . . (in therapy) . . . one that often leads to a negative therapeutic reaction, is our need to cling to the internal objects we have constructed" (Sandler & Sandler, 1998, p. 140). For the therapist, then, it is tremendously informative to know what early and perhaps ongoing attachment relationship patterns are exerting such a strong pull on the patient's loyalty. From the perspective of a patient's AAI, unreasonable, odd, and sometimes highly damaging behaviors in the present (e.g., compulsive caregiving or aggressive outbursts) can often be understood as the repetition of a past attachment pattern that may be deeply familiar and all too easily activated. Listening, then, to a speaker's response to the AAI (most commonly via reading the transcription) provides powerful clues as to the gravitational pulls on his or her attention, emotion, and behavior.

6. Use of the AAI as an Aid (among Other Information) in Placement, Parole, or Custody Decisions

So often in our applied or clinical work we are called upon to make a potentially life-changing recommendation. Should a parent be permitted to keep a child around whom there are documented child welfare concerns? As persons assigned to watch over a child's welfare, should we believe that trust in a given parent has been earned?

First, it should be clear that we do not advocate basing a parole or a placement decision regarding a child on an assessment of a person's response to the AAI alone. However, in the context of other kinds of interviews with parents (or prisoners), direct observations, and clinician and other assessment measures, the AAI offers an additional, vital contribution on its own (see Jones, Chapter 7, this volume). As we elucidate directly below, for example, one indication that an abused person *may not* go on to abuse his or her own child (here the AAI is, again, only one assessment among others) is when the speaker seems both to accept having been abused, and attempts to understand (and, in a few cases, even forgive) the abuser. But it is unlikely that understanding and accepting that one was abused, and that the abuser was another fallible, understandable person, can have taken place in a vacuum. As an illustration, a particular AAI question is relevant here (i.e., "Were there any other adults around in your childhood who played a caregiving role, like parents, but they were not parents?"). This question, late in the AAI sequence, sometimes brings to light some compensatory attachment figure (e.g., a grandmother). Often this is someone the speaker has not yet recalled in the AAI. And it is someone, perhaps the only one, who played a vital positive role by demonstrating that there was someone on whom the child could rely on for a humorous, considerate, and attentive response. This 'unsung' hero in the life history of the adult often needs to be unearthed, and the positive influence of this adult may come as a pleasant surprise to the speaker. We say more about this in the seventh clinical use of the AAI, under the heading 'Identifying the

Angel in the Nursery." Here we address the issue of what it may mean to resolve abuse experiences, a supreme challenge.

It is obviously a positive sign in the AAI when a speaker demonstrates that he or she has not left unresolved a past trauma. Indeed, in the nonclinical population whose childhood experiences have involved trauma, it is not uncommonly the case that the speaker conveys a sense of moving beyond the fear he or she felt so often as a child. Additionally, such speakers are capable of going some way toward understanding, though not necessarily forgiving, *caregiving* figure(s) who perpetrated abuse against them as children. In these circumstances, the interview often reveals a robust sense of self, interpersonal awareness, and valuing of attachment, so that the therapist entertains the hope that this adult, who was abused, is not likely to become an abuser. Such resilience typically emerges because the individual discovered one or more secure bases or refuges beyond the abusive relationship, such as an immediate or extended family member, but also perhaps a friend, a teacher, a spouse, or a therapist. Against this background, the AAI may be seen to provide important additional information in making life-changing recommendations (to parole boards or family courts), not least of which may be recommending therapy that helps a patient grasp vital attachment difficulties that arise in the interview.

7. Identifying the Angel in the Nursery

The way loss or trauma in the mind inevitably impinge upon a parent's relationship with his or her baby was captured by Fraiberg, Adelson, and Shapiro (1975), who wrote about how, in every nursery, there are "ghosts" from the past lives of the parents. And the AAI can be seen as a reliable and valid way to "measure the ghost in the nursery" (Fonagy, Steele, Moran, Steele, & Higgitt, 1993). Yet, as we suggested earlier, there is also much evidence that the AAI can be used to identify "angels in the nursery" (Lieberman, Padrón, Van Horn, & Harris, 2005). Evidence of such angels may appear at any point in the interview, though the specific question relevant to this comes late in the set of AAI questions, at a time when the speaker is about as relaxed as he or she is likely to be in thinking about childhood, and often this calls to mind the most positive adult figure in a speaker's childhood. It is frequently a grandmother (see Hrdy [1999] regarding how the grandmother's role in assisting in the care of her offspring's offspring may help in accounting, in evolutionary terms, for her own extended life). And whereas mention of the benevolent influence of this person may be brief in an AAI, the story often represents a shining light in an otherwise dense and dark net of memories. One of the particular clinical applications we envision is relying on the AAI as a source of information and support in parent–infant therapy (see Baradon & Steele, Chapter 8, this volume; Jones, Chapter 7, this volume; Steele & Baradon, 2004).

We know from much developmental research that having just one safe haven and secure base in one's childhood, perhaps not even for an extended period, is enough to make a momentous difference. For the therapist, knowing about this "angel" may provide a powerful ally in clinical work in which one might otherwise despair (with the patient).

8. The AAI Permits Reliable Observation of Reflective Functioning

The concept of reflective functioning arose out of an infrequently observed phenomenon in some AAIs, that, is the state-of-mind scale known as meta-cognition, which is defined as monitoring and correcting one's own speech and thoughts (Main et al., 2003; Main et al., Chapter 2, this volume). In the 200 AAIs that began our longitudinal study of attachment (Steele & Steele, 2005), we found it necessary to enlarge our rating of metacognition to include monitoring not only one's own speech but also the observation and monitoring of others' speech, thought, and emotions. Over time, this came to be called *reflective functioning* (RF), broadly defined as (1) awareness of the nature of mental states in the self *and* others, (2) the mutual influences at work between mental states and behavior, (3) the necessity of a developmental perspective, and (4) the need to be sensitive to the current conversational context (Fonagy, Target, Steele, & Steele, 1998[8]; Steele & Steele, 2008). This elaboration on metacognition led us to examine whether individual differences in RF were linked to individual differences in infant–parent attachment (Fonagy, Steele, Steele, Moran, & Higgitt, 1991). We found that this was particularly true for parents who had experienced significant adversity during childhood *and* *showed* high RF in their AAIs. RF was a marker of resilience in these parents (Fonagy, Steele, Steele, Higgitt, & Target, 1994). RF expresses itself most clearly in response to AAI questions that demand reflection (e.g., "Why do you think your parents behaved the way they did during your childhood?"). The speaker who is interested in this question is likely to find psychotherapy attractive but may need help to reign in his or her seemingly analytic stance, and structure thoughts and feelings, lest he or she become stuck in a low mode of RF termed *hyperactive*. The patient who finds nothing of interest or value in this question and is limited to absenting him- or herself from responsibility for knowing (e.g., "My parents behavior? How should I know? Ask them!") presents a different set of challenges to the therapist, who must aim to cultivate the inhibited reflective process, lest the patient be stuck in an RF mode termed *disavowal* or—lower yet—*hostile*. Mentalization-based treatment takes this as the core aim of clinical work (Fonagy, Target, Gergely, & Jurist, 2002). Here, it is important to note that the validity of the RF concept is based on rating it in AAIs, and although therapy may lead to increases in RF, this may not mediate improvements in child–parent outcome (see Toth et al., Chapter 6, this volume).

9. Selection and Training of clinicians

Another useful application of the AAI for clinicians involves the role of the therapist in the clinical domain. Here we propose that the AAI may have a potentially important role, namely, in helping clinicians in a training or supervisory position to work with candidate clinicians, as well as clinicians in training.

In case this seems too radical a proposal, it should be noted that the psychoanalytic tradition especially has taken this idea very seriously: Most training involves undergoing personal analysis. This is done in part not only to offer a unique form of assessment and aid to the budding clinician but also to assist the candidate in getting "his or her own house in order" before offering help to others. Although we do not advocate use of the AAI as a sole method for selection of candidates, it may be helpful in identifying the challenges that a given applicant needs to address and resolve.

A most pertinent study by Zegers, Schuengel, van IJzendoorn, and Janssens (2006) compared AAIs of clinicians working with emotionally and behaviorally disturbed adolescents in an inpatient setting. Zegers and colleagues found that secure attachment, as identified in AAIs given to the clinicians, was predictive of an increase over time in the adolescents' perception of their mentors as psychologically available. This intriguing area of research is in its early stages, but given the pressure to deliver evidence-based treatments and to measure fidelity to models, it would seem a natural next step to use the AAI to assist in identifying the presence of the relevant qualities of clinicians delivering treatment.

The use of the AAI in an earlier study that compared the AAIs of clinicians and patients alongside therapeutic outcome was also highly revealing (Tyrrell, Dozier, Teague, & Fallot, 1999). This study examined dismissing/preoccupied strategies on a continuum, not unlike the AAI security subgroup scores described earlier, with some classifications on the border with dismissal (F1–F2), and others on the border with preoccupation (F4–F5). They found that a mismatch between therapist and patient predicted better outcomes than did a match (i.e., those secure therapists whose scores bordered on dismissing worked better with patients who scored high on preoccupation and vice versa). The cases of mismatches seemed best suited to promoting a positive therapeutic outcome, because the therapist was best able to challenge the patient's habitual mode of relating. This work, and our rendering of it, echoes suggestions by Slade (1999) concerning adult psychotherapy and the AAI. She argues that precoccupied patients need someone to provide structure and boundaries, whereas dismissing patients need to be encouraged to cross boundaries to which they adhere too rigidly, and to adopt a more liberal, accepting attitude toward themselves and others. Patients can, and do of course, move from preoccupied to dismissing stances or the other way around (see Ammaniti, Dazzi, & Muscetta, Chapter 10, this volume).

10. Assessing Relevant Therapeutic Outcome

There has been a recent increase in both case studies and systematic research, including randomized, controlled treatment trials. Representative examples of this important work are briefly considered below. The findings are promising and point to the immense relevance of the AAI as a tool for tracking treatment progress and outcomes.

The randomized, controlled treatment trial of note is that reported by Levy and colleagues (2006) involving 90 outpatients with borderline personality disorder, randomly assigned either to transference-focused psychotherapy (TFP), a modified psychodynamic supportive psychotherapy, or dialectical behavior therapy. Treatment was delivered by therapists trained to high levels of competence in these manualized approaches, and each received weekly supervision from acknowledged experts in each approach (see Diamond, Yeomans, Clarkin, Levy, & Kernberg, Chapter 11, this volume, for a case illustration of this program of work). AAIs were administered prior to beginning treatment and 1 year into treatment by independent assessors (not the therapist). This approach, yielded rewards insofar as AAI coherence increased significantly over the year of treatment, as did RF, and the frequency of secure AAI classifications increased threefold, from 5 to 15%, but only for patients treated with TFP. Reading how these authors phrase the goal of TFP, one can easily imagine AAI security, coherence, or high RF being described: "The patient develops the capacity to think more coherently and reflectively, with more realistic, complex, and differentiated appraisals of the thoughts, feelings, intentions, and desires of self and others" (Levy et al., 2006, p. 1037). By contrast, the focus—and mechanisms of change operating in—dialectical behavior therapy and supportive psychotherapy appear somewhat tangential to the AAI; hence, they are less effective in terms of assisting a patient to acquire secure autonomy—at least in this study.

The case studies literature includes repeat administrations of the AAI that provide a detailed window on changes in the internal world that occur in psychoanalytic psychotherapy across years of treatment (see, e.g., Ammanitti et al., Chapter 10, this volume). Coherence is clearly shown to improve in one patient, whereas other patients are shown to shift from deeply insecure modes of feeling, thinking, and relating to less insecure, more organized modes of functioning. Given the extent to which mental health in adulthood is correlated with AAI security and resolution of loss or trauma (see van IJzendoorn & Bakermans-Kranenburg, Chapter 3, this volume), we can expect continued growth in research and case study reports that rely on the AAI as an indicator of change and therapy outcomes.

Conclusion

It is vital to remember that the use of the AAI in clinical contexts encompasses an interdisciplinary approach. Although the underlying theoretical constructs are clearly rooted in psychoanalytic theorizing, as constructed by John Bowlby, analysis of the AAI includes elements of linguistic discourse analyses alongside contemporary developmental psychological research that may otherwise be outside the domain of most clinicians. From the protocol itself one understands what may usefully begin a therapeutic relationship in terms of lis-tening carefully for global descriptions in contrast to recounting specific inci-dents, or paying special attention to discussions of hurt, rejection, separations, and, most obviously, loss and/or trauma.

The centrality of the concept of coherence is a widely appreciated goal of clinical work, which familiarity with the AAI uniquely highlights and expands (see Main et al., Chapter 2, this volume). Understanding the sophistication involved in measuring coherence and the obvious connection to Bowlby's writings on defensive exclusion of painful material that characterize many (incoherent) psychotherapeutic encounters can illuminate the clinical process. And this process itself can be facilitated by understanding the role of the ther-apist as providing a secure base for the client. From this base, clients are encouraged to explore their various states of mind, many of which are con-nected to their attachment figures, and some of which they would rather avoid and not think about, let alone put into words. Attending to the deviations that ensue from a coherent and unencumbered narrative can potentially provide the therapist with important clues on how best to proceed. In particular, via familiarity with the AAI coding system, and the particular AAI response(s) provided by the patient, the therapist is likely to arrive at an improved under-standing both of transference and countertransference reactions.

Thus, there are many lessons for clinicians to be derived from the AAI protocol, the coding system, and the expansive literature that has arisen out of the move to the level of representation in developmental research ushered in by Main and her colleagues (George, Kaplan, & Main, 1985; Main et al., 1985; Main, Goldwyn, & Hesse, 2003). It is our hope that this chapter has provided the reader with an appreciation for how this move initiated with the AAI delivered attachment theory and research back to the clinical domain from which it initially evolved (Bowlby, 1949, 1988), and promises—particularly as new applications of the AAI are uncovered and elucidated—further growth in the future.

Notes

1. Google Scholar, January 24, 2008, cited 1,291 times.
2. See Chapter 3, this volume, in which van IJzendoorn and Bakermans-Kranenburg report on the explosive growth in the number of clinical studies ($n = 61$) and on results garnered from over 4,200 AAIs from published work, and remark on some 9,000 AAIs having been collected and analyzed as of August 2006.
3. We borrow freely here from Main et al. (2003) in providing this overview of the principal AAI classifications and subclassifications. More details are provided by Main et al. in Chapter 2, this volume.
4. Markers of speech that signal a lack of resolution of mourning concerning past loss or trauma are described in the next section of this chapter, and also in (Main et al., Chapter 2, this volume) on the rating and classification system. Additionally, fur-ther chapters in this book rely on this clinically relevant set of criteria.

5. Guidelines for transcription are available from Mary Main or Erik Hesse, Psychology Department, University of California, Berkeley.
6. Full guidelines for how to administer the AAI are available from Mary Main or Erik Hesse, Psychology Department, University of California, Berkeley.
7. See Bretherton and Mulholland (1999) for a full discussion of Bowlby's term *defensive exclusion* and its origins in Piagetian thinking, information-processing theory, and Bowlby's rendering of psychoanalytic theory in terms of how real-world experiences with parents shape the internal working model of the developing child.
8. The unpublished RF manual elaborates at length on how to score RF or mentalization as it may appear across the whole AAI, not simply one or other question. An overall score on a scale ranging from −1 to 9 is assigned.

References

Agid, O., Shapira, B., Zislin, J., Ritsner, M., Hanin, B., Murad, H., et al. (1999). Environment and vulnerability to major psychiatric illness: A case control study of early parental loss in major depression, bipolar disorder and schizophrenia. *Molecular Psychiatry, 4*, 163–72.

Ainsworth, M. D. S. (1967). *Infancy in Uganda: Infant care and the growth of love.* Baltimore: Johns Hopkins Press.

Ainsworth, M. D. S., & Bell, S. M. (1969). Some contemporary patterns of mother–infant interaction in the feeding situation. In A. Ambrose (Ed.), *Stimulation in early infancy* (pp. 133–170). London: Academic Pres.

Ainsworth, M. D. S., Blehar, M. C., Waters, E., & Wall, S. (1978). *Patterns of attachment: Assessed in the Strange Situation and at home.* Hillsdale, NJ: Erlbaum.

Ainsworth, M. D. S., & Marvin, R. S. (1995). On the shaping of attachment theory and research: An interview with Mary D. S. Ainsworth. *Monographs of the Society for Research in Child Development, 60*(2/3), 2–21.

Benoit, D., & Parker, K. C. H. (1994). Stability and transmission of attachment across three generations. *Child Development, 65*, 1444–1456.

Berger, P., & Luckmann, T. (1966). *The social construction of reality: A treatise in the sociology of knowledge.* Garden City, NY: Doubleday.

Blehar, M. C., Lieberman, A. F., & Ainsworth, M. D. S. (1977). Early face-to-face interaction and its relation to later infant–mother attachment. *Child Development, 48*, 182–194.

Bowlby, J. (1949). The study and reduction of group tensions in the family. *Human Relations, 2*, 123–128.

Bowlby, J. (1973). *Attachment and loss: Vol. 2. Separation.* New York: Basic Books.

Bowlby, J. (1979). *The making and breaking affectional bonds.* London: Tavistock.

Bowlby, J. (1982). *Attachment and loss: Vol. 1. Attachment.* London: Hogarth Press. (Original work published 1969)

Bowlby, J. (1988). *A secure base: Clinical applications of attachment theory.* London: Routledge.

Bretherton, I., & Mulholland, K. (1999). Internal working models in attachment relationships: A construct revisited. In J. Cassidy & P. R. Shaver (Eds.), *Handbook of attachment: Theory, research, and clinical applications* (pp. 89–114). New York: Guilford Press.

Brown, G. W., & Harris, T. O. (1978). *The social origins of depression: A study of psychiatric disorder in women*. New York: Free Press.

Bruner, J. (1991). The narrative construction of reality. *Critical Inquiry, 18*, 1–21.

Carlson, E. A. (1998). A prospective longitudinal study of attachment disorganization/disorientation. *Child Development, 69*, 1107–1128.

Cohen, J. (1992). A power primer. *Psychological Bulletin, 112*, 155–159.

Conway, M. A., & Pleydell-Pearce, C. W. (2000). The construction of autobiographical memories in the self-memory system. *Psychological Review, 107*, 261–288.

De Wolff, M. S., & van IJzendoorn, M. H. (1997). Sensitivity and attachment: A meta-analysis on parental antecedents of infant attachment. *Child Development, 68*, 571–591.

Dozier, M., & Kobak, R. R. (1992). Psychophysiology in attachment interviews: Converging evidence for deactivating strategies. *Child Development, 63*, 1473–1480.

Fonagy, P., Gergely, G., Jurist, E. J., & Target, M. (2002). *Affect regulation, mentalization, and the development of the self*. New York: Other Press.

Fonagy, P., Steele, H., & Steele, M. (1991). Maternal representations of attachment during pregnancy predict the organisation of infant–mother attachment at one year. *Child Development, 62*, 891–905.

Fonagy, P., Steele, M., Moran, G., Steele, H., & Higgitt, A. (1993). Measuring the ghost in the nursery: An empirical study of the relation between parents' mental representations of childhood experiences and their infants' security of attachment. *Journal of the American Psychoanalytic Association, 41*, 957–989.

Fonagy, P., Steele, M., Steele, H., Higgitt, A., & Target, M. (1994). The Emmanuel Miller Memorial Lecture 1992: The theory and practice of resilience. *Journal of Child Psychology and Psychiatry, 35*, 231–257.

Fonagy, P., Steele, M., Steele, H., Moran, G., & Higgitt, A. (1991). The capacity for understanding mental states: The reflective self in parent and child and its significance for security of attachment. *Infant Mental Health Journal, 12*, 201–218.

Fonagy, P., Target, M., Steele, H., & Steele, M. (1998). *Reflective-Functioning Manual, version 5.2, for application to Adult Attachment Interviews*. London: University College London.

Fraiberg, S., Adelson, E., & Shapiro, V. (1975). Ghosts in the nursery: A psychoanalytic approach to the problems of impaired infant–mother relationships. *Journal of the American Academy of Child Psychiatry, 14*, 387–421.

Freud, A. (1946). *The ego and the mechanisms of defence*. New York: International Universities Press. (Original work published 1936)

Freud, S. (1923). The ego and the id. In J. Strachey (Ed.), *The standard edition of the complete psychological works of Sigmund Freud* (Vol. 19, pp. 1–66). London: Hogarth Press.

George, C., Kaplan, N., & Main, M. (1984). *Adult Attachment Interview protocol*. Unpublished manuscript, University of California, Berkeley.

George, C., Kaplan, N., & Main, M., (1985). *Adult Attachment Intreview protocol* (2nd ed.). Unpublished manuscript, University of California, Berkeley.

George, C., Kaplan, N., & Main, M., (1985). *Adult Attachment Intreview protocol* (3rd ed.). Unpublished manuscript, University of California, Berkeley.

Hesse, E. (1999). The Adult Attachment Interview: Historical and current perspectives. In J. Cassidy & P. R. Shaver (Eds.), *Handbook of attachment: Theory, research and clinical applications* (pp. 395–433). New York: Guilford Press.

Hesse, E., & Main, M. (2000). Disorganized infant, child, and adult attachment: Collapse in behavioral and attentional strategies. *Journal of the American Psychoanalytic Association*, 48, 1097–1127.

Hesse, E., & Main, M. (2006). Frightened, threatening, and dissociative parental behavior in low-risk samples: Description, discussion, and interpretations. *Developmental Psychopathology*, 18, 309–343.

Hesse, E., & van IJzendoorn, M. H. (1999). Propensities towards absorption are related to lapses in the monitoring of reasoning or discourse during the Adult Attachment Interview: A preliminary investigation. *Attachment and Human Development*, 1, 67–91.

Holmes, J. (1992). *Between art and science*. London: Routledge.

Holmes, J. (1993). *John Bowlby and attachment theory*. London: Routledge.

Hrdy, S. B. (1999). *Mother Nature: A history of mothers, infants and natural selection*. New York: Pantheon.

Korfmacher, J., Adam, E., Ogawa, J., & Egeland, B. (1997). Adult Attachment: Implications for the therapeutic process in a home visitation intervention. *Applied Developmental Science*, 1, 43–52.

Levy, K. N., Kelly, K. M., Meehan, K. B., Reynoso, J. S., Clarkin, J. F., Lenzenweger, M. F., et al. (2006). Change in attachment and reflective function in the treatment of borderline personality disorder with transference focused psychotherapy. *Journal of Consulting and Clinical Psychology*, 74, 1027–1040.

Lieberman, A. F., Padrón, E., Van Horn, P. V., & Harris, W. W. (2005). Angels in the nursery: The intergenerational transmission of benevolent parental influences. *Infant Mental Health Journal, 26*, 504–520.

Lyons-Ruth, K., & Jacobvitz, D. (1999). Attachment disorganization: Unresolved loss, relational violence, and lapses in behavioral and attentional strategies. In J. Cassidy & P. R. Shaver (Eds.), *Handbook of attachment: Theory, research, and clinical applications* (pp. 520–554). New York: Guilford Press.

Main, M., & Goldwyn, R. (1984). Predicting rejection of her infant from mother's representation of her own experience: Implications for the abused–abusing intergenerational cycle. *Child Abuse and Neglect*, 8, 203–217.

Main, M., & Hesse, E. (1990). Parents' unresolved traumatic experiences are related to infant disorganized attachment status: Is frightened and/or frightening parental behavior the linking mechanism? In M. T. Greenberg, D. Cicchetti, & E. M. Cummings (Eds.), *Attachment in the preschool years: Theory, research, and intervention* (pp. 161–182). Chicago: University of Chicago Press.

Main, M., Hesse, E., & Goldwyn, R. (2003). *Adult Attachment Classification System version 7.2*. Unpublished manuscript, University of California, Berkeley.

Main, M., Kaplan, N., & Cassidy, J. (1985). Security in infancy, childhood, and adulthood: A move to the level of representation. *Monographs of the Society for Research in Child Development*, 50(1–2, Serial No. 209), 66–104.

Main, M., & Solomon, J. (1990). Procedures for identifying infants as disorganized/disoriented during the Ainsworth Strange Situation. In M. T. Greenberg, D. Cicchetti, & E. M. Cummings (Eds.), *Attachment in the preschool years* (pp. 121–160). Chicago: University of Chicago Press.

Routh, C. P. , Hill, J. W., Steele, H., Elliott, C. E., & Dewey, M. (1995). Maternal attachment status, psychosocial stressors and problem behaviour: Follow-up after parent training courses for conduct disorder. *Journal of Child Psychology and Psychiatry*, 36, 1179–1198.

Sandler, J., & Sandler, A. M. (1998). *Internal objects revisited*. London: Karnac.

Slade, A. (1999). Attachment theory and research: Implications for the theory and practice of individual psychotherapy with adults. In J. Cassidy & P. R. Shaver (Eds.), *Handbook of attachment* (pp. 575–594). New York: Guilford Press.

Sroufe, L. A., Egeland, B., Carlson, E., & Collins, W. A. (2005). *The development of the person: The Minnesota Study of risk and adaptation from birth to adulthood*. New York: Guilford Press.

Steele, H. (2003). Unrelenting catastrophic trauma within the family: When every secure base is abusive. *Attachment and Human Development, 5*, 353–366.

Steele, H., & Steele, M. (2005). Understanding and resolving emotional conflict: The view from 12 years of attachment research across generations and across childhood. In K. E. Grossmann, K. Grossmann, & E. Waters (Eds.), *Attachment from infancy to adulthood: The major longitudinal studies* (pp. 137–164). New York: Guilford Press.

Steele, H., & Steele, M. (2008). On the origins of reflective functioning. In F. Busch (Ed.), *Mentalization: Theoretical considerations, research findings, and clinical implications* (pp. 133–156). New York: Analytic Press.

Steele, H., Steele, M., & Fonagy, P. (1996). Associations among attachment classifications of mothers, fathers, and their infants. *Child Development, 67*, 541–555.

Steele, M., & Baradon, T. (2004). Clinical uses of the Adult Attachment Interview in parent–infant psychotherapy. *Infant Mental Health Journal, 25*, 284–299.

Stern, D. (1985). *The interpersonal world of the infant*. New York: Basic Books.

Tulving, E. (1972). Episodic and semantic memory. In E. Tulving & W. Donaldson (Eds.), *Organization of memory* (pp. 381–403). New York: Academic Press.

Tulving, E. (1983). *Elements of episodic memory*. New York: Oxford University Press.

Tyrrell, C., Dozier, M., Teague, G. B., & Fallot, R. D. (1999). Effective treatment relationships for persons with serious psychiatric disorders: The importance of attachment states of mind. *Journal of Consulting and Clinical Psychology, 67*, 725–733.

van IJzendoorn, M. H. (1995). Adult attachment representations, parental responsiveness, and infant attachment: A meta-analysis on the predictive validity of the Adult Attachment Interview. *Psychological Bulletin, 117*(3), 387–403.

van IJzendoorn, M. H., & Sagi, A. (1999). Cross-cultural patterns of attachment: Universal and contextual dimensions. In J. Cassidy & P. R. Shaver (Eds.), *Handbook of attachment: Theory, research, and clinical applications* (pp. 713–734). New York: Guilford Press.

van IJzendoorn, M. H., Schuengel, C., & Bakermans-Kranenburg, M. J. (1999). Disorganized attachment in early childhood: Meta-analysis of precursors, concomitants, and sequelae. *Development and Psychopathology, 11*, 225–249.

Ward, M. J., & Carlson, E. A. (1994). Associations among adult attachment representations, maternal sensitivity, and infant–mother attachment in a sample of adolescent mothers. *Child Development, 66*, 69–79.

West, M., & George, C. (1999). Abuse and violence in intimate adult relationships: New perspectives from attachment history. *Attachment and Human Development, 1*, 137–156.

Zegers, M. A., Janssens, J. M., Van IJzendoorn, M. H., & Schuengel, C. (2006). Attachment representations of institutionalized adolescents and their professional caregivers: Predicting the development of therapeutic relationships. *American Journal of Orthopsychiatry, 76*, 325–334.

2

Studying Differences in Language Usage in Recounting Attachment History

An Introduction to the AAI

MARY MAIN, ERIK HESSE, and RUTH GOLDWYN

This chapter provides a comprehensive overview of the questions that comprise the Adult Attachment Interview (AAI) protocol, together with its associated scoring and classification system. Familiarity with the interview and the system with which it is analyzed supplies the reader with an essential port of entrée into understanding the chapters that follow. As well, it provides a background for use of the AAI in clinical contexts (AAI protocol: George, Kaplan, & Main, 1985, 1996; system of analysis: Main & Goldwyn, 1984b, 1988; Main, Goldwyn, & Hesse, 2003).

The AAI scoring and classification system focuses on the patterns of speech that emerge in the individual asked to respond to a series of 20 questions that comprise the interview protocol. Many of these concern childhood experiences with primary caregivers. Other questions address individuals' thoughts and feelings about the influence of childhood experiences upon his or her adult personality, the possible reasons caregivers may have behaved as they did when the speaker was a child, and the nature of the current relationships with the caregivers/parents. Questions regarding major loss experiences, as well as any overwhelmingly frightening or traumatic experiences occurring throughout the individual's lifetime, are included. The interview ends by asking what wishes the speaker would have for his or her children's (or imagined children's) future, and what he or she hopes the children would have learned from his or her parenting.

Following an extensive study of the initial texts gleaned from this protocol, Main and Goldwyn (1984a, 1984b) discovered three basic and relatively organized ways of recounting life history with respect to attachment. Each of these appeared to reflect what they termed a particular "state of mind" with respect to attachment, namely, (1) *secure–autonomous* (valuing of attachment, but seemingly objective regarding any particular experience or relationship), (2) *dismissing of attachment* (dismissing or devaluing the importance of attachment relationships and experiences), and (3) *preoccupied* (preoccupied with or by past attachment relationships and/or experiences).

The central finding first reported was the remarkable degree of overlap between these "organized" states of mind with respect to attachment, as seen in a parent's AAI and the infant's response to that parent during a brief separation-and-reunion procedure known as the Ainsworth Strange Situation (Ainsworth, Blehar, Waters, & Wall, 1978). Specifically, in the original study of a Bay Area sample (Main, 1985; Main & Goldwyn, 1984b; Main, Kaplan, & Cassidy, 1985; see Steele & Steele, Chapter 1, this volume), and later in many other regions and countries, parents classified as secure–autonomous by the AAI were found to be much more likely than others to have infants who— during the Strange Situation—behaved in ways that indicated the presence of a secure attachment to that same parent. Thus, the infants of secure–autonomous parents typically explored energetically in the parent's presence, and showed distress or called for the parent during his or her absence. Having actively established proximity or contact immediately upon reunion, however, they soon settled down and returned to play. Parents who dismissed the importance of attachment relationships during the AAI were more likely to have infants classified as *avoidant*—that is, infants who showed little or no distress on separation from them, then actively avoided and ignored them on reunion. Parents who were preoccupied with their own parents had infants who behaved in an *ambivalent/resistant* manner; these infants failed to explore even prior to the first separation, and became extremely, rather than moderately, distressed when separated. On reunion, they alternately clung to and expressed anger toward the parent, and were unable to "settle" and turn to play.

These findings were initially reported in the 1980s, and by 1995, a combined overview of existing studies conducted by van IJzendoorn showed replication across 18 samples, including 854 parent–infant pairs from six different countries. This overview revealed that 75% of secure–autonomous parents had secure infants, a finding that also held when the interview was conducted prior to the birth of the first child (e.g., London: Fonagy, Steele, & Steele, 1991; Steele, Steele, & Fonagy, 1996; Toronto: Benoit & Parker, 1994; inner-city New York: Ward & Carlson, 1995). Additionally, as would be expected, van IJzendoorn's (1995) overview showed that across studies, secure–autonomous parents were more sensitive and responsive to their infants than were parents whose AAI texts had been judged as dismissing or preoccupied. Later, it would be shown that placement in the three organized categories was (a) stable when the AAI was given to the same person twice, even if across several years, and (b) unrelated to the individual's assessed general intelligence or memory abilities (see Hesse, 1999).

Eventually, Main and Hesse (1990) discovered that disorganized lapses in speech or reasoning occurred during the discussion of loss or abuse in some speakers, including a substantial minority drawn from low-risk community samples. This led to the development of a fourth AAI category termed *unresolved/disorganized*. These lapses in the monitoring of speech or reasoning were attributed to the arousal of, and interference from, partially dissociated *fear* connected with the experience under discussion (Hesse & Main, 2000, 2006). Shortly thereafter, it was recognized that some interview texts could not be classified in terms of any singular organized category, because either "contradictory" strategies were present or the interview was otherwise virtually formless. This led to the development of a fifth, *cannot classify*, category (Hesse, 1996).

In the case of parent–child dyads, both cannot classify and unresolved/disorganized interviews are associated with the *disorganized/disoriented* infant Strange Situation classification (Main & Solomon, 1986, 1990). Infants are placed in this fourth Strange Situation category when they fail to maintain the behavioral organization that characterizes those judged secure, avoidant, or ambivalent/resistant. Infants are categorized as disorganized/disoriented when, for example, they approach the parent with the head averted, put a hand to the mouth in a gesture indicative of apprehension immediately upon reunion, or rise to approach the parent, then fall prone to the floor. Infants are also termed disorganized/disoriented when, for example, they freeze all movement with arms elevated or become still, with a trance-like expression. Disorganized Strange Situation behavior has been found to be associated with frightened, frightening, dissociative, and other forms of anomalous parental behavior (Hesse & Main, 2006; Lyons-Ruth, Bronfman, & Parson, 1999; Main & Hesse, 1990). Both the cannot classify and unresolved/disorganized AAI categories have proven especially predominant in clinical samples (van IJzendoorn & Bakermans-Kranenburg, 1996), and infant disorganized attachment with the mother has been linked with psychopathology assessed in the same individuals in young adulthood (Carlson, 1998), especially in the event of intervening trauma (Ogawa, Sroufe, Weinfield, Carlson, & Egeland, 1997). Disorganized attachment status is seen in the majority of infants in maltreatment samples (Carlson, Cicchetti, Barnett, & Braunwald, 1989; Lyons-Ruth, Connell, Zoll, & Stahl, 1987) and has been found associated with both externalizing and internalizing disorders in low-risk samples (e.g., Solomon, George, & DeJong, 1995).

Before moving on to a description of the protocol and system of analysis, it is critical to consider the strong relation between the AAI and the thinking of John Bowlby (1969/1982, 1973, 1980). These ideas fall broadly within the object relations school of thought as Bowlby (1969/1982) readily acknowledged (Balint, 1939/1949; Fairbairn, 1952; Spitz, 1965; Winnicott, 1953). First, from his early works forward, one of the fundamental premises guiding Bowlby's thinking about the origins of an individual's emotional difficulties was insistence on the need to take into account, as fully as possible, *actual* experiences that occurred in that individual's childhood (Bowlby, 1979). Second, Bowlby proposed that one must pay special attention to the way these experiences are (re)presented by the individual, and—whether historically accurate or not—presently form his or her "internal working model" or "state of mind" with respect to the self, and the self in relation to parents and important others.

The first of these two fundamental aspects of Bowlby's thinking with regard to the development of emotional difficulties is addressed by those AAI questions that call directly for the speaker's descriptions of real-life experiences. Although historical events can never be known retrospectively, experiences with each parent as primarily loving or unloving during childhood are "inferred" or estimated from the full verbatim AAI transcript. Here, the AAI scoring system powerfully complements most of the existing self-report screening instruments aimed at identifying problematic features of childhood experiences, because it does not take at face value the individual's direct evaluations or report. The AAI also gives emphasis to Bowlby's focus on other aspects of real-life experiences (i.e., those involving traumatic loss or abuse), allowing coders to estimate the extent to which loss or abuse experiences may be core unsettling experiences that complicate adult functioning, including vital health and relationship domains.

Bowlby's second focus was the mental representations a person forms of his or her attachment-related experiences, termed *states of mind* or *representational/working models* (1973, p. 203). Here, Bowlby was concerned with the representational model of self, other, and the relation between them. The AAI addresses this second focus by repeatedly querying individuals regarding their *present* thoughts and feelings about specific aspects of their past. In the AAI, these phenomena are approached in terms of what to the coder appears to be guiding the speaker in appraising and interpreting attachment-relevant information in the interview context.

Against this background, we now turn to a description of the questions that comprise the AAI protocol, then move on to present the rating scales alongside the overall classification system, which is more familiar in the published literature. The tendency to publish reports regarding AAI data at the level of overall classification (i.e., secure as opposed to insecure [dismissing or preoccupied], and separately, unclassifiable, and unresolved or not unresolved concerning past loss or trauma) has also inevitably been maintained by the majority of the contributors in this volume. In this chapter, however, we also focus on the continuous scales that are assigned to all AAI texts, and that contribute critically to the delineation of the five major AAI classifications. Finally, the three organized AAI categories are also associated with specific constellations of features indicating different overall "attitudes toward attachment," as we discuss below.

A central focus that runs throughout this chapter is an elaboration of the definitions of narrative *coherence* versus *incoherence*. That a speaker responding to the AAI is coherent and collaborative in describing his or her attachment-related experiences is critical to the judgment that an AAI is secure–autonomous, and as such is a consistent correlate of mental health in adulthood and childhood (van IJzendoorn & Bakermans-Kranenburg, Chapter 3, this volume). Here the reader gains entrée to the work of the linguistic philosopher H. P. Grice (1975), who provided several principles or *maxims* that speakers must follow to be considered to be participating in cooperative, rational discourse. It appeared, then, that speakers who could maintain cooperative, coherent, and rational discourse throughout the AAI (adhering to each of Grice's *conversational maxims*) were likely to have secure babies. In contrast, those speakers whose conversations went astray in various specifiable ways would have infants who, in the Strange Situation, were classified as either insecure–avoidant or insecure–ambivalent, in accordance with the specific maxims that had been violated.

The AAI Protocol: An Overview of the Questions

All persons have their own individual approach to telling their life story, and the way they do so may vary dramatically depending on their resources, history, and the demand characteristics of the situation. As a set series of questions with follow-up probes, the AAI calls upon speakers to answer direct and challenging queries regarding their life history, the great majority of which they never have been asked before. This is done at a relatively rapid pace and within approximately an hour. Ample opportunities are thereby created for speakers to contradict themselves, to find themselves unable to answer questions clearly, or to be led into excessively lengthy discussions of particular topics (e.g., recent experiences, events, conflicts) that may stray from the request that has just been stated. Moreover, a speaker must not only address the question at hand but also be able to remember what he or she has already said, in order to integrate the overall presentation as it emerges. The central tasks of the AAI, then, are to (1) produce and reflect upon relationships and experiences related to attachment history, *while simultaneously* (2) maintaining coherent conversation with the interviewer (Hesse, 1996).

It is striking that despite the fact that the interviewee is always informed in some detail regarding the overall topic of the interview prior to its administration, actually engaging in the process often appears to be a far more powerful experience than the speaker had anticipated. This is consistent with clinical observations from Freud's and Janet's day forward—that speaking to another person regarding highly personal or emotional topics in a clinical or other professional setting is a unique and potentially profound experience. This given, the protocol is deliberately arranged to elicit structural variations in the ways that speakers organize and present their attachment-related history, together with an evaluation of its influence upon their present personality and functioning. Therefore, interviewers must skillfully ensure that the timing of their queries and the nature of their own discourse serves only to highlight, not to alter, the participant's natural volition to respond in particular ways (as seen earlier in Steele & Steele, Chapter 1, this volume). In this way, trained coders who later read the transcription are best able to arrive at a probabilistic estimate of "what happened" during the adult speaker's childhood.[1] To this aim, the interview opens with a request for a brief overview of the persons with whom the participant lived, and whether he or she lived with persons other than the parents. In this case, the interviewer asks, "Who would you say raised you?" If persons other than biological or adoptive parents are named, then they are subsequently included in the central queries. The interviewer next asks for a general description of relationships to parents/parental figures in childhood:

> "I'd like you to try to describe your relationship with your parents as a young child if you could; start from as far back as you can remember."

This question is unusual and can be difficult to answer, as is the next question, which unfolds in directions particularly likely to "surprise the unconscious" (George et al., 1985). This comprises a request for five adjectives, words, or phrases that best represent the relationship with each parent or parental figure (hereafter, *parent*). After adjectives have been provided, the speaker is probed for specific *episodic* memories (ideally, memories specific to time and place) that illustrate or support each descriptor choice. For example, the interviewer may say:

> "You used *caring* as your first adjective for your relationship with your mother. I wonder whether you could give me some incidents or memories from your childhood that would tell me why you chose that adjective."[2]

Once this process has been completed for the mother, it is then repeated for the father, and, when applicable, for anyone else the speaker named as having raised him or her. The interviewee is asked which parent he or she felt closer to, and why, then what he or she did when emotionally upset, physically hurt, or ill—times when we would expect the attachment system to be especially activated—and how the parents responded. Another important query refers to personal or family responses to separation experiences, a topic to which Bowlby (1973) devoted an entire volume. The interviewee is also asked about possible experiences of rejection, and any threats regarding discipline.

Other questions concern potentially traumatic experiences. Each major loss, whether it occurred in childhood or later, is extensively probed, such that speakers are asked to describe (1) how the death occurred, (2) their reactions to the loss at the time, (3) any funeral or memorial service attended, (4) changes in feelings regarding the loss over time, (5) what they see as effects upon their adult personality and functioning, and, finally, for parents (6) any effects the loss may have had on their behavior with their children. In the case of persons with multiple losses, interviewers restrict their queries to those that seem the most significant.

Losses are not the only potentially traumatic events probed. The interviewer also seeks a description of abuse (or any other overwhelmingly frightening experiences that may have occurred throughout the lifetime). In cases of abuse, the interviewer sensitively attempts to establish its extent and frequency. However, the guide to the protocol suggests that—except when the interview is administered by well-trained individuals with clinical skills—sexual and physical abuse should not be as extensively probed as loss. For some participants, this will be the first discussion of such experiences, and the interviewer's aim should be to leave the individual free from undue distress or regret on account of what he or she may have disclosed.

The speaker is then asked about the overall effects of the experiences with parents on his or her present personality; whether any experiences constituted a significant setback to development; and why he or she believes the parents behaved as they did. These latter questions in particular are useful in elucidating the individual's capacity for reflective functioning (Fonagy, Steele, Steele, Moran, & Higgitt, 1991; see also Steele & Steele, Chapter 1, this volume), or ability to put him- or herself in the caregiver's place and to consider the thoughts and feelings that motivated the parent's behavior. An important question following upon the above (see Jacobvitz's Afterword, this volume) is whether there were any other adults to whom the speaker felt especially close, like parents, when he or she was a child.

Toward the close of the interview, speakers are asked about the nature of the current relationship with parents (if living). In addition, whether or not speakers have children, they are questioned as to how they feel (or imagine they would feel if they had a child) about being separated from their child at this time, and how experiences of being parented may have affected responses (or imagined responses) to their own child. Finally, speakers are invited to speculate regarding wishes for their real or imagined child 20 years from now. These questions offer insight into aspects of the individuals' representations of themselves as (real or prospective) parents. They are placed at the end of the interview to move toward a sense of closure in response to the earlier, often more penetrating questions focused on childhood experiences.

The AAI protocol, then, is designed and structured to bring into relief individual differences in deeply internalized strategies for regulating emotion and attention in response to the discussion of attachment. This is achieved despite the fact that although interview transcriptions have recorded the full verbatim exchange, they are nonetheless devoid of reference to body movement or facial expression or intonation, all of which, of course, can be observed in the clinical setting. The AAI coder is then free to look at (rather than *behind* or *through*; see Capps & Oakes, 1995) the speaker's language usage in response to each of the interview questions. Remarkably, on the basis of language use alone, the AAI coder is able in many cases to predict how the speaker will behave with others, including, perhaps most importantly, his or her own offspring in the earliest years of life.

The Organized Categories of the AAI
Viewed in Terms of Attentional Flexibility

As the reader is now aware, the historical roots of the AAI scoring and classification system lie first in the match between the three central or *organized* forms of parental responses to the AAI interview queries (secure–autonomous, dismissing, or preoccupied), and the three central or *organized* forms of infant response to that parent in the Strange Situation (respectively, secure, avoidant, or preoccupied). The term *organized* originated in Main's (1990) observation that infants in these original three Strange Situation categories differed with respect to the flexibility versus inflexibility of attention to (1) parent and (2) inanimate environment they exhibited during Ainsworth's separation-and-reunion procedure. *Attentional flexibility* was ascribed to secure babies, in that they readily alternated between attachment and exploratory behavior across the episodes of the Strange Situation, exploring in the parent's presence, and showing attachment behavior (e.g., crying, calling) in his or her absence and again immediately upon reunion (e.g., by seeking proximity and contact). Attentional *inflexibility*—attending almost exclusively either to the inanimate environment or to the parent—was seen in insecure–avoidant infants, who persistently focused *away from* the parent and on the toys, as well as in insecure–ambivalent/resistant infants, who focused persistently *toward* the parent and, typically, away from the toys.

As we would later realize (e.g., Main, 1993), the organized categories of the AAI can also be interpreted in terms of the attentional flexibility observed in secure–autonomous parents as they alternately present their attachment-related experiences and respond to the requirement to evaluate their influence (Hesse, 1996). In contrast, attentional inflexibility is seen (1) in dismissing responses to the AAI, in which the linguistic focus is persistently *away from* past attachment relationships and their influences, and (2) in preoccupied responses to the AAI, in which the focus is insistently, albeit confusedly, so strongly oriented *toward* attachment relationships and experiences that it prevents appropriate responses to queries. Main (1993, 1995, 2000; Main, Hesse, & Kaplan, 2005) has proposed that inflexibility of attention is closely allied to "working" defensive processes. It should be noted, however, that insofar as inflexibilities of attention are stable across the AAI or the Strange Situation, they still—like flexible responses—remain relatively, *and singularly*, organized.

Before moving further into the analysis of the AAI, we turn to a brief review of the work of the linguistic philosopher H. P. Grice (1975, 1989). This introduction to Grice gives the reader a clearer understanding of our presentation of differing "organized" language usages within the AAI. It also facilitates an understanding of what is actually being assessed when coherence versus incoherence within a given text is under consideration.

Although the AAI interviewer presents the exact interview questions and their accompanying probes as faithfully as possible, there are in fact two people involved in this talk exchange. This means that this interview is in many ways far closer to being a conversation than a spoken autobiography. Thus, by focusing especially upon the interviewee, the AAI can be analyzed in terms of the degree to which his or her responses approximate those that meet the "Gricean" requirements for an ideally rational and cooperative conversation.

These requirements were put forward by Grice in terms of four *maxims*, or principles, to which, he suggested, any cooperative, coherent, and rational conversationalists will naturally "adhere" or follow. To the extent that these principles or maxims are "violated," the conversation veers away from this ideal. Of course, in any conversation, one or both speakers may be inconsistent and untruthful, long-winded or rudely terse, veer off on tangents, or become confusing, unclear, and disorderly. To be classified as secure–autonomous within the AAI, however, coherent, cooperative, and rational discourse is normally[3] maintained by interviewees. This holds true even when they are responding to queries about the most vital, and for some, the saddest, most frightening, and most confusing elements within their history. The four maxims follow.

1. *Quality: "Be truthful, and have evidence for what you say."* This maxim is violated when, for example, a parent is described in highly positive general terms, but the specific biographical episodes that the interviewer calls for actively contradict (or simply fail to support) the interviewee's adjectival choices. Such an interview can also be said to be internally inconsistent, and failures in internal consistency of the type just described appear most frequently in dismissing AAI texts.

2. *Quantity: "Be succinct, yet complete."* This maxim calls for conversational turns of reasonable length (i.e., neither too short nor too long). By requiring speakers to be sufficiently "complete," Grice is saying that excessively short answers are not normally acceptable. This occurs when, for example, "I don't remember" and/or "I don't know" becomes the response to several queries in sequence, and no effort to explain or express regret for this apparent lack of recall is undertaken. Excessively terse responses are often seen in dismissing texts.

Conversely, by requiring as well that responses—so long as they are complete—be sufficiently succinct, the maxim of (appropriate) quantity is also violated when a speaker takes excessively long conversational turns. Here, the interviewee may take the floor for several minutes, perhaps wandering off topic or else giving details that become increasingly unnecessary. This form of quantity violation is found in many preoccupied texts.

3. *Relation: "Be relevant to the topic as presented."* Adherence to this maxim is necessary to every conversation: Otherwise, the speakers are

engaged in solipsistic enterprises that not only fail to move ideas forward but also in fact do not require two persons. Thus, the maxim of relation is violated when queries regarding the childhood relationship with the speaker's mother are met with discussions of current interactions with the mother, or with descriptions of the speaker's relationship with his or her own children. Violations of relevance occur not infrequently in preoccupied texts and, indeed, may in themselves be indicative of a preoccupation that—once aroused by queries regarding attachment history—thereafter forbids a satisfactory exchange with the interviewer.

4. *Manner: "Be clear and orderly."* This maxim is violated when, for example, speech becomes grammatically entangled, psychological "jargon" is used, vague terms appear repeatedly, or the speaker fails to complete sentences that have been fully started. Violations of manner are particularly striking in preoccupied texts.

Having concluded this discussion of Grice's conversational maxims:

1. We take our readers through several specific interview queries in a manner that permits them to "listen" to responses that typically would be associated with each of the three organized categories of the AAI. Here, we point out when specific maxims are being violated (or, in the case of secure–coherent speakers, when the speaker has adhered to specific maxims).

2. We then present the state-of-mind scales associated with each of the organized adult attachment categories. These provide an astonishing fit to Grice's maxims, even though Main and Goldwyn devised each of the relevant scales several years before learning of his work (Main et al., 2005).

3. Finally, we review the strongly differing general features or content characteristics that Main and Goldwyn first identified as reflective of implicit or explicit attitudes toward attachment, and whose presence is carefully noted by coders. Here, too, additional illustrative examples are taken from AAI texts.

Exemplar Responses to Specific Interview Questions

Possibly the earliest point in the interview that calls for especially close attention to a speaker's response is when he or she is addressed as follows (question 3):

> "Now I'd like you choose five adjectives or words that reflect your relationship with your mother, starting as far back as you can remember in early childhood—as early as you can go, but say, age 5 to 12 is fine. I know this may take a bit of time, so go ahead and think for a minute . . . then I'll ask you why you chose them. I'll write each one down as you give them to me."

Note that this question, briefly mentioned earlier, is comprised of two parts that operate at different "mental levels": a *semantic* level (the five descriptors or adjectives themselves, devoid of space–time particulars) and an *episodic* level (the probes for "why you chose them," i.e., for what specifically tended to happen, and if possible, a specific example). Once the interviewee has completed his or her choice of descriptors and has also responded to the call for specific incidents from childhood to help explain why each was chosen, the trained coder examines the text for the extent of fit or match between them.

In essence, the set of "adjectives or words" supplied by the speaker comprises his or her synopsis, whether consciously or unconsciously derived, of the overall nature of his or her childhood relationship with the particular parent figure being discussed. Thus, once the first part of the question has been answered (i.e., the five[4] descriptors have been provided), the speaker has for all intents and purposes "taken a stance" as to the kind of relationship he or she had with this particular parent. The adjectives can, of course, vary from the extremely negative to the extremely positive, with perhaps a mixed constellation being most common. For example, with respect to the mother, if the adjective choices were "very loving, very caring, supportive, trustworthy, and warm," the speaker is clearly attempting to convey a history of highly positive interactions. In contrast, an adjectival constellation that comprises the words "interfering, warm, unpredictable, rule maker, and caring" leads to the impression of a relationship that had both positive and negative qualities.

In the follow-up probes, the interviewee is asked for a specific memory that would illustrate why each particular word or adjective had been selected. This is, of course, the portion of the question in which the participant is asked to begin drawing on episodic memory; hence, even if the adjectives produced by two different speakers were identical, the narrative that emerged could take an entirely different form.

As an example, let us consider a constellation that began with *loving*. The interviewer is now required to probe as follows:

"You described your childhood relationship with your mother [father] as *loving*. Can you think of a memory or an incident that would illustrate why you chose *loving* to describe the relationship?"

The range of possible answers is virtually infinite, yet even at this early point in an AAI, the response given already reveals information that can be approached with a view toward ultimate scoring and classification. It is likely that the speaker's response bears deeply on the degree of his or her own self-awareness and, in some cases, whether or not the speaker is conscious of it, upon the motivation to convey a particular impression to the interviewer.

Consider as an example, then, the following, not at all uncommon, response to the interviewer's probe calling for specific memories or incidents (in this case, to support *loving*).

RESPONSE: I don't remember . . . (*5-second pause*) Well, because she was kind, and generous. And supportive, she was also supportive. [Note that here the speaker is simply using similar words to describe previous words. In essence, rather than providing memories or incidents, the speaker is simply substituting one word for another.]

INTERVIEWER: Well, this can be difficult, because a lot of people haven't thought about these things for a long time, but take a minute and see if you can think of an incident or example.

RESPONSE: (*10-second pause*) Well . . . (*5-second pause*) I guess like, well, you know, she was always giving things, giving things to the community, baking cakes, or volunteering her time for charitable causes . . . that sort of thing. . . . That's all I recall.

INTERVIEWER: Thank you. And, I just wonder whether there might be another example?

RRESPONSE: Just that . . . everyone saw how generous and loving she was . . . that's all.

From this brief exchange, many tentative hypotheses can be made about the possible direction the interview will follow, and we can already see that the speaker is attempting to convey a positive impression of the mother. However, concerning the proposition that the speaker had a loving relationship with her during childhood, we have been given no real supporting evidence. Instead, the speaker has elected to discuss his or her estimate of the impression that may have been gained by the community as a whole. Perhaps convincingly loving interactions will be recalled later in the interview, but at this point, we can say that if the speaker continues along these lines (i.e., seeming to attempt to create a positive picture of childhood experiences with the mother, but in fact frequently blocking discourse yielding a paucity of support for the positive adjectives chosen), there is a good likelihood that the transcript as a whole will be classified as dismissing. Thus, dismissing speakers, as noted, violate Grice's *quality–truthfulness* maxim in failing to provide evidence for what they have claimed.

Now let us consider a second speaker, who has also begun the description of his or her childhood relation to the mother with *loving*.

RESPONSE: Ah . . . sure, well I, when I was really little and had nightmares she would come into my room and sit with me until I felt better, just talk to me until she pretty much took away my fears. And if I was sick, she was always right there, guess she coddled me a bit then if I played it up right.

INTERVIEWER: OK, well, I wonder if you remember a specific time or incident where you found her loving.

RESPONSE: That's hard. . . . Oh, I remember once I had been mean, no question, to another kid I was mad at in my class, and had spoiled his chemistry experiment, and the teacher punished me. She was right, too. Well when I got home, my mom asked me what was wrong, and we talked about it. She said I should apologize to the other kid, and she called his parents for me, and somehow it wasn't too hard to apologize with her sitting there. I guess she dealt with the teacher on her own, I never heard too much more about it.

If the interview continues in this vein, with well-supported statements regarding parenting, including specific episodic memories, we begin to suspect that the transcript would eventually be coded as secure–autonomous. This interviewee has given a coherent response, one in which his or her adjectival choice and support for it fit well together.

Finally, we give an example of a third interviewee who has also chosen *loving* as the first adjective for her childhood relationship with his or her mother, and is now asked for childhood incidents supporting that memory:

INTERVIEWER: Are there any memories or incidents that come to mind with respect to loving?

RESPONSE: Really some loving things, like she'd take me shopping. I remember her asking me how the makeup looked that she'd put on in the store and how a dress or blouse fit. Mommy was so beautiful. Then we'd get home and she'd be tired dadadadadada yeah, oh, . . . bring her stuff and that . . . kind of slip away to her my room, liked my room, it was cozy and that . . . and ah, what was the question?

Although speech of the type exemplified here is uncommon, it gives an example of part of an AAI text that, if continued in this style, points to the passively preoccupied subclassification (subtype E1; see Chapter 1, this volume). Here we see a slight violation of expected manner when the speaker refers to her mother as "Mommy." We also see more marked violations (i.e., elusive additions to already completed sentences ["and that"], nonsense speech ["dadadadadada"], and the mix-up of personal pronouns regarding whose room was whose ["her my"]).

But now let us look at speakers who have begun with a negative descriptor for the childhood relationship with the mother—in this case, *difficult*. The interviewer again will have set the stage as follows:

"*Difficult*. Are there any memories or incidents that come to mind with respect to *difficult*?"

Here is a response taken from a first speaker who, should responses continue as they do here, will not be classified as secure.

RESPONSE: Difficult. Weak person, cried, difficult. Fell apart at funerals.

INTERVIEWER: OK, well, I wonder if you have any specific memory of times you found difficult?

RESPONSE: When she was weak, when she cried. Sobbed through our neighbor's funeral. Embarrassing, couldn't wait to get away from her. Next question?

This response is likely to have come from a dismissing speaker. However, this speaker dismisses attachment relationships not through an inability to focus on them in the personal way called for, as shown by the first (probably) dismissing speaker described, but rather by casting the parent aside and refusing discussion. Responses of this kind tend to come from interviewees who fall in the derogating subclassification of the dismissing AAI category (Ds2; see Steele & Steele, Chapter 1, this volume). Note that like the previous dismissing speaker who gave only brief responses and failed to support *loving* as an adjectival choice, this speaker also has little to say—or, in Gricean terms, violates expected "quantity" for the conversation in being overly succinct.

Let us now consider a second speaker who has also selected *difficult* as her first adjective describing her childhood relationship with her mother:

"Difficult. Well, she was difficult, no question. I had three siblings and I'd say it's likely that all of us found her difficult. She had a harsh voice most of the time, I remember that, and she also had a harsh hand. But like I said, my father left when I was 4, and she was the sole breadwinner, and she was trying hard to keep us on the straight and narrow. The time she spanked me the hardest was the day when she came home and I wasn't there. I was over at our neighbor's house. I think it scared her. So she was a difficult mother for me."

This speaker is responding coherently, in that her entire discussion is relevant and sufficiently elaborated. In addition, she gives a specific example ("the time she spanked me the hardest") within her discussion. There is no difficulty in following her reply; hence, there are no violations of manner.

Finally, here is a third speaker who has been asked to support *difficult* as the first adjective given for her relation with her mother in childhood:

"Uh, yeah. . . . Wait 'til your dad comes home. . . . There were some bad times with her, you know she called me up the other day and . . . like, what did I think of her new boyfriend? Like who needs this? But yeah, difficult, like when she does come over she can be impossible with her grandson, and I'm the only one who's got her a grandchild. She should be grateful."

This speaker has gone immediately off topic, hence violating the maxim of relevance. She is talking about the present relationship with her mother, and moving on to her mother's behavior with her grandson, when the task, of course, was to describe the *difficult* aspect of her childhood relationship with her mother. There are also some violations of manner. Thus, she slips into the parent's voice in her opening by suddenly stating, "Wait 'til your dad gets home." This is indicative of preoccupation generally, because the speaker appears to be addressing herself in the parent's voice rather than talking to the interviewer in the present. In addition, in that the passage as a whole indicates a lack of monitoring of the discourse context, from a Gricean point of view this speaker is not cooperative.

These initial examples are relatively "prototypical" for insecure–dismissing, secure–autonomous, and insecure–preoccupied transcripts, and are, of course, far too brief for interview classification. They do, however, demonstrate distinctly different forms of discourse response to the same interview question that—if predominating in type across the text as a whole—would lead to placement in different AAI categories. We now continue through different responses to several other interview questions.

Question 10 focuses on the speaker's view of the overall effects that experiences with the parents may have had on his or her personality, and includes a follow-up probe regarding possible setbacks to development. At this point in the AAI, to answer the question in a way that "fits properly" with the earlier description of life history presented thus far, the speaker must be able to recall and evaluate what he or she said and provide an answer that is consonant with that presentation.

In short, question 10 asks that the interviewee engage in integrated thinking or *mentalizing*, a component of the Reflective Functioning Scale for the AAI (Fonagy et al., 1991; Steele & Steele, Chapter 1, this volume). The Reflective Functioning Scale also places special emphasis on still another question near interview midpoint:

> "Why do you think your parents behaved as they did during your childhood?"

With respect to this question, speakers across all the major AAI categories may discuss their parents' parents (their grandparents), and the ways their parents may have been influenced by them in growing up. However, some secure–autonomous speakers' responses are impressively complex. Other secure–autonomous speakers' responses can, of course, be more mundane, but they seldom give "automatic" or simplistic answers to this query, and may leave room for error in their reconstruction. For example, an especially thoughtful secure–autonomous speaker might reply as follows:

> "I know a lot was going on for my parents when we were little, just problems with my dad's job, and my mother always finding herself in new places and having to make new friends, and everything else that goes with constant moving around. And I think maybe my mother's mother didn't give her the kind of security she should have had, you know, confidence. She sort of had to learn to parent as she went."

This speaker seems to be thinking through how to answer the question in the moment, evidencing the "freshness" of speech that is characteristic of secure–autonomous speakers. In contrast, speakers whose transcripts will be judged dismissing or preoccupied are more likely to give "rote" answers. A dismissing speaker might simply say, "Because they were just normal parents behaving like everybody in the neighborhood, just like their own parents did, doing what was right." Another example of a different kind of "rote" answer seen in some preoccupied speakers is overly psychological, such as "Because of the way they were treated by their parents, definitely, they carried that baggage their parents handed down, and that's why they handed it down to me too."

As Steele and Steele have already indicated (Chapter 1, this volume), secure–autonomous speakers seem to be able to stay in the present, not only in response to queries that directly call for current evaluations but also across the interview as a whole. We therefore consider a question that comes near the close of the interview and sometimes raises issues involving anger. But, as we have emphasized throughout this chapter, it is the form rather than the content of speech that provides the interview analyst with an index of the speaker's current state of mind with respect to attachment.

This time, let us imagine we are speaking to late adolescents, perhaps just at the ending of college (Question 16):

> "Now I'd like to ask you, what is your relationship with your parents [or remaining parent in cases of loss] like for you now as an adult? Here I'm asking about your current relationship."

A first response then—this one taken from a secure–autonomous speaker— might be as follows:

> "I'd have to say it hasn't changed much since I was a child, and all the things I've been telling you are pretty much the same. My relationship with my mother is still pretty good, and she sends me regular care packages to college, and I'm probably still a little too dependent on her, 'cause I call her pretty often, especially if I've had a bad day at school. And my relationship with my father, it's still strained, and he's still distant. We . . . still can't think what to say to each other . . . and I still get more angry with him than I should at times. I'll probably be over it by next week, and things were fine last week, but we had a blow up just now over Thanksgiving break, and I yelled and stormed out of the room. So, basically no change—and me already way past childhood!"

This speaker is certainly sufficiently coherent, but we can also see some aspects of the "attitudes toward attachment" (discussed below) that typify secure speakers, including acceptance of imperfections in the self—and implicitly, in others. Note as well that the speaker *remains simply descriptive* of an argument and bout of angry behavior toward her father. She does not become preoccupied by it, and she ends with humor.

Among dismissing young speakers, we often see answers of the following kind.

> "Current relationship. Well, I think it's gotten even better now that I'm older. They respect me more now that I'm in college, and they leave me alone more, and there's not so much interference from my mother. I had had a tendency to blame my dad sometimes for not paying attention to me when I was 14, 15, but now I know he was just trying to help me grow up. So, it's fine right now."

In this portion of his interview, this dismissing speaker is being clear in manner and is not notably violating coherence, quantity, or relevance. On the other hand, he appears to view his father's neglect and his parents' tendency to leave him alone as ultimately desirable, because it has fostered his independence. However, this kind of response also shows the sadness that may underlie dismissing mental states and has sometimes been associated with depression (Ivarsson, Chapter 9, this volume).

Finally, we turn to an answer that might be found in a young insecure–preoccupied speaker, this time one who is passively preoccupied (E1). Again, of course, the interviewer has called for a description of the current relationship with parents.

> "Uh, not so easy, not easy at all. Saw 'em just last week. My grades were really hard on them; they weren't good grades and that hurt them again. Good people, but there's still that lack of fit. Fit, yeah, something about my temperament just isn't right for my mother, never has been, and my grades just, uh, uh."

This passage is not especially incoherent. But a trained coder would nonetheless be alert to consider preoccupation, and especially the passive subclass of preoccupation because of the violation of manner (the speech is not fully clear and orderly) and the presence of attitudinal features (described in a forthcoming section) indicative of passive preoccupation, evidenced by strong and unbalanced self-blame accompanied by an apparently unexamined sense of having failed to please the parents. As in the dismissing discussion of current relationships given previously, the speaker's sadness is also implicitly evident.

Analyzing AAI Texts for Placement in the "Organized" Classifications

Every AAI text is assigned to one of the three organized classifications (*secure*, *dismissing*, or *preoccupied*), whether it is primarily either of the *unresolved/disorganized* or *cannot classify* categories that were briefly described earlier and are elaborated upon below. We now proceed to review the three readings or steps taken by AAI coders as they set out to determine a text's best-fitting organized category placement. The process begins with the use of two sets of 9-point rating scales. Starting with the first of these, the coder attempts to ascertain (1) the speaker's probable childhood experiences with each parent. A second set of scales (2) is then applied to assess the speaker's current state of mind with respect to attachment-related experiences, as revealed in the specifics of particular conversational/discourse usages. Once these state-of-mind scale scores are assigned to the interview text, the transcript is studied a third time (3) using features representative of the speaker's implicit or explicit attitudes toward attachment (Main et al., 2003).

First Reading: Examining a Speaker's Inferred Experiences with Parental Figures

In the first review of an interview text, the coder assigns ratings to each parent on five 9-point scales. Here 9 is a high rating, and 1 indicates that the transcript is sufficiently elaborated to allow the coder to infer that this experience was not present. (Where information is simply unavailable, rather than attempting a score, the coder records "n.i." for no information.) These include four scales for negative parental behavior (rejecting of attachment, role-inverting, neglecting, and pressuring to achieve) and a summary "loving" scale. Experience scores are assigned via the coder's own assessment of probable experiences, rather than what the interviewee states directly.

Each scale is introduced with exemplars of "what qualifies" as, for example, loving parental behavior, and qualifications for scores of 1, 3, 5, 7, and 9 are spelled out. Coders are urged to use the extremes of the scales as well as the middle ranges. With respect to "loving" parental behavior, for example, a rating of 9 (*Very loving*) can be assigned in the face of occasional untoward behavior. Similarly, a parent who provides for a child's physical well-being, academic, and material success, without any indications of personal attention or emotional availability, is rated a 1 (*Absence of loving behavior*). In this first experience-oriented pass through the text, coders record any significant losses, as well as abuse or other frightening events. A record is also made of moves from the original home, divorce, and the presence of any stepparents.

The eventual assignment of a transcript to an overall "organized" state of mind classification has no direct or consistent link to a speaker's probable experiences, except perhaps that when high loving scores are assigned to both parents, the overall classification most often is secure–autonomous. At the same time, low loving scores for both parents do not dictate an insecure classification, because placement in the secure–autonomous category is based exclusively on the overall coherence of the text. Because coherence can change, whereas life-history cannot, this latter point is no doubt of special import to all those involved in intervention.

Second Reading: Assigning Ratings on the "State-of-Mind" Interview Scales

Once the coder has assigned scores for probable experiences with each parent during childhood, he or she assigns scores on the several 9-point scales for language usage as it pertains to states of mind with respect to attachment. As we show below, when scores on particular state-of-mind scales are especially high, the coder is further directed to place the interview text in a particular, associated organized category. Before describing these scales and providing illustrations of the way they are utilized, we pause to consider them in terms of Grice's maxims (1975, 1989). This discussion clarifies how and why the state-of-mind scales are critical to determining AAI category placement. Whereas speakers who adhere to Grice's maxims for cooperative discourse are identified as secure, difficulties with particular maxims identify the two "organized" forms of insecurity:

1. Dismissing speakers largely violate Grice's maxim of quality ("Be truthful, and have evidence for what you say"), especially via high scores for *idealization* of the parent(s). Many dismissing speakers are also overly succinct, thus violating quantity. Excessive brevity is seen when the speaker implies that a given attachment figure is beneath discussion, via curt, contemptuous remarks, and receives high scores on the scale identifying *derogation*. Cutting short the conversational exchange can also occur via the use of statements such as an unelaborated "I don't remember," which is scored on the scale for *insistence on lack of memory for childhood*.

2. Preoccupied speakers, unlike dismissing speakers, usually adhere to the maxim of quality insofar as the coder is likely to agree if the speaker asserts that childhood experiences have been challenging. Where preoccupied speakers drift from and violate Grice's maxims is in terms of relevance (straying from the topic), quantity (going on at unnecessary length), and manner (showing peculiar, confusing, and noncollaborative speech). Violations pointing to the preoccupied classification are scored on the continuous scales identifying *passivity or vagueness of discourse* (violating manner) and *involved/involving anger* (often simultaneously violating relevance, quantity, and manner).

Scales Associated with the Dismissing Adult Attachment Category

Three scales are normally[5] associated with the dismissing adult attachment classification. Scores above a 5 on either idealization of an attachment figure or contemptuous derogation require that the text be assigned to the dismissing category. Insistence on lack of memory for childhood is also associated with this category and, as noted, often occurs in conjunction with idealization (and sometimes with derogation).

Idealization of a Primary Attachment Figure. This scale assesses the discrepancy between the overall view of the parent taken from the subject's speech at the abstract or semantic level, and the interviewer's inferences regarding the probable behavior of the parent. Because the speaker's actual history is, of course, unknown, any discrepancies come from within the transcript itself. For the higher ratings, there is a marked lack of unity between estimates of the speaker's probable experience with the primary attachment figure(s) and his or her positive to highly positive generalized or "semantic" descriptions. Thus, despite low scores assigned to a particular parent for loving behavior during childhood, the portrait presented is consistently positive. Additionally, gratuitous praise of the parents may be offered (e.g., references to "wonderful" or "excellent" parents).

As an illustration, we quote from one transcript wherein the adolescent speaker used only positive adjectives to describe his relationship with his mother. Later he would reveal that she nevertheless had both repeatedly threatened him and placed him in foster care in his early teens. At the outset of the interview, however, one of his adjectives for his mother had been *outstanding*.

INTERVIEWER: What about *outstanding*? You used that word to describe your relationship with your mother.

RESPONSE: Um, my mother is an outstanding person. She knows what is going on inside my head and she can understand me better than anyone else in the world and she just, oh, how can I describe it? She has always been there for me and I do find that outstanding.

As noted elsewhere in the transcript, this young person had referred to repeated threats to place him in care, and an actual placement in care. Nonetheless he responded as follows to the question regarding rejection:

INTERVIEWER: Did you ever feel pushed away or ignored by your parents?

RESPONSE: No, never.

INTERVIEWER: Your mom and dad?

RESPONSE: No, they have always been there. They've never pushed me away. They have never ignored me. They have always had to listen to what I've got to say. They have always seen what I've done and yeah, no.

The strong discrepancy between what he described his parents as having done (i.e., given him away to others) and his saying they had "always been there" and "never pushed me away" led to a high idealization score for this speaker.

Insistence on Lack of Memory for Childhood. This scale assesses the speaker's insistence upon her inability to recall her childhood, especially when she uses this to block further queries or discourse. The scale focuses on the subject's direct references to lack of memory. High ratings are given to speakers whose first response to numerous interview queries is "I don't remember," especially when this reply is repeated or remains firmly unelaborated.

> INTERVIEWER: I'd like you to try to describe your relationship with your parents as a young child ... if you could start from as far back as you can remember?
>
> RESPONSE: I don't remember.
>
> INTERVIEWER: Well, it can be hard. Just, well, why don't you just take a minute to think.
>
> RESPONSE: I don't remember that far back. Just normal.
>
> INTERVIEWER: Does anything come to mind?
>
> RESPONSE: No.

Active, Derogating Dismissal of Attachment-Related Experiences and/or Relationships. This scale deals with the cool, contemptuous dismissal of attachment relationships or experiences and their import, in which the speaker gives the impression that attention to attachment-related experiences (e.g., a friend's loss of a parent) or that one or more parental figures are foolish, laughable, or not worth the time.[6] As an example, an adopted teenager, who had experienced disrupted attachments and was currently being seen for significant attachment difficulties, used derogating statements throughout the interview to describe her difficult relationship with her mother.

> INTERVIEWER: What would be another word or phrase to describe your relationship with your mother?
>
> RESPONSE: Well, from 6 onwards I just thought she was a total cow and I hated her.

Asked later to about the nature of her current relationship with her mother, she replied as follows:

> RESPONSE: Um ... the same for ages, um, not talking to her, um ... still hate her.
>
> INTERVIEWER: You still hate her.
>
> RESPONSE: The same as it has been for god knows how many years.
>
> INTERVIEWER: So it has not changed a whole lot?
>
> RESPONSE: No.
>
> INTERVIEWER: What thing satisfies you most about your relationship with your mother?
>
> RESPONSE: When she is out of my way ... [Goldwyn, 2005].

Scales Associated with the Preoccupied Adult Attachment Category

High scores on either of the following state-of-mind scales—involving anger and passivity of discourse—lead to placement in the preoccupied category.

Involved/Involving Anger Expressed toward the Primary Attachment Figure(s). Accurate ratings on this scale depend on close attention to a particular form discourse can take when anger toward a particular attachment figure is implied or expressed. Importantly, direct descriptions of angry episodes involving past behavior ("I got so angry I picked her favorite magazine and threw it at her") or direct descriptions of current feelings of anger ("I'll try to discuss my current relationship with my mother, but I should let you know I'm really angry at her right now") would receive a rating of 1 on this scale. In contrast, high ratings are assigned to speech that includes, for example, run-on, grammatically entangled sentences describing situations involving the offending parent; subtle efforts to enlist interviewer agreement; unlicensed, extensive discussion of surprisingly small recent parental offenses; extensive use of psychological jargon (e.g., "My mother had a lot of material around that issue"); angrily addressing the parent as though he or she were present; and, in an angry context, slipping into unmarked quotations from the parent. Thus, when asked about his current relationship with his parents, one man responded with significantly angry preoccupied discourse that wandered from the topic. Below, he is asked to elaborate on why his current relationship with his father makes him sad.

> INTERVIEWER: And what's the part with your dad that is the most disappointing for you, that makes you sad?
>
> RESPONSE: When he smokes and drinks, I don't like it when he does that, well it is up to him what he does with his health but you know, I just think if he wants to waste his life away then he is doing that perfectly isn't he, that is just my opinion you know, his is probably "I like a few drinks and you know I can't help smoking because I've got addicted" and it's like well "You can always get someone to help you because you have done it before and you could always cut back on the amount of beer that you have every night or whatever" you you, so but he don't, he don't drink too much but he does drink a bit it's like the fridge is just clogged with alcohol it just like get the alcohol away it's like if you want to drink something just go and open a bottle of wine and I will be happy to drink that because beer is awful [Goldwyn, 2005].

Passivity or Vagueness in Discourse. High scores are assigned when, in many places within the transcript, the speaker seems unable to find words, seize on a meaning, or focus on a topic. Vague expressions or even nonsense words may be used, or a vague ending may be added to an already completed sentence (”I sat on his lap, *and that*”). Discourse is also considered vague/passive with respect to intrusions from irrelevant topics or slips into pronoun confusion between the self and the parent. In addition, as though absorbed into early childhood states or memories, the interviewee may inadvertently speak as a very young child ("I runned very fast") or describe experiences as they are described to a young child ("My mother washed my little feet"). Vague discourse should not be confused with restarts, hesitations, or dysfluency. The following passage would be assigned a high score for passivity:

> INTERVIEWER: Could you tell me a little bit more about why you used the word *close* to describe the relationship?

> RESPONSE: Well my mom, you know like she kind of shaded me in her. And I remember mornings I runned to be with her uh walking the . . . well the dog had a leash and I guess she had to go fast 'cause the dog was pulling on her, leash was like this big long leather thing I don't know whether you can still get those I haven't seen one long like that since I was little but a lot's changed since then, you know even when you think about like just going downtown and you look at the storefronts and things and the way the signs are and the lights and this and that and the other it's like a different world now (*continues . . .*).

Scales Associated with the Secure–Autonomous Adult Attachment Category

Coherence of Transcript. For high ratings, the speaker exhibits a steady and developing flow of ideas regarding attachment. The person may be reflective and slow to speak, with some pauses and hesitations, or speak quickly with a rapid flow of ideas. Overall, however, the person seems at ease with the topic, and discussions often have a quality of freshness. Although verbatim transcripts never look like written narratives, there are few significant violations of Grice's maxims of quantity, quality, relation, and manner. The reader has the impression that, on the whole, this text provides a "singular" as opposed to a "multiple" model of the speaker's experiences and their effects (as discussed by Main, 1991).

We supplied some examples of speech indicative of coherence in a secure–autonomous speaker's well-elaborated (hence, internally consistent) support for the term *loving* (pp. 41–42), and also when we referenced another speaker's care in venturing to describe why his or her parents may have behaved as they did (p. 45).

Although Grice's maxims are not notably violated by secure speakers (i.e., there is an absence of substantial indices of coherence violations), Main and colleagues' (2003) scoring system for the AAI in fact also includes positive indices of coherence that were not specifically described by Grice. Some of these add to the integrated nature of the text as a whole, such as when a speaker forewarns something the interviewer may want to ask about at a later time:

> "Well, in my childhood, my relationship with my parents was pretty good, like I guess I'll be saying, but when I was about 15, which I guess is you're calling out of childhood, it changed. Actually. And you may want to ask me more about that later."

Or the alert interviewee may not only struggle actively to answer a difficult question but also refuse to allow a tired or inattentive interviewer to (very incorrectly; see George et al., 1996) "put words in his mouth," as in the following example:

> RESPONSE: This last adjective is a hard one, um, something good, like *glad*, um, I know what I'm thinking but I just can't . . . I can't get it yet, wait, I . . .
>
> INTERVIEWER: (*breaking in*) Loving?
>
> RESPONSE: No. Not *loving*. It wasn't really a loving relationship, it's just there were times when we were um, well, happy with each other. Put down *happy at times*.

Metacognitive Monitoring or "Thinking about Thinking in the Moment" (Full Scale Development Still in Progress). For high ratings on this scale, evidence of active monitoring of thinking and recall is evident in several places within the interview. Thus, the speaker may comment on logical or factual contradictions in the account of his or her history, possible erroneous biases, and/or the fallibility of personal memory. Underlying metacognitive monitoring (Forguson & Gopnik, 1988) is active recognition and acceptance of an *appearance–reality distinction* (the speaker acknowledges that experiences may not have occurred as they are being presented), *representational diversity* (the speaker remarks that a sibling does not share his or her view of the father), and *representational change* (the speaker remarks that what is said today might not have been said yesterday). Here are some examples:

> "That's how I see it at least. But come to think of it, my father might see our childhood relationship entirely differently. It's been a while since we saw each other."

> "Rejected? No, I didn't feel rejected. No. Well . . . I say 'no' but, um, maybe I'm just not admitting it [7-second pause]. OK, if I look back on it, back then I—I guess I did feel rejected."

Coherence of Mind. Ratings on this scale are assigned only after scores for all other state-of-mind scales have been undertaken. As an example, a speaker who stumbles sufficiently to be unclear in places, and whose transcript includes many dysfluencies and restarted sentences—yet whose underlying thinking is nonetheless readily comprehensible when carefully read—may receive a higher score on coherence of mind than on coherence of transcript. In a second, contrasting example, a speaker who is generally coherent and fits to the secure–autonomous classification may also be unresolved/disorganized (e.g., having elevated scores for lapses in reasoning regarding dead–not-dead status of a loved one, see below). Although the unresolved/disorganized status may have been derived from just a few sentences, it is clear that the global coherence of this speaker's "mind" is lower than the linguistic coherence seen in the transcript as a whole.

Once a transcript has been assigned scores on each of the aforementioned scales, the coder consults a table within the AAI manual (Main et al., 2003) that ordinarily allows the coder to turn any particular configuration of scores into a best-fitting classification. Thus, if scores for idealization of one or both parents are high, as are scores for insistence on lack of memory, the dismissing classification is assigned. This process of moving from individual scale scores to the various configurations of scores that point to placement in one of the three organized categories is informally termed the *bottom-up* approach to AAI classification.

Third Reading: Classifying AAI Texts via Apparent Attitudes toward Attachment (a "Feature Analysis")

In this final step in identifying an organized category, coders determine the applicability of all features associated with each major classification (and later, subclassification; see Steele & Steele, Chapter 1, this volume) to the transcript at hand. These features are delineated in a section of the scoring and classification manual designed exclusively for this purpose. In completing their work with this aspect of the transcript, coders indicate whether each feature is present to a strong, moderate, or weak degree.

Here, we elaborate upon some of the features that point to particular AAI classifications. In the analysis actually undertaken, some of the features listed in the manual guidelines are *required* for classification placement, whereas others are simply noted as frequent correlates. Features leading to a particular categorical/classificatory placement are informally termed the *top-down* approach to text analysis, and should dovetail with the classification derived from the *bottom-up* configurations produced by the state-of-mind scales.

Insofar as is possible, this final step is undertaken independently of consideration of the continuous scale scores. This makes a cross-check available: If the *bottom-up* (scales) and *top-down* (overall features) analyses do not point to the same classification, then the interview transcript is rechecked. Provided that the coder still considers his or her discordant judgments accurate following this rechecking, then the interview transcript is placed in the "cannot classify" category (below).

Attitudes toward Attachment Leading to Secure–Autonomous Category Placement

As always, the reader should remember that for parents, the AAI classifications are predictive of the quality of their infant's attachment to them. Hence, in pointing to features identified with each of the three AAI classifications, we are essentially highlighting attitudes toward attachment that predominate in persons who raise infants falling in particular organized attachment categories. Due to space limitations, we outline only some of the most striking and distinguishing features associated with each organized category.

The following features would point to a secure–autonomous category placement:

• Whether openly or subtly, the speaker indicates the capacity for missing, needing, and depending on others. At places in the interview, the speaker states that attachment-related experiences have affected his or her development or functioning.

Statements applicable to these features could include:

"And I really missed her, more than I even expected. I was so happy to see her, and actually, when we've been apart awhile, I still feel that way now."

"I guess one setback was the way I took my mother's criticism to heart. I think it made me a little paranoid and I try too hard to be 'perfect' even now."

• The interviewee seems open and "free to explore" the attachment-related interview topic, treating the recounting and evaluation of his or her life history with respect to attachment as neither "closed" nor "foreign." The speaker can flexibly change his or her view of person or event, even while interview is in progress, suggesting autonomy and ultimate objectivity.

A statement fitting to these headings could include:

"OK, well I guess I'd have to say closer to my father than my mother. I know I said I saw a lot more of my mother and that's true, but the way I felt—inside, I guess, I did, I felt closer to my father. That's not how I ever saw myself up to now, but with all the things we've been discussing."

• A sense of balance, proportion, or humor.

"OK, my dad was flawed, I was flawed, we've discussed it backwards and forwards. Sometimes he flagellates himself over his inadequacies, but then just when I'm feeling pretty righteous he rears up again and flagellates me over mine. Sometimes we end up laughing. I guess neither of us is quite housebroken."

• Seems at ease with imperfections in the self. Relatedly, there is explicit or implicit forgiveness of/compassion for/acceptance of parents' failings.

"I try to call my parents a lot and I should, I really should, but my wife and kids and my work—well, I attend to them and sometimes that means I put my parents second, even though they're getting old now. I do keep trying to look in on them more often now. And they're still very difficult people, guess that how it's going to stay, that hasn't changed."

• Ruefully cites untoward flawed behavior of self appearing at times despite conscious intentions or efforts.

"When I'm with [child] I try hard not to be like my mom was with me, and most of the time I guess I succeed most days. But sometimes I act just like her. I feel so bad but I do. I hear her raging, screaming voice in mine. But I try to catch myself, and when I do, I apologize."

Attitudes toward Attachment Leading to Placement in the Dismissing Category

• Self is described positively as being strong, independent, or normal, with little or no articulation of hurt, distress, or feelings of needing or depending on others. The speaker minimizes or downplays descriptions of negative experiences, and may interpret such experiences positively, in that they have made the self stronger.

"My parents raised me strictly. They used the belt on me when I needed it, didn't with my little brother. I'm, a lot stronger than he is because of it. I handle stress at work a lot better than he does, and I'm more independent, I've noticed."

• Responses are abstract, and seem remote from present or remembered feelings, or memories, and the topic of the interview seems foreign. Often, for example, the speaker may emphasize fun or activities with parents, or presents and other material objects when asked about relationships.

"My relationship with my parents in childhood. Um, lots of toys, lots of fun things, piles of toys at Christmas, pretty much spoiled me with toys I'd have to say. So . . . I'd say, both of them, really great parents."

• Identifies with negative aspects of the parent's behavior.

"They didn't go visit my sister at boarding school because we knew she didn't need it. She was 8 that year, like I was when I left for boarding school. Time for her to learn like I did."

Attitudes toward Attachment Leading to Placement
in the Preoccupied Category

• The topic of the interview is addressed, but it seems inflexible and closed. Interview responses may seem memorized.

> "Yeah, from my early life with my parents, I've realized they were totally dysfunctional, and why they were. I could tell you all about that."

• Responses to the interview are persistently tied to experiences with the parents, even when these experiences are not the topic of inquiry.

> "What would I hope for my child's future? To begin with, not to turn out to be the kind of parent my parents were."

• The speaker may attempt to involve the interviewer in agreement regarding the parent's faults.

> "She was impossible, just selfish and impossible. You know the type I mean, right?"

• The speaker may oscillate repeatedly and indecisively in evaluations of parents, sometimes within the same sentence.

> "Great mother—well, not really. Mothering wasn't her area. No, I mean actually, really grateful to her, except when she . . . "

• Unbalanced, excessive blaming of either the parents or the self.

> "My mother had a hard time with me when I was little. I had a hard temperament to deal with. Guess I was too much for her . . ."

The Cannot Classify and Unresolved/Disorganized AAI Categories: Global and Local Breakdowns in Discourse Strategy

As noted in our introduction to this chapter, the *cannot classify* and *unresolved/disorganized* categories had not been discovered when the AAI scoring and classification system was first developed. This was probably due to their subtlety and complexity, which left them unrecognized until the three organized categories were well understood. As is often true, "exceptions to the rule" only become apparent after much basic experience with a particular phenomenon has been obtained.

As soon as these two categories began to appear within AAI manuals in the late 1980s, they were found to be especially prevalent among persons in severe psychological difficulty—for example, patients diagnosed with borderline, dissociative, and obsessive–compulsive disorders, as well as psychiatrically distressed forensic populations (for overviews, see van IJzendoorn & Bakermans-Kranenburg, 1996; Chapter 3, this volume). Thus, an understanding of these two latter AAI categories is inevitably of special relevance to clinicians.

We first discuss the *cannot classify* category, which represents contradictions and anomalies usually seen throughout the transcript. The unresolved/disorganized category differs from the cannot classify category in that it is identified via brief or "local" disruptions in discourse during the discussion of loss or other potential trauma.

The Cannot Classify (Unorganized) Interview Category

The cannot classify category emerged in the early 1990s as expert judges began noting a small percentage of transcripts that failed to meet criteria for placement in one of the three central or organized attachment categories. This was first observed in transcripts where, for example, an unsupported positive description of one of the parents led to a relatively high idealization score, yet in direct contradiction to the expected accompanying global patterning, this same parent was later discussed in an angrily preoccupied manner. Thus, although a high score for idealization would have called for placement in the dismissing category, at the same time speech indicative of preoccupation was also evident at high levels in other places. It was therefore concluded (see Hesse, 1996) that these transcripts were unclassifiable and should be placed in a separate group.

To illustrate an AAI transcript designated as cannot classify, we use extracts from a text originally presented by Hesse (1996). In part of his interview the speaker, Mr. K, indicated that he had suffered neglect, rejection, and physical abuse from his parents, and that he still had a scar "from one of the beatings." Nonetheless, at the opening of the interview he had described his relationship with his parents as "pretty good . . . everything was fine . . . I didn't have any problems." He used the following five descriptors for his relationship with his mother: *placid*, *friendly*, *uninvolved*, *easy*, and *tensionless*. Mr. K said that these five adjectives would describe his relationship with his father as well. This degree of "semantic–episodic" discrepancy (see p. 50), of course, led to very high scores for idealization, and fit the dismissing AAI category.

However, in a strong departure from the dismissing stance just described, this interview also contained substantial lapses into angrily preoccupied speech that led to a high score for involved/involving anger. Hence, placement in the preoccupied category was warranted as well. The following examples are excerpts from three consecutive pages of preoccupied speech within Mr. K's AAI:

"But my father got off easy, since he wasn't the religious fanatic and he wasn't on this really horrible power trip. . . . And so my mother had this

... and it was reinforced constantly as I was growing up that my mother had a very warped view of sex, and she thought it was dirty and nasty and evil and horrible and, you know, disgusting. ... But see whenever she told us anything it was just really stupid things and so, like . . . and . . . I would try and make her feel better and then she would kind of get hysterical on me saying that I should be like this when obviously I was trying to make her feel better, and I did not want to be told how I should be like and how I should live the way she wanted me to live, and have the same attitudes."

As the reader can see, this approach to the interview task reveals two incompatible strategies for the organization of information relevant to attachment that lead to scores forcing placement in two opposing insecure categories; therefore, it is assigned to the cannot classify category.

A second type of unclassifiable transcript was identified in the same year (Minde & Hesse, 1996), when Hesse was asked to analyze an AAI text without knowing that the speaker was a woman being seen in therapy. The patient, Mrs. A, had been noted by her therapist to be unusual in several ways (e.g., in demanding successfully to have her infant removed from her body at fetal age 8 months, and—immediately following birth, when her infant was necessarily placed in intensive care—in visiting continually and demanding to breast-feed against the requests of the nurses).

It was concluded that the interview text of Mrs. A—like that of Mr. K—should also be considered unclassifiable, in this case due to overall low coherence of transcript in the absence of elevated insecure state-of-mind scores. Therefore, Mrs. A's AAI was described as presenting a second type of unclassifiable or cannot classify text. Interestingly, however, despite the lack of observable contradictory strategies within the text, Mrs. A's therapist observed that long after the postnatal period, her caregiving behavior still alternated startlingly between minimizing/dismissing and maximizing/preoccupied behavior.

Although emerging within journal articles as early as 1996, this second subtype of the cannot classify category has only recently been added to the AAI scoring and classification manual and—given the articulation of new guidelines (Main et al., 2003)—used by advanced coders (e.g., Ivarsson, Chapter 9, this volume). The reason for this delay had been the far greater difficulty involved in learning how to recognize texts of this latter kind, and it is still recommended that only highly practiced coders attempt this type of cannot classify identification.

However, it does appear that "low coherence" transcripts of this newer kind, like those displaying "contradictory strategies," do predict disorganized and unclassifiable offspring responses (Behrens, Hesse, & Main, 2007). Other AAI researchers have also found convincing and intriguing reasons why certain texts do not fit to the earlier "contradictory strategies" approach to identifying unclassifiability. These have included, for example, apparent complete absence of attachment representations in a Holocaust survivor (Koren-Karie,

Sagi-Schwartz, & Joels, 2003), and *self-derogation* (for which there is as yet no scale) seen in forensic populations (Turton et al., 2001). It is not known yet whether these same texts will also fit to the "low coherence" formulations of the newer manuals.

The Unresolved/Disorganized Attachment Category

Main and Goldwyn had noted as early as 1984 that the parents of disorganized/disoriented infants often spoke in unusual ways regarding loss experiences. Thus, these speakers seemed "unresolved," but the particulars of how and why were as yet difficult to specify or articulate. Over time, however, it would become increasingly clear that what the parents of disorganized infants exhibited could be termed *lapses in the monitoring of reasoning or discourse* during discussions of loss or other potentially traumatic experiences. These discourse–reasoning lapses suggested temporary alterations in consciousness, and are now believed to represent either interference from normally dissociated memory or belief systems, or unusual absorptions involving memories triggered by the discussion of traumatic events (Hesse & Main, 2006).

Lapses in the monitoring of *reasoning* are manifested in statements that appear to violate our usual understanding of physical causality or time–space relations. Marked examples of reasoning lapses are seen when speakers make statements indicating that a deceased person is believed to be simultaneously dead and not dead in the physical sense, for example:

> "It was almost better when she died, because then she could get on with being dead and I could get on with raising my family."

This statement implies a belief, operative at least in that moment, that the deceased remains alive in the physical sense (albeit perhaps in a parallel world). Statements of this kind may indicate the existence of incompatible belief and memory systems that, normally dissociated or segregated from one another, have intruded into consciousness simultaneously as a result of the interviewer's questions. Another example of a lapse in reasoning would include a statement such as the following:

> "I'm still afraid he died that night because I forgot to think about him. I promised to think about him and I did, but that night I went out, and so he died."

Lapses in the monitoring of discourse, in contrast, sometimes suggest that the topic has triggered a "state shift" indicative of considerable absorption, that frequently appears to involve entrance into peculiar, compartmentalized, or even partially dissociated/segregated states of mind (Hesse & Main, 2006). Thus, for example, an abrupt alteration or shift in speech register inappropriate to the discourse context occurs when a speaker moves from his or her ordinary conversational style into a eulogistic or funereal manner of speaking, or pays excessive attention to detail. Some specific examples include the following:

"She was young, she was lovely, she was dearly beloved by all who knew her, and who witnessed her as she was torn from us by that most dreaded of diseases, tuberculosis. And then, like a flower torn from the ground at its moment of splendor . . . "

"He died 32 years ago last month, on March 1, a Monday, right before his 32nd birthday. It was a spring day, and I remember when I rode to the hospital, I took the bus, and then I got off at LaForge Street, and then I turned down Gamercy, and then suddenly I was there at Washington, and . . . "

Both state shifts and the sudden appearance of incompatible ideas suggest momentary but qualitative changes in consciousness. Thus, they appear to represent temporary/local as opposed to global breakdowns in the speaker's discourse strategy. Discourse–reasoning lapses of the kinds just described often occur in high-functioning individuals and are normally not representative of a speaker's overall conversational style. For this reason, among others, transcripts assigned to the unresolved/disorganized (hereafter, *unresolved*) category are given a best-fitting alternate classification (e.g., unresolved/dismissing).

In 1990, Main and Hesse showed for the first time that unresolved AAI status in a parent was markedly predictive of infant disorganized attachment status as assigned by independent coders when parent and infant had been observed within the Strange Situation procedure 5 years previously. Nine-point scales for both indices of unresolved loss and abuse were later devised, and this original result linking disorganization in parental AAI texts and infant disorganized Strange Situation behavior has been well replicated in later studies (van IJzendoorn, Schungel, & Bakermans-Kranenburg, 1999). More recent studies have continued to show significant relations between these adult and infant phenomena. Some important extensions of the links between infant disorganization and a parent's unresolved mental state have been, for example, reported in studies involving the next-born child following miscarriage (Bakermans-Kranenburg, Schuengel, & van IJzendoorn, 1999), and stillbirth (Hughes, Turton, Hopper, McGauley, & Fonagy, 2001).

We end this discussion of disorganized AAI texts by referring once more to the speaker's likely concomitant experiences of fear (Hesse & Main, 1999, 2000, 2006; see also Main & Hesse, 1990). As we noted at the outset in this chapter, infant disorganized Strange Situation behavior has been found associated with frightened, frightening, dissociative, and other forms of anomalous parental behavior (Hesse & Main, 1999, 2000, 2006; Lyons-Ruth et al., 1999; Main & Hesse, 1990). More recently, direct relations have been established between unresolved/disorganized and cannot classify parental status, and the exhibition of such behaviors in the presence of the offspring. Like lapses in the monitoring of speech or reasoning seen within AAI texts, such behaviors may result from the effects of fear upon the maintenance of normal consciousness. Thus, for unresolved and cannot classify parents, fear may intrude upon interactions with the infant in the form of (often inadvertently) frightening behaviors (Abrams, Rifkin, & Hesse, 2006; Jacobvitz, Leon, & Hazen, 2006), leading to disorganization and disorientation in the infant under stress.

Conclusion

The AAI is a semistructured protocol that focuses on an individual's description and evaluation of salient early attachment experiences, and the ways these experiences are perceived to have affected current personality and functioning. The verbatim interview text is analyzed via an accompanying scoring and classification system, which serves to identify five differing "states of mind with respect to attachment," each corresponding to a particular category of offspring Strange Situation response to the speaker. The continuous scales that assist in identifying classificatory status were found some years following their development to have a striking conceptual fit to those aspects of the work of H.P. Grice, which pertained to the ideal of cooperative, rational discourse. Perhaps the most critical finding regarding Grice's approach to the analysis of language as adapted for use with the AAI is that *the parents of insecure infants seldom appear able to discuss their own attachment-related experiences without significantly violating one or more of Grice's conversational maxims.* In contrast, the maintenance of coherence and collaboration during these discussions has repeatedly been shown to predict secure infant attachment. Additionally (see van IJzendoorn & Bakermans-Kranenburg, Chapter 3, this volume), cooperative, coherent discourse maintained during the AAI is associated with emotional health, while uncooperative, incoherent discourse is associated with clinical levels of difficulties. However, as Levy and his colleagues demonstrated in their study of borderline patients (see Preface, p. xviii), 1 year of psychotherapy—which cannot alter a person's life history, but may engender changes in the way it is described and evaluated—can significantly increase both the degree of coherence seen in AAI narratives and the proportion of patients who are judged secure-autonomous.

Finally, we note that the tradition of AAI research conforms closely to vital aspects of the consulting room, where clinicians listen to what a patient says, paying careful attention to what is said, to how it is said, and as well to what is not said. This way of listening is likely to be significantly enhanced by familiarity with the AAI and the expanding body of literature related to it. In turn, as increasing numbers of individuals utilize the protocol and learn[7] its accompanying system of analysis, new avenues for refining and improving upon clinical interventions will likely be created—as this volume attests.

Acknowledgments

We are grateful to Howard and Miriam Steele not only for excouraging us through many rereadings of this chapter, but as well for their careful explication of the relation between the AAI and Bowlby's original thinking, utilized within our introduction. They have gone far beyond the usual editorial role in contributing to this chapter.

Notes

1. This, of course, is estimated from the judge's study of the full text rather than simply the speaker's overt attempts at presentation; even then, it will be subject to inaccuracies (Hesse, 1999, 2008).
2. Occasionally, a speaker may be unfamiliar with the word *adjective* (e.g., owing to lack of schooling); in such cases the interviewer speaks instead of *words* or *phrases* that describe what the relationship was like.
3. Violations of these maxims are permitted when "licensed" by the speaker (see Grice [1989] and Mura [1983]). An excessively long speech turn can, for example be licensed if the speaker begins, "Well, I'm afraid this is going to be quite a long story," whereas a very short turn can be licensed by "I'm really sorry, but I don't feel able to discuss this right now."
4. Although the interviewer encourages the speaker to provide five adjectives, and indicates readiness to wait, not all speakers provide this many. This early in the interview it is not necessarily indicative of insecure attachment status, especially given that a fuller description of interactions with a given parent may appear later on.
5. High scores on a scale for *fear of loss from an unknown source* are used to place speakers in the dismissing category (subcategory Ds4). This subcategory is sufficiently rare that the scale is not detailed in this chapter.
6. Derogation is rare in low-risk samples but is more prevalent in clinical samples. Derogating statements are noted for their dismissing brevity and the speaker's the apparent intent of casting the individual or topic aside (see recent discussions by Goldwyn, 2005; Turton, McGauley, Marin-Avellan, & Hughes, 2001; Wallis & Steele, 2001).
7. Training in the analysis of the Adult Attachment Interview takes place through a 2-week institute involving one or two certified trainers and 15–20 participants. Usually about seven institutes are offered per year, and are taught only by those who have been certified to train via (1) participation in two full conventional institutes, and (2) 2–3 weeks of participation in "training-to-train" institutes held by Main and Hesse. Those interested in obtaining training in the analysis of the AAI should contact any or several of the following 11 certified trainers regarding upcoming institutes: Anders Broberg, *Anders.Broberg@psy.gu.se*; Nino Dazzi, *Nino.Dazzi@uniroma1.it*; Sonia Gojman de Millán, *sgojman@yahoo.com*; Erik Hesse, Fax: (510) 642-5293; Tord Ivarsson, *Tord.Ivarsson@vgregion. se*; Deborah Jacobvitz, *debj@mail.utexas.edu*; Nancy Kaplan, *Nancy_Kaplan@hotmail.com*; Mary Main, Fax: (510) 642-5293; David and Deanne Pederson, *Pederson@uwo.ca*; and June Sroufe, *jsroufe@visi.com*. Trainings are frequently offered in the United States, as well as Canada, the United Kingdom, Italy, Scandinavia, Mexico, and occasionally in other regions and countries.

The AAI protocol is available from Main and Hesse at University of California, Berkeley (fax number above). Those wishing to be trained and certified in the analysis of AAI transcripts must not only attend an AAI institute with one of the trainers listed above, but also be found reliable via a reliability check in which agreement is established with Main and Hesse across 30 transcripts. The certification rate is high, and 50 new coders—among them, of course, practicing clinicians—were certified in 2007.

References

Abrams, K.Y., Rifkin, A., & Hesse, E. (2006). Examining the role of parental frightened/frightening sub-types in predicting disorganized attachment within a brief observational procedure. *Development and Psychopathology, 18*, 345–361.

Ainsworth, M. D., Blehar, M. C., Waters, E., & Wall, S. (1978). *Patterns of attachment: Assessed in the Strange Situation and at home.* Hillsdale, NJ: Erlbaum.

Bakermans-Kranenburg, M. J., Schuengel, C., & van IJzendoorn, M. H. (1999). Unresolved loss due to miscarriage: An addition to the Adult Attachment Interview. *Attachment and Human Development, 1*, 157–170.

Balint, A. (1949). Love for the mother and mother-love. *International Journal of Psychoanalysis, 30*, 251–259. (Original work published 1939)

Behrens, K. Y., Hesse, E., & Main, M. (2007). Mothers' attachment status as determined by the Adult Attachment Interview predicts their 6-year-olds' reunion responses: A study conducted in Japan. *Developmental Psychology, 43*, 1553–1567.

Benoit, D., & Parker, K. (1994). Stability and transmission of attachment across three generations. *Child Development, 55*, 706–717.

Bowlby, J. (1973). *Attachment and loss: Vol. 2. Separation.* New York: Basic Books.

Bowlby, J. (1979). *The making and breaking of affectional bonds.* London: Tavistock.

Bowlby, J. (1980). *Attachment and loss: Vol. 3. Loss.* New York: Basic Books.

Bowlby, J. (1982). *Attachment and loss: Vol. 1. Attachment.* London: Hogarth Press. (Original work published 1969)

Capps, L., & Oakes, E. (1995). *Constructing panic: The discourse of agoraphobia.* Cambridge, MA: Harvard University Press.

Carlson, E. A. (1998). A prospective longitudinal study of disorganized/disoriented attachment. *Child Development, 69*, 1107–1128.

Fairbairn, W. R. D. (1952). *Psychoanalytic studies of the personality.* London: Routledge.

Fonagy, P., Steele, H., & Steele, M. (1991). Maternal representations of attachment during pregnancy predict the organisation of infant–mother attachment at one-year. *Child Development, 62*, 891–905.

Fonagy, P., Steele, M., Steele, H., Moran, G., & Higgitt, A. (1991). The capacity for understanding mental states: The reflective self in parent and child and its significance for security of attachment. *Infant Mental Health Journal, 12*, 201–218.

Forguson, L., & Gopnik, A. (1988). The ontogeny of common sense. In J. W. Astington & P. L. Harris (Eds.), *Developing theories of mind* (pp. 226–243). New York: Cambridge University Press.

George, C., Kaplan N., & Main, M. (1985). *The Adult Attachment Interview.* Unpublished manuscript, University of California, Berkeley.

George, C., Kaplan, N., & Main, M. (1996). *The Adult Attachment Interview.* Unpublished manuscript, University of California, Berkeley.

Goldwyn, R. (2005). *What can the Adult Attachment Interview contribute to the assessment of attachment disorders and difficulties in adolescence: A pilot study.* Unpublished doctoral thesis, Academic Unit of Psychiatry and Behavioural Sciences, University of Leeds, Leeds, UK.

Grice, H. P. (1975). Logic and conversation. In P. Cole & J. L. Moran (Eds.), *Syntax and semantics* (Vol. 3, pp. 41–58). New York: Academic Press.

Grice, H. P. (1989). *Studies in the way of words.* Cambridge, MA: Harvard University Press.

Hesse, E. (1996). Discourse, memory and the Adult Attachment Interview: A note with emphasis on the emerging cannot classify category. *Infant Mental Health Journal, 17,* 4–11.

Hesse, E. (1999). The Adult Attachment Interview: Historical and current perspectives. In J. Cassidy & P. R. Shaver (Eds.), *Handbook of attachment: Theory, research, and clinical applications* (pp. 395–433). New York: Guilford Press.

Hesse, E. (2008). The Adult Attachment Interview: An overview. In J. Cassidy & P. R. Shaver (Eds.), *Handbook of attachment: Theory, research, and clinical applications.* New York: Guilford Press.

Hesse, E., & Main, M. (1999). Second-generation effects of unresolved trauma in nonmaltreating parents: Dissociated, frightened, and threatening parental behavior. *Psychoanalytic Inquiry, 19,* 481–540.

Hesse, E., & Main, M. (2000). Disorganized infant, child, and adult attachment: Collapse in behavioral and attentional strategies. *Journal of the American Psychoanalytic Association, 48*(4), 1097–1127.

Hesse, E., & Main, M. (2006). Frightened, threatening, and dissociative parental behavior in low-risk samples: Description, discussion, and interpretations. *Development and Psychopathology, 18,* 309–343.

Hughes, P., Turton, P., Hopper, E., McGauley, G. A., & Fonagy, P. (2001). Disorganized attachment behavior among infants born subsequent to stillbirth. *Journal of Child Psychology and Psychiatry, 42,* 791–801.

Jacobvitz, D., Leon, K., & Hazen, N. (2006). Does expectant mothers' unresolved trauma predict frightened/frightening maternal behavior?: Risk and protective factors. *Development and Psychopathology, 18,* 363–380.

Koren-Karie, N., Sagi-Schewartz, A., & Joels, T. (2003). Absence of attachment representations (AAR) in the adult years: The emergence of a new AAI classification in catastrophically traumatized Holocaust child survivors. *Attachment and Human Development, 4,* 381–397.

Lyons-Ruth, K., Bronfman, E., & Parsons, E. (1999). Maternal frightened, frightening or atypical behavior and disorganized infant attachment patterns. *Monographs of the Society for Research in Child Development, 64*(3), 67–96.

Lyons-Ruth, K., Connell, D. B., Zoll, D., & Stahl, J. (1987). Infants at social risk: Relations among infant maltreatment, maternal behavior, and infant behavior. *Developmental Psychology, 23,* 223–232.

Main, M. (1985, April). *A move to the level of representation: The Adult Attachment Interview.* Paper presented at the meeting of the Society for Research in Child Development, Toronto, Canada.

Main, M. (1990). Cross-cultural studies of attachment organization: Recent studies, changing methodologies, and the concept of conditional strategies. *Human Development*, *33*, 48–61.

Main, M. (1991). Metacognitive knowledge, metacognitive monitoring, and singular (coherent) versus multiple (incoherent) models of attachment: Findings and directions for future research. In C. M. Parkes, J. Stevenson-Hinde, & P. Marris (Eds.), *Attachment across the life cycle* (pp. 127–159). London: Routledge.

Main, M. (1993). Discourse, prediction, and recent studies in attachment: Implications for psychoanalysis. *Journal of the American Psychoanalytic Association*, *41*(Suppl.), 209–244.

Main, M. (1995). Recent studies in attachment: Overview, with implications for clinical work. In S. Goldberg, R. Muir, & J. Kerr (Eds.), *Attachment theory: Social, developmental, and clinical perspectives* (pp. 407–474). Hillsdale, NJ: Analytic Press.

Main, M. (2000). The Adult Attachment Interview: Fear, attention, safety, and discourse processes. *Journal of the American Psychoanalytic Association*, *48*, 1055–1096.

Main, M., & Goldwyn, R. (1984a). *Adult attachment scoring and classification system*. Unpublished manuscript, University of California, Berkeley.

Main, M., & Goldwyn, R. (1984b). Predicting rejection of her infant from mother's representation of her own experience: Implications for the abused-abusing intergenerational cycle. *Child Abuse and Neglect*, *8*, 203–217.

Main, M., & Goldwyn, R. (1988). Unpublished data, University of California, Berkeley.

Main, M., Goldwyn, R., & Hesse, E. (2003). *Adult Attachment Classification System version 7.2*. Unpublished manuscript, University of California, Berkeley.

Main, M., & Hesse, E. (1990). Parents' unresolved traumatic experiences are related to infant disorganized attachment status: Is frightened/frightening parental behavior the linking mechanism? In M. T. Greenberg, D. Cicchetti, & E. M. Cummings (Eds.), *Attachment in the preschool years: Theory, research, and intervention* (pp. 161–182). Chicago: University of Chicago Press.

Main, M., Hesse, E., & Kaplan, N. (2005). Predictability of attachment behavior and representational processes at 1, 6, and 19 years of age: The Berkeley Longitudinal Study: Attachment. In K. E. Grossmann, K. Grossmann, & E. Waters (Eds.), *Attachment from infancy to adulthood: The major longitudinal studies* (pp. 245–304). New York: Guilford Press.

Main, M., Kaplan, N., & Cassidy, J. (1985). Security in infancy, childhood and adulthood: A move to the level of representation. *Monographs of the Society for Research in Child Development*, *50*(1–2, Serial No. 209), 66–104.

Main, M., & Solomon, J. (1986). Discovery of a new, insecure-disorganized/ disoriented attachment pattern. In T. B. Brazelton & M. Yogman (Eds.), Affective development in infancy (pp. 95–124). Norwood, NJ: Ablex.

Main, M., & Solomon, J. (1990). Procedures for identifying infants as disorganized/ disoriented during the Ainsworth Strange Situation. In M. T. Greenberg, D. Cichetti, & E. M. Cummings (Eds.), *Attachment in the preschool years* (pp. 121–160). Chicago: University of Chicago Press.

Minde, K., & Hesse, E. (1996). The role of the Adult Attachment Interview in parent–infant psychotherapy: A case presentation. *Infant Mental Health Journal*, *17*(2), 115–126.

Mura, S. S. (1983). Licensing violations: Legitimate violations of Grice's conversational principle. In R. T. Craig & K. Tracy (Eds.), *Conversational coherence:
Form, structure and strategy.* Beverly Hills, CA: Sage.

Ogawa, J. R., Sroufe, A. L., Weinfield, N. S., Carlson, E. A., & Egeland, B. (1997).
Development and the fragmented self: Longitudinal study of dissociative symptoms in a non-clinical sample. *Development and Psychopathology, 9,* 855–879.

Solomon, J., George, C., & DeJong, A. (1995). Children classified as controlling at age
six: Evidence for disorganized representational strategies and aggression at home
and at school. *Development and Psychopathology, 7,* 447–463.

Spitz, R. (1965). *The first year of life.* New York: International Universities Press.

Steele, H., Steele, M., & Fonagy, P. (1996). Associations among attachment classifications of mothers, fathers, and their infants. *Child Development, 67,* 541–555.

Turton, P., McGauley, G., Marin-Avellan, L., & Hughes, P. (2001). The Adult Attachment Interview: Rating and classification problems posed by non-normative samples. *Attachment and Human Development, 3*(3), 284–303.

van IJzendoorn, M. (1995). Adult attachment representations, parental responsiveness,
and infant attachment: A meta-analysis on the predictive validity of the Adult
Attachment Interview. *Psychological Bulletin, 117*(3), 387–403.

van IJzendoorn, M. H., & Bakermans-Kranenburg, M. J. (1996). Attachment representations in mothers, fathers, adolescents, and clinical groups: A meta-analytic
search for normative data. *Journal of Consulting and Clinical Psychology, 64,* 8–
21.

van IJzendoorn, M. H., Schuengel, C., & Bakermans-Kranenburg, M. J. (1999). Disorganized attachment in early childhood: Meta-analysis of precursors, concomitants, and sequelae. *Development and Psychopathology, 11,* 225–249.

Wallis, P., & Steele, H. (2001). Attachment representations in adolescence: Further evidence from psychiatric residential settings. *Attachment and Human Development, 3*(3), 259–268.

Ward, M. J., & Carlson, E. A. (1995). Associations among adult attachment representations, maternal sensitivity, and infant–mother attachment in a sample of adolescent mothers. *Child Development, 66,* 69–79.

Winnicott, D. W. (1953). Transitional objects and transitional phenomena. *International Journal of Psychoanalysis, 34,* 1–9.

3

==

The Distribution of Adult Attachment Representations in Clinical Groups

A Meta-Analytic Search for Patterns of Attachment in 105 AAI Studies

MARINUS H. VAN IJZENDOORN
and MARIAN J. BAKERMANS-KRANENBURG

How are attachment representations associated with psychological disorders? Some 10 years ago Dozier suggested that preoccupied attachment representations might be associated with felt experience of distress and be expressed in internalizing disorders such as depression or borderline personality disorder, whereas dismissing representations might be associated with more externalizing indices of distress, such as eating disorders, conduct disorders, and hard-drug use (Dozier, Chase Stovall, & Albus, 1999; Dozier & Tyrrell, 1997). In recent years the role of disorganized or disoriented attachment representations has been stressed. Unresolved attachments are suggested to be important in the emergence of disorders with a dissociative component, such as posttraumatic stress disorder, and to make individuals more vulnerable to developing psychopathology (Harari, Bakermans-Kranenburg, & van IJzendoorn, 2007; Hesse, 1999b; Liotti, 2004; Sroufe, Egeland, Carlson, & Collins, 2005).

Here we draw on the accumulated data collected with the Adult Attachment Interview (AAI; George, Kaplan, & Main, 1985; Main, Kaplan, & Cassidy, 1985; see Bakermans-Kranenburg & van IJzendoorn, 1993, for the first psychometric validation) to test the hypothesis that in clinical groups insecure attachment categories are overrepresented, in particular the insecure–unresolved category. Furthermore, we explore systematic patterns in the association between attachment representations and clinical disorders, in particular the potential link between dismissing attachments and externalizing problems compared to the possible overrepresentation of preoccupied and unresolved classifications in the case of internalizing disorders. Our previous meta-analysis focusing on these issues was conducted more than a decade ago (van IJzendoorn & Bakermans-Kranenburg, 1996). Because the number of AAI studies has increased dramatically (more than 9,000 individuals participated in the AAI since its inception), it is now time to take stock of the available evidence for a more grounded association between attachment representations and clinical disorders.

Central Questions

Although most research on the psychometrics of the AAI has been conducted in normal, nonclinical groups, it has also been applied in numerous clinical samples. More than 10 years ago we published a meta-analysis of the limited number of clinical AAI studies available at that time. Because of this limited number we were not able to conclude with any certainty the presence or absence of systematic relations between clinical status and type of attachment representations. Although we found an overwhelming overrepresentation of insecure and unresolved attachments in clinical samples, we were unable to establish linkages between specific syndromes and specific type of attachment strategies (i.e., the minimizing of attachment strategy displayed by dismissing individuals vs. the maximizing attachment strategy of preoccupied individuals). Moreover, some research involved yet incomplete studies in progress (e.g., Hesse, van IJzendoorn, & Main, 1993), and the normal comparison group contained both mothers and expectant mothers (Benoit & Parker, 1994; Fonagy, Steele, & Steele, 1991), and samples with an overrepresentation of mothers of insecure children (Main & Goldwyn, 1991). On the one hand, with more pertinent studies available, we may now be able to select more strictly studies with nonclinical, nonrisk, middle to high socioeconomic status (SES) mothers with at least some caregiving experience taking care of their own children, to achieve a normative distribution based on a reasonable combined sample size to which other samples can be compared. On the other hand, with more clinical studies on a broader range of clinical disorders, we may now be in a better position to address some of the issues of the previous meta-analysis.

Following the approach of the 1996 meta-analysis, we review the currently available studies on normative and clinical groups to derive updated normative data and to uncover important trends. The present meta-analysis focuses on several interrelated questions. First, how are the AAI classifications distributed in samples of nonclinical mothers, that is, in community samples that were not selected with the purpose of including clinical or at risk participants? In these "normal" samples, we expect to find a majority of secure–autonomous classifications and an overall distribution comparable with the global distribution of infant–mother attachment classifications, with a somewhat higher percentage of insecure–dismissing attachments than insecure–preoccupied classifications, and about 15% of unresolved attachment representations (van IJzendoorn, Goldberg, Kroonenberg, & Frenkel, 1992; van IJzendoorn, Schuengel, & Bakermans-Kranenburg, 1999). We expect the clinical groups to deviate from this norm distribution, with a majority of insecure classifications of both organized and disorganized kinds.

The second question concerns adolescent attachment representations: How are AAI classifications distributed in samples of adolescents without children? Because adolescents have had less time to work through their childhood attachment experiences, and might still find themselves in a struggle for independence, they may show fewer secure–autonomous representations and more insecure–dismissing attachments than adults. This relative overrepresentation of insecure–dismissing attachments might be reflected in even larger numbers of dismissing adolescents in clinically disturbed samples.

Third, how are AAI classifications distributed in groups with physical handicaps such as deafness or blindness? As Keller (1933, cited in McKinnon, Moran, & Pederson, 2004) suggested, blindness shuts individuals off from the natural world, whereas deafness separates them from the social world. Nevertheless, we hypothesize that physically handicapped persons without psychiatric symptoms show similar attachment representations to norm groups, analogous to the attachment distribution of physically handicapped children in the Strange Situation procedure, which is similar to the distribution of nonclinical children (van IJzendoorn et al., 1992).

Fourth, dependent on the type of disorder, an overrepresentation of dismissing and preoccupied representations might be expected. Rosenstein and Horowitz (1996) and Dozier and Tyrrell (1997; Dozier et al., 1999), for example, supposed that internalizing problems such as borderline disorders would co-occur with preoccupied attachment representations, whereas externalizing problems, such as antisocial disorders, would co-occur with a dismissing representation of attachment experiences. Dozier and colleagues (1999) speculated that mood disorders would show a more complicated picture, because some types of more externalizing mood disorders may move attention away from the person (bipolar depression), whereas others focus attention on the person's inner world (as in unipolar depression).

Fifth, in any clinical group with an elevated chance of having experienced abuse in childhood, we expect to find an overrepresentation of unresolved classifications as a consequence of loss or trauma of other kinds, as in borderline or suicidal groups.

Last, we suppose that parents of clinically disturbed children more often show insecure attachment representations only when the children have psychological problems instead of physical illnesses.

Relevant Studies

Pertinent studies were selected through Web of Science (WoS, Institute for Scientific Information) and PsycLIT (search terms: "AAI," "Adult Attachment Interview"; citation of George, Kaplan, & Main, 1985; Main & Goldwyn, 1991; van IJzendoorn & Bakermans-Kranenburg, 1996; and their references to clinical AAI studies) websites, and through systematic search of pertinent references to AAI studies in the *Handbook of Attachment* (Cassidy & Shaver, 1999). We included only published studies using the AAI and its original coding system (Main & Goldwyn, 1991), leaving out the numerous studies conducted on basis of the Q-sort processing of the interview material (Kobak, Cole, Ferenz-Gillies, & Fleming, 1993; Zimmermann, Becker-Stoll, Grossmann, Grossmann, Scheuerer-Englisch, & Wartner, 2000), as well as studies conducted with (semi)projective or paper-and-pencil measures (e.g., Bartholomew, 1994). We do not mean to suggest that these latter studies are not relevant or sound, but we wanted to limit the clinical adult attachment studies to those presenting three- and/or four-way classifications of attachment representations across various clinical groups. For these types of studies extensive psychometric validation has been conducted, and the standardized coding of the interview material across research teams has been guaranteed through a system of regularly organized training workshops coordinated by Main and Hesse, so that comparability of the studies' findings is maximized.

This selection approach resulted in a set of 28 samples with nonclinical mothers, 61 clinical samples, and 16 samples with adolescents. In some cases, more than one sample was included in a study (e.g., Tyrrell & Dozier, 1997; Tyrrell, Dozier, Teague, & Fallot, 1999); on the other hand, some papers concerned the same sample (e.g., Sagi et al., 1994, 1997). The current (quantitative) review, therefore, covers data from more than 4,200 participants who completed the AAI. A large subset of studies reported on not only the three-way dismissing (Ds), secure–autonomous (F), and preoccupied (E) classifications but also on the four-way classifications involving the unresolved (U) category. Because of the relevance of this category for clinical and theoretical purposes, we analyzed our data for both the three- and four-way distributions. Unfortunately, only part of the studies reported on the cannot classify (CC) category as a separate classification. Therefore, we combined the U and CC classification into one category in the four-way categorization. In this chapter we include only studies on clinical groups compared to nonclinical normative groups. We do not discuss the numerous studies on groups at risk (adolescent mothers), groups with low SES, or non–European American backgrounds.

This material will be presented in an article (in preparation) in which we also provide more statistical details of the quantitative analyses conducted here.

Narrative Review of Clinical AAI Studies

In this narrative review we briefly discuss AAI studies conducted in clinical groups with diagnoses derived from the fourth edition of the *Diagnostic and Statistical Manual of Mental Disorders* (DSM-IV; American Psychiatric Association, 1996) and similar diagnostic tools. We differentiate between Axis I clinical disorders and Axis II personality disorders. Researchers investigated several types of Axis I disorders more or less defined by the DSM-IV categories of mood, anxiety, eating, and somatoform disorders, as well as substance abuse and schizophrenia. AAI researchers devoted their attention to Axis II antisocial and borderline personality disorders. Furthermore, samples with a high risk for suicidal behavior were studied, as well as those with abused subjects or abusive parents who committed some type of family violence. In contrast to these evidently psychologically disturbed groups, researchers also focused on individuals with visual or auditory handicaps, and on parents of children with psychological or physical problems in the clinical range. We present one or two examples of studies in each of the two DSM diagnostic axes before we turn to the search for some quantitative evidence for a systematic association between attachment representations and clinical disorder.

Mood Disorders

According to DSM-IV, mood disorders are multifaceted and differentiated. Major depressive disorder, dysthymic disorder, bipolar I disorder, bipolar II disorder, and cyclothymic disorder are classified under the same heading of mood disorders, although phenotypically they differ rather substantially. Major depressive disorder is characterized by one or more major depressive episodes, with at least two weeks of depressed mood or loss of interest accompanied by at least four additional symptoms of depression, such as reduced appetite and insomnia. Dysthymic disorder is the less severe type of major depression, whereas the bipolar disorders are characterized by (hypo-)manic episodes, along with depressive episodes. Attachment representations in persons with mood disorders have been studied by several research teams (Ammaniti et al., 2006; Murray, Halligan, Adam, Patterson, & Goodyer, 2006; Rosenstein & Horowitz, 1996; Patrick, Hobson, Castle, Howard, & Maughan, 1994; Tyrrell & Dozier, 1997). As an example, Patrick and colleagues (1994) studied attachment representations in a group of 12 dysthymic subjects who fulfilled the DSM criteria and served as comparisons for a group of patients with borderline personality disorder. They found only two (17%) secure–autonomous subjects, but also only two participants (17%) with unre-

solved representations. The relative overrepresentation of dismissing attachments (n = 5, 42%) in this dysthymic group might indicate a turning of their
attention away from (rejecting) past attachment experiences and from reflection on the self in relation to these experiences.

Anxiety Disorders

Anxiety disorders comprise a heterogeneous category with various types of
anxiety disorders, such as agoraphobia, social phobia, panic disorders, and
posttraumatic stress disorder (PTSD). Panic attacks comprise discrete periods,
with a sudden onset of intense fearfulness and symptoms such as shortness of
breath, palpitations, or chest pains. Agoraphobia is anxiety about places or
situations from which escape seems difficult. PTSD is characterized by
reexperiencing an extremely traumatic event, with symptoms of increased
arousal or avoidance of stimuli associated with the trauma. From the
perspective of attachment representations, thus far only panic disorders with
and without agoraphobia (Zeijlmans van Emmichoven, van IJzendoorn,
De Ruiter, & Brosschot, 2003) and PTSD (Stovall-McClough & Cloitre,
2006) have been studied. Zeijlmans van Emmichoven and colleagues (2003)
examined 28 outpatients with anxiety disorder who met DSM-IV criteria for a
primary diagnosis of anxiety disorder. The majority of the patients had panic
disorder with agoraphobia (n = 19). The anxiety disorder group showed more
dismissing attachments than expected (12 Ds, 43%), but only three (11%) U
classifications. In contrast, the PTSD group studied by Stovall-McClough and
Cloitre (2006) showed a strong overrepresentation of U subjects (19 of 30
participants, 63%), which may be related to their past experiences with abuse,
because the patients were selected on the basis of abuse experiences, as well as
PTSD. For quantitative analysis, we decided to categorize this study in the
cluster with clinically disturbed abused groups.

Eating Disorders

Eating disorders are characterized by severe disturbances in eating behavior,
with anorexia nervosa indicating a refusal to maintain a minimally normal
body weight, and bulimia nervosa indicating alternations of binge eating and
self-induced vomiting. Ramacciotti and colleagues (2000) hypothesized that
lack of self-confidence, which is pervasive among persons with anorexia or
bulimia, may be a result of insecure relationships experienced in their childhood. They examined 13 outpatients with a primary DSM-IV diagnosis of eating disorder (mainly anorexia) and without comorbid Axis I or II diagnoses.
They found more Ds attachments (n = 5, 38%) than expected, and no U representations. Candelori and Ciocca (cited in Ward, Ramsay, & Treasure, 2000)
studied three types of eating disorders separately, namely, anorexia nervosa,
anorexia with bingeing and purging, and bulimia (12 patients in each category). Attachment distributions were strikingly different between groups. Of

subjects in the anorexia nervosa group, seven (58%) had Ds attachments, and only one (8%) had an E attachment, whereas the other types showed a strong overrepresentation of the E classification. The authors suggest that individuals with the restricting anorexia tend to be dismissive, focusing attention away from their emotional problems onto bodily issues, whereas the patients with bulimic behaviors (anorexia or bulimia) tend to be preoccupied, focusing attention on their subjective feelings. It should be noted that subgroups of patients with eating disorders were too small to make reliable differentiations.

Somatoform Disorders

The common characteristic of somatoform disorders is the presence of unexplained physical symptoms that cause clinically significant distress but, in contrast to factitious disorders, are not intentional. They may lead to high health care utilization and conflict-ridden interactions with health care providers. Waller, Scheidt, and Hartmann (2004) studied 35 patients with diagnoses of a somatoform disorder according to *International Classification of Diseases* (ICD-10) criteria; a secondary psychiatric diagnosis was necessary in 60% of the patients (anxiety, depression, adjustment, and personality disorders). Almost half of the patients with somatoform disorders ($n = 17, 49\%$) showed Ds attachments, and nine (26%) patients were classified as E. A relatively large number of patients appeared to be secure ($n = 9, 26\%$). The authors speculated that the repression of affect and diminished affect awareness involved in somatoform disorders may be interpreted as concordant with an attachment strategy of diverting away from and avoiding internal feelings of distress, and may in this respect be similar to eating disorders. They also stressed that frequent comorbidity, and the heterogeneity of the somatoform diagnosis itself, might be responsible for both dismissing and preoccupied strategies in their sample.

Substance Abuse

The core feature of substance dependence is the presence of cognitive, behavioral, and physiological symptoms indicating that the individual continues use of the substance despite significant substance-related problems. Repeated self-administration of drugs leads to tolerance, withdrawal, and compulsive drug-taking behavior. Simonelli and Vizziello (2002) examined attachment representations in a sample of 28 mothers with drug addiction. Only one subject (4%) was classified as secure–autonomous; more than half were considered preoccupied with their past attachment experiences, and in 39% of the cases the addicted women were classified as unresolved. Drug abuse seems to be a disorder that escapes the externalizing characterization of those disorders (e.g., eating disorders) that lead to avoidance of attention to self and emotions (Dozier et al., 1999); drug abuse does not necessarily seem to imply distraction from reflections on negative attachment experiences. It may come as no surprise that the children of these mothers were in most (81%) cases insecurely attached.

Schizophrenia

Schizophrenia, a disturbance with psychotic episodes in which the patient loses contact with reality, includes delusions, disorganized speech, and/or grossly disorganized or catatonic behavior. Schizophrenia is widely considered a genetically based disease, but disordered, overly critical communication in the family has also been implicated in the onset, if not also the etiology, of this most severe Axis I disorder. To our knowledge, only one AAI study was conducted on a small group of 28 patients diagnosed with schizophrenia (Tyrrell & Dozier, 1997; also cited in Dozier et al., 1999). Most patients with schizophrenia showed Ds attachment (24 of 27, 89%), and 12 patients (43%) in the four-way classification system were classified as U. Dozier and colleagues (1999) correctly note that these distributions do not tell much about the etiology of the disorder, because disoriented speech is characteristic of patients with schizophrenia when they talk about not only attachment-related issues but also other topics. The Ds strategy used in the AAI may not be considered a cause of the disorder, but it may alert the therapist to a specific type of communication about emotions that the patients are prone to display.

Antisocial Personality Disorder

The core of antisocial personality disorder is a pervasive pattern of disregard for, and violation of, the rights of others that typically starts with childhood conduct disorders and continues into adulthood. Antisocial persons often are irresponsible, impulsive and aggressive, and may be deceitful and manipulative for personal profit or pleasure. DSM-IV indicates that child abuse or neglect, erratic parenting, or inconsistent discipline may increase the chance of a person becoming antisocial. These possible parenting causes of antisocial personality disorder may have triggered several attachment research teams to focus their work on this specific disorder, often in a forensic or prison environment (Fonagy et al., 1997; Frodi, Dernevik, Sepa, Philipson, & Bragesjö, 2001; Lamott & Pfäfflin, 2001; Levinson & Fonagy, 1997, 2002; Marin-Avellan, McGauley, Campbell, & Fonagy, 2005; Rosenstein & Horowitz, 1996; van IJzendoorn et al., 1997). van IJzendoorn and colleagues (1997) studied 40 violent criminal offenders with personality disorders in two Dutch forensic psychiatric hospitals, and found that attachment representations were highly insecure. Only 5% were classified as autonomous. The large number of comorbid disorders in this forensic group may be the reason for the presence of minimizing (Ds, 23%) as well as maximizing (E, 20%) attachment strategies. Also worthy of note was the high percentage (53%) of U and CC subjects (25% U and 28% CC). Many offenders had experienced separation from or had lost their parents, or had been institutionalized during childhood. Subjects who had experienced more attachment disruptions were more insecure in their attachment representations, which reminds one of Bowlby's (1944) first empirical study on juvenile thieves whose affectionless personalities he traced back to their early childhood experiences of recurrent separations from attachment figures.

Borderline Personality Disorder

A pervasive pattern of instability of interpersonal relationships, self-image, and affects, and marked impulsivity is characteristic of borderline personality disorder. Persons with this disorder make frantic efforts to avoid real or imagined abandonments, and this may involve impulsive actions, such as self-mutilation or suicidal behaviors. They tend to shift dramatically from idealizing to devaluing partners who are perceived as rejecting or abandoning. This ambivalent relationship pattern resembles the preoccupied anger that transpires from AAI studies about parents who are described as rejecting and unloving by individuals who are classified as displaying preoccupied speech. Barone (2003) studied prospective outpatients at a major university hospital that specialized in the treatment of personality disorders. Patients were diagnosed with the Structured Clinical Interview for DSM-IV (SCID), and all subjects met DSM-IV criteria for borderline personality disorder. In addition, 14 persons also were diagnosed with histrionic, 10 with narcissistic, 3 with antisocial, and another 4 with combined borderline, narcissistic, and histrionic personality disorders. Only 9 (23%) patients were classified as preoccupied, and nearly the same number ($n = 8$, 20%) received a classification as dismissive. Half of the sample subjects ($n = 20$) were unresolved. Contrary to our expectation, preoccupied state of mind is not characteristic of the borderline personality disorder exclusively, and unresolved loss or trauma seems more descriptive of this syndrome. The large number of comorbid individuals might have been responsible for the mixture of E, U, and Ds attachment representations in this clinical group. The complexities of psychotherapy with persons with borderline personality disorder, including an account of how the AAI contributes to understanding this disorder, may be found elsewhere in this volume (Ammaniti, Dazzi, & Muscetta in Chapter 10, and Diamond, Yeomans, Clarkin, Levy, & Kernberg in Chapter 11).

In summary, the AAI studies on the various Axis I and Axis II disorders do not seem to allow for easy generalizations and conclusions about patterns of attachment in clinical groups with diverging diagnoses. It is clear that heterogeneity and comorbidity of the samples may be one of the reasons for this lack of clear-cut and systematic associations between type of disorder and type of attachment representation. However, the significance of an underlying dimension of more internalizing versus more externalizing expression (Dozier et al., 1999) might be more fruitfully tested quantitatively.

Quantitative Review of Clinical AAI Studies

Categorical Data Analysis

To address our central questions about attachment classification distributions in various clinical groups compared to normal groups in a systematic, quantitative way, we used a specific meta-analytic approach based on correspondence analysis that has been used in the past to review attachment studies (van IJzendoorn & Bakermans-Kranenburg, 1996; van IJzendoorn & Kroonenberg, 1988; van IJzendoorn et al., 1992). This categorical data-analytic approach allows simultaneous inspection of configurations of attachment classifications and types of clinical groups, and a search for specific patterns of attachment in relation to particular types of clinical disorders.

Following our earlier article on this topic (van IJzendoorn & Bakermans-Kranenburg, 1996), we used correspondence analysis to describe similarities and differences in sample distributions (Greenacre, 1985). Correspondence analysis, or ANACOR, permits simultaneous analysis of both sample and category profiles. Its solution is obtained through singular value decomposition of the standardized residuals and a weighting of the singular vectors by the square root of the singular values multiplied by the inverse square root of n participants in a sample. In the graphical representation of the results of ANACOR, the origin represents the marginal distribution of both categories and samples. The maximum number of independent dimensions of such graphical representations is equal to the minimum number of row and column categories minus 1. Thus, the standardized residuals for the Ds, F, and E distributions can be perfectly represented in two dimensions, and those for the Ds, F, E, and U distributions, in three dimensions, but a two-dimensional solution may in some cases also adequately represent the variation in the data.

The graphical representation shows which samples have similar distributions over categories and which categories have similar distributions over samples, as well as which categories and which samples deviate strongly from their baseline distribution. The method was applied to the nonclinical mothers samples to create a baseline. The total of normal adolescent samples, clinical adult samples, and clinical adolescent samples have been projected into the graphical representation of the samples of nonclinical mothers by using regression-type procedures (Greenacre, 1985). Also, DSM-IV clusters of clinical samples into syndromes have been projected into this graphical space, as well as the clusters of samples into more internalizing versus externalizing problems. The computations were performed using the ANACOR procedures of the Statistical Package for the Social Sciences (SPSS) categories. The advantage of the ANACOR approach is that the patterns of distributions rather than the separate category frequencies are investigated and compared. The graphic ANACOR display provides a complete overview of the similarities and differences among the distributions of the samples, and between the samples and the normative total nonclinical mothers distribution.

For meta-analytic purposes we used the methods of categorical data analysis instead of the more traditional meta-analytic approach in which effect sizes are combined across studies and specific hypotheses about associations between the AAI and other variables are tested (van IJzendoorn, 1995). This traditional, confirmatory approach does not yield the descriptive information that we are searching for in the current meta-analytic study, and it cannot be applied to our explorations of differences and similarities between the AAI classification distributions of various (clinical) samples and some nonclinical baseline. Therefore, the current approach preserves the unique nature of every single study and outlines its position against the background of the total nonclinical mothers distribution.

Attachment Representations in Nonclinical Mothers and Adolescents

In the combined sample of $n = 1,012$ nonclinical mothers, 25.4% were classified as Ds, 56.3% as F, and 18.3% as E. A majority of the nonclinical mothers—albeit a small majority—were classified as secure–autonomous. With the category U included, the combined sample of $n = 889$ nonclinical mothers showed the following distribution: 19.6% classified as Ds, 55.2% as F, 10.4% as E, and 14.9% as U/CC. These figures are marginally different from the percentages published in our 1996 article on the first wave of AAI studies, with about half of the participants included.

We had expected that adolescents might show less autonomy and more dismissiveness, because they would still need time to work through their childhood attachment experiences and might be in the process of distancing themselves from their parents. We anticipated that they also might show less unresolved loss or trauma, simply because of their lower chance of having experienced significant losses compared to adults. These contentions were not borne out by our data. The nonclinical adolescent AAI classification distribution of 32.7% Ds, 56.4% F, and 10.5% E differed only slightly from the nonclinical mothers distribution, with a marginal overrepresentation of the dismissing category and an underrepresentation of the preoccupied category among nonclinical adolescents. The four-way distributions (27.7% Ds, 47.5% F, 8.3% E, and 16.5% U/CC) showed some overrepresentation of the insecure–dismissing attachments and, contrary to our expectations, the percentage of unresolved adolescents was not lower than that of the normative nonclinical mothers group.

Attachment Representations in Clinical Samples

We hypothesized that adolescents and adults with clinical problems would show more insecure attachment representations, and that children's disturbed social–emotional development would be related to parents' own insecure—Ds, E, or U—attachment biographies. We expected individuals with physical handicaps, however, to be more similar to the normal group. In Figures 3.1 to 3.4, 61 samples (or subsamples) have been presented with a variety of problems.

As expected, the combined clinical groups showed extreme deviation in distribution of AAI classifications. In the combined clinical samples of adult subjects (n = 685), 35% were classified as Ds, 27% as F, and 38% as E. Thus, a large majority (73%) of the clinical adults were classified as insecure. With the category U included, the combined sample of clinical adults (n = 605) showed the following distribution: 21% classified as Ds, 26% as F, 13% as E, and 41% as U/CC. The U category was strongly overrepresented in the combined clinical group, as was—to a lesser extent—the E category.

The subset of parents of clinical children showed an overrepresentation of insecure attachment representations. In the case of the four-way classifications, parents of children with physical problems appeared to deviate even somewhat more from the nonclinical baseline than the sample of parents of children with psychological problems, but the small number of studies in the former subgroup precludes any firm conclusions.

In Figures 3.5 and 3.6, the clinical groups have been projected into the plot of AAI distributions of the samples of nonclinical mothers. The center of the plot at the intersection of the Ds, F, and E vectors represents the distribution of nonclinical mothers samples. The first dimension of Figure 3.5 shows an overrepresentation of E classifications on the right and an overrepresentation of Ds classifications on the left. The second dimension (y axis) shows an overrepresentation of Ds classifications to the bottom. Thus, in Figure 3.3, the two dimensions neatly differentiate both insecure categories from each other and from the secure category. The first dimension in Figure 3.6 sets the secure category at the right side of the graphical display, apart from the other categories, and the second dimension shows the contrast between U classifications (to the top) and the other classifications. The third dimension was considered too weak to be included in the graphic display.

In Figure 3.5, all clinical groups except groups with physical handicaps are located at the right side of the graph, away from the F vector, indicating an overrepresentation of insecure (Ds and E) attachment representations. The center of gravity of the clinical participants is located quite some distance away from the center of the plot, showing an overrepresentation of both Ds and E participants. In Figure 3.6, most clinical groups are located in the upper left part of the graph, indicating an overrepresentation of participants classified as E and U. Some clinical (clusters of) samples (e.g., eating disorders, depression, and anxiety) deviate to the lower left part of the graph, which means that they showed an overrepresentation of participants classified as Ds and/or E, without an overrepresentation of the U category. In contrast, the centers of gravity for the combined nonclinical adolescents and the combined physically handicapped groups are located quite near the origin, showing their similarity to the distribution of the combined nonclinical mothers groups for both the three-way and four-way distributions.

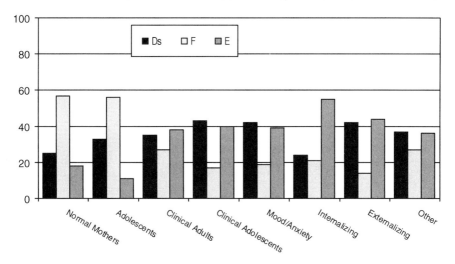

FIGURE 3.1. Three-way distributions of AAI classifications (%).

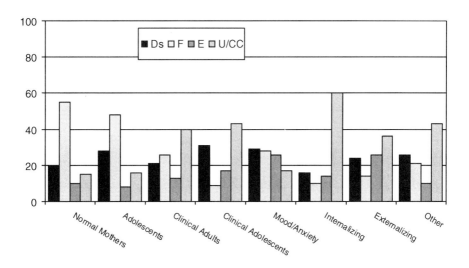

FIGURE 3.2. Four-way distributions of AAI classifications (%).

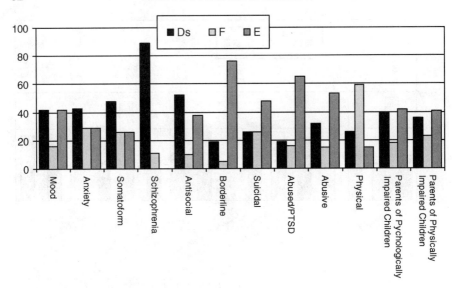

FIGURE 3.3. Three-way distributions of AAI classifications in various clinical groups (%).

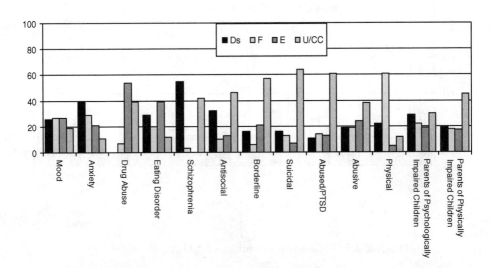

FIGURE 3.4. Four-way distributions of AAI classifications in various clinical groups (%).

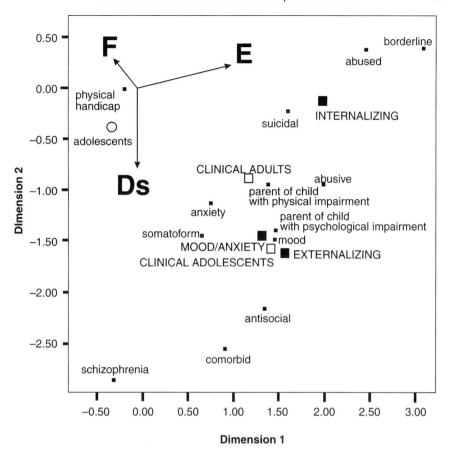

FIGURE 3.5. Correspondence analysis solution for the three-way AAI classifications.

The correspondence analyses facilitate the search for systematic relations between diagnosis and AAI classifications distribution. First, from Figure 3.5 we see that the center of gravity for the clinical groups indicates an over-representation of both E and Ds classifications. Therefore, globally, clinical status is not related to a specific organized insecure adult attachment category. Looking at more detailed divisions within the global clinical group, however, we find that individuals with borderline personality disorder with experiences of abuse and suicidal individuals more often show preoccupied attachment representations. Individuals with more internalizing clinical problems show an overrepresentation of preoccupied attachments, as was suggested by Dozier and colleagues (1999).

In contrast, some of the more externalizing problems and disorders, such as antisocial personality disorder and other conduct disorders, and somatoform disorder, seem to be characterized by an overrepresentation of Ds attachments. Patients with schizophrenia almost always display Ds attachment representations, at least in the one and only (rather small) AAI study of schizophrenia thus far (Tyrrell & Dozier, 1997, as cited in Dozier et al., 1999). However, the center of gravity for the more externalizing problems is located between the Ds and E vectors, meaning that these samples are characterized by a mixture of Ds and E subjects. Abusive adults, for example, display not only Ds strategies but also quite a bit more E representations than the nonclinical normal group (see Figure 3.5). Thus, Dozier and colleagues' (1999) hypothesis of a linkage between Ds attachments and externalizing problems can only be partly confirmed: Subjects with externalizing problems of various kinds show both Ds and E strategies in dealing with their past attachment experiences.

Other groups with overrepresentations of both Ds and E classifications are those with mood disorders, and parents of children with psychological or physical problems. Dozier and colleagues (1999) had already suggested that mood disorders are potentially heterogeneous in their orientation: Inwardly focused patients with chronic unipolar depression might be different than outwardly focused patients with bipolar depression. Relevant studies, however, are either too small for quantitative analysis or they do not allow for a differentiation in these subtypes of depression. That parents of children with psychological problems show more insecure attachments than the normal group may indicate some (environmental or genetic) parental contribution in the emergence of these problems. Contrary to our expectation, however, a similar overrepresentation of Ds and E attachments is also visible in the position of the parents of children with physical problems such as growth failure or respiratory illnesses. One might speculate that the parental role, in addition to other causes, in such problems is important (see Benoit, Zeanah, & Barton, 1989; Benoit, Zeanah, Boucher, & Minde, 1992; Cassibba, van IJzendoorn, Bruno, & Coppola, 2004).

Taking into account the U classifications (see Figure 3.6), we notice an extremely strong association with some psychological problems and disorders, such as borderline personality disorder, abuse, or suicide. Thus, these types of internalizing problems seem to be strongly associated with unresolved loss or trauma. In contrast, elevated rates of U attachments are absent in groups of patients with eating disorders and in those with mood disorders. Between these two extremes are positioned some of the groups with externalizing problems, such as groups with antisocial disorders and abusive individuals, the small group with schizophrenia, and the hybrid group with comorbid diagnoses of various kinds. This same pattern of overrepresented insecurely organized strategies and unresolved attachments seems to be characteristic of parents of children with clinical problems. Thus, it is important to note that clinical status is not exclusively related to the seemingly most disturbed adult attachment category, the U category, including the CC cases (Hesse et al., 1993). The center of gravity for the clinical groups suggests an overrepresentation of participants with the U classification, as well as those with an E

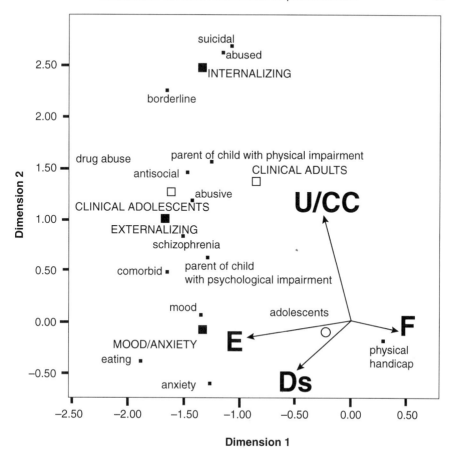

FIGURE 3.6. Correspondence analysis solution for the four-way AAI classifications.

classification (Figure 3.4). As Dozier and colleagues (1999) stated, the unresolved category is important for some disorders, in particular disorders related to dissociative tendencies, but not for eating and mood disorders.

Discussion and Conclusions

This narrative and quantitative review of 105 studies, including more than 4,200 AAI classifications, presents distributions of AAI classifications in samples of nonclinical mothers, adolescents, and various clinical groups. The distribution of nonclinical mothers is as follows: 20% Ds, 55% F, and 10% E. About 15% of the nonclinical mothers are unresolved with respect to loss or trauma of other kinds. The field of adult attachment research is developing with remarkable speed. The AAI is one of the most time-consuming instruments in the area of developmental and clinical psychology, and developmental psychopathology. It requires extensive training and practice, careful verbatim transcription of 1-hour interviews, and mastery of a laborious coding procedure. Nevertheless, in two decades, research groups from many different countries have produced a large body of data addressing several important developmental and clinical issues. As far as we know, more than 9,000 AAIs had been collected and processed as of August 2006. In this review, we surveyed the clinically relevant part of the available studies and tried to derive normative data, as well as evidence to test some clinically relevant ideas and hypotheses.

Major Findings

Our first question was how the AAI classifications are distributed in samples of nonclinical mothers, that is, in community samples not selected with the purpose of including clinical participants. The majority of these mothers are classified as securely attached (56%), with about one-quarter of the mothers being classified as insecure–Ds, and almost one-fifth as insecure–E. In addition, some 15% of the nonclinical mothers display unresolved attachment representations. Nonclinical populations may be less "healthy" than one might expect. A study of self-proclaimed healthy volunteers supports the occurrence of a considerable number of U cases in "normal" samples from a different perspective (Halbreich et al., 1989). In this respect, it is important to note that the nonclinical samples were community samples not screened for clinical symptoms. The adult attachment distributions are remarkably similar to the distributions of infant–mother attachment classifications, with a somewhat higher percentage of insecure–avoidant than insecure–resistant attachment classifications, and about 15% of disorganized attachment representations (van IJzendoorn et al., 1992, 1999). The nonclinical mothers groups' attachment distributions served as normative baselines against which we examined attachment distributions in adolescent and a variety of clinical groups.

Our second question concerned adolescent attachment representations. The steep increase we found in AAI studies of nonclinical and clinically disturbed adolescents in the past decade makes it easier to come to some firm conclusions about their attachment representations. The AAI might be considered a viable alternative to observational attachment assessments that are still lacking for this age group. Because most adolescents either live with their parents or have just left their home, they have had less time to work through their childhood attachment experiences, and may still find themselves in a struggle for independence. Therefore, they may show fewer secure–autonomous representations and more insecure–dismissive attachments than adults. However, adolescent attachment distributions are rather similar to adult distributions, with somewhat more Ds attachments and somewhat fewer E attachments in the forced, three-way distribution. The percentage of unresolved representations in adolescents (16.5%) is close to the corresponding percentage in adults.

Our third question pertained to attachment representations in groups with physical handicaps such as deafness or blindness. The distributions are strikingly similar to those in the normal groups. If anything, secure–autonomous representations seem to be present somewhat more often in adults with these physical handicaps. This is an important corroboration of the discriminant validity of the AAI and its attachment classifications: Only psychological problems and disorders seem to be associated with deviant attachment distributions, not physical handicaps unrelated to psychosocial causes. The finding of a normative attachment distribution in physically handicapped adults nicely converges with the outcome of an earlier meta-analysis on physically handicapped children that showed a regular distribution of Strange Situation attachment classifications in early childhood (van IJzendoorn et al., 1992).

Fourth, we examined not only whether insecure and U attachments would be prevalent in clinical groups, but also whether specific patterns of insecure attachments would be associated with particular kinds of disorders. In accordance with the predictions (Dozier et al., 1999), we found that internalizing problems such as borderline disorders tend to co-occur with preoccupied attachment representations. However, contrary to expectation, externalizing problems such as antisocial disorders not only co-occur with dismissive representations of attachment experiences but also include quite a few subjects with preoccupied attachment representations. We suggest that the excessive comorbidity in several samples of criminals with antisocial personality disorders (e.g., Levinson & Fonagy, 2002; Marin-Avellan et al., 2005; van IJzendoorn et al., 1997) may be responsible for this complicated picture of Ds and E strategies related to antisocial disorders. Dozier and colleagues' (1999) contention that mood disorders would also show a complicated combination of Ds and E strategies seems to be borne out by the current dataset. Some mood disorders may indeed be more externalizing given that their presence implies moving attention away from the person (as in bipolar depression), whereas others lead to more exclusive attention on the person's inner world (as in unipolar depression).

Fifth, subjects who have experienced abuse and suicidal individuals often appear to be unresolved when they speak about past experiences of loss or other trauma. In their basal (three-way) attachment strategy they show more often E attachment representations, maximizing their attachment concerns. With this profile they are remarkably similar to the cluster of groups with internalizing problems. Unlike persons with eating disorders, drug abuse, or somatoform disorders, which also involve some kind of physical harm to the self, suicidal individuals seem to be self-focused in calling upon attention from (potentially supportive) others as they maximize attachment-related behaviors. Of course, many suicidal patients have underlying chronic depression as a core diagnosis, which may be related to preoccupation with past attachment experiences of a negative nature.

Our last question concerned the parents of clinically disturbed children. In a previous meta-analysis we showed that parental responsiveness compensated for children's physical impairments and did not lead to skewed Strange Situation attachment classification distributions (van IJzendoorn et al., 1992). Therefore, we expected that parents of physically ill children would not differ from nonclinical mothers in the normal groups. However, parents of both physically and psychologically disturbed children showed rather strongly deviating attachment patterns, with overrepresentations of both insecure–organized strategies and the unresolved classification. The only group difference between the parents of physically versus psychologically disturbed children seems to be the relative overrepresentation of the unresolved category in the former, who show a lack of resolution of mourning about the loss of their ideal child, and still show signs of unresolved responses to the diagnosis of their children's illnesses (Pianta, Marvin, Britner, & Borowitz, 1996). We should also note that the kinds of physical illnesses subsumed under this heading—failure to thrive, asthma—may not exclude some social–emotional component in the emergence or development of the symptoms (Benoit et al., 1989, 1992; Cassibba et al., 2004).

Limitations

The current review is limited in several ways. The quantitative part of the review is not an epidemiologically valid survey, and our normative data on clinical groups are based on sometimes quite modest numbers of rather small studies. For this reason we stressed the exploratory and descriptive nature of our analyses, and refrained from too much statistical testing. Our speculations about the associations between types of attachment insecurity and types of clinical problems are speculative in two ways: First, we need more data (i.e., clinical samples) to establish these associations more firmly. In several cases, disorders were represented with only one study group, which restricts generalizability. Second, to detect clear-cut patterns of attachment representations in clinical groups, clinical diagnoses should be uniform and valid, and comorbidity should be avoided. Of course, it is unrealistic to expect both of these requirements to be implemented in the foreseeable future, although in this respect the DSM-IV approach to diagnosis has resulted in significant progress. In terms of the DSM-IV multiaxial assessment categories, it is also clear that not all relevant diagnostic classifications have received the same attention from the clinical researchers. Adult attachment information on most Axis II personality disorders is lacking, because research efforts have focused so far on antisocial and borderline disorders, and have neglected the other disorders, such as obsessive–compulsive, avoidant, or paranoid personality disorders. Clinical disorders of Axis I have been covered more adequately, but important diagnoses, such as dissociative identity, factitious, anxiety, and sleep disorders, have been examined insufficiently.

A second limitation arises from the inherent ethical and practical considerations guiding the primary clinical attachment studies. It is difficult to study attachment-related issues in clinical samples without knowledge of subjects' backgrounds. Complete blindness about the kind of diagnosis is almost impossible to achieve in clinical attachment research, because the patient's life history is part of the AAI. The AAI would be invalid if an abused group of patients' abuse experiences were deleted from the transcript to guarantee blind coding. Random selection of participants with clinical disorders is often not feasible, and most clinical samples are convenience samples that became available through cooperation with a few therapists or therapeutic centers. Matching of these patients with nonclinical comparisons has been done quite often and in a careful way, but the number of potentially important matching variables is too large to be covered in relatively small groups. These necessary weaknesses in primary studies translate into limitations of our quantitative approach, although aggregation of data may contribute to more valid insights into underlying patterns.

Clinical Implications

The clinical use of the AAI and its classifications of attachment representations may still be considered limited. To us the most important use seems to be the perspective of attachment theory on the importance of childhood attachment experiences, and the new vocabulary to express and communicate this perspective. The crucial role of the current representations of attachment instead of the actual past experiences—although the two are interrelated—takes into account the constructive or "working" nature of autobiographical memory (Roisman, Fortuna, & Holland, 2006; Roisman, Padrón, Sroufe, & Egeland, 2002), and creates room for change. The dimension of minimizing versus maximizing attachment concerns may be at least as important for understanding patients as the internalizing versus externalizing continuum, and the two dimensions may in fact be complementary rather than (entirely) overlapping. We speculate that internalizing problems may coexist with minimizing attachment concerns, whereas externalizing problems may in some cases go together with maximizing attachment concerns. Crossing the two dimensions yields four categories that may all be important to describe the complex reality of clinical patients with comorbid features.

Although unresolved loss or trauma does not play the most important role in every clinical disorder, it remains an important factor in understanding patients with various clinical diagnoses. In previous research, we found that maternal attachment security served as a protective factor in shielding the child from becoming disorganized because of the mother's continuing unresolved loss (Schuengel, Bakermans-Kranenburg, & van IJzendoorn, 1999). We suggest that maternal attachment insecurity may therefore be addressed before focusing on the loss or trauma, to decrease the occurrence of frightening behavior and ensuing disorganization (Byng-Hall, 1999). Most attachment-based intervention studies have not aimed exclusively at prevention of attachment disorganization; rather, the child's attachment disorganization was included as an outcome measure. In a recent meta-analysis of 15 attachment-based intervention studies, we showed that sensitivity-focused interventions with the aim of increasing the mother's sensitivity to her infant's needs and signals were most effective in preventing infant attachment disorganization. We speculated that these interventions may have successfully affected the mother's attentional processes, promoting the focusing of attention on the child. As a consequence of a stronger focus on the child, the mother would experience fewer intrusions of traumatic experiences in the presence of the child and show less frightening–frightened behavior (Bakermans-Kranenburg, van IJzendoorn, & Juffer, 2005; Hesse & Main, 2006; Juffer, Bakermans-Kranenburg, & van IJzendoorn, 2005; Madigan et al., 2006). In the case of depressive or suicidal patients, a similar focus on interactive behavior may leave less room for dissociative ruminations about the self.

Because therapies promoting security of attachment in parents indirectly lower the risk of attachment disorganization in their children, it is worthwhile considering the influence of both client and clinician attachment in the context of corrective emotional experience. Bernier and Dozier (2002) found that case managers with a secure attachment representation were better able to respond to the needs of clients, whether these clients were using Ds or E strategies. An example of a preoccupied strategy in the context of therapy is presenting oneself as very vulnerable, thus eliciting caretaking in the therapist. An example of a Ds strategy is presenting oneself as strong and self-reliant, thus creating a business-like atmosphere or even a cold animosity in the relationship with the case manager or therapist. Analyzing the phenomenon of corrective emotional experience, Bernier and Dozier stated that the most effective combinations are probably those of secure but somewhat dismissive therapists with preoccupied clients, and secure but somewhat preoccupied therapists with dismissive clients. The counterbalancing of the client's attachment bias to dismissiveness or preoccupation appeared to provide the best fit between therapist and client (Bernier & Dozier, 2002; Dozier, Cue, & Barnett, 1994). They hypothesized that the therapist's natural style helps him or her to resist the pull to react to the client in a complementary way. Thus the client's often rigid strategies are not reinforced, and the therapist creates an opportunity to change and adapt strategies (see also Harari et al., 2007).

We need more intervention studies demonstrating the effectiveness of specific therapies for the improvement of attachment security in persons with clinical disorders. Most attachment-based studies of clinical samples are descriptive and correlational, and it is logically impossible to differentiate cause and effect in the associations between attachment representation and clinical disorder. Although we are inclined to see attachment representations as antecedents of the emergence of clinical disorders, it might easily be the other way around, and attachment representation may be seen as an epiphenomenon of the more fundamental disorder. Longitudinal studies may shed some light on the causal relations between attachment and clinical disorder. Allen, Hauser, and Borman-Spurrell (1996) assessed attachment representations in adolescent patients and in a matched control group. Ten years later, criminality and hard drug use were measured and found to be predicted by Ds and U states of mind in adolescence, even after controlling for previous hospitalization. Definite evidence for causal relations between attachment and disorder can only be produced in experimental studies (e.g., therapeutic evaluations). In a pioneering study, Fonagy and colleagues (1996) evaluated the influence of psychotherapy on inpatients with personality disorders who were interviewed with the AAI upon admission to the psychiatric hospital. Fonagy and colleagues found that dismissive patients showed most improvement from admission to discharge, and that no other psychometric or clinical assessment could better predict therapeutic success. It is only through these types of intervention studies that we may see more clearly the causal role of adult attachment in the emergence and disappearance of clinical disorders.

In summary, clinical subjects' distributions of attachment classifications deviate markedly, with a strong overrepresentation of insecure and unresolved attachment representations. People whose disorders have an internalizing dimension (e.g., borderline personality disorder) seem to show more preoccupied and unresolved attachments, whereas people whose disorders have an externalizing dimension (e.g., antisocial personality disorder) display more Ds and E attachments, with fewer signs of unresolved loss or trauma. However, most disorders have been studied only rarely, groups are often heterogeneous, and individuals may have more than one disorder, so that systematic relations between clinical diagnosis and type of insecurity remain elusive.

For clinical applications, it may be important to differentiate the unresolved category into various subtypes of disoriented discourse, starting with different labels for unresolved loss and abuse, which may easily be associated with diverging clinical consequences. Hesse's (1996, 1999a, 1999b) introduction of the CC category may also fulfill an important role in the prediction of clinical disorders and the effectiveness of their treatment (Minde & Hesse, 1996), but the CC category has not yet been included systematically in all clinical attachment studies. In most clinical studies there were patients with secure–autonomous attachment representations, even in the most psychiatrically disturbed groups of criminal offenders in maximum security hospitals (Levinson & Fonagy, 2002; van IJzendoorn et al., 1997). These counterintuitive and intriguing cases deserve more of our attention, even though they may be rare, because they may point the way to unexpected resilience or to unanticipated problems in the application of the AAI to (some) clinical populations (Turton, McGauley, Marin-Avellan, & Hughes, 2001).

Above all, we need more clinical attachment studies to confirm the preliminary findings. Most disorders have been studied only rarely, and systematic relations between clinical diagnosis and type of insecurity remain elusive. The increasing popularity of the AAI in the clinical arena guarantees a broader database for interpretation of the findings in the future.

Acknowledgments

Support from the Netherlands Organization for Scientific Research to the first author (NWO SPINOZA award) and to the second author (NWO VIDI grant) is gratefully acknowledged. We also acknowledge the contributions of Reineke Mom, Anne Rutgers, and Marielle Beijersbergen in collecting and archiving the primary studies.

References

Allen, J. P., Hauser, S. T., & Borman-Spurrell, E. (1996). Attachment theory as a framework for understanding sequelae of severe adolescent psychopathology: An 11-year follow-up study. *Journal of Consulting and Clinical Psychology, 64,* 254–263.

American Psychiatric Association. (1996). *Diagnostic and statistical manual of mental disorders* (4th ed.). Washington, DC: Author.

Ammaniti, M., Speranza, A. M., Tambelli, R., Muscetta, S., Lucarelli, L., Vismara, L., et al. (2006). A prevention and promotion intervention program in the field of mother–infant relationship. *Infant Mental Health Journal, 27,* 70–90.

Bakermans-Kranenburg, M. J., & van IJzendoorn, M. H. (1993). A psychometric study of the Adult Attachment Interview: Reliability and discriminant validity. *Developmental Psychology, 29,* 870—880.

Bakermans-Kranenburg, M. J., van IJzendoorn, M. H., & Juffer, F. (2005). Disorganized infant attachment and preventive interventions: A review and meta-analysis. *Infant Mental Health Journal, 26,* 191–216.

Barone, L. (2003). Developmental protective and risk factors in borderline personality disorder: A study using the Adult Attachment Interview. *Attachment and Human Development, 5,* 64–77.

Bartholomew, K. (1994). Assessment of individual differences in adult attachment. *Psychological Inquiry, 5,* 23–27.

Benoit, D., & Parker, K. C. H. (1994). Stability and transmission of attachment across three generations. *Child Development, 65,* 1444—1457.

Benoit, D., Zeanah, C. H., & Barton, M. L. (1989). Maternal attachment disturbances and failure to thrive. *Infant Mental Health Journal, 10,* 185—202.

Benoit, D., Zeanah, C. H., Boucher, C., & Minde, K. (1992). Sleep disorders in early childhood: Association with insecure maternal attachment. *Journal of the American Academy of Child and Adolescent Psychiatry, 31,* 86—93.

Bernier, A., & Dozier, M. (2002). The client–counselor match and the corrective emotional experience: Evidence from interpersonal and attachment research. *Psychotherapy: Theory, Research, Practice and Training, 39,* 32–43.

Bowlby, J. (1944). Forty-four juvenile thieves: Their characters and home life. *International Journal of Psychoanalysis, 25,* 19–52, 107–127.

Byng-Hall, J. (1999). Family and couple therapy: Toward greater security. In J. Cassidy & P. R. Shaver (Eds.), *Handbook of attachment: Theory, research, and clinical applications* (pp. 625–646). New York: Guilford Press.

Cassibba, R., van IJzendoorn, M. H., Bruno, S., & Coppola, G. (2004). Attachment of mothers and children with recurrent asthmatic bronchitis. *Journal of Asthma, 41,* 419–431.

Cassidy, J., & Shaver, P. R. (Eds.). (1999). *Handbook of attachment: Theory, research, and clinical applications.* New York: Guilford Press.

Dozier, M., Chase Stovall, K., & Albus, K. E. (1999). Attachment and psychopathology in adulthood. In J. Cassidy & P. R. Shaver (Eds.), *Handbook of attachment: Theory, research, and clinical applications* (pp. 497–519). New York: Guilford Press.

Dozier, M., Cue, K. L., & Barnett, L. (1994). Clinicians as caregivers: Role of attachment organization in treatment. *Journal of Consulting and Clinical Psychology, 62*(4), 793–800.

Dozier, M., & Tyrrell, C. (1997). The role of attachment in therapeutic relationships. In J. A. Simpson & W. S. Rholes (Eds.), *Attachment theory and close relationships* (pp. 221–248). New York: Guilford Press.

Fonagy, P., Leigh, T., Steele, M., Steele, H., Kennedy, R., Mattoon, G., et al. (1996). The relation of attachment status, psychiatric classification, and response to psychotherapy. *Journal of Counseling and Clinical Psychology, 64,* 22–31.

Fonagy, P., Steele, H., & Steele, M. (1991). Maternal representations of attachment during pregnancy predict the organization of infant–mother attachment at one year of age. *Child Development, 62,* 891—905.

Fonagy, P., Target, M., Steele, M., Steele, H., Leigh, T., Levinson, A., et al. (1997). Crime and attachment: Morality, disruptive behavior, borderline personality disorder, crime, and their relationships to security of attachment. In L. Atkinson & K. J. Zucker (Eds.), *Attachment and psychopathology* (pp. 223–274). New York: Guilford Press.

Frodi, A., Dernevik, M., Sepa, A., Philipson, J., & Bragesjö, M. (2001). Current attachment representations of incarcerated offenders varying in degree of psychopathy. *Attachment and Human Development, 3,* 269–283.

George, C., Kaplan, N., & Main, M. (1985). *Adult Attachment Interview.* Unpublished manuscript, University of California, Berkeley.

Greenacre, M. J. (1985). *Theory and applications of correspondence analysis.* London: Academic Press.

Halbreich, U., Bakhai, Y., Bacon, K. B., Goldstein, S., Asnis, G. M., Endicott, J., et al. (1989). The normalcy of self-proclaimed "normal" volunteers. *American Journal of Psychiatry, 146,* 1052—1055.

Harari, D., Bakermans-Kranenburg, M. J., & van IJzendoorn, M. H. (2007). Attachment and dissociation. In E. Vermetten, M. Dorahy, & D. Spiegel (Eds.), *Traumatic dissociation: Neurobiology and treatment* (pp. 31–54). Arlington, VA: American Psychiatric Publishing.

Hesse, E. (1996). Discourse, memory, and the Adult Attachment Interview: A note with emphasis on the emerging Cannot Classify category. *Infant Mental Health Journal, 17,* 4–11.

Hesse, E. (1999a). The Adult Attachment Interview: Historical and current perspectives. In J. Cassidy & P. R. Shaver (Eds.), *Handbook of attachment: Theory, research, and clinical applications* (pp. 395–433). New York: Guilford Press.

Hesse, E. (1999b). *Unclassifiable and disorganized responses in the Adult Attachment Interview and in the Infant Strange Situation Procedure: Theoretical proposals and empirical findings.* Unpublished dissertation, Leiden University, The Netherlands.

Hesse, E., & Main, M. (2006). Frightened, threatening, and dissociative parental behavior in low-risk samples: Description, discussion, and interpretations. *Development and Psychopathology, 18,* 309–343.

Hesse, E., van IJzendoorn, M. H., & Main, M. (1993, March). *Developing the BLAAQ self-report inventory concerning attachment organization: A conceptual overview.* Paper presented at the biennial meeting of the Society for Research in Child Development, New Orleans, LA.

Juffer, F., Bakermans-Kranenburg, M. J., & van IJzendoorn, M. H. (2005). The importance of parenting in the development of disorganized attachment: Evidence from a preventive intervention study in adoptive families. *Journal of Child Psychology and Psychiatry, 46,* 263–274.

Kobak, R. R., Cole, H. E., Ferenz-Gillies, R., & Fleming, W. S. (1993). Attachment and emotion regulation during mother–teen problem solving: A control theory analysis. *Child Development, 64,* 231–245.

Lamott, F., & Pfäfflin, F. (2001). Bindungsrepräsentationen von Frauen, die getötet haben [Attachment representations in female murderers]. *Monatsschrift für Kriminologie, 84,* 10–24.

Levinson, A., & Fonagy, P. (2002). Offending and attachment: The relationship awareness and offending in a prison population with psychiatric disorder. *Canadian Journal of Psychoanalysis, 32,* 225–251.

Liotti, G. (2004). Trauma, dissociation, and disorganized attachment: Three strands of a single braid. *Psychotherapy, 41,* 472–486.

Madigan, S., Bakermans-Kranenburg, M. J., van IJzendoorn, M. H., Moran, G., Pederson, D. R., & Benoit, D. (2006). Unresolved states of mind, anomalous parental behavior, and disorganized attachment: A review and meta-analysis of a transmission gap. *Attachment and Human Development, 8,* 89–111.

Main, M., & Goldwyn, R. (1991). *Adult Attachment Classification System.* Unpublished manuscript, Berkeley, University of California.

Main, M., Kaplan, N., & Cassidy, J. (1985). Security in infancy, childhood and adulthood: A move to the level of representation. *Monographs of the Society for Research in Child Development, 50*(1–2, Serial No. 209), 66–104.

Marin-Avellan, L. E., McGauley, G., Campbell, C., & Fonagy, P. (2005). Using the SWAP-200 in a personality-disordered forensic population: Is it valid, reliable and useful? *Criminal Behaviour and Mental Health, 15,* 28–45.

McKinnon, C. C., Moran, G., & Pederson, D. (2004). Attachment representations of deaf adults. *Journal of Deaf Studies and Deaf Education, 9,* 366–386.

Minde, K., & Hesse, E. (1996). The role of the adult attachment interview in parent–infant psychotherapy: A case presentation. *Infant Mental Health Journal, 17,* 115–126.

Murray, L., Halligan, S. L., Adams, G., Patterson, P., & Goodyer, I. M. (2006). Socioemotional development in adolescents at risk for depression: The role of maternal depression and attachment style. *Development and Psychopathology, 18,* 489–516.

Patrick, M., Hobson, R. P., Castle, P., Howard, R., & Maughan, B. (1994). Personality disorder and the mental representation of early social experience. *Development and Psychopathology, 6,* 375—388.

Pianta, R. C., Marvin, R. S., Britner, P. A., & Borowitz, K. C. (1996). Mothers' resolution of their children's diagnosis: Organized patterns of caregiving representations. *Infant Mental Health Journal, 17,* 239–256.

Ramacciotti, A., Sorbello, M., Pazzagli, A., Vismara, L., Mancone, A., & Pallanti, S. (2000). Attachment processes in eating disorders. *Eating and Weight Disorders, 6,* 166–170.

Roisman, G. I., Fortuna, K., & Holland, A. (2006). An experimental manipulation of retrospectively defined earned and continuous attachment security. *Child Development, 77,* 59–71.

Roisman, G. I., Padrón, E., Sroufe, L. A., & Egeland, B. (2002). Earned secure attachment status in retrospect and prospect. *Child Development, 73,* 1204–1219.

Rosenstein, D. S., & Horowitz, H. A. (1996). Adolescent attachment and psychopathology. *Journal of Consulting and Clinical Psychology, 64,* 244–253.

Sagi, A., van IJzendoorn, M. H., Scharf, M., Joels, T., Koren-Karie, N., Mayseless, O., et al. (1997). Ecological constraints for intergenerational transmission of attachment. *International Journal of Behavioral Development, 20,* 287–299.

Sagi, A., van IJzendoorn, M. H., Scharf, M., Koren-Karie, N., Joels, T., & Mayseless, O. (1994). Stability and discriminant validity of the Adult Attachment Interview: A psychometric study in young Israeli adults. *Developmental Psychology, 30,* 988–1000.

Schuengel, C., Bakermans-Kranenburg, M. J., & van IJzendoorn, M. H. (1999). Frightening maternal behavior linking unresolved loss and disorganized infant attachment. *Journal of Consulting and Clinical Psychology, 67,* 54–63.

Simonelli, A., & Vizziello, G. F. (2002). La qualita delle rappresentazioni di attaccamento in madri tossicodipendenti come fattore di rischio per lo sviluppo affettivo del bambino [Internal working models of attachment in drug-addicted mothers as a risk factor in infant affective development]. *Eà Evolutiva, 72,* 54–60.

Sroufe, L. A., Egeland, B., Carlson, E., & Collins, W. A. (2005). *The development of the person: The Minnesota study of risk and adaptation from birth to adulthood.* New York: Guilford Press.

Stovall-McClough, K. C., & Cloitre, M. (2006). Unresolved attachment, PTSD, and dissociation in women with childhood abuse histories. *Journal of Consulting and Clinical Psychology, 74,* 219–228.

Turton, P., McGauley, G., Marin-Avellan, L., & Hughes, P. (2001). The Adult Attachment Interview: Rating and classification problems posed by non-normative samples. *Attachment and Human Development, 3,* 284–303.

Tyrrell, C., & Dozier, M. (1997, April). *The role of attachment in the therapeutic process and outcome for adults with serious psychiatric disorders.* Paper presented at the biennial meeting of the Society for Research in Child Development, Washington, DC.

Tyrrell, C. L., Dozier, M., Teague, G. B., & Fallot, R. D. (1999). Effective treatment relationships for persons with serious psychiatric disorders: The importance of attachment states of mind. *Journal of Consulting and Clinical Psychology, 67,* 725–733.

van IJzendoorn, M. H. (1995). Adult attachment representations, parental responsiveness, and infant attachment: A meta-analysis on the predictive validity of the Adult Attachment Interview. *Psychological Bulletin, 117,* 387–403.

van IJzendoorn, M. H., & Bakermans-Kranenburg, M. J. (1996). Attachment representations in mothers, fathers, adolescents, and clinical groups: A meta-analytic search for normative data. *Journal of Consulting and Clinical Psychology, 64*, 8–21.

van IJzendoorn, M. H., Feldbrugge, J. T., Derks, F. C., De Ruiter, C., Verhagen, M. F., Philipse, M. W., et al. (1997). Attachment representations of personality-disordered criminal offenders. *American Journal for Orthopsychiatry, 67*, 449–459.

van IJzendoorn, M. H., Goldberg, S., Kroonenberg, P. M., & Frenkel, O. J. (1992). The relative effects of maternal and child problems on the quality of attachment: A meta-analysis of attachment in clinical samples. *Child Development, 63*, 840–858.

van IJzendoorn, M. H., & Kroonenberg, P. M. (1988). Cross-cultural patterns of attachment: A meta-analysis of the Strange Situation. *Child Development, 59*, 147–156.

van IJzendoorn, M. H., Schuengel, C., & Bakermans-Kranenburg, M. J. (1999). Disorganized attachment in early childhood: Meta-analysis of precursors, concomitants, and sequelae. *Development and Psychopathology, 11*, 225–249.

Waller, E., Scheidt, C. E., & Hartmann, A. (2004). Attachment representation and illness behavior in somatoform disorders. *Journal of Nervous and Mental Disease, 192*, 200–209.

Ward, A., Ramsay, R., & Treasure, J. (2000). Attachment research in eating disorders. *British Journal of Medical Psychology, 73*, 35–51.

Zeijlmans van Emmichoven, I. A., van IJzendoorn, M. H., De Ruiter, C., & Brosschot, J. F. (2003). Selective processing of threatening information: Effects of attachment representation and anxiety disorder on attention and memory. *Development and Psychopathology, 15*, 219–237.

Zimmermann, P., Becker-Stoll, F., Grossmann, K., Grossmann, K. E., Scheuerer-Englisch, H., & Wartner, U. (2000). Longitudinal attachment development from infancy through adolescence. *Psychologie in Erziehung und Unterricht, 47*, 99–117.

II

Intervention Research with Mothers, Infants, and Toddlers

4

The AAI Anticipates the Outcome of a Relation-Based Early Intervention

CHRISTOPH M. HEINICKE and MÓNICA SUSANA LEVINE

In this chapter, our first goal is to show how mothers' prebirth Adult Attachment Interview (AAI; Main, Goldwyn, & Hesse, 2003) classification *anticipated* their involvement in and ability to work in a relation-based home intervention (the UCLA Family Development Project) and how, together with variations in that involvement, their AAI status also *anticipated* the 6- to 24-month mother–child and child social–emotional development. Mothers identified by the AAI as secure–autonomous in their relationship potential could effectively establish a positive, trusting relationship with the home visitor to work on a variety of issues in a range of ways. Similarly, this capacity for relating to the visitor was a significant factor in the formation of a positive relationship to their children and their children's positive social–emotional development.

Consistent with goals of this volume in relation to these results, we highlight the clinical context of the use of the AAI in two ways. Thus, as part of the delineation of the development of the first and second intervention studies, we elaborate the reasons for choosing the AAI as opposed to a general personality interview to formulate and test our hypotheses. We also demonstrate the power of the AAI in identifying mothers who struggle with the effects of unresolved issues but are capable and motivated to work on resolving these issues in therapy.

Our second goal in this chapter is to show how the AAI anticipated key issues in the treatment of a first-time, at-risk parent. Components of a young mother's relationship to her parents and her reactions to the loss of her grandmother were delineated during the AAI, then replicated and worked on/ resolved during a 2½-year intervention.

Background

Previous research has demonstrated the impact of the UCLA Family Development Project early intervention that focuses on a home visitation and mother–infant group mode of delivery. In a randomized trial, significant effects (effect sizes) were found for the following family, mother–child, and child areas of functioning: (1) quality of mother's partner support; (2) mother–child relationship aspects, such as responsiveness to need, the mother's encouragement of autonomy, as well as her appropriate and positive forms of control; and (3) child aspects, such as security of attachment, autonomy, and a positive response to maternal control (Heinicke, Fineman, Ponce, & Guthrie, 2001). Even though group differences between those who received the intervention and those who did not were significant and striking, there were also variations within the intervention group mothers' involvement in the work of the home-based intervention and the outcome of functioning as listed earlier. Given these variations in outcome, we sought to determine the factors likely to anticipate them.

An extensive research review of the impact of prebirth and ongoing antecedents on family development (Heinicke, 2002) started with the six-domain family systems model of parenting articulated by Cowan, Powell, and Cowan (1997). These authors stressed the significance of one domain influencing another, including their interaction over time, with parent personality functioning impacting both couple and parent–child interactions, as well as child development.

Accordingly, our preliminary study (n = 46) of mothers' and fathers' personalities as antecedents of variations in family development focused on their adaptation competence, capacity for positive sustained relationships, and self-development (Heinicke et al., 2000). Citations of the research literature defining these concepts are given in Heinicke (2002, pp. 365–366).

These personality antecedents, assessed at 3 months by the Personality Disorder Evaluation (Loranger, 1988), were part of a profile of antecedents of variations in outcome at 12 months. Heinicke and colleagues (2000) found that the mother's responsiveness to the needs of her infant at 1 month, aspects of her personality, infant irritability at 1 month, partner and family support at 6 months, and the extent of the mother's involvement in the work of the intervention significantly anticipated the child's attachment security at 12 months (as assessed by Q-sort and expectation of being cared for), as well as the mother's responsiveness (for the results of the full regression model, see Heinicke et al., 2000). Thus, a family systems model of the antecedents of parenting, an extensive literature review, and a preliminary study led to the hypotheses guiding the study summarized in this chapter.

We also reasoned that a more specific assessment of the mother's capacity to enhance her child's secure attachment, before interaction with her child influenced its development—namely, a prebirth assessment of her functioning—would give a clearer picture of the influence of that antecedent. Specifically, in the study of 57 families reported in this chapter, the AAI (Main et al., 2003) was administered to all mothers during the third trimester of pregnancy. Indeed, in the already cited research review (Heinicke, 2002) linking prebirth assessments and postbirth development, most frequently replicated result is the link between the mother's secure–autonomous development, as assessed by the AAI before her child's birth and her child's secure (vs. insecure) attachment at approximately 1 year of age. As part of a meta-analysis of the predictive validity of the AAI, van IJzendoorn (1995) summarized the findings linking three forms of prebirth maternal representations assessed by the AAI to three postbirth attachment security classifications; he found a 69% correspondence for the three-way classifications.

By adding the AAI to our assessments of the mother before her child is born, we could determine in our intervention sample whether the mother's secure–autonomous status also anticipated her child's secure attachment, and whether involvement in the intervention was an additional, independent factor influencing that development.

The longitudinal studies of at-risk families by Sroufe, Egeland, Carlson, and Collins (2005) provide data and a framework for interpreting the impact of our intervention on developmental trajectories. In characterizing 2-year outcome as guided self-regulation, their theoretical emphasis is consistent with the focus on the three mother–child relationship qualities assessed and analyzed in this study—namely, mother's responsiveness–child's security, mother's encouragement of autonomy–child's autonomy, and mother's appropriate use of control–child's positive response to control (see Table 4.1). "As was true for infants, toddlers require responsive and consistent involvement by caregivers to remain regulated. Caregivers provide scaffolding for regulation and a protective envelope within which the toddler can freely explore new capacities and desires" (Sroufe et al., 2005, p. 107).

The 2-year outcome used by Sroufe and colleagues (2005)—Experience in the Session—measured guided self-regulation in a child–parent task situation. In a multifactor longitudinal approach, Sroufe and colleagues found that the Experience in the Session Scale was significantly anticipated by each of the following: (1) ratings from an interview with the mother covering her early family relationship (e.g., positive identification with a competent mother); (2) a composite, 3-month measure of infant irritability, with particular emphasis on predicting caregiver behavior; (3) a history of stable secure attachments from 12 to 18 months, interpreted as reflecting stability in the parent–child relationship; and (4) the cumulative support experienced by the mother in the first 2 years of her child's life. These antecedents are consistent with those used in this study.

TABLE 4.1. Outcome Trends for Three Subgroups of a Sample of 57, Defined by Prebirth Maternal Adult Attachment Classifications

	Assessment point			Significance levels		
Outcome	0–6 months	7–12 months	13–24 months	Intergroup	Time	Time × group
Average work						
F	2.42	2.69	2.69[a,b]	.008	.076	.036
Ud/F	2.65	3.20[c]	3.38[c]			
Ud/E, Ud/Ds, E, Ds	2.40	2.36	2.05			
Average sessions						
F	18.67	16.52[b]	18.33	.037	.0001	.038
Ud/F	22.00	18.30[c]	23.08[c]			
Ud/E, Ud/Ds, E, Ds	19.78	11.52	13.91			
Mother responsiveness to need						
F	5.37	5.84	5.63	.001[b,c]	.769	.220
Ud/F	5.42	5.42	5.75			
Ud/E, Ud/Ds, E, Ds	4.91	4.32	4.50			
Mother encourage autonomy						
F	5.05	5.58	5.47	.008[b,c]	.402	.156
Ud/F	5.17	5.50	5.50			
Ud/E, Ud/Ds, E, Ds	4.82	4.55	4.55			
Mother appropriate control						
F			5.53	.001[b,c]		
Ud/F			5.67			
Ud/E, Ud/Ds, E, Ds			4.36			
Child expects care						
F	5.89	6.21	6.21	.001[b,c]	.422	.287
Ud/F	6.25	6.25	6.17			
Ud/E, Ud/Ds, E, Ds	5.64	5.45	5.18			
Child sense of separate self						
F	5.05	5.58	5.74	.173	.002	.205
Ud/F	5.17	5.92	5.92			
Ud/E, Ud/Ds, E, Ds	5.00	5.18	5.18			
Child externalize control						
F			2.74	.002[b,c]		
Ud/F			2.25			
Ud/E, Ud/Ds, E, Ds			3.55			

[a] F group significantly different from Ud/F group.
[b] F group significantly different from Ud, E, Ud/Ds, E, and Ds group.
[c] Ud/F group significantly different from Ud/E, Ud/Ds, E, and Ds group.

Plan of Analysis

Guided by the general hypothesis that both the mother's prebirth attachment status and the extent of involvement in the work of the home-based intervention would impact outcome independently, we first studied the impact of the mother's attachment status by dividing the total sample into subsamples of varying adult attachment status, then presented the average outcome assessments for these subsamples when the child was 6, 12, and 24 months of age in a repeated measures analysis of variance model. Taking advantage of the categorical judgment derived from the AAI, we defined a subsample of secure–autonomous (F), unresolved trauma (U) with a secure–autonomous secondary scoring (F), and a third group of Insecure classifications: preoccupied, dismissing, and U, with secondary scoring of preoccupied (E) and dismissing (Ds). The assessment of the mother's involvement in the work of the home visit was based on the number of home visits completed in a given time interval, and the average of the 5-point work ratings made by the home visitor after each home visit. The time intervals for these assessments were birth–6 months, 7–12 months, and 13–24 months.

To study the combined effect of these two major antecedents, as well as others, on outcome at child age 2 years, we then applied a stepwise regression model. To allow comparison with the other prebirth dimensions, the mother's responses to the AAI were represented in dimensional form. We used three summary (state-of-mind) ratings as part of the AAI: Coherence of the Narrative, Extent of Unresolved Physical and Sexual Trauma, and Extent of Unresolved Loss. Entered into a factor analysis with other prebirth variables, these three ratings constituted one of the prebirth factors that emerged; the others were Depression/Anxiety, Quality of Partner Support, and IQ/Ego Functioning.

Methods

Identification of Subjects

As standard procedure, the site coordinators at three West Los Angeles prenatal clinics administer the Comprehensive Prenatal Services Program Interview (CPSPI) to the women during regularly scheduled prenatal visits. This interview, as well as the total record of the prenatal visits, provided information on seven eligibility and 12 risk characteristics. Poverty, emotional and sexual abuse, and mental health issues were key selection criteria (for further definitions, see Heinicke et al., 2006).

Interventions Used

The intervention services offered included the following:

1. *Home visiting* to address personal, parent–child, and child development issues. These issues were defined and understood, and alternate solutions were proposed and followed up. The personal issues most frequently involved relationships, finances, and work. Home visits occurred once a week during the first year, then every other week the second year. Visits lasted for 1 hour (for further details, see the operational manual [Heinicke, 2000]).
2. A *mother–infant group* to share parenting issues and to enhance knowledge of child development. Group sessions with five to eight mother–infant pairs lasting 1½ hours occurred once a week from infant ages 2 to 18 months (for further details, see Heinicke, 2000).
3. *Advocacy* at the parent's request and in addition to the visit. Home visitors intervene on behalf of the families regarding issues of child care, work, health care delivery, preschool, or other social systems as part of the intervention.
4. *Referral* to community agencies as needed (e.g., child care, issues around additional medical and/or counseling services, help with housing, job application, and training).

Measures

The measures used in this presentation and listed below are drawn from a larger set, including parallel and correlated indices. Procedures used and reliability assessments of all measures are described in Heinicke and colleagues (2006) and Heinicke (2004). Particularly relevant to the outcome measures used in this presentation is the extensive documentation of the reliability and cross-situational validity of the mother–child and child ratings made by an independent observer in the home (see Heinicke et al., 2006, pp. 106–108).

Prebirth Maternal Capacity for Relationships

The AAI classifications (Main et al., 2003) are the primary measures of the mother's relationship capacity and, more specifically, the level of her security–autonomy as opposed to various forms of insecurity. As described in detail by Hesse (1999), the AAI is a semistructured, hour-long protocol comprising 20 questions. The transcribed and scored interview yields the following states of mind in respect to attachment: secure–autonomous (F), dismissing (Ds), preoccupied (E), and unresolved/disorganized (Ud).

The standard classifications (F, Ds, E, Ud, and CC [cannot classify]) were assigned, as well as secondary scorings (e.g., Ud/F). Moreover, all the Experience and Mind Scales were scored. The scorer, Christoph Heinicke was certified as scorer of the AAI by Mary Main and Erik Hesse following a 2-week training institute led by Deborah Jacobvitz.

Prebirth Maternal Adaptation

Two self-report inventories reflect the mother's adaptation: the Beck Depression Inventory (Beck, Ward, Mendelson, Mock, & Erbaugh, 1961) yields a depression score. The Spielberger Anxiety Scale (Spielberger, 1977) assesses the experienced calm or tension of the mother.

Prebirth Maternal Cognitive Functioning

Profiles of each mother's functioning on the Shipley Institute of Living Scale (Shipley, 1940) and the Loevinger Test of Ego Development (Loevinger & Wessler, 1983) are assessed in the third trimester of pregnancy. From these profiles, we use the estimate of the Full Scale IQ and the overall Rating of Ego Functioning.

Maternal Partner and Family Support: Prebirth to 24 Months

We devised a recorded semistructured interview of the mother using four lead questions and follow-up probes that provide information for 5-point ratings on the extent of contact and quality of support experienced from (1) her partner and (2) family and friends. Ratings by an independent rater of the amount of contact and quality of support from these two sources yield four reliable measurements.

This assessment is supplemented by two inventories. The Cutrona Support Inventory score (Cutrona, 1984) supplements the assessment with a rating of the general level of support, and the summary score from the Locke–Wallace Inventory (Locke & Wallace, 1959) supplements the interview-based ratings describing the mother's satisfaction with her partner. The total scores derived from these two inventories are used.

Mother Responsiveness: 6, 12, and 24 Months

The primary measure of this construct is the 7-point global rating by the independent observer in the home (home observer) of the Mother's Responsiveness and Efficiency in Meeting the Child's Needs: To what extent can the parent (1) perceive the child's cues of his or her needs and rhythms, (2) take appropriate action to meet these needs, and (3) do so efficiently, without excessive expenditure of time or strain on either infant or caretaker? The home observations on which the global ratings are based last 90 minutes and include filming 15 minutes of mother–child free play.

Child's Security of Attachment: 6, 12, and 24 Months

The primary measure of this construct is the 7-point global rating entitled Expectation of Being Cared For at 6, 12, and 24 Months. This rating by the home observer refers to the infant's expectation that his or her needs will be acknowledged and responded to with immediacy and effectiveness. Another measure of the child's security that is also used as an outcome measure is the Attachment Q-Set (AQS; Waters, 1986). Computer scoring yields both a Security and a Dependency Score at 12 and 24 months. A meta-analysis of the observer AQS has shown that it is a valid measure of attachment (van IJzendoorn, Vereijken, Bakermans-Kranenburg, & Riksen-Walraven, 2004).

Mother Encouragement of Autonomy: 6, 12, and 24 Months

The primary measure of the mother encouragement of autonomy construct is the home observer 7-point rating of Encouragement of Optimal Separation and Moves toward Autonomy. This scale focuses on the extent to which the caregiver encourages experiences that promote the child's independent functioning and sense of autonomy.

Child Autonomy: 6, 12, and 24 Months

The primary measure of this construct is the home observer 7-point global rating Sense of Separate Self. To what extent has the child achieved a sense of self, separate from and individuated from the primary caretaker?

Mother Appropriate Control: 24 Months

The primary measure of the mother's appropriate control is the home-observer 7-point global rating Appropriateness of Maternal Control Efforts. This scale focuses on the extent to which the caregiver is appropriate in her method(s) of control with her 2-year-old. Appropriateness includes four main elements: an accurate reading of the child's need for control, promptness of response, confident nature of response, and fit of the response to the nature of the child's externalizing behavior.

Child's Self-Regulation and Response to Control: 24 Months

The primary measure of the child's self-regulation is the home observer 7-point global rating Child's Externalization of Control: 2–4 Years of Age. Two dimensions are used in formulating the global ratings and the definition of the rating points 1 through 7: the number of times the child's behavior calls for control, and the type of behavior requiring control.

Infant Characteristic: Irritability at 1 Month

This rating by the independent home observer defines the amount of time the infant is distressed in reaction to routine events. It ranges from 1 (*Almost no fuss*) to 5 (*Crying most of the observation time*).

Maternal Involvement in the Home Visit:
Ratings of the Quality of the Mother's Involvement

Indices of the mother's involvement in the intervention were derived from the 62-item rating by the intervenor after each home visit. These were organized in relation to three major aspects of the home visits: (1) the consolidation of the relationship with the mother; (2) the frequency and quality of the interventions; and (3) how the mother made use of the intervention (see the operational manual defining intervention and ratings; Heinicke, 2000).

In addition to these specific ratings, three summary, 5-point ratings captured the mother's involvement in the intervention process: Positive Connection, Trust in the Intervenor, and Extent of Work.

1. *Positive Connection*: A quality of the relationship between intervenor and mother (parent) that expresses through words, feelings, and actions the wish to be with each other and to continue that contact.

2. *Trust*: The mother's expectation that the intervenor (a) can be counted on to help her (relationship-gratification expectation), (b) will respect her goals and desires (respect for autonomy expectation), and (c) will create a sense of safety, allowing the mother to reveal her inner world (promotion of security expectation).

3. *Work*: the mother's ability to (a) confront a psychological issue, (b) elaborate the components of the issue, (c) arrive at an understanding of the issue, and (d) plan a course of action in relation to that issue.

These ratings after each session were averaged for the intervals 0–6, 7–12, and 13–24 months intervals.

Maternal Involvement in the Home Visit: A Quantitative Index

The number of sessions completed by the mother in a given time interval provides a quantitative index of involvement. For the intervals 7–12 and 13–24 months, number of sessions correlates, respectively, with the extent of work ratings $(.598^{.0001}$ and $.607^{.0001})$.

Results

Outcome Trends as a Function
of the Prebirth Maternal Adult Attachment Classification

The first hypothesis of our study was that a mother classified on the AAI as secure–autonomous (F and/or Ud/F), as opposed to insecure, before the birth of her child would be more involved in the work of the home intervention, and would by child age 24 months be more responsive to the needs of her child, encourage autonomy, and use verbal and positive forms of control. In this relationship context, the 2-year-olds would expect to be cared for, would show more autonomy, and would respond positively to the mother's control.

The trend analysis of repeated measures of the outcome provides the clearest picture of the development of the families from pregnancy to 2 years as a function of maternal attachment, and grouping the AAI classification as antecedents reflects the important qualitative distinctions of that assessment. Accordingly, to capture the qualitative distinctions of the AAI and to demonstrate their impact on outcome, our trend analysis comprised three groupings: (1) secure–autonomous (F, n = 21); (2) unresolved/disorganized with respect to trauma or loss (Ud), with a secondary scoring of secure–autonomous (F, n = 13); and (3) the remaining insecure classifications not fitting either of the first two groupings (Ud/E, Ud/Ds, E, and Ds [n = 23]). The Ud/F group was separated because in this population, mothers in an unresolved state regarding trauma and/or loss who presented a coherent transcript and state of mind were judged to be more capable of overcoming the impact of the unresolved trauma. The interpretation of the Ud/F classification as representing a possible protective factor is consistent with the finding that mothers classified as Ud, with a secondary scoring of secure showed less frightening behavior than Ud mothers with a secondary scoring of insecure (Schuengel, van IJzendoorn, & Bakermans-Kranenburg, 1999). Further supporting the validity of distinguishing Ud–secure and Ud–insecure mothers are the results reported by Jacobvitz, Leon, and Hazen (2006). Ud mothers with a secondary scoring of secure in pregnancy showed less frightening behavior at 8 months than Ud mothers with a secondary scoring of insecure. Moreover, when combined with their respective non-Ud–secure and non-Ud–insecure groupings, the secure mothers were more sensitive to their infants at 8 months than those in the total insecure group. In the study reported here, the secure mothers, including the Ud–secure mothers, were significantly more sensitive than the insecure mothers, including the Ud–insecure mothers.

The Mother's Prebirth Attachment and Involvement in the Work of the Intervention

Regarding the impact of the mother's secure–autonomous status on her involvement in the work of intervention, Table 4.1 presents the average work ratings and average sessions completed for the intervals 0–6, 7–12, and 13–24 months for those mothers classified as secure–autonomous (F), those who presented evidence for an unresolved/disorganized trauma in the context of a coherent narrative (Ud/F), and the remaining classifications of insecure functioning (Ud/E, Ud/Ds, E, Ds). Application of the repeated measures analysis of variance to the *work ratings* for the sample of 57 revealed a group effect ($Pr < F$ .008) and a group × time interval effect ($Pr < F$ .036). Table 4.1 also reveals the results of cross-sectional t-test comparisons. In summary, mothers classified as continuing to be unresolved in regard to past trauma (abuse or loss), but generally presenting a coherent narrative of their past relationships, were most involved in the work of the intervention, and increasingly so. By contrast, those classified in various insecure categories were less, and decreasingly, involved in the intervention.

Repeated measures analysis of variance of the *average number of sessions* attended by the mothers in the three time intervals also suggests that those in the Ud/F group were the most involved. There was a significant group effect (*Pr < F* .037), a significant time interval effect (*Pr < F* .0001), and a significant group × time interval effect (*Pr < F* .038). Results of cross-sectional *t*-tests are listed in Table 4.1.

The Mother's Prebirth Attachment and Her Child's Social–Emotional Development

The average ratings of the *child's expectation of being cared for* are shown in Table 4.1 for the three attachment classification at the 6, 12, and 24-month time points. Applying repeated measures analysis of variance, there was a significant group difference (*Pr < F* .001). Children of the mothers classified as F and Ud/F both differed in respect to the expectation of being cared for from the children of the mothers in the Ud/E, Ud/Ds, E, and Ds groups (*Pr < /t/* .0008 and *Pr < /t/* .003, respectively). The children of the mothers in the F and Ud/F groups did not differ. Indeed, except for child sense of separate self where there were no group differences, the F and Ud/F groups did not differ on any of the 2-year outcome indices, but each differed significantly from the insecure group.

Application of repeated measures analysis of variance to the average ratings of the *child's development of a separate self* (see Table 4.1) showed no significant impact of the mother's prebirth attachment status. The *child rating of the externalization of control* at the 24-month point (see Table 4.1) revealed a group difference as a function of the mother's prebirth attachment classification (*Pr < F* .002).

The Mother's Prebirth Attachment and Her Relationship to Her Child

The average ratings of the *mother's responsiveness* to her child as a function of her prebirth attachment classification are also given in Table 4.1. Application of the repeated measures analysis of variance shows a highly significant group difference (*Pr < F* .001).

The average ratings of the *mother's encouragement of her child's autonomy* as a function of her prebirth attachment classification also are given in Table 4.1. Application of the repeated measures analysis of variance shows a significant group difference (*Pr < F* .008).

The rating of *mother's verbal and positive control of her child*, done at the 24-month point only, revealed a group difference as a function of the mother's prebirth attachment classification (*Pr < .001*).

Two-Year Outcome as a Function of Various Antecedents

If this repeated measures analysis of variance displays the considerable impact of adult attachment on the mother's involvement in the work of the intervention and on the longitudinal development of mother–child and child outcome measures, what other antecedents may have an additional impact on mother–child and child outcomes? This time we focused on the 24-month child and the mother–child outcome assessments.

We hypothesized that in a hierarchical regression mode of analysis, including the mother's prebirth adult attachment, the following would be additional (unique) predictors of the 2-year outcome measures:

- The 1-month mother responsiveness to the needs of her infant and the infant's irritability.
- The quality of the 6-month mother's partner and family support.
- The extent of the mother's involvement in the work of the home visitor's intervention in the 7- to 12-month period.

To make a linear form of the maternal attachment assessment available and to place it in the context of the other assessments during the third trimester of the pregnancy, we derived a factor score for that quality as follows: Given the categorical distinctions found for this sample of at-risk mothers, we decided first to distinguish between secure and insecure mothers by including the central rating of that distinction, namely, coherence of the narrative. To represent variations in the reaction to trauma and/or loss, the two ratings representing those variations also were included. Thus, the three state-of-mind scales from the AAI were Coherence of Narrative, Unresolved Response to Past Physical and Sexual Trauma, and Unresolved Response to Past Loss (Main et al., 2003).

The other prebirth measures were as follows: Ratings from the semistructured support interview focused on the extent and quality of the mother's contact with her partner, family, and friends. The Locke–Wallace Inventory also yielded a score in this domain (Locke & Wallace, 1959). Two ratings from the Spielberger Anxiety Scale—Calm and Tense—assessed this dimension (Spielberger, 1977), and the Beck Depression Inventory (Beck et al., 1961) yielded a total depression score. The Loevinger Sentence Completion Test for Ego Development (Loevinger & Wessler, 1983) yielded a summary score of ego functioning, and the mother's IQ was measured by the Shipley Institute of Living Scale (Shipley, 1940). A principal components analysis performed on the aforementioned 14 variables resulted in four principal components. One factor called unresolved trauma/incoherence was loaded on the three AAI state-of-mind scales—negatively on Coherence and positively on Unresolved Response to Trauma and Loss—and used for further analysis representing (negatively) the secure–autonomous dimension, which by definition was independent of the other three factors: anxiety/depression, quality of partner relationship, and IQ/ego functioning (see Heinicke et al., 2006 for further description). To determine their anticipation of the 24-month outcome assessment results, each of the six hypothesized antecedents—the prebirth maternal unresolved trauma/incoherence factor score; the 1-month mother responsiveness to need and infant irritability; the 6-month family and partner support; and the 7- to 12-month involvement in the work—were entered into stepwise regression analyses of six outcomes. Results are listed in Table 4.2.

Consistent with a review of existing longitudinal research, the 24-month measures of the child's expectation of being cared for and the mother's responsiveness to the needs of her child, her encouragement of the child's autonomy, and her use of positive and verbal controls are all anticipated by an index reflecting her prebirth AAI status. Striking is the fact that after all other antecedents are entered, the extent of involvement in the work of the home visit in the 7- to 12-month interval remains as a unique antecedent of all six outcome measures. Both the prebirth AAI status and the involvement in the work of the home visit also are significant antecedents when the observer AQS is used as a 24-month outcome measure (Heinicke, 2002).

In addition to the influence of an aspect of the mother's prebirth capacity for sustained relationship (her attachment status) and her capacity to make use of the intervention (the work from the 7- to 12-month interval), her support system (6-month family and partner support) also anticipated certain 24-month mother–child and child outcomes. Two 24-month child outcomes (expectation of being cared for and sense of separate self) and one mother–child interaction outcome (maternal positive and verbal control) were anticipated by the mother's 6-month level of support.

The hypotheses of the study also asked whether the earliest (1 month) status of the infant and mother–infant responsiveness to the infant's needs may influence the previous interacting antecedents. Variations in the 24-month outcome of the child's AQS, sense of separate self, and the mother's use of positive and verbal control were anticipated (negatively) by the infant's irritability.

Summary and Discussion of Findings on Variations in Outcome

The most consistent finding of this study is that all six 24-month child and mother–child outcome measures were significantly impacted by the variations in the mother's involvement in the work of the home visit intervention during the 7- to 12-month period of her infant's life. Equally significant, the trends from birth to 24 months in this involvement in all but one of the outcome measures were significantly different and more positive for the mothers classified as secure (F and Ud/F) as opposed to insecure (Ud/Ds, Ud/E, Ds, and E). The exception was the child's development of a sense of separate self.

TABLE 4.2. Antecedents of 24-Month Child and Mother–Child Outcome

Dependent variable: The child's expectation of being cared for at 24 Months

Antecedent variable:	Partial R^2	F	$Pr < F$
Unresolved trauma/incoherence	.18	12.02	.001
Work 7–12 months	.10	7.57	.008
6-month quality of partner support	.07	5.73	.020
6-month quality of family support	.06	4.99	.030

Total model R^2 = .41, df = 4, 52, p < .001; antecedents df = 1, 52

Dependent variable: The observer attachment Q-sort at 24 months

Antecedent variable:	Partial R^2	F	$Pr < F$
Unresolved trauma/incoherence	.17	11.51	.001
Work 7–12 months	.07	5.41	.024
1-month infant irritability	.05	3.72	.059

Total model R^2 = .30, df = 3, 53, p < .001; antecedents df = 1, 53

Dependent variable: The child's sense of separate self at 24 months

Antecedent variable:	Partial R^2	F	$Pr < F$
6-month quality of family support	.21	15.00	.0003
Work 7–12 months	.08	5.82	.019
1-month infant irritability	.05	3.78	.057

Total model R^2 = .34, df = 3, 53; antecedents df = 1, 53

Dependent variable: The child's positive response to control at 24 months

Antecedent variable:	Partial R^2	F	$Pr < F$
Work 7–12 months	.13	7.90	.007

Total model R^2 = .13, df = 1, 56; antecedents df = 1, 56

Dependent variable: Maternal responsiveness to the needs of her child at 24 months

Antecedent variable:	Partial R^2	F	$Pr < F$
Work 7–12 months	.16	10.83	.002
Unresolved trauma/incoherence	.09	6.13	.016
1-month mother responsive to need	.04	2.95	.092

Total model R^2 = .29, df = 3, 53; antecedents df = 1, 53

Dependent variable: Maternal encouragement of child's autonomy at 24 months

Antecedent variable:	Partial R^2	F	$Pr < F$
Work 7–12 months	.16	10.75	.002
Unresolved trauma/incoherence	.09	6.12	.016
1-month responsiveness to need	.04	3.02	.088
6-month quality of family support	.04	3.33	.074

Total model R^2 = .33, df = 4, 52; antecedents df = 1, 52

Dependent variable: Maternal positive and verbal control at 24 months

Antecedent variable:	Partial R^2	F	$Pr < F$
Work 7–12 months	.23	16.33	.0002
6-month quality of family support	.11	8.78	.004
1-month infant irritability	.09	8.19	.006
Unresolved trauma/incoherence	.03	3.63	.062

Total model R^2 = .46, df = 4, 52; antecedents df = 1, 52

Among trends showing a group difference as a function of the prebirth maternal security (intergroup), two also showed divergent trends over time (group × time); that is, the two measures of maternal involvement were not significantly different from birth to 6 months, but they diverged after 6 months as a function of the mother having been classified as secure versus insecure before her child was born. As noted in the previous study (Heinicke et al., 2000), the priority of the home visit intervention in the first 6 months is on building the mother's positive connection to, and trust in, the home visitor. Work is also initiated in the first 6 months, but the involvement in the work varied and continued, as opposed to decreasing, only for those mothers classified as secure–autonomous. Most important in classifying mothers as secure was the coherence of their narrative. This was true for those who had resolved past trauma and for those who had not. Thus, the same secure–autonomous state that anticipated the mother's involvement in the work of the intervention also helped to sustain it as more difficult emotional issues were confronted in the emerging relationship after 6 months. Moreover, this ability to sustain involvement with the intervenor was then linked to the 2-year outcome.

Case Presentation: Unresolved Response to Loss in the Context of a Coherent Narrative and the Capacity to Sustain a Relationship—Ud Loss, Trauma, F4b

Just as the AAI anticipated involvement in the work and outcome of our sample of 57 families, it also anticipated the foci of treatment in a single case. Thus, one goal of this case presentation is to illustrate how components of a young mother's relationship to her parents and her reactions to the loss of her grandmother were delineated during the AAI interview, then replicated and worked on/resolved during a 2½-year intervention in various contexts, but also very specifically in relation to the therapist. The mother's transference and the therapist's counter feeling reaction were salient and the subject of much therapeutic work.

A second goal of the case presentation is to illustrate that as the relationship and reaction to loss issues were progressively resolved, the therapy increasingly facilitated the mother's adaptation to her partner, her fulfillment as a parent, her pursuit of a college education, and her need to support herself.

Introductory Profile of the Mother, Partner, and Infant

The young mother, MJ, was initially referred to the project by the health care provider in the third trimester of her pregnancy. Of the several criteria for inclusion in the project she met, participation in mental health services in the past was the most significant.

She and her partner, both relatively new to the area, were still adjusting to their new environment. She felt close to some of her immediate family members who lived nearby—mother, younger sister, and a maternal aunt—and had almost daily contact with them. Conversely, her partner did not have any family in the area, although he had close friends. They had met the year before and had soon begun a relationship. In preparation for the birth of their baby, the couple moved into a comfortable apartment together and decorated it as an expression of who they were. The pregnancy and delivery were normal, with no complications following the birth. Pediatric examination revealed a healthy baby.

Depiction of MJ's Relationship to Her Parents and Her Reaction to the Loss of Her Grandmother

Although necessarily selective, the following quotes suggest an AAI profile that was replicated, elaborated, and worked on/resolved in MJ's therapy. [Interviewer comments during MJ's dialogue are in parentheses.]

From early in the interview:

INTERVIEWER: So there were resentments?

MJ: Yes. I think there were.

INTERVIEWER: What would you say hurt the most?

MJ: Umm . . . [2 seconds] for some reason, I just felt like my mom could have been warmer than she was. She was kind of just cold and, which she probably, I realize now she kind of had to be because she had all these, she had four children going through teenage life at the same time (Yeah) and she, she was dealing with a lot.

From later in the interview:

INTERVIEWER: You have mentioned this already. How did you experience your grandmother's loss?

MJ: I was 15 when her cancer was diagnosed. It was very difficult. Yeah, just because she was that one, I wouldn't, yeah. I would say it was more difficult for me than my mom because that's all, all I looked at her was like this big ball of love that you could just always go to. (Yeah) She'd never be mad at you or, and we were very close. Yeah, we, she was constantly in my life like every year of my . . . (Every year) Yeah. So . . . [2 seconds] Yeah so, that, that was hard, but we all, you know, did it, mourned through her death as a family and (*Together*) yeah. She got sick and we knew it was coming and (1 second) yeah. I went through probably about 6 months of helping my grandmother. (Mmm) Like cleaning for her, getting things together and I didn't know she was sick at the time, but now that I look back, I could see that it was her like getting ready for the death. When she died, I was terribly upset.

INTERVIEWER: Were you depressed?

MJ: I didn't remember feeling depressed that early, but I started focusing my energy like on diets that prevented cancer or supposedly did and the whole idea of cancer started to freak me out, so I just started eating different and became a vegetarian.

INTERVIEWER: You linked [eating and cancer] at the time?

MJ: Yeah.

INTERVIEWER: And then what did you feel?

MJ: Umm, I think as the eating disorder took over (Mmm), umm, and I started to feel out of control. (Mmm) That's when I started to feel the depression. Yeah.

INTERVIEWER: Did you experience any kind of physiological change at that time?

MJ: It sure felt like it. Yeah.

INTERVIEWER: Were you in any kind of danger?

MJ: What do you mean? From a doctor's point of view?

INTERVIEWER: Yes.

MJ: Yeah. I had to go into hospital.

INTERVIEWER: A difficult time.

MJ: Yeah that was really, that was really difficult.

INTERVIEWER: How did you see yourself coming out of this?

MJ: When I met my aunt [Dad's sister], who helped me out of it and just introduced me to spirituality. Deeper level than just therapy. Then again I was older.

INTERVIEWER: Did the depression return at all?

MJ: Yeah. I lived with the depression for a while. Umm, and actually I went on some medication, Zoloft, but I actually didn't pull out of the depression until I got pregnant. Which kind of scares me for after I'm pregnant, but hopefully with lifestyle changes it will get better.

Framework for Joining of Select Components of MJ's Functioning, as Documented by the AAI, to the Phases and Content of the Intervention

In summary, the AAI depicted MJ's parents as supportive but not emotionally close. It became clear in the AAI that our future mother compensated for this as a child by turning to her grandmother—a ball of love. The AAI documents MJ's melancholic response to the loss of her grandmother; identification with the grandmother, leading to attempts to prevent her own cancer death through nutritional means; and the subsequent eating disorder and depression. As we demonstrate later, aspects of these issues were replicated and specifically resolved as part of the grief work that occurred during the treatment. MJ's constant search was for the ideal person and solution, as well as the acceptance of her current support, and attempts at greater emotional closeness with her mother.

Aside from the specific description, the AAI provides a general assessment of the future mother's coherence of narrative and of mind, demonstrated by her consistent use of the therapeutic relationship opportunity. With the help of that relationship MJ could then organize herself to meet the challenges of a changing partnership, to become a competent parent, and to finish a full semester of college and support herself financially.

Given the excerpts from the AAI and an initial framework for linking the detailed description to the content and phases of the therapy, we next present the narrative of that therapy.

The Phases and Content of the Therapeutic Intervention with MJ

Commitment to Participation in the Project and Personal Goals

As part of MJ's written consent to participate in the project, including the details of the services provided and the evaluations to be conducted, she volunteered that she "has problems with commitments." The implication was that making a commitment, and being helped to keep that commitment to the project, would also be generally beneficial.

Having been told that, if needed, psychiatric services were available, MJ responded, "With my history of depression, this service will be good for me." Thus, although MJ was not referred for these specific problems, their presence could well be seen as a motivation for treatment.

Positive Connection and Trust in Intervenor Associated with Organizing MJ as a Parent and Her General Sense of Self-Efficacy: The First 6 Months

The first 6 months of treatment solidified the relationship that enabled MJ to work on her issues. As is typical for mothers participating in the UCLA Family Development Project intervention, the positive connection and trust was initially greatly enhanced by sharing certain experiences. In this case, sharing for MJ comprised offering tea to the home visitor, admiring and observing the baby, strolling around the neighborhood, and going to the coffee shop when there was no privacy at home.

This period of the intervention focused on MJ's preoccupation with being a mother, enhancing her self-efficacy, and confronting her lack of self-assertion. Difficulties around establishing a comfortable breast-feeding–sleep cycle became one area for enhancing MJ's self-efficacy. She had been told by her pediatrician to feed the baby every 2 hours and to wake him if necessary. This was not working. What did the home visitor think? Extensive discussion was directed toward MJ trusting her own judgment and, in this and other ways, increasing her sense of self-efficacy. The affirmation of her parenting skills continued throughout the intervention.

Issues around doing the right thing emerged in relation to both MJ's mother and the intervenor. The relationship with her mother was woven throughout the treatment and experienced alternatively as critical, supportive, and distant. Her mother's criticism of MJ's educational/occupational choices caused a big fight. The intervenor suggested that MJ might be worried that, like her mother, she (the therapist) would tell MJ that she was "not doing it right." "No," was MJ's reply. "You wouldn't do that. You are cool."

In subsequent discussions, MJ turned on herself, distressed that she could not really assert herself. For example, why did she not tell her boss she needed time to pump her milk? Rather than asserting herself, MJ required others to divine her needs. Thus, the boss should have offered MJ time to pump her breasts. The issue of self-assertion also focused on MJ organizing herself to reach her goals of optimal parenting, going to school, and earning a living. Increasingly, this meant saying "no" to certain people.

As she initiated the separation from her partner DM, MJ had initially hoped the therapist could "fix" things. She encouraged his Alcoholic Anonymous (AA) attendance and hoped he would change. But her expectations of her partner were clearly being disappointed. He continued to drink and did not take care of her the way he had when they first met and he trained her for a job in a coffee shop. MJ felt she had to leave him, and she worked toward making the separation amiable and protective of their child.

Before turning to the further account of MJ's search for other, ideal caretakers, the intervenor's continuing assistance in practical matters, such as starting classes and obtaining financial aid, should be noted. It clearly facilitated MJ's adaptation. MJ feared that the intervenor was bored with these practical details and that she (MJ) should not expect too much. They discussed these feelings and their transference implications, as well as MJ's fears that she would not stick to her own commitments, that is, to the classes. To understand MJ's therapeutic progress we also need to acknowledge the value of her mother's daily support and availability as MJ addressed emerging conflicts.

The Search for the Ideal Solution—MJ's Partner Is Inadequate and Her Therapist Must Be Like the Grandmother to Defend against Anger Generated by the Lack of Emotional Closeness to Her Mother: The Second 6 Months

The Conflict about Her Partner. In the context of the search for an ideal partner, MJ not only felt very let down but also guilty that she had not tried hard enough to keep the partnership a positive one. She did not want her son to be exposed to a father who was drinking, but she did want him to have some contact with DM. If she trusted the therapist, could the therapist really fix the problem? MJ was openly angry that her partner had let her down. Should she push DM into therapy? She could not stand his drinking; also she generally did not feel fulfilled by him. Distressed by the conflicted feelings, MJ wanted the therapist to tell her what to do. She could not trust herself, because she was not as spiritual as her aunt. She indicated that her grandmother would have found a solution.

As MJ became clearer about her wish to separate from DM, the therapist offered to see both of them, primarily to help them discuss how best to achieve such a separation. The meetings were constructive and both MJ and DM expressed the wish to maintain the contact between father and son. MJ's expectations of his caring for her and their son again emerged; again, she felt that a deeper connection was missing.

The Search for the Ideal Caretaker Appears as a Transference Resistance. The therapeutic sessions were next marked by the therapist needing to try many avenues and questions before MJ was able to respond. MJ noted that her grandmother had been in the theater, and through play and questioning had been able to draw her out. Whereas her twin sister was more forward in their family interactions, MJ studied and stayed in the background. However, MJ's grandmother made her feel important. MJ held back and was slow to initiate work on difficult issues until the therapist had "drawn her out." As they discussed this, MJ for the first time shared her art with the therapist. So the reenactment with an older person (the therapist) revealed how MJ's relationship with her grandmother helped to counter her anger at not having been closer to her mother in childhood.

Indeed, her mother continued to be a source of conflict for MJ. They shared an apartment, and MJ relied on her mother for babysitting while she attended classes in the evenings. However, her mother's criticism of MJ's parenting, as well as their lack of intimacy, continued to disappoint MJ. As she reacted angrily with her mother, her guilt over her earlier behavior in adolescence was revived. She berated herself for not being able to live up to the selfless ideal of care and love portrayed by other members of her family—grandmother, paternal aunt, younger sister.

DM continued to disappoint her. MJ wanted her son to have a father, but when she arranged a visit, DM arrived drunk. She did persist in arranging visits, but she felt very angry that DM did not try harder.

The Search Continues: "If I Give, Will I Get Enough Back?" Increasingly MJ was able to articulate her fears. If she truly trusted the therapist, would she be disappointed? Did the therapist really understand her loneliness and depression? Having fallen for a man who drank, how could MJ trust herself in general? Still searching for the answer and dealing with her uncomfortable feelings, MJ turned to a psychic, as she had in the past. Interestingly, the psychic told MJ to trust an older person with her best interests at heart. After thinking about the statement, MJ announced in the next session that she understood the older person to be the therapist.

This period was also characterized by an increased desire on MJ's part to understand herself, but she feared that she would not, in the end, feel the way her grandmother had made her feel (special). Over a number of sessions, MJ and the therapist discussed MJ's constant search to reexperience "that special feeling" she had with her grandmother and to find "the solution with the therapist and elsewhere." She responded self-critically: "Well, shouldn't I be over that? I've been working on it quite a while." In addressing this issue, MJ's response and subsequent dream material marked the beginning of further mourning over the loss of the grandmother. MJ recalled that after the death of her grandmother, she repeatedly dreamt that the grandmother was still alive in the basement of her house and giving off a putrid odor that she could remember upon waking. MJ also shared a dream from the previous night, in which her grandmother, grandfather (who was still alive), and her partner were all dead. In further elaboration of this dream, she noted that she was happy that she was telling the therapist about this. It was as if she had to finish a relationship to move further ahead.

MJ's Progressive Adaptation, Irritation, and Greater Emotional Closeness with Her Mother

It is very likely that the wish to move forward was part of MJ's incentive to take further steps to finance her college education. At the same time, her feelings toward her mother and the therapist also emerged more clearly. When MJ's younger brother stayed with them, her mother took over making breakfast, a task usually performed by MJ. Even more egregiously, the mother made toast for her son, but MJ had to make her own. She was irritated but could not really tell her mother. In an effort to elucidate her feelings and encourage self-reflection, the therapist suggested that MJ might be irritated that the therapist had not done more to help her, but was afraid to express her feelings. MJ replied quickly, "If I was irritated with you, I could tell you."

Further work addressed the disappointment that MJ feared; that she will not get enough back if she reaches out for greater intimacy. When the therapist took a 1-week vacation, MJ turned to a book for solutions. In the next session, as this "continuing search" was interpreted, MJ reported that she got a knot in her stomach. Furthermore, she was afraid that the therapist was "coming out of duty." On the other hand, if the therapist enjoyed coming, then MJ would feel worthy. MJ recognized that her grandmother had in the past been an emotional replacement for what MJ had not experienced with her mother. She also noted that even though they currently shared an apartment, she did not kiss her mother. Her mother would really have liked that. As it happened, when the mother became ill, MJ took care of her. When she was better, MJ told her mother that she was happy she was better and gave her a kiss. Shortly afterward, MJ dreamed that her son's head was bashed in by her grandfather. In the dream, MJ did not want her son to wake and feel pain, so she asked her mother to do something. To ease her grandson's pain, the grandmother twice smashed his head with a ladle and then MJ woke up. In her associations, MJ observed, "As I get closer to a person, something in me needs to be smashed so I can keep getting closer. The dream was eerie."

Further Resolution of Past Conflicts, Including MJ's Eating Disorder and Her Relationship with Her Father, Occurs in the Context of Further Adaptation, and MJ Begins Two Classes: The Third 6 Months

This period was marked by the intensity of MJ's transference manifestations. Her longing to be taken care of and her fears that the therapist would not take care of her again emerged. To ward off these feelings, she turned elsewhere for the answer, primarily to books. The therapist struggled with MJ's return to prolonged silences in the session and her increasing irritation because things still had not changed for her. The implication was that the therapist had not done enough to help MJ overcome her uncomfortable feelings.

In contrast to previous diminution of herself, MJ recognized that she was working hard, and that her mother was happy with her. However, her son's sleep rhythm was still disturbed, and MJ became angry that her ex-partner did not offer much help with the new pressures of studying and working. MJ complained of being tired, of having no adult time, and of often feeling out of control—often sad, worried over schoolwork, and berating herself for not spending more quality time with her son. "I am glad I am telling you," she added. "Other therapists would recommend medication." The therapist's not recommending medication, as had been MJ's previous experiences with therapy, became an important point in the treatment, leading to MJ's increased ability to trust the therapist, because she felt special and that she mattered. MJ cried as she talked about her isolation and that needing "adult time" did not mean that she was not a good mother. MJ again realized that she needed to be more assertive in asking for help. Perhaps she could depend on others, such as her sister or aunt who lived nearby, for help with babysitting in the evenings to give her time to study and to do yoga.

As MJ reflected on her own anxiety when starting new situations, she realized that being overwhelmed was impacting her son's sleep rhythm. She could eventually be firmer and not respond to all of her son's crying. She realized that somehow eliminating all crying did not constitute being a perfect mother.

During this time, MJ continued her grief work, accepting the loss of both her grandmother and her partner. Given her increasing ability to meet the various challenges—her grief work, responding to her son's needs, living with her mother, holding down a part-time job, and asking for help—MJ organized herself to find enough study time and did very well in her two classes.

As MJ Further Organizes Herself to Take a Full Load of Classes, She Harasses Herself for Not Finding the Ideal Day Care Situation: The Fourth 6 Months

Preparation for the Full Semester: Meeting Reality—Day Care, Budgets, Studying. MJ's search for the ideal caretaking situation focused on finding the ideal day care for her son. MJ again and again blamed herself for not being with her son enough and not doing the right thing. When she finally chose a day care provider, her son settled in well and was happy to see her when she picked him up.

Parallel issues of taking care of herself and being taken care of emerged at this time. MJ's new friend noticed that she seemed underweight and coaxed her to eat fruit. Actually, she was "eating a ton, but was still skinny." Even though she was afraid to talk about her eating disorder because it would drive others away, MJ sought reassurance from her aunt and her mother that the eating disorder was not returning.

As she once more juggled all the pressures to prepare for the full semester, MJ dreamt that she was harassing herself because she had had a drink with her twin sister. Discussion with the therapist led to the realization that MJ generally harassed herself, that she could not accept her achievements because they were not perfect. Given this tendency toward self-criticism, MJ had become afraid to move ahead; whatever she did would not be good enough.

Starts Full Semester: The Emphasis on Organizing Herself. Many of the previous areas of concern continued to emerge as MJ started her first full semester of college. If MJ asserted herself by telling her mother not to yell at the baby when he pooped on the floor, would her mother continue to support her? If she could not make small talk, could she hold down her coffee shop job? But most important, the therapist now focused on the task of organizing MJ's day and week. This intervention clearly helped MJ "to keep her mind from racing." As MJ improved, the baby's sleep patterns, which had again been disrupted, also improved. Her continuing efforts to improve the relationship with her mother and sister led to greater support from them; they increasingly enjoyed taking care of her son. As she and the therapist reviewed these multiple issues, MJ was afraid that the therapist would see her as a "drama queen." Interpretation and discussion allowed her to work on these and other concerns, including her feelings about termination.

Further Progress and Termination

Although the therapist reminded MJ that their last session was fast approaching, and MJ knew that the regular home visiting contacts were limited to 2 years from the date of the infant's birth, MJ could not initially discuss her feelings about it. However, she displayed the well-known reactions to treatment termination: communicating that nothing had been solved, while displaying striking instances of progress. She reported feeling desperate and intensely disliking her life, going to school, and not having enough time to spend with her son. She thought of moving to join her brother in another state. The therapist's major intervention to counter these feelings was to point out what MJ had achieved both as a college student and as a parent. Moving far away would clearly disrupt the continuity of the education for which she had fought so hard.

Initially, MJ responded by indeed continuing her progress. She registered for the spring semester, considered local moves that would improve their housing situation, and joined the mother–toddler group, which would potentially connect her to the project for another year. Her feelings about ending the regular visits also gradually emerged. During a session, when only four regular contacts remained, MJ wanted to discuss two topics: her experience of date rape when she was 18 years old, and how currently to approach a man in the coffee shop that she found attractive. She decided to postpone dealing with the "date rape," as if the therapy needed to continue since it had not dealt with this important event. In regard to approaching the man to whom she was attracted, her mother said, "Just see where it goes." A discussion with the therapist led MJ to conclude that it might first be best to have several conversations with this man. MJ remarked on what a good sounding board the therapist was, then asked who would be her sounding board in the future? The therapist noted MJ's ability to reflect on potential directions, reaffirming her availability on an ad hoc basis in the future.

The therapist admired MJ's outstanding test and grade performance at the end of the semester. As if again holding on to the view that all was not perfect, MJ wondered whether all the pressure she had endured was worth it, and whether the therapist would help her apply to a preschool for her son.

Discussion of the Case

Examining both the excerpts from the AAI and the phases of the treatment, certain conclusions seem warranted. The interpretation of the Ud/F categorization indicating both a capacity for positive relationships and motivation to resolve issues of adaptation is supported on a general level by the overall course of the intervention. MJ was able to organize herself to make use of the relationship with the home visitor and the associated services relative to issues that concerned her. As she developed a positive connection and trust in the therapist, enhanced particularly by sharing experiences and positive mutual affirmation, MJ could both reflect on and attain more effective adaptation in regard to issues focusing on herself, her partner, her family, and her infant.

This therapy illustrates various intervention modes that constitute the overall treatment approach: empathic listening, clarifying, enhancement of understanding, and at times interpreting the issues and conflicts that emerge. Specifically, many of the therapeutic sessions focused on elucidating how MJ had in childhood turned from the "support" of her parents to the emotional closeness (ball of love) of her grandmother. This was depicted by the AAI, as was the reaction to the loss of the grandmother (i.e., an eating disorder and depression). The recapitulation of turning from "just support" to the idealized love object in the relationship with the therapist provided the motivation and setting for MJ to find alternative adaptations to that loss. In this context, MJ faced the loss of her grandmother in the past and of her current partner, enabling the grief work to begin.

The recapitulation of the salient issues in the relationship with the therapist (transference) also elicited MJ's strength to find alternative adaptations to these issues. The therapist, like her grandmother, had to "draw her out" and tell MJ "what she should do" about her conflicted feelings toward the father of her son. Resolving these transference issues involved, first of all, recognizing and accepting them. MJ shared her idealizations, disappointments, and fears. Once MJ accessed these relationships and their associated feelings, the therapist encouraged her to reflect on their meaning. The narrative suggests that this reflection facilitated better adaptation to the challenges MJ was facing. Closely related to this process was the actual availability and "support" of MJ's mother and MJ's ability to work on her ambivalent feelings to the point of being able to take care of her own ill mother and give her a kiss when she got better.

Although always influenced by an understanding of the nature of MJ's functioning and relationships, the therapist also focused specifically on the adaptation to certain problems. The questions concerned how to view the problem, available alternative options, and the evaluation of solutions once an option had been chosen. What specific solutions would enable MJ to separate from her partner, yet encourage his contact with his son? How could the emergence of her son's irregular sleep pattern be related to her anxiety? Equally important, how could she deal with it? After she addressed her feelings about not getting more help, how could MJ organize her day to maximize her study time?

Both advocacy and direct assistance were part of the treatment profile. In this case, the therapist helped in filling out forms (e.g., to enter MJ's son into preschool, and to make MJ aware of potential financial help). Finally, throughout the treatment both general and specific positive reinforcement played a critical role in developing MJ's sense of worth and effectiveness.

Reflecting the complexity of the developmental trajectories (Sroufe et al., 2005), the therapist pursued salient issues that related to MJ's functioning, her relationship with her child, and the child's development. As indicated earlier, the therapist used different interventions to promote developmental progress and adaptation.

Concluding Remarks

We started with a focus on 2-year mother–child qualities, such as the mother's responsiveness to her child's needs and the child's security of attachment, that were impacted by the UCLA Family Development Project intervention in a randomized trial. We next observed great variations in that outcome *within* the intervention group. A preliminary study revealed that the personality characteristics of the mother, her support system, and 1-month infant and mother–child qualities were likely to anticipate these variations.

Given the emphasis on a relationship-based intervention and likely variations in the mother's capacity to make use of that relationship, the AAI is seen as a powerful assessment measure of that capacity in this study of 57 families. The choice of the prebirth AAI was also particularly relevant because of its known power in predicting security of attachment in nonintervention populations. Indeed, our study shows that the AAI *anticipated* mothers' capacity to make use of the intervention, and that both the AAI and involvement in the work of the intervention were unique predictors of 2-year social–emotional development. We have also illustrated how the profile of issues defined by the AAI *anticipated* key issues in treatment of first-time at-risk parents.

References

Beck, A. T., Ward, C. H., Mendelson, M., Mock, J., & Erbaugh, J. (1961). An inventory for measuring depression. *Archives of General Psychiatry, 4*, 561–569.

Cowan, P. A., Powell, D., & Cowan, C. P. (1997). Parenting interventions: A family systems perspective. In I. E. Sigel & K. A. Renninger (Eds.), *Handbook of child psychology: Vol. 4. Child psychology in practice* (5th ed., pp. 3–72). New York: Wiley.

Cutrona, C. E. (1984). Social support and stress in the transition to parenthood. *Journal of Abnormal Psychology, 93*(4), 378–390.

Heinicke, C. M. (2000). *UCLA Family Development Project: Operational manual for preventive intervention plan* (rev. ed.). Los Angeles: University of California, Department of Psychiatry and Biobehavioral Sciences. (Available from Christoph M. Heinicke, Jane and Terry Semel Institute for Neuroscience and Human Behavior, 760 Westwood Plaza, Room 68-237B, Los Angeles, CA 90024-1759)

Heinicke, C. M. (2002). Transition to parenting. In M. H. Bornstein (Ed.), *Handbook of parenting* (Vol. 3, 2nd ed., pp. 363–388). Mahwah, NJ: Erlbaum.

Heinicke, C. M. (2004). *Manual for global ratings of infant and caregiver–infant relationship from 6 to 24 months.* Los Angeles: University of California, Department of Psychiatry and Biobehavioral Sciences. (Available from Christoph M. Heinicke, Jane and Terry Semel Institute for Neuroscience and Human Behavior, 760 Westwood Plaza, Room 68-237B, Los Angeles, CA 90024-1759)

Heinicke, C. M., Fineman, N. R., Ponce, V. A., & Guthrie, D. (2001). Relationship based intervention with at-risk mothers: Outcome in the second year of life. *Infant Mental Health Journal, 22*(4), 431–462.

Heinicke, C. M., Goorsky, M., Levine, M., Ponce, V., Ruth, G., Silverman, M., et al.

(2006). Pre and postnatal antecedents of a home visiting intervention and family developmental outcome. *Infant Mental Health Journal, 27*(1), 91–119.

Heinicke, C. M., Goorsky, M., Moscov, S., Dudley, K., Gordon, J., Schneider, C., et al. (2000). Relationship based intervention with at-risk mothers: Factors affecting variations in outcome. *Infant Mental Health Journal, 21*(3), 133–155.

Hesse, E. (1999). The Adult Attachment Interview: Historical and current perspectives. In J. Cassidy & P. R. Shaver (Eds.), *Handbook of attachment: Theory, research and clinical applications* (pp. 395–433). New York: Guilford Press.

Jacobvitz, D., Leon, K., & Hazen, N. (2006). Does expectant mother's unresolved trauma predict frightened/frightening maternal behavior?: Risk and protective factors. *Development and Psychopathology, 18,* 363–379.

Locke, H., & Wallace, K. (1959). Short marital adjustment and prediction tests: Their reliability and validity. *Marriage and Family Living, 21,* 251–255.

Loevinger, J., & Wessler, R. (1983). *Measuring ego development: Volume 1. Construction and use of a sentence completion test.* San Francisco: Jossey-Bass.

Loranger, H. W. (1988). *Personality Disorder Examination (PDE) manual.* Yonkers, NY: DV Communications.

Main, M., Goldwyn, R., & Hesse, E. (2003). *Adult attachment scoring and classification systems* (Manual in draft: Version 7.2). Unpublished manuscript, Department of Psychology, University of California, Berkeley.

Schuengel, C., van IJzendoorn, M., & Bakermans-Kranenburg, M. (1999). Frightening, maternal behavior linking unresolved loss and disorganized infant attachment. *Journal of Consulting and Clinical Psychology, 67,* 54–63.

Shipley, W. C. (1940). A self-administering scale for measuring intellectual impairment and deterioration. *Journal of Psychology, 9,* 371–377.

Spielberger, C. D. (1977). *Self-evaluation questionnaire.* Palo Alto, CA: Consulting Psychologists Press.

Sroufe, A. L., Egeland, B., Carlson, E. A., & Collins, A. W. (2005). *The development of the person: The Minnesota study of risk and adaptation from birth to adulthood.* New York: Guilford Press.

van IJzendoorn, M. H. (1995). Adult attachment representations, parental responsiveness, and infant attachment: A meta-analysis on the predictive validity of the adult attachment interview. *Psychological Bulletin, 117,* 387–403.

van IJzendoorn, M. H., Vereijken, C. M., Bakermans-Kranenburg, M. J., & Riksen-Walraven, J. M. (2004). Assessing attachment security with the Attachment Q-Sort: Meta-analytic evidence for the validity of the Observer AQS. *Child Development, 75*(4), 1188–1213.

Waters, E. (1986). *Attachment Behavior Q-Set: Revision 2.0.* Unpublished manuscript, State University of New York, Stony Brook.

5

Adult Attachment, Parental Commitment to Early Intervention, and Developmental Outcomes in an African American Sample

DOUGLAS M. TETI, LAUREN A. KILLEEN, MARGO CANDELARIA, WENDY MILLER, CHRISTINE REINER HESS, and MELISSA O'CONNELL

As this volume attests, adult state of mind regarding attachment has increasingly become a focus in clinical work, particularly in terms of whether states of mind can be altered in response to psychotherapy (Levy et al., 2006; Steele & Baradon, 2004). In this chapter, we examine the role of attachment states of mind in organizing parental receptivity and engagement to an early intervention program for premature infants, the majority of whom were reared in socioeconomically disadvantaged circumstances. Intervention for such infants, and identifying predictors of parental commitment to intervention, is clearly warranted. Premature birth comprised 12.5% of all yearly births in the United States in 2004 (Martin, Hamilton, Menacker, Sutton, & Matthews, 2005), and children born prematurely are at significantly higher risk than full-term infants for chronic medical conditions and developmental delays in physical growth, language, intellectual and socioemotional functioning (Aylward, 2005; Hack, Klein, & Taylor, 1995, Reichman, 2005; Salt & Redshaw, 2006; Singer et al., 2001; Taylor, Burant, Holding, Klein, & Hack, 2002; Taylor, Minich, Bangert, Flilipek, & Hack, 2004), and for parent–infant interactional difficulties that appear to be linked with deficits in preterm infants' communicative capacities and parental distress related to having an infant born too soon (Miles & Holditch-Davis, 1995; Teti, O'Connell, & Reiner, 1996). These problems are more pronounced among very premature ($\leq$ 32 weeks gestational age) and extremely premature ($\leq$ 28 weeks gestational age) infants, the latter of whom have been found to be at extreme risk for developmental delay by 30 months of age (Aylward, 2005; Hack et al., 1995). Developmental prognoses of premature infants may be further compromised when premature infants are born to socioeconomically disadvantaged families. Indeed, poverty exacts its own heavy toll on child development (McLoyd, 1998), and children reared in poverty are at high risk for significant developmental delays in language, cognitive, and social development (Baroody, Lai, & Mix, 2006; Duncan & Magnuson, 2005; Evans, 2004; Magnuson & Waldfogel, 2005; Rouse, Brooks-Gunn, & McLanahan, 2005; Ryan, Fauth, & Brooks-Gunn, 2006). Thus, preterm infants born into poverty are at "double jeopardy," because their development can be adversely affected by both medical and environmental risks.

Infants born prematurely (< 37 weeks gestational age) have been repeated, frequent targets of intervention over the past three decades (e.g., Bromwich & Parmelee, 1979; Brooks-Gunn et al., 1994; Browne & Talmi, 2005; Mahoney & Cohen, 2005; Rauh, Achenbach, Nurcombe, Howell, & Teti, 1988). Although a full review of these programs is beyond the scope of this chapter, the brief, targeted intervention package described herein is consistent with the kind of short-term, focused interventions, identified from meta-analyses by Bakermans-Kranenburg and colleagues, that have a high likelihood of success in promoting parental sensitivity (Bakermans-Kranenburg, van IJzendoorn, & Bradley, 2005; Bakermans-Kranenburg, van IJzendoorn, & Juffer, 2003; see also Bakermans-Kranenburg, van IJzendoorn, & Juffer, 2005). Our intervention comprised three components, each of which was successful in improving parental sensitivity in earlier work: The first involved parent-delivered, infant-focused, systematically delivered tactile/kinesthetic stimulation, which we expected to promote parents' awareness of infant bodily and social cues, and their skills, confidence, and sensitivity during interactions with the infant (Cullen, Field, Escalona, & Hartshorn, 2000; Ferber et al., 2005; Onzawa, Glover, Adams, Modi, & Kumar, 2001). The second made use of the Neonatal Behavioral Assessment Scale (NBAS; Brazelton & Nugent, 1995) as an intervention tool with parents. NBAS demonstrations with parents, especially when repeated, have been found to promote parental knowledge of infant capabilities and weaknesses, and to establish mutually positive infant–parent transactions and improved parental responsivity (Anderson & Sawin, 1983; Brazelton & Nugent, 1995; Das Eiden & Reifman, 1996; Rauh et al., 1988; Widmayer & Field, 1980; Worobey & Belsky, 1982). Finally, the intervention employed a brief (20-minute) psychoeducational video (*Premie Talk: Understanding Your Premature Baby's Behavior*; Cusson & DeWeese, 1992) about infants' perceptual and interactive capacities, and specific parental practices to foster infant connections with the environment. Cusson, Viscardi, Tyhala, Yin, and Okunski (1996) found that African American mothers exposed to two showings of this video prior to infant hospital discharge had improved knowledge about basic infant care and improved sensitivity with their babies at 6 months of age, relative to controls.

There is reason to believe that attachment states of mind regarding attachment can play an important role in organizing parental responses to and engagement with an intervention of this kind. First, it is intuitive to expect that mothers with secure states of mind, defined in part by the high value placed on attachment relationships, would commit more strongly to intervention efforts aimed toward improving quality of parenting and the parent–infant relationship than would parents with insecure states of mind. Second, because autonomously attached adults have successfully integrated past attachment experience with current emotions, mothers with autonomous states of mind would be expected to interpret and respond to intervention messages with greater openness, objectivity, and veridicality, and with less defensiveness and distortion, than would mothers with nonautonomous states of mind. The few studies that have assessed the role of Adult Attachment Interview (AAI)–indexed states of mind regarding attachment in organizing receptivity to intervention support these expectations, especially when comparing individuals with autonomous versus dismissing, attachment-deactivating strategies (George, Kaplan, & Main, 1996; Main & Hesse, 1990). Dozier (1990; Dozier & Tyrrell, 1998) found clients with autonomous states of mind to be more receptive to and engaged with psychotherapy than clients with dismissing states of mind, reflected by the finding that autonomous clients were more receptive and committed to carrying out therapeutic "tasks" (e.g., taking prescribed medicines) and to discussing ongoing concerns as they arose, and less likely to miss scheduled appointments than were dismissing clients. Furthermore, Dozier, Lomax, Tyrrell, and Lee (2001) found that psychiatrically disturbed clients with dismissing strategies were less likely than clients with preoccupied strategies to remain "on task" with case managers. In at least one home intervention study (the Minnesota Steps toward Effective, Enjoyable Parenting [STEEP] Project), which targeted environmentally high-risk mothers, autonomous mothers showed greater receptivity to and compliance with a home visiting intervention protocol than did dismissing mothers (Korfmacher, Adam, Ogawa, & Egeland, 1997). Korfmacher and colleagues (1997) also reported that mothers classified as unresolved were less committed to the intervention program and to working with interventionists than were mothers with "organized" states of mind.

Parental commitment to early intervention, however, is multiply determined. Some studies have examined the predictive power of parental personality and psychiatric factors (e.g., coping strategies, depression) (Gavidia-Payne & Stoneman, 1997; Ireys, De Vet, & Chernoff, 2001), and intervention program characteristics (Bailey, Buysse, Edmondson, & Smith, 1992; Logan & Caruso, 1997), with varying degrees of success. A far larger literature, however, has documented linkages between family socioeconomic resources and parental commitment, with most studies demonstrating that parental engagement with early intervention is positively associated with higher family income and parental education, and smaller family size (Arcia, Keyes, Gallagher, & Herrick, 1993; Gavidia-Payne & Stoneman, 1997; Kochanek & Buka, 1995; Kuchler-O'Shea, Kritikos, & Kahn, 1999; Liaw, Meisels, & Brooks-Gunn, 1995; Mahoney & Filer, 1996). The associations between low socioeconomic resources and both major and minor life stressors, such as transportation difficulties, unstable housing, marital discord, or single parenthood, may make it more difficult for parents to engage effectively with early intervention services (Allen, Affleck, McGrade, & McQueeney, 1984; Beckman, Robinson, Rosenberg, & Filer, 1994; Dunst, Trivette, & Deal, 1988; Rickel, 1986).

Nevertheless, many low-income, environmentally stressed parents *do* effectively engage with early intervention programs (e.g., Minke & Scott, 1995), suggesting that factors other than socioeconomics and perhaps, in particular, factors intrinsic to the parent, figure importantly in motivating parental involvement. In this chapter we explore one such possibility, maternal state of mind regarding attachment, in predicting mothers' commitment to early intervention in a predominantly urban-dwelling, low-income sample of African American mothers of premature infants. We proposed the following hypotheses:

1. Autonomous mothers will commit more strongly to the intervention than will nonautonomous mothers, which is consistent with prior work on the quality of adults' engagement with psychotherapy (Dozier, 1990) and with a nurse home visiting program (Korfmacher et al., 1997).

2. Maternal commitment to intervention will be positively associated with more favorable socioeconomic indicators (e.g., higher incomes and educational attainment), which is consistent with earlier work demonstrating such linkages (e.g., Arcia et al., 1993; Gavidia-Payne & Stoneman, 1997; Kochanek & Buka, 1995; Kuchler-O'Shea et al., 1999).

3. Differences between autonomous and nonautonomous mothers in parental commitment will persist after we statistically control for socioeconomic variables.

4. Both autonomous attachments and maternal commitment to intervention will be predictive of more sensitive mothering and improved infant developmental outcomes at 3–4, 12, and 24 months of infant age, corrected for prematurity.

5. Finally, relative to examining relations between maternal commitment to intervention, intervention outcomes, and whether mothers' states of mind are resolved or unresolved, although theoretical links between unresolved states of mind and commitment to intervention are not straightforward, several studies suggest that unresolved states of mind, regardless of underlying attachment classification, may be particularly unresponsive to brief interventions and to psychotherapy

(Moran, Bailey, Gleason, DeOliveira, & Pederson, Chapter 15, this volume; Routh, Hill, Steele, Elliott, & Dewey 1995); thus, we would anticipate that mothers with unresolved states of mind would be unlikely to respond effectively to our intervention.

Methods

Participants

This present study focuses on a subsample of mothers ($n = 83$) participating in a larger, ongoing study funded by the National Institute of Child Health and Human Development (R01-38982) to implement and evaluate the efficacy of a 20-week, eight-session early intervention protocol designed to promote infant development and the parent–infant relationship. All participants in this and in a larger study ($n = 173$) were predominantly urban-dwelling and low-income African Americans recruited from the neonatal intensive care units (NICUs) in four hospitals in the Baltimore/Washington, DC area. No recruitment took place until infants were at least 32 weeks postconceptual age (PCA) to ensure their medical stability and viability. Families were not recruited if there was a maternal drug problem in evidence (from toxicology screening), if mothers were less than 18 years of age, or if the infant had diagnosable chromosomal abnormalities. This information was obtained from NICU personnel prior to any contact with the families.

Within 48 hours of recruitment, families were assigned randomly to the intervention or control groups. Only mothers and infants in the intervention group were examined in this study. Among the 83 mothers recruited into this group, 18 had dropped out of the study by 3–4 months of infant age, an additional participant had dropped out by 12 months (19 total), and an additional 14 had dropped out by 24 months (33 total). We conducted attrition analyses to determine whether the families who had dropped out of the study by 3–4, 12, and 24 months of infant age were in any way different, in terms of sociodemographics and infant medical data, from participants who remained in the study at those age points. Mothers who dropped out of the study by the time their infants were 2 years of age were more likely to be on public assistance [$\chi^2(1) = 8.22$, $p = .004$] and less likely to be employed [$\chi^2(1) = 4.11$, $p = .043$] than were mothers who completed the study. No differences at any age point were found for infant gender, mothers' educational attainment, yearly family income, maternal age, marital status, infant birthweight, infant gestational age at birth, and infant length of stay in the hospital before discharge.

Of the 67 mothers and infants who had completed the intervention by 3–4 months of infant age, technical difficulties in recording the AAI were encountered for five mothers. Table 5.1 presents sociodemographic and infant medical data on the 62 participants who completed the intervention and had a codable AAI.

As shown in Table 5.1, slightly more female than male infants, and a wide distribution of gestational age (GA) and birthweights (BW) is represented, with minimal skewness (GA = –0.28; BW = 0.01). Although the mean length of infant stay in the hospital prior to discharge was about 36 days, this distribution was positively skewed (1.12), with a median of 28 days. Thus, about 50% of the infants in this sample were hospitalized 4 weeks or more prior to discharge. Approximately 82% of the mothers in this inner-city sample had graduated high school, and a few of them (about 15%) went on to attain a bachelor's degree or higher. Although some socioeconomic diversity was apparent in this sample, the majority of families were low-income, with

TABLE 5.1. Sociodemographic and Infant Medical Information on the Present Intervention Sample of African American Mothers and Their Preterm Infants

Variable	Percent	Mean	SD	Range
Infant data				
Gender (female)	53.2			
Gestational age (weeks)		30.71	3.23	23–37
Birthweight (grams)		1459.95	509.49	540–2,555
Length of hospital stay (days)		35.97	25.22	4–123
Maternal data				
Age (years)		25.84	5.92	18–43
Parity (primiparous)	53.2			
Education				
Did not graduate high school	17.7			
High school diploma	37.1			
Some college	27.4			
Associate's degree	3.2			
Bachelor's degree	12.9			
Master's degree	1.6			
Yearly family income				
< $10,000	31.6			
$10,000–19,999	15.8			
$20,000–29,999	15.8			
$30,000–39,999	8.8			
$40,000–49,999	7.0			
$50,000–59,999	5.3			
$60,000 or above	15.8			
Receiving state/federal assistance	79.0			
Marital status				
Single	58.1			
Married/living with partner	41.9			
Currently employed	32.3			

Note. n = 62.

about 63% reporting yearly family incomes of under $30,000 and 79% receiving some form of public assistance.

Procedure

An initial baseline home visit was scheduled following recruitment to obtain sociodemographic information from the mothers and to conduct the AAI. These visits took place when infants were between 32 and 36 weeks PCA, prior to the onset of the intervention, and were typically done before infants had been discharged from the hospital. The AAI was administered by a trained interviewer. Outcome assessments of the infants were obtained at three points postintervention: 3–4 months, 12 months, and 24 months of infant age, corrected for prematurity.

Administration of the AAI

The AAI was administered to mothers by an interviewer who was trained on the AAI interviewing protocol by Douglas Teti. Prior experience with the population under study prompted some minor changes to the very beginning of the AAI protocol to take into account the possibility that mothers in the sample were reared in father-absent homes, and that mothers may have formed significant attachments in childhood to caregivers other than just their mothers. Thus, the interviewer began each interview by asking the mother: "Can you tell me a little bit about your family when you were growing up? Who would you say raised you?" The interviewer would then proceed to ask the mother to describe her relationship with each caregiver she named. We also wished to remain open to the possibility that even when a mother was reared in a father-absent home, she nevertheless could have developed a relationship with her father in other contexts. Indeed, this was not uncommon in our sample. Thus, we made a point to inquire about whether the mother had any relationship with her father, even though he might have spent relatively little time living at home. If it was clear that some kind of relationship was established, the interviewer proceeded to ask the mother to describe her relationship with her father as well.

Aside from these minor modifications, AAI interviews with the mothers followed the standard format (George et al., 1996). Each mother was asked to provide some general and contextual information about family and early childhood, and to talk a little more specifically about early relationships with caregivers. The mother was then asked to provide up to five adjectives to describe her relationships with the named caregivers and, if warranted, with her father, and to provide support for each descriptor with a specific memory. Each mother was also asked about the following: to which caregiver she felt closest, and why; what she as a child would do when upset; what her first separation experience was like; whether she ever felt rejected or threatened in childhood and her impressions of why the caregiver behaved as he or she did;

information pertaining to loss (past and present) and to abuse; information about any changes in the current relationships with caregivers; how she felt about separating from her own infant; what three wishes she would have for her baby in 20 years; and what she hoped her child would learn from being parented by her.

Interviews were videotaped and audiorecorded, and typically took between 45 and 60 minutes to complete. The audiocassettes were then transcribed verbatim, carefully following AAI transcription guidelines.

Two trained coders, each certified in the AAI classification system by Mary Main and Erik Hesse, classified the 62 mothers' AAI transcripts. Both coders, completely blind to any additional data on the mothers and infants, established interrater reliability on 38 transcripts from the larger, ongoing study, with 84% intercoder agreement ($\kappa = .64$) on autonomous versus nonautonomous classifications, and 89% agreement ($\kappa = .71$) on whether mothers were unresolved with respect to loss/trauma. In this study sample, 34 AAIs were classified as autonomous, 26 as dismissing, 1 as preoccupied, and 1 as cannot classify. Thirteen of the 62 mothers in this sample received an additional classification of unresolved, primarily to do with a past loss; these interviews were alternatively classified as dismissing in six cases, preoccupied in zero cases, and autonomous in six cases, and cannot classify in one case. Given the small numbers in the preoccupied and cannot classify groups, results below are based primarily on comparison of dismissing and autonomous groups. We also discuss our lack of findings when comparing the unresolved with resolved groups.

The Intervention

The proposed eight-session, 20-week intervention integrated two psychoeducational components and one parent-administered, infant tactile stimulation component into a transportable (from the NICU to the home) package that was justified theoretically and empirically. The intervention's theoretical basis derived from the transactional model of development (Sameroff, 1975) in that its aims were expected to establish positive, reciprocal transactions between infants and their caregivers to facilitate developmental outcomes, and from attachment theory (Ainsworth, Blehar, Waters, & Wall, 1978; Bowlby, 1969/1982), in that the quality of infants' attachment to parents should be enhanced in intervention subjects via improved parental sensitivity to infants' social cues. The relatively short-term, behaviorally oriented intervention was similar to interventions identified by van IJzendoorn, Juffer, and Duyvesteyn (1995) that have been successful in promoting parental sensitivity and infant–parent attachment. The intervention was conducted by a doctoral-level intervention coordinator (Christine Reiner Hess) and three interventionists, beginning at 32 weeks PCA for infants less than 32 weeks GA, and between 32 and 36 weeks PCA for infants greater than 32 weeks GA. Intervention onset co-occurred with the development of suck–swallow coordination and cardio-

TABLE 5.2. Timeline of Intervention Activities

Infant postconceptual age in weeks	Intervention Activities
32–36	Introduction video, *Premie Talk*, in hospital
34–38	Second showing of *Premie Talk*; first NBAS demo, in hospital or in home
36–40	Introduction to massage therapy; second NBAS demo, in hospital or in home
38–42	Massage therapy; third NBAS demo, in hospital or in home
40–44	Massage therapy; fourth NBAS demo, in hospital or in home
44–48	Massage therapy; fifth NBAS demo, in home
48–52	Massage therapy; sixth NBAS demo, in home
52–56	Massage therapy; seventh NBAS demo, in home

Note. NBAS, Neonatal Behavioral Assessment Scale. With each successive demonstration of the NBAS, both mothers and fathers were increasingly encouraged to participate in its administration.

respiratory control in preterms, which emerge at approximately 34 weeks GA. Thus, the initial intervention sessions coincided with the transition between gavage (tube) and oral feedings, and with increased parental involvement with the baby's feedings in turn. Interventionists and the intervention coordinator were certified NBAS examiners and working toward a master's- or doctoral-level degree in applied developmental psychology (ADP) at the University of Maryland, Baltimore County. Each family was assigned one interventionist during the 20-week intervention period. Each intervention session lasted between 1 and 2 hours. Table 5.2 depicts intervention activities across the 4-month intervention period.

Intervention Components

The 20-week intervention protocol integrated the following three components:

1. *Premie Talk: Understanding Your Premature Baby's Behavior* (Cusson & DeWeese, 1992). This 20-minute videotape was shown to parents when their infants were 32–36 and 34–38 weeks PCA in a private room in the NICU or, if the infant had been discharged, in the home. Viewing of the video was followed by a 40-minute review of its contents. Discussions at 32–36 weeks covered the following points: (a) Premature infants are sensitive to the world around them and use behavior to communicate with parents; (b) the NICU is an unfamiliar, noisy, overstimulating environment to the preterm baby; (c) preterm infants tend to sleep a lot and are not as responsive as full-term babies; (d) preterm babies respond best to gentle stimulation; (e) preterm

babies have three basic states of consciousness: asleep, awake and alert, and fussy; (f) the awake and alert state is best for social interaction; and (g) preterm infants are not all the same—some are healthier; therefore, they can do more than others. An additional 20-minute discussion included parents' general questions about any of these points and about their newborns. Two weeks later, at 34–38 weeks PCA, the videotape was shown again to parents, and the interventionist reviewed the points covered at 32–36 weeks PCA and responded to additional questions parents had about that material. The following additional points were then covered: (a) Preterm babies use engagement cues to indicate when they are ready to interact, and disengagement cues to signal when they "need a break"; (b) common engagement cues; (c) common disengagement cues; (d) what to do when the baby shows disengagement cues during interaction; (e) how to awaken a drowsy baby for a feeding; (f) how to calm a fussy baby; and (g) review and recap of major points, and responses to any questions parents may have.

2. *NBAS demonstrations with increasing parental involvement.* Following the second viewing of the videotape at 34–38 weeks PCA, the interventionist administered the Brazelton NBAS for the first time to the infant in the NICU, if the infant had not yet been discharged, or in the home, if the infant had been discharged. The parents were observers during this first NBAS administration, and the interventionist discussed the administration and results of the exam openly with the parents, emphasizing infant capacities, as well as areas of special need. Because the NBAS can be stressful for preterm infants, who frequently exhibit heightened levels of physiological and state disorganization (Brazelton & Nugent, 1995), only selected items of the NBAS were administered when infants were less than 40 weeks PCA. These items were chosen because (a) they were less physically stimulating and aversive to the infant, (b) they indicated some basic infant reflexes that many parents found intrinsically interesting, and (c) they directly demonstrated simple but important skills for parents in their early interactions with their newborns. These included the plantar, Babinski, rooting, sucking, and palmar reflexes; social interactive (orienting and following) to face and to voice; cuddling; and consoling maneuvers. Administration of more physically stimulating reflex/motor items such as the glabellar, ankle clonus, placing, standing, walking, crawling, incurvation, spin, nystagmus, defensive movement, tonic neck, and Moro reflexes, and habituation to the light, rattle, and bell, were postponed until 40 weeks PCA. Parental attention was called not only to the infant's current and ongoing state changes, color changes, motor maturity, spontaneous versus elicited activity, hand-to-mouth activity, self-quieting actions, smiles, startles, and tremors, but also to the infant's general alertness, robustness, and endurance, with discussion about what these characteristics reflected about the infant's capacities. NBAS administrations were repeated at 36–40, 38–42, 40–44, 44–48, 48–52, and 52–56 weeks PCA, and parents were encouraged to repeat the administration of NBAS items with their infants, with the goal of being able, with guidance from the interventionist, to complete the full exam

by 44–48 weeks. The interventionist became a full partner with parents, reviewing and discussing the infant's capacities in response to specific NBAS items, and highlighting the developmental changes in the infant that occur with maturation.

3. *Infant massage.* Massage therapy was introduced in the intervention at 36–40 weeks PCA and in each intervention session thereafter, with the NBAS administration following massage. At 36–40 weeks PCA, the examiner demonstrated a protocol of infant massage techniques based on methods outlined by Field (2001; Field, Grizzle, Scafidi, Abrams, & Richardson, 1996), and gave the parents a copy of the protocol to review. The protocol involved alternate, 5-minute phases of tactile (first and third phases) and kinesthetic (second phase) stimulation. Parents were taught gentle tactile stimulation of the prone infant's head and neck, shoulder, back and waist, thigh and foot, and arm regions, stroking each region with six 10-second strokes, using the fingers of both hands. In the kinesthetic phase, with the infant in a supine position, parents were taught to administer five 1-minute segments of gentle, passive flexing and extending of the infant's right arm, left arm, right leg, left leg, and both legs simultaneously. Massage demonstrations, with parental involvement, were given again at 38–42, 42–44, 44–48, 48–52, and 52–56 weeks PCA, followed each time by NBAS administration. The interventionist and parents reviewed and practiced the massage protocol with the infant during these visits, acting as partners in this process. Parents were encouraged to engage in 10- to 15-minute massage sessions with their babies two to three times a day and to keep a daily record of how often they massaged their babies. Intervention fidelity and any ongoing intervention issues were monitored during weekly meetings between Douglas Teti, the intervention coordinator, the project coordinator, and the interventionists.

Assessment of Parental Commitment to Intervention

Several measures of commitment to intervention were derived. Beginning at 36–40 weeks PCA and at each intervention visit thereafter, interventionists reviewed the parents' infant massage log and recorded the number of times the infant was massaged by the mothers and any other caregivers (e.g., fathers, grandmothers) since the last intervention session, and calculated the total number of massages given to infants across the entire intervention. Higher frequencies of infant massage were taken as an index of maternal commitment to the intervention, in that mothers were instructed to massage their infants two or three times daily in between intervention visits.

A second, more qualitative measure of maternal commitment was obtained with a rating scale system based on the work of Korfmacher and Olds (Korfmacher et al., 1997; Korfmacher, Kitzman, & Olds, 1998). Five 5-point scales from the Korfmacher and colleagues' New Mother Project were rated for each mother after each intervention session: maternal involvement, conflict with material, understanding of intervention material, environmental distractions, and preoccupation with other events or crises. Training on these ratings was provided to the interventionists by the intervention coordinator. Interrater reliability on the Korfmacher and colleagues ratings was established between the intervention coordinator and the three interventionists on 22 families (seven families for two of the three interventionists, and eight for the third). Intraclass correlations, based on absolute agreement between the intervention coordinator and the interventionists, were .87 for maternal involvement, .12 for conflict with material, .73 for understanding of intervention material, .56 for environmental distractions, and .85 for preoccupation with other events or crises. Because of the low reliability obtained for conflict with material, this variable was omitted from further analysis.

A composite, summary measure of interventionists' ratings of maternal commitment to intervention, averaged across the entire intervention, was then derived for each mother by (1) reverse-scoring the environmental distractions and preoccupation with other events/crises score distributions, so that higher scores reflected higher commitment to intervention; (2) creating after each visit a composite commitment to intervention score by summing scores on involvement, understanding of intervention material, environmental distractions, and preoccupation with other events/crises; (3) summing composite scores across all intervention sessions in which the mother participated; and (4) dividing the resulting sum by the total number of intervention sessions in which the mother participated—usually eight ($n = 54$), but in some cases six ($n = 4$) or seven ($n = 9$). This procedure yielded a mean maternal commitment to intervention score for each mother, averaged across the entire intervention, which served as the unit of analysis. Cronbach's alpha for this commitment score, derived from the full sample of 64 mothers, was quite adequate ($\alpha = .89$). In addition, interrater reliability for this measure between the intervention coordinator and the three interventionists, derived from the interrater reliability subsample of 22 families (discussed previously), was high (intraclass correlation = .91, based on absolute agreement).

All interventionists were completely blind to mothers' AAI classifications (in most cases, AAIs were classified after the intervention was completed).

Three additional measures of commitment pertained more directly to the efforts mothers made to keep their intervention appointments: (1) the number of canceled intervention visits; (2) the number of "no-shows" without clear reason/explanation (i.e., the number of times interventionists showed up at the family's home for a scheduled home visit and the mother was not at home, after which she provided no clear reason for not being home); and (3) the number of "no-shows" that were followed by a clear reason/explanation.

These five measures of maternal commitment (frequency of infant massage, interventionists' ratings of commitment, number of canceled visits, number of "no-shows" without clear reason/explanation, and number of "no-shows" with a clear reason/explanation) were only modestly intercorrelated (see Table 5.3) and were analyzed individually.

TABLE 5.3. Intercorrelations among Commitment to Intervention Indices

	Mother involvement	Total number of infant massages	Total number of no-shows for clear/ legitimate reason	Total number of no-shows for unclear/ poor reason	Total number of canceled visits
Mother involvement	1.00				
Total number of infant massages	.33*	1.00			
Total number of no-shows for clear/ legitimate reason	.08	−.14	1.00		
Total number of no-shows for unclear/poor reason	−.42**	−.24†	.20	1.00	
Total number of canceled visits	−.20	−.24†	−.13	.03	1.00

$*p < .05$; $**p < .001$; $†p < .10$.

Outcome Assessments

Several mother and infant outcome assessments were obtained postinter-vention. These included the Maternal Behavior Q-Sort (MBQ; Pederson & Moran, 1995), used to measure maternal sensitivity during naturalistic obser-vations (1–2 hours) of mother–infant interaction at 3–4, 12, and 24 months of infant age. The MBQ is a well-established measure of maternal sensitivity that correlates significantly with attachment and the Ainsworth rating scales of maternal sensitivity (Pederson, Moran, Sitko, Campbell, Ghesquire, & Acton, 1990). Interrater reliability was obtained between the project coordinator and three graduate research assistants on 32 mother–infant observations, yielding a mean intraclass correlation of .82.

Infant–mother attachment security assessed at 12 and 24 months with the Attachment Q-Sort (AQS; Waters, 1995). The AQS, a measure of attachment for infants and preschoolers, is designed to capture the affective and behavior-al dimensions of the quality of children's attachment to a specific caregiver. AQS scores have been found to relate significantly to Strange Situation classi-fications (van IJzendoorn, Vereijken, Bakersman-Kranenburg, & Riksen-Walraven, 2004). Interrater reliability between the project coordinator and three graduate student "blind" observers was obtained with a procedure simi-lar to that used for the MBQ on 27 mother–infant observations, with a mean intraclass correlation of .87.

Infant mental development at 3–4, 12, and 24 months was assessed with the second edition of the Bayley Scales of Infant Development Mental Development Index (MDI), highly regarded as a valid and reliable standardized infant assessment tool with well-established psychometrics (Bayley, 1993). At a given infant age, the scores for the MDI have a mean of 100 and a standard deviation of 15. Finally, infant behavior problems and behavioral competencies were assessed at 12 and 24 months with the Brief Infant–Toddler Social and Emotional Assessment (BITSEA; Briggs-Gowan & Carter, 2002). The BITSEA has forty-two 3-point scale items, and parents are asked to rate each item in terms of how descriptive it is of their child (0, *Not true/rarely* to 2, *Very true/often*). Thirty-one items comprise the problem domain (e.g., "Hits, bites, or kicks you"), and 11 items comprise the competence domain ("Can pay attention for a long time"). The BITSEA has good test–retest reliability and convergent and discriminate validity (Briggs-Gowan, Carter, Irwin, Wachtel, & Cicchetti, 2004).

Results

Hypothesis 1

We conducted a one-way analysis of variance (ANOVA), with mothers' major attachment classification as the grouping variable (autonomous vs. dismissing), to test the hypothesis that mothers with an autonomous state of mind would commit more strongly to the intervention than would mothers with a nonautonomous (dismissing) state of mind. Analyses indicated that interventionists rated autonomous mothers as significantly more involved in the intervention than dismissing mothers [$F(1, 58) = 8.83, p = .004$], and a marginally significant group difference indicated that autonomous mothers massaged their infants more frequently than did dismissing mothers [$F(1, 58) = 3.59, p = .063$; see Table 5.4 for means and standard deviations]. There were no signifi-

TABLE 5.4. Group Differences (Autonomous vs. Dismissing State of Mind) in Commitment to Intervention Indices

	AAI state of mind	
	Autonomous	Dismissing
Commitment to Intervention Dependent Variables	M (SD)	M (SD)
Mother involvement*	4.46 (0.66)	3.87 (0.86)
Total number of infant massages†	70.66 (44.02)	49.85 (39.54)
Total number no-shows for clear/legitimate reason	0.21 (0.54)	0.23 (0.43)
Total number no-shows for unclear/poor reason	0.32 (0.73)	0.65 (1.29)
Total number of canceled visits	1.18 (1.71)	1.85 (1.47)

Note. Autonomous, $n = 34$; dismissing, $n = 26$.
*$p < .01$; †$p < .10$.

cant differences between autonomous and dismissing mothers on the other indicators of commitment to intervention: total number of no-shows for a clear or legitimate reason, total number of no-shows for an unclear or poor reason, and total number of canceled visits. A similar ANOVA comparing resolved and unresolved mothers with respect to loss or trauma, found no significant group differences on any commitment to intervention index. Thus, the following analyses report only autonomous versus dismissing comparisons.

Hypothesis 2

We conducted correlational analyses to test the hypothesis that maternal commitment to intervention would be positively associated with more favorable socioeconomic indicators. Mothers rated by interventionists as more involved in the intervention completed higher levels of education [$r(58) = .42, p < .001$], had a higher family income [$r(58) = .29, p < .05$], and were less likely to be dependent on public assistance [point biserial $r(58) = -.28, p < .05$]. The frequency of times mothers were not home when interventionists came to visit but provided a rational explanation ("no-shows" for clear/legitimate reasons) was inversely associated with family income [$r(58) = -.29, p < .05$], and the frequency of no-shows without clear/legitimate reasons was inversely associated with both family income [$r(58) = -.32, p < .05$] and maternal education [$r(58) = -.38, p < .01$].

Interestingly, mothers' major attachment classification was also significantly related to several key socioeconomic variables. Autonomous mothers completed a higher level of education (averaging some college experience) than did dismissing mothers (averaging a high school diploma or general equivalency degree [GED]) [$F(1, 58) = 6.36, p = .014$] and had a higher yearly family income (averaging \$30,000–39,999) than dismissing mothers (averaging \$10,000–19,999) [$F(1, 54) = 12.72, p = .001$]. Additionally, autonomous mothers were more likely to be independent of public assistance than were dismissing mothers [$\chi^2(1) = 11.47, p = .001$].

Hypothesis 3

To test the hypothesis that differences between autonomous and nonautonomous (dismissing) mothers in maternal commitment to intervention would persist after statistically controlling for socioeconomic variables, we conducted analyses of covariance (ANCOVAs), with mothers' major attachment classification as the grouping variable. These analyses indicated that group differences in mother involvement between autonomous and dismissing mothers remained significant when we statistically controlled for the highest level of education completed [$F(1, 57) = 4.46, p = .039$], yearly family income [$F(1, 53) = 4.26, p = .044$], and dependence on public assistance [$F(1, 57) = 4.75, p = .034$]. Additionally, after controlling for dependence on public assistance, autonomous mothers had fewer canceled visits (M = 1.18, SD = 1.71) than did dismissing mothers [M = 1.85, SD = 1.41, $F(1, 57)$ = 4.68, p = .035].

Hypothesis 4

We conducted one-way ANOVAs, with mothers' major attachment classification as the grouping variable (autonomous vs. dismissing), to test the hypothesis that mothers with an autonomous state of mind would be more sensitive in their mothering and have infants with better developmental outcomes than would mothers with a dismissing state of mind (see Table 5.5).

Table 5.5 shows that autonomous mothers exhibited significantly more sensitive maternal behavior at 24 months of infant age than did dismissing mothers [$F(1, 38)$ = 10.62, p = .002], a slightly smaller difference in the same direction that approached significance at 12 months but no differences at 3–4 months. Autonomous mothers also had children who were more securely attached at 24 months than did dismissing mothers [$F(1, 36)$ = 12.86, p = .001], but no such differences were observed at 12 months. There were no significant group differences in other infant developmental outcomes, including the Bayley MDI, and Maternally Reported Infant Behavior Problems and Competencies (from the BITSEA).

We repeated these analyses, statistically controlling for socioeconomic status, because AAI state of mind (autonomous vs. dismissing) was related to socioeconomic status indices, as previously reported. These analyses indicated that there continued to be significant group differences between autonomous

TABLE 5.5. Group Differences (Autonomous vs. Dismissing State of Mind) in Parent–Infant Outcomes

| | AAI state of mind | |
| | Autonomous | Dismissing |
Parenting and attachment dependent variables	M (SD)	M (SD)
Maternal behavior Q-sort 3–4 months of infant corrected age	1.42 (0.55)	1.25 (0.75)
Maternal behavior Q-sort 12 months of infant corrected age†	1.44 (0.42)	1.21 (0.50)
Maternal behavior Q-sort 24 months of infant corrected age*	1.59 (0.43)	1.15 (0.31)
Attachment Q-set z-score 12 months of infant corrected age	0.90 (0.35)	0.83 (0.43)
Attachment Q-set 24 months of infant corrected age**	1.12 (0.37)	0.62 (0.47)

Note. Autonomous, n = 34; dismissing, n = 26.
*p < .01; **p < .001; †p < .10.

and dismissing mothers on sensitive maternal behavior toward infants at 24 months when we statistically controlled for the highest level of education completed [$F(1, 37) = 8.83$, $p = .005$], yearly family income [$F(1, 34) = 9.87$, $p = .003$], and dependence on public assistance [$F(1, 37) = 5.50$, $p = .024$]. Furthermore, group differences on child–mother attachment at 24 months remained significant when we controlled for the highest level of education completed [$F(1, 35) = 12.25$, $p = .001$], yearly family income [$F(1, 32) = 6.35$, $p = .017$], and dependence on public assistance [$F(1, 35) = 10.31$, $p = .003$].

Hypothesis 5

To test the hypothesis that mothers who were more committed to the intervention would be more sensitive in their mothering and have infants with better developmental outcomes than mothers who were less committed to the intervention, we used correlational analyses (see Table 5.6) to examine the relations between the commitment to intervention indices and (1) sensitive maternal behavior at 3–4, 12, and 24 months of infant age; (2) infant–mother attachment at 12 and 24 months; (3) Bayley MDI scores at 3–4, 12, and 24 months; and (4) infant behavioral problems and competencies as reported by mothers on the BITSEA at 12 and 24 months.

Greater mother involvement in the intervention, as rated by the interventionists, was significantly related to more sensitive maternal behavior toward infants at 12 months of age, and relations approached significance between this measure of involvement and maternal sensitivity at 3–4 and 24 months, and infant behavior problems (inversely) at 24 months. Frequency of infant massages given by the mother was significantly and positively related to more sensitive maternal behavior at child age 3–4 and 12 months, and to higher Bayley MDI scores at child age 3–4 months. Similar positive associations that approached significance were found between infant massage frequency and maternal sensitivity at 24 months, Bayley MDI scores at 12 months, and infant behavior problems (inversely) at 12 months. Frequency of no-shows for unclear/poor reasons related inversely to maternal sensitivity and infant–mother attachment security at 12 months and positively at 24 months to infant behavior problems. Finally, total number of canceled intervention visits was negatively predictive of Bayley MDI scores at 3–4 months.

Some of these significant correlations became nonsignificant when we repeated these analyses, controlling for mothers' highest level of education. However, interventionists' ratings of maternal involvement remained significantly associated with maternal sensitivity at 12 months. In addition, total number of infant massages was significantly associated with 12-month Bayley MDI scores. The inverse association between frequency of no-shows for unclear/poor reasons and infant–mother attachment security at 12 months, and the positive association between no-shows for unclear/poor reasons and 24-month infant behavior problems, continued to be significant after controlling for maternal education. Finally, number of canceled intervention visits

TABLE 5.6. Correlations between Commitment to Intervention Indices and Child Outcomes

	Maternal behavior Q-sort 3–4 mo corrected age	Maternal behavior Q-sort 12 mo corrected age	Maternal behavior Q-sort 24 mo corrected age	Attachment Q-set 12 mo corrected age	Attachment Q-set 24 mo corrected age	Bayley MDI 3–4 mo corrected age	Bayley MDI 12 mo corrected age	Bayley MDI 24 mo corrected age	12-mo infant behavior problems (BITSEA)	12-mo infant behavioral competencies (BITSEA)	24-mo infant behavior problems (BITSEA)	24-mo infant behavioral competencies (BITSEA)
Mother involvement	.25†	.44***	.28†	.14	.21	.12	.11	–.03	–.16	–.10	–.29†	–.08
Total number of infant massages	.29*	.28*	.30†	.22	.12	.28*	.27†	.25	–.25†	.13	–.14	.10
Total number of no-shows for clear/legitimate reason	–.14	–.04	–.01	.07	–.04	.11	–.14	–.15	.12	.17	–.14	.25
Total number of no-shows for unclear/poor reason	–.20	–.37**	–.23	–.30*	–.01	–.16	–.13	.07	.15	.15	.38*	–.04
Total number of canceled visits	.17	0.05	.08	.08	–.09	–.36**	–.12	–.17	.14	–.20	.14	–.22

*p < .05; **p .01; ***p < .001; †p < .10.

143

remained significantly and negatively associated with 3- to 4-month Bayley MDI scores when we controlled for maternal education.

Discussion

Our findings supported the hypothesis that an autonomous state of mind regarding attachment would be associated with stronger maternal commitment to an early intervention program than would nonautonomous (in this study, dismissing) attachment. We found to be true in particular for the composite measure of maternal commitment, derived from interventionists' ratings of the mothers, and at a trend level for mothers' reports of the frequency of infant massages across the entire intervention. These results support earlier work by Dozier (1990), who found that autonomous clients committed more fully to a psychotherapeutic intervention than did nonautonomous clients, and by Korfmacher and colleagues (1997), who found that autonomous states of mind in mothers were associated with greater receptivity to a home visiting intervention program. In addition, our results support the premise that mothers with an autonomous state of mind regarding attachment intuitively value an intervention that purports to improve the mother–infant relationship, and respond to it with greater openness and objectivity, and less defensiveness and distortion than do mothers with nonautonomous attachments. Important in this regard was our finding that autonomous attachment continued to predict stronger maternal commitment to intervention even after we controlled for socioeconomic marker variables, which themselves were associated with maternal commitment in our study and in earlier work (Arcia et al., 1993; Gavidia-Payne & Stoneman, 1997; Kochanek & Buka, 1995; Kuchler-O'Shea et al., 1999; Mahoney & Filer, 1996), and with mothers' attachment states of mind in our study.

As we hypothesized, autonomous states of mind were predictive of maternal sensitivity and security of infant–mother attachment, particularly among mothers of 24-month-old infants, but not earlier. It is possible that AAI-linked differences in maternal sensitivity were not readily observable at 12 months and early on in our sample of infants at risk for developmental delay, two-thirds of whom were born at 32 weeks GA or younger. Importantly, this relation approached significance at 12 months ($p < .10$), and was the same at 3–4 months, albeit not statistically significant. These results, of course, support earlier work demonstrating linkages between autonomous states of mind and parental sensitivity (Crowell & Feldman, 1991; Hesse, 1999; Pederson, Gleason, Moran, & Bento, 1998; van IJzendoorn, 1995; Ward & Carlson, 1995). Importantly, however, these predictive associations remained after we controlled for socioeconomic variables, emphasizing the unique role of maternal states of mind regarding attachment in organizing quality of mothering, even under adverse socioeconomic circumstances.

Links between maternal attachment status and infant developmental outcomes, however, were limited to infant–mother attachment and did not extend to infant Bayley MDI performance at any age, or to mothers' reports of infant behavioral problems or competencies at 12 and 24 months. Although these results are consistent with attachment theory, they beg the question: Why, in the face of such linkages, were no predictive associations found between AAI classifications and nonattachment outcomes? In light of our belief that infant–mother attachment outcomes are *formative* rather than *summative* in nature, we surmise that such associations, perhaps particularly between maternal states of mind and social–emotional outcomes, such as infant behavioral problems and competencies, may yet be found with further developments in the mother–infant relationship and in the children's social-cognitive and behavioral repertoires. More consistently predictive of nonattachment infant outcomes, however, was maternal commitment to intervention, even after we statistically controlled for maternal education. Mothers' engagement with the intervention was, as expected, predicted by socioeconomic variables (education, income, dependence on public assistance), and by mothers' states of mind regarding attachment, even after we controlled for socioeconomic variables. It behooves interventionists implementing attachment-based intervention protocols to think carefully about how to approach and to "hook" parents who, because of lower socioeconomic status, high life stress, and nonautonomous attachments, are less likely to be motivated to engage in intervention efforts to improve parent–child relationships. With such parents, intervention approaches with the parent–child relationship as the focal point may need to be more intensive in terms of increasing in frequency of intervention visits, systematic monitoring of whether and how well parents are implementing the intervention between visits, and perhaps incorporating systematic efforts to understand specific parental developmental needs and insights about their infants and themselves, and parents' developmental histories (Azar, 2003; Minde & Hesse, 1996; Steele & Baradon, 2004).

Consistent with earlier work (Arcia et al., 1993; Gavidia-Payne & Stoneman, 1997; Kochanek & Buka, 1995; Kuchler-O'Shea et al., 1999; Liaw et al., 1995; Mahoney & Filer, 1996), socioeconomic background was a significant predictor of mothers' quality of engagement in the intervention. Of particular interest in this study was our finding that mothers with autonomous states of mind were significantly more highly educated, reported more family income, and were less likely to be on public assistance than were mothers with nonautonomous (dismissing) attachments. These linkages made it all the more compelling to control statistically for socioeconomic variables when we assessed associations between maternal AAI status and maternal commitment. At the same time, these relations were unexpected. Research with the AAI typically has not reported associations between parent AAI classifications, educational attainment, and family income. The small amount of work so far has not found significant linkages (Constantino, 1996; Tarabulsy et al., 2005), although in a meta-analysis van IJzendoorn and Bakermans-Kranenburg (1996) found that mothers of low socioeconomic status were more likely than middle-class mothers to be classified as dismissing. Unlike most earlier work, however, this study targeted an exclusively African American, predominantly (but not exclusively) low-income, high-risk adult sample recruited from inner-city hospitals in Baltimore and Washington, DC. The significant associations between AAI classifications and socioeconomic markers in this study can be readily explained if socioeconomic differences between the autonomous and dismissing mothers have persisted since childhood, making it more likely for dismissing mothers to have experienced a history of harsher parenting while growing up than that experienced by the autonomous mothers. Such an explanation would be consistent with McLoyd's (1998) premise that a primary mechanism by which poverty and the stressors associated with it affect children's social–emotional development is through harsh parenting. What is clear, however, is that the mechanisms by which social-ecological variables influence the development of adult attachment representations remain poorly understood. Our findings suggest that much can be learned about such mechanisms by examining the antecedents of adult attachments (e.g., quality of caregiving in childhood by mothers and other attachment figures) in samples with low-income or wide-ranging socioeconomic status.

The fact that autonomous mothers in our study committed more strongly to the intervention than did dismissing mothers should not be taken as unequivocal support for the hypothesis that intervention will be more efficacious with autonomous mothers than with dismissing mothers. Importantly, Fonagy and colleagues (1996) found that it was dismissing, not autonomous clients, who appeared to benefit most in terms of quality of global functioning from a yearlong psychotherapeutic intervention. Fonagy and colleagues targeted a population and employed an intervention quite different from those in our study, and they did not systematically assess clients' commitment to intervention; their results, however, raise caution about making strong predictions that the present early intervention program will be more beneficial for autonomous mothers than for dismissing mothers and their infants. Analyses of intervention effects on quality of parenting and infant development await additional follow-up analysis of this sample.

Unlike Korfmacher and colleagues (1997), we found no linkages between resolved and unresolved mothers and parental commitment to intervention. The reasons for this discrepancy are unclear. We note that Korfmacher and colleagues who also targeted a predominantly low-income, high-risk sample, identified a substantial proportion of mothers who were unresolved with respect to past trauma. By contrast, only 8% (one mother) of the 13 unresolved mothers in our sample was unresolved with respect to trauma, an unexpectedly low proportion in light of the higher rates of child abuse and harsh parenting associated with very low social class (Gelles, 1992; Pelton, 1994). We speculate that histories of trauma in the present sample—and the likelihood of being classified as unresolved with respect to trauma—may have been underreported, which in turn may have led to a reduction in the proportion of mothers classified as unresolved. This may have resulted from our efforts to comply with human subjects' protection recommendations made by the institutional review boards (IRBs) overseeing this study, which required that all mothers be notified, during informed consent and before being interviewed, that research project personnel were obligated by law to report to local child protection agencies any past reports of child abuse that might be divulged during the administration of the AAI. As a result, mothers in our study may have been less likely to report severe, significant trauma experiences in their AAIs. It remains unclear, of course, whether a greater proportion of unresolved mothers with respect to trauma, and an overall increase in unresolved mothers overall, would have mattered in terms of finding unresolved and resolved differences in maternal commitment. We call attention to this point, however, given the discrepancies between our study and that of Korfmacher and colleagues in the proportion of trauma-based unresolved mothers.

Our results are limited to mothers with major AAI classifications of either autonomous and dismissing, due to the fact that only one mother in this study was classified as preoccupied (group E). Although earlier work (e.g., Dozier, 1990) suggests that preoccupied mothers would commit less strongly to intervention than would autonomous mothers, our study was simply unable to provide any useful information about how preoccupation is linked with mothers' level of commitment to the intervention. Another limitation is that we had no choice but to rely on mothers' reports of how frequently they and other family members massaged their infants in between intervention visits; thus, there is no guarantee that these reports were not distorted or inflated. We are heartened, however, by the fact that both the composite measure of maternal commitment, derived from interventionists' ratings, and the maternally reported frequency of infant massage related in expected ways to mothers' major attachment classifications.

Our results add to a small but growing body of literature that suggests states of mind regarding attachment organize parental responses to early intervention efforts to promote the quality of infant–parent relationships. To the extent to which parental engagement in such efforts promotes mothering and infant development, our findings suggest that the AAI may serve as a useful screening tool to identify parents who may be less inclined to commit fully to early intervention protocols. Interventionists in turn may need to be prepared to work harder, longer, and more intensively with nonautonomous mothers than with autonomous mothers to promote intervention effects. Additional research might well be directed toward understanding how interventionists can differentially approach and tailor an early intervention program for mothers (and fathers) with different states of mind regarding attachment, so as to optimize parents' engagement with intervention and, in the long term, children's development.

Acknowledgments

This study was supported by a grant from the National Institute of Child Health and Human Development (Grant No. R01 HD38982), awarded to Douglas Teti. We wish to thank the many graduate and undergraduate research assistants who contributed to this study. Special thanks are given to the families who served as participants in this study, who donated their time so openly and unselfishly.

References

Ainsworth, M. D. S., Blehar, M. C., Waters, E., & Wall, S. (1978). *Patterns of attachment: A psychological study of the strange situation.* Hillsdale, NJ: Erlbaum.

Allen, D. A., Affleck, G., McGrade, B. J., & McQueeney, M. (1984). Factors in the effectiveness of early childhood intervention for low socioeconomic status families. *Education and Training of the Mentally Retarded, 19,* 254–260.

Anderson, C. J., & Sawin, D. B. (1983). Enhancing responsiveness in mother–infant interaction. *Infant Behavior and Development, 6*(3), 361–368.

Arcia, E., Keyes, L., Gallagher, J. J., & Herrick, H. (1993). National portrait of sociodemographic factors associated with underutilization of services: Relevance to early intervention. *Journal of Early Intervention, 17,* 23–32.

Aylward, G. P. (2005). Neurodevelopmental outcomes of infants born prematurely. *Journal of Developmental and Behavioral Pediatrics, 26*(6), 427–440.

Azar, S. (2003). Adult development and parenthood: A social-cognitive perspective. In J. Demick & C. Andreoletti (Eds.), *Handbook of adult development* (pp. 391–415). New York: Kluwer Academic/Plenum Press.

Bailey, B. B., Buysse, V., Edmondson, R., & Smith, T. M. (1992). Creating family-centered services in early intervention: Perceptions of professionals in four states. *Exceptional Child, 58,* 298–309.

Bakermans-Kranenburg, M. J., van IJzendoorn, M. H., & Bradley, R. H. (2005). Those who have, receive: The Matthew Effect in early childhood intervention in the home environment. *Review of Educational Research, 75*(1), 1–26.

Bakermans-Kranenburg, M. J., van IJzendoorn, M. H., & Juffer, F. (2003). Less is more: Meta-analyses of sensitivity and attachment interventions in early childhood. *Psychological Bulletin, 129*(2), 195–215.

Bakermans-Kranenburg, M. J., van IJzendoorn, M. H., & Juffer, F. (2005). Disorganized infant attachment and preventive interventions: A review and meta-analysis. *Infant Mental Health Journal, 26*(3), 191–216.

Baroody, A. J., Lai, M.-L., & Mix, K. S. (2006). The development of young children's early number and operation sense and its implications for early childhood education. In B. Spodek & O. N. Saracho (Eds.), *Handbook of research on the education of young children* (2nd ed., pp. 187–220). Mahwah, NJ: Erlbaum.

Bayley, N. (1993). *Bayley Scales of Infant Development* (2nd ed.). San Antonio, TX: Psychological Corporation.

Beckman, P. J., Robinson, C. C., Rosenberg, S., & Filer, J. (1994). Family involvement in early intervention: The evolution of family-centered services. In L. J. Johnson, R. J. Callagher, M. J. LaMontagne, J. B. Jordan, J. J. Gallagher, P. L. Huninger, & M. B. Karnes (Eds.), *Meeting early intervention challenges: Issues from birth to three* (pp. 67–513). Baltimore: Brookes.

Bowlby, J. (1982). *Attachment and loss: Vol. 1. Attachment*. New York: Basic Books. (Original work published 1969)

Brazelton, T. B., & Nugent, J. K. (1995). *Neonatal Behavioral Assessment Scale* (3rd ed.). London: MacKeith Press.

Briggs-Gowan, M. J., & Carter, A. S. (2002). *Brief Infant–Toddler Social and Emotional Assessment (BITSEA) manual, Version 2.0.* New Haven, CT: Yale University Press.

Briggs-Gowan, M. J., Carter, A. S., Irwin, J. R., Wachtel, K., & Cicchetti, D. V. (2004). The Brief Infant–Toddler Social and Emotional Assessment: Screening for social–emotional problems and delays in competence. *Journal of Pediatric Psychology, 29*(2), 143–155.

Bromwich, R., & Parmelee, A. H. (1979). An intervention program for preterm infants. In T. M. Field, A. S. Sostek, S. Goldberg, & H. H. Shuman (Eds.), *Infants born at risk* (pp. 389–411). New York: Spectrum.

Brooks-Gunn, J., McCarton, C. M., Casey, P. H., McCormick, M. C., Bauer, C. R., Bernbaum, J. C., et al. (1994). Early intervention in low-birth-weight premature infants: Results through age 5 years from the Infant Health and Development Program. *Journal of the American Medical Association, 272,* 1257–1262.

Browne, J. V., & Talmi, A. (2005). Family-based intervention to enhance infant–parent relationships in the neonatal intensive care unit. *Journal of Pediatric Psychology, 30*(8), 667–677.

Constantino, J. N. (1996). Intergenerational aspects of the development of aggression: A preliminary report. *Journal of Developmental and Behavioral Pediatrics, 17,* 176–182.

Crowell, J. A., & Feldman, S. S. (1991). Mothers' working models of attachment relationships and mother and child behavior during separation and reunion. *Developmental Psychology, 27,* 597–605.

Cullen, C., Field, T., Escalona, A., & Hartshorn, K. (2000). Father–infant interactions are enhanced by massage therapy. *Early Child Development and Care, 164,* 41–47.

Cusson, R. M., & DeWeese, M. (1992). *Premie talk: Understanding your premature baby's behavior.* Videotape produced by the School of Nursing, University of Maryland, Baltimore.

Cusson, R. M., Viscardi, R. M., Tyhala, L., Yin, T., & Okunski, G. (1996, April). *Enhancing parenting of preterm infants with a video-assisted maternal education program.* Paper presented at the biennial International Conference on Infant Studies, Providence, RI.

Das Eiden, R., & Reifman, A. (1996). Effects of Brazelton demonstrations on later parenting: A meta-analysis. *Journal of Pediatric Psychology, 21*(6), 857–868.

Dozier, M. (1990). Attachment organization and treatment use for adults with serious psychopathological disorders. *Development and Psychopathology, 2,* 47–60.

Dozier, M., Lomax, L., Tyrell, C. L., & Lee, S. W. (2001). The challenge of treatment for clients with dismissing states of mind. *Attachment and Human Development, 3*(1), 62–76.

Dozier, M., & Tyrrell, C. (1998). The role of attachment in therapeutic relationships. In J. A. Simpson & W. S. Rholes (Eds.), *Attachment theory and close relationships* (pp. 221–248). New York: Guilford Press.

Duncan, G. J., & Magnuson, K. A. (2005). Can family socioeconomic resources account for racial and ethnic test score gaps? *The Future of Children, 15(1)*, 35–54.

Dunst, C. J., Trivette, C. M., & Deal, A. G. (1988). *Enabling and empowering families.* Cambridge, MA: Brookline Books.

Evans, G. W. (2004). The environment of child poverty. *American Psychologist, 59(2)*, 77–92.

Ferber, S. G., Feldman, R., Kohelet, D., Kuint, J., Dollberg, S., Arbel, E., et al. (2005). Massage therapy facilitates mother–infant interaction in premature infants. *Infant Behavior and Development, 28(1)*, 74–81.

Field, T. (2001). Massage therapy facilitates weight gain in preterm infants. *Current Directions in Psychological Science, 10*, 51–54.

Field, T. Grizzle, N., Scafidi, F., Abrams, S., & Richardson, S. (1996). Massage therapy for infants of depressed mothers. *Infant Behavior and Development, 19*, 107–112.

Fonagy, P., Leigh, T., Steele, M., Steele, H., Kennedy, R., Mattoon, G., et al. (1996). The relation of attachment status, psychiatric classification, and response to psychotherapy. *Journal of Consulting and Clinical Psychology, 64*, 22–31.

Gavidia-Payne, S., & Stoneman, Z. (1997). Family predictors of maternal and paternal involvement in programs for young children with disabilities. *Child Development, 68(4)*, 701–717.

Gelles, R. J. (1992). Child abuse and violence in single-parent families: Parent absence and economic deprivation. *American Journal of Orthopsychiatry, 59*, 492–501.

George, C., Kaplan, N., & Main, M. (1996). *Adult Attachment Interview, third edition.* Unpublished manuscript, University of California, Department of Psychology, Berkeley.

Hack, M., Klein, N. K., & Taylor, H. G. (1995). Long-term developmental outcomes of low-birth weight infants. *The Future of Children, 5(1)*, 176–196.

Hesse, E. (1999). The Adult Attachment Interview: Historical and current perspectives. In J. Cassidy & P. R. Shaver (Eds.), *Handbook of attachment: Theory, research, and clinical applications* (pp. 395–433). New York: Guilford Press.

Ireys, H. T., De Vet, K. A., & Chernoff, R. (2001). Who joins a preventive intervention?: How risk status predicts enrollment. *Journal of Community Psychology, 29*, 417–427.

Kochanek, T. T., & Buka, S. L. (1995). *Socio-demographic influences on services used by infants with disabilities and their families.* Providence, RI: Early Childhood Research Institution Service Utilization. (ERIC Document Reproduction Service No. ED 386899)

Korfmacher, J., Adam, E., Ogawa, J., & Egeland, B. (1997). Adult attachment: Implications for the therapeutic process in a home visitation intervention. *Applied Developmental Science, 1*, 43–52.

Korfmacher, J., Kitzman, H., & Olds, D. (1998). Intervention processes as predictors of outcomes in a preventive home-visitation program. *Journal of Community Psychology, 26*, 49–64.

Kuchler-O'Shea, R., Kritikos, E. P., & Kahn, J. V. (1999). Factors influencing attendance of children in an early intervention program. *Infant–Toddler Intervention, 9*, 61–68.

Levy, K. N., Meehan, K. B., Kelly, K. M., Reynoso, J. S., Weber, M., & Clarkin, J. F., et al. (2006). Change in attachment patterns and reflective function in a randomized control trial of transference-focused psychotherapy for borderline personality disorder. *Journal of Consulting and Clinical Psychology, 74*(6), 1027–1040.

Liaw, F., Meisels, S. J., & Brooks-Gunn, J. (1995). The effects of experience of early intervention on low birth weight, premature children: The Infant Health and Development Program. *Early Childhood Research Quarterly, 10*(4), 405–431.

Logan, K. J., & Caruso, A. J. (1997). Parents as partners in the treatment of childhood stuttering. *Seminars in Speech and Language, 18*, 309–326.

Magnuson, K. A., & Waldfogel, J. (2005). Early childhood care and education: Effects on ethnic and racial gaps in school readiness. *The Future of Children, 15*(1), 169–196.

Mahoney, G., & Filer, J. (1996). How responsive is early intervention to the priorities and needs of families? *Topics in Early Childhood Special Education, 16*, 437–457.

Mahoney, M. C., & Cohen, M. I. (2005). Effectiveness of developmental intervention in the neonatal intensive care unit: Implications for neonatal physical therapy. *Pediatric Physical Therapy, 17*(3), 194–208.

Main, M., & Hesse, E. (1990). Parents' unresolved traumatic experiences are related to infant disorganized attachment status: Is frightening and/or frightened parental behavior the linking mechanisms? In M. T. Greenberg, D. Cicchetti, & E. M. Cummings (Eds.), *Attachment in the preschool years* (pp. 121–160). Chicago: University of Chicago Press.

Main, M., Kaplan, N., & Cassidy, J. (1985). Security in infancy, childhood, and adulthood: A move to the level of representation. *Monographs of the Society for Research in Child Development, 50*(1–2, Serial No. 209), 66–104.

Martin, J. A., Hamilton, B. E., Menacker, F., Sutton, P. D., & Matthews, T. J. (2005). *Preliminary births for 2004: Infant and maternal health: Health E-stats.* Hyattsville, MD: National Center for Health Statistics.

McLoyd, V. (1998). Socioeconomic disadvantage and child development. *American Psychologist, 53*, 185–204.

Miles, M. S., & Holditch-Davis, D. (1995). Compensatory parenting: How mothers describing parenting their 3-year-old, prematurely born children. *Journal of Pediatric Nursing, 10*, 243–253.

Minde, K., & Hesse, E. (1996). The role of the adult attachment interview in parent–infant psychotherapy: A case presentation. *Infant Mental Health Journal, 17*(2), 115–126.

Minke, D. M., & Scott, M. M. (1995). Parent–professional relationships in early intervention: A qualitative investigation. *Topics in Early Childhood Special Education, 15*, 335–352.

Onzawa, K., Glover, V., Adams, D., Modi, N., & Kumar, R. C. (2001). Infant massage improves mother–infant interaction for mothers with postnatal depression. *Journal of Affective Disorders, 63*(1), 201–207.

Pederson, D. R., Gleason, K. E., Moran, G., & Bento, S. (1998). Maternal attachment representations, maternal sensitivity, and the infant–mother attachment relationship. *Developmental Psychology, 34*, 925–933.

Pederson, D. R., & Moran, G. (1995). A categorical description of infant–mother relationships in the home and its relation to Q-sort measures of infant–mother interaction. *Monographs of the Society for Research in Child Development, 60*(2), 111–132.

Pederson, D. R., Moran, G., Sitko, C., Campbell, K., Ghesquire, K., & Acton, H.

(1990). Maternal sensitivity and the security of infant–mother attachment: A Q-sort study. *Child Development, 61*(6), 1974–1983.

Pelton, L. (1994). Thee role of material factors in child abuse and neglect. In G. B. Melton & F. D. Barry (Eds.), *Protecting children from abuse and neglect: Foundations for a new strategy* (pp. 131–181). New York: Guilford Press.

Rauh, V. A., Achenbach, T. M., Nurcombe, B., Howell, C. T., & Teti, D. M. (1988). Minimizing adverse effects of low birthweight: Four-year results of an early intervention program. *Child Development, 59*(3), 544–553.

Reichman, N. E. (2005). Low birth weight and school readiness. *The Future of Children, 15*(1), 91–116.

Rickel, A. (1986). Prescription for a new generation: Early life interventions. *American Journal of Community Psychology, 14*, 1–15.

Rouse, C., Brooks-Gunn, J., & McLanahan, S. (2005). Introducing the issue. *The Future of Children, 15*(1), 5–14.

Routh, C., Hill, J., Steele, H., Steele, M., Elliot, C., & Dewey, M. (1995). Maternal attachment status and psychosocial stressors are associated with the outcome of parent training courses for conduct disorder. *Journal of Child Psychology and Psychiatry, 36*, 1179–1198.

Ryan, R. M., Fauth, R. C., & Brooks-Gunn, J. (2006). Childhood poverty: Implications for school readiness and early childhood education. In B. Spodek & O. N. Saracho (Eds.), *Handbook of research on the education of young children* (2nd ed., pp. 323–346). Mahwah, NJ: Erlbaum.

Salt, A., & Redshaw, M. (2006). Neurodevelopmental follow-up after preterm birth: Follow up after two years. *Early Human Development, 82*(3), 185–197.

Sameroff, A. J. (1975). Early influences on development: Fact or fancy? *Merrill–Palmer Quarterly, 21*, 267–294.

Singer, L. T., Siegel, A. C., Lewis, B., Hawkins, S., Yamishita, T., & Baley, J. (2001). Preschool language outcomes of children with history of bronchopulmonary dysplasia and very low birth weight. *Journal of Developmental and Behavioral Pediatrics, 22*(1), 19–26.

Steele, M., & Baradon, T. (2004). The clinical use of the adult attachment interview in parent–infant psychotherapy [Special issue]. *Infant Mental Health Journal, 25*(4), 284–299.

Tarabulsy, G. M., Bernier, A., Provost, M. A., Maranda, J., Larose, S., Moss, E., et al. (2005). Another look inside the gap: Ecological contributions to the transmission of attachment in a sample of adolescent mother–infant dyads. *Developmental Psychology, 41*, 212–224.

Taylor, H. G., Burant, C. J., Holding, P. A., Klein, N., & Hack, M. (2002). Sources of variability in sequelae of very low birth weight. *Child Neuropsychology, 8*(3), 163–178.

Taylor, H. G., Minich, N., Bangert, B., Flilipek, P., & Hack, M. (2004). Long-term neuropsychological outcomes of very low birth weight: Associations with early risks for periventricular brain insults. *Journal of the International Neuropsychological Society, 10*(7), 987–1004.

Teti, D. M., O'Connell, M. A., & Reiner, C.D. (1996). Parental sensitivity, parental depression, and child health: The mediational role of parental self-efficacy. *Early Development and Parenting, 5*, 237–250.

van IJzendoorn, M. H. (1995). Adult attachment representations, parental responsiveness, and infant attachment: A meta-analysis on the predictive validity of the Adult Attachment Interview. *Psychological Bulletin, 117,* 1–17.

van IJzendoorn, M. H., & Bakermans-Kranenburg, M. J. (1996). Attachment representations in mothers, fathers, adolescents, and clinical groups: A meta-analytic search for normative data. *Journal of Consulting and Clinical Psychology, 64,* 8–21.

van IJzendoorn, M. H., Juffer, F., & Duyvesteyn, M. G. C. (1995). Breaking the intergenerational cycle of insecure attachment: A review of the effects of attachment-based interventions on maternal sensitivity and infant security. *Journal of Child Psychology and Psychiatry, and Allied Disciplines, 36*(2), 225–248.

van IJzendoorn, M. H., Vereijken, C. M., Bakermans-Kranenburg, M. J., & Riksen-Walraven, J. M. (2004). Assessing attachment security with the attachment Q-Sort: Meta-analytic evidence for the validity of the observer AQS. *Child Development, 75*(4), 1188–1213.

Ward, M. J., & Carlson, E. A. (1995). Associations among adult attachment representations, maternal sensitivity, and infant–mother attachment in a sample of adolescent mothers. *Child Development, 66,* 69–79.

Waters, E. (1995). The Attachment Q-Set (Version 3.0). *Monographs of the Society for Research in Child Development, 60*(Serial No. 244, Nos. 2–3), 234–246.

Widmayer, S. M., & Field, T. M. (1980). Effects of Brazelton demonstrations on early interactions of preterm infants and their teenage mothers. *Infant Behavior and Development, 3*(1), 79–89.

Worobey, J., & Belsky, J. (1982). Employing the Brazelton Scale to influence mothering: An experimental comparison of three strategies. *Developmental Psychology, 18*(5), 736–743.

6

Attachment-Theory-Informed Intervention
and Reflective Functioning
in Depressed Mothers

SHEREE L. TOTH, FRED A. ROGOSCH, and DANTE CICCHETTI

Attachment theory imparts a powerful framework for investigating the nature of the relationship between early caregiving experiences and child developmental outcome (Ainsworth, Blehar, Waters, & Wall, 1978; Crittenden, 1992; George & Solomon, 1999; Main, Kaplan, & Cassidy, 1985; Sroufe, 1983). John Bowlby (1977a, 1977b, 1988b) emphasized the potential of attachment theory's contribution to understanding the pathways by which early experiences of caregiving contribute to positive mental health or, conversely, to psychopathology. Moreover, Bowlby believed that attachment theory could facilitate the implementation of therapeutic interventions. Although Bowlby's ideas were coolly received by the clinical field at the time of their publication, attachment theory as a framework for clinical intervention has gained increasing acceptance (Oppenheim, 2004), in no small way because of the immense clinical relevance of the Adult Attachment Interview (AAI; George, Kaplan, & Main, 1985), and the affiliated rating and classification system (Main, Goldwyn, & Hesse, 2002), as well as extensions to this, such as the manual for rating reflective functioning in AAIs (Fonagy, Target, Steele, & Steele, 1998).

In this chapter, we describe how the AAI helped inform and demonstrate the effectiveness of child–parent psychotherapy (Lieberman & Van Horn, 2005), and discuss its implementation in the provision and evaluation of an intervention designed for the toddler offspring of depressed mothers. We then present outcome data on the efficacy of the preventive intervention. To gain insight into the mechanisms through which successful outcome was attained, we focus on changes in reflective functioning (RF) among mothers who participated in the intervention. Clinical exemplars of pre- and postintervention AAIs (George et al., 1985) are provided to illustrate features of the treatment process that may have contributed to higher levels of maternal RF and increased child attachment security. Examples of RF from therapy sessions, including increases in a mother's mentalizing in relation to her child, also are presented.

Attachment in the Offspring of Depressed Mothers

Maternal depression has been shown to impede the caregiving that mothers provide to their offspring. In particular, features of major depressive disorder (MDD), including anhedonia, helplessness, hopelessness, sleep disruptions, and feelings of worthlessness, may contribute to a relational context that impairs the development of the mother–child relationship and future child development. Linkages between depressive disorders and difficulties in mothers' own childhood experiences of caregiving also conspire to increase the likelihood that a negative relational history may be transmitted across generations (Arieti & Bemporad, 1978; Bowlby, 1980, 1988a; Mahler, 1968; Sandler & Joffe, 1965). In fact, retrospective studies have found that depressed adults report histories replete with inadequate or abusive care (Bemporad & Romano, 1992). Thus, insecure childhood attachment relationships may contribute to mothers' depression and may also influence the way in which such mothers are able to relate to their offspring. In the current work, use of the AAI allowed us to investigate the extent to which insecure childhood experiences (e.g., neglect or rejection) were particularly characteristic of those mothers presenting with depression.

From the perspective of attachment theory, maternal physical absence is likely to be less significant for the child than experiencing the parent as psychologically unavailable. Because the offspring of a depressed mother is likely to experience periods during which the caregiver is overwhelmed and emotionally unavailable, the development of a secure attachment relationship between mother and child may be impeded.

Although results have varied as a function of sample characteristics, investigations of attachment security in infants, toddlers, and preschoolers with depressed caregivers coalesce to suggest that offspring of depressed mothers are at increased risk for the development of insecure attachment relationships (Cicchetti, Toth, & Rogosch, 1999; Gaensbauer, Harmon, Cytryn, & McKnew, 1984; Lyons-Ruth, Connell, Grunebaum, & Botein, 1990). Therefore, the provision and evaluation of the efficacy of interventions to prevent insecure attachment between mothers with MDD and their offspring assume clinical importance.

A Preventive Intervention for Toddlers with Depressed Mothers

It is not uncommon for depressed women to receive interventions directed toward the amelioration of their depression. However, it is much less likely that such interventions deal with influences that such depression may exert on the broader familial context (Cicchetti, Toth, & Rogosch, 2004). Failure to address the evolving relationship between mother and child may increase the risk of an insecure attachment relationship for the child.

The intervention approach reported herein was developed with the goal of improving the quality of the mother–child relationship for the offspring of women who had experienced an episode of MDD at some time subsequent to the birth of their child. Toddler–parent psychotherapy (TPP; also referred to as child–parent psychotherapy [CPP]) has its roots in the work of Selma Fraiberg (1980), who described the pernicious influences that a negative parental past can exert on caregiving and, subsequently, on the parent–child relationship. To modify a potentially negative trajectory from a maternal unresolved caregiving history to depression, to insensitive caregiving and, ultimately, to an insecure attachment relationship, mothers and their toddler offspring were seen in conjoint therapy sessions.

According to Lieberman and VanHorn (2005), CPP is based on a number of conceptual premises:

- The attachment system is the primary organizer of children's responses to danger during the first five years of life (Ainsworth & Wittig, 1969; Ainsworth et al., 1978; Bowlby, 1969/1982).
- Emotional and behavioral difficulties in the early years need to be addressed in the context of the child's primary attachment relationships (Fraiberg, 1980; Lieberman, Silverman, & Pawl, 2000).
- During the first 5 years of life, risk factors, including insecure attachments, operate in the context of transactions between children and their social ecologies, including the family, neighborhood, community, and society (Cicchetti & Lynch, 1993).
- The therapeutic relationship is a necessary component of treatment.

The structure of TPP is unique in that mothers and their toddlers are seen in conjoint therapy sessions. Through joint observation of the mother and the child, opportunities arise to understand the influence of maternal representations on the character of interactions between mother and child. Therapists must attend to both the interactional and the representational levels as they are manifested in the dyadic therapy sessions. Not only are representations that have evolved from the mother's relationship history viewed as affecting the character of the interactions between herself and her child, but also interactions and toddler behaviors evoke maternal representations that influence the mother's reactions to the toddler and her experience of self. Ordinary behaviors between a mother and toddler during therapy sessions are regarded as behavioral manifestations of relationship themes. Through the use of observation and empathic comments, the therapist works toward assisting the mother to recognize how she experiences and perceives her toddler and herself, thereby allowing for correction of distorted perceptions and alterations in how she experiences the toddler and herself. The therapist also attends to the nature of the interactions that occur between mother and toddler, mother and therapist, and therapist and toddler. Interactions in one relationship pair tend to elicit parallel interactions in other relationship pairs, and therapist attention to this parallel process in interactions across relationships and the influence of representations on these interactions provides templates for modifying maternal representations as they are enacted behaviorally in the mother–child relationship.

In the course of this intervention, TPP is designed to provide the mother with a corrective emotional experience in the context of the relationship with the therapist. Through empathy, respect, concern, accommodation, and positive regard, a context is provided for the mother and the toddler, in which the mother can internalize new experiences of self in relation to others and to the toddler. If a mother has a generalized negative representational model of self and relationships, then a therapeutic goal is to help her to utilize more specific representations with regard to various relationship partners, including the toddler. Evolving positive representations of the therapist can be contrasted with maternal representations of self in relation to parents. As the mother is able to reconstruct representations of self in relation to others through the therapeutic relationship, she also is able to reconstruct and internalize new representations of herself in relation to her child.

As the therapist highlights, clarifies, and restructures the dynamic balance between representational and interactional contributions to the quality of the mother–child relationship, the quality of maternal and child relationship capacities improves. Moreover, the reorganization of maternal representations of self and of self in relation to others provides a framework for ongoing optimization of mother–child relationship functioning. Thus, therapeutic change occurs through expansion of the mother's understanding of the effects of prior relationships on her current feelings and interactions. The expectation is that through the development of more positive representational models of self and of self in relation to others, maternal sensitivity, responsivity, and attunement to the child increase.

In this investigation, TPP was initiated after the completion of baseline research assessments and the randomization to the depressed intervention (DI) group. All therapists utilized an intervention manual that specified the principles and procedures for the TPP implementations. The length of the intervention period averaged 58.19 weeks ($SD = 10.00$), and ranged from 42 to 79 weeks. The mean number of intervention sessions was 45.24 ($SD = 11.16$, range = 30–75). The quality of the implementation of TPP was monitored through weekly individual supervision, weekly group presentations and discussions of videotaped therapy sessions, and monthly monitoring of videotaped sessions for each case by one of the authors (Dante Cicchetti), who was not providing direct supervision of therapists and was able to assess adherence to the TPP model objectively. An adherence checklist was utilized, and any deviations from the standard intervention were immediately addressed with the therapist's supervisor. These procedures ensured the fidelity of the implementation of TPP.

As expected, prior to the initiation of the intervention, mothers with a history of MDD evidenced significant emotional, cognitive, interpersonal, and representational difficulties (Cicchetti, Rogosch, & Toth, 1998). Across diverse measurements, mothers in the DI group and mothers randomized to the depressed control (DC) group did not differ from each other, but they differed consistently from the nondepressed normal control (NC) group. Although not all mothers who had experienced MDD were depressed at the beginning of the investigation, the vulnerabilities in the depressed groups were substantial and exceeded the confines of depressive episodes. In examining the microsystem contextual features associated with maternal depression, we found that families with depressed mothers evidenced greater stress and reported more frequent parenting hassles. Depressed mothers also reported less social support, less companionship, and less assistance in their daily lives. Finally, the marriages of depressed women in the DI and DC groups were less harmonious and satisfying, with greater levels of conflict than were present in the NC group (Cicchetti et al., 1998).

Given the centrality of attachment to the theoretical underpinnings and delivery of the preventive intervention, a number of methods for assessing the quality of attachment were utilized. These included the Strange Situation (Ainsworth & Wittig, 1969), the AAI (George et al., 1985), and the Parent Attachment Interview (PAI, Bretherton, Biringen, Ridgeway, Maslin, & Sherman, 1989). All were administered prior to and upon the completion of the intervention. For our purposes in this chapter, we focus on the RF code from the AAI and on the Strange Situation classifications.

Consistent with theory and empirical research, mothers with a history of MDD in our sample at the baseline assessments were found to disclose greater adversity in their childhood relationships with their parents. In particular, the Loving, Rejecting, and Neglecting Probable Experience subscales from the AAI were examined. Not only did depressed mothers reveal less loving, and more rejecting and neglecting relationships with their mothers on the AAI compared to nondepressed mothers, but also these differences were even more pronounced in depressed mothers' recollections of their relationships with their fathers. Thus, the representations of childhood relationships with parents among mothers with MDD were dominated by memories and feelings of deficits in affection and care, suggesting a high likelihood of insecure attachment relationships with their mothers and/or fathers earlier in life.

We also examined the degree of stability in the Probable Experience subscales from the baseline to the postintervention follow-up AAI assessments, and whether there was evidence of any differential change depending on treatment group membership. Among the mother and father subscales, only one, Father Rejecting, demonstrated an effect of time, such that mothers in the study were rated as representing their fathers as somewhat less rejecting at follow-up. However, none of the group × time interactions was significant, indicating that the memories mothers reported about their early relationships were not differentially altered at follow-up based on study group membership. Thus, general stability in the Loving, Rejecting, and Neglecting Probable Experience subscales across time indicated that memories and impressions of early experiences of relationships with mothers and fathers had continuity, and that the TPP intervention did not alter what mothers remembered about their early relationships with parents. Given these findings, we were particularly interested in determining whether the level of complexity in thinking about early experiences may have been influenced by TPP, rather than by an alteration of memories of early experience per se.

Reflective Functioning

Although investigators have consistently found that maternal capacity to regulate and organize thoughts and feelings about caregiving history is linked to the ability to regulate, organize, and respond sensitively to children's needs for comfort, proximity, and safety (Carlson & Sroufe, 1995; Main, 1995, 2000; van IJzendoorn, 1995), the mechanisms underlying the intergenerational transmission of attachment remain unclear (van IJzendoorn, 1995). For many years, it was assumed that maternal behavior accounted for the transmission of attachment. Specifically, mothers who were secure with respect to their states of mind regarding their caregiving histories were expected to respond to their children's needs for comfort and proximity in a sensitive fashion. Conversely, mothers with insecure states of mind regarding their caregiving histories were expected to reject or fail to respond sensitively to their children's needs. Despite the theoretical credibility of these propositions, empirically only weak links between maternal attachment, maternal behavior, and infant attachment have been found (van IJzendoorn, 1995).

Therefore, efforts to identify possible mechanisms accounting for the intergenerational transmission of attachment have broadened. Drawing on a psychoanalytic tradition, in conjunction with cognitive theorists' notions of intentionality, Fonagy and his colleagues (1995) shifted the emphasis from "thinking about one's own thinking" to the interpersonal and intersubjective mechanisms operative in thinking about one's own and others' internal, mental, and explicitly affective experiences. The construct of "mentalization" (Fonagy, Steele, Moran, Steele, & Higgitt, 1991; Fonagy et al., 1995) is defined as the capacity to understand the behaviors of self and others in terms of underlying mental states and intentions. According to this conceptualization, a mother's capacity to hold complex mental states in mind allows her to hold her child's internal affective experience in mind, thereby enabling her to understand her child's behavior with respect to his or her feelings and intentions. By imparting meaning to the child's affective experiences and helping the child to experience affects in a regulated fashion, the mother fosters security and safety (Fonagy et al., 1995). As such, "reflective functioning" (RF), the overt manifestation in narrative form of an individual's mentalizing capacity, refers to the core capacity that enables parents to access the emotions and memories of their own attachment experiences coherently and to provide a secure base for their children. Although all humans are born with the ability to mentalize, early caregiving relationships provide children with the opportunity to learn about mental states and to determine the depth to which the social environment can be understood (Fonagy, Gergely, Jurist, & Target, 2002).

Reflective Functioning among Depressed Mothers

In our study, RF was coded from the AAI at both the initial and post-intervention assessments for all participants. RF on the AAI refers to adults' abilities to reflect upon the mental states and intentions of their own care-givers in attachment-relevant situations (Fonagy et al., 1998). RF can occur at any point in the AAI, which typically last 45–75 minutes. However, the RF scale particularly assesses responses to questions late in the interview that demand reflection on complex unobservable mental states, such as "Why do you think your parents behaved the way they did?" and "What kind of effect did your childhood experiences have upon your development and personality?" Answers to questions such as these yield an evaluation of the capacity to think about one's caregivers' internal affective experiences and to describe their impact on the development of one's self-experience. The 11-point scale describes a range from bizarre (–1) to high (+9) RF. RF is coded based on the adult's (1) awareness of the nature of mental states, (2) explicit effort to tease out mental states underlying behavior, (3) recognition of the developmental aspects of mental states, and (4) recognition of mental states in relation to the interviewer (Fonagy et al., 1998).

Mothers in the sample varied widely at both time points in their level of RF, with scores ranging from 0 to 7. Average scores for the sample were 3.44 initially and 3.97 at follow-up. Interestingly, the Probable Experience subscales demonstrated some relations with both baseline RF and change in RF at follow-up. Mothers with more loving, less rejecting, and less neglecting experiences in parent–child relationships had higher baseline RF scores. In turn, greater adversity in childhood relationships was correlated positively with RF increases from baseline to follow-up. There may have been greater opportunity for expansion of mentalization in regard to their parents for mothers who had experienced more difficult early relationships, and who continued to struggle to come to terms with those experiences.

To evaluate group differences in RF, as well as changes in RF in response to the TPP intervention, RF scores were evaluated in a repeated measures analysis of variance (ANOVA). In contrast to the findings for the Probable Experience subscales from the AAI discussed previously, the results revealed both a significant effect of time and a significant group by time interaction. At the initial assessment, the DI (depressed intervention), DC (depressed control), and NC (normal control) groups did not differ in their respective mean RF levels. The sample as a whole evidenced an increase in RF from the initial to postintervention assessments. However, the degree of change varied by group. The DI group had the largest increase in RF, whereas the NC group demonstrated virtually no change. The DC group showed an increase in RF intermediate to increases in the DI and NC groups. The level of RF achieved by the DI group at postintervention was significantly higher than that of the NC group, but only marginally significantly higher than the level of the DC group. Paired *t*-tests also were used to compare initial and postintervention levels within each of the groups. The increase in RF was very significant in the DI group but only marginally significant in the DC group; the change in the NC group was not significant. Thus, the DI group stood out in terms of gains made in RF by the end of the TPP intervention.

Because there was a considerable range of RF scores in each of the groups, we wanted to examine more closely the number of mothers in each group who demonstrated low versus high levels of RF at each of the time points, and patterns of change. Scores of 4 and above were considered high levels of RF, with scores below 4 categorized as low RF levels. Consistent with the lack of mean RF group differences prior to the intervention, there were no group differences in the rate of high RF in the first assessment. Across the groups, 43% of the mothers evidenced high RF levels. In contrast, at postintervention follow-up, there were significant differences in the proportion of mothers in each group with high RF levels. In the DI group, 80.5% of the mothers evidenced high RF levels, in contrast to 60.5% in the DC group and 41.5% in the NC group. The high RF rate in the DI group was significantly greater than the rate in the DC and the NC groups.

We also considered patterns of change in RF across the three groups by classifying each participant into one of four patterns: low-level RF at both time points, decline from high to low levels, increase from low to high RF, and high RF at both time points. The distribution of mothers in these change patterns differed significantly across the intervention groups. Notably, 48.8% of the mothers in the DI group showed improvement in RF from low to high levels, in contrast to only 27.9% in the DC group and 24.1% in the NC group showing this pattern. Moreover, only 12.2% of the DI mothers were low in RF at both time points, whereas 27.9% of DC mothers and 31.0% of NC mothers had this pattern.

Toddler Attachment Organization

In addition to the changes in RF observed among depressed mothers participating in the TPP, we also evaluated the toddlers' attachment organization with the Strange Situation prior to and following the intervention. At the initial evaluation, insecure attachments predominated in both the DI and the DC groups relative to the NC group. Whereas 55.9% of the toddlers in the NC group were classified as secure, significantly fewer toddlers in the DI group (16.7%) and DC group (21.9%) demonstrated secure attachment relationships with their mothers. The rate of avoidant attachments (36.4 and 28.1%, for DI and DC groups, respectively), contrasted with 19.1% in the NC group; only the difference between the DI and NC groups was significant. Although the low rates of resistant attachment precluded comparison, substantial significant differences existed for disorganized attachment, with rates of 37.9% in the DI group and 40.6% in the DC group, contrasted with 19.1% in the NC group. Thus, consistent with expectations, insecure attachment, including substantial rates of disorganized attachment, was frequently observed in the two depressed groups at twice the rate observed in the children of non-depressed mothers (Toth, Rogosch, Manly, & Cicchetti, 2006).

When the children were 3 years old, and the mothers and toddlers assigned to the DI group had completed TPP, follow-up assessments with the Strange Situation were again conducted. The results indicated that there had been substantial change in the distribution of attachment classifications in the DI group. The rates of secure attachment had increased dramatically to 67.4%. In contrast, virtually no change occurred in the DC group, with only 16.7% of children in this group demonstrating secure attachment organizations. In fact, the rate of secure attachment in the DI group was significantly greater than that in both the DC group and the NC group (47.6%), whereas the NC group continued to have significantly higher rates of secure attachment than the DC group. Similarly, the rate of disorganized attachment in the DI group had decreased to 10.6%, whereas significantly more (40.7%) of children in the DC group had disorganized attachments at follow-up. Overall, in the absence of the TPP intervention, stability of attachment security–insecurity was more common in the DC and NC groups. Stable insecure attachment was most common in the DC group (72.2%). In the NC group, 33.3% of the group were secure at both time periods, and 31.7% were insecure at both assessments. However, the most prevalent pattern in the DI group was change from insecure to secure attachment (54.3%). Thus, dramatic improvement in the rate of secure attachment was evident in the DI group following completion of TPP (Toth et al., 2006).

Maternal Reflective Functioning as a Mediator of Attachment Outcomes

The results presented indicate that the TPP intervention achieved important positive outcomes for young offspring and their depressed mothers. Because altering maternal representational models, as reflected in the positive change in RF, was a desired goal of TPP, we anticipated that improvement in maternal RF might be an intervening process that could explain the process whereby improvements in toddler attachment organization occurred in the DI group. Thus, we expected that maternal RF would serve as a mediator of the intervention results for attachment. For this to be the case, we needed to demonstrate that improvement in maternal RF was linked to actual change in attachment security. To be viable, a mediating variable in intervention outcome studies also needs to be a process that has demonstrated change in the intervention group but not in the nonintervention group (Hinshaw, 2002). Thus, given the larger increase in RF in the DI group relative to the DC group, RF seemed to be an appropriate candidate for explaining intervention results for toddlers' attachment on both conceptual and statistical grounds. In contrast, given the lack of time × intervention group interaction effects for the probable experience subscales of the AAI, changes in the representation of loving, rejecting, and neglecting relationship features were precluded as possible processes accounting for the intervention outcomes for child attachment.

At the initial assessment, mean maternal RF did not differ for children classified as secure versus insecure. Similarly, there were no significant group differences in RF for children classified as secure, ambivalent, resistant, and disorganized. When maternal RF was examined at postintervention follow-up, again, no group mean differences were observed for secure versus insecure children on the four-category attachment classifications. Thus, we did not find evidence that maternal RF differed by child attachment classification prior to or following the intervention.

We also conducted a repeated measures ANOVA to determine whether membership in stability and change groups of child attachment (stable–secure, insecure to secure, secure to insecure, and stable–insecure) for the three intervention groups related differentially to change in RF. Of particular interest was whether the interaction of attachment change pattern group and intervention group was significant. However, this interaction was not significant, suggesting that change–stability in attachment security across the intervention groups was not differentially or reliably associated with change in RF.

We further probed to determine whether high versus low maternal RF rather than average levels of maternal RF was important for influencing attachment security. At postintervention, we examined mothers who either had high RF levels at both time periods or changed from low to high levels following intervention versus mothers who had low RF levels at both time periods or declined from high to low levels at follow-up. These outcome RF groups were contrasted with child attachment change patterns (stable–secure, insecure to secure, secure to insecure, and stable–insecure). A χ^2 analysis was not significant, indicating no differential effects of maternal high RF levels on attachment change patterns. The percentage of mothers having high RF levels at follow-up ranged from 55.2% for the stable–secure group to 66.7% for mothers in the insecure to secure group. The percentage of mothers with high RF levels in the secure to insecure group was 61.1% and 55.9% in the stable–insecure group. Moreover, when the χ^2 analyses were conducted separately within each intervention group, again, no significant effects were observed.

Overall, the findings indicate substantial improvement in toddler attachment security in response to the TPP intervention, as well as improvements in RF levels for mothers in the DI group. However, we did not find evidence that the increases in the prevalence of secure attachment in the DI group could be explained as a consequence of improvements in maternal RF levels. Accordingly, it appears that the two positive outcomes of TPP were relatively independent despite our anticipation that increasing mothers' RF levels would contribute to improving the attachment organization of offspring.

These results are particularly interesting in the context of recent work that has examined maternal RF with respect to offspring (cf. Slade, 2005). Rather than focusing on maternal RF with respect to one's own caregiving history, the author proposed that maternal reflective capacities need to be examined directly as they emerge within the mother–child relationship. By directly assessing mothers' capacities to understand their children's experiences and their own experiences as parents in mental state terms, Slade hypothesized that a more direct examination of the intergenerational transmission of attachment might be attained. As such, our findings involving RF assessed in relation to mothers' thinking about their own parents and relationships in childhood may have been a step removed. Although it might be assumed that RF capacities assessed in regard to one's parents would correspond to and promote RF in regard to one's child, this need not be the case. RF may vary in regard to the types of relationships assessed, as may be observed with different patterns of attachment to one's mother and one's father. Furthermore, whereas RF has been conceptualized as an undergirding feature of maternal sensitivity (Fonagy & Target, 1997), more sophisticated mentalization in general may not necessarily equate with more effective relational responding to the child, particularly in clinical samples. In effect, not only is it important for a mother to understand her child in mental state terms, but also she must be able to relate to her child in a manner adaptively consistent with her understanding of him or her. In times of distress, for example, the sensitive mother needs to appreciate and mirror the emotional experience of her child, as well as to modulate effectively the intensity of negative emotion. Maternal depression may interfere with the mother's capacity to respond to the child's affective experience, even in the context of higher levels of RF.

In addition to the AAI, PAIs also were obtained prior to and following the TPP intervention. These interviews remain to be coded; however, we anticipate that RF assessed by focusing more specifically on the mother's experience and understanding of her child may be more strongly linked to child attachment organization. Moreover, given the explicit focus on expanding the mother's perception, experience, and understanding of her child within the context of the TPP sessions, we would expect that the DI group would evince substantial elaboration of RF capacities as a result of the intervention, whereas the DC and NC groups would not. Additionally, TPP allows the mother to "experiment" with relating to her child in new ways within the context of the security afforded by the conjoint therapy sessions. This feature of

TPP may promote the mother's capacity not only to understand her child more deeply in mental state terms but also to relate to her child in a manner that corresponds sensitively to the child's emotional experience. Thus, we expect that such changes advanced through TPP may constitute the processes through which major gains in attachment security were achieved in the DI group. Our future research agenda involves examination of these relations.

Clinical Illustration

To elucidate better the course of therapy, attachment organization, and intervention efficacy, we next provide background information on one of the representative DI cases. In particular, we focus on maternal and child attachment organization pre- and postintervention, and provide exemplars of RF derived from the AAI and from therapy sessions.

Rita, the 32-year-old mother of 18-month-old Karen, was referred to the TPP program by the psychiatrist she was seeing to monitor her antidepressant medication. Rita had a history of MDD dating to adolescence, and had been on antidepressant medication for 1 year prior to her pregnancy with Karen. Rita had continued on her medication throughout her pregnancy and was concerned that the medication had adversely affected Karen.

In her baseline AAI, Rita described a caregiving history that involved violence. She reported that after her mother told her biological father that she wanted a divorce, he raped her and was put in jail for attempting to murder her the night Rita was conceived. Rita reported that she had never met her biological father, and that her mother had been involved with her stepfather from the time of her birth, eventually marrying him when Rita was 8 years old. Rita went on to state that she had never met her biological father, because he was violent. As she continued to describe her childhood years, it was apparent that "violence" was also a characteristic of Rita's stepfather.

Despite the fact that Rita stated that her mother was loving and "always there for [her]," this recollection was contradicted at several points in the AAI. Most significantly, with regard to maternal unavailability, Rita reported that a neighbor sexually molested her when she was 4 or 5 years of age, prior to her mother's marriage to her stepfather. Rita did not inform her mother of the sexual abuse until she reached adulthood.

In reviewing Rita's preintervention AAI, it was clear that she continued to struggle with considerable confusion stemming from her childhood years. Rita's inability to resolve her childhood experiences was especially evident in her discussion of her stepfather's death. After stating that she continued to have difficulty dealing with his death, Rita, in an emotion-laden voice, stated:

"You have a lotta confused thoughts, you know? . . . Umm, finally when, when you've reached the point after so many years when you can say to each other that you love each other and that you're sorry for the things you've done, and then he's no longer there. . . . I was in a lot of pain. I was angered. I was, I felt, I felt, uh, guilty. I felt guilty because I had wished him dead earlier. Not now. Not once we knew each other in, in a normal sense. But, uh, relieved. Relieved because I knew that he couldn't get me anymore. He couldn't get to my mother anymore. Very confusing."

The guilt, unreasonable uncertainty around playing a causal role in the loss, and overall confusion that emerged as Rita discussed her childhood abuse and the death of her abusive stepfather resulted in the classification of Rita's AAI as unresolved/disorganized (Ud). In accord with recommendations and practices regarding providing an alternative forced classification for AAIs categorized as U (Main, 1995), Rita's AAI also had features consistent with a preoccupied/entangled classification. Specifically, Rita's experience of a weak mother who failed to protect her from abuse, the role reversal in relation to her mother, her seeming inability to move beyond a sense of self as entangled in her childhood relationships, and her guilt and conflicted feelings over anger toward her parents are consistent with a preoccupied/entangled attachment organization.

In a review of the RF level in the baseline AAI, Rita evidenced a low to moderate degree of RF. When asked if any aspects of her early experiences were a setback in her development, Rita replied that her father used to tell her how homely she was, and that she believed him. She went on to say, "When you hear that when you're a little girl, then you don't think that anybody is going to want to be with you because you're homely. And, if you're homely, and you can't bring any friends home, then you don't have any friends." When describing her grandmother's funeral when Rita was 12 years old, very little RF was evident. "Everybody was real sad. When I went to the funeral, everything was so black. And it was a rainy day, and I say everything was so black, but I guess it was 'cause everybody was wearing black, probably. Umm, everybody was crying. Umm, it was real sad and everybody cried a lot. And I didn't cry, I didn't cry." When queried as to whether the loss had an effect on her adult personality, Rita stated, "No. It was my first interaction with death, but, umm, it wasn't a bad one." In discussing the death of her stepfather, Rita admitted that the loss had affected her adult personality. However, when asked whether it affected her approach to Karen, she stated, "No, I don't think so. I think umm, it's only, it's only me that, that it affects." In describing her current relationship with her mother, Rita said, "It's more normal now. I understand why she put up with the [abuse]. I don't know why, but I understand. And just because she would put up with it doesn't mean I would."

In Rita and Karen's preintervention Strange Situation, Karen presented as quite wary of the stranger. Although Karen did not protest Rita's departure, when alone during the second separation her facial expression was disoriented, and freezing and stilling were noted. Although disorganized/disoriented behavior cannot be classified in the absence of the mother, these occurrences were interesting and atypical of more securely attached toddlers. Additionally, other indices of disorganization were observed. During the first reunion with Rita, Karen aborted an approach to Rita and made little eye contact with her, and shared positive affect between mother and toddler was not evident. During the second reunion, Karen approached Rita with a wide-mouthed smile, but backed away and eventually engaged in a sideways approach to Rita. Again, no shared positive affect was present. With regard to attachment classification, Karen meets criteria for a disorganized/disoriented attachment pattern. When trying to force-classify Karen into one of the three organized attachment categories as recommended by Main and Solomon (1986, 1990), her attachment was most consistent with the insecure–avoidant classification.

Course of Intervention for Rita and Karen

Over the course of therapy, the pervasive influence of Rita's childhood experiences on her parenting of Karen became very clear. Rita mentioned that during her childhood, her mother had attempted suicide several times, and that she had learned to avoid upsetting her mother out of fear of causing her to harm herself. At the time she entered therapy, Rita and her husband rented a home from her mother, adjacent to her mother's own home. Rita also relied on her mother for all of her transportation needs, because she had not renewed her driver's license when she was pregnant with Karen. It appeared that the prospect of parenthood served to further the enmeshment between Rita and her mother. Rita had extreme difficulty in asserting herself in any way, a characteristic that, again, was seemingly attributable to her stance in relation to her mother. She chose to blame herself and to experience guilt when she had any strivings for self-care or self-determination.

During early dyadic sessions, Karen generally avoided interacting with Rita. Karen's play was disconnected and haphazard, and her motor skills seemed to be awkward. She was difficult to engage and often would stare off into space for long periods of time, a presentation consistent with the disorganized/disoriented classification of the Strange Situation. Although Rita reported that she feared that her use of medication had resulted in developmental delays for Karen, she simultaneously expressed fear that Karen would be "smarter" than she. At these times, she seemed oblivious to Karen's needs and her tone was characterized by veiled anger. Rita also mentioned that she often did not feel like Karen's mother, because her own mother had tried to fill that role, and she resented this.

Therapy sessions focused on helping Rita to resolve her conflicted emotional experiences, to assert herself, and to thereby become freer to parent and to enjoy Karen's developmental progress. A significant component of this process involved helping Rita to recount childhood experiences and to express her anger rather than holding onto feelings of responsibility for her mother and guilt for failing to meet all of her mother's needs.

With respect to RF during therapy sessions, initially a relatively low RF level was present. Rita noted in the initial session that Karen was happy all the time, an observation that was very discrepant from the somber-faced little girl seen by the therapist. Rita also was quite concrete in her interactions with Karen, relabeling Karen's "slide" as a "block." Despite the fact that Karen was able to communicate her needs, including requesting milk during an early session, Rita spent most of the session talking about how Karen could not communicate her own needs.

In an early session Rita also reported that whereas Karen always used to say "yes" to anything that she was asked, she now said "no." To emphasize her point, Rita animatedly asked Karen if she wanted to take a nap. Much to Rita's dismay, Karen replied, "Yes." Rita disagreed with the therapist's input that perhaps Karen was responding to the tone of her voice, and she remained perplexed over Karen's style of communication. When describing her current pregnancy to Karen, Rita stated that she told Karen that she was having the baby for her. She added that Karen sometimes patted her tummy and jumped in her lap, "so I don't know how she feels about it." These examples highlight Rita's limited RF at the initiation of treatment.

Approximately 7 months into treatment, changes in Rita's RF, particularly with respect to Karen, were evident. During a session in which Rita noted that she had recently had many visitors to her home, she acknowledged that Karen had difficulty adjusting to the presence of so many visitors. Rita's insight into the effect of guests in the home on Karen was a significant sign of progress with respect to her ability to think about how other adults impacted Karen. Near the end of therapy, in a wonderful example of Rita's increased RF, Rita asked Karen to tell the therapist what they had discussed earlier in the day. Karen stated that she had told her mother that she didn't want to go to the center because of a prior fire drill and her fear that another would occur. Rita reported telling Karen that she understood her fears, and that they could discuss them with the therapist. She assured Karen that once at the center, if she felt unsafe, then they could go home. This exchange highlighted Rita's increased sensitivity to Karen's internal states and the ability to negotiate a goal-corrected partnership with her daughter.

At the termination of therapy, Rita and Karen were again seen in the Strange Situation. Although there were similarities between the Strange Situations conducted when Karen was 18 and 36 months of age, there also were significant differences. Karen's affect was much more positive, she made more eye contact with Rita, and there was considerable synchrony of affective tone between mother and daughter. Although Karen again took no real notice of her mother's departure, upon reunion she approached her mother immediately and offered her a puzzle. The aborted approaches noted at 18 months were no longer evident. Overall, a much more positive relationship was exhibited, and Karen was classified as securely attached to her mother.

Finally, Rita's postintervention AAI, though continuing to contain elements of unresolved abuse (U), was classified as secure–autonomous (F).

Although Rita continued to have some preoccupying anger about her childhood, the postintervention AAI differed from the previous AAI with respect to Rita's presentation of a more balanced view of her early experiences, as well as her descriptions of efforts to resolve conflicts with her mother.

Importantly, significant RF increases were evident in Rita's postintervention AAI. In discussing her current relationship with her mother, Rita stated:

> "I have a difficult time telling my mother exactly how I feel. I'm afraid that it's going to hurt her. Uh, she's been hurt enough. Finally, one particular day I came right out and asked her if she thought that if I didn't say things to her because I was afraid she was gonna go and kill herself. And she said yes. And so she knew that I had that feeling. I was afraid to hurt her, because if I hurt her she was gonna go home and kill herself. She's assured me that that's not going to happen. So, it was a very growth-oriented conversation, because I don't feel so concerned anymore with hurting her feelings because she'll deal with 'em."

Although in the baseline AAI Rita denied worrying about Karen when they were separated, a considerable shift was noted on the postintervention AAI. "I worry that something can happen to her that I'm not gonna know, probably because it happened to me and I never told my mother."

Summary

In summary, the preventive intervention provided for offspring of depressed mothers illustrates the impact of TPP on RF. Although differences did emerge on the Probable Experience scales of the AAI, with mothers with a history of MDD reporting more adverse experiences with both mothers and fathers than did women with no history of MDD, these scales did not change over time. Mothers who reported more childhood adversity also were more likely to show changes in RF over time. However, the probable experiences variables could not serve as mediators of intervention effects. Interestingly, although both RF and attachment security improved as a function of the intervention, RF did not mediate security of attachment. However, the examples of RF derived from the therapy sessions do reveal improvement in maternal capacities to understand the child in mental state terms, highlighting the types of changes that occurred over the course of the intervention. In future work it will be important to examine changes in maternal RF, specifically in regard to the child, to determine further the role of RF as a mediator of intervention efficacy. Moreover, this investigation highlights the importance of providing interventions that address the child's need to have a caregiver who is mindful of what is on the child's mind. The absence of mentalization in the parent–child relationship places children at heightened risk for future psychopathology.

References

Ainsworth, M. D. S., Blehar, M. C., Waters, E., & Wall, S. (1978). *Patterns of attachment: A psychological study of the Strange Situation.* Hillsdale, NJ: Erlbaum.

Ainsworth, M. D. S., & Wittig, B. A. (1969). Attachment and the exploratory behavior of one-year-olds in a Strange Situation. In B. M. Foss (Ed.), *Determinants of infant behavior* (Vol. 4, pp. 113–136). London: Methuen.

Arieti, S., & Bemporad, J. (1978). *Severe and mild depression.* New York: Basic Books.

Bemporad, J. R., & Romano, S. J. (1992). Childhood maltreatment and adult depression: A review of research. In D. Cicchetti & S. L. Toth (Eds.), *Rochester Symposium on Developmental Psychopathology: Developmental perspectives on depression* (Vol. 4, pp. 351–376). Rochester, NY: University of Rochester Press.

Bowlby, J. (1977a). The making and breaking of affectional bonds: I. Aetiology and psychopathology in the light of attachment theory. *British Journal of Psychiatry, 130,* 201–210.

Bowlby, J. (1977b). The making and breaking of affectional bonds: II. Some principles of psychotherapy. *British Journal of Psychiatry, 130,* 421–431.

Bowlby, J. (1980). *Attachment and loss: Vol. 3. Loss, sadness, and depression.* New York: Basic Books.

Bowlby, J. (1982). *Attachment and loss: Vol. 1. Attachment.* New York: Basic Books. (Original work published 1969)

Bowlby, J. (1988a). *A secure base.* New York: Basic Books.

Bowlby, J. (1988b). Developmental psychiatry comes to age. *American Journal of Psychiatry, 145,* 1–10.

Bretherton, I., Biringen, Z., Ridgeway, D., Maslin, M., & Sherman, M. (1989). Attachment: The parental perspective. *Infant Mental Health Journal, 10,* 203–220.

Carlson, E. A., & Sroufe, L. A. (1995). Contribution of attachment theory to developmental psychopathology. In D. Cicchetti & D. J. Cohen (Eds.), *Developmental psychopathology: Theory and methods* (Vol. 1, pp. 581–617). New York: Wiley.

Cicchetti, D., & Lynch, M. (1993). Toward an ecological/transactional model of community violence and child maltreatment: Consequences for children's development. *Psychiatry, 56,* 96–118.

Cicchetti, D., Rogosch, F. A., & Toth, S. L. (1998). Maternal depressive disorder and contextual risk: Contributions to the development of attachment insecurity and behavior problems in toddlerhood. *Development and Psychopathology, 10,* 283–300.

Cicchetti, D., Toth, S. L., & Rogosch, F. A. (1999). The efficacy of toddler–parent psychotherapy to increase attachment security in offspring of depressed mothers. *Attachment and Human Development, 1,* 34–66.

Cicchetti, D., Toth, S. L., & Rogosch, F. A. (2004). Toddler–parent psychotherapy for depressed mothers and their offspring: Implications for attachment theory. In L. Atkinson & S. Goldberg (Eds.), *Clinical applications of attachment* (pp. 229–275). Mahwah, NJ: Erlbaum.

Crittenden, P. M. (1992). Quality of attachment in the preschool years. *Development and Psychopathology, 4,* 209–241.

Fonagy, P., Gergely, G., Jurist, E., & Target, M. (2002). *Affect regulation, mentalization, and the development of the self.* New York: Other Press.

Fonagy, P., Steele, M., Moran, G., Steele, H., & Higgitt, A. (1991). The capacity for understanding mental states: The reflective self in parent and child and its significance for security of attachment. *Infant Mental Health Journal, 13*, 200–217.

Fonagy, P., Steele, M., Steele, H., Leigh, T., Kennedy, R., Mattoon, G., et al. (1995). Attachment, the reflective self, and borderline states: The predictive specificity of the Adult Attachment Interview and pathological emotional development. In S. Goldberg, R. Muir, & J. Kerr (Eds.), *Attachment theory: Social, developmental and clinical perspectives.* Hillside, NJ: Analytic Press.

Fonagy, P., & Target, M. (1997). Attachment and reflective function: Their role in self-organization. *Development and Psychopathology, 9*(4), 679–700.

Fonagy, P., Target, M., Steele, H., & Steele, M. (1998). *Reflective functioning manual, version 5.0, for application to Adult Attachment Interviews.* London: University College London.

Fraiberg, S. (1980). *Clinical studies in infant mental health.* New York: Basic Books.

Gaensbauer, T. J., Harmon, R. J., Cytryn, L., & McKnew, D. (1984). Social and affective development in infants with a manic–depressive parent. *American Journal of Psychiatry, 141*, 223–229.

George, C., Kaplan, N., & Main, M. (1985). *The Adult Attachment Interview, unpublished protocol* (3rd ed.). Berkeley: Department of Psychology, University of California.

George, C., & Solomon, J. (1999). The development of caregiving: A comparison of attachment theory and psychoanalytic approaches to mothering. *Psychoanalytic Inquiry, 19*, 618–646.

Hinshaw, S. P. (2002). Intervention research, theoretical mechanisms, and causal processes related to externalizing behavior problems. *Development and Psychopathology, 14*(4), 789–818.

Lieberman, A. F., Silverman, R., & Pawl, J. H. (2000). Infant–parent psychotherapy: Core concepts and current approaches. In C. H. Zeanah (Ed.), *Handbook of infant mental health* (2nd ed., pp. 472–484). New York: Guilford Press.

Lieberman, A. F., & Van Horn, P. (2005). *"Don't hit my mommy!": A manual for child–parent psychotherapy for young witnesses of family violence.* Washington, DC: Zero to Three.

Lyons-Ruth, K., Connell, D., Grunebaum, H., & Botein, S. (1990). Infants at social risk: Maternal depression and family support services as mediators of infant development and security of attachment. *Child Development, 61*, 85–98.

Mahler, M. (1968). *On human symbiosis and the vicissitudes of individuation: Infantile psychosis* (Vol. 1). New York: International Universities Press.

Main, M. (1995). Recent studies in attachment: Overview, with selected implications for clinical work. In S. Goldberg, R. Muir, & J. Kerr (Eds.), *Attachment theory: Social, developmental, and clinical perspectives* (pp. 407–474). Hillsdale, NJ: Analytic Press.

Main, M. (2000). The organized categories of infant, child, and adult attachment: Flexible vs. inflexible attention under attachment-related stress. *Journal of the American Psychological Association, 48*, 1055–1096.

Main, M., Goldwyn, R., & Hesse, E. (2002). *Adult attachment scoring and classification system.* Unpublished manuscript, University of California, Department of Psychology, Berkeley.

Main, M., Kaplan, N., & Cassidy, J. C. (1985). Security in infancy, childhood and adulthood: A move to the level of representation. *Monographs of the Society for Research in Child Development Monograph, 50*(1–2, Serial No. 209), 66–104.

Main, M., & Solomon, J. (1986). Discovery of a disorganized/disoriented attachment pattern. In T. B. Brazelton & M. W. Yogman (Eds.), *Affective development in infancy* (pp. 95–124). Norwood, NJ: Ablex.

Main, M., & Solomon, J. (1990). Procedures for identifying infants as disorganized/disoriented during the Ainsworth Strange Situation. In M. Greenberg, D. Cicchetti, & E. M. Cummings (Eds.), *Attachment in the preschool years* (pp. 121–160). Chicago: University of Chicago Press.

Oppenheim, D. (2004). The added value of attachment theory and research for clinical work: Introduction to the Special Issue. *Infant Mental Health Journal, 25*(4), 267–268.

Sandler, L., & Joffe, W. G. (1965). Notes on childhood depression. *International Journal of Psychoanalysis, 46,* 88–96.

Slade, A. (2005). Parental reflective functioning: An introduction. *Attachment and Human Development, 7*(3), 269–281.

Sroufe, L. A. (1983). Infant–caregiver attachment and patterns of adaptation in preschool: The roots of maladaptation and competence. In M. Perlmutter (Ed.), *Minnesota Symposium in Child Psychology* (Vol. 16, pp. 41–83). Hillsdale, NJ: Erlbaum.

Toth, S. L., Rogosch, F. A., Manly, J. T., & Cicchetti, D. (2006). The efficacy of toddler–parent psychotherapy to reorganize attachment in the young offspring of mothers with major depressive disorder: A randomized clinical trial. *Journal of Consulting and Clinical Psychology, 74,* 1006–1016.

van IJzendoorn, M. H. (1995). Adult attachment representations, parental responsiveness, and infant attachment: A meta-analysis on the predictive validity of the Adult Attachment Interview. *Psychological Bulletin, 117,* 387–403.

Parent–Infant Relationships, Adolescents, and Adults in Psychotherapy

7

The AAI as a Clinical Tool

AMANDA JONES

This chapter explores a case in which the Adult Attachment Interview (AAI) was a powerful clinical tool. I decided to use the AAI several months into treatment with a father who had previously been convicted of several offenses against his first two children, and who now had a 1-year-old son by another partner. I use material from the work to elaborate George, Kaplan, and Main's (1985) description of how the AAI can *surprise the unconscious* and provide valuable clues for how to proceed with clinical interventions. Answering the AAI questions rendered visible how the father used denial and excessive projection to protect himself from emotional conflict and pain. His answers also gave clues as to why he did so. In the ensuing work these defensive processes became more readily available. Gradually, as the father began to reclaim the projected aspects of himself, risk to his son lessened. The father began to recognize the impact his emotions and assumptions had on others. I describe how the AAI contributed to developing this father's *reflective functioning* (Fonagy, Target, Steele, & Steele, 1998). Hypotheses about attachment theory are addressed throughout the text, then pulled together at the end. I consider how, in psychodynamic parent–infant psychotherapy (Baradon et al., 2005; Jones, 2006), the AAI can contribute to the therapist and parent's metaphorical development as a fresh and restorative sexual couple, both in terms of the parent's history and in relation to how the parent conceives of the baby in his or her mind (both consciously and unconsciously).

Parent–Infant Psychotherapy

There are many innovative ways to work with parents and babies, approaches that address different levels of difficulty and choose different ports of entry.[1] In the Parent–Infant Mental Health Service, in which the work I describe took place, individuals present with myriad forms of pathology. It is a free National Health Service and referrals need to meet criteria of serious pathology, difficulties that have not responded to primary or secondary care interventions. In many cases the adult parent presents with personality difficulties. The case I describe was referred by Child Protection Services.

I decided to use the AAI some months into treatment because I was experiencing an impasse. The 20-year-old mother Kate was referred with her 1-year-old son Rick. The father, Pete,[2] was in his late 30s and was not referred. He was a "Schedule 1 Offender."[3] Until recently in the United Kingdom this label was used for someone convicted of sexual and/or physical offenses against children. It has recently been discontinued and replaced by the term "Risk to Children" for adults identified as posing an ongoing risk to children. Pete had been convicted for several offenses. At age 17 he exposed himself to two young teenage girls in a park and tried to touch one of them. In his late 20s, he was convicted of physically abusing his two sons. There had also been severe domestic violence in his marriage, and his former wife had accused him of sexually abusing one of their sons. Although these allegations were not substantiated, Pete had not been allowed contact with his children for 10 years. He also had been in prison for stealing and assault.

When Pete moved to our area, he was still on parole. He came to the attention of social services when his new partner Kate became pregnant. There is a statutory requirement in the United Kingdom to have a prebirth child protection meeting when a Schedule 1 Offender is one of the parents or lives in the home of the new baby. After the birth, Rick was placed on the child protection register, because Pete was still considered a substantial risk. At first he was allowed only supervised contact with Rick in the presence of Kate and her mother, and he was not allowed to live with them.

Pete evoked two strong emotions in the social services system: disgust and fear. His behavior toward professionals was aggressive and dismissive, and he could be deliberately intimidating. He was uncooperative and showed no willingness to take responsibility for any of his previous offenses, tending instead to blame the damage he did on his first wife. Alarm bells were also ringing because Kate was young.

The referral to the Parent–Infant Mental Health Service was framed in the following way: The social worker requested therapy for Kate and Rick, with the aim that I should help Kate "come to her senses" and terminate the relationship with Pete. In the social worker's view, Rick could only be safe if Pete was deleted from the picture. I said that parent–infant psychotherapy focused on improving the attachment relationship between parent(s) and baby; I was unsure whether I could help but agreed, in the first instance, to meet with Kate.

In the first meeting Kate's narrative was full of contradictions: She explained she had planned to become pregnant without telling Pete, emphasizing how she wanted her baby to have a father he knew, and how Pete had never been violent to them. Her own father had left her mother shortly after Kate's birth; she knew nothing of him and felt forbidden to ask. Although Kate wanted her son to know his father, she had chosen an older man who was likely to be forbidden contact with his child. Powerful unconscious forces operating in Kate included urges to help and heal a damaged (and damaging man), and the strong possibility of a repetition of the "absent father" for her son. Kate was also heavily involved with her mother, in such a way that she seemed like a husband substitute.

I asked whether Kate would want Pete to be involved in parent–infant therapy. She said that she wanted therapy but that Pete hated professionals. I contacted the social worker to say I would start to work with Kate and Rick to aid Kate's adjustment to being a first-time mother in the context of considerable pressures, but that I could not follow the request to encourage Kate to end the relationship with Pete. Kate would have the opportunity to explore the meaning of her choice to be with Pete. I said that in time Kate and Pete might want to come to therapy together to think about how they were contributing to Rick's development. It was a difficult conversation: I found myself saying that I did not think that being a "Schedule 1 Offender" precluded the offender from access to treatment. The social worker said it would be complicated to arrange therapeutic meetings: Pete would have to arrive after Kate for sessions and leave before, and so forth. I said that although it might never happen, we needed to anticipate it, because, from the baby's point of view, it was important to offer treatment to both parents.

Four sessions later, Kate and Pete came to therapy together. Pete was a large man who emanated hostility and made no eye contact with me. He was restless and verbally aggressive, swearing frequently, especially about the social worker. But I noticed that Kate was not afraid, just fed up. Pete did manage to communicate uncertainty as to *how to play* with Rick when he was allowed to see him. I said that we could look at that in parent–infant psychotherapy and, if they wanted, videotape some play interactions. Pete became interested. I was the first professional who communicated an invitation for him to be with his son.

The social worker, albeit reluctantly, agreed to weekly family sessions. In the next six sessions we worked on the interactions between Pete and Rick. Following Beebe's (2003) model of working with video feedback, I filmed each parent for 5 minutes (and sometimes both together) playing with Rick. The following week we would watch the film. I invited the parents to comment freely on what they saw. What did they feel and think? What did they imagine Rick was feeling and thinking? Pete quickly noticed how he dominated the play and played as if Rick were not present. For example, in one clip, Pete built a brick wall and ignored Rick's interest; he could not register Rick's communications for contact. But when Pete watched the videotape, he could see how he ignored Rick. He linked this to imagining how he had always played alone as a child. A few fragments of his childhood came into consciousness. Pete said he had been beaten "black and blue" as a child: "I didn't want to play with no one." But he would not pursue his observations; a steel guard of denial came down. I noticed how Pete became visibly uncomfortable. He laughed sardonically and said, "What does it matter anyway?"

Although his interactions with Rick improved, with other professionals Pete's abusive and denigrating behavior persisted. I commented on the unhelpfulness of his hatred and suggested that we have some individual sessions to consider what got stirred up in him when faced with authority. Kate was keen on the idea; Pete reluctantly agreed. At first we met every 2 weeks. The most virulent fury burst forth in Pete, solely toward professionals. He blocked any attempt I made to inquire more about his own parents, swearing at me frequently. When I probed more about what had happened with his sons and former wife, it became even worse. On several occasions he got up to hit me, or stormed out of the room. (Unbeknownst to Pete, I had access to an alarm to signal for help, with a team that knew the nature of the work, so I managed to contain my fear in those moments.)

I felt we had reached an impasse because Pete stuck to his narrative about "bad professionals," and his refusal to offer more information about his background also prevented exploration of meaning. I felt controlled by him, yet caught in a paradox: Although everything and everyone was bad in Pete's eyes, somehow he managed to have a nonviolent relationship with Kate, he agreed to see me, and he was trying to have a relationship with Rick. He had also managed to comply with the child protection care plan. I could not make sense of him.

But by this stage I had enough information to hypothesize the following: Pete generated considerable anxiety in others; people became afraid in his presence. This begged the question as to why. Why did others experience Pete as this powerfully cruel figure? It was clear that others became anxious and frightened when with him. From a psychoanalytic perspective, one way of understanding this would be to consider that Pete drew upon defensive strategies when faced with situations in which he felt threatened. His behavior indicated that somehow he identified with an inner experience of a cruel, aggressive, and powerful figure (A. Freud, 1936/1993). Thus, he became frightening and felt no fear; in synchrony, others became fearful. It seemed that Pete coped with his fear and anxiety by inducing in others the very feelings he was trying to avoid himself. The social worker admitted to being terrified of him. I only had hints that Pete might also have been a terrified child. In Priscilla Roth's (2005) words, "a complicated series of identifications, introjections, projections, more identifications" (p. 204) appeared to take place when Pete felt threatened. "Projective identification," although an unwieldy term, was originally used by Melanie Klein (1946/1975b) to describe a defensive way of managing intolerable feelings, whereby the unbearable feeling is split off and somehow imagined to reside in *the other* person.[4]

With Pete, I could see how others were rendered frightened and worthless, while he felt immune from pain. Theoretically, it would make sense to consider that Pete relied on projective identification because he could not bear to feel frightened or worthless himself, and somehow needed to create these feelings in others to reassure himself that he was untouched by harm. A contemporary view of this process suggests that the *recipient of the projected state* is likely to feel as if something "unstoppable" is going on (Cimino & Correale, 2005, p. 51); the social worker felt assailed and frightened. This process was also prevalent in the therapy: if I struck a nerve with Pete, quick as a flash, I experienced fear of punishment. These feelings were incongruent with what I had been feeling earlier in the day, or even earlier in the session, which led me to think they were connected to the defensive response my question triggered in Pete (as well as my own idiosyncratic ways of managing worry). With hindsight I now realize that when I asked about his sons, I reminded Pete of his own childhood, evoking a defensive response in which his childhood vulnerability not only had to be decimated and denied but also engendered in me. I often ended the sessions feeling shaken, little, and deskilled, while Pete would sometimes leave in a dismissive, almost triumphant state. So Pete related to me as if I were frightened and bad, feelings that perhaps he found hard to accept as his own.

The other side was that Pete did not just generate fear; people hated him and wanted to punish him. The subject of child abuse, especially sexual abuse (whether substantiated or not), does stir up vehement responses. So individuals within the social services system had to manage strong feelings toward Pete. After a conversation with one child protection police officer, I felt somehow implicated in child abuse because I was willing to treat a "Schedule 1 Offender." The point is this: Pete stimulated people's superegos into action, and not in a helpful way. Far from the superego responses acting like firm but fair internal policemen or teacher figures, more punishing and unforgiving dynamics occurred (Freud, 1923/1949, 1935/1975a; Green, 2005; Klein, 1935/1975a). Although Pete seemed without conscience, I came to learn that he was actually highly critical of himself, and he did have the potential for remorse. I thought a particular aspect of Pete's own harsh superego was in some ways split off and projected into professionals. I examine in greater detail (Jones, 2006) the influence of unconscious processes and the role of the superego in parent–infant psychotherapy. I noticed that Pete felt perpetually criticized and judged by professionals. Moreover, the nature of Pete's offenses ensured that his projections found fertile grounds in which to take root.

Given these characteristics, I thought Pete still posed considerable risk. Rick was relatively safe so long as Pete could aim his hatred at "bad professionals." But if the system were not present, where would such feelings go? I imagined that Pete's other sons had become the target of powerful and pathological projections: particularly his need to induce fear in others to feel power-ful himself. I knew that if therapy was to lessen his potential to harm again, Pete would need to reclaim aspects of these projections. Although we had made a therapeutic alliance, I saw no evidence that this was happening.

I had heard of other parent–infant clinicians using the AAI (e.g., at the Parent–Infant Project at the Anna Freud Centre, London). In a discussion with Howard Steele, I thought the AAI might offer a way to get more information about Pete's background, and that his responses might also demonstrate more about how he protected himself when attachment-related feelings were stirred. I already had evidence to suggest that Pete *identified with an aggressor* (A. Freud, 1936/1993): He projected aspects of himself for which he did not want to take responsibility; he denied his own complex emotions; and he found it impossible to imagine that other people might be having thoughts or feelings other than those he ascribed to them. He lived in a black-and-white world, splitting easily into "good" and "bad," with most of the external world being bad. But I felt at a loss to understand more fully his *internal working models*. I imagined that he had experienced considerable trauma as a child, yet I had no narrative of this. My hypotheses were based on how he behaved with me and the feelings I had when in his presence. I needed to know more to proceed. So I introduced the AAI by saying that I knew Pete did not want to talk about his childhood, but that to help him more with Rick, it would help to know about his early experiences, and that a well-researched interview would help me gather information I needed to keep helping him. I made clear how it might stir up feelings with which I would help him (by this time, although stormy, we did have a therapeutic frame). I reiterated Pete's motivation to be a better father with Rick, at which point he nodded and, after a few moments of look-ing down at the carpet, agreed to do it. The tone of his voice was weary and worried. We conducted the interview the following week (which I audio-taped). I did not anticipate what would come forth.

Pete had consistently refused to talk about his mother. Right at the begin-ning, the AAI puts this crucial relationship in the spotlight. What Pete revealed was an intense description of both the internal relationship he contin-ued to have with his mother in his mind *and* the defensive processes he needed to use when faced with talking about his relationship with her—defenses he had possibly developed during his childhood that were now almost "aspects of character" (Waddell, 1998, p. 43).

> THERAPIST: So when thinking about your mother, can you think of five words or adjectives that you might choose to describe your relation-ship with her as a small boy?
>
> PETE: I don't know actually because I never had one—never had a rela-tionship with Mum, period—so I don't know how to describe it really, it's none, nonexistent, really nonexistent, because there was-n't, there was never a relationship there at all so. Never felt anything,

don't want anything either, so I haven't missed out on anything. (*He laughed.*)

This response conveyed Pete's use of denial and how he needed to isolate feelings about his mother, so that he made the relationship sound as if it were denuded of meaning. He appeared to have mastered feeling unwanted or unloved by adopting a defensive posture whereby he behaved as if he needed and wanted no one. He was, so to speak, self-sufficient (this way of being has been described in the psychoanalytic literature as adopting a phallic defense; see Birksted-Breen, 1996). My response was to feel derailed; an important relationship was *nonexistent*. The *emotion* was incongruent: What Pete was describing was awful, yet he laughed. I persisted.

> THERAPIST: So would any kind of emotional words come to mind to describe the relationship with her?
>
> PETE: I couldn't say it on tape. I wouldn't like to. No, nonexistent, it's . . . I don't feel anything. I don't know how to describe it. It's a hard one, innit? (*He laughed.*) I've never really thought about it. I know it's nonexistent, nonexistent. . . . I never think about it, first time I've thought about it. I've never really thought about it, I just push it back in my mind and leave it there, leave it buried.

I felt emptiness and despair listening to Pete say, "It's a hard one, innit?" The way he reiterated how he "never really thought about it" and how it was the "first time I've thought about it" indicated that it felt risky to think about it. I saw this as intrinsically linked to Pete's first comment, "I couldn't say it on tape." In a few words, Pete conveyed his hostility and hatred toward his mother, the very feelings that had probably soared to life uncontrollably with his first wife. Pete hinted at the strategies he had used *not to know* his thoughts and feelings: *pushing* it to the back of his mind, *burying* it. But Pete was thinking, albeit with difficulty.

> THERAPIST: And if I asked you for five words to describe you relationship with your father?
>
> PETE: Exactly the same, no different. Nothing whatsoever. Never got on, nothing, there was no, no bond there at all. Nothing whatsoever. Nothing, nothing at all—nonexistent as far as that one goes as well. It didn't bother me once I got to 14 or 15. Then I was going out, it didn't bother me. That's probably why I was going out nicking, attention seeking, I suppose.

I felt numb. In the context of my numbed state—perhaps previously Pete's–he showed a shift in his capacity to think about his behavior from a slightly new perspective: His "nicking" had meaning, stealing attention in a way. Pete had never made an *observation about himself* before. The abject neglect of the existence of his emotional reality was starkly apparent in minutes, as were his ways of defending himself from thinking and feeling about it. Pete's words vividly depicted a bleak, loveless world. It made sense that he had not wanted to talk about it before. Perhaps his repeated use of the term "nonexistent" conveyed his perception that his emotional reality had not existed for his parents. This probably contributed to Pete's dismissal of his feelings with me, and in a way he needed me to feel it too. I did feel momentarily numbed. Pete needed to deny that his parents had meaning. I now knew that Pete did not feel loved by his primary attachment figures. A little later, I asked how his parents disciplined him. He looked at me with dull eyes.

> PETE: I'd get beaten, maybe just beaten with belts, *so that's what they'd do*. Hit me with a leather belt, or anything, a bit of a wood. . . . The old man would use anything to hit me, so. (*His affect was flat.*)
>
> THERAPIST: Do you remember the youngest age you were when that happened?
>
> PETE: It started from the age of 7, I think. (*long pause.*)
>
> THERAPIST: You were very small.

It is part of the interview protocol not to comment on the respondent's answers, but almost without thinking, I said, "You were very small." I said it very quietly to this large man sitting in front of me and, in the context of his deadened affect, I felt intensely moved by him. He looked at me, as if surprised, and his next association indicated that my emotional response somehow helped him to open up.

> PETE: I think that's why it screwed my head up, I think. (*He looked upset.*)
>
> THERAPIST: What screwed your head up?

It is important to look at this moment in detail. As I said, I was moved by what Pete was telling me. I felt *for* him, which I had not done before. Throughout the earlier treatment, I had worked out of a superego demand to offer a therapeutic intervention to a man who had not been treated before; it had not been connected to my desire to be involved. But as he allowed me closer, different feelings came alive. It sounded as if Pete was saying the physical abuse from his father had "screwed" his head up, but when I asked (in a slightly disoriented way), "What screwed your head up?", Pete's associations were of another incident of abuse, this time a sexual one. I do not think he had had any prior intention of telling me, but the fact that he said, "I think that's why it screwed my head up, I think," indicated that Pete was starting to think, to reflect on his experience. I think *my asking* (and feeling for him) made the difference.

PETE: When I got abused—when I was 14—I got abused by two blokes. They [his parents] called me a liar. So that's why I never went to the police. I kept it to myself. They didn't want to know, so I just left it. It's hard to deal with something like that, but I managed, so I don't think about it anyway, so.

The merger of earlier neglect and a later experience of abuse came forth. Pete was having an opinion about the care he had received as a child, and then as an adolescent. When he was raped in a public toilet by two grown men, Pete tried to tell his parents and his request for help was utterly rejected. The intensity of his hatred toward authority figures began to make sense, and I was getting an insight into his defensive strategies: not to think, not to feel, not to mind, not to want. I had seen research that suggested Pete was likely to have experienced ongoing primary "cumulative trauma" (Khan, 1963/1974a) as an infant because he had no sense of an empathic, loving mother to help him endure, and to give meaning to the microtraumatic moments that every infant experiences when faced with overwhelming internal and external stimuli. This appeared to have left Pete psychically vulnerable and unable to protect himself from later abuse. These later traumatic events, in terms of being physically beaten by both parents and raped by strangers in his childhood and adolescence, combined with the earlier cumulative trauma, rendered Pete highly prone to feeling persecuted by both his feelings and his belief that others wanted to harm him.

THERAPIST: That leads into the next question. How you feel the experiences you had as a child with your parents have affected you, your adult personality?

PETE: Well it's affected me a lot, you know, it's affected me. I mean I know I can look at what I've done to my boys, right? Probably physically and mentally, it should never have happened. That's why I, that's why I can't make the same mistakes with Rick, so I blame my parents for that.

By this point, Pete's defenses were lowered, and for the first time he spoke as if he were able to take some responsibility for what happened with his sons, but he could only do so if it were seen in the context of what he experienced with his parents—experiences he had refused to share before. I think he felt closer to me.

A little later I asked about losses.

THERAPIST: Was there anybody else at all that you felt close to, any other adult?

PETE: Only me nan [grandmother]. And that was it. There was only her. The only one I could talk to. Apart from her, that was it, and I couldn't always go to her. It wouldn't be fair going to her all the time.

THERAPIST: Can you describe to me your relationship with her?

PETE: You know, with my nan, my old man's mum. It was like, umm, a mother and son relationship. I looked to her more like a mum. They'd treat me right. If I'd go round there and I'd be crying, they'd sit down and ask me what was wrong, they wouldn't automatically jump on me—do you know what I mean?—and say, "Oh, it's your fault." But when they died it just went stale inside. And I weren't even allowed to go to the funeral, I was, er, 14, I was nearly 15 when she died. Me old man didn't even want me to go to the funeral, because he knew I was getting on better with them than he was.

This new information allowed me to understand how it was possible that Pete had managed to sustain a relationship with me, and why he was trying to have a relationship with Kate. Someone had valued him—his nan. The comment "but when they died it just went stale inside" stopped me in my tracks. Pete, who had existed by denying his emotional reality, suddenly used a graphic metaphor to describe his internal state. The room went quiet and, after a few minutes he sniffed, took off his glasses and rubbed his eyes. Pete had lost his grandparents in the same year that he was raped and felt abandoned by his own parents. The atmosphere between us was intense. Given what Pete had told me, there had clearly been significant trauma in his early life and adolescence. So later, when I came to the question on trauma, I asked Pete what had been most difficult for him in his life.

THERAPIST: What would you describe or highlight as particularly traumatic that's happened in your life?

PETE: Having two kids, that's been traumatic in my life. What I've done to them, that's a traumatic thing in my life. Nothing else matters really.

The shift, by this point, was considerable. Here was a man who could now, albeit tentatively, own the fact that he had hurt his children, and this knowledge was traumatic for him.

PETE: And my parents not bringing me up the way, the way they should have done, basically, I think they made terrible mistakes. They'd never admit it but they made terrible mistakes. I started to make the mistakes with my boys and I'm not going to make them again. It's cost me my two kids, so.

By the end of the interview Pete was able to balance both realities: the fact that it mattered to him that his parents had made "terrible mistakes" and the fact that repeating such mistakes with his own sons had resulted in his losing them. Although the interview only lasted for some 45 minutes, I felt I knew Pete very differently by the end. I think Pete felt heard by me, and this started in him the process of being able to hear the cries of his own sons.

Howard Steele read, rated, and classified the transcription of the interview. Outstandingly high scores for having been rejected and neglected by both parents, and similarly ceiling high scores for derogation of these parents, led to a primary classification of dismissing. Additionally, the dismissing/derogating (Ds2) subtype, rare in nonclinical samples, was readily identified as appropriate. This applies when attachment figures are derogated and the self is elevated. Despite Pete's past experiences of sexual abuse and significant loss (of beloved grandparents) he was not judged to be unresolved. There was a qualification to this insecure–dismissing profile at the end of the interview, as noted, when Pete was mildly reflective and identified his own abusive behavior (not just that of his parents) as a terrible mistake, along with the determination not to repeat this behavior in the future. This was certainly a hopeful sign.

After the interview, therapeutic sessions continued—1 week individually with Pete and the next with Pete, Kate, and Rick. Pete managed to persist with the themes that emerged in the AAI: his feelings about his parents, about being raped, his jealousy about a favored younger brother, and how all these feelings led to behavior that placed his first wife and children at risk. In terms of the possibility for transformation and change, of particular pertinence was the restoration of his nan as someone who had loved him, but whom he lost too soon. In talking about her, his self-hatred softened. The internalization of her superego started to come into the fore. It was gentler, more understanding. Pete slowly started to be able to listen to other people's points of view. I could see that I had somehow managed to access and align with the transferential potential linked with Pete's nan, whereas the social worker (and other professionals) came up against the transference of his much hated mother and/or father. I asked Pete if I could meet with the social worker and share some thoughts about the dynamics that seemed to thwart progress. He agreed, and I shared with the social worker the hypothesis about the transference dynamics. She was visibly relieved: It now made sense where the hatred came from, and she broadened her imagination about Pete. He was no longer just a child abuser. Although the situation was still tricky, they started to work together more productively.

The AAI helped me to be able to imagine Pete as a child. His defenses had forbidden me to do so before. In the context of my imagination, Pete started to think more about it too. In the therapy relationship, I think Pete felt that all of his disturbing ways of being had value, without my ever condoning abusive behavior. This is what the therapeutic frame offers: willingness to *hold in mind* all of a patient's ways of being, to tolerate uncertainty (e.g., could he ever be safe with a baby?), and to cope with difficult projections. Winnicott (1955/1965) emphasized the crucial parental provision of "holding the baby in mind." In describing an infant's need to be held both physically and emotionally, Winnicott wrote, "Here is absolute dependence, and environmental failure at this very early stage cannot be defended against, except by a hold-up of the developmental process" (pp. 147–148). In the therapy relationship with Pete, this entailed being able to think about him as a human being separate from me, a person who had been so injured and so dangerous. By providing appropriate ego support (through psychological and emotional holding), over time the process allowed him to develop the capacity to integrate these polarized (yet connected) experiences. I think Pete did start to integrate these different aspects of himself: his capacity to be abusive, his vulnerability. He allowed me to care for his well-being because maybe somewhere our relationship reminded him of his nan.

In the meantime, Pete's relationship with Kate changed. This is hard to write about. Kate had never felt the need for therapy herself. Although I thought differently, she was not willing to explore her own relationship with her mother, a relationship in which I thought she seemed to play the role of a husband substitute. I came to understand that it suited Kate to have a distant but present father for her son, but that actually she never intended to live independently of her mother. Pete's wants changed. In the context of the therapeutic work, his wishes for a more mutual relationship developed. Rick, I realized, was never going to have a fully present father, and I could do nothing about that other than try to help Kate and Pete find ways to include Pete in Rick's life. I saw Pete and Kate for several sessions together, in which they decided to separate as partners but wanted to find a way to be decent parents for Rick. During this time, Rick was taken off the child protection register, and Pete had some affirmation that he had somehow grown and moved on, and become less of a risk to others.

I certainly felt this in the therapy sessions. I rarely felt intimidated by Pete anymore. The sense of being controlled dissipated; instead I felt free to question him about anything, and Pete became much more able to free associate with me. His use of projective identification changed: He could think about his own frightened states and feel cared for while doing so, and in light of that he no longer needed to induce terror in others. As we progressed, what came increasingly to the fore was Pete's chronic and enduring low self-esteem, linked to his experiences of not feeling loved, particularly by his mother (which I described earlier as "primary cumulative trauma"). He was much more depressed than he had let himself know and feel before. As his use of denial and projective identification changed, inevitably he hurt more, especially when facing the harm he had done to his two sons, and his loss of them (they persisted in not wanting to see him). At this point I suggested to Pete that he be assessed by an adult psychiatrist in case some form of antidepressant medication could act as an adjunct to the therapy. He was prescribed fluoxetine, which he thought helped him cope with his blackest moments. It was extraordinarily complex work, lasting some 4 years. My commitment to Pete was solid and, unlike his nan, I did not die or leave him too soon. This, I think, was essential for him.

Eventually Pete found a new relationship with a woman named Beth, who was more mature and not from a difficult background. He asked me to work with the two of them, which I did for 6 months. Kate was furious about this, wanting Pete to remain a distant provider *solely* for herself and Rick. There were difficult altercations, and Pete began to realize that contact with Rick would continually stir difficult feelings for Kate. Yet he persisted in accepting the possibilities Kate offered in order for him to see Rick. Kate's envy in relation to his growth was hard for Pete and his new partner to manage.

I could see that a new and more satisfying relationship was growing between Pete and Beth. They worked hard with me about how to manage intimacy as a couple. Beth suffered from epilepsy, and it was touching to observe Pete take the role of protector in relation to her physical vulnerability. Then Beth became pregnant, which heightened her medical risk. The same scenario was repeated: Social services had to become involved, but this time it was different. Everyone could recognize the hard work Pete had done. He was fully involved in the antenatal process (which was more complicated due to Beth's epilepsy), and their new baby son was off the child protection register within a month. It warmed me to hear that the child protection Chair had smiled at Pete and said, "Well done and good luck." Pete was proud of himself.

I then worked for several months with Pete, Beth, now his wife, and new baby son together (in proper parent–infant psychotherapy in which the baby is central to the sessions). What I witnessed was Pete's capacity to fall in love with a vulnerable baby, his new son Ben, and his son with him. I saw a transgenerational pattern change: Ben had two protective parents who provided a consistent-enough empathic love. As a baby, his microtraumatic moments were responded to and contained. He internalized his parents as a "protective shield" (Khan, 1964/1974b). I saw him with Pete and Beth recently for a review. They are flourishing and Ben, who is 18 months old, is in my view securely and passionately attached to his father.

Reflections about the Work and the Theme of Conception

How did the AAI contribute to the process of change? There was an advent of "mentalization" during the AAI interview (Bateman & Fonagy, 2004, pp. 75–82). Pete demonstrated *an awareness of his children's mental states*, and an awareness of himself as having thoughts and feelings that might in turn affect his children. I think this was the beginning of Pete facing the damage he had done and, as I described, the immense guilt he was to experience during the therapy. This emerged in the context of *his* emotional state as a child being given meaning by me. For example, in the AAI interview I spontaneously said about the physical abuse Pete endured, "You were very small." But in the ensuing work I was also in touch with his sons' experience of being small and terrified with an enraged Pete. I provided a metaphorical scaffold for Pete to bear considering his and their experiences. The seesaw was constant: Pete as an abused angry child, humiliated and injured, and what he had done to his first two sons. Although at times I felt provoked into becoming a punishing and neglectful mother, Pete and I managed not to fall into an intransigent, destructive dynamic. I thank supervision for this: The presence of benign and supportive external views helped me manage my own responses so that I could, on the whole, albeit imperfectly, provide Pete with my own receptive, yet discerning, mind.

Two things were important: First, without Pete knowing it, for several months prior to administering the AAI I had been providing him with a *mentalizing, caring mind*. My *reflective function* was working hard—with Pete and with the wider system. I cared about him and tried to keep in people's minds the notion that emotions and mental states underlie behavior, that historical contexts exert unseen pressures (Faimberg, 2005), and that feelings and mental states can change (Bateman & Fonagy, 1999, 2000). I think this contributed to Pete being able to use the AAI to start to explore the significance of his own childhood. He could then imagine himself as having suffered, and take some responsibility for the suffering his sons had endured. The compulsion to repeat pain changed. Fonagy, Gergely, Jurist, and Target (2002) suggest that insecure attachment "may be seen as the infant's identification with the caregiver's defensive behaviour" (p. 43). The defensive behavior of withdrawing from, and denying the reality of, difficult feelings appeared to have been in play first between Pete's parents and Pete as an infant and child, then between Pete and his partners and, crucially, his children. Such *patterns of relatedness* tell as-yet silent stories that, so to speak, are often unconscious.[5] In *Remembering, Repeating and Working Through* Freud (1914/1958) emphasized how "we may say that the patient does not *remember* anything of what he has forgotten and repressed, but *acts* it out. He reproduces it not as a memory but as an action; he *repeats* it, without, of course, knowing that he is repeating it . . . and in the end we understand that this is his way of remembering" (p. 150, original emphasis). In parent–infant psychotherapy the repetition of defensive responses is often pivotal to the therapeutic process. I think Pete's defensive use of projective identification, which had enabled him *not to remember what he had repressed and suppressed in words*, changed. This helped him take responsibility for harming his sons.

Second, after the AAI, Pete became focused on the idea that therapy was about working on aspects of his personality that troubled him rather than locating all problems in others. He recognized that he had a problem with his impulsive temper and effortful control. Bateman and Fonagy (2004) point out that "the capacity to inhibit a dominant response in place of a sub-dominant one is a key achievement of early development. . . . Mentalizing involves setting aside immediate physical reality in favour of a less compelling reality of the other's internal state" (p. 78). Pete's propensity to use violent language and behavior changed in light of his being able to push a metaphorical pause button and consider the views of others. This could only happen once he felt less persecuted. He began to realize that the views of others could be helpful, like the views of his grandparents. I think the AAI offered Pete the opportunity to take an *observer position*, whereby he could look at the relationships in which he had participated from a different perspective (Birksted-Breen, 1996; Britton, 1989), with his therapist embodying a supportive and concerned *auxiliary superego* (Strachey, 1934). Pete could then find in his new partner relationship aspects of what he had found with me. He could be vulnerable with her and courageously honest about his difficulties.

The case has been worth recounting in detail because I have evidence that change has been sustained, and that Pete's newest son is securely attached to his father. This implies that a previously compelling transmission of violence and abuse has been transformed. I had four therapeutic tools:

- The developmental thrust inherent in the perinatal period (Slade, 2002).
- Appropriate medication to support the therapy work.
- My commitment to Pete and compassion for his thwarted potential.
- The impact of the AAI.

The AAI's Influence on the Restorative Sexuality of the Therapist–Parent Relationship

The perinatal period is, in Arietta Slade's (2002) words, "a highly vulnerable time, filled with the potential for transformation, and with the even greater potential for repeating old patterns of relatedness and intimacy" (p. 10). Pete had no idea that the birth of his sons would rouse unforeseen ghosts that would threaten to obstruct his children's development (Fraiberg, Adelson, & Shapiro, 1975). Inevitably, when a baby is born, a crucial sexual act has taken place and culminated in a conception: The parent's feelings about this may reveal much about his or her own sexual development—information that could be salient to how the current baby is represented in the parent's mind. Pete, I think, felt fundamentally threatened and confused by the conception of his three sons. A detailed analysis of Pete's sexuality is not possible in this chapter. But Slade (2002) depicted the danger of the *repetition* of old patterns of relatedness and intimacy, and on this I can comment in relation to violence and rape. In Pete's family, pseudointimacy was achieved in violent interactions. Could therapy transform this pattern—that of a violent parental couple, violent to themselves and to their child?

How therapist and parent interact as a fresh and restorative sexual couple is, as a subject, somewhat neglected in the current literature on parent–infant psychotherapy. I emphasize here that the gender of the therapist exerts an influence on the process, but often, as a female therapist, I am experienced as a potent male presence that enables a mother to conceive of her baby (and possibly the parental relationship) differently. As a therapist one always has to be available to a multitude of transferential relationships. To conclude, I offer some ideas on how administering the AAI when I did might have influenced Pete and myself as a metaphorical sexual couple at two levels:

- The level in which Pete could be conceived anew as a baby, with myself in the maternal and paternal roles.
- The level at which Pete and I could conceive his children differently, with us working together as a parental couple.

These two levels were, I think, in dynamic interaction: Pete's new conception occurred in *our* minds during the interview; thus, it contextualized, in the intercourse of the interview, his capacity to occupy a different position as a father. I was emotionally moved during the interview in such a way that I felt differently about Pete. This, I think, helped Pete feel differently about his children.

I have chosen this case to demonstrate how the AAI questions can bring into the room (in the present, during the interview) important repressed themes and *new* sexual dynamics. In this case the interview helped Pete and myself to have a different and meaningful interchange. As a couple, we had an emotional intercourse in which a new closeness could be conceived and new ideas produced. I think the AAI helped us move out of what had felt like the persistent pull to enter into unhelpful sadomasochistic exchanges, a dynamic that I think had been in play between Pete's parents and reenacted in Pete's own sexual relationships, and in his relationships with his children. During the interview, Pete could experience reparative urges in relation to his children. How come?

As noted earlier, the AAI was administered at a point when I had already established a meaningful therapeutic relationship. In light of this, perhaps the *structure* of the AAI questions acted like a potent paternal function. The questions are, in themselves, potent, offering the *potential* to penetrate and challenge many levels of psychic experience. They provided the reality of order, limits, and positional difference, with myself as the interviewer *in charge* and Pete as interviewee. In contrast, simultaneously I then received and experienced Pete's answers, providing a receptive maternal function, while also holding in mind the history of my relationship with Pete (thus, my mind had to provide a dynamic maternal–paternal bisexual function). I think I *conceived* Pete freshly again during the interview: I understood him differently; I *wanted* to invest in him and help him after it. This *want* had not been alive in me before. I believe Pete sensed this, and that it helped him to connect to a desire to repair damage, to be a different kind of father, in an emotionally alive way.

From a psychoanalytic perspective, Lebovici (1988) wrote about how the desire (or not) for maternity starts to come alive early in a child's life, when the girl is identified with her mother and wanting (or not) to give a child to her father. Thus, a present conception and pregnancy have unconscious links to earlier times. For Pete, perhaps the natural unconscious wish to make a baby with his mother was tragically damaged. Pete's feeling that his mother had never loved or wanted him appeared to contribute to his belief that he could *never* produce a valuable baby; after all, he had utterly devalued himself, and his babies were at risk of abuse (enacted repetition of devaluation). But I can imagine that as a small boy Pete's mind and body might frequently have felt overpowered by violent impulses and/or physical pain. His intrapsychic conflicts about his parents, and their relationship as a couple, continued to have a destructive influence in his mind. Although in the AAI we learned how Pete had tried to "bury" his feelings throughout his life, when he became involved in a relationship and then became a father, all his unresolved issues started to exert an influence. The AAI quickly bought these conflicts into view. What I did not anticipate was how the structure of the interview would enable us to experience a different potency as a couple, both about Pete *and* about his children (as *his* valuable, though lost productions, in relation to his first two sons).

Conclusion

Psychodynamic, systemically sensitive parent–infant psychotherapy is a powerful intervention offered during a vulnerable time. I have shown how the AAI, as a clinical tool, can in some cases be an important therapeutic aid. My emotional experience while conducting the interview was critical in terms of the therapeutic process and, like Steele and Baradon (2004), I found that the AAI—used within the context of a secure therapeutic relationship—helped to "promote integration and reflective capacities" (p. 297) and loosen the noose of constraining defensive processes. In light of this, if the work is ongoing, then I suggest that a baby can benefit and potentially flourish (Ricoeur, 1996) if the therapist–parent couple is sufficiently ready to enter into a new creative (metaphorically sexual) encounter. In clinical work, the point—in terms of timing—at which the therapist administers the AAI is perhaps pertinent in relation to what it can produce.

Acknowledgments

This work would not have been possible without the clinical wisdom of Juliet Hopkins, child psychotherapist and family psychotherapist; Angela Joyce, adult and child psychoanalyst; and Trudie Rossouw, child psychiatrist, psychoanalyst, and Associate Medical Director of Specialist Services for North East Mental Health Trust. I would also like to thank Paula Doran and Loxford Sure Start UK for funding the collaborative work with Howard Steele. I am grateful for his contribution in relation to classifying Pete's AAI, and his consistent interest and support as my ongoing PhD supervisor. Finally, I thank Pete, Kate, Beth, Rick, and Ben.

Notes

1. For example, see Bakermans-Kranenburg, van IJzendoorn, and Juffer (2005); Baradon et al. (2005); Beebe (2003); Cramer (1997); Fivaz-Depeursinge and Corboz-Warnery (1999); Fraiberg, Adelson, and Shapiro (1975); Puckering, Mills, Rogers, Cox, and Mattsson-Graff (1994); and Sameroff, McDonough, and Rosenblum (2004). My preference for grappling with unconscious dynamics leads me to highlight the importance of defensive processes in this chapter (Jones, 2005, 2006, 2007) but that does not preclude the usefulness of other, more behavioral models.
2. Although anonymity has been preserved and some details changed, I have the father's consent to share aspects of his therapy relating to the use of the AAI.
3. "Schedule 1 Offender" was a label for life, with no review procedure; the new "Risk to Children" label is intended to encourage agencies to examine the changing contexts of risk-posing behavior.
4. This concept has been elaborated by others, including Bion (1957/1988, 1959/1988), Rosenfeld (1949/1997, 1952/1965), and Sandler (1988).
5. See Faimberg's (2005) *The Telescoping of Generations: Listening to the Narcissistic Links between Generations* for a contemporary psychoanalytic account of the influence of unconscious influences between generations.

References

Bakermans-Kranenburg, M. J., van IJzendoorn, M. H., & Juffer, F. (2005). Disorganized infant attachment and preventative interventions: A review and meta-analysis. *Infant Mental Health Journal, 26*(3), 191–216.

Baradon, T., Broughton, C., Gibbs, I., James, J., Joyce, A., & Woodhead, J. (2005). *The practice of psychoanalytic parent–infant psychotherapy: Claiming the baby.* London: Routledge.

Bateman, A., & Fonagy, P. (1999). The effectiveness of partial hospitalization in the treatment of borderline personality disorder: A randomized controlled trial. *American Journal of Psychiatry, 156,* 1563–1569.

Bateman, A., & Fonagy, P. (2000). Effectiveness of psychotherapeutic treatment of personality disorder. *British Journal of Psychiatry, 177,* 138–143.

Bateman, A., & Fonagy, P. (2004). *Psychotherapy for borderline personality disorder: Mentalization-based treatment.* Oxford, UK: Oxford University Press.

Beebe, B. (2003). Brief mother–infant treatment: Psychoanalytically informed video feedback. *Infant Mental Health Journal, 24*(1), 24–52.

Bion, W. R. (1988). Differentiation of the psychotic from the non-psychotic personalities. In E. B. Spillius (Ed.), *Melanie Klein today* (Vol. 1). London: Routledge. (Original work published 1957)

Bion, W. R. (1988). Attacks on linking. In E. B. Spillius (Ed.), *Melanie Klein today* (Vol. 1). London: Routledge. (Original work published 1959)

Birksted-Breen, D. (1996). Phallus, penis and mental space. *International Journal of Psychoanalysis, 77,* 649–657.

Britton, R. (1989). The missing link: Parental sexuality in the Oedipus complex. In R. Britton, M. Feldman, & E. O'Shaughnessy (Eds.), *The Oedipus complex today: Clinical implications.* London: Karnac Books.

Cimino, C., & Correale, A. (2005). Projective identification and consciousness alteration: A bridge between psychoanalytis and neuroscience? *International Journal of Psychoanalysis*, 86(1), 51–61.

Cramer, B. (1997). Psychodynamic perspectives on the treatment of postpartum depression. In L. Murray & P. J. Cooper (Eds.), *Postpartum depression and child development*. New York: Guilford Press.

Faimberg, H. (2005). *The telescoping of generations: Listening to the narcissistic links between generations*. Hove, UK: Brunner-Routledge.

Fivaz-Depeursinge, E., & Corboz-Warnery, A. (1999). *The primary triangle: A developmental, systems view of father, mothers and infants*. New York: Basic Books.

Fonagy, P., Gergely, G., Jurist, E. L., & Target, M. (2002). *Affect regulation, mentalization, and the development of the self*. New York: Other Press.

Fonagy, P., Target, M., Steele, H., & Steele, M. (1998). *Reflective-functioning manual, version 5.0, for application to Adult Attachment Interviews*. London: University College London.

Fraiberg, S., Adelson, E., & Shapiro, V. (1975). Ghosts in the nursery: A psychoanalytic approach to the problem of impaired infant–mother relationships. *Journal of the American Academy of Child Psychiatry*, 14, 387–422.

Freud, A. (1993). Identification with the aggressor. In *The ego and the mechanisms of defence* (pp. 109–121). London: Karnac Books. (Original work published 1936)

Freud, S. (1949). *The ego and the id*. In J. Strachey (Ed. & Trans.), *The standard edition of the complete psychological works of Sigmund Freud* (Vol. 19, pp. 3–66). London: Hogarth Press. (Original work published 1923)

Freud, S. (1958). Remembering, repeating and working through. In J. Strachey (Ed. & Trans.), *The standard edition of the complete psychological works of Sigmund Freud* (Vol. 12, pp. 145–156). London: Hogarth Press. (Original work published 1914)

Freud, S. (1975). *New introductory lectures on psycho-analysis*. In J. Strachey (Ed. & Trans.), *The standard edition of the complete psychological works of Sigmund Freud* (Vol. 22). London: Hogarth Press. (Original work published 1933)

George, C., Kaplan, N., & Main, M. (1985). *Adult Attachment Interview* (2nd ed.). Unpublished manuscript, University of California, Berkeley.

Green, A. (2005). *Key ideas for a contemporary psychoanalysis: Misrecognition and recognition of the unconscious*. London: Routledge.

Jones, A. (2005). *The process of change in parent–infant psychotherapy*. Unpublished doctoral dissertation, Tavistock Centre, London.

Jones, A. (2006). How video can bring to view pathological defensive processes and facilitate the creation of triangular space in perinatal parent–infant psychotherapy. *Infant Observation*, 9(2), 109–123.

Jones, A. (2007). Levels of change in parent–infant psychotherapy. *Journal of Child Psychotherapy*, 32(3), 295–311.

Khan, M. (1974a). The concept of cumulative trauma. In *The privacy of the self*. London: Hogarth Press. (Original work published 1963)

Khan, M. (1974b). Ego-distortion, cumulative trauma and the role of reconstruction in the analytic situation. In *The privacy of the self* (pp. 59–68). London: Hogarth Press. (Original work published 1964)

Klein, M. (1975a). The early development of conscience in the child. In M. Klein, *Love, guilt, and reparation & other works, 1921–1945*. London: Hogarth Press. (Original work published 1935)

Klein, M. (1975b). Notes on some schizoid mechanisms. In M. Klein, *Envy and grati-*

tude & other works, 1946–1963. London: Hogarth Press. (Original work published 1946)

Lebovici, S. (1988). Fantasmatic interaction and intergenerational transmission. *Infant Mental Health Journal, 9*(1), 10–19.

Puckering, C., Mills, M., Rogers, J., Cox, A. D., & Mattsson-Graff, M. (1994). Mellow mothering: Process and evaluation of a group intervention for mothers with parenting difficulties. *Child Abuse Review, 3*, 299–310.

Ricoeur, P. (1996). Fragility and responsibility. In E. Iwanowski Trans. & R. Kearney (Ed.), *Paul Ricoeur: The hermeneutics of action*. London: Sage.

Rosenfeld, H. A. (1965). *Psychotic states: A psychoanalytical approach*. London: Karnac Books. (Original work published 1952)

Rosenfeld, H. A. (1997). Remarks on the relation of male homosexuality to paranoia. In M. Klein, *Envy and gratitude & other works, 1946–1963* (pp. 1–24). London: Vintage. (Original work published 1946)

Roth, P. (2005). Projective identification. In S. Budd & R. Rushbridger (Eds.), *Introducing psychoanalysis: Essential themes and topics* (pp. 200–211). Hove, UK: Routledge.

Sameroff, A. J., McDonough, S. C., & Rosenblum, K. L. (Eds.). (2004). *Treating parent–infant relationship problems*. New York: Guilford Press.

Sandler, J. (1988). *Projection, identification, projective identification*. London: Karnac Books.

Slade, A. (2002, June/July). Keeping the baby in mind: A critical factor in perinatal mental health. *Zero to Three*, pp. 10–16.

Steele, M., & Baradon, T. (2004). Clinical use of the Adult Attachment Interview in parent–infant psychotherapy. *Infant Mental Health Journal, 25*(4), 284–299.

Strachey, J. (1934). On the therapeutic effect of psycho-analysis. *International Journal of Psychoanalysis, 15*, 127–159.

Waddell, M. (1998). *Inside lives: Psychoanalysis and the development of the personality*. London: Duckworth.

Winnicott, D. W. (1965). Group influences and the maladjusted child. In *The family and individual development* (pp. 146–154). London: Tavistock. (Original work published 1955)

8

Integrating the AAI in the Clinical Process of Psychoanalytic Parent–Infant Psychotherapy in a Case of Relational Trauma

TESSA BARADON and MIRIAM STEELE

Unresolved intergenerational relational trauma—wherein the "ghosts" (Fraiberg, Adelson, & Shapiro, 1975) of pain and brutality are passed down the generations—challenge the heuristic and applied frameworks of clinicians and researchers alike. The Adult Attachment Interview (AAI) can be a central tool for exploring reported trauma and identifying unresolved trauma from the parent's past. Psychoanalytic parent–infant psychotherapy is a clinical modality that aims to modify the process by which the traumatic ghosts of the past revisit a parent's relationship with his or her own baby. This chapter illustrates the use of the AAI in applied psychoanalytic work with parents and infants in a case of relational trauma, by way of linking themes from the AAI with parent–infant interactions and clinical process. The material reported here is part of work in progress in the Parent–Infant Project at the Anna Freud Centre, London, where infants (under 12 months) and their parents are seen when typically occurring attachment processes are compromised, and early attachment troubles threaten the infant's development. Since we collaborated with therapists in the Project team to introduce the AAI, there has been work over some years to hone its integration within the clinical–therapeutic process. To date we have conducted the AAI with over 280 parents seen at the Anna Freud Centre. This chapter details an interview we obtained from one mother and shows how it facilitated understanding of relational trauma and progress toward resolution in the therapeutic work that followed.

Relational trauma (Schore, 2001), which is seen frequently in clinicians' consulting rooms, is characterized, in our experience, by extreme volatility in the parent's state of mind in relation to the infant that is enacted in neglectful or abusive behaviors interspersed with genuine care and contingent responsivity. The parent's lability is apparently random and entirely unpredictable to the infant. Thus, the infant, who at times experiences a caring and contingently respondent parent develops ways of being with the parent, when the parent is in this state of mind, that approximate secure attachment patterns. Yet suddenly the infant may be in the presence of a frightened–frightening person and is put in the position described by Main and Hesse (1990, p. 180) as "an irresolvable paradox wherein the haven of safety is at once the source of alarm," a situation of "fright without solution" (Hesse & Main, 1999, p. 484). In more extreme cases, the infant, so dangerously dependent on what Winnicott described as the caretaker's ability to "know what the infant feels like and so be able to provide almost exactly what the infant needs" (1965a, p. 54) may suffer extreme distress, a "sense of going to pieces," of "falling forever" (Winnicott, 1965b), and so be forced into psychic survival through dissociation (Perry, 1997; Schore, 1994, 2002). As Main and Hesse first theorized (1990), it seems possible that these are the infants who cannot develop a coherent, consistent defense against frightening or inconsistent relational intrusions, and who go on to develop a disorganized pattern of attachment (Abrams, Rifkin, & Hesse, 2006; Hesse & Main, 1999, 2006; Lyons-Ruth, Bronfman, & Parsons, 1999; Madigan, Moran, & Pederson, 2006; Madigan, Bakermans-Kranenburg, van IJzendoorn, Moran, Pederson, & Benoit, 2006).

Our aim in this chapter is twofold: (1) to illustrate how the AAI can focus the therapist's dynamic formulation regarding the parent's attachment state of mind and the observed difficulties in the relationship, and (2) present to the reader a "behind the scenes" perspective of the *process* of therapeutic intervention in parent–infant psychotherapy. By straddling clinical observations of trauma in the moment-to-moment transactions between parent and their infant, and the narrative evidence of experienced trauma in the parent's childhood, the chapter illustrates how a mother's state of mind concerning attachment is enacted in her interactions with her baby and his responses to her, and the therapeutic encounter. In particular, the chapter looks at the expressions of relational trauma in the parent–infant interactions, in the infant's affects and behaviors, and the clinical material—representational and enactive—of the parent.

The first session with a new family is a relatively unstructured experience of being-together and is devoted to the questions "What has brought you here?" and "What can we offer you?" The clinician administers the AAI in the second or third session (remaining faithful to the guidelines for conducting the AAI; George, Kaplan, & Main, 1985). The AAI process is used to highlight central intergenerational themes and mental functioning in the parent–infant psychotherapeutic context. Where the AAI is clinically contraindicated because of a highly fragile emotional economy in the parent, the attachment history is left to evolve as appropriate in the free flow of the verbal and procedural material unfolding in therapy.[1]

Case Illustration

The case and AAI material presented is taken from therapeutic work[2] with a mother (Alice) and infant (Jacob) whose relationship was characterized by intergenerational relational trauma.

First Session

The following extract is from the therapist's process notes from the first session:

> I met 10-month-old Jacob, peering from his large buggy, in the corridor. Alice had needed the toilet and asked the receptionist if she could leave him. He was looking askance when I came through, and I tried to speak soothingly to him. It took a few minutes for him to build up a cry, although he certainly did not find it easy to be with a stranger. Just as he started screaming, Alice returned and Jacob was quickly comforted.
>
> Jacob was very apprehensive of me as we settled in the room, and he clung to his mother. I commented that he had met me while she was out of sight and now was associating me with Mummy's departure. Alice thought he might be hungry and put him to the breast. He fed for a while.
>
> I invited her to tell me what brought them here. Her response was "It's a long history how I ended up here. He was born and I didn't feel any joy about having a baby. I was expecting that I would be happy and I wasn't. It was related to the moment after birth when I felt all that hard work for nothing, no reward. Ever since then I just wish he would disappear or I could make it go back and never became pregnant."
>
> I was leaning forward, listening intently. Alice was looking thoughtful; her tone of voice was mostly even, although at one point there was a slight tremor. From time to time she glanced at Jacob at the breast. One of his hands was against her back, the other seemed slack. When Alice finished speaking she stroked Jacob's hair, looking down at him. In other circumstances I would have thought that she was looking at him tenderly. I asked something and Jacob, hearing my voice, turned his head toward me. I leaned forward and said, "We are talking about you, Jacob."
>
> By this point in the session my interest was really aroused. I was observing very different interactions between mother and infant from the words that I was hearing. While the words depicted a desperate situation, the bodily transactions were reassuring. Jacob seemed to display the same contradictions in his approach and use of mother. On the one hand social referencing her in the presence of the stranger—myself, and on the other hand inhibiting all zestful possession of her. In the countertransference I did not know where I stood."

Conducting the AAI

In the next session the AAI was administered by the therapist.

Alice presented a coherent picture of her childhood relationships with her parents. Her mother was presented in positive terms; her father was described in a derogatory way as absent and neglectful. There seemed sufficient "specific examples," and the therapist was speculating that it would could code as secure. Then, midway in the interview, there was a dramatic turn in response to a probe about further separations. Out of the blue, Alice stated that when she was about 16, her mother "fell into a psychosis" and was extremely disturbed. Following detailed descriptions of her mother's psychotic behavior there was a change in her descriptions of earlier experiences, with an emphasis on her mother's singularly erratic behavior that marked her home as different from others. From this point on in the interview coherence plummeted.

At the end of the AAI, the therapist spends unstructured time with the parent to make links between important themes brought up in the interview and what he or she may previously have observed in the interactions between parent and baby. With Alice, the therapist raised the disjunction in her representations of her mother in the AAI, and wondered about a link to the "different mothers" she had observed in Alice in relation to Jacob. With her clinical hat on, she also thought Alice was still preoccupied and aggrieved (clinically unresolved) with regard to her mother's changing personas and her own loss of the "good mother" to the ill one.

Commentary of the AAI Coder[3]

This interview begins with Alice attempting to be a collaborative subject who demonstrates that she understands the interview context by describing her childhood experiences so that they can be understood by someone who obviously is unfamiliar with them. For example, in response to being asked for some details about her family (e.g., who lived with her and where), Alice describes the various members of her family, how old each sibling was, and when the many location moves occurred. She describes her relationship with her mother as "emotional, very intimate . . . not very intellectual." She goes on to say, "I also found that she knew everything and she was the best and the cleverest of all and, you know, I would believe what she would say. I wouldn't say I adored her, but I did think that she was, you know, a great person and I respected her and yeah." With this we find evidence of Alice's idealizing stance toward her mother; whereas she tries to temper her over-the-top description by adding that she would believe what her mother said to her, we are left wondering whether this may mean that now, as an adult, she is able to evaluate this esteem differently than she did as a child. A more reflective explanation was not forthcoming. Instead, Alice contradicts herself in the next sentence by saying, "I wouldn't say I adored her, but I did think that she was, you know, a great person and I respected her and yeah." Ending her sentence with "and yeah" also makes us wonder what her next thought might have been, because she leaves the listener/reader dangling. This is a common feature of a passively preoccupied (E1) interview, a subclass of preoccupied interviews described earlier by Main, Hesse, and Goldwyn (Chapter 2, this volume). Here the speaker shows how dependent she is on the listener and, by extension, many others in her attachment history. She seems to have more to say, yet grows too vague of mind to be able to say it, or else loses track of her speech and becomes ineffectual/passive.

Yet there are indeed secure–autonomous elements in the AAI, as indicated by the therapist's process notes on the early interactions between Alice and Jacob on the first visit. These sentences show that Alice is able to support some of her positive descriptions of her relationship with her mother very well—indeed, with fairly strong examples taken from the parental "loving" scale of the AAI. When asked, "When you were upset as a child, what would you do?", she says, "I'd cry and I would go to my mum and she'd give me a big hug, and she would ask what happened and she would talk to me about it." Alice elaborates further and comments that "with that feeling of being upset or hurt or disappointed, she'd give it room, she wouldn't 'shush' me and say oh, you know, that's all right, now and go back and play." Alice is able to describe a specific incident of this after she was bullied at school: "I talked to my mum about it and she tried to comfort and see that I'd feel good, although it didn't solve the problem, but she did comfort me."

On the other hand, when asked to describe her relationship with her father, Alice conveys a derogating stance. One of the adjectives she chooses to describe their relationship is "indifferent," which she elaborates upon by saying, "I don't remember missing him when he was away for work. . . . It wasn't that when he opened the door and all the kids came storming, saying 'Daddy's home.' It wasn't like that at all. It never meant that much to me that he got to spend time with us." Alice reveals her representations of her father as less than ideal and, in fact, despite them seems to persevere with representations of mother as understanding and available. But halfway through the interview a different picture emerges. First, in response to having experienced rejection at the hands of her parents, Alice describes being left by them in a relatively unsupervised context when the three children, ages 16, 14, and 10 (Alice), were left at home alone while the parents vacationed. Alice, without adequate supervision, ran away; she was gone "only a few hours but enough to cause a lot of trouble." Asked how she felt about the experience, Alice responds, "I felt very very very lonely. Deep inside I felt that nobody understands me and nobody knows me and nobody can actually get to me." While these descriptions begin to pave the way for indications of less than optimal experiences during Alice's childhood, what follows next in response to the AAI question "Can you tell me about any separations from your parents?" is a detailed account of trauma she experienced from early childhood through the adolescent years. Alice tells us, "Yeah, there was one when I was much older so would have been about 16 and my mum fell into psychosis and she was very unwell." She goes on to describe her mother's serious mental illness, then, even more bizarrely, how her father joined in the paranoid delusions. When asked if this was the first time Alice knew about her mother's severe mental illness, Alice says, "No, there were two other times. My dad noticed because a couple of years before, she'd been unwell, and my dad kind of got sucked into it and he joined in, and about 2 or 3 days into it was very hard time, because they were in the heaviest psycho state you could imagine and they would lock all the doors in the house, and they were very paranoid and they would shut all the curtains and they'd talk weird things, really bizarre and complex things." From this point in the interview, coherence diminishes and with it the transcript becomes somewhat of a challenge to comprehend, yet the confusion exists alongside passages that convey what it was like to grow up with such challenging experiences. For example, Alice describes her mother: "She'd be different or she'd use different language to people or she'd behaved differently. I didn't mind as a child but I did notice that my mum is a bit different. So although that was the first stage of psychosis I've actually seen her in, it didn't come as a shock, I felt, oh, all right, something has exploded that's always been there."

In coding this interview one strong candidate assignment was a classification of lack of resolution of mourning with regard to loss and/or trauma, because of the obvious adversity inherent in growing up with a parent with such obvious mental illness. This type of trauma is well captured in the manual, where one index of abuse is when a "parent exhibits bizarre and frightening behavior in front of the child, even if not directed at the child" (Main, Goldwyn, & Hesse, 2003, p. 149). How does Alice represent the persistent experience of a frequently psychotic and paranoid set of parents throughout her childhood? Her chief strategy is to minimize the overall effect, such as when she says, "It didn't come as a shock, it was bad, umm, just one of those things I felt, yeah," and later flatly rules out the experience of abuse when asked if there was any such experience, including *emotional* abuse. This suggests a denial of the intensity of the experience of abuse that occurs alongside a clear report of the experience of being a child, then an adolescent, living in a house run by parents with paranoid delusions. These delusions included the belief that only by staying in the house was the family safe from the violent reach of the Mafia or abusive grandparents. Given the frequency of these traumatic events it is surprising that they are not mentioned until some 400 lines into the interview, when Alice is asked about experiences of separation. One can infer that these experiences of being with mentally disturbed parents made Alice feel, at times, acutely separate from them. In any case, the minimizing stance she takes toward this prominent aspect of her experience is consistent with her dismissing side, and also with her lack of resolution of the trauma, scored at 7 on the 9-point scale, in this unsuccessful denial of the occurrence, nature, and intensity of the abuse.

In addition to Alice's interview being unresolved (U) relative to abuse, it was classified as cannot classify (CC) on account of the coexistence of preoccupied and dismissing features (see Main et al., Chapter 2, this volume). Alice's narrative shows evidence of her E3 classification, typified by being "fearfully preoccupied by traumatic events" including psychosis in a parent, in which the speaker has become and presently remains confused, fearful, and overwhelmed. Moreover, the manual describes these E3 interviews as containing references to traumatic/frightening experiences that *repeatedly enter the interview out of context*. This was certainly the case in this interview. Interestingly, however, alongside the narrative indicators of passive preoccupation (E1, discussed earlier), Alice adopts a contrasting dismissing/derogating stance, especially when discussing her father, but also in more general descriptions in which her state of mind regarding attachment is characteristic of dismissing interviews. Like the E1 subclassification among preoccupied (E) interviews, dismissing/derogating (subclassified as Ds2; see Main et al., Chapter 2, this volume) is rare. When most speakers are being dismissing, they "idealize" their parent, escaping "real" consideration of attachment troubles (hence, dismissing it), saying "It was fine" or "It was great." With respect to her father, however, Alice dismisses attachment in another way by speaking of him with direct contempt (an illustrative, although extreme example not taken from Alice in particular would be "My [parent]? Nothing, just a nerd. Didn't mean anything to me. Might as well put [parent] down as dead").

This interview exemplifies the way in which complex elements of a parent's state of mind with regard to attachment may enrich the clinician's dynamic formulations relative to observing the parent's interactions with the infant. What follows is the presentation of clinical material that reflects the quality of the mother's conflicting, fluctuating attention to her infant, and the infant's concomitant response to these perturbations in intersubjectivity. Moreover, the reader is offered a unique 'window" into the therapeutic process by being exposed to the mind of the therapist as she reveals her thoughts and feelings during her work in helping this mother develop a more reflective stance, and in involving the infant in a meeting of minds.

Clinical Process

From the first contact it was clear that both mother and baby were in pain in their relationship and wanted it to change. From one session to the next, both separately and together, they were avidly engaged in the therapeutic process. The therapist also felt deeply invested in this piece of work in response to their commitment, and was rewarded as she beheld and was part of liveliness, pleasure, and zest that slowly took root in the relationship.

Yet even as the emotional work deepened, Jacob and Alice kept close rein on their relationship with each other and with the therapist, as though experiences of intimacy were not to be risked. The therapist became aware of their acute sensitivity to the slightest shift in the other, and the interweaving of responsivity and withdrawal. By age 10 months (at referral) the procedures of being-with-the-other were well established in Jacob.

This is illustrated in material from Session 5, when Jacob was 11.5 months old.

Observation of Parent–Infant Interaction and the Concomitant Process of Construction of a Dynamic Formulation

The following extract is from the therapist's sessional notes.

> We were on cushions on the floor, as usual, with Jacob approximately half a meter in front of his mother, his back to her. Alice, long hair tied back, had her hands on her knees. Her back was curved, draping Jacob from a distance. I was seated across the mat. Jacob appeared engrossed in play, in which he placed a small doll in a container and took it out again. Alice, now reporting that she was more bonded with Jacob, was casting her mind back to her feelings in the early months. I raised the question of her disappointment and anger.

Observation[4]

ALICE: But, yes, it is that deeper permanent feeling of anger and not so much at him but at nature. I felt betrayed and disappointed (*her voice rises*) that somebody had promised me that wonderful baby and now it's not wonderful at all.

Her voices drops. Jacob leans forward to reach for another, larger, container

So I felt that somebody had tricked me into something and now, you know, what I expected or what I was promised is not there.

Alice is talking in a louder, animated way and waves her hands a bit. She looks at me, conveying the intensity of her feelings.

Jacob sits down again and looks at the toys he is holding. He glances at me.

Inferred meaning[5]

As Jacob is faced with his mother's rejection of him, expressed in her voice, gestures, and facial expression, he keeps his focus firmly on his own activities. He makes no movement to contact her, thus informing me how much he is inhibiting his propensities to act on a wish for closeness.

I find myself drawn to her narrative, ignoring for the instant, Jacob, who appears absorbed.

Because I am convinced that Jacob is in fact tracking his mother's state of mind very carefully, I am concerned that he is so adept at maintaining his apparently cut off position from his mother. I miss what on later examination of the video proved to be his glance at me—his mute plea, perhaps, for help?

Alice has slumped into silence and Jacob places the doll in the smaller container and tries to put them both in the bigger one. Despite his advanced fine-motor skills, he is struggling to manage the simple task of putting the dolls into containers, where they in fact fit easily.

Jacob expresses his wish for containment in his play, but his fragility is concretely expressed in his failure to place the one container in the other. I feel the sadness and hopelessness in them both.

There is a slight pause. I am gathering my thoughts, and look up at the ceiling as I do so.

I am only peripherally aware of staring at the ceiling, but in retrospect, I recognize this as an unconscious maneuver to regulate my own feelings in the face of the subterranean rage and pain in Alice and defense in Jacob.

TB: Do you think, though, that being cross at nature . . . ?

My train of thought is leading to a suggestion that anger with "nature" is a way of protecting Jacob from her disappointment, but I do not complete this intervention.

Jacob looks at me as I begin to speak, then follows my gaze and also looks up at the light.

I choose to privilege Jacob's slight movement and to interpret it as a wish to join with me.

I notice Jacob's movement and break off in midsentence. I lean toward him, resting my elbows on the floor and talk to him.

TB: (*to Jacob*) These are very serious things we are talking about, Jacob.

Jacob stills as I talk and looks down. One of the containers drops from his hand.

My response has been too strong for him. I feel he has momentarily withdrawn to the point of cutting off.

TB: (*Repeats, very gently this time*) Aren't they, very serious?

Intuitively, my voice becomes more modulated and prosodic to call him back into relatedness with me.

And you are busy putting the doll in and out. Are you also finding out what belongs inside and what belongs outside?

I am addressing both Jacob and his mother.

Jacob places the doll into the container he is still holding and looks at me briefly.

He and I are in "conversation" now.

Yes?

I am inviting the next step.

His mother leans over, head sideways so that she can see his face.

His mother, too, now risks joining in.

Jacob shakes the container and doll, and it makes a rattling noise. I mirror his action by shaking my hand, so that my bracelets rattle. Jacob looks at me seriously.

Jacob takes the initiative and I follow, but extend his gesture from the toys to my hands and bracelets— making them available also for his exploration.

He shakes the toys again. Alice smiles and murmurs "Mmm."

We are exploring a three-way space.

TB: Again?

Is it safe for us to create a playful dance together? Will it be two or three players?

I shake my hand again and rattle the bracelets.

Jacob reaches for the second container but fails to encompass the smaller container and doll in it.

I think about his possible wish for a threesome that may yield for him a much needed sense of containment.

TB: Yes. You can put that one on top. Look.

I reach out and place the larger container over both.

I am eager in my wish to carry this forward.

Jacob turns his body away from me, and moves to nestle into his mother.

My eagerness has been experienced as intrusive. I frighten Jacob with my volition, and he turns toward his primary figure.

Alice draws back from Jacob, although her head still reclines to the side to look at him.

A procedural communication of rejection.

Jacob stills.

I contemplate momentary dissociation in the face of her withdrawal at the very point when he seeks her succor.

TB: Where has it gone?

I am talking concretely about the hidden doll and container, and symbolically about his retreat from me, and Alice's retreat from him.

TB: (*Playfully, as though speaking for Jacob*) Mmm, don't get too close to me, Tessa.

I put the threat into words: "Close" is both physical and emotional.

Alice laughs as I say this, and Jacob lets the container I had placed fall to the floor.

Alice seems to recognize it, and also to be pleased to locate the "badness" in me (rather than in herself?).

I move back into a sitting position, so that, in fact, my body is also withdrawn from the closer, more intimate triangle of a minute ago.

TB: You're not so sure.

There is a pause. Jacob focuses again on the toys and his mother, and I watch in silence.

He glances up at the light.

(*I whisper playfully.*) Do you like the light?

Jacob looks at me and then up again.

TB: Is it OK again, now that I'm leaning back?

My voice is still light.

Was I coming too close?

Alice laughs, her hand is now resting very lightly on Jacob's hip.

ALICE: That was "yes."

I acknowledge this with a little smile and nod.

There is a pause.

TB: What do you think that's about?

Alice turns to me; looks bewildered.
ALICE: What?

(*There is a brief pause.*)

Jacob continues playing with the toys as though he had not noticed we resumed talking.

I feel they need space and am uncomfortable with a feeling of having unwittingly intruded.

I am addressing the anxiety in both of them, and I wait while they both self-regulate.

I take this as an invitation to reengage.

This time, I am keeping my verbal "touch" as "light" as I can.

Alice and I have shifted positions, and she is "lightly" claiming her baby and allowing him some "feather light" physical holding.

She identifies with Jacob.

I convey my acceptance.

We are adjusting to the different positioning.

I invite Alice to join me in thinking about her son's state of mind underpinning his behaviors.

It seems that Alice has "slipped" away—is it into deep thought or dissociation?—and my voice called her back—perhaps shocking, frightening, shaming her?

I am taken aback by her "other" state of mind.

Based on my countertransference to Alice, I imagine Jacob is highly disregulated at that point and is self-regulating through the play.

TB: him turning into you when I came close . . . ?

I notice that Alice's hand are now back on her lap.

ALICE: I don't know. He's not normally like that with other people. Maybe it's because we're here and it's quiet, whereas if we're in playgroup, he'll always interact with other kids or other people, but because this is so serious . . .

She is talking in a detached, informative way.

I, like Jacob, carry on as though nothing has happened!

At what point she had she withdrawn them from Jacob?

I am thinking that this environment is too emotionally intense, and that a relationship with someone who is focused on the emotions of that relationship (myself), is intensely evocative and scary, and requires stringent regulation.

It seems that the interaction between Alice and Jacob is characterized by their fear of destructive intimacy and a very subtle dance of entering and exiting self- and mutual regulation (Beebe, 2000; Beebe & Lachman, 1998). In his behaviors, Jacob makes no demands on his mother. Knowing how frightened he must feel by her emotional disregulation, the therapist imagines that singular effort is going into the inhibition of his attachment needs for security and reassurance. At this point in the clinical process it is the therapist who responds more overtly to the inevitable pull of intersubjective needs. This may be understood as both the conscious therapeutic task and "innately encoded responses to signals re[garding] attachment" (Pally, 2001, p. 90). Neuroscience data also inform us that the same nonverbal regulatory mechanisms (of voice, facial expression, posture, touch) between mother and infant "occur between adults to facilitate attachment, regulate affect and physiology and to provide a sense of being understood" (Pally, 2001, p. 71). Thus, through the interventions in the room, the mother is intermittently able to bring into the encounter with her infant her procedures of comforting, containing, caretaking—such as when she holds him lightly.

The therapist also assumed that Jacob's preoccupation (as expressed in his play with the containers) reflected a process that was taking place also for his mother—that of gaining an understanding of what belonged to the internal world as opposed to the external, including that of the other person–"the mother." At that point, however, she and I had not yet made the link with another aspect of the therapy that was on her mind.

Addressing Past and Present in the Therapy

An area of work in the Parent–Infant Project that is regarded as essential (Baradon et al., 2005) was completely rejected by Alice. In the direct work with the baby, the therapists verbalize affects, intentions, and anxieties that they see or assume in the baby. Through this, therapists scaffold the infant's internal experience when the parent is not yet able to do this, and represents the baby's state of mind to both baby and parent. As therapy progresses, this function is usually taken over by the parent.

In this work, Jacob appeared to relish this activity with the therapist. He would stare intently at her eyes and mouth, carefully regulating the intensity of contact by looking down. She would wait for him to be ready to reengage, which he invariably did, his facial expression almost transfixed. Alice, on the other hand, closed down. Initially, the therapist thought that perhaps Alice felt they were in competition to "know" her baby, and that the therapist was thereby clumsily evoking envy. Then she began to recognize that Alice had closed her conscious mind to intuitions and hypotheses of what Jacob might be feeling and was not allowing herself to use her own experiences as a baby to imaginatively understand Jacob (normal projection). The therapist put this to Alice, who was dismissive of the possibility that one can know what a baby is really saying or feeling, and stated that things could be interpreted any way one wishes.

During this conversation, Jacob was playing with a ball in which protruding faces can be pushed and made to disappear. The therapist wondered whether this was symbolic of the many faces of "Mother" and the unpredictable changes in her emotional stance and availability. The intergenerational trajectories were becoming clearer: Alice's bodily and declaratively represented experiences of her own mother's changeability were being repeated in Jacob's experiences with her as a sometimes embracing and, at other times, a shut down and intentionally "not knowing" mother.

Therapeutic Progress

The exploration of maternal changeability and how this is experienced by the young child was extended within, and through, the therapeutic encounter. The following extract is from the therapist's process notes from Session 7 (Jacob, 12.1 months old).

> Jacob was giving me wooing, but teasing little smiles. Despite his interest in me he kept his distance. Alice thought maybe he just didn't like me, although she had no explanation for why this might be. I suggested that she, too, had reservations about me, but she denied this. I spelled out that she was perhaps afraid I might put her in touch with very strong feelings that would get out of control and unbalance the applecart of her relationships. In this way coming to therapy was not only helpful but also dangerous. Alice admitted that she felt frustrated with our work. She noted that she used to feel that what her mother said to her were intrusions and thought this might be happening with me. She said she had an immediate response of "No, you are wrong," when I made any kind of suggestion about what Jacob might be feeling. I commented that she did not have an image of the other mind as being helpfully inquiring and not just intrusive, and reiterated that I had come to represent danger as well as relief.

At this point Alice blurted, "That feeling that I get inside I can't put it into words . . . it's that fear that I get when she gets that look on her face, the sound of her voice that suddenly tips . . . I hear that a lot. So what exactly the fear is about I don't. . . . It's just there." She was speaking about the ongoing tyranny of her terrifying childhood relationship with her mother, an enactment of her U-abuse/ CC/E3 status as revealed in her AAI. I felt extremely moved by her predicament. Alice reached her arms to Jacob, and he came over to her and sat on her lap. She cradled him and he relaxed into her. It seemed to me that what had transpired between Alice and myself enabled her to imagine her son's feelings and take them into her cogitation/reverie. This was expressed in her initiative and embrace. Later in the session Alice confirmed that it was the first time she had been able to be in touch with her awful feelings and convey them to someone else.

This discourse heralded a transition from procedural memory to symbolic representation. With it came Alice's ability to begin to symbolize her baby's experiences.

Discussion

This material demonstrates links between parental representations, verbal and procedural interactions with the infant, (presumed) infant experiences, evolving procedures of being-with-parent, and developing representations of self with other. In a prior report we highlighted the joint contributions to clinical work with parents and infants of becoming familiar with the parent's attachment representations, and of concomitant defenses and patterns of emotion regulation inferred from the AAI (Steele & Baradon, 2004). We argued that "one of the main contributions of the AAI in parent–infant psychotherapy is its sensitivity to the parent's mental functioning in relation to unresolved attachment issues that could be unconsciously repeated in interactions with their infants" (p. 288). The report also highlighted that the very process of conducting the AAI communicates a therapeutic assumption about the influences from the past upon the current relationship between the parent and infant, and can provide the parent with an affectively meaningful and scaffolded experience (Lyons-Ruth et al., 1999) discourse about their own attachment experiences (see also Jones, Chapter 7, this volume). The material is this chapter exemplifies further the contributions made to the clinical work with trauma by linking detailed observation of parent–infant interactions and the adult representations presented through the AAI. The clinician's holding of information from both sources can inform (1) how parental representations of traumatic attachment experiences are expressed procedurally with the infant, and (2) the process of co-construction of relational knowing between parent and infant.

Procedural expression of parental representations is a central (arguably *the* central; see Stern, 2004; Stern et al., 1998) area of intervention in parent–infant psychotherapy. It is in the implicit domain that knowledge of how relationships work and the unconscious repetitions of traumatic attachments reside. It is axiomatically characteristic of the implicit domain that this knowledge cannot be accessed symbolically and is expressed through action and enactment (Davis, 2001; Solms & Turnbull, 2002). While information about the parents' procedures of being with their infant is derived from observation of their interactions, and from the therapist's own responses to the encounter, the clinician's understanding of the unconscious influences of parental representations and defenses is enhanced by the understanding of the material and coherence of the AAI. This understanding remains in the clinician's preconscious and guide interventions, whether or not the clinician chooses actively to discuss the AAI material with the parent. In this case, Alice was a willing investigator of her past and intuitively accepted the influences of her unresolved trauma on the parenting of her baby. Therefore, the therapist was able to capitalize on the experience and the narrative of the AAI to address the unwelcome "ghosts" that were invading Alice's transference to Jacob and derailing his attachment to her.

In particular, the therapist could monitor the minute adjustment each made in the transactions to accommodate the central dilemma of regulation of intimacy and distance, and the co-construction of defenses against overwhelming attachment needs. Yet, observing Jacob's attachment compromises, the therapist felt his struggles acutely in the countertransference. She saw that Alice's physical responsivity acted as a mesmerizing promise, keeping alive his desire for genuine intersubjective experience and preventing the development of a dismissive stance. At the same time, her depression and rejection forced him into precocious self-sufficiency that collapsed at times into moments of dissociation. As readers will no doubt infer for themselves, although we did not conduct a Strange Situation, had we done so at intake, Jacob may well have been classified as disorganized/disoriented (D) on the basis of the dissociative collapses observed in our play sessions, and alternatively, as avoidant on the basis of his precocious self-sufficiency, again as observed in our play sessions. As we have noted, of course, Jacob's observed precocious self-sufficiency in the play sessions also reflects the strong dismissing tendencies in the mother's AAI text (hence, the baby–mother attachment would probably have been D/A or disorganized/avoidant). However, the mother's text also reflected preoccupation, which would predict some resistant–ambivalent behavior (hence, an additional CC classification) when her infant was under acute stress, leading to a D/CC infant classification under stress—a situation that we take steps to avoid during our therapy. CC AAIs in parents have in fact been found linked to D, as well as to CC in infants and young children (Behrens, Hesse, & Main, in press; Hesse & Main, 2006). This imagined Strange Situation outcome for Jacob would, we hope, only have been identifiable at intake, because considerable progress was made during the parent–infant therapy.

Administering the AAI with Alice early in the treatment enabled her to "bring" (in surprising the unconscious) her own early relational trauma into the discourse with the therapist before consciously understanding its significance for relationship with her baby. It is interesting, however, that whereas the AAI introduced the relational trauma, recognition and an ability to work with it only came later in the therapy. Indeed, this suggests that although the AAI can focus the therapist's mind on the salient features of attachment experiences and states of mind, the material can only be used when it is emotionally alive for the patient in a safe relationship with the therapist.

What has also emerged from the work, and is highlighted in this chapter, is that the differences between the clinical understanding of relational trauma and its impact on the baby, and the definitions of trauma and abuse for the purposes of coding the AAI do not detract from the usefulness of the AAI within the therapeutic process. Moreover, conducting the AAI, in our experience, can cultivate the attachment process between the parent and the therapist, which is essential for change (Stern, 2004). The patient often experiences the combination of unstructured sessions and the AAI as an evocative way to become known and understood. From the therapist's point of view, the process of conducting the Interview and the emotional information received can centrally shape empathic understanding of, and countertransference to, the parent. This contributes to the therapist's ability to hold the parent's vulnerability in mind when observing and experiencing the traumas she or he may be unwittingly imposing on the baby. In this way, the AAI can provide an important holding framework in which revisiting the past and present "ghosts" can begin.

Notes

1. For further discussion of clinical counter-indications to conducting the AAI in parent infant psychotherapy, see Steele and Baradon (2004).
2. The therapy was conducted by Tessa Baradon.
3. The interview was coded by Miriam Steele.
4. The observation as described was checked against a video recording of the session, and interactions "missed" by the therapist during the session were supplemented from this.
5. The inferred meaning describes the therapist's feelings and thinking, which feed into her dynamic formulations regarding the therapeutic process.

References

Abrams, K., Rifkin, A., & Hesse, E. (2006). Examining the role of parental frightened/frightening subtypes in predicting disorganized attachment within a brief observation procedure. *Development and Psychopathology, 18*, 345–361.

Baradon, T., Broughton, C., Gibbs, I., James, J., Joyce, A., & Woodhead, J. (2005). *The practice of psychoanalytic parent–infant psychotherapy: Claiming the baby.* London: Routledge.

Beebe, B. (2000). Co-constructing mother–infant distress: The microsynchrony of maternal impingement and infant avoidance in the face-to-face encounter. *Psychoanalytic Enquiry, 20*(3), 421–440.

Beebe, B., & Lachman, F. (1998). Co-constructing inner and relational processes: Self and mutual regulation in infant research and adult treatment. *Psychoanalytic Psychology, 15*, 1–37.

Behrens, K., Hesse, E., & Main, M. (in press). Mothers' attachment status as determined by the Adult Attachment Interview predicts their 6-year-olds' reunion responses: A study conducted in Japan. *Developmental Psychology.*

Davis, T. J. (2001). Revising psychoanalytic interpretations of the past: An examination of declarative and non-declarative memory processes. *International Journal of Psychoanalysis, 82*, 449–462.

Fraiberg, S., Adelson, E., & Shapiro, V. (1975). Ghosts in the nursery: A psychoanalytic approach to the problems of impaired infant–mother relationships. *Journal of the American Academy of Psychiatry, 14*, 387–421. ᵛ

George, C., Kaplan, N., & Main, M. (1985). *Adult Attachment Interview* (2nd ed.). Unpublished manuscript, University of California, Berkley.

Hesse, E. (1999). The Adult Attachment Interview: Historical and current perspectives. In J. Cassidy & P. R. Shaver (Eds.), *Handbook of attachment* (pp. 395–433). New York: Guilford Press.

Hesse, E., & Main, M. (1999). Second-generation effects of unresolved trauma in nonmaltreating parents: Dissociated, frightened, and threatening parental behavior. *Psychoanalytical Inquiry, 19*, 481–540.

Hesse, E., & Main, M. (2006). Frightened, threatening, and dissociative (FR) parental behavior as related to infant D attachment in low-risk samples: Description, discussion, and interpretations. *Development and Psychopathology, 18*, 309–343.

Lyons-Ruth, K., Bronfman, E., & Parsons, E. (1999). Atypical attachment in infancy and early childhood amongst children at developmental risk: Part IV. Maternal frightened, frightening, or atypical behaviour and disorganised infant attachment patterns. In J. Vondra & D. Barnett (Eds.), Atypical patterns of infant attachment: Theory, research and current directions. *Monographs of the Society for Research in Child Development, 64*(3), 67–96.

Madigan, S., Bakermans-Kranenburg, M. J., van IJzendoorn, M. H., Moran, G., Pederson, D. R., & Benoit, D. (2006). Unresolved states of mind, anomalous parental behaviour, and disorganised attachment: A review and meta-analysis of a transmission gap. *Attachment and Human Development, 8*(2), 89–111.

Madigan, S., Moran, G., & Pederson, D. R. (2006). Unresolved states of mind, disorganised attachment relationships, and disrupted interactions of adolescent mothers and their infants. *Developmental Psychopathology, 42*(2), 293–304.

Main, M., Goldwyn, R., & Hesse, E. (2003). *Adult attachment scoring and classification systems, version 7.2.* Unpublished manual, University of California, Berkeley.

Main M., & Hesse, E. (1990). Parents' unresolved traumatic experiences are related to infant disorganised attachment status. In M. T. Greenberg, D. Cicchetti, & E. M. Cummings (Eds.), *Attachment in the preschool years: Theory, research, and intervention* (pp. 161–182). Chicago: University of Chicago Press.

Pally, R. (2001). A primary role for nonverbal communication in psychoanalysis. *Psychoanalytic Inquiry, 21*, 71–93.

Perry, B. D. (1997). Incubated in terror: Neurodevelopmental factors in the "cycle of violence." In J. D. Osofsky (Ed.), *Children in a violent society* (pp. 124–149). New York: Guilford Press.

Schore, A. N. (1994). *Affect regulation and the origins of the self*. Hillsdale, NJ: Erlbaum.

Schore, A. N. (2001). The effect of early relational trauma on right brain development, affect regulation, and infant mental health. *Infant Mental Health Journal*, 22, 210–269.

Schore, A. N. (2002). Dysregulation of the right brain: A fundamental mechanism of traumatic attachment and the psychopathogenesis of posttraumatic stress disorder. *Australian and New Zealand Journal of Psychiatry*, 36, 9–30.

Solms, M., & Turnbull, O. (2004). *The brain and the inner world*. London: Karnac Books.

Steele, M., & Baradon, T. (2004). The clinical use of the Adult Attachment Interview in parent–infant psychotherapy. *Infant Mental Health Journal*, 25(4), 284–299.

Stern, D., Sander, L., Nahum, J., Harrison, A., Lyons-Ruth, K., Morgan, A., et al. (1998). Non-interpretive mechanisms in psychoanalytic therapy: The "something more" than interpretation. *International Journal of Psychoanalysis*, 79, 903–921.

Stern, D. N. (2004). *The present moment in psychotherapy and everyday life*. New York: Norton.

Winnicott, D. W. (1965a). The relationship of a mother to her baby at the beginning. In D. W. Winnicott (Ed.), *The family and individual development* (pp. 15–20). London: Tavistock.

Winnicott, D. W. (1965b). The theory of the parent–infant relationship. In D. W. Winnicott (Ed.), *Maturational processes and the facilitating environment* (pp. 37–55). London: Hogarth Press and the Institute of Psycho-Analysis.

9

Obsessive–Compulsive Disorder in Adolescence

An AAI Perspective

TORD IVARSSON

Built on the foundations of the biological sciences—with chief emphases upon ethology and evolution (Bowlby, 1969/1982)—attachment theory offers an understanding of how different children have learned to cope with the activation of their brains' fear system, which is believed inevitably to activate tendencies to attempt to obtain proximity to or contact with the attachment figure. The consideration of an individual's attachment history and/or current "state of mind with respect to attachment" is currently improving our understanding of a wide variation of developmental outcomes, including instances of marked psychopathology (e.g., Carlson, 1998; Sroufe, Egeland, Carlson, & Collins, 2005). Attachment research methods, particularly the Adult Attachment Interview (AAI; George, Kaplan, & Main, 1985, 1996) together with the corollary rating and classification system (Main, Goldwyn, & Hesse, 2003; Main, Hesse, & Goldwyn, Chapter 2, this volume), have given us new tools in our attempts to understand developmental pathways and outcomes, normal and pathological.

This chapter provides an initial report taken from an ongoing clinical and research investigation of AAI patterns among adolescents with obsessive–compulsive disorder (OCD) and, to our knowledge (see van IJzendoorn & Bakermans-Kranenburg, Chapter 3, this volume), is the first study to approach OCD using the AAI. As OCD in adolescence frequently is comorbid with depression, depressed adolescents were studied as well (Ivarsson, 2007). OCD is considered an anxiety disorder, and it can be assumed that the fear system is frequently activated in these individuals without ready availability of an external (or internal) secure base or haven of safety (Ainsworth, Blehar, Waters, & Wall, 1978) that might assuage the acute fears and anxieties that implode upon them. The chapter first provides a brief overview of these clinical problems, including as well contemporary accounts regarding etiology and treatment. The chapter then illustrates the potential relevance of the adolescent's attachment status, as seen in the AAI, to understanding one of several factors potentially contributing to aspects of OCD (and depression), as well as the relation of an individual's attachment status, again, as seen in the AAI, to possible treatments. Consideration of the probable distinct developmental pathways leading to OCD, or depression, are discussed in the context of presenting preliminary findings of the AAI profiles observed in each group.

Anxiety Disorders in Adolescence

OCD is defined by the presence of obsessions and compulsions which are time consuming, associated with functional deficits or suffering (American Psychiatric Association, 1994). Obsessions are thoughts, ideas, pictures, or impulses that are not simply worries over real-life problems, such as concern that an already worrisome situation may turn catastrophic (e.g., that a sick sibling might die). Their intensity, frequency, and content are things that the individual with OCD recognizes (mostly) as irrational. Like adults with the disorder, children's symptoms include obsessions (e.g., thoughts of contamination, fear of harming others, or feeling shamefully bad) and compulsions (behaviors in the typical broad categories of repetitive washing or various checking rituals). Whereas insight into the irrationality of such thoughts and behaviors is required for the diagnosis of OCD in adults, diagnostic requirements do not require that children have full insight, even if most of them do. Moreover, a peculiar quality to obsessions (regardless of the age of the patient) is that they are so intrusive and frightful that the individual with OCD feels the need to cope actively on his or her own with the thoughts (if the situation eliciting them cannot be avoided). This gives rise to "compulsions" that serve as the main way for the children or adolescents (as for adults) to cope with the ensuing anxiety. Children with a germ obsession, for example, typically perceive the situation to be such that they compulsively wash their hands to get rid of the germs, expecting that this will alleviate the anxiety. However, some patients start washing their hands even before thoughts of germs or dirt have emerged, wishing to protect themselves against the pernicious influence of the anticipated anxiety. The apparently central role of anxiety within most OCD cases has led to placement of OCD within the anxiety disorders (and it is classified as such in the fourth edition of the *Diagnostic and Statistical Manual of Mental Disorders* [DSM-IV; American Psychiatric Association, 1994]). However, as we discuss later, not all patients fit in with this paradigm (McKay et al., 2004).

OCD in childhood and adolescence is not common, with the highest point prevalence of 0.6% in early adolescence and lower prevalence rates during middle childhood (0.2%) and the preschool years (0.02%) (Heyman et al., 2001). Some studies have, however, indicated higher prevalence, with a lifetime (0–18 years) prevalence close to 2–3% (Valleni-Basile et al., 1994; Zohar et al., 1992).

The seemingly senseless, repetitive fear of one's own thoughts, fear of a loved one's death, fear of contamination, and so forth, and the irrational and sometimes bizarre compulsions and odd behaviors of patients with OCD have stimulated almost endless speculations about the origins of the condition within psychiatry and psychology. Some of these have centered on the possible contribution of attachment issues to the disorder (De Ruiter, 1994; Ehiobuche, 1988). One speculation concerned the ambivalence that is characteristic of many patients with OCD traced to the possible co-occurrence of a parental style of both rejection and overprotection (De Ruiter, 1994). However, available data were inconsistent with regard to support for the proposed link. In a recent review article concerning the issue, Doron and Kyrios (2005) argued for the contribution of insecure internal working models to negative self-schemas or individual differences in worldview as a cognitive vulnerability to OCD, making some patients more prone to self-blame in the event of, for example, intrusions of aggressive thoughts or impulses. Moreover, they speculated that insecurity during childhood might hamper learning from experience, particularly for the child with anxious–ambivalent/resistant attachments, creating a situation in which attachment is frequently activated without immediate satisfaction, thus preventing the healthy activation of exploration. For example, children with ambivalent/resistant attachment patterns tend to be focused inflexibly on the parent, and consequently have difficulties in assimilating later experience into their self-schema. However, the bearing this has on the development of obsessions and compulsions rather than, for example, depression, is not clear.

It seems unlikely, as Doron and Kyrios (2005) suggest, that one type of link between attachment and OCD would prove to be true and applicable in all cases. This is an especially important assumption given the heterogeneity of the disorder (Ivarsson & Valderhaug, 2006). Also, the success of the biological sciences in illuminating parts of the neurobiology and neurochemistry of the disorder (Rosenberg, Keshavan, O'Hearn, et al., 1997; Rosenberg et al., 2000; Russell et al., 2003; Szeszko, MacMillan, McMeniman, Lorch, et al., 2004)—as seen in, for example, the successful use of the learning-based paradigm in the psychological treatment of OCD (Abramowitz, Whiteside, & Deacon, 2005), together with the successful use of medications (Geller et al., 2003)—has moved the field from observations and generalizations, based on individual patients, to broader issues that concern empirical scientific approaches to understanding and treating the disorder. Furthermore, it is clear from family studies that genetics contributes in a decisive way to the etiology of the disorder (Grados et al., 2001; Himle, Curtis, & Gillespie, 2005; Pauls,

Alsobrook, Goodman, Rasmussen, & Leckman, 1995; Reddy et al., 2001; Yang & Liu, 1998). For example, a twin study (Hudziak et al., 2004) has furthered insight into the importance of heredity (roughly 50% additive genetic effects) and demonstrated that models for any impact of psychosocial factors must rise beyond simplistic models (the remaining variance was largely explained by unique environmental effects) except for the younger age group (12-year-olds), for which there were some shared environmental effects. Also, a biological environmental influence such as beta-hemolytic streptococcal infection (Swedo et al., 1998) has also been present in some cases. Thus, the etiology of OCD is complicated, and there is as yet little knowledge about the relationship between OCD subgroups and etiology. Moreover, little is known regarding interactions between genetics and environmental factors, something that ought to be expected and has been shown to occur in both conduct disorder (Caspi et al., 2002) and depression (Eley et al., 2004).

The evidence for ambivalent/resistant attachment patterns contributing to the development of anxiety has been shown in younger children (Shamir-Essakow, Ungerer, & Rapee, 2005). High levels of anxiety symptoms were associated with not only the inhibited temperament type, something that has been observed in many studies (e.g., Biederman et al., 1990; Hirshfeld et al., 1992; Rosenbaum et al., 1993) but also ambivalent/resistant attachment (Shamir-Essakow et al., 2005). As might be expected, having two risk factors instead of one engendered even greater risk for anxiety disorder. A longitudinal link between ambivalent/resistant attachment during infancy and OCD during adolescence comes from the Minnesota Study (Warren, Huston, Egeland, & Sroufe, 1997). OCD was one of the rarer forms in the study of combined anxiety disorders groups that were highly likely to have a history of anxious–resistant attachment. But the small number of adolescents with OCD in the Warren and colleagues (1997) study, and the lack of information about their current attachment status, calls for an AAI-based study with a substantial group of adolescents with OCD to explore further the link between attachment and one or more of the various OCD subtypes. Finally, it should be noted that in Warren's study of infant Strange Situation behavior with the mother, the "disorganized" (Main & Solomon, 1990) classification was not utilized.

As indicated earlier, however, OCD is a heterogeneous disorder that encompasses different symptom patterns in different patients (Ivarsson & Valderhaug, 2006; McKay et al., 2006). Moreover, different patterns of other clinical features that might influence etiology, such as comorbidity (Geller et al., 2004; Ivarsson, Melin, & Wallin, in press), age of onset (Hanna, 1995; Hanna, Fischer, Chadha, Himle, & Van Etten, 2005), familiar or sporadic type (Hanna, Fischer, et al., 2005), and familial context (Grados et al., 2001; Hanna, Himle, Curtis, & Gillespie, 2005; Pauls et al., 1995) occur. Given this level of complexity within OCD, we cannot expect that an environmental factor such as attachment (Bokhorst et al., 2003) would be equally important in all cases (i.e., that the same "mechanisms" would be important in all cases of

OCD). For example, a pediatric patient with OCD, who has obsessions concerning how the parent might be harmed, needs the parent as haven of safety in a more pronounced way than does the patient with mainly symmetry obsessions and ordering compulsions. The parents are, of course, important even for the latter patient, but we would not expect the fear system to be involved. Neither would the attachment system necessarily be involved in regulating the child's feelings of the ordering being not "just right" except in extreme situations, when the child might be overwhelmed with negative feelings and high stress levels. In many patients with OCD, especially those with comorbid tic disorders, OCD symptoms are driven by sensory incompleteness, without any inherent, rational cognitive meaning in terms of the fear system. For patients with more clear-cut anxiety and fears involving issues of safety for either the self or the parent, and compulsions involving various safety-promoting behaviors, we should expect the fear system to be involved more intensely and for such problems to tax the attachment system, devoted as it is to coping with anxiety and fear.

The high degree of comorbidity in OCD (Geller et al., 2000; Ivarsson et al., in press) makes specific attributions of causality difficult when it comes to the associations between OCD and attachment. Many patients with OCD, especially adolescents, are depressed (Geller et al., 2000; Ivarsson et al., in press), and depression itself is associated with attachment insecurity, as has been shown previously (Rosenstein & Horowitz, 1996).

In our study, reported below, we have aimed to investigate attachment issues in adolescents with OCD. Simultaneously, we try to disentangle possible contributions from depression (a common comorbidity in adolescent OCD), in the process of examining the possible association between insecure attachment and OCD.

The Gothenburg Study of Attachment in OCD and Depression

Adolescents with OCD who sought treatment from the OCD Clinic at the Queen Silvia Children's Hospital (where I am medical director) were asked to enroll in the study. The subspecialized unit is available to patients with OCD within the Gothenburg area. Many adolescents with OCD were also depressed, allowing us to examine three groups of patients: adolescents with OCD only; adolescents with OCD and depression; and, as a clinical control group, adolescents with depression only. A second, low-risk control group was drawn from a community sample. We used DSM-IV criteria for OCD and/or depression (major or minor) as inclusion criteria, and semistructured interviews in the diagnostic procedure.

Patients with depression without OCD came from various sources, mostly from different child psychiatric outpatient units within the Gothenburg area. The control group from various schools in the Gothenburg area comprised adolescents who were not being seen in clinics and were not known to have emotional difficulties or disorders. Additionally, this control group was chosen to match the clinical groups in terms of both urban and nonurban origins, and both lower- and upper-level socioeconomic backgrounds.

Some Preliminary Results

Our study of 100 adolescent patients, ages 13–17 years, is now completed, so some "rough" figures in our data can be disclosed. The AAI interviews have been coded by a rater—trained and certified in the Main, Goldwyn, and Hesse (2003) system—who was kept blind as to membership in any of the four groups, each consisting of 25 subjects. A reliability test showed acceptable agreement and the figures cited below, concerning group differences, were statistically significant. In the control group, somewhat more than 50% of the AAIs were secure–autonomous (F), slightly more than 10% were unresolved trauma/loss (U), and the remaining interviews were insecure–dismissing of attachment (Ds). No control group interview was insecure–preoccupied. These proportions are not far from the current nonclinical norms (van IJzendoorn & Bakermans-Kranenburg, Chapter 3, this volume). Our OCD patients tended to have Ds interviews (OCD-only somewhat more, and OCD + DD somewhat less than 50%). The remaining interviews in the OCD-only group had about equal proportions of F, U, and CC (cannot classify, the newer "low-coherence" form appearing in the most recent AAI manual; Main et al., 2003). One interview was judged to be insecure-preoccupied (E). In contrast, the OCD + DD group had a high proportion of unresolved (U) interviews, similarly to the DD-only group (circa 40% in both groups). Another common feature in these two groups was an elevated proportion of CC interviews (circa 20% in both groups). Interviews coded F or E were present, though not so common in the two groups with depression, less than 10%. A full report of the data can be found in Ivarsson, Granqvist, Broberg, and Gillberg (2007).

The secure–autonomous transcripts of the OCD, DD, and control groups were very similar. They contained rich biographical memories with details about events (leading to high scores for coherence of transcript and coherence of mind). A clear majority of the interviews from young people with OCD (with or without comorbid depression) were judged to be Ds. Common features of these interviews were that the respondents used moderately positive adjectives for their parents, emphasizing on fun and activities in which they engaged with the parents, yet presented very few "memories" that were evidence of loving parental behavior, and frequently insisted on a lack of memory for childhood experiences. They generally appeared to have very little memory for events (this constellation results in moderate-to-high idealization scores plus an insistence on difficulty with lack of recall typical of the fairly common Ds subtype). Few transcripts in the OCD or the OCD + DD group were classified as insecure–preoccupied, not even when forced classifications were used (i.e., the structure underlying a U or CC classification); in these cases, Ds or F were more common secondary classifications.

So it seems as though the Ds state of mind is a characteristic feature of the OCD clinical groups. However, this cannot be taken to imply that we know that the adolescents' attachment experience during childhood was uniformly one of rejection of attachment. It is well established that a Ds state of mind may arise from a rejecting experience at the hands of caregivers (i.e., having one's bids for care and comfort turned away) leading to a preference to believe this was not the case, thus "dismissing" the truth. Alternatively, a Ds state of mind may arise from an involving/role reversal experience with a caregiver (i.e., the caregiver who communicates to the child, "I need you to take care of me"; Main et al., 2003), as well as from a frightening one. Given that OCD is seen as an anxiety disorder, the latter is an especially interesting possibility, because frightened or frightening parental behavior has repeatedly been found to be associated with infant disorganization (Hesse & Main, 2006; Madigan et al., 2006; Main & Solomon, 1990). Moreover, about half of the Ds adolescents seen in both the Bay Area and Minnesota samples were disorganized with the mother during infancy, a classification traditionally associated with fright (see Main, Hesse, & Kaplan, 2005). Thus, not only rejection but also a combination of rejection and over-involvement, and frightened or frightening behavior on the part of the mother during infancy and early childhood are not ruled out.

Although the experience of our patients during childhood is reported retrospectively, not assessed directly, and always referenced as "probable" experience in the AAI coding manual (Main et al., 2003), the data in our sample indicate a role for involving/role reversal experience mainly in cases of depression without OCD. Mean scores for involving/role reversal experiences in the DD group were just below the midpoint (5) of the 9-point scale and significantly higher than those of the other three groups, which had scores grouped in the lower end of the scale (1–3). Rejection scores were at similar high levels (5–7) in all the three clinical groups, whereas the control group had low scores (1–3). In terms of the state-of-mind scale scores, it is interesting that AAIs from the DD group without OCD received significantly elevated (though still moderate) E scores for involving anger toward both mother and father as compared to the other three groups, which had scores in the lower end of the scale. Elevated anger scores are linked to the Insecure–angry/preoccupied subtype (E2) but may appear in CC interviews that are at once Ds and, in the same interview, E2. The Insecure–passive/preoccupied subtype (E1) is linked to high scores for passive speech. On this scale, patients with OCD + DD scored higher than the other three groups, but the only significant difference for passive speech was that between OCD + DD and controls.

The AAIs from the DD group, regardless of the presence of OCD, as indicated earlier, were associated with unresolved trauma or loss in a substantial proportion of the cases (about 40% in both groups). Although the real-life experiences of an individual are not taken as established within responses to the AAI (Hesse, 1996), perhaps we can nonetheless presume, given the very high proportions and the sharp contrast to the two control groups, that traumatic experience and loss are for many depressed adolescents important components of the etiological pathway. However, the two groups differed in that adolescents with OCD + DD had only suffered loss, while abusive experience was an important component of the U-transcripts from the DD group. Abuse or traumatic experiences ranged from watching a parental suicide attempt to frank maltreatment. However, while the parents were involved in many cases, in several cases, maltreatment was perpetrated by adults other than attachment figures or by other youths. The AAI classification "beyond" or alternative to the U in depressed cases, was mostly a dismissing one (i.e., U/Ds) rather than preoccupied or secure. In the other U cases among the DD group and in the OCD + DD group, where Ds was not the primary classification "beyond" or "secondary to" the unresolved status, CC was often observed (U/CC; i.e., these transcripts show no coherent strategy with which the adolescents have been able to handle the difficult events in their lives).

In other cases (OCD, OCD + DD, and DD) CC was present against a background of Ds or as in the vignette below, which shows F features so mixed with Ds that the selected final category is determined as CC (Main et al., 2003; expanded CC system). We have less understanding of why this should be so. A lack of "mentalizing" language is a characteristic trait in these interviews, and the paucity is such that the reader suspects that there might be theory of mind deficits, as described in autism spectrum disorders (ASDs), at least in some cases. In fact autistic features are common in OCD (somewhat less than 1 out of 10 as a diagnosis; Ivarsson et al., in press) and even more as a dimensional construct (Ivarsson & Melin, in press). It is tempting to speculate that these features might play a role in the low levels of mentalizing language in the interviews of this subgroup. However, this issue has not been studied explicitly yet.

Our data indicate that attachment issues in adolescent depression seem to be more directly involved, and that unresolved trauma and loss (with concomitant "local" disorganization in speech or reasoning when adolescents are queried regarding such experiences; see Hesse, 1996) is common, as is CC ("global" disorganization due to the presence of both Ds and E speech seen throughout the interview [Hesse, 1996] or more recently, due to simple low coherence absent elevated scales pointing to Ds or E [Main et al., 2003]).

Our preliminary data, which indicate that a slim majority of AAIs from adolescents with OCD have Ds states of mind about attachment, nonetheless also indicate a minority with a secure state of mind with respect to attachment. The presence of some young persons with OCD who are nonetheless secure on the AAI lend support to Warren and colleagues' (1997) retrospective findings about young people with anxiety disorders. In findings from the Minnesota Study, whereas insecure–anxious/ambivalent responses to the Strange Situation were markedly associated with anxiety disorders (again, infant disorganized attachment status was not assessed in this study), there were also young people with anxiety disorders who had been secure with their mothers during infancy. Considering the Warren and colleagues findings and our own together, then, it does seem that both early security, as assessed in the Strange Situation procedure, and a secure–autonomous state of mind during adolescence, *can* in some cases clearly be linked to anxiety disorders. However, the studies differ in that our OCD (DSM-IV anxiety disordered) youngsters were mostly dismissing of attachment, whereas Warren and colleagues' study indicated a substantial role for early resistant/ambivalent attachment. Confounding factors (e.g., that, as noted, attachment in the Warren and colleagues group was assessed with the Strange Situation in infancy, and that few of these cases had OCD) might be responsible for the discrepancies. The other study that offers some grounds for comparisons (Manassis, Bradley, Goldberg, Hood, & Swinson, 1994) indicated that mothers with anxiety disorders had fewer than expected secure children and more than expected resistant and disorganized children. However, for present purposes of understanding correlates and causes of OCD in adolescence, it is not clear whether OCD was among the anxiety disorders suffered by the mothers in the Manassis and colleagues study.

To permit further insight into the AAIs of the adolescents studied in this investigation, the next section of this chapter provides verbatim excerpts or vignettes from the interviews.

Illustrative Vignettes from the AAIs

A Boy with OCD Found to Be Dismissing on the AAI

An adolescent boy with OCD (mostly with not only obsession about harm to self or others and checking compulsions, but also repetition compulsions until things felt right) used the term "pretty close" to describe the relationship with his mother. Prompted by the interviewer, he said: "Well, we have always been able to talk about everything and that. (*Mmm* [*interviewer encouraging sound; all interviewer sounds and questions are within parentheses and in italics*]) Yes. [*The interviewer asks for a special episode, an event that could help him understand why the adolescent used that term.*] Well, I don't know. There is no special memory about that. It's just that we have always been able to talk about everything [*Mmm*] so there is no special event that I can tell you."

This vignette shows a lack of episodic memories and the lack of concern about not being able to provide a memory (leading to a high score for idealization; i.e., the discrepancy that arises between positive semantic general descriptions for a relationship and the biographical memories from childhood that substantiate the claims, ultimately leading to a classification of dismissing of attachment [Ds1]).

By definition, to be identified as such, an older patient with OCD must have some insight into the degree to which the obsessions and compulsive behaviors are exaggerated. However, this insight does not extend to the use of a metacognitive stance to, as a matter of course, to evaluate the mental content. Do we see indications that this absence of metacognitive faculties has been "trained" or learned within the attachment relationship?

A Girl with OCD Found to Be Dismissing on the AAI

A 14-year-old girl used the word "nice" about her relationship with her mother. Her main obsessions were fears of illness and dirt, with concomitant reassurance rituals and exaggerated handwashing. Asked to think about some childhood memories that could give the interviewer a sense of how her mother was "nice," she answered: "Mmm {sighs} play games, talks, go for walks. It hasn't happened very often. (*Mmm. Could you tell me about some special time it happened?*) Mmm no, not any special time, but it . . . (*Well, just think of any ordinary day, when you and your mom might have done something like that? Could you think of a time that happened?*) She helped me with my homework. (*Yes.*) That is nice, that is—nice. (*Yes.*) Is with me and plays . . . the, the a guitar. (*Mmm.*) So, I think she is nice, is nice and so (*Mmm.*) do you want me to continue? (*Mmm . . . yes. So, this is something that happens most days?*) Yes. (*Yes, could you tell me about another childhood memory that could help me understand how she was nice?*) {3-second pause} No, we biked to my daycare when we lived in [City] (*Yes*) often and then we talked. (*Yes.*) And that was nice, I think. (*Yes, could you think of a special time?*) I don't remember much (*No*) from [City]. (*No.*)

This excerpt illustrates the small degree to which many of these adolescents with OCD appear to be oriented toward relationships, even apart from their insistence that they do not remember childhood events. The events are tersely described, and feelings and needs for security, as well as valuing attachment, are not described directly. The excerpt illustrates that there can also be a concrete quality to the essential parts of the answer (e.g., the word "play" seems to lead to thoughts about the guitar). Using the reflective functioning (RF) framework (Fonagy, Steele, Steele, Target, & Schacter, 1997), these patients may lack mentalization; that is, they do not talk as though their own and their parents' thoughts, feelings, and mental states are important ingredients in a story. However, these Ds features and the lack of RF is not a necessary component of OCD (i.e., it is not a feature of the disorder), because some adolescents, even those with severe OCD, can be secure–autonomous with regard to their state of mind in the AAI.

A Girl with OCD Found to Be Secure–Autonomous on the AAI

In our clinic, we saw a 15-year-old girl with OCD who harbored mainly aggressive obsessions that something disastrous might happen, or that she might inadvertently harm someone. These fears were accompanied by checking, reassurance, and mental rituals. As well, this adolescent was depressed.

This young girl described her mother as "loving," and provided good support for use of this adjective. She recalled, when prompted for a memory, how she and her friends in school had made a "bullying club" against a new-comer, and she was selected to act as a spy. However, somebody leaked out the plot, and a teacher took her to task about the whole thing. She said: "And the teacher scolded me severely, and I felt so stupid and sad and all the other kids who had been in on it kept quiet about it, so I was the only one who was scolded. And I was very agitated like . . . when I came home, I talked with my mom and she called the teacher and talked with her and so. . . . (*How did it all end for you?*) "Oh it felt much better, because my mom had taken care of it."

Although this girl spoke a bit tersely, the essential feature of her mom as a haven of safety for her is apparent in the tale. The girl could tell her mother about the bad thing she had done and successfully enlist her mother's support in a situation she could not manage on her own, and the mother's actions then made her feel better. To recall being able to tell a parent of a time when one was bad, and feeling nonetheless supported, is a primary index of loving behavior on the part of the parent in the AAI manual (Main et al., 2003).

A Boy with OCD Found to Be CC/F/Ds in the AAI

In some cases of OCD the AAI transcripts are designated cannot classify (CC is used for texts unclassifiable as F, Ds, or E). In one such adolescent from the OCD group, with obsessions about stealing and doing something wrong, checking and rereading rituals, a general lack of memories, a terse story, little idealization (weakly positive general descriptors that were actually substantiated), and general lack of a coherent tale, the interview was judged to be CC against a background of F with some added Ds features. This new way of identifying CC has been extended by Main and colleagues (2003) to permit some texts that are globally anomalous but do not show contradictory (Ds, and simultaneously E) strategies (as was required in previous editions of the system) to be placed in this category. In this example, then, the coherence score is too low for a fit to F, and CC/F is now utilized in such cases, as is CC/F/Ds seen here.

Ah, your fourth word was that {3-second pause} *your mum did not object against things.* (Yes [patient response]). *Ah, could you tell me a memory—something from your childhood, a memory that—that could help me understand that she wasn't against things, that she was not against what you did?*)

"Ah! Mmm {5-second pause} Noo. She thinks I should do some more naughty things . . . a little . . . (*Mmm*) . . . more [*Mmm.*] Always, so, just a little, (*Mmm*) not be so good all the time. (*Yes, yes.*) But, it could be such a thing that (*Yes*) she thinks (*Yeah*) that. She's said that scores of times, that she wouldn't mind if I do something {*giggles*} that would be (*Yes*) a bit more naughty than I use to do. (*Oh, yeah,* {*giggles*} *yes.*) Play a trick, or something. (*Yes.*)

This boy had been overly cautious and inhibited all his life, so his mother's wish for him to be a little more daring, expressed in a tentative, passive, and sparse way, was certainly very reasonable. This fits with other CC narratives inclining toward the Ds stance, with a general lack of memory for childhood and weakly positive or neutral general descriptors. Thus, the adolescents neither try to impress the interviewer with a positive childhood (as in Ds), nor fault their parent (as in E), and the narratives show little indication of love and secure base memories. These interviews are very terse, and in some cases interview questions elicit angry retorts (e.g., "Do you have to ask such ridiculous questions?"), revealing a derogatory attitude toward attachment (not to mention the interviewer).

In contrast, many of the narratives of our depressed patients indicated difficult life experiences and the more "classic" form of CC could be applied when patients expressed contradictory views about these experiences.

A Girl with Depression Found to Be CC/E1/Ds2 on the AAI

In one AAI, a depressed girl, on the general question about childhood relationships, talked for quite a while and ended with the following: "But ah, {3-second pause} I don't know, but my relationship with my mom has been, well quite . . . good, though in the later years, I have become irritated on. She has like. . . . It feels like she has tried to do, to turn me against Dad a little. (*Mmm*) Ah . . . and so . . . it is I guess, yes. {3-second pause} Yes, as I grew older, then, or (*Mmm*) perhaps when I-I was 6 years old perhaps then—started (*Mmm*) it to be like. . . . Because as I started to fight with her so, because when one is little—is small—my mom fought with me about little things (the Swedish word she used meant "insignificant things") and then when she (*Mmm*) turned to me, it was a little more that one like [*Mmm*] . . . No, I don't know. So I became. But I and Dad fought a lot and then it was like my mother took, like took my side and she started to say bad things about Dad and—like I thought that was quite good because—then I could say bad things too . . . or like it's difficult to say bad things about him, and so Mom and I were against Dad and so. (*Mmm*.) Like that. And I am quite happy about that. Now, I can see that is, is hellishly . . . stupid or like . . . it is my dad that my mom is so. [*Mmm*]. And so she takes care of herself. Now, I think she is stupid. On the other hand, Dad is very stupid at times. I don't stay with him so often now (?) to (?) and so." (*Mmm mmm, mmm, mmm*.)

Later, asked to provide five adjectives or a short sentence to describe her relationship with her dad when she was a child, she used the word "defended" about her dad, and when asked for a childhood memory, she became angrily preoccupied: "Last week my brother came home and—been very sad because Dad had like raised his hand like this and almost hit him. (*Mmm*) And that want. I don't know, it can well have happened, but . . . I don't think he would ever have hit him but perhaps he kind of . . . threatened a little, kind of. And Mom just started right on that 'I don't like that you go there' and . . . it became like he is no good and blah-blah-blah and like . . . and she is no better herself like that. (*Mmm*) She tries like to . . . smear him like and. . . . That like she doesn't see that it is our dad she talks about, like. Like, I mean, half of me."

In this case, the speech used is all over the map of attachment-related difficulties reliably identified in the Berkeley scoring system (Main et al., 2003). The excerpt provided would receive, for example, high scores for passive speech (e.g., "blah, blah, blah," a correlate of overall preoccupation linked to the E1 subtype) and for derogation of both parents described as "stupid" (a correlate of an overall Ds state of mind linked to the Ds2 subtype). This combination of incompatible states of mind leads to the CC designation.

The preceding excerpts from our clinic patients' AAIs indicate that in building a model of the contribution of attachment theory to OCD etiology, we need to hypothesize a more indirect link or, rather, different indirect links between attachment and OCD, because all these insecure, unresolved, and CC forms of response to the AAI have been observed in troubled adolescents without OCD (e.g., Wallis & Steele, 2001; for use of the "new" form of CC in a Japanese sample, see also Behrens, Hesse, & Main, 2007). Furthermore, different indirect links between attachment and OCD are called for because OCD is a heterogeneous disorder with small subgroups, which makes any subgroup rather uncommon (perhaps 0.1–0.2%) in the general population compared to, for example, the Ds form of attachment classifications, which is very common (20–25%) with respect to prevalence. With regard to depression (without OCD), on the other hand, the traumatic events and the anomalous attachment experience that many (but not all) described might indicate a more direct link between attachment issues and expression, as stated earlier.

Attachment and OCD

How then should one understand the possible contribution of attachment difficulties to OCD? In view of the success of the behaviorally based treatments, at least with respect to short-term (Abramowitz et al., 2005) and intermediate-term results (Barrett, Farrell, Dadds, & Boulter, 2005), we believe that any link must (1) be compatible with the learning theory paradigm (LTP), which includes at its core exposure and response prevention (see Stovall-McClough, Cloitre, & McClough, Chapter 13, this volume, i.e., it should not replace attachment theory but rather aid us in understanding why OCD symptoms develop and get reinforced over time), using the LTP and attachment theory; (2) aid us in understanding why many OCD symptoms, such as reassurance rituals, involve the parents; (3) show how insecure–nonautonomous forms of attachment might be a nonspecific risk-factor for the development of OCD; and finally (4) possibly help us understand why some patients do not respond well to cognitive-behavioral therapy (CBT).

In clinical work with patients with OCD, I have had much experience with patients whose attachment issues have been apparent. Clinical experience must enhance our discussion of the possible links.

Secure–Autonomous Attachment

The presence of secure–autonomous attachment in a minority of cases is well in accordance with our experience that many parents of our patients are able to function as both a secure base and safe haven for their children and that OCD, just as has previously been shown with regard to adult depression (Fonagy, Leigh, Steele, & Steele, 1996), can be associated with secure–autonomous attachment. From not only a twin study (Hudziak et al., 2004) but also the wealth of biological studies (Arnold et al., 2004; Fitzgerald, MacMaster, Paulson, & Rosenberg, 1999; Rosenberg, Keshavan, Dick, et al., 1997; Rosenberg, Keshavan, O'Hearn, et al., 1997; Rosenberg et al., 2004; Szeszko, MacMillan, McMeniman, Chen, et al., 2004) it is clear that biological factors play an important role in the etiology of OCD, and our preliminary results imply that these factors may in some cases be expressed without any contribution from attachment insecurity. However, less optimal parenting strategies that do not lead to insecurity might still play a role (Manassis, 2001). Parenting that includes less effective modeling in coping with stressful events or maternal overconcern with the child's safety because the mother has an anxiety disorder herself have been suggested as possible contributions. These plausible suppositions await empirical confirmation. Clinically, we find that some parents find it easier than others not to collude with reassurance rituals, or at least they are able to disentangle themselves, once they have been advised to do so. The parent of a child with aggressive obsessions about the mother dying during the night, for example, is advised to tell the child that she knows he or she is scared, that it is unlikely that she will die during the night, and although she cannot know for sure, the danger is so slight that she feels it is OK. However, this is done at the proper stage in CBT, when addressing obsessions about mother dying in the context of exposing the impoverished evidence base for the child's beliefs. In optimal circumstance, this results in decreased anxiety (i.e., habituation or getting used to more reasonable belief structure with an evidence base), and the child agrees to stop that ritual (i.e., response prevention). It is my contention that when this is done sensitively and appropriately to good effect, it is likely that we are working with a securely attached child.

Insecure Attachment

There may be different causal links between different attachment strategies (Ds, E, and U/CC) and OCD, with different developmental pathways. So far, our own clinic data indicate a substantial role for Ds attachment in adolescent with OCD.

Why should increased rates of Ds attachment strategies be associated with OCD? First, I agree with Doron and Kyrios (2005) that an insecure state of mind with respect to attachment experiences might be a nonspecific risk factor for the development of OCD. A nonspecific risk factor would in our model be concerned with three aspects. First, a lack of skills in emotional regulation would leave the child with emerging OCD symptoms in a situation where he or she has insufficient skills to cope with the increased anxiety. Thus, overwhelmed with anxiety, the child discovers that excessive behavior (e.g., handwashing) relieves the anxiety about germs for the time being; thus, this behavior is reinforced according to the LTP. Moreover, Doron and Kyrios have proposed that cognitive structures that evolve through an insecure attachment are an important facet of the process leading to OCD. Clinicians would rather see this as one aspect of the lack of emotional regulation skills in the children (i.e., where negative self-schemas about their own competence in eliciting support from others, their own worthiness in getting support, and lack of positive self-talk make the individual vulnerable to worsened OCD symptoms once subclinical symptoms have emerged).

Second, recognizing the immaturity of children and adolescents, we believe that having access to the parent in time of need as a haven of safety is an important asset in such a situation. Emotional access to the parent is the most active buffer for anxiety in children's lives according to attachment theory, and there is no reason to believe that patients with OCD would not try to turn to their parent when anxious—in fact, we know they do. Being able to return to the haven of safety, the child or adolescent would also benefits from the parent's feedback concerning the actual danger of germs on the hands, the anxiety involved in having inappropriate sexual thoughts about the parent, or frightening thoughts about harming the parent with a knife. In our experience with children in such situations, it is crucial that parents have the ability to harbor their own unpleasant affect and fears in such a situation, something that might be difficult for anyone, and that for insecure dyads is especially difficult. According to our experience, different dyads act differently in these situations. Thus, the common pattern in which the child tries to cope on his or her own and the parent remains comparatively uninvolved (the Ds stance) until a breaking point occurs and the child demands reassurance, soon evolves into rituals. In other dyads (fewer), we find that anxiety tends to run wildly, with each partner reinforcing anxiety in the other. Some dyads even end up with role-reversal, in which the child starts to support or instruct the parent (I think this may be common in CC dyads).

Third, as shown in several of the cases described in this chapter, and our own data from the subset with OCD + DD in a previous report (Ivarsson, 1998), many patients with OCD and depression lack mentalizing abilities (reflective functioning). Deficits in this area (i.e., thinking about their own and others' thinking and feelings) may be detrimental in a situation where anxiety-provoking thoughts and impulses arise from the OCD. Thus, youngsters take their thoughts and feelings at face value and do not monitor them as a matter of course. And, as I mentioned earlier, although adult OCD is defined as the patient having some insight into the irrationality of the symptoms, this is not required to reach a diagnosis of OCD in children. In fact, insight varies across cases with different symptom patterns (Ivarsson & Valderhaug, 2006), and also across time in the same youngster (i.e., better when discussing the OCD symptoms in the doctor's office but much less useful in anxiety-provoking situations).

These three aspects might be seen as different facets of the lack of emotional regulation in insecure children and would, according to my view, be a correlate of insufficient control of the amygdala structure (the most important aspect of the fear system) by the orbitofrontal cortex, and especially the gyrus orbitalis, that are parts of the corticostriatal–thalamocortical functional loops that current biological models of OCD implicate (Carlsson, 2000). Lack of control of such loops could then ensue from different biological/genetic sources, as Carlsson suggests, and/or in interaction with impaired attachment relationships, as I propose. The situation is then analogous to the development (or lack thereof) of effortful control (Kochanska & Murray, 2003), a control that is needed both for the inhibition of inappropriate response and for the substitution of better coping behaviors in emotion-provoking situations. It would be of great interest to assess more objectively the interplay between these brain structures, both from the functional (using functional magnetic resonance imaging [fMRI]) and neurochemical (using magnetic resonance spectroscopy) viewpoints.

A more specific link between attachment insecurity and some OCD behaviors that are acted out within the attachment relationship can be seen in the presence of reassurance rituals, as described earlier. When the full dataset is analyzed, it will be possible to test empirically whether these kinds of rituals are among the more prevalent and significant rituals in insecure youngsters. In this hypothesis, reassurance rituals are seen as a breakdown of the Ds strategy in both partners of the dyads. Thus, reassurance rituals could be reinforced for two reasons: (1) their immediate anxiety-relieving function in accordance with the LTP and/or (2) the child's attachment-related requirements are met in a time of dire need, providing a parental response for attachment behaviors that are rewarding in itself for any child.

In fact, in some reassurance rituals, the child does not just demand that the parent reassure him or her that, for example, no thief will break in during the night; the parent must also use the exactly right tone of voice. By itself, as the LTP paradigm states, increased attention itself leads to positive reinforcement, and adding the motivation that ensues from the attachment system further strengthens these behaviors. I believe this is one reason that reassurance rituals are so common in patients with OCD (i.e., they are both positively and negatively reinforced). To clarify, the negative reinforcement results from the anxiety-relieving function of the ritual (Rasmussen & Eisen, 1990), increasing the likelihood that the child will use the same behavior in the future when confronted with the same situation. Positive reinforcement is the result of the reward (in the neurobiological sense) of getting the parent's attention, closeness, and aid when in need (which is the developmental task of the attachment system).

Using the LTP model for OCD, which has proved so useful in daily therapeutic work with these patients, I suggest a model in which the attachment system might act to reinforce OCD behaviors in the broadest sense. Thus, I argue, different patients with OCD might be associated with insecure forms of attachment through different combinations of these developmental pathways, in which the contribution of each could vary substantially. Other characteristics of comorbidity in OCD (e.g., with ASDs) would lead to certain aspects of the pathogenesis being more prominent, because autistic traits (mostly as a diagnosis of pervasive developmental disorder not otherwise specified) would lead to the lack of metacognition, one of the more important aspects in such a case, while the actual buffering capacity of the parent might be more within the normal range. Although our data indicate that rejection of attachment behavior would be present in the developmental trajectory of many patients, this cannot be incorporated into the model as a direct acting etiological factor, except as part of the current Ds stance, with deficits of "buffering capacity" online. Hypothesizing that CC attachment status is associated with a severe deficit in emotional and behavioral regulation could easily be incorporated in the model.

Depression in OCD, according to these data, is similar to depression without OCD with regard to the presence of U, as well as CC. However, in other cases, it might be that the depression in OCD is intrinsically linked with the OCD disorder itself through several links. The most obvious link is that the depressed state would constitute a "demoralization syndrome" (Gittelman-Klein & Klein, 1971; i.e., having a severe anxiety disorder leads to a poor quality of life and consequently to depression). Supportive evidence is the observation that depression is usually subsequent to the anxiety disorder (Kovacs, Gatsonis, & Paulauskas, 1989). However, there might be more specific links between depression and OCD. Goodyer suggested as much when he coined the term "obsessional depression" (Goodyer, Herbert, Secher, & Pearson, 1997) for cases of persistent depression in which a strong predictor of continued depression was found to be comorbid OCD. Our preliminary results indicate that the process leading to depression in OCD in many cases does not follow severe negative life events and/or abnormal attachment relationships that lead to U and/or CC attachment classifications, but, from the attachment point of view, from the everyday play of rejection of attachment behaviors in combination with the OCD. Thus, as in OCD generally, we hypothesize that for OCD and depression, the insecure attachment relationships lead to problems in emotional regulation, negative self-schemas, and a limited epistemic space with lack of metacognitive monitoring that could counteract both the OCD and the depressive cognitions.

Intervention

Could these considerations lead to improved treatment? Today, few people would argue against, or not recommend CBT with exposure and response prevention (ERP) for OCD symptoms. However, although CBT is an evidence-based treatment with good studies showing its efficacy (Abramowitz et al.,

2005), not all children and adolescents get well, and a substantial minority either do not respond well or respond hardly at all, and in many of these cases, issues within the family need to be dealt with (among them, those related to attachment).

It is our contention and experience that many of these unresponsive or partially responsive patients need family interventions that, among other things, increase parents' capacity to be both the secure base and the safe haven. Especially those dyads that feature role reversal need intervention that must include the attachment perspective. In our clinic we have used attachment-based interventions when needed to enable treatment with CBT in selected cases, mostly with younger children. However, because attachment-based assessments have not been widely available in that age range, our supposition (of insecure attachment) is uncertain. Clearly, further research within this area will be facilitated by the development of attachment assessment methods covering the full age range. Another possible line of intervention might address the lack of epistemic space or mentalizing in many of these youngsters. Although the CBT is helpful in teaching patients to identify and understand both troublesome emotions and thoughts, because of the focus of CBT on ERP, it might be that for CBT nonresponders, therapeutic techniques that enhance mentalizing might be fruitful, as suggested by Fonagy (2006) with respect to eating disorders.

In conclusion, some data from our clinic's study indicate that attachment insecurity may play a role in the etiology of the OCD in many, but not all, patients. In secure–autonomous patients including those classified CC/F, presumably, the biological factors are stronger, leading to overt OCD in spite of the youngster having access to more resources, both individual and interpersonal. What this entails for the long-term outcome is an empirical question that needs to be elucidated. We also argue that attachment insecurity might influence different developmental pathways leading to overt OCD symptoms. Our preliminary data indicate that attachment does not play a direct role (as might be the case in adolescent depression), but acts within the confines of other risk factors, as expressed earlier. Finally, there is need for further research to specify these developmental pathways, in the interests of determining how attachment insecurity interacts with different risk factors within the LTP.

Clearly, much more research is needed, using better research strategies than the current cross-sectional design with retrospective inferences regarding attachment experience. A longitudinal study following children with a high risk of developing OCD (i.e., children of adults with OCD or Tourette's syndrome from infancy or alternatively, siblings of pediatric OCD patients) from early school age, assessing attachment and other factors associated with mastery or risk, similar to the Minnesota Study (Sroufe et al., 2005), would be the ultimate test of these ideas. Also, such a longitudinal investigation could study prevention strategies, both primary (by promoting attachment security, among other things) and secondary (by early detection and intervention).

References

Abramowitz, J. S., Whiteside, S. P., & Deacon, B. J. (2005). The effectiveness of treatment for pediatric obsessive–compulsive disorder. *Behavior Therapy, 36*, 55–63.

Ainsworth, M. D. S., Blehar, M. C., Waters, E., & Wall, S. (1978). *Patterns of attachment.* Hillsdale, NJ: Erlbaum.

American Psychiatric Association. (1994). *Diagnostic and statistical manual of mental disorders* (4th ed.). Washington, DC: Author.

Arnold, P. D., Rosenberg, D. R., Mundo, E., Tharmalingam, S., Kennedy, J. L., & Richter, M. A. (2004). Association of a glutamate (NMDA) subunit receptor gene (*GRIN2B*) with obsessive–compulsive disorder: A preliminary study. *Psychopharmacology (Berlin) , 174*, 530–538.

Barrett, P., Farrell, L., Dadds, M., & Boulter, N. (2005). Cognitive-behavioral family treatment of childhood obsessive–compulsive disorder: long-term follow-up and predictors of outcome. *Journal of the American Academy of Child and Adolescent Psychiatry, 44*, 1005–1014.

Behrens, K. Y., Hesse, E., & Main, M. (2007). Mothers' attachment status as determined by the Adult Attachment Interview predicts their 6-year-olds' reunion responses: A study conducted in Japan. *Developmental Psychology, 43*, 1553–1567.

Biederman, J., Rosenbaum, J. F., Hirshfeld, D. R., Faraone, S. V., Bolduc, E. A., Gersten, M., et al. (1990). Psychiatric correlates of behavioral inhibition in young children of parents with and without psychiatric disorders. *Archives of General Psychiatry, 47*, 21–26.

Bokhorst, C. L., Bakermans-Kranenburg, M. J., Fearon, R. M., van IJzendoorn, M. H., Fonagy, P., & Schuengel, C. (2003). The importance of shared environment in mother–infant attachment security: A behavioral genetic study. *Child Development, 74*, 1769–1782.

Bowlby, J. (1982). *Attachment and loss: Vol. 1. Attachment* (2nd ed.). New York: Pelican Books. (Original work published 1969)

Carlson, E. A. (1998). A prospective longitudinal study of attachment disorganization/disorientation. *Child Development, 69*, 1107–1128.

Carlsson, M. L. (2000). On the role of cortical glutamate in obsessive–compulsive disorder and attention-deficit hyperactivity disorder, two phenomenologically antithetical conditions. *Acta Psychiatrica Scandinavica, 102*, 401–413.

Caspi, A., McClay, J., Moffitt, T. E., Mill, J., Martin, J., Craig, I. W., et al. (2002). Role of genotype in the cycle of violence in maltreated children. *Science, 297*, 851–854.

De Ruiter, C. (1994). Anxious attachment in agarophobia and obsessive–compulsive disorder: A literature review and treatment implications. In C. Perris, W. A. Arrindell, & M. Eisemann (Eds.), *Parenting and psychopathology* (pp. 281–307). Chichester, UK: Wiley.

Doron, G., & Kyrios, M. (2005). Obsessive compulsive disorder: A review of possible specific internal representations within a broader cognitive theory. *Clinical Psychology Review, 25*, 415–432.

Ehiobuche, I. (1988). Obsessive–compulsive neurosis in relation to parental child-rearing patterns amongst the Greek, Italian and Anglo-Australian subjects. *Acta Psychiatrica Scandinavica, 78*, 115–120.

Eley, T. C., Sugden, K., Corsico, A., Gregory, A. M., Sham, P., McGuffin, P., et al.

(2004). Gene–environment interaction analysis of serotonin system markers with adolescent depression. *Molecular Psychiatry, 9,* 908–915.

Fitzgerald, K. D., MacMaster, F. P., Paulson, L. D., & Rosenberg, D. R. (1999). Neurobiology of childhood obsessive–compulsive disorder. *Child and Adolescent Psychiatric Clinics of North America, 8,* 533–575, ix.

Fonagy, P. (2006, October). *Adolescence and mentalisation: The nature of adolescent eating disorders and dysfunctional attachment.* Paper presented at the annual meeting of the American Association of Child and Adolescent Psychiatry, San Diego, CA.

Fonagy, P., Leigh, T., Steele, M., & Steele, H. (1996). The relation of attachment status, psychiatric classification, and response to psychotherapy. *Journal of Consulting and Clinical Psychology, 64,* 22–31.

Fonagy, P., Steele, M., Steele, H., Target, M., & Schachter, A. (1997). *Reflective functioning manual for application to Adult Attachment Interviews (Version 4.1).* Unpublished manuscript, University College London, London.

Geller, D., Biederman, J., Faraone, S. V., Frazier, J., Coffey, B. J., Kim, G., et al. (2000). Clinical correlates of obsessive–compulsive disorder in children and adolescents referred to specialized and non-specialized clinical settings. *Depression and Anxiety, 11,* 163–168.

Geller, D. A., Biederman, J., Faraone, S., Spencer, T., Doyle, R., Mullin, B., et al. (2004). Re-examining comorbidity of obsessive compulsive and attention-deficit hyperactivity disorder using an empirically derived taxonomy. *European Child and Adolescent Psychiatry, 13,* 83–91.

Geller, D. A., Biederman, J., Stewart, S. E., Mullin, B., Martin, A., Spencer, T., et al. (2003). Which SSRI?: A meta-analysis of pharmacotherapy trials in pediatric obsessive–compulsive disorder. *American Journal of Psychiatry, 160,* 1919–1928.

George, C., Kaplan, N., & Main, M. (1985, 1996). Unpublished data, University of California at Berkeley.

Gittelman-Klein, R., & Klein, D. F. (1971). Controlled imipramine treatment of school phobia. *Archives of General Psychiatry, 25,* 204–207.

Goodyer, I. M., Herbert, J., Secher, S. M., & Pearson, J. (1997). Short-term outcome of major depression: I. Comorbidity and severity at presentation as predictors of persistent disorder. *Journal of the American Academy of Child and Adolescent Psychiatry, 36,* 179–187.

Grados, M. A., Riddle, M. A., Samuels, J. F., Liang, K. Y., Hoehn-Saric, R., Bienvenu, O. J., et al. (2001). The familial phenotype of obsessive–compulsive disorder in relation to tic disorders: The Hopkins OCD family study. *Biological Psychiatry, 50,* 559–565.

Hanna, G. L. (1995). Demographic and clinical features of obsessive–compulsive disorder in children and adolescents. *Journal of the American Academy of Child and Adolescent Psychiatry, 34,* 19–27.

Hanna, G. L., Fischer, D. J., Chadha, K. R., Himle, J. A., & Van Etten, M. (2005). Familial and sporadic subtypes of early-onset obsessive–compulsive disorder. *Biological Psychiatry, 57,* 895–900.

Hanna, G. L., Himle, J. A., Curtis, G. C., & Gillespie, B. W. (2005). A family study of obsessive–compulsive disorder with pediatric probands. *American Journal of Medical Genetics: B. Neuropsychiatric Genetics, 134,* 13–19.

Hesse, E. (1996). Discourse, memory, and the Adult Attachment Interview: A note with emphasis on the emerging cannot classify category. *Infant Mental Health Journal, 17,* 4–11.

Hesse, E., & Main, M. (2006). Frightened, threatening, and dissociative parental behavior in low-risk samples: Description, discussion, and interpretations. *Development and Psychopathology, 18*(2), 309–343.

Heyman, I., Fombonne, E., Simmons, H., Ford, T., Meltzer, H., & Goodman, R. (2001). Prevalence of obsessive–compulsive disorder in the British nationwide survey of child mental health. *British Journal of Psychiatry, 179,* 324–329.

Hirshfeld, D. R., Rosenbaum, J. F., Biederman, J., Bolduc, E. A., Faraone, S. V., Snidman, N., et al. (1992). Stable behavioral inhibition and its association with anxiety disorder. *Journal of the American Academy of Child and Adolescent Psychiatry, 31,* 103–111.

Hudziak, J. J., Van Beijsterveldt, C. E., Althoff, R. R., Stanger, C., Rettew, D. C., Nelson, E. C., et al. (2004). Genetic and environmental contributions to the Child Behavior Checklist Obsessive–Compulsive Scale: A cross-cultural twin study. *Archives of General Psychiatry, 61,* 608–616.

Ivarsson, T. (1998). *Depression and depressive symptoms in adolescence: Clinical and epidemiological studies.* Unpublished dissertation, Gothenburg University, Gothenburg, Sweden.

Ivarsson, T., Granqvist, P., Broberg, A., & Gillberg, C. (2007). *Attachment organisation using the Adult Attachment Interview in adolescents with obsessive-compulsive disorder (OCD), OCD with depression and depression without OCD.* Manuscript to be submitted.

Ivarsson, T., & Melin, K. (in press). Autism spectrum traits in children and adolescents with obsessive–compulsive disorder (OCD). *Journal of Anxiety Disorders.*

Ivarsson, T., Melin, K., & Wallin, L. (in press). Categorical and dimensional aspects of co-morbidity in obsessive–compulsive disorder (OCD). *European Child and Adolescent Psychiatry.*

Ivarsson, T., & Valderhaug, R. (2006). Symptom patterns in children and adolescents with obsessive–compulsive disorder (OCD). *Behaviour Research and Therapy, 44,* 1105–1116.

Kochanska, G., & Murray, K. (2003). Inhibitory control in young children and its role in emerging internalization. *Child Development, 67,* 490–507.

Kovacs, M., Gatsonis, C., & Paulauskas, S. L. (1989). Depressive disorders in childhood: IV. A longitudinal study of comorbidity with and risk for anxiety disorders. *Archives of General Psychiatry, 46,* 776–782.

Madigan, S., Bakermans-Kranenburg, M. J., van IJzendoorn, M. H., Moran, G., Pederson, D. R., & Benoit, D. (2006). Unresolved states of mind, anomalous parental behavior, and disorganized attachment: A review and meta-analysis of a transmission gap. *Attachment and Human Development, 8,* 89–111.

Main, M., Goldwyn, R., & Hesse, E. (2003). Adult attachment scoring and classification system. In M. Main (Ed.), *Assessing attachment through discourse, drawings and reunion situations.* New York: Cambridge University Press.

Main, M., Hesse, E., & Kaplan, N. (2005). Predictability of attachment behavior and representational processes at 1, 16, and 19 years of age: The Berkeley Longitudinal Study. In K. E. Grossmann, K. Grossmann, & E. Waters (Eds.), *Attachment from infancy to childhood: The major longitudinal studies* (pp. 245–304). New York: Guilford Press.

Main, M., & Solomon, R. (1990). Procedures for identifying infants as disorganized/disoriented during the Ainsworth Strange Situation. In M. T. Greenberg, D. Cicchetti, & E. M. Cummings (Eds.), *Attachment in the preschool years: Theory, research and intervention* (pp. 121–160). Chicago: University of Chicago Press.

Manassis, K. (2001). Child–parent relations: attachment and anxiety disorders. In W. K. Silverman & P. D. Treffers (Eds.), *Anxiety disorders in children and adolescents* (pp. 255–272). Cambridge, UK: Cambridge University Press.

Manassis, K., Bradley, S., Goldberg, S., Hood, J., & Swinson, R. P. (1994). Attachment in mothers with anxiety disorders and their children. *Journal of the American Academy of Child and Adolescent Psychiatry, 33,* 1106–1113.

McKay, D., Abramowitz, J. S., Calamari, J. E., Kyrios, M., Radomsky, A., Sookman, D., et al. (2004). A critical evaluation of obsessive–compulsive disorder subtypes: Symptoms versus mechanisms. *Clinical Psychology Review, 24,* 283–313.

McKay, D., Piacentini, J., Greisberg, S., Graae, F., Jaffer, M., & Miller, J. (2006). The structure of childhood obsessions and compulsions: Dimensions in an outpatient sample. *Behaviour Research Therapy, 44,* 137–146.

Pauls, D. L., Alsobrook, J. P., Goodman, W. K., Rasmussen, S. A., & Leckman, J. F. (1995). A family study of obsessive–compulsive disorder. *American Journal of Psychiatry, 152,* 76–84.

Rasmussen, S. A., & Eisen, J. L. (1990). Epidemiology and clinical features of obsessive–compulsive disorder. In M. A. Jenike, L. Baer, & W. E. Minichiello (Eds.), *Obsessive–compulsive disorders: Theory and management* (2nd ed., pp. 10–27). St. Louis, MO: Mosby.

Reddy, P. S., Reddy, Y. C., Srinath, S., Khanna, S., Sheshadri, S. P., & Girimaji, S. R. (2001). A family study of juvenile obsessive–compulsive disorder. *Canadian Journal of Psychiatry, 46,* 346–351.

Rosenbaum, J. F., Biederman, J., Bolduc-Murphy, E. A., Faraone, S. V., Chaloff, J., Hirshfeld, D. R., et al. (1993). Behavioral inhibition in childhood: A risk factor for anxiety disorders. *Harvard Review of Psychiatry, 1,* 2–16.

Rosenberg, D. R., Keshavan, M. S., Dick, E. L., Bagwell, W. W., MacMaster, F. P., & Birmaher, B. (1997). Corpus callosal morphology in treatment-naive pediatric obsessive compulsive disorder. *Progress in Neuro-Psychopharmacology and Biological Psychiatry, 21,* 1269–1283.

Rosenberg, D. R., Keshavan, M. S., O'Hearn, K. M., Dick, E. L., Bagwell, W. W., Seymour, A. B., et al. (1997). Frontostriatal measurement in treatment-naive children with obsessive–compulsive disorder. *Archives of General Psychiatry, 54,* 824–830.

Rosenberg, D. R., MacMaster, F. P., Keshavan, M. S., Fitzgerald, K. D., Stewart, C. M., & Moore, G. J. (2000). Decrease in caudate glutamatergic concentrations in pediatric obsessive–compulsive disorder patients taking paroxetine. *Journal of the American Academy of Child and Adolescent Psychiatry, 39,* 1096–1103.

Rosenberg, D. R., Mirza, Y., Russell, A., Tang, J., Smith, J. M., Banerjee, S. P., et al. (2004). Reduced anterior cingulate glutamatergic concentrations in childhood OCD and major depression versus healthy controls. *Journal of the American Academy of Child and Adolescent Psychiatry, 43,* 1146–1153.

Rosenstein, D. S., & Horowitz, H. A. (1996). Adolescent attachment and psychopathology. *Journal of Consulting and Clinical Psychology, 64,* 244–253.

Russell, A., Cortese, B., Lorch, E., Ivey, J., Banerjee, S. P., Moore, G. J., et al. (2003). Localized functional neurochemical marker abnormalities in dorsolateral prefrontal cortex in pediatric obsessive–compulsive disorder. *Journal of Child and Adolescent Psychopharmacology, 13*(Suppl. 1), S31–S38.

Shamir-Essakow, G., Ungerer, J. A., & Rapee, R. M. (2005). Attachment, behavioral inhibition, and anxiety in preschool children. *Journal of Abnormal Child Psychology, 33*, 131–143.

Sroufe, L. A., Egeland, B., Carlson, E. A., & Collins, W. A. (2005). *The development of the person: The Minnesota Study of risk and adaptation from birth to adulthood.* New York: Guilford Press.

Swedo, S. E., Leonard, H. L., Garvey, M., Mittleman, B., Allen, A. J., Perlmutter, S., et al. (1998). Pediatric autoimmune neuropsychiatric disorders associated with streptococcal infections: Clinical description of the first 50 cases [published erratum appears in *American Journal of Psychiatry*, 1998, *155*(4), 578]. *American Journal of Psychiatry, 155*, 264–271.

Szeszko, P. R., MacMillan, S., McMeniman, M., Chen, S., Baribault, K., Lim, K. O., et al. (2004). Brain structural abnormalities in psychotropic drug-naive pediatric patients with obsessive–compulsive disorder. *American Journal of Psychiatry, 161*, 1049–1056.

Szeszko, P. R., MacMillan, S., McMeniman, M., Lorch, E., Madden, R., Ivey, J., et al. (2004). Amygdala volume reductions in pediatric patients with obsessive–compulsive disorder treated with paroxetine: Preliminary findings. *Neuropsychopharmacology, 29*, 826–832.

Valleni-Basile, L. A., Garrison, C. Z., Jackson, K. L., Waller, J. L., McKeown, R. E., Addy, C. L., et al. (1994). Frequency of obsessive–compulsive disorder in a community sample of young adolescents. *Journal of the American Academy of Child and Adolescent Psychiatry, 33*, 782–791.

Wallis, P., & Steele, H. (2001). Attachment representations in adolescence: Further evidence from psychiatric residential settings. *Attachment and Human Development, 3*, 259–268.

Warren, S. L., Huston, L., Egeland, B., & Sroufe, L. A. (1997). Child and adolescent anxiety disorders and early attachment. *Journal of the American Academy of Child and Adolescent Psychiatry, 36*, 637–644.

Yang, Y., & Liu, X. (1998). A family study of obsessive–compulsive disorder. *Zhonghua Yi Xue Yi Chuan Xue Za Zhi, 15*, 303–306.

Zohar, A. H., Ratzoni, G., Pauls, D. L., Apter, A., Bleich, A., Kron, S., et al. (1992). An epidemiological study of obsessive–compulsive disorder and related disorders in Israeli adolescents. *Journal of the American Academy of Child and Adolescent Psychiatry, 31*, 1057–1061.

10

The AAI in a Clinical Context

Some Experiences and Illustrations

MASSIMO AMMANITI, NINO DAZZI, and SERGIO MUSCETTA

This chapter provides a detailed overview of how we arrived at a deep appreciation for the usefulness of the Adult Attachment Interview (AAI) in clinical work. We do this by presenting fragments from three clinical cases in which the interview material helped us to understand the relational and intrapsychic dynamics of the patients concerned. In the first of these cases, we apply the AAI dimensional concept of coherence to psychotherapy sessions and observe an increase in coherence over time, as well as rely on interviews from the mother and young adult in therapy to explicate the process of intergenerational transmission in the context of early losses in one generation impacting upon the developmental trajectory of the next. The second clinical case involves a young man in which repeated administrations of the interview served to both forecast the course and chart progress observed in therapy. The third case involves a young woman with features of borderline personality disorder.

In the AAI, the way patients talk about their personal histories, not only with regard to content, but also with respect to the *way* they narrate them, is a useful reinforcement of the traditional clinical "way of listening." In particular, an important source of information is the extent to which speakers are open to their past experiences: whether they are organized, collaborative, and able to convey a "fresh" approach while talking about their past attachment relationships, or whether they are preoccupied with their past histories or minimize important emotional events, and/or idealize their parents. These and other features of AAI narratives help the therapist form hypotheses as to the probable early relational models underlying the patient's character. They also enhance clinician identification of the defensive styles on which patients rely during treatment. In this way, the clinician's attention is systematically drawn to

> listening for changes in voice; for contradictions, lapses, irrelevancies, and break-downs in meaning; and for the subtle, ongoing disruptions and fluctuations in the structure and organization of discourse. Indeed, these ways of listening for moments when experience cannot be contemplated or mentalized offer the therapist a view of how the patient defends himself or herself against the intrusion of unacceptable feelings or memories into conscious thought. (Slade, 1999, p. 582)

Listening for these variations in patients' levels of coherence allows us to make informed assumptions about how early empathic failures of caregivers influence patients' histories. Similarly, this way of listening facilitates the identification of elements of past affective experiences that have been dissociated or have not yet been fully integrated. Therefore, it is possible to understand the specific function played by certain models of affect and thoughts, and the way they protect the patient from intolerable experiences and elicit specific actions and thoughts in others (both within and outside of therapy). In summary, paying attention to the narrative process from the perspective of the AAI (George, Kaplan, & Main, 1985) and its corollary rating system (Main, Hesse, & Goldwyn, Chapter 2, this volume; Main, Goldwyn, & Hesse, 2002) allows the therapist to organize more systematically what has always been inherent in good clinical "listening."

A Model for Use of the AAI in Our Clinical work

Ever since we began administering the AAI in the evaluation phase of treatment, we have refrained from embarking on any possible therapeutic project without it. At the end of the first session, the patient is asked to participate in an audio-recorded interview. The patient is told that it is important not only to record the facts she relates but also the way she experiences them subjectively. The patient is also told that the audio recording is necessary to understand the material better in this initial stage of the therapeutic encounter. If the patient agrees, the AAI is administered in the second session. The third session is mainly devoted to understanding the effect the interview has had on the patient, whether she thought about it afterward and, if so, how. In this context, a clinical restitution of the interview is carried out and after that the normal clinical listening resumes. An example may render our type of intervention clearer. If the patient states during the interview that whenever he was upset as a child he went to his room and cried alone, then it would be important to verify whether not resorting to people for help was general mode for him. The patient may be led to reflect that this way of not relating to others when in need may be an obstacle to the development of a relationship with the therapist.

Why devote the third section to understanding the effect of the interview? Because we have noticed that allowing the patient to express his or her experience of the interview is important. The interview stimulates and activates in some patients a process of reflection and reinterpretation of their past. This promotion of insight is clearly an unpredictable consequence of the clinical use of the AAI, which was originally developed and applied in research with nonclinical populations. Furthermore, we have noticed that some patients' therapeutic progress is accompanied by a change in the AAI classification, evident upon the second or further interviews. In summary, we use this interview for different reasons:

1. It represents an accurate and systematic way either to explore the developmental context of the patient or to get a story that is based on a continuous movement back and forth between daily experiences related not only to "stressful" situations (separations, diseases, accidents, losses) but also to the quality of the care received.
2. It gives the therapist a quick picture of the patient's relational patterns that may be enacted within the therapeutic relationship.
3. It is possible by means of a follow-up interview for the therapist to observe changes in the attachment pattern influenced by the treatment.

We want to stress that rather than being in conflict with the psychoanalytic "way of listening," this approach is very much in concert with it. The framework organizes our observations, and centrally includes an ongoing evaluation of the way patients describe and talk about their current and past attachment experiences. Invariably, we form expectations of the clinical process that will develop in early work with a patient. When administered early in treatment, the AAI may confirm or give new structure to these expectations, giving the therapist vital clues as to what is likely to follow: For instance, a dismissing and devaluing attitude could point to a patient's difficulty linking past and present or to a general transference resistance. On the contrary, a preoccupied or involving attitude from a patient who seems to be collaborative might organize his or her resistance by either overwhelming the therapist with a range of highly emotive material or wandering to irrelevant topics without focusing on a coherent, clinically useful topic.

To illustrate the extent to which, and how, we rely on the AAI in our clinical work, we next provide a description of our basic approach to clinical work. In monitoring the patient's AAI experience and information later shared with the therapist, we aim to link a person's memories of everyday life to past stressful conditions that Bowlby considered relevant for the attachment system (separations, accidents, illnesses, bereavements), and to the quality of caregiving experienced in the past (whether the patient received cold but attentive caregiving, whether he or she had an affectionate caregiver as well, or whether role reversal was present). As is well known, it is not the facts themselves that are telling. Rather, it is more relevant to know how the real experiences were subjectively experienced and processed, and are currently represented in the conversational and linguistic features of the patient's narrative. Indeed, there are sometimes indications of real traumatic experiences that have been worked through well, whereas other, less conspicuous aspects of early caregiving leave deleterious marks on the organization of the mind of the patient.

The Use of the AAI in the Clinical Setting: The Case of "Z"

The first time one of us used the AAI was with an adolescent patient who manifested dissociative symptoms (Muscetta, Dazzi, De Coro, Ortu, & Speranza, 1999). From the mother's account we would have reason to predict that the youngster would have been classified as disorganized as a young child, and his AAI at the time of intake at age 15 was classified unresolved/dismissing (unresolved with regard to past loss and dismissing/restricted in feeling). Also, an interview conducted with his mother was classified as "unresolved/cannot classify" (see Main et al., Chapter 2, this volume). In this case the AAI was helpful in generating a hypothesis about the connection between intergenerational transmission of the incapacity to work and experiences of loss. Analyzing the transcripts of six sessions of psychotherapy with this boy also made it possible to analyze the evolution of coherence.

At the time treatment began, Z was 15 years old, the third son in his family. His eldest brother was 25 years old and lived on his own. The second brother, 22 years old, was a university student in another town. The mother asked for a consultation because of Z's passivity and absent-mindedness, as well as his poor school performance. His passivity in relation to his schoolwork contrasted with his performance on his football (soccer) team, where he enjoyed leadership status. Both parents were disoriented by Z, whose mother described him as so different from his older siblings.

The lengthy telephone conversation resulted in a plan for a consultation in which two psychotherapists would meet the parents with their son in the first session. One psychotherapist would continue meeting with the parents, whereas the other would continue with the boy. A final joint session was planned. All the sessions would be audio-recorded to let both psychotherapists know what was going on.

During the first session, the mother, a 57-year-old teacher, monopolized the conversation. She gave a lot of information, often more than was required. Sometimes she gave the impression that she was lost in her memories, which she described in great detail. On occasion she described events that had occurred 12 years earlier as though they had happened the day before. The psychotherapists, often confused by her way of speaking, were obliged to ask for clarification. The 63-year-old father of Z had difficulty intervening but managed to add brief comments and personal opinions about the facts and memories discussed by his wife. The boy was nearly silent throughout the session. Z's history was described meticulously, although not in an orderly fashion by the mother. In early infancy, during the breast-feeding stage, Z's sleep–wake patterns were irregular: The baby withdrew by sleeping, so that nursing was solicited more often by the mother (who felt the need to empty her breasts) than by the baby's spontaneous request. As an adolescent, Z continued to use sleep as a way to withdraw from relationships. This generally happened after he was pressured by his mother or others who wanted him to study or to pay attention to something. Since early infancy, he had used another "escaping" reaction to distressing situations: In some instances, he became absentminded, showing a sort of "dissociation" that worried his family and teachers. Z was almost completely silent during the first months of the first year of elementary school. His mother described him as follows: "He used to look out of the window. . . . He looked as if he was attracted by the outside. . . . His attention wandered and he had a vacant look on his face. . . . The teacher was really worried."

During this joint session, Z was dressed in the formal attire of an old man and appeared almost spiritless. He hardly replied to specific questions asked of him by the psychotherapists, who hoped to avoid a situation in which the boy felt abandoned or pushed into a corner. Z's answers, while concise and appropriate, were delivered in a weak voice.

During his first individual session, Z spoke casually without much of a problem. The therapist began by asking Z if he wanted to say something after the session with his parents. He proposed to speak about what had happened since they had last seen each other. Z made an accurate report of his days devoted to the preparation for the end of the school quarter: oral and written examinations, hours of study, home work. The tone of Z's voice, the richness of detail in his account, and his tendency to use very long pauses were difficult for the psychotherapist. He felt bored as he noticed that Z could gradually drift into a silent zone, similar to that in which he was confined by the mother's insistence on discussing his school problems during the first consultation. The psychotherapist was very curious about his own boredom: He had no personal reason to be tired or bored, and so he considered his boredom to be something that belonged to the patient, according to the hypothesis that Z was not able to express this feeling and/or was not conscious of it. In other words, the psychotherapist decided to consider his own feeling as a communication coming from the patient, who was probably bored because he was obliged to dedicate all his time to school. The therapist started to comment on this emotion. As Z was giving details of his days and his homework, the therapist started to make comments on the situation during the pauses, at the same time noting the sad and resigned expression on the boy's face, the thin tone of his voice, and the overall lifeless attitude of his body[2]: "What a pain! Every day really looks the day before. It is not possible just to study all day long."

This kind of intervention seemed to give a little life to the boy. It became clearly evident that Z spent so much time doing homework because his concentration was continuously disturbed by an idea that appeared to be a compulsive one: "Tomorrow there is the oral test." Such obsessive ideas also disturbed him in different situations. On the previous Saturday evening, when Z was watching a movie with his brother, he was not able to wholly enjoy it because he was continuously thinking," On Monday I have a mathematics exam."

The psychotherapist described this phenomenon as a kind of "screen" that interfered in Z's life and in his experiences. This could be the explanation for the difficulty he had in doing all sorts of things; the "screen" kept every experience at a distance, as if it could always be a kind of danger for him.

THERAPIST: As far as you can remember, when was the first time you noticed something like this?

Z: It always happened to me. . . . Actually, I don't remember.

THERAPIST: You really can't give me just the first episode when something similar to this happened?

Z: I was playing football. I was 12 or 13 years old. . . . I really don't remember . . . and I started to miss the ball.

THERAPIST: Perhaps something which can happen also here, now, when I speak to you?

Z agreed with this last comment by the therapist and communicated with a painful look that throughout the session he had the recurring disturbing thought: "Afterwards I have still to do my homework."

To avoid the phenomenon of decreased attention during the five sessions, it was necessary for the therapist to alternate interaction initiatives with occasions in which he respected unusually long pauses (more than 50 seconds). The therapist believed that this strategy helped diminish the patient's recurring dissociative or "disorganized/disoriented" behavior in the relationship. Below, we first give some more data from Z's history, then describe facets of his symptomatology, and the improvements and changes that took place during this brief treatment.

Z's Early Infancy

Z's sleep–wake patterns were irregular. When Z was 2–3 years old, he began having *pavor nocturnus* (night terror) crises that lasted until he was 13 years old. Z was conceived just a few months after his mother lost her own mother. Moreover, his mother had two tragic pregnancies prior to Z's conception: a newborn sister who died just after delivery and another child lost in the sixth month of pregnancy. Throughout the entire pregnancy with Z, his mother was profoundly disturbed and awaited his birth in a state of terror. Her internal representations of the new baby were practically inhibited to the degree that she could hardly anticipate what her relationship with this son would be like. She experienced the pregnancy, as well as the first year of life with Z, in a state of suspension, without a sense of time passing.

Z's Current Symptomatology

Z had two completely different ways of being absentminded: Sometimes he was just daydreaming, but at other times he felt that he had no more thoughts in his mind. Z felt really disoriented and frightened by these moments, because he felt that he was different from other people.

> "I can be absentminded even when I play in football matches. In fact the coach tries to wake me up, because he thinks I am looking some place other than where the action is. It is as if my brain wants to have a rest: I am not thinking any more. That's the difference: Other people are day-dreaming, they still do have thoughts, and I am spellbound."

This lack of continuity in Z's mental functioning also appeared in one dream:

> "It was summertime. . . . I was in a village in which my parents have a holiday house, and I was going down some steps toward a terrace with a wonderful view of the sea. Suddenly everything turned black. . . . I was-n't able to see anymore . . . everything disappeared. . . . In any case, I continued to go down but the steps looked broken, so that I was obliged to jump, and when I was jumping blackouts were alternating with moments of normal vision."

In parallel with the therapist's modifications in his relational approach, Z began to take the initiative in the conversation more frequently. Gradually his depressive attitude seemed to decrease, and Z reported being more active in school. At the same time, after some encouragement in therapy to give voice to his feelings, Z showed a new ability to think in an organized way about the motivations that guided his behavior. An example of this new mode of relating is presented in the following:

> "When I've done my homework after dinner, often I just go straight to bed, not only because I've finished studying, since I could watch televi-sion perhaps, but just because of some fear, I don't know . . . anxiety. When I have done homework also in the evening, I don't like to do any-

thing more, and I go to sleep and I sponge [block] out everything I've done during the day, I mean I try to sponge it out at night."

In these short sentences we recognize some of those "metacognitive processes" that are believed to be reliable indicators of an ability "to reflect on the validity, nature and source" of one's own mental representation of experience (Main, 1991). In Z's case, such metacognitive monitoring of activities suggests the possibility that Z is reorganizing his past experiences (we want to emphasize that Z's sleep consistently had been connected to disengagement strategies in his past) and, consequently, his thoughts about himself and how his mind worked.

The changes in the teacher's evaluation of Z were also reported by Z's mother, together with the great change in the relationship between herself and her son. [Z's comments, as reported by his mother, are in brackets.]

"Yes, he behaves . . . that is . . . he is really nervous at the moment. In the past he was more quiet, although his quietness was probably only apparent . . . but he managed to be quiet. . . . Now he easily flies in a rage . . . and he is getting a little rebellious. ['It's not possible! . . . I can't study all week, including the weekend.'] And yesterday he was fixing his bike . . . and he started to kick it because he wasn't able to insert a screw. He can be violent. I have never seen him like he is at the moment . . . and also now, when he comes back from school, he comes in the kitchen where I am cooking. ['Stop, Mom, you have to listen to me.'] He has been like this for 20 days . . . and he starts speaking of the school, what's happened. ['They are preparing a school trip to Paris.'] The teacher promised them and da da and da da. He speaks and he speaks. . . . He never did this in the past. And also in school . . . the teachers found a way to let him speak and participate, assuming that a normal oral test is difficult. . . . Now he starts to ask to speak and to intervene on different topics, so that they know that he studied."

The mother was really pleased, because Z finally spoke to her. Their relationship improved, and there were fewer moments in which the boy was absentminded, a behavior that, as we mentioned already, was very frightening to her.

AAI Classifications of Z and His Mother

Z's AAI

With regard to the category of attachment assigned to Z's AAI, all judges agreed to classify this interview as Ud/Ds3: Unresolved–disorganized–restricted. The U category is assigned when indices of lack of resolution of mourning are present, specifically, lapses in the monitoring of speech or reasoning, leading to incoherence and confused statements. When these emerge during the discussion of events surrounding the loss of an attachment figure, as was the case in Z's interview, the transcript received a score of 7 on the relevant 9-point scale (where a score of 6 or above automatically leads the rater to judge the interview as belonging to the U category). In Z's interview, this judgment was based on his absorbed/confused/disorganized retelling of the death of his four grandparents, including his maternal grandmother, who had died before his birth. The Ds classification was assigned on the basis of Z's continuous attempts to limit the influence of attachment relationships and experiences. The adolescent's organization of thought appeared to permit attachment to remain relatively deactivated through idealization of his parents and strong discrepancies between his semantic evaluation of his past (as normal or positive) and the probable episodic (adverse) details of his past experience. The Ds3 subcategory "restricted in feeling" was justified by Z's moderate insistence on lack of memory for childhood, yet he was able to report negative experiences; a "feeling" response to such memories, however, appeared to be absent, and Z repeatedly disavowed any negative influence on himself. The score for coherence of transcript of this AAI was 3. Metacognitive processes were found to be completely absent (1).

The Mother's AAI

The mother's AAI was classified as unresolved/cannot classify (U/CC): This latter category has been justified by the presence of an unusual mixture of mental states with respect to attachment: while the descriptors of the state of mind relevant to her past relationship with her mother met the Ds subcategory (Ds3, "restricted in feeling"), memories and representations of her father seemed instead to be organized in a markedly "preoccupied" (E) manner, in which she demonstrated an angry, involved state of mind (subcategory E2, "angry/conflicted"), which was even more noticeable since her father had died, many years earlier, when she was 8 years old. In this case, demonstrating in one interview two distinct and incompatible insecure states of mind (e.g., Ds and E) led to the CC assignment. (For a full discussion of considerations regarding CC, see Main et al., Chapter 2, this volume.) The score for coherence of this transcript was very low (2), partly justified by a very high score on the scale of "unresolved loss" (8). Low levels of metacognitive processes were scored on the basis of a limited ability to reflect about her present relationships with her husband and sons (2).

From the attachment interviews of both Z and his mother, a peculiar inability to cope with loss seemed to be transmitted from mother to son, as evident in the speech patterns of each when discussing the same losses. We want to report here two examples of incoherence on the AAI regarding past experiences of loss, from Z and from his mother, respectively, to point out the surprising similarities in their mental organization of such experiences.

Example of Incoherence in Z's AAI

THERAPIST: When you were a little child, did you see your grandparents?

Z: Umm, no, because they were already dead. No . . . wait a moment . . . my father's father was still alive . . . but he lived in Naples, so. . . . My mother's parents instead . . . umm, no . . . but we knew each other better (maternal grandparents), because during the summer we are all together and so we are all together for 3 months.

THERAPIST: Ah . . .

Z: *We see* each other,[3] but I didn't see them.

(Note Z's sudden change to use of the *present tense* in speaking about long since dead grandparents—a lapse in the monitoring of reasoning.)

Example of Incoherence in the Mother's AAI

THERAPIST: Did you see your grandparents when you were little?

MOTHER: Yes . . . so . . . yes, in V. Indeed they are dead, three . . . no, my father's mother . . . no, she had died by delivery, then no, they were left orphans, so not . . . but my maternal grandparents and my paternal grandfather . . . we lived all together in V., yes, I remember it very, well. From my mother's part . . . umm . . . I always saw . . . the relationship with my mother was somewhat . . . strange: Mom *is* a very silent woman, very reserved. . . . I don't know. . . . She doesn't like . . . I can't tell you.

(Note the mother's sudden change to speaking of her dead mother's qualities in the *present tense*.)

Example of Avoidance in Z's Therapy Discourse

THERAPIST: Yes, this we saw also the other time: This idea of homework is a sort of obsessive thought which never leaves you. It disturbs you perhaps and doesn't allow you to do what you want to, because you are always thinking of what is going to happen. Also now, as you were coming in, you were already thinking of your lesson and what you have to do afterwards.

Z: But I'm a little happy, because my brother is coming. So there is some happiness.

(Note how Z does not respond to the therapist's remarks, and instead shifts focus and changes the subject.)

Two points are of interest for scoring the coherence of transcripts of the therapeutic sessions involving Z. The first is the relatively steady decrease in incoherence scores, observed via close study of the psychotherapy transcripts rated in terms of the extent to which Z violated the Gricean maxim, the cooperation principle in conversation; that is, session by session, through the to-and-fro conversation with his therapist, Z became less "incoherent." This is most evident in the newly organized way he narrated his personal experience, feelings, and emotions.

The second point is that Z appeared to have changed something in his prevailing conversational strategies. In scoring the six psychotherapy transcripts on these two dimensions (Ds and E) we found that whereas the Ds scores of incoherence, which were clearly dominant in his style of conversation during the interview, tended to decrease, the E scores tended to remain stable and even to increase slightly across the sessions. Such scores were assigned mostly for indicators of "oscillations" in Z's point of view and of some run-on and confusing sentences, in which he reported direct quotations from his parents' speech. Whereas some may view the shift from incoherence with a Ds quality to incoherence with more of an E quality as less than optimal, in clinical work with disturbed patients, the pendulum can swing from a range of attachment states of mind and, we hope, converge on a road to more autonomous–secure, balanced representations.

Discussion of Z and His Mother

Mother's Traumatic Experiences, Early Empathic Failures, and Z's Probable Attachment Status: Underpinning Links to the Adolescent's Troubles

We conceptualized Z's maladaptive behavior, as well as his symptomatology, as linked to the difficulties his mother had in establishing the good affective attunement with him in infancy, something that could easily be connected with the mother's mourning the loss of her own mother and the loss of two previous babies from which she seemed unable to recover.

There are many different ways of processing loss of a loved person. Sometimes a pregnancy is a kind of reaction to the loss of a loved person. In these cases, a particular kind of ambiguous dead–live internal object seems to be created, and the loss is processed through projective substitutions: The newborn becomes a designated loss carrier. This may have been the fate of Z, at least insofar as his early development was concerned.

The concept of a frightening–frightened mother (Main & Hesse, 1990) is useful in understanding the situation described by Z's mother (her history, that of her child, and her relationship with him), as well as Z's symptomatology and his relationship with the psychotherapist. Main (1981) emphasized the importance of fear in the activation of attachment behavior. The parent is a safety figure for the child, and if he or she frightens the child, a paradoxical situation takes place: The source of danger (from which the child is supposed to escape) is at the same time meant to be the child's secure base. This paradoxical situation, which cannot be resolved behaviorally, provokes a breakdown of the child's behavioral and attention strategies. The frightened and/or frightening behavior of Z's mother (which is easily imaginable if one remembers her description of her peculiar way to breast-feed) could be the linking mechanism that helps us understand Z's disoriented/disorganized behavior, which presumably began in infancy and was still present at the time of the consultation.

Examples we gave from AAIs of both Z and his mother support the hypothesis of an intergenerational transmission of pronounced difficulties with resolving mourning and, in a more general way, with processing information in an organized and coherent fashion. As Hesse elaborates:

> Lapses may in various ways represent either interference from normally dissociated memory systems or unusual absorptions involving memories triggered by the discussion of traumatic events. Lapses in reasoning and in the monitoring of discourse suggest the possibility of "states shifts" where the individual has entered a peculiar, compartmentalized state of mind involving a particular traumatic experience. Both lapses and the sudden appearance of incompatible ideas suggest momentary but qualitative changes in the influence of memory upon consciousness. (1996, p. 4)

"The peculiar breast-feeding" (as defined by Z's mother) could perhaps be considered a precursor to many disengagement processes Z later used to avoid difficult situations. When Z was a baby, his incredibly long sleeping periods (10–15 hours) could also be described in terms of adaptive behavior to a threatening environment that awaited him when awake. It is well known that a breast-feeding mother gives her baby much more than just milk. The emotional availability systems in the mother and child go some way in explaining the reciprocal nature of rewards that can generally be detected in parent–infant interactions. Because of the loss of her own mother and that of her two previous children, Z's mother was evidently so anxious that she was not able to imagine Z in the future. She was always close to a state of terror, fearing what could possibly happen. This would have inhibited her normal interaction with the child. Z, faced with his anxious mother, avoided the uncomfortable situation by sleeping, further aggravating his mother's anxiety about breast-feeding when her breasts became painfully filled with milk. At this point, she might well have blamed the infant Z for her discomfort ("He refuses to eat, so I am in pain"), only worsening her relationship with Z. Between feedings, Z's mother was absent from the relationship, lost in her memories and panicking about the future.

> "It was really very strange. . . . I was looking at Z and I knew that he was growing up, but I couldn't really see him growing. . . . The delivery took place in February, but I don't remember the months from February to June. It was June and for me it was always February. I wasn't able to think that Z was capable of growing up. I was seeing him always in that

specific time . . . as if I had been able to stop time every time I was looking at him. I do imagine my other two children in the future. . . . I am
capable of imagining them. This does not happen with Z. He is what he
is in this specific moment. . . . This has been the way I accepted him
from the very beginning. I panicked about 'the day after.' . . . Since the
pregnancy started I had fear of time and I wanted to stop it. Then the
delivery . . . and every day I was looking at him and I used to tell to
myself: 'I am not able to imagine him when he will walk.' I didn't have a
'process of anticipation' about his future . . . I don't know . . . I had fear.
I don't know if any of this has been transmitted to Z. . . . I don't believe
so because I have never spoken with him about this. I don't know . . .
and yet they say that if during pregnancy. . . . I don't know."

   Whereas most of the mother's behavior was related to her own traumatic
experiences rather than to aspects of the ongoing interaction with Z, this did
not ameliorate the situation, as has been emphasized by Main and Hesse
(1992), because the mother was not comprehensible to the child and "owing
to the fact that what is producing fear in the parent is attachment-related, the
infant may occasionally become confused in the parent's mind either with the
parent herself or with those attachment figures whose death or behavior produced the original trauma" (p. 86). The parent behavior can be particularly
frightening to the child, especially when the parent is in a kind of trance
status—"He is there and not there"—and this can force the child to develop a
frightening internal representation whose source is not available (Main &
Hesse, 1992).
   The continuous exposure to situations in which ambiguity, confusion,
and fear characterize the mother–infant relationship can determine that particular disoriented behavior observed in the Strange Situation. This behavior
may well persist, as it appears to have done in Z's case, and whereas his
behavior was not overtly disorganized (as we see in a preverbal infant), it indicated a lack of orientation toward the surrounding environment, which Z,
with an amazed expression on his face, seemed to perceive as being immov-
able. It is plausible that the episodes of absentmindedness described by the
mother, and Z's own propensities in this direction, represent the continuation
of Z's early terrifying and disorganizing interactions with his mother.

Infant Disorganized Attachment Status and Vulnerability to Dissociative Disorders

Liotti, who suggested (1992) that people who were disorganized/disoriented
(D) during infancy are more prone to develop later dissociative disorders, provided empirical evidence to support and extend this suggestion.
   According to DSM-IV the essential feature in the dissociative disorders is
a disruption in the usually integrated functions of consciousness, memory,
identity, or perception of the environment. It is well known that trauma is a

central element in the etiology of dissociative disorders. Not just major traumas are considered as possible starting points for dissociative disorders: Our clinical material suggests the possibility of extending the notion of trauma to disadaptive caregiving relationships. In fact, the parents of Z were not abusive in the strict sense of the word, but they were inconsistent as caregivers.

According to Liotti (1992), there is a connection between a mother's mourning experiences during the perinatal life of a child and the presence of disorders in the child's state of consciousness, which may be the main area involved in that individual's psychopathology as an adult. Liotti also considers dissociative disorders to be similar to hypnotic states, noting that a "trance status" results when the patient is not able to integrate an inescapable interpersonal situation with his or her cognitive schema. The situation is similar to that in which a child cannot avoid the activation of the attachment system during the interaction with a frightening and/or frightened caregiver.

Thus, from this initial exploration of the clinical usefulness of the AAI with Z and his mother, we were inspired to rely on the AAI in further clinical work involving diverse mental ill-health. In each case, the AAI has helped forge a therapeutic alliance, illuminated the inner world of the interviewed patient, and played a vital role in shaping, monitoring, and evaluating clinical progress. We continue with a detailed case study showing how the AAI may help a clinician understand the developmental origins of complex pathology, and to operate at multiple levels in the service of clinical progress.

Marco's Case: Obsessive–Compulsive Disorder in an Alexithimic and Dissociative Patient

When Marco was 22 years old, he began treatment twice a week, the first stage of which lasted for 5 months. Treatment was interrupted for some months but resumed, with the patient attending four sessions a week.

Marco's parents were professionals, and he lost his mother when he was 10 years old. When the therapist saw Marco for the first time, he had been attending a university for more than 2 years but had yet to take any exams. His social life seemed to be on the wane; every time he was to see friends (which occurred less and less) there were frequent arguments concerning his behavior: He was often late and unreliable.

During the first session Marco gave the therapist a very contradictory picture of his difficulties in studying: On the one hand, he emphatically pointed out his interests in the subjects and the faculty; on the other, when the therapist tried to learn the reason why Marco had not taken an exam yet, Marco assumed a "skiver" (idle, lazy) attitude: "I don't wanna study. I try, but then I get bored."

After his wife's death, Marco's father lived with him until he was 18 years old, then he remarried and moved into another apartment. He now had a 2-year-old child, but Marco could not stand this situation, because seeing his stepmother, Francesca, reminded him of his mother and made him think about his past, which in turn saddened him. So he avoided seeing both his step-mother and his half-brother. Once a week his father stays in the apartment where Marco has been living with his nanny since he was 4 years old.

From the first session, the therapist realized that Marco would be a tough nut to crack, because his contradictory attitude toward studying was also present in the relationship with the therapist. He asked the therapist to help him, but at the same time conveyed a wish not to speak, because he was not able to bear anything related to his own past, of which he seems to remember little.

However, his phobia, concerning past memories, along with the issue of his mother's loss, were severe and diffuse. Marco had developed a defensive barrier against all things that could make him think of his past. During sessions Marco strongly defended himself against any kind of interpretations that the therapist tried to give to his words or behavior. Because of Marco's critical, hostile, rejecting attitude, kidding him had become a kind of game for the therapist—a game that Marco began to appreciate, to expect, and to antici-pate.

This avoidance of childhood matters was also clearly anticipated in Marco's AAI. Two AAI raters, who knew nothing about Marco's case, both pointed out three features supporting the classification of unresolved mourning/cannot classify/fearfully preoccupied/dismissing–idealizing (U/CC/E3b/Ds1) These classifications describe Marco's (1) traumatic memory loss; (2) unresolved loss; and (3) an idealized picture of his father and an impover-ished memory for childhood. The following passages of the interview are related to Marco's (1) being bothered by recalling past fearful experiences; (2) poor episodic memory; (3) metacognitive processes, evident in a couple of pas-sages, that emphasize how the questions themselves began to activate a pro-cess of insight; and (4) linguistic and conversational features supporting the two judges' unresolved loss classification.

Excerpts from Marco's AAI

THERAPIST: I would like you to describe your relationship with your par-ents as a young child, starting as far back as you can remember.

MARCO: Here we go (smiles). Beside the fact is that I don't remember very well, I have to tell you that it's very hard for me. . . . It's hard because it bothers me; looking back at my past bothers me . . . ask-ing myself questions about those times, about how and why, well . . . you know, it does really bother me. . . . I have a barrier and I don't know either why or where it came up. I don't know the reason. . . . I have nothing against anybody . . . but the annoyance is there and it's a real one. It bothers me to talk about the good relationship, it's that.

THERAPIST: Was it a good one?

MARCO: Yes . . . no, not too good, no. . . . It's that there were things that shocked me when I was a child, I don't know, like the typical china pot that falls down on your head (*he laughs*). No, no, everything goes well. It's all good, but let's put it this way: I don't wanna talk about it, that's it. I know I have to talk about it; otherwise you will not have anything to work on.

THERAPIST: Can't you do it?

MARCO: (*Clears his throat*) No, well . . . well . . . it bothers me.

THERAPIST: Does it bother you to recall these things?

MARCO: Yes . . . yes, it does. . . . Yes, it does bother me . . . any . . . anything. . . . It bothers me to recall everything related to that period . . . I mean, now I'm fine, so why do I have to remember things that make me upset? . . . I mean, it's like getting myself in trouble. That's why I have overcome these memories. I mean, it bothers me.

Marco's preference for positive words to describe his attachment history and his pronounced difficulty with actually remembering (the feature of his transcript leading to the Ds1 classification) are further evident when he tries to answer the question and probes concerning his representation of his relationship with his mother as a young child.

THERAPIST: Could you pick five adjectives that would describe your relationship as a young child with your mother?

MARCO: (*Pauses*) Well, the relationship was great! (*smiles*)

THERAPIST: So, you have said *great*. Then we'll see about the other adjectives . . .

MARCO: Well, great! I mean, great, good, all those positive adjectives that one could choose.

THERAPIST: Well, now would you give me a specific memory from your childhood, just one, so that I could see why the relationship was great?

MARCO: Well great, great . . . great, 'cause I say so, obviously? Obviously, there is a reason, I say so because, obviously, even if I don't remember certain things. I mean, however, there is. . . . It's obvious, I say it's great not just to say it, I say it because it's great, I know. I mean, do you know what I mean?

THERAPIST: Do you mean it in general?

MARCO: Of course, I know it's great.

THERAPIST: Can you give me an example?

MARCO: An example! Like it's not . . . well, I mean not great because . . . I don't know. . . . He took me to the toy store, great because we were fine . . . for this reason. And you would ask me what was this "we were fine"? An example . . .

THERAPIST: When . . .

MARCO: An example . . . I have so many memories . . . like . . . we used to make jokes, although . . . it bothers me.

THERAPIST: That you used to make jokes, it's a general thing?

MARCO: Yeah, I know. But I don't remember.

THERAPIST: Don't you remember even an episode?

MARCO: No, not a specific one.

THERAPIST: A memory, the memory of an episode?

MARCO: No, not really, not a specific one.

THERAPIST: Not a specific one?

MARCO: No. . . . I don't . . . no, not a specific one . . . I mean, not words. I remember that . . . we were fine but I don't remember words, exchanges of words . . . but in the end it's like . . . it's like a chapter of my life was closed, it's like I want to split it in two parts. Just take away everything that really bothers me. . . . I see myself as a different one. Do you understand me?

Once in a while Marco seemed to be able to recognize the discrepancy between the description of his own past experiences as being perfect and the sorrow he was actually feeling:

"Yeah . . . yeah . . . great, even though recalling my own past bothers me. It's weird 'cause it was great. . . . Why does this bother me? No, I don't understand. It's nonsense, I can't explain it. I, I would say . . . if it were a bad thing . . . while, on the contrary . . . it was . . . I don't know, I have no idea."

Since the coherence of his answers was quite low, this metacognitive activity was striking. When Marco realized that the therapist's questions confront him with the discrepancies between his representation of the past and his emotional reactions, Marco began to get in trouble. For instance, although he believed he got over the loss of his mother thanks to his father's dedication to him (although he also felt that it lacked the sincerity he deserved), he answered questions about his mother's death.

MARCO: And yet, I have been helped a lot. I mean, I have a good dad, so I wonder why, what was I missing? Nothing, he was a father and a mother to me, so why did I feel empty? Yes, maybe it's not the same but . . . it was good. I don't ask for, I mean I don't ask . . . I mean, of course I feel bad (*his tone of voice becomes more mellow*), but maybe I'm fine this way, and it bothers me to recall and to analyze, too. . . . It bothers me to recall the dialogues we had.

THERAPIST: Do you remember any of them?

MARCO: No, I remember when my mother and I were having fun.

THERAPIST: And how old were you at that time?

MARCO: Well, I don't know. Ten. Bho!

THERAPIST: And before 10 years old?

MARCO: Ah, when I was a young child?

THERAPIST: Yeah, when you were 5, 6 years old?

MARCO: No, I don't remember! I don't say it on purpose. . . . It's 'cause . . . there's a blank.

The lack of episodic memory is less evident concerning Marco's relationship with his father. However, even in this situation, what emerges is a vague memory of the relationship as emphatically positive, but without access to a specific episode. When Marco is asked to give an example of the good relationship, he describes an episode charged with emotional content, not all of which was positive, as in the following dialogue about Marco's mother's death:

THERAPIST: I would like to ask you about the loss of your mother. How old were you when . . . ?

MARCO: Well, I was . . . it was summer, last year of high . . . it happened on July 19th, last year of elementary, well, elementary school was over. . . . What do you want me to tell you? Where did I learn about it?

THERAPIST: Where did you learn about it and how did you react? Do you remember it?

MARCO: This is important for you, isn't it? Well, I went to bed. (*His tone of voice has already changed; he is anxious and speaks fast.*) I knew she was at the hospital, but I couldn't even think about it. (*He laughs.*)

THERAPIST: Why at the hospital?

MARCO: I don't know, I really don't know . . . and you know, nothing has been hidden to me. I was staying at my aunt's. She's another character you should know about. It's important, she's a real aunt, she's my father's sister, she's very smart. It's incredible. . . . She's the one who made me go for treatment, she's the one who gave me this suggestion . . . well, hmm . . . what was I talking about? Ah, about the loss, yeah!

THERAPIST: You were saying that you were staying at your aunt's.

MARCO: That I was staying at my aunt's. . . . Well, that day I found out that in the morning, well, they had already learnt about it at eight o'clock . . . and they told me that my uncle had already learnt about it but he had to pretend he didn't know . . . and then my aunt drove me to my grandma's. . . . It sure is hard! It's hard to talk about it.

THERAPIST: Was it unexpected?

MARCO: Yeah, yes it's hard, it's hard, and this is really hard. (*He sighs.*) I found out through my grandmother, and everybody else behaved as if nothing had happened . . . obviously. Dad came . . . and he said it to me. Well, it bothers me. Do you know that even to talk about this, it bothers me? It's also because I see you, I mean, I know I have to talk about it, but it bothers me.

THERAPIST: Didn't you talk about it with anybody else before?

MARCO: Of course not, it's something I don't want to . . . what's the purpose of describing how I mourned? Here is the reason, I'll say it! I know it in other situations! And clearly . . . and then they are private things, they are things that . . . obviously they are sad, even though everything went smooth after all. Hmm . . . they are things . . . I mean, I know it would help you more, but it bothers me even though . . . I mean it was my father that told me about it. . . . He told me. He came into my room. . . . He burst into tears and me too. Mom is dead and . . . then, then everything was fine. I mean he has been really . . . and then he, we took off for a beautiful trip to Mexico for 21 days . . . beautiful and from there . . . from there nothing. Everything was fine and then I went, I started the sixth grade, seventh, eighth, great during the eighth grade. I used to study with my father, spend time with him, travel with him. I used to go out. I used to go out with my friends. I liked it a lot, I used to go out a lot. I mean with the right curfew I started to go to the disco. During my junior and senior years . . . in the afternoon, you know? Hmm, and then everything was a bed of roses.

The authors of the AAI coding manual (Main et al., 2002) consider narratives that wander to irrelevant topics and suddenly change topic, rooted in a lack of monitoring of one's own speech, as noted in the earlier indices of Marco's unresolved loss. Thus, Marco's interview is assigned to the U category regarding past loss. A related feature of unresolved mourning that is a factor in a fearfully preoccupied state of mind (E3b), as was the case in Marco's interview, is evidence of the ongoing impact of traumatic memory loss from childhood. "Yeah . . . yes, memories bother me. That's the reason why I get rid of them when they come up."

Thus, it may be clear, from the speech examples above, why Marco's AAI was classified variously as U/CC/E3b/Ds1.

After a month of working together, Marco revealed to the therapist that he actually had particular memories that he called "photograms," which slipped into his mind like unwelcome guests, to stop his normal ideative process, and make him shake his head and squeeze his eyes while he tried to get rid of them. Marco's life had become a nightmare; on the one hand, he was frightened by these "photograms" undermining his capacity to study; on the other hand, complex obsessive rituals emerged, especially when he needed to get dressed. Actually this was why, in addition to his blunting and lack of attention, Marco was always late. The interview revealed not only traumatic memory loss, which the therapist thought was a result of Marco's loss of his mother, but also a kind of "hyperamnesia" made of "photograms" and filled with perceptual details.

As previously stated, the first phase of treatment was interrupted after 5 months, when Marco had to leave for military service because he had not taken any exams at university. Those few difficult months were characterized by Marco's strong annoyance with any kind of interpretation the therapist made, which in turn provoked Marco's obsessive ideation, "photograms," shaking his head, and bluntness. Sometimes he could not even speak about what he had done during the day. He tried but he soon stopped, telling the therapist, "I don't wanna go to the psychiatrist. . . . No . . . for God's sake, you are nice . . . but I don't wanna." Although he was often late, Marco never missed a session and he continued to attend. A mutual positive relationship was established. The therapist was very careful because Marco tried to seduce and flatter him to remain distant from his own problems. The overall atmosphere of the therapeutic situation was characterized by idealization that Marco seemed intent upon recreating on the heels of the idealized relationship with his father. Aware that only a lively environment could protect Marco against the possible reoccurrence of negative experiences, the therapist made the decision to give Marco space for an essentially supportive relationship, focusing on quick, short answers and making remarks about what was happening in the here and now. One of the therapist's main practical goals—one that was not always achieved—was to keep Marco from reexperiencing traumas within the sessions. The therapist came to realize more and more that Marco's poor collaboration and oppositional stance was a strategy aimed at dismissing his severe inability to use his own mind—a mind that tended to fall apart and withdraw from any kind of relationship with the therapist.

When Marco resumed treatment, many things had changed in the meantime. The "photograms" seemed to have faded, and Marco had decided to visit his father's new apartment. However, the return of obsessive thoughts bothered Marco, and he was able to note that they arose especially when "Francesca was there . . . and not my mother." He also had an affair with a girl that lasted a few months, during which Marco first had sexual intercourse. When this affair ended, he deteriorated greatly. While Marco was dating this girl, many dissociative episodes occurred. Any little thing was enough to unleash long phases of narrow-mindedness and withdrawal, all signs that, along with the loss of erection, were experienced by the girl as index of his lack of interest and love. Actually it was worry over failure of this relationship that induced Marco to ask for treatment the second time.

There was also an ambiguous statement in the first AAI. The therapist discovered that Marco's mother had had severe depression that probably started during pregnancy and continued into his infancy. She had been on medication for many years but with little success. Marco also showed the therapist a photo album that indicated his mother's beauty before her pregnancy, and showed how her face became swollen and lacked any emotional expression after she was medicated. His mother's intensive care and hospitalizations were so traumatic for Marco that even now he claimed not to know why she had died. So which of so many possibly threatening experiences was the core traumatic experience for Marco? Was it the loss of his mother? Why did he keep on getting confused about the day of her death, saying that he was 12 years old, when she died while he was actually 10? What happened when he was 12 years old? The therapist began to think that the loss of his mother was not the *origin* of Marco's difficulties, but something that had happened long before that.

At 12 years, Marco had his first ejaculation, so his pubertal development may have been difficult. Perhaps when he was 12 years old, it was not the real mother who died but the mother of his childhood, the mother of his infantile self. Could entrance into puberty be considered "traumatic" in the same manner as the development of sexuality, as Laufer, Moses, and Laufer (1984) and Laufer (1984) suggested, or might the onset of new cognitive skills, as Piaget (1936) (1936) studied in such detail, and which nowadays Fonagy, Gergely, Jurist, and Target (2002) highlighted, have been an important time for the emergence of the mentalization abilities? The emergence of abstract thinking, as these authors suggest, can create a considerable tension in the mental system of the adolescent. This strong enhancement of the themes connected to developmental discontinuity can certainly help us in understanding the severe obsessive symptomatology from puberty on.

A second turning point occurred after the summer break in treatment. Marco decided to enroll in another major, statistics, and for some months seemed to be another person. He attended lectures with real interest and punctuality, took notes, and studied. His father, who had given him up as lost, could not believe his eyes. Marco began taking care of himself and, above all, he passed two exams with flying colors. Marco often visited his father and was an affectionate big brother. The university was not only a place for studying, but there was also lots of opportunity for contact with other students and the patient's harsh defenses were severely put to the test. All this newness was too much for him. He was used to living in his own private world, surrounded by capsules of obsessive ideas. Difficulties in studying arose again, but this time, so did a new social life. Marco hung out with fellow students and had an affair with a girl that lasted 1 month and was characterized by a reassuring, intense, and satisfying sexual relationship. However, his improvements were always followed by a new emergence of obsessive and dissociative symptoms, though they were less and less severe.

At the beginning of every session Marco tried to gauge the therapist's mood. "How are you?" was frequently his first question, and soon afterward he would scan the therapist's face in a worried and at the same time suspicious way. This effort in monitoring the therapist's mood was reminiscent of what a blind man does when he touches someone else's face with his hands to get a picture of what the person whom he cannot see looks like. It was also reminiscent of the need to monitor, evaluate, and control the (feared) relational partner, which is well documented in the literature on developmental sequelae of infant disorganization. Marco's expectations were seldom correct: Although they were not necessarily projections, most of the time they were random and confused. Marco's inability to monitor his therapist's mood adequately reflected his incapacity to read his own mental states.

Marco discovered a new sensation, namely, that he felt lonely. This was the result of his move toward living in his apartment on his own. Helped by some friends, he was able to prepare the apartment and learn how to select an appropriate roommate. However, the more things Marco did, the more clearly his inadequacy to deal with his life became evident. He also became aware of feeling an emotion he said he never felt before: fear. Whatever he decided to do—for example, whether or not to have a chat with a potential roommate, whether or not to talk with a worker in charge of remodeling the apartment, whether or not to go to the university to study with his colleagues at the library—Marco was always afraid and he now understood that this might be the reason he refused to face the realities of everyday life.

In the first AAI, Marco showed a strong idealization of his father. However, this idealized relationship was no longer defendable, causing a series of conflictual situations between Marco and his father. Treatment was undermined by either Marco's idealized relationship with the therapist or an unempathic controversy with his father, who became very critical and started saying that Marco was getting worse and always talking back. Marco replied that his father did not "know a damn" about him and that he felt he was getting better while strongly defending his new discoveries related to feeling lonely, scared, and nervous: "It's an improvement; I couldn't feel anything before." This relational awkwardness was not just in relation to his father: Marco also behaved provocatively toward the therapist and other people (friends, potential girlfriends, acquaintances) in a way that easily triggered arguments, offenses, irritation, and misunderstandings that in turn could have led to the breakup of relationships and emotional links. At the same time, Marco was involved with other people in a much more engaging way than had previously been possible.

The Readministration of the AAI

The AAI, administered once again after 2 years of treatment, showed a change in Marco's attachment classification, moving from a deeply troubled U/CC/E3b/Ds1 initial classification to a much more organized, albeit insecure–fearfully and passively preoccupied (E1/E3) state of mind.

This shift in classification importantly demonstrated a reduction in the level of traumatic memory or unresolved loss, a change with obvious implications for Marco's possible future children in terms of the buffer it provides against the otherwise probable transmission across generations of unresolved–disorganized attachment patterns. The "photogram" memories gradually lost their perceptual liveliness and were replaced with thoughts characterized by more typical obsessive ideation. Altogether, Marco had become alive to emotion in himself and others, and while not yet autonomous–secure in his AAI, he had achieved an organized state of mind with respect to attachment. Over time, this strategy of preoccupation might be expected to lead to a more settled emotional state. Therapy seemed to have helped Marco make the vital step toward resolution of the loss of his mother, and launch him on a path that might lead to greater ease with his adult sexual self.

Discussion

In terms of Marco's severe incapacity to recognize his own and others' feelings, which could be traced to a relational failure, we could also see this as representing severe impairment of a mental function that is essential for adequate development of the socialization process. As Bruner suggested in the early 1980s, an adult's parenting quality is represented by his or her tendency to try to look at all the child's signals and gestures in terms of intentional communications: Mother always knows the reason why the child is crying or laughing. The child cries because he or she needs to sleep, because he or she is hungry or cold, and this mirroring of the child as an intentional being forces him or her to understand not only others' mental states but also his or her own. A mother's sensibility seems to be more and more an external organizing factor of the child's biobehavioral regulation. It is the right hemisphere that seems to store the inner working model of the attachment relationship, recorded in the implicit memory system, and that determines the subject's early affect regulation within coping and survival strategies. In Marco's case, a relational trauma clearly occurred, probably connected to his mother's depression during his first and second year of life. Long-term effects of the earliest relational traumas bring a new light to the concept of critical or sensitive phase development (12–18 months). During this period of rapid maturation anatomical structures link up with attachment behavior and affect regulation. The probable brain locations of these developments are the right orbitofrontal and corticolimbic systems. Therefore, we must entertain as a likely possibility that relational trauma early in life may prevent the right hemisphere from reaching adequate maturation. Moreover there are dramatic consequences for the semantic processing of all data that come from the right hemisphere and have to be transferred to the left one. This seems to represent the neuroanatomical process accounting for the severe incapacity of abused children to talk about their own emotions and inner states. This represents the first expression of "alexithymia," the inability to put emotions into words, which is also a typical symptom among patients (like Marco) who have had early traumatic experiences.

There appear to be many similarities between the neuroendocrine patterns seen in posttraumatic stress disorder and alexithymia. Alexithymic personalities show impaired affect symbolization capacity, a tendency toward impulsive behaviors, and avoidance of social relations, along with poor self-caring and self-regulating capacities. In our opinion, all these things lead to a picture that is quite similar to the one represented by Marco.

Marco's metacognitive capacity was gradually reinforced, and he is now making further and significant improvements: He has been involved in a stable, intimate relationship for many months; at the same time, he has passed 17 exams at his university. Marco arrives on time for sessions, and a third recently administered AAI showed further changes in his attachment classification (Ds3/Ds2), to a dismissing stance involving restriction of feeling and some derogation of attachment figures (i.e., the previously idealized father). This suggests that the emotional pendulum for Marco had swung away from hyperactivation and preoccupation to (over)containment and reserve (another organized, albeit insecure, state of mind), with a turning of aggression outward instead of at himself. Over time, given all the changes Marco has shown in therapy, we would expect him to settle still closer to the autonomous–secure center of social and emotional life. Coming from the E3/E1 position suggested by his second AAI, a move to Ds3 (restricted in feeling) can arguably be seen as an advance and move away from prior difficulties. Ds3 speakers are only moderately incoherent, and the speaker often appears relatively well focused, with some normalizing of difficult attachment experiences. Certainly, the progress Marco has shown in therapy and in his work and social life, speaks volumes for the human potential to overcome early disorganizing experiences.

Maria's Case: Borderline Personality Organization

Maria was 39 years old when she was referred by her aunt, who said that her niece had had a psychotic breakdown during which she had shown delusional, paranoid thoughts and a state of confusion with intense aggressive reactions. Within a few days, thanks to pharmacological treatment, Maria was able to recover relatively good psychological functioning and seemed to be more connected to reality.

During the first interview she expressed conflicting attitudes. On the one hand, she presented herself as a successful woman, both in her professional and social life. Maria talked about her previous experience in New York, where she worked as a successful fashion designer. However, she then vacillated, talking about how oppressed she felt by her mother, who forced her to come back to Rome, where she was now living, financially supported by her mother.

Maria's Initial AAI

We now provide excerpts from Maria's AAI, with a view toward discussing themes that arose and were then mirrored in her psychotherapy sessions.

> THERAPIST: So, how would you describe the relationship with your mother?
>
> MARIA: I am sorry, I'm sorry. Since she has never taken care of me personally, either when I was anorexic or as a child, and she has never given me the love that one needs from her mother, she is now neurotically trying to reestablish some sort of relationship with me. And this gets on my nerve.
>
> THERAPIST: Yes, I am asking you something about your childhood.
>
> MARIA: And it was like that when I was a child, too.
>
> THERAPIST: You talked about an overprotective relationship with your mother.
>
> MARIA: No, it's now that it has become overprotective; well, it's not overprotective, it's sick. In any case, it's not overprotective. (*She sounds irritated.*)
>
> THERAPIST: So, what do you mean?
>
> MARIA: It's sick. It is not in the right quantity, it is not in the right way [referring to overprotectiveness].
>
> THERAPIST: All right.
>
> MARIA: To protect a child is a right thing to do, even if to be overprotective is still better than to insult her or to hold her to ransom . . . or threaten her, "If you don't do this, I won't give you that" (*still in a tense tone of voice*).
>
> THERAPIST: Could you give me an example of this?
>
> MARIA: Yes, for instance, "If you don't undergo therapy, I won't provide you with a living."
>
> THERAPIST: And as a child?
>
> MARIA: Or she tells me, "If you talk to me this way, it means you are attached to my money and I'll kill myself." That's what she says to me.
>
> THERAPIST: And as a child. Do you remember which kind of attitude your mother used to have with you?
>
> MARIA: Oh, she also used to hit me. She beat me, she batter . . . how do you say that?
>
> THERAPIST: An example as a child?
>
> MARIA: Another way a relationship can be sick, for instance, that I am getting clean from medication and my mother comes to visit me in

America and I don't want her home with me and she . . . I feel sick, I feel ashamed to be seen when I throw up, I kindly ask her to go for a walk, but she won't go, just because she can't stand the city. It is a sick relationship.

Maria's demonstrated difficulty in remembering the past without referring to her current involved relationship with her mother in highly typical interviews judged to be in the preoccupied category. Maria's thoughts and resentment seem to indicate that she has forgotten the context of the interview and the questions she is being asked. She talks as if her mother were in front of her, and overwhelmed by rage and resentment, she does not respect the turn taking with the interviewer, all resulting in a very low score for narrative coherence, and a high score for current anger toward mother. Her reference to being beaten during childhood by her mother also alerts the reader to the probable experience of abuse (one would first want to ascertain the severity and frequency of the beatings, as was done later in the interview when abuse was specifically probed), and a corollary requirement to rate the extent to which the trauma has been resolved.

THERAPIST: Which kind of relationship did you have with your father?

MARIA: I didn't have any relationship at all with him.

THERAPIST: Oh, you didn't, and does any other adjective come to your mind, anyway?

MARIA: My father was really ill, I mean mentally. It was only later when he also got physically ill. I didn't have any decent relationship with whomever.

THERAPIST: Does any memory come to your mind?

MARIA: Yes, but they are not nice at all.

THERAPIST: Sorry?

MARIA: I feel like crying now. Don't you see my nice makeup today? I'd prefer not to talk about that. Can we talk about it next session?

THERAPIST: It's all right, all right. But you were talking about whom . . .

MARIA: (*Interrupts.*) It's not the makeup, I was only joking. It's that this [referring to the father] he died a little time ago and it hurts me so much.

In terms of the relationship with her father, we observe a dismissing, devaluing attitude. Indeed, Maria did not acknowledge any relationship with him whatsoever referring to him as "this," as if to cancel his identity. As the interview goes on, Maria is unable to answer the questions, because she was so involved in the relationship with her mother that she lost track of interviewer's questions. This distancing from father and high involvement with mother is suggestive of a CC quality.

Maria seems to be still very entangled with and angry with her parents, and the efforts to detach herself defensively from past negative experiences cannot prevent her from feeling really hurt. Her capacity to reflect upon her childhood experiences was very limited, and memories came up in an unmodified form. She was unable to respond to the question "Why do you think your mother has behaved in the way she did?" This would demand an evaluation of the probable origins of her mother's character, from which Maria is not sufficiently removed. Her limited reflective functioning emerged when she answered the question "Do you think these experiences have affected your personality?" by saying, "I do think so. They hurt me and made me feel angry . . . and kept me from trusting a person with whom I lived together."

Regarding the attachment classification (Main et al., 2002) we have agreed upon a CC assignment, with primary classifications of preoccupied/enmeshed (E2) and dismissing (Ds2), that is to say, evidence of both enmeshed and detaching features within Maria's mind concerning attachment. As already pointed out (Main et al., 2002, p. 207), "the 'Cannot Classify' category is always utilized when no single state of mind with respect to attachment is predominant" (see also Main ct al., Chapter 2, this volume).

We can study the same AAI from Maria by using the Hostile–Helpless (HH) Coding System (Lyons-Ruth, Yellin, Melnick, & Atwood, 2003; Melnick, Finger, Hans, Patrick, & Lyons-Ruth, Chapter 16, this volume) which has been developed as an extension rather than a substitution for the work of Main and Goldwyn (1985) and Hesse (1999) by creating additional interview-wide codes to capture indicators of pervasively nonintegrated mental states with respect to attachment and secondary to chronic relational trauma, including sexual, physical, and emotional abuse. According to this coding system, Maria's interview fits with the hostile–helpless mixed classification (HH2). This is applied to interviews, like Maria's, that comprise a mixed picture in which indices of hostile, helpless, and fearful states of mind coexist.

Maria's initial interview included a global devaluation of the maternal figure, whereas the representations of the father conveyed more of a helpless quality, such as when he was described as a sick person indulging in alcohol. Fitting with the HH coding system (Lyons-Ruth & Melnick, 2005), Maria's malevolent representation of her mother continues to be active in the present and seems not to have been mitigated during adulthood. The references to global devaluing of the mother are quite numerous, more than five, confirming the observations reported in a sample of patients with borderline personality disorder (BPD) (Lyons-Ruth, Melnick, Patrick, & Hobson, 2007).

After the initial evaluation, which supported the BPD diagnosis, the patient agreed to twice-weekly psychotherapy and psychopharmacological treatment. Maria's narrative responses to the AAI concurred with her presentation in psychotherapy sessions. Maria seemed to accept the relationship with the therapist, in which she felt some reassurance, but she also repeatedly asked him to reproach her mother. If the therapist failed to comply with the request, Maria accused him of taking the mother's side. Maria repeatedly threatened to interrupt treatment that her mother forced her to undertake, and that she probably would not have undertaken on her own.

Because Maria was unemployed and did not have personal income, one of the recurrent topics was her economic issues. Beside her apartment, her mother gave her a considerable amount of money on a monthly basis. The patient gave the impression of living a life in which she felt like a hostage to her mother, who controlled and blackmailed her, thereby keeping her in a position of subjection. Paranoid anxieties, which she could not manage, appeared.

On the other hand, the therapist realized that apart from the missed sessions and ongoing interferences throughout the treatment, he and Maria had established quite a stable relationship that gave her psychological support and prevented possible relapses. The course of treatment was often marked by acting out, through which Maria tried to make the therapist side with her and ask Maria's mother to give her more money or to let her move to another country where, unlike Rome, she would have more chances in finding work. The therapist's emotional resonance was fairly strong, because he felt compelled and even manipulated by the patient, who threatened to interrupt the treatment if he did not do as she wished. It was evident how massively Maria employed splitting mechanisms. She ascribed all the negative and violent aspects to the mother, while presenting herself as the only person within her family to tell the truth and behave honestly.

The AAI after 3 Years of Psychotherapy

After 3 years the therapist suggested to Maria that an AAI be readministered to verify whether the structure of her attachment bonds had significantly changed during the treatment. The suggestion was not welcomed by Maria, who did not want to relive the past, which she considered too painful. However, Maria initially agreed to undertake the interview. After the first questions concerning the adjectives about parents, Maria had strong emotional reactions and cried angrily and desperately. Her responses to the questions regarding representation of her mother overlapped with those given during the first administration. Specifically, she described her mother as a malevolent, violent figure who had always neglected and abandoned her to the nannies that "were changed as often as my mother's blouses."

Maria described how her mother had never done anything to protect her; for instance, when her mother's common-law husband used to kick Maria or put her head in a sink full of water, her mother never said anything. Although the same traumatic memories regarding childhood experiences with her parents emerged again, "detaching" mechanisms Maria had utilized before to keep traumatic memories at a distance were much more limited. For instance, a crucial point was reached when Maria was asked to report episodes from infancy to support the adjectives she had just used to describe her relationship with her mother. For this reason the interview was not completed, because the patient's negative emotional state seemed to be so strongly activated that the therapist himself was wondering whether it would be useful to finish.

Features of the attachment coding had not dramatically changed. Evidence of involvement with the attachment figures continued to predominate consistent with the classification of preoccupied/enmeshed (E2), with E3 (fearfully preoccupied by traumatic events) as an alternate classification.

The transcript analyzed within the HH system (Lyons-Ruth et al., 2003) showed evidence of the mixed-category HH2, in which hostility and helpless aspects coexist. Maria seems identified with the hostile attachment figure, for instance, when she devalues and violently attacks other people, yet seems helpless when she reports feeling trapped and a hostage to an attachment figure that she cannot escape.

As treatment progressed, it seemed that the evoked memories of the past, alongside "detaching mechanisms" that were active at the beginning of the treatment, faded partially away, although it remained clear that Maria would like to cancel the past and live in a present dimension in which she would have no need for others.

The AAI after 5 Years of Psychotherapy

In the following years, Maria's therapy proceeded on a more regular and stable basis, although she occasionally dropped some sessions, pretending to have health problems. At the same time, the figure of the psychotherapist became more and more important to her, because he was able to share Maria's difficulties. Overall, the climate of the sessions improved as Maria was less resentful and rageful toward her mother. Depressive reactions that at times occurred involved her life in general and, in particular, her difficulties in finding a job and growing concerns about her body. These concerns were further elicited by a series of accidents that had some consequences for her health.

After 5 years of psychotherapy, the therapist thought it time for a new evaluation of Maria's state of mind concerning attachment. Maria was willing to submit herself to the new administration of the AAI, hardly remembering having already done it. When asked to provide five adjectives to describe her relationship as a child with her mother, Maria answered "sad," because she had spent a lot of time on her own, frequently entrusted to babysitters and the like. She then added "panicked, frightened, and nausea."

When asked to report specific episodes as evidence for the adjectives chosen, Maria responded that her mother used to slap her face, and that she often witnessed violent interactions between her parents, because both used to drink a lot of alcohol. As for the nausea, Maria reported that she had had anorexia from virtually her birth until adolescence. As a consequence, her mother used to lose her temper and stuff her with food that Maria had not eaten in the preceding meal.

Maria expressed her sorrow for not having positive memories of her mother, even when her mother did something good for her, such as buying Maria a scooter, because her mother would take advantage of this to force Maria to comply with her requests and expectations. With respect to her mother, a new element emerged in Maria's narrative: "I know my mother did not hate me, but she was only annoyed by me. Figure it out, I was anorexic from birth. I was a disturbance in her life." Maria's narrative was now more coherent, and she seemed more able to control her feelings without being flooded by rage. Unlike the previous interviews, she did not mention the current relationship with her mother, except in the final part of the interview, when she commented that her mother wanted her to leave her apartment and move to a smaller one, and asked the therapist for help with this specific issue.

As to the adjectives concerning the father, Maria said: "We never had physical contact and he used to throw up a lot, since he was an alcoholic, although I think he cared for me." As to the grandmother who had already been presented as a positive figure in her childhood, Maria described her as "good, very generous, ill, and sadly concerned about me." Maria seemed very involved emotionally when speaking about her, explaining that her grandmother had helped her get over anorexia during adolescence, "because she trusted me; whenever I didn't feel like eating she didn't insist as my mother would do." This enlarged appreciation for her grandmother appeared to provide a conscious root to some of Maria's current adaptive functioning. It may be that the experience of the AAI interview directed Maria's attention to this little thought about grandmother, who was an important source of learning that an attachment figure can be benevolent and caring (see Jones, Chapter 7, this volume, for a further illustration of this "power" of the AAI).

Overall, the interview showed a degree of evolution in Maria's state of mind: with the AAI rater ascribing to her the E3 classification (fearfully preoccupied by traumatic events). However, Maria seemed more able to speak about the traumatic events and to understand the relational dynamics underlying these experiences, acknowledging that she was a "difficult child" who caused her mother emotional strain. Given this evolution facilitated, we hope, by the therapeutic work, an alternative final classification of F5 (somewhat resentful/conflicted, while accepting of continuing involvement) (Main et al., 2002) was proposed, since Maria showed an adequate level of coherence in her attachment narrative; moreover, there was a good degree of emotional self-containment and the presence of some humor.

Discussion

From a clinical point of view, Maria showed a complex and serious mental disorder involving severe personal impairment, with a pervasive pattern of instability of mood, interpersonal relationships, and self-image. The actual clinical disturbances were rooted in Maria's infancy, when she showed marked mood reactivity with intense dysphoria, anger, irritability, and anxiety.

In the histories of patients with BPD, as in Maria's case, the caregivers often inadequately mirror and respond to the infant's distress, manifested by a hostile–helpless attitude (Lyons-Ruth et al., 2003) and dissociated or disorganized, frightened or frightening behavior (Jacobvitz, Hazen, & Riggs, 1997; Schuengel, Bakermans-Kranenburg, & van IJzendoorn, 1999). These children experience their distress as a danger signal for abandonment, because their parents tend to withdraw from them in a state of anxiety or rage, to which the children react with a complementary dissociative response (Liotti, 1999). From the developmental point of view the internal experiences of the child remain neither contained nor organized, and the child incorporates a representation of the other into his or her emerging self-structure. In this case, what is incorporated in the structure of the self is nonreflective, neglectful, or abusive. This can create disorganized attachment, which is considered an important risk factor (Barone, 2003) in predicting negative reaction to traumas, separations, or losses (Adam, Keller, & West, 1995). In this case, Maria's history of disorganized attachment seemed fairly pervasive.

It is well known (Bowlby, 1969, 1984) that relational trauma interferes with integrated attachment by the activation of dissociative defenses that serve as a protection against the overwhelming and depersonalizing experience connected to the reoccurrence of trauma (Bromberg, 1996). Maria's initially highly incoherent narrative and impoverished affect regulation skills were clearly linked to early and ongoing relational trauma. During the vicissitudes of psychotherapy, for a number of years, Maria would frequently reenact the relationship with her mother, while perceiving the psychotherapist as a dangerous and hostile figure; had she reenacted the relationship with her father, she would have perceived the therapist as a helpless figure, totally dominated by her mother (a role she herself frequently assumed). Over time, drawing on the secure relationship with her grandmother, Maria came to see that the therapist sought to protect her and had her interests in mind, and that she was deserving of the benevolent interests of others. In therapy, the goal with Maria was to mitigate both the menacing and involving experience with the mother, and the helpless and depressing experience with the father. Some distance toward this goal had been achieved by the 5-year follow-up AAI.

More generally, use of the AAI can broaden the methodology of clinical assessment, showing clearly a patient's attachment dynamics, and psychotherapeutic treatment (Ammaniti, 1999). From a psychotherapeutic point of view, administration of the AAI and discussion of the states of mind activated by the questions may be helpful in promoting in the patient both self-reflection and personal integration by drawing attention to mental states and providing a secure base from which to explore these states.

Notes

1. The authors of this chapter have been working in Rome, mainly at the University of Rome "Sapienza," for many years. They all share the same clinical and research interest in the field of attachment, as witnessed by their longitudinal studies from infancy to adolescence, as well as clinical applications of attachment framework and studies on attachment in twin pairs. The following list includes some of the more accessible publications that appear in English journals and books:

> Ammaniti, M. (1999). How attachment theory can contribute to the understanding of affective functioning in psychoanalysis. *Psychoanalytic Inquiry*, *19*(5), 784–796.
> Ammaniti, M., van IJzendoorn, M. H., Speranza, A. M., & Tambelli, R. (2000). Internal working models of attachment during late childhood and early adolescence: An exploration of stability and change. *Attachment and Human Development*, *2*, 328–346.
> Ammaniti, M., & Sergi, G. (2003). Clinical dynamics during adolescence: Psychoanalytic and attachment perspectives. *Psychoanalytic Inquiry*, *23*(1), 54–80.
> Ammaniti, M., Speranza, A. M., & Fedele, S. (2005). Attachment in infancy and in early and late childhood. In K. A. Kerns & R. A. Richardson (Eds.), *Attachment in middle childhood* (pp. 115–136). New York: Guilford Press.
> Muscetta, S., Dazzi, N., De Coro, A., Ortu, F., & Speranza, A. M. (1999). States of mind with respect to attachment and change in a psychotherapeutic relationship: A study of the coherence of transcript in a short-term psychotherapy with an adolescent. *Psychoanalytic Inquiry*, *19*(5), 885–921.

2. We believe that the main task of a psychotherapist is to try consistently to assign meaning to both the patient's verbal and nonverbal communications.
3. Z's maternal grandmother died 1 year before his birth.

References

Adam, K. S., Keller, A. E., & West, M. (1995). Attachment organization and vulnerability to loss, separation, and abuse in disturbed adolescents. In S. Goldberg, R. Muir, & J. Kerr (Eds.), *Attachment theory: Social, developmental, and clinical perspectives* (pp. 309–341). Hillsdale, NJ: Analytic Press.

Ammaniti, M. (1999). How attachment theory can contribute to the understanding of affective functioning in psychoanalysis. *Psychoanalytic Inquiry*, *19*(5), 784–796.

Barone, L. (2003). Developmental protective and risk factors in borderline personality disorder: A study using the Adult Attachment Interview. *Attachment and Human Development*, *5*(1), 64–77.

Bowlby, J. (1969). *Attachment and loss: Vol. 1. Attachment.* New York: Basic Books.

Bowlby, J. (1984). Psychoanalysis as a natural science. *Psychoanalytic Psychology*, *1*, 7–22.

Bromberg, P. M. (1996). *Standing in the spaces: Essays on clinical process, trauma, and dissociation.* Hillsdale, NJ: Analytic Press.

Fonagy, P., Gergely, G., Jurist, E., & Target, M. (Eds.). (2002). *Affect regulation, mentalization, and the development of the self*. New York: Other Press.

George, C., Kaplan, N., & Main, M. (1985). *Adult Attachment Interview protocol*. Unpublished manuscript, University of California, Berkeley.

Hesse, E. (1996). Discourse, memory and the Adult Attachment Interview: A note with emphasis onthe emerging "Cannot Classify" category. *Infant Mental Health Journal, 17*(1), 4–11.

Hesse, E. (1999). The Adult Attachment Interview: Historical and current perspectives. In J. Cassidy & P. R. Shaver (Eds.), *Handbook of attachment: Theory, research, and clinical applications* (pp. 395–433). New York: Guilford Press.

Jacobvitz, D., Hazen, N., & Riggs, S. (1997). *Disorganized mental processes in mothers, frightening/frightened caregiving, and disoriented/disorganized behavior in infancy*. In D. Jacobvitz (Chair), Caregiving correlates and longitudinal outcomes of disorganized attachments in infants. Symposium conducted at the biennial meeting of the Society for Research in Child Development, Washington, DC.

Laufer, M., Moses, E., & Laufer. (1984). *Adolescence and developmental breakdown. A psychoanalytic view*. New Haven, CT: Yale University Press.

Liotti, G. (1992). Disorganizzazione dell'attaccamento e predisposizione allo sviluppo di disturbi funzionali [Disorganization of attachment and development of functional disorders]. In M. Ammaniti & N. Dazzi (Eds.), *Attaccamento e psicoanalisi* [Attachment and psychoanalysis] (pp. 219–232). Bari, Italy: Laterza.

Liotti, G. (1999). Disorganization of attachment as a model for understanding dissociative psychopathology. In J. Solomon & C. C. George (Eds.), *Attachment disorganization* (pp. 291–317). New York: Guilford Press.

Lyons-Ruth, K., & Melnick, S. (2005). *Pervasively unintegrated, highly defended/helpless states of mind on the Adult Attachment Interview* (Classification and coding manual, version 4). Unpublished manuscript.

Lyons-Ruth, K., Melnick, S., Patrick, M., & Hobson, P. (2007). A controlled study of hostile–helpless states of mind among borderline and dysthymic women. *Attavhment and Human Development, 9*(1), 1–16.

Lyons-Ruth, K., Yellin, C., Melnick, S., & Atwood, G. (2003). Childhood experiences of trauma and loss have different relations to maternal unresolved and hostile–helpless states of mind on the AAI. *Attachment and Human Development, 5*(4), 330–352.

Main, M. (1981). Avoidance in the service of attachment: A working paper. In K. Immelman, G. Barlow, M. Main, & L. Petrinovitch (Eds.), *Behavioral development: The Bielefeld Interdisciplinary Project*. New York: Cambridge University Press.

Main, M. (1991). Metacognitive knowledge, metacognitive monitoring and singular (coherent) versus multiple (incoherent) models of attachment: Findings and direction for future research. In C. M. Parkes, J. Stevenson-Hinde, & P. Marris (Eds.), *Attachment across the life cycle* (pp. 124–159). London: Tavistock/Routledge.

Main, M., & Goldwyn, R. (1985). *Adult attachment scoring and classification systems*. Unpublished classification manual, University of California, Berkeley.

Main, M., Goldwyn, R., & Hesse, E. (2002). *Adult attachment scoring and classification systems* (Version 7.1). Unpublished manual, University of California, Berkeley.

Main, M., & Hesse, E. (1990). Parents' unresolved traumatic experiences are related to infant disorganized status: Is frightened and/or frightening parental behavior the linking mechanism? In M. T. Greenberg, D. Cicchetti, & E. M. Cummings (Eds.), *Attachment in the preschool years: Theory, research and intervention* (pp. 161–182). Chicago: University of Chicago Press.

Main, M., & Hesse, E. (1992). Disorganized/disoriented infant behavior in the Strange Situation, lapses in the monitoring of reasoning and discourse during the parent's A.A.I. and dissociative states. In M. Ammaniti & D. Stern (Eds.), *Attaccamento e psicoanalisi* [Attachment and psychoanalysis] (pp. 86–140). Bari, Italy: Laterza.

Muscetta, S., Dazzi, N., De Coro, A., Ortu, F., & Speranza, A. M. (1999). States of mind with respect to attachment and change in a psychotherapeutic relationship: A study of the coherence of transcript in a short-term psychotherapy with an adolescent. *Psychoanalytic Inquiry, 19*, 885–921.

Piaget, J. (1936). *The origins of intelligence in children.* New York: International University Press.

Schuengel, C., Bakermans-Kranenburg, M., & van IJzendoorn, M. (1999). Frightening maternal behavior linking unresolved loss and disorganized infant attachment. *Journal of Consulting and Clinical Psychology, 67*, 54–63.

Slade, A. (1999). Attachment theory and research: Implications for the theory and practice of individual psychotherapy with adults. In J. Cassidy & P. R. Shaver (Eds.), *Handbook of attachment* (pp. 575–594). New York: Guilford Press.

11

The Reciprocal Impact of Attachment and Transference-Focused Psychotherapy with Borderline Patients

DIANA DIAMOND, FRANK E. YEOMANS, JOHN F. CLARKIN,
KENNETH N. LEVY, and OTTO F. KERNBERG

In this chapter we attempt to illustrate the utility of attachment concepts for clinical work by presenting one case from a longitudinal study on changes in attachment status and reflective function in borderline patients over the course of 1 year of transference-focused psychotherapy (TFP), a form of psychoanalytic psychotherapy based on object relations theory (Kernberg, 1975, 1976). All of us who treat borderline patients know that disorders of attachment are central in borderline conditions. The attachments formed by borderline patients in and out of the consulting room are turbulent and chaotic, with unpredictable shifts between clinging and repudiation, intense idealization and scathing devaluation, and alternating intrusions into the therapist's life and sudden unilateral rejection of others, including the therapist. Object relations theorists believe that this chaos stems from an underlying lack of integration in the patient's psychological structure in that unstable and polarized self and object representations, associated with highly charged and poorly modulated affect states, determine the individual's experience of self and others, and perception of reality. The nonintegration of the different representations of self and other leads to identity diffusion, a state of discontinuity and confusion in the individual's relations to self, others, and the external world. However, even if borderline patients share a lack of internal integration, we know that attachments formed by borderline patients are not just of one type: They may be characterized as much by dismissing devaluation of attachment relationships as by terrors of aloneness and persistent cravings for connection. Adding considerations of attachment status to the fundamental state of identity diffusion may help us in understanding the different clinical presentations of borderline personality, and how they may change differentially in the course of treatment.

A number of previous studies have identified insecure attachment organization (Diamond, Clarkin, Levine, et al., 1999; Fonagy, Gergely, Jurist, & Target, 2002; Fonagy, Leigh, et al., 1996; Fonagy, Steele, et al., 1995; Gunderson, 1996; Levy, Blatt, & Shaver, 1998; Patrick, Hobson, Castle, Howard, & Maughan, 1994; Slade, 1999; Steele & Steele, 1998) and deficits in reflective functioning, or the capacity to think in mental state terms (Bateman & Fonagy, 2004; Diamond, Stouvall-McClough, Clarkin, & Levy, 2003b; Fonagy, 1991, 1998, 2001; Fonagy et al., 2002; Levy et al., 2006) in borderline patients, thereby expanding our understanding of the object relations features of borderline pathology. From an object relations point of view, these insecure states of mind with respect to attachment stem both from basic internal identity diffusion, a state that provides no stable internal representation of self or object, and from the structure and nature of the predominant object representations; that is, from the strong presence of negatively valenced or persecutory representations in the patient's conscious experience of self and others, along with the lack of integration of positive and negative aspects of the representational world. Attachment concepts and measures, including the concept of attachment security or insecurity as measured by the Adult Attachment Interview (Main & Goldwyn, 1998) and mentalization as measured by the Reflective Function Scale (Fonagy, Steele, Steele, & Target, 1997), have provided ways of assessing change in aspects of the representational world of borderline patients. Recent investigations have shown significant improvement in attachment representations or internal working models as well as mentalization or reflective function in borderline patients over the course of 1 year of transference-focusing psychotherapy (TFP; Levy et al., 2006).

Transference-Focused Psychotherapy

TFP is a psychodynamic treatment designed for patients with borderline personality disorder (BPD) and borderline personality organization (BPO) and has been delineated in a series of treatment manuals (Clarkin, Yeomans, & Kernberg, 2006; Kernberg, Selzer, Koenigsberg, Carr, & Appelbaum, 1989; Koenigsberg et al., 2000, Yeomans, Clarkin, & Kernberg, 2002). TFP is based on a model of borderline pathology that integrates Kernberg's object relations model of the structural organization of personality (Kernberg, 1984; Kernberg & Caligor, 2004) with an understanding of the interaction between behavior and neurobiological aspects of the individual (Depue & Lenzenweger, 2005;

Posner et al., 2002, 2003). Whereas the psychoanalytic view of borderline per-sonality organization has been essential in understanding the psychological experience of the patient and guiding treatment (Yeomans et al., 2002), our model of BPD posits a dynamic interaction of temperament, especially a pre-ponderance of negative affect over positive affect; low effortful control; and an absence of a coherent sense of self and others in the context of an insecure model of attachment. Furthermore, we recognize that difficulties in processing negative affect, faulty and ineffective conflict resolution, insecure (primarily anxious/preoccupied and/or disorganized/unresolved attachment organization (Bateman & Fonagy, 2004; Fonagy et al., 1996), and low effortful control all contribute to the deficits in affect regulation and information processing that are at the heart of BPD (Clarkin & Posner, 2005; Posner et al., 2003).

Hence, our model of BPD posits that temperament and environment combine to establish the split psychological structure of borderline patients that evolves in the course of early development. From an object relations per-spective, mental representations of frustrating others in relation to a helpless deprived self are internalized and split off from mental representations of grat-ifying others in relation to a satisfied self. These opposite self–object dyads are imbued with intense affects, both hateful (in association with the frustrating other) and loving (in association with the gratifying other). Early interper-sonal experiences are cumulatively internalized in the individual's mind and become established in cognitive-affective structures or "object relations dyads"—units that combine a specific representation of the self in relation to the other, linked by specific affects that in the case of the borderline individual are somewhat loosely and chaotically organized in relation to each other. In addition, these dyads are not exact, accurate representations of historical real-ity, although they bear the imprint of interpersonal transactions with early attachment figures. In our view, however, the representational world is not delimited by mental representations of self in relation to attachment figures, although the internal working models of attachment based on the child's expe-rience of early parent–child attachment transactions, such as the parents' responses to the child in times of threat, danger, and illness, may form the bedrock of the representational world. The representational world is also patterned by temperament, biological capacities and limitations, impulses, wishes, conflicts, and fantasies that derive from the myriad behavioral systems of sexuality, aggression, exploration, affiliation, and caregiving that Bowlby and others have posited in addition to attachment (Bowlby, 1969/1982). Although a more complete discussion of the relationship between internal working models of attachment and psychoanalytic theories of the representa-tional world is beyond the scope of this chapter and can be found elsewhere, both are thought to operate outside of awareness and to be resistant to change (see Diamond & Blatt, 1994; Eagle, 1997, 2003; Levy et al., 1998; Main, 1995; Main, Kaplan, & Cassidy, 1985; Steele & Steele, 1998).

For borderline individuals in the course of early development, separate object relations dyads, associated with sharply different affects are defensively split off from one another and determine the lack of continuity of the border-line patient's subjective experience in life. Although the patient has no conscious awareness of the defensive aspects of this split internal world, the idealized and persecutory facets of his or her experience remain consciously available at different times, but defensively sequestered from each other, which accounts for the typical symptoms of borderline personality: chaotic interpersonal relations; emotional lability; polarized, black-and-white thinking; and proneness to lapses in reality testing.

The treatment focuses on the transference, because the patient lives out his or her predominant object relations dyads in the transference, as in other relations. The core task in TFP is to identify the patient's various internal object relations dyads or internal working models of attachment (which are often multiple in the case of the borderline patient), and to help modulate and integrate them into unified, coherent representations of self and other. The combination of understanding and affective experience in the therapy leads to the integration of the split off representations and the creation of an integrated identity and experience of others.

Thus, in TFP, the therapist must attend to (1) the degree of identity diffusion versus integration, and (2) the specific predominant dyads (self- and object representations). These attachment features of borderline pathology are particularly evident in the transference, which in TFP can be seen as the vehicle for mobilizing and transforming the insecure attachment behaviors and their associated internal working models of attachment. The attachment perspective diverges somewhat from TFP's object relations' foundations, which gives more emphasis to dynamic conflicts and particularly the role of aggression as an impediment to the integration of the internal world, and the formation and maintenance of secure attachment bonds, including that with the therapist. However, despite these differences, TFP, like most treatments for BPD, gives centrality to the consolidation of an attachment relationship to the therapist and to the development of increased capacity for reflective function, or the ability to think in mental state terms, that is, to comprehend the intentions, thoughts, feelings, beliefs, and motivations of self and others (Bateman & Fonagy, 2004; Kernberg, Diamond, Yeomans, Clarkin, & Levy, in press).

Attachment Theory and TFP for Patients with BPD

Our research and clinical investigations at the Personality Disorders Institute at Weill Medical College of Cornell University, where TFP was developed, have been influenced by the increasing attention to the application of the writings of Bowlby (1969/1982, 1973, 1980, 1988) and his followers (Fonagy et al., 1995, 1996; Main, 1995). Specifically, the interest in applying attachment constructs to the therapeutic relationship and process (see Diamond et al., 2002; Fonagy, 2001) is central to our work. Bowlby hypothesized that the attachment behavioral system, by which he meant the innate proclivity of young children to seek proximity and caretaking from an adult member of the species, is active throughout the life cycle, particularly in situations where an individual who is ill and in distress seeks protection or contact with someone deemed older or wiser. Increasingly this model has been applied to the therapeutic situation. Bowlby stated that the chief role of the therapist was to provide "the patient with a temporary attachment figure" (1975, p. 306). In this process, the therapist's own internal working models of attachment, or sets of rules and expectations regarding the interactive attributes of early caregivers, are mobilized along with those of the patient. Like all attachment relationships, the therapeutic one was thought by Bowlby (1969/1982, 1973) to be inherently bidirectional, with attachment-seeking behaviors (proximity seeking, smiling, calling) tending to evoke corresponding adult attachment or caretaking behaviors (soothing, holding, protecting). Allan Schore's reading of the neuroscience literature (2001, 2003a, 2003b) suggests that just as the infant's right hemisphere is involved in the development of the attachment behavioral system, so also is the caretaker's right hemisphere activated in comforting and protecting functions (see also Siegel, 1999). As Schore points out, attachment "is an active dyadic process that occurs between two brains that are co-generating synchronized emotional communications with each other" (2001, p. 23), and we might apply this formulation to psychotherapy as well. Bowlby (1978, 1988) conceptualized all attachment relationships, including the therapeutic one, as inherently bidirectional, with attachment-seeking behaviors (proximity seeking, smiling, calling) tending to evoke corresponding adult attachment or caretaking behaviors (soothing, holding, protecting).

Bowlby (1988) hypothesized that transference inevitably involves patients' recapitulation of their early attachment history and patterns in the therapeutic arena. Furthermore, Bowlby (1978, 1988) believed that the developmental findings of attachment theory and research would illuminate our understanding of the transference–countertransference dynamics of more severely disturbed patients, particularly those with borderline and narcissistic pathology. In the case of patients with insecure states of mind with respect to early attachment relationships, the internal working models of early attachment relationships are likely to be multiple, contradictory, and unintegrated, leading to complex and sometimes chaotic transferences and countertransferences (Bowlby, 1988; Farber, Lippert, & Nevas, 1995; Holmes, 1996; Main, 1991, 1995, 1999). Bowlby (1988) observed that patients alternately cast the therapist in the role of an early attachment figure and assume the role of that attachment figure themselves in relationship to the therapist, and that the more disturbed the patient, the more chaotic, rigid, and resistant to change such internal working models are likely to be. Hence, in Racker's (1968) terms, the therapist may experience both complementary and concordant forms of countertransference that together provide an important source of insight into the nature of the patient's internal working models of attachment. Particularly with the more severely disturbed patient, the therapist may be able to comprehend fully the patient's often complex and contradictory representational states with respect to attachment only by objectively sorting through his or her own welter of internal responses to the patient.

In our own research, we have been observing change toward increased coherence and security of internal working models of attachment in patients with BPD over 1 year of TFP (Diamond, Stovall-McClough, Clarkin, & Levy, 2003b; Diamond et al., 1999; Levy et al., 2006). We have also found that the patient's attachment status or current state of mind regarding early attachment relationships, as assessed on the Adult Attachment Interview (AAI), is a major characteristic that affects the course of TFP for patients with BPD, from the initial stages of establishing a treatment contract to the patients' characteristic responses to separations and endings, and to the nature of the dominant object relations dyads enacted in the transference (see Diamond et al., 1999; Koenigsberg et al., 2000).

We have also been investigating the impact of patient and therapist states of mind with respect to attachment in the therapeutic relationship, through an interview adapted from the AAI, the Patient–Therapist Adult Attachment Interview (PT-AAI) (George et al., 1999). In TFP the transference functions as a metanarrative that shapes the therapeutic interactions, both verbal and nonverbal, and becomes the vehicle through which the patient's attachment narrative(s) emerges and changes. Indeed, in developing the PT-AAI, we have been inspired by previous clinical and empirical investigations linking attachment status to (1) transference–countertransference dynamics (Dozier & Tyrrell, 1998; Fonagy, 1991; Holmes, 1995, 1996; Szajnberg & Crittenden, 1997), (2) the quality and nature of the therapeutic alliance (Bordin, 1994; Dozier & Tyrrell, 1998; Eagle, 2003; Mackie, 1981), (3) patients' characteristic responses to endings and separations from the therapist (Gunderson, 1996; Holmes, 1995, 1996, 1998), and (4) patterns of patient–therapist discourse (Fonagy, 1991, 1998, 2001; Slade, 1999). Our initial investigations with the PT-AAI (Diamond et al., 2002, 2003b) suggest that it is a useful instrument to track one aspect of the transference, the attachment state of mind with respect to the therapist, and to investigate the ways in which it recapitulates aspects of the attachment state of mind on the AAI with respect to the parents. The PT-AAI, like the AAI, is scored for attachment classification, using an adaptation of the five-way adult attachment scoring and classification system (Diamond et al., 2003a; Main & Goldwyn, 1998).

Research Findings

In this section we summarize the three major TFP research studies to place the clinical case in the context of our general outcome data, including data changes in attachment status and reflective function over the course of 1 year of TFP. We have conducted a series of three related studies to investigate the impact of TFP on the symptomatology, social adjustment, utilization of psychiatric and medical services, attachment organization, and reflective function of patients with BPD. With the assistance of a treatment development grant from the National Institute of Mental Health (NIMH; John F. Clarkin, P.I.), we generated initial effect sizes of the treatment over a 1-year period (Clarkin et al., 2001). Women with BPD who had at least two incidents of suicidal or self-injurious behavior in the previous year were selected for treatment. TFP demonstrated significant changes for the patients in a number of crucial areas. There was a significant decrease in the average medical risk of parasuicidal acts and improvement in the average physical condition following these acts. After 12 months of treatment, 52.9% of the subjects no longer met criteria for BPD. There were significantly fewer emergency room visits, hospitalizations, and days hospitalized.

Subsequent to this initial study, we compared the results of patients with BPD treated with TFP to those who received 1-year treatment as usual (TAU) in our own clinical setting. Psychiatric emergency room visits and hospitalizations during the treatment year were significantly lower in the TFP group compared to the TAU group. Patients who completed TFP showed an increase in global functioning, whereas those in TAU did not. All of the within- and between-subject effect sizes for TFP treatment participants indicated significant change, whereas effect sizes for the TAU group either deteriorated or were small (Levy, Clarkin, Schiavi, Foelsch, & Kernberg, 2007).

Encouraged by these initial results, we conducted a randomized clinical trial of TFP (Clarkin, Levy, Lenzenweger, & Kernberg, 2004) comparing our object relations treatment with dialectical behavior therapy (DBT) and a supportive psychodynamic therapy (SPT). Results indicate that patients in all three manualized treatments showed significant clinical change in many domains of functioning after 1 year of treatment, including diminution of depression and anxiety and improved psychosocial or interpersonal functioning. In the domain of suicidality, patients in both TFP and DBT showed significant reductions in suicidality, whereas those in SPT did not. Interestingly, only patients in TFP showed a marked diminution of factors related to aggression such as impulsivity and verbal and direct assault (Clarkin, Levy, Lenzenweger, & Kernberg, 2007).

We were also interested in examining the mechanisms of change, that is, how TFP brings about change, compared to the other treatments (Levy et al., 2006). For this research question, we used the reflective functioning (RF) score (Fonagy et al., 1997), an attachment-based index of mentalization, obtained from the AAI (George, Kaplan, & Main, 1985/1998), given prior to and after 1 year of treatment for patients in all treatment conditions. The AAI interviews are also rated for RF on an 11-point scale that ranges from –1, active repudiation or bizarre formulations of mental states, to 9, the formulation of unusual, highly elaborated, original and multifaceted depictions of mental states of self and others, with a midpoint of 5, which shows a clear, explicit, if somewhat ordinary, capacity to think in mental state terms. After 1 year of treatment, RF increased significantly in a positive direction for patients in the TFP group but did not change for patients in either the DBT or SPT groups. In addition, we also assessed narrative coherence on the AAI (Grice,

1975). The Narrative Coherence subscale of the AAI has been found to be the best predictor of attachment security ($r = .96$, $p = .001$) (Waters, Treboux, Crowell, Fyffe, & Crowell, 2001). Patients in the TFP group showed significant increases in narrative coherence after 1 year, whereas those in the other two groups did not. For patients in TFP, narrative coherence scores improved to a level just short of indicating attachment security. Finally, after 1 year of treatment, there was a significant increase in the number of TFP patients classified with secure states of mind with respect to attachment, but not in DBT or STP patients. It should be noted that of the 90 patients in the randomized control trial, 31.7% were initially classified as unresolved, while 18% were rated as cannot classify (Levy et al., 2006).

Case Illustration

We present a patient from our study. Although we focus on how her state of mind with respect to attachment and RF capacity might have shaped aspects of the therapeutic process and the therapeutic relationship during the first year of psychotherapy, our clinical description of the case extends to 4 years of treatment. The patient, whom we will call Nicole, is in her early 30s. She is in her fourth year of TFP with a senior therapist in the project who had over 10 years of experience in treating borderline patients, and was judged independently to be both adherent and competent in TFP. Like all the patients in the study, she was diagnosed with BPO (Kernberg, 1975) and BPD (American Psychiatric Association, 1994), and had a history of parasuicidal behaviors and multiple prior inpatient and outpatient treatments. In addition, like the majority of patients (60%) in the initial sample of which she was a part, her primary attachment classification on the AAI was unresolved with respect to loss and trauma (Diamond et al., 2003b). Also like the majority of the patients in our two initial studies, she was considered a treatment success in that she showed diminution of symptoms, including self-injurious urges and behaviors, fewer hospitalizations, and improved psychosocial functioning after the 1 year of treatment required by the research study (Clarkin et al., 2001). After the research year, she chose to continue with her therapist at a reduced fee.

   At 4 months, and then at 1 year, after beginning treatment, Nicole, like the other patients in our study, was given the AAI. At 1 year, both the patient and the therapist were given the PT-AAI. Both interviews were scored for attachment classification by raters who were blind to identifying characteristics and time of administration of the interviews. In the following section we illustrate the clinical utility of the research data for understanding aspects of the course of treatment for challenging and treatment-resistant patients with BPD such as Nicole.

   Nicole's personal history was one of unrelenting loss, abuse, and neglect. The mother developed a severe degenerative illness after the patient was born. Nicole remembers her mother being "angry all the time" and describes her as alternately neglectful and abusive. When Nicole was 3 years old, the father left the family (which also included two older brothers) for another woman, whom he married, and who discouraged all contact with his children. Nicole's mother subsequently deteriorated substantially and had to be hospitalized on numerous occasions for both emotional and physical disorders. When Nicole was 7, her mother became a paraplegic and was hospitalized until her death several years later. Nicole and her siblings were shuffled among their relatives, because their father refused to care for them and in fact failed to pick them up the day of the mother's death. Significantly, Nicole's earliest memory, at age 3, is of her father forgetting to pick her up to take her out for her birthday when her mother was in the hospital, and of feeling as though she would "perish and die." In adolescence, she developed anorexia and was hospitalized on several occasions for eating disorder and self-destructive behaviors. She married in her early 20s and had a son with her first husband. Her self-destructive behaviors, such as cutting, suicide attempts, and abusive behaviors toward her family (particularly her husband) led to a number of inpatient hospitalizations and failed outpatient treatments. About 6 years prior to the current treatment, she engaged in sexual relations with her therapist at the time. After that experience she became repulsed by sex. Her husband divorced Nicole because of her sexual involvement with her therapist. She remarried but almost immediately began an affair with her son's teacher, which led to a pregnancy and abortion. Her suicidality and destructive behaviors escalated, and after she attacked her husband's car with a baseball bat, Nicole was rehospitalized and subsequently referred to the borderline project.

Course of Treatment

Given Nicole's history of failed treatments and boundary violations, it is not surprising that the course of therapy was not only extremely stormy right from the beginning but also filled with dramatic, self-destructive enactments. She began treatment with a defiant, oppositional, and dismissing attitude, saying, "I don't want you or this treatment, but I need to get over my stupid symptoms so that I won't need anybody in my life and can live totally on my own." Based on his model of borderline pathology, the therapist understood this initial negative therapeutic reaction as representative of only part, albeit the dominant part, of Nicole's internal world. He listened to her in the first weeks of therapy with the intention of more fully comprehending and eliciting the full scope of her internal representational world. More data were provided by Nicole's way of dealing with the treatment contract. Initially, she gave lip service to the contract, but without reflection or intention to follow it, as evidenced by the fact that she refused to go the emergency room to be evaluated when she overdosed. Throughout the first 6 months, Nicole continued to drink intermittently, to overdose periodically, and to engage in other destructive and self-destructive behaviors that represented a challenge to the treatment contract and to the continuance of the therapy itself. During this period, Nicole's aggression toward herself and her therapist were interchangeable, such as an incident in which she surreptitiously tried to cut herself in a session, then began beating her therapist on the chest with her fists when he tried to intervene.

Nonetheless, over the first year of therapy, Nicole's suspicious, denigrating stance devolved into kaleidoscopic shifts between persistent devaluation and rejection of the therapist, and intense preoccupation with closeness to and caring from the therapist. Her strivings for contact and emotional engagement quickly elicited fears of rejection and abandonment that led to retreat into devaluation of the therapist and the treatment. Interspersed with her alternations between distancing devaluation and fearful clinging were dramatic enactments of a sexual and aggressive nature. There were multiple episodes in which she acted out within the sessions in a sexually aggressive manner, sometimes attempting to climb in the therapist's lap, unbutton his shirt, or undress herself in the sessions. These enactments represented an accretion of elements, including her conviction that others were objects to be exploited and abused as she herself had been exploited and abused. At times she acted out this object relational dyad with her therapist, as in the incident when she cut herself in the session, then beat her therapist on the chest for intervening, or when she made overt sexual advances toward the therapist. His firm but empathic refusal and containment of her sexual overtures gradually led her to relinquish her persistent beliefs that his interest in her was based primarily on sexual exploitation. Nicole's relentless attempts to seduce the therapist sexually, along with her initial glib acceptance, then blatant disregard of the treatment contract, represented also a manifestation of her antisocial traits that had contributed to the destruction of other treatment relationships.

By the end of the first year, Nicole began to respond well to the structure of the therapy, and her acting out gradually diminished. In the second and third years of therapy, sexual acting out inside and outside the sessions ceased, and she developed the capacity for more mature interdependence that was evident in her relationship with her husband, whom she began to value and relate to more fully, both emotionally and sexually. In addition, her functioning at work improved markedly in that she was capable of more sustained effort and took more pleasure in her success than she had previously.

Nevertheless, in Nicole's fourth year of therapy, destructive acting out returned, bringing renewed challenges to the treatment frame and contract. After she broke her contract by drinking and overdosing on her medications 2 days in a row, the therapist told Nicole that it was impossible for him to continue with her as an outpatient (as he had explained would be the case after the first overdose, if she did not go to a hospital). He told her that she would have to be hospitalized at that point, with the understanding that she could reenter therapy after 2 months provided that she demonstrate she could follow the hospital staff's treatment recommendations and be willing to adhere to the terms of a new treatment contract.

After 2 months, Nicole did resume treatment with the therapist with a more stringent treatment contract. Since that time she has ceased such self-destructive and destructive acting out, and has begun to explore a number of issues, including her excruciating history of loss and abuse, her guilt about her past affairs and abortion, as well as her sense of self as irrevocably bad and evil. Therapeutic exploration of her regression revealed that Nicole had felt only "half better" and that she feared improvement would lead to the loss of the therapist, for which she was unprepared. Her acceptance of the frame, and acknowledgment of the finitude and limits of therapy, have also led to mourning the loss of her past idealized expectations of therapy, as evidenced by her statement, "I've gotten a lot better in this therapy, but you've taken something away from me. Before I could believe in a perfect ideal love and now I see it's not possible. . . . I've accepted that." In accepting that her fantasy of ideal all-gratifying love with the therapist was not possible, Nicole showed marked progress in increasing her capacity for intimacy and gratitude in relation to the significant others in her life, including the therapist.

AAI Ratings

Nicole's state of mind with respect to attachment on the AAI, as assessed four months into treatment, predicted the chaotic treatment course and kaleidoscope of transferences that ensued. She was initially classified with a primary state of mind of Unresolved (U) because she showed severe lapses in discourse and logic and dramatic behavioral reactions in response to questions on loss and trauma. In addition, she received a secondary classification of Cannot Classify (CC) because she oscillated among different mental states with respect to attachment, using both dismissing/derogating (Ds2) and preoccupied/enmeshed (E2) strategies. We are presenting a patient with such a complex admixture of attachment states of mind because, in our experience, even those patients who show a dominant and consistent discourse strategy in their research interviews (AAI) often show a mixture of dismissing (Ds), preoccupied (E), and unresolved (U) strategies in the narratives that are the stuff of clinical reality. We provide some examples from the AAI transcripts to illustrate the characteristics of narrative discourse captured by these classifications. Although Nicole was able to complete the first AAI interview, her discourse and collaboration deteriorated markedly during the questions on loss and abuse. When asked about past experiences of abuse, for example, she acknowledged that her mother (and brothers) had abused her during childhood, but then alternated between acknowledgment and denial of the abuse. Nicole's speech became fragmented, disorganized, and incoherent, and she appeared to dissociate with regard to her memories surrounding her mother's abusiveness, stating, "She wasn't there," and "I just wish I was related to someone else." Similarly, when asked about her mother's death, she withdrew from the interviewer, began to mutter incoherently, made gestures to scratch herself, and ultimately lapsed into a mute, frozen state reminiscent of the freezing or trance-like behaviors of infants judged disoriented/disorganized in the Ainsworth Strange Situation. Such an extreme behavioral reaction, together with cognitive and linguistic disorganization, is indicative of lack of resolution of traumatic experiences on the AAI (Main & Goldwyn, 1998). In summary, Nicole's narrative was disrupted and fragmented by unmetabolized pain about past traumatic experiences.

At other points in the interview, Nicole oscillated among different attachment states of mind. As is characteristic of dismissing speakers, she initially strove to curtail the influence of attachment on her thoughts and feelings by approaching the interview tasks on an abstract level. When asked to give five words to describe her mother, for example, she first provided somewhat idealized words such as "understanding," "supportive," and "friendship." However, when prompted to provide specific memories to illustrate these words, she stated that she misunderstood the task and had thought she was supposed to describe the "ideal" mother. She then abruptly switched her descriptors to five words that were unrelentingly negative: "unloving," "unkind," "not understanding," "not supportive," and "definitely not a friend." She was mostly unable to provide specific memories to illustrate these words, instead giving general and vague statements, such as "She was always angry at me; she was always critical of me" (her elaboration of unloving). When asked to choose five words to describe her relationship with her father, Nicole also initially dismissed him in a derogating and contemptuous manner, stating, "I didn't have a relationship with him," and "I guess, stranger." But in elaborating on these words, she became overwhelmed by involving anger, which broadened to include both parents, losing the boundary between past and present, self and other, as the following passage indicates.

> "I, my memory of him is when he was telling me he was leaving. . . . And I started, I, I was sitting on his lap; he was in the kitchen and I started to cry. And he thought I was crying because I, because he was, because he, I thought, he thought that I thought he was leaving right then and there. And, like, I knew what he meant. . . . I can't, I can't do this. I can't. I'm sorry if I inconvenienced you . . . like, I don't even know why I'm crying, 'cause normally it doesn't bother me at all. I mean, I could care less. It's just makes me think, like, I just can't believe how, like, people could be like, so—like, how can you beat your kids, they're like, your life, and how could you like, mistreat them? And, then, like, I, I, I—he's not a bad person—I, I just think that . . . you know, and my mother was the same way toward me, but not my brothers. You know, so I just, like, I can't. Because of that, I know how I love my kids. You know, and nothing anyone can do could ever make me feel differently toward them, even if they grew up to be like, killing. . . . So how could my mom and father do that to me? And, so there must be something wrong with me if they're not like that toward other people."

Nicole's angry/preoccupied state of mind was evident in the run-on, garbled sentences listing the failings of her parents, in the way that she brought current feelings about her own children into the interview during queries regarding the past, and in her attempts to engage the preoccupation of the interviewer by insisting that she was unable to continue with the interview. In summary, on her AAI, Nicole initially strove to deactivate thoughts and feelings related to early attachment experiences, but ultimately she became overwhelmed by angry preoccupation toward attachment figures and at times retreated into a dissociated state in which she enacted through repetitive, self-destructive gestures her history of early traumatic loss and abuse. Thus, this interplay of Ds, U, and E states of mind with respect to attachment in the AAI paralleled the configuration of transference and countertransference that emerged in the clinical process, as described earlier and on the PT-AAI interviews at 1 year.

PT-AAI: Patient

Just as Nicole had initially maintained a stance of rejection and devaluation in the therapeutic area, when asked on the PT-AAI to describe her relationship with the therapist, she initially replied in a scathing and derogatory fashion, "I don't understand when you say relationship, cause there's no, like, relationship." She then retreated into a positive wrap-up, typical of dismissing speakers, stating, "No, it's uh, he's fine. He's helped me with like, stuff. . . . I mean, I just, I see him twice a week." Nicole's dismissing state of mind was also evident in that derogation of the significance of attachment relationships alternated with idealizing tendencies (Ds1). The words that she ultimately gave to describe the therapist were uniformly positive (e.g., "nice," "patient," "mellow," "caring," and "professional"), but she provided unconvincing and/or contradictory examples to back them up, as is typical of dismissing speakers. For instance, when asked what experiences come to mind about his being patient, she replied:

> "I don't know . . . I just can't like really, it's like, that I hate him, but I really don't hate him. . . . He always tries to help me. Like, he'll try and help me speak, like, and sometimes I don't trust him at all. But . . . it's like sometimes I trust him, sometimes I don't trust him."

The pervasively fearful preoccupation with traumatic thoughts and experiences (E3 rating) was evident in Nicole's use of frightening imagery about cutting herself and in her catastrophic fantasies about the death of the therapist during separations. She reported, "I hate when he goes away on vacation. . . . It makes me sick . . . 'cause, like I think about, like, a plane crash or something . . . like he's never coming back."

On the PT-AAI, Nicole was also found to be still struggling with a great deal of current involving anger toward the therapist (E2). For example, in elaborating on her descriptor of her therapist as "patient," she lapsed into garbled run-on sentences and entangled anger typical of preoccupied speakers, stating:

"Like I just need and um—and I can't really talk, and—or I'll get like really angry or, or then I just . . . like, a part of me gets, like, stupid. And, like, like if he says, you know, like every thing he says I'll just like—like, I'll, I'll fight with him, but like, there's a part of me that doesn't, is like, saying, 'Well, OK, well, you'll just struggle and . . . " I don't know, I just can't like, really. It's like, that I hate him, but I really don't hate him, I don't hate anyone. I hate the Pope for some reason. But when, when I start getting like that—I, I um, I have a hard time."

Thus, on the PT-AAI at 1 year, Nicole was alternately dismissing, devaluing, angrily preoccupied, or fearfully preoccupied in her state of mind with respect to the therapist, just as she had been with respect to early attachment figures on the first AAI, leading to a PT-AAI classification of cannot classify (CC/Ds1/Ds2/E2/E3).

In addition to capturing the recapitulation of her predominant attachment states of mind with respect to the parents in the therapeutic relationship, Nicole's responses on the PT-AAI also delineated shifts in her states of mind as a result of the therapeutic work. For example, there was some evidence that the therapeutic relationship provided her with the stability to begin to modulate her inchoate anger toward attachment figures. She reported drawing on her relationship with the therapist in regulating her affect and behavior during a recent argument with her husband, as follows:

"I feel like, that I understand him [the therapist], because he can, um, sometimes he'll say things that—that, like, are exactly the way I think, or feel something about. Or, um, or he'll say things that I'm not aware of, and then when he says it I'm like, 'Wow, yeah, that's. . . .' And then, so then, when it happens again to me, like, then like, I think about it like more. Like, I'm able to like think. . . . So then sometimes I can, um, like diffuse the situation, like, instead of like, I mean, it's not often but it's getting better, but, like, instead of like, um, like I, I had an argument with my husband yesterday, but I didn't, like I, I didn't touch, like usually I would punch him, kick him, or throw things. (*Mmm hmm*) But, I didn't. I mean, I was going, like I wanted to, but I just didn't."

Nicole reported that her work with the therapist has enabled her to "go with the flow of things, instead of, like, taking everything so personally," suggesting that through her therapeutic work she has become less paranoid and untrusting. That these shifts devolve in part from her internalization of the therapist and his reflective capacities is indicated by the following response to the question about whether she thinks of the therapist outside of sessions:

"Yeah, sometimes when I'm alone. Like, something he, he had said about—like, if he brings up something and then, like, I'm in that situation, and then I realize what I'm doing isn't the right thing, and then I'll think about, like, what he had said. . . . Yeah, yeah, I hear, like, his voice."

This internalization of aspects of the therapist was evident in the improvement in Nicole's capacity for mentalization on the PT-AAI at 1 year. The AAI at admission was rated as severely deficient or lacking in reflective function (–1 on the RF scale), because she retreated into silence, burst into tears, or gave hostile remarks or gestures on the demand RF questions. But on the PT-AAI at 1 year, she showed some limited capacity for consideration of mental states, albeit at a rudimentary level, leading to a rating of low or rudimentary RF (3). For example, in the following passage, in which she reflects on how the therapeutic work has affected her, Nicole demonstrates some capacity to take a developmental perspective on mental states:

"It's helped me because . . . I'm able to see like, more things that he's done. . . . I'm kind of like, maturing. . . . I just feel like I see things better than I did because of the therapy. Like, I, I don't see it so bad. . . . I've grown up, you know . . . it's like, I'm old, but I don't feel that way. Like, sometimes I feel real . . . mature.

The interview indicated that she drew on her rudimentary identification with and even imitation of her therapist's reflective capacity to help her to recognize her own thoughts, feelings, desires, wishes, and impulses as intentional mental states that can be explored and modulated in the therapeutic encounter. That she remained somewhat deficient in her capacity to explore the mind of the therapist and others is evidenced by her laconic and unreflective reply to the question about why she thinks the therapist does therapy the way he does: "He probably works with everyone like that. That's just his, the way he was taught to do therapy, I guess. I don't know."

PT-AAI: Therapist

When asked initially on the PT-AAI interview to describe his relationship with the patient, the therapist presented a contradictory picture of a patient who is alternately volatile, seductive, destructive, and withdrawn, paralleling the patient's CC attachment status on the AAI and PT-AAI. He acknowledged that her contradictory presentation posed a challenge for him even as an experienced clinician, and shaped an equally complex set of countertransference reactions. The therapist began his interview by comparing the treatment to Shakespeare's play *The Taming of the Shrew*, stating that this "fiery patient kind of pulls for . . . a kind of involvement." The therapist also stated that there was a "contrast between how fiery she could be at times and how sometimes she just looked like the shell of a person, almost like a ghost, and you wondered where the person in her went to." Just as the patient presented in starkly contradictory ways, so the therapist vacillated between feeling hopelessly frustrated by the patient and finding the work "quite gratifying," because, as he said, "I think she's beginning to get better and certainly the sessions are a lot easier with her." The five words he gave to describe Nicole—"intense," "ambivalent," "scary," "gratifying," and "fun"—convey the combination of captivation and aversion that characterized his interview. He elaborated on the word "intense" by describing her sexual overtures toward him:

> "Even more intense were those instances when she was trying to physically seduce me. She would get up from her chair, come over, try to sit in my lap, and I would have to stand up so she couldn't sit, and once she actually got into my lap before I realized. . . . I've never had this happen. So she sat in my lap and I would have to, you know, sort of fight— 'struggle' perhaps is a better word—to disengage her physically from me. . . . It was quite difficult to do, of course. Even if I did it gently, she experienced it as a total rejection. . . . It's stopped now and, I hope, for good . . . and, you know, I, I mean, on the one hand, that was assaultive to me; on the other hand, I think it was very humiliating for her. So it was a fine line."

In short, the therapist's words to describe the patient capture his contradictory and complex countertransference feelings, which in turn reflect the oscillations in the transference evident in the patient's CC PT-AAI rating. However, because the therapist was able to describe his somewhat conflictual, angry, and overinvolved feelings toward Nicole in a coherent, contained, and humorous fashion, his interview was rated as secure–autonomous (resentful/conflicted, while accepting of future involvement [F5]), albeit on the preoccupied end of secure.

Interestingly enough, given the therapist's concern about rejecting the patient, there were also intense feelings of rejection by the patient, providing evidence of an object relation of a rejecting, abusive other and a desperate self that we might see as an example of projective identification. That the therapist struggled with such difficult, conflictual feelings elicited by the object relations dyads that emerged in the transference is evident in his affirmative response to the question "Have you ever felt rejected by this patient?"

> "Yeah. Uh, it's interesting because I think there's a great sort of strong attachment from her to me. So I, I shouldn't feel rejected because every time she says she's going to drop out it, it um, it's like a child, you know, who says they're going to run away from home. But at, at the beginning, I didn't realize it . . . and at first I would think, you know, all my effort, and you're just going to, you know, turn your back on it. So I felt rejected at those times. Then I just realized that she says it but she's very attached and she probably won't really leave."

The therapist described the experience of separation from Nicole as anxiety provoking. He reported that although she initially denied having any feelings about separations, as treatment progressed, she sometimes threatened suicide or demanded that he give her personal possessions, such as his necktie, to keep during his absence. Nonetheless, the therapist maintained a high level of RF capacity (7) about the transference distortions that fueled her acting out and treatment-threatening behaviors, along with an understanding of how his mental states were causally related to those of the patient and vice versa. For example, when asked why he believed the patient acted the way she did and how she felt about him, he vividly described the complex admixture of idealization and paranoid distortion that characterized the transference, along with some playful acknowledgment of his own role in her internal world:

> "I think she's very attached to me. I think she, um, considers me some sort of savior. She doesn't understand me because she, like, she says she doesn't understand why anybody would be good, and I think she basically sees me as good when she's not being paranoid and thinking that's a mask behind which evil is lurking. Um, and I think at times, I mean she's really, uh, there's been this mixture of idealization . . . thinking that the only way somebody could care about her is if she offered herself sexually, and then a certain amount of sexual aggression toward me. . . . 'Cause um, well, how did she feel about me? Um, I think . . . in some ways she'd like to dump her husband and have me as her husband instead."

In reflecting on what he has learned from the experience with this patient on the PT-AAI, the therapist stated that he had never seen such a "clear-cut case of a paranoid transference" and that his work with Nicole had helped him to understand better the ways in which such a transference may represent a defense against the developing attachment to the therapist. Furthermore, he stated quite candidly that his work with the patient had helped him to grow as a therapist, in that it made him pay more attention to "what goes on with the affect in the room" after "you've got the theory and technique down." He concluded, "So, if there's been a change in me, it's sort of realizing you can't do this work without a certain amount of personal engagement, but you have to be careful how much."

Evolution of Transferences

Through the therapist and patient's retrospective accounts of the treatment on the PT-AAI, we can piece together the mosaic of the antisocial, perverse, paranoid, and depressive transference manifestations (Kernberg, 1992) that emerged in the course of treatment. In the initial phases of TFP, Nicole accepted the treatment contract in bad faith, without reflection, and without any intention to follow it. Such conscious, deliberate deceptiveness is characteristic of antisocial transferences (Yeomans et al., 2002). Although antisocial patients have the worst prognosis of all patients with personality disorders (Kernberg, 1984), the therapist maintained some hope in this case, because he saw Nicole as borderline with narcissistic, paranoid, and antisocial traits rather than as a full-fledged antisocial personality. He interpreted her deceptiveness and disregard for the contract, her insistence that she did not need anybody, and her initial indifference to separations as attempts to objectify him to avoid and contain the unmetabolized pain associated with unresolved attachment traumas that led to breakdowns in discourse and logic on the initial AAI. As stated earlier, the therapist observed that approximately 4 months into the treatment, Nicole began to manifest yearnings and need for emotional closeness to him. She experienced these longings for emotional contact with him as intolerable and quite quickly reverted to perverse enactments in the therapy, culminating in her attempt to seduce the therapist, and also evident in her cutting herself in sessions. The therapist conceptualized this stage of transference development as the chaotic alternation between two principal object relations dyads: one in which Nicole came across as a fierce "tiger lady," and the other in which she experienced herself as a desperately needy child. Such perverse transferences, which often entail enactments involving a confluence of sexual and aggressive wishes, are motivated by the patient's relentless desire to corrupt the therapeutic situation, to infiltrate it with hatred and destructiveness, and to destroy the helpfulness of the therapist. In true antisocial personalities, these actions would be motivated solely by the pleasure of triumph over others; in Nicole, they were largely to protect herself from the betrayal she feared if she let her longing show through. From an attachment perspective such a perverse transference also reflects the patient's underlying unresolved state of mind with respect to early losses and attachment traumas that, because they cannot be verbalized coherently, erupted in extreme behavioral reactions in the therapeutic arena. Kernberg (2004) has observed that in the course of their resolution, both psychopathic and perverse transferences tend to shift into paranoid transferences. As we saw earlier, the therapist described Nicole as in the grip of a "clear-cut, chronic paranoid transference." At one point this paranoid transference reached delusional proportions, when she thought her therapist might be the devil in disguise. Shortly thereafter, she hallucinated the presence of the devil in her bedroom, exposing a transient paranoid regression in the transference (Kernberg et al., 1989).

However, from an attachment perspective, one might also see the paranoid transference as the activation, through the intense closeness of the therapeutic relationship, of Nicole's dominant attachment state of mind, which the therapist characterized as her conviction that "worse than evil, you can't trust anyone, and you can't expect real kindness or caring from anybody." Hence, the therapist saw the paranoid transference as defending against its opposite—an intense attachment that Nicole could not allow herself to experience. The paranoid transference may also be seen as the externalization in the therapeutic relationship of a part of the self that the patient cannot accept, specifically, identification with the abusing, rejecting other that Nicole could not tolerate experiencing as part of herself, but expressed in aggressive enactments toward self and others. Since she could not tolerate awareness or exploration of this split-off, internal aspect of herself, she was driven to projects it onto others.[1]

Repeated interpretations to this effect led eventually to the emergence of signs of a depressive transference involving guilt and concern about the therapist, and remorse over past failures and transgressions toward others. One sees glimmerings of such depressive anxieties and object relational patterns on the PT-AAI in Nicole's statements about her strivings to contain her anger at her husband, in her assertion that she draws on the therapist's internal presence to regulate and modulate her affect, in her acknowledgment that she is growing old and maturing, in her regrets about the tremendous damage she has wrought on her body through cutting, and her fears that her children might be affected adversely by her destructive and self-destructive activities. Such depressive themes have formed an increasingly major aspect of the treatment from the end of the first year, when the PT-AAI assessment was conducted, to the present.

With regard to major developments over the course of the therapy, we can speculate as to the significance of the interruption of the treatment when the patient's acting out flared up in the fourth year. Whereas, on a superficial level, the patient claimed that the therapist abandoned her, one might surmise that his insistence on the limits and structure necessary for the continuance of therapy contributed to Nicole achieving a more integrated and modulated view of him, as one who is not omniscient or omnipotent, but who has limits in his capacities, and can be hurt and injured. Yet enough of a positive transference—which in Freud's (1914/1958) view involved the process of "attaching him [the patient] to the treatment and to the person of the doctor" (p. 139)—had developed in the meantime that the destruction was not total, and Nicole could hold on to a positive image of him even during the period when therapy was suspended. The resumption of therapy was followed by a period in which the patient presented as depressed, apathetic, and without enough energy to perform daily tasks. Though tempted to rely on antidepressant medication, the therapist addressed this by interpretation, suggesting that Nicole was experiencing guilt and concern over the ways in which loved and needed objects were threatened by her aggression, evident as well in her fears that her children might also have been harmed by her destructive acting out toward self and others. Most recently, Nicole has also been exploring guilt over her affair and her abortion, which she fears have branded her as murderously evil. Therapeutic exploration at this stage focused on the linkage between these negative self-representations and the effects of guilt and remorse that she was beginning to experience and her ongoing identification with powerful, punitive internal object representations that she had previously projected onto others. By identifying the guilt and remorse behind Nicole's depressive, apathetic state, her therapist brought her to reflect on it and become aware that it did not define her totally. She came to realize that just as she had once split off and projected her identification with hostile internal objects, she now was splitting off and denying the libidinal side of her self.

This reflection assisted her in integrating her loving and hateful feelings toward the therapist, manifested in increased capacity for mature dependency and collaborative work, and in the extension of this capacity to relationships outside the treatment setting. This integration took place both gradually and unevenly. As is typical in the midphases of therapy, movement toward integration was often followed by a temporary regression to the paranoid constructions in the transference; but with each cycle, the regressions were less intense and briefer (Clarkin et al., 2006). The patient's experience of trust and deepening attachment to the therapist would set off a renewed fear of vulnerability and risk that had to be explored. Ultimately, as Nicole's internal integration solidified, the dialogue in the therapy sessions became a mutual exchange in which patient and therapist could explore the meanings of the patient's experience in the transference. In summary, Nicole's case indicates how, in the course of TFP treatment, the patient may oscillate among psychopathic, perverse, paranoid, and depressive transferences that parallel to some extent the fluctuations among different states of mind with respect to attachment on the AAI and the PT-AAI.

Conclusion

This chapter has illustrated some of the major issues that have arisen in attempts to apply attachment concepts and attachment research to therapeutic work with more severely disturbed patients, which was one of Bowlby's (1988) original goals for attachment theory. Specifically, the case demonstrates how systematic investigation that through the AAI provide us with a blueprint about the patient's attachment state of mind, may both predict and be complemented by clinical investigations through the transference, providing a more nuanced view of the often chaotic and contradictory, distorted, and fragmented internal working models of attachment in clinical groups. This patient dramatically illustrates how more disturbed patients often have multiple, contradictory, oscillating states of mind with respect to attachment (Main, 1991, 1999) necessitating a CC rating on the AAI or PT-AAI. Furthermore, the PT-AAI may capture the therapist's contradictory and complex countertransference feelings toward a patient with clear oscillatory tendencies in the transference. Knowledge of the AAI (and PT-AAI) and their scoring systems may help the clinician in practice to listen for multiple, conflictual, and contradictory attachment states of mind, including fleeting secure states that may emerge from an exploration of the patient's history and from here-and-now interactions with the therapist. Our investigations with the AAI have expanded our understanding of the split internal world of the patient with BPD that, from an object relations perspective, is thought to be a fundamental aspect of the pathology. Indeed, this chapter illustrates that it is through such creative syntheses of empirical and clinical investigations that advances in the application of attachment theory and research to clinical groups will be made.

Acknowledgments

An abbreviated version of this chapter was presented at the conference, Transference-Focused Psychotherapy for Borderline Personality, Weill Cornell Medical College, New York City, November 16, 2002. The research presented in this chapter was supported by grants from the National Institute of Mental Health (Grant No. MH53705, John F. Clarkin, PI; Grant No. MH12530, Kenneth N. Levy, PI), the International Psychoanalytic Association (Diana Diamond, PI; Kenneth N. Levy, PI), the Research Foundation of CUNY (Diana Diamond, PI), the Köhler-Stiftung Foundation of Munich (Kenneth N. Levy, PI; Diana Diamond, Pamela Foelsch, and Otto Kernberg, co-PIs), and a grant from the Borderline Personality Disorder Research Foundation (BPDRF; Otto F. Kernberg, PI). We thank the BPDRF founder and executive officer, Marco Stoffel, and the scientific board for their advice and encouragement. We gratefully acknowledge the assistance of our colleagues in the Personality Disorders Institute at Weill Cornell Medical College and our students at City College and Hunter College of the City University of New York.

Note

1. A related, but somewhat different, formulation would be that the paranoid transference was the patient's way of managing the "alien self" (Fonagy et al., 2002). Fonagy sees the alien self as an element that "colonizes" the mind of the patient without being a part of it and that, therefore, does not need to be integrated, but can "dissolve" as the patient's capacity to mentalize self and other improves. We think, rather, in terms of a bad or aggression-laden internal objects linked to the preponderance of negative affect, particularly aggression, and/or engendered by traumatic or problematic experiences with attachment figures, that needs to be integrated so that it can be mastered and used in appropriate ways, such as ambitious or competitive strivings.

References

American Psychiatric Association. (1994). *Diagnostic and statistical manual of mental disorders* (4th ed.). Washington, DC: Author.
Bateman, A., & Fonagy, P. (2004). *Psychotherapy for borderline personality disorder: Mentalization-based treatment*. New York: Oxford University Press.
Bordin, E. S. (1994). Theory and research on the therapeutic working alliance: New directions. In A. O. Horvath & L. S. Greenberg (Eds.), *The working alliance: Theory, research and practice* (pp. 13–37). New York: Wiley.
Bowlby, J. (1973). *Attachment and loss: Vol. 2. Separation*. New York: Basic Books.
Bowlby, J. (1975). Attachment theory, separation anxiety and mourning. In D. A. Hamburg & K. H. Brodie (Eds.), *American handbook of psychiatry* (2nd ed., Vol. 6, pp. 292–309). New York: Basic Books.
Bowlby, J. (1978). *Attachment theory and its therapeutic implications*. Chicago: University of Chicago Press.
Bowlby, J. (1980). *Attachment and loss: Vol. 3. Loss, sadness and depression*. New York: Basic Books.

Bowlby, J. (1982). *Attachment and loss: Vol. 1. Attachment.* New York: Basic Books. (Original work published 1969)

Bowlby, J. (1988). *A secure base: Parent–child attachment and healthy human development.* New York: Basic Books.

Clarkin, J. F., Foelsch, P. A., Levy, K. N., Hull, J. W., Delaney, J. C., & Kernberg, O. F. (2001). The development of a psychoanalytic treatment for patient with borderline personality disorder: A preliminary study of behavioral change. *Journal of Personality Disorders, 15,* 487–495.

Clarkin, J. F., Levy, K. N., Lenzenweger, M. F., & Kernberg, O. F. (2004). The Personality Disorders Institute/Borderline Personality Disorder Research Foundation randomized control trial for borderline personality disorder: Rationale, methods, and patient characteristics. *Journal of Personality Disorders, 18*(1), 52–72.

Clarkin, J. F., Levy, K, N., Lenzenweger, M, & Kernberg, O. F. (2007). Evaluating three treatments for borderline personality disorder: A multiwave study. *American Journal of Psychiatry, 164,* 922–928.

Clarkin, J. F., & Posner, M. (2005). Defining the mechanisms of borderline personality disorder. *Psychopathology, 38,* 56–63.

Clarkin, J. F., Yeomans, F., & Kernberg, O. S. (1999). *Transference-focused psychodynamic therapy for borderline personality disorder patients.* New York: Wiley.

Clarkin, J. F., Yeomans, F., & Kernberg, O. F. (2006). *Psychotherapy for borderline personality: Focusing on object relations.* Washington, DC: American Psychiatric Publishing.

Depue, R. A., & Lenzenweger, M. F. (2005). A neurobehavioral dimensional model of personality disturbance. In M. F. Lenzenweger & J. F. Clarkin (Eds.), *Major theories of personality disorder* (2nd ed., pp. 391–453). New York: Guilford Press.

Diamond, D., & Blatt, S. J. (1994). Internal working models of attachment and psychoanalytic theories of the representational world: A comparison and critique. In M. B. Sperling & W. H. Berman (Eds.), *Attachment in adults: Clinical and developmental perspectives* (pp. 72–97). New York: Guilford Press.

Diamond, D., Clarkin, J., Levine, H., Levy, K., Foelsch, P., & Yeomans, F. (1999). Borderline conditions and attachment: A preliminary report. *Psychoanalytic Inquiry, 19*(5), 831–884.

Diamond, D., Clarkin, J. F., Levy, K. N., Levine, H., & Kotov, K. (1999). *The Patient–Therapist Adult Attachment Interview (PT-AAI).* Unpublished manuscript, Department of Psychology, City University of New York.

Diamond, D., Clarkin, J. F., Stovall-McClough, C., Levy, K. N., Foelsch, P., Levine, H., et al. (2002). Patient–therapist attachment: Impact on the therapeutic process and outcome. In M. Cortina & M. Marone (Eds.), *Attachment theory and the psychoanalytic process* (pp. 127–178). London: Whurr Press.

Diamond, D., Stovall-McClough, C., Clarkin, J. F., & Levy, K. N. (2003a). *Patient–therapist adult attachment scoring and classification systems.* Unpublished research manual, Department of Psychology, City University of New York.

Diamond, D., Stovall-McClough, C., Clarkin, J. F., & Levy, K. N. (2003b). Patient–therapist attachment in the treatment of borderline personality disorder. *Bulletin of the Menninger Clinic, 67*(3), 224–257.

Dozier, M., & Tyrrell, C. (1998). The role of attachment in the therapeutic relationship. In J. A. Simpson & W. S. Rholes (Eds.), *Attachment theory and close relationships* (pp. 221–248). New York: Guilford Press.

Eagle, M. (1997). Attachment and psychoanalysis. *British Journal of Medical Psychology, 70*, 217–229.

Eagle, M. (2003). Clinical implications of attachment theory. *Psychoanalytic Inquiry, 23*, 12–27.

Farber, B. A., Lippert, R. A., & Nevas, D. B. (1995). The therapist as attachment figure. *Psychotherapy, 32*, 204–212.

Fonagy, P. (1991). Thinking about thinking. *International Journal of Psychoanalysis, 72*, 639–656.

Fonagy, P. (1998). An attachment theory approach to the treatment of the difficult patient. *Bulletin of the Menninger Clinic, 62*, 147–168.

Fonagy, P. (2001). *Attachment theory and psychoanalysis*. New York: Other Press.

Fonagy, P., Gergely, G., Jurist, E., & Target, M. (2002). *Affect regulation, mentalization, and the development of the self*. New York: Other Press.

Fonagy, P., Leigh, T., Steele, M., Steele, H., Kennedy, R., Mattoon, G., et al. (1996). The relation of attachment status, psychiatric classification and response to psychotherapy. *Journal of Consulting and Clinical Psychology, 64*, 22–31.

Fonagy, P., Steele, M., Steele, H., Leigh, T., Kennedy, R., Mattoon, G., et al. (1995). Attachment, the reflective self and borderline states: The predictive specificity of the Adult Attachment Interview and pathological emotional development. In S. Goldberg, R. Muir, & J. Kerr (Eds.), *Attachment theory: Social, developmental and clinical perspectives* (pp. 233–279). Hillsdale, NJ: Analytic Press.

Fonagy, P., Steele, M., Steele, H., & Target, M. (1997). *Reflective-Functioning Manual: Version 4.1: For Application to the Adult Attachment Interviews*. Unpublished manuscript, University College London.

Freud, S. (1958). The dynamics of transference. In J. Strachey (Ed. & Trans.), *The standard edition of the complete psychological works of Sigmund Freud* (Vol. 12, pp. 97–108). London: Hogarth Press. (Original work published 1914)

George, C., Kaplan, N., & Main, M. (1998). *The Berkeley Adult Attachment Interview*. Unpublished manuscript, Department of Psychology, University of California, Berkeley.

George, C., Kaplan, N., Main, M., Diamond, D., Clarkin, J., Levy, K., et al. (1999). *The Patient–Therapist Adult Attachment Interview (PT-AAI)*. Unpublished manuscript, Department of Psychology, City University of New York.

Grice, H. P. (1975). Logic and conversation. In R. Cole & J. Morgan (Eds.), *Syntax and semantics: Speech acts* (pp. 41–58). New York: Academic Press.

Gunderson, J. (1996). The borderline patient's intolerance of aloneness: Insecure attachments and therapist's availability. *American Journal of Psychiatry, 153*, 752–758.

Hesse, E. (1999). The Adult Attachment Interview. In J. Cassidy & P. R. Shaver (Eds.), *Handbook of attachment: Theory, research, and clinical applications* (pp. 395–433). New York: Guilford Press.

Holmes, J. (1995). Something there is that doesn't love a wall: John Bowlby, attachment theory and psychoanalysis. In S. Goldberg, R. Muir, & J. Kerr (Eds.), *Attachment theory: Social, developmental and clinical perspectives* (pp. 19–43). Hillsdale, NJ: Analytic Press.

Holmes, J. (1996). *Attachment, intimacy and autonomy: Using attachment theory in adult psychotherapy*. Northvale, NJ: Aronson.

Holmes, J. (1998). The changing aims of psychoanalytic psychotherapy. *International Journal of Psychoanalysis, 79*, 227–240.

Kernberg, O. (2004). *Aggressivity, narcissism, and self-destructiveness in the psycho-therapeutic relationship: New developments in the psychopathology and psychotherapy of severe personality disorders.* New Haven, CT: Yale University Press.

Kernberg, O. F. (1975). *Borderline conditions and pathological narcissism.* New York: Aronson.

Kernberg, O. F. (1976). *Object relations theory and clinical psychoanalysis.* New York: Aronson.

Kernberg, O. F. (1984). *Severe personality disorders: Psychotherapeutic strategies.* New Haven, CT: Yale University Press.

Kernberg, O. F. (1992). Psychopathic, paranoid and depressive transferences. *International Journal of Psychoanalysis, 73,* 13–28.

Kernberg, O. F., & Caligor, E. (2004). A psychoanalytic theory of personality disorders. In M. F. Lenzenweger & J. F. Clarkin (Eds.), *Major theories of personality disorder* (2nd ed., pp. 114–156). New York: Guilford Press.

Kernberg, O. F., Diamond, D., Yeomans, F., Clarkin, J., & Levy, K. (in press). Mentalization and attachment in borderline patients in transference focused psychotherapy. In E. Jurist & A. Slade (Eds.), *Reflecting on the future of psychoanalysis: Mentalization, internalization and representation.* New York: Other Press.

Kernberg, O. F., Selzer, M. A., Koenigsberg, H. W., Carr, A. C., & Appelbaum, A. H. (1989). *Psychodynamic psychotherapy Of borderline patients.* New York: Basic Books.

Koenigsberg, H. W., Kernberg, O. F., Stone, M. H., Appelbaum, A. H., Yeomans, F. E., & Diamond, D. (2000). *Borderline patients: Extending the limits of treatability.* New York: Basic Books.

Levy, K. N., Blatt, S. J., & Shaver, P. (1998). Attachment styles and parental representations. *Journal of Personality and Social Psychology, 74,* 407–419.

Levy, K. N., Kelly, K. M., Meehan, K. B., Reynoso, J. S., Clarkin, J. F., Lenzenweger, M. F., et al. (2006). Change in attachment and reflective function in the treatment of borderline personality disorder with transference focused psychotherapy. *Journal of Consulting and Clinical Psychology, 74,* 1027–1040.

Levy, K. N., Schiavi, J. M., Clarkin, J. F., Foelsch, P. A., & Kernberg, O. F. (2007). *Transference focused psychotherapy of patients with borderline personality disorder: Comparison of a treatment as usual cohort.* Unpublished manuscript.

Mackie, A. J. (1981). Attachment theory: It's relevance to the therapeutic alliance. *British Journal of Medical Psychology, 54,* 201–212.

Main, M. (1991). Metacognitive knowledge, metacognitive monitoring, and singular (coherent) vs. multiple (incoherent) models of attachment: Findings and directions for future research. In C. M. Parkes, J. Stevenson-Hinde, & P. Marris (Eds.), *Attachment across the life cycle* (pp. 127–159). London: Routledge.

Main, M. (1995). Recent studies of attachment: Overview with selected implications for clinical work. In S. Goldberg, R. Muir, & J. Kerr (Eds.), *Attachment theory: Social, developmental, and clinical perspectives* (pp. 407–454). Hillsdale, NJ: Analytic Press.

Main, M. (1999). Epilogue: Attachment theory: Eighteen points with suggestions for future studies. In J. Cassidy & P. R. Shaver (Eds.), *Handbook of attachment: Theory, research, and clinical applications* (pp. 845–887). New York: Guilford Press.

Main, M. & Goldwyn, R. (1998). *Adult attachment scoring and classifications system.* Unpublished scoring manual, Department of Psychology, University of California, Berkeley.

Main, M., Kaplan, N., & Cassidy, J. (1985). Security in infancy, childhood, and adulthood: A move to the level of representation. In I. Bretherton & E. Waters (Eds.), Growing points in attachment theory and research. *Monographs for the Society for Research in Child Development, 50*(1–2, Serial No. 209), 66–104.

Patrick, M., Hobson, P., Castle, D., Howard, R., & Maughan, B. (1994). Personality disorder and the mental representation of early social experience. *Development and Psychopathology, 6,* 375–388.

Posner, M. I., Rothbart, M. K., Vizueta, N., Levy, K., Thomas, K. M., & Clarkin, J. (2002). Attentional mechanisms of borderline personality disorder. *Proceedings of the National Academy of Sciences USA, 99,* 16366–16370.

Posner, M. I., Rothbart, M. K., Vizueta, N., Thomas, K. M., Levy, K. N., Fossella, J., et al. (2003). An approach to the psychobiology of personality disorders. *Development and Psychopathology, 15,* 1093–1106.

Racker, H. (1968). *Transference and countertransference.* London: Maresfield Library.

Schore, A. N. (2001). Effects of a secure attachment relationship on right brain development, affect regulation and infant mental health. *Infant Mental Health Journal, 22,* 7–66.

Schore, A. N. (2003a). *Affect dysregulation and disorders of the self.* New York: Norton.

Schore, A. N. (2003b). *Affect regulation and repair of the self.* New York: Norton.

Siegel, D. J. (1999). *The developing mind: How relationships and the brain interact to shape who we are.* New York: Guilford Press.

Slade, A. (1999). Attachment theory and research: Implications for theory and practice of individual psychotherapy. In J. Cassidy & P. Shaver (Eds.), *Handbook of attachment: Theory, research, and clinical applications* (pp. 575–594). New York: Guilford Press.

Szajnberg, N. M., & Crittenden, P. M. (1997). The transference refracted through the lens of attachment. *Journal of the American Academy of Psychoanalysis, 25*(3), 409–438.

Steele, H., & Steele, M. (1998). Attachment and psychoanalysis: Time for a reunion. *Social Development, 7,* 92–119.

Waters, E., Treboux, D., Fyffe, C., & Crowell, J. (2001). *Secure versus insecure and dismissing versus preoccupied attachment representation scored as continuous variables from AAI state of mind scales.* Manuscript submitted for publication.

Yeomans, F. E., Clarkin, J. F., & Kernberg, O. F. (2002). *A primer of transference focused psychotherapy for the borderline patient.* Northvale, NJ: Aronson.

IV

The AAI and Trauma

12

The AAI and Its Contribution to a Therapeutic Intervention Project for Violent, Traumatized, and Suicidal Cases

SONIA GOJMAN DE MILLÁN and SALVADOR MILLÁN

An Adult Attachment Interview (AAI) assessment of teenage mothers who live and work in the streets contributed significantly to a social-psychological intervention project. The Seminario de Sociopsicoanálisis A.C. (SEMSOAC) developed this project to support and supervise the work of art teachers and instructors who had established a voluntary day center in Mexico City that facilitated access to graphic arts, artistic creation, and therapeutic listening for self-employed youngsters living on the streets, who were either at risk of abandoning or had already abandoned their family homes.

The Center,[1] established in the heart of one of the poorest and most densely populated neighborhoods in the city, provided a refuge for these young people whenever they felt like dropping in. It became evident soon after the Center's creation that some of the girls who attended were pregnant, and that others had already given birth to infants. Special conditions and support were necessary to provide for these teenage parents, and special attention was given to their particular needs and caregiving practices.

By presenting some examples of these cases of multiple traumas, we intend to convey how the AAIs of teenage mothers can orient the understanding of characteristically difficult life experiences and of the diverse mental processes forged in them.

We argue that clinical intervention projects with populations that are very difficult to engage can benefit from the knowledge obtained through the

AAI. A coherent account of their difficulties and states of mind can facilitate the complex interactive processes developed through the intervention and support the appropriate participation of the staff members who conduct them.

A large part of the world's population has been swept up by the dramatic changes taking place in the global socioeconomic system. One specific effect—not limited to poor countries—has been the polarization of social structures and standards of living, a phenomenon that has thrown much of the world's population into a life of extreme poverty (Sanchez Diaz de Rivera & Almeida Acosta, 2005).

The children and teenagers who live and work in the streets have gone out in search of their means of survival. They are part of what UNICEF has recently called "invisible children" (UNICEF, 2006). Although the numbers reported by different institutions vary widely, it is well known that "tens of millions of children live on the streets in plain sight, but paradoxically are among the most invisible, their plight ignored, and their needs neglected. Street children are vulnerable to all forms of exploitation and abuse" (UNICEF, 2006).

The phenomenon has become ever more serious and complex, because crime organizations use the youngsters' vulnerability to involve them in prostitution; robbery; violence; and the transportation, distribution, and consumption of drugs (Artistas por la Calle, 2005).

More than 30,000 youngsters are estimated to be living in the streets of Mexico City (V. Espinosa, personal communication, October 3, 2005). Very seldom do institutions try to face the youngsters' unique conditions, and most of these put them into shelters whose strict discipline programs feel to the children like prisons, from which they systematically escape.

A voluntary day center to facilitate street children's access to food, primary health services, and orientation for reentering school, while encouraging their creative expression in workshops as an integral developmental opportunity, was established by the nongovernment organization Artistas por la Calle A.C., with extremely inconsistent support from the federal government. It struggled to remain open despite continuous economic crisis. More than 400 youngsters had established some kind of contact with the Center; 100–150 of them had developed a close steady relationship. About 20 of these girls had infants, 12 of which were born during the 3 years that the project had been in existence.

SEMSOAC was invited to take part in this project by developing a "social character" study[2] (Gojman de Millán, 2000; Gojman de Millán & Millán, 2004) and immediately thereafter established a therapeutic space for children and teenagers at the Center.

Weekly group therapy sessions were held by two clinicians from the SEMSOAC, one psychoanalyst and one candidate[3] in each of four groups: one for children, one for women from the surrounding community, one for childless teenagers, and one for teenage parents. This group therapy, which initially lasted for 6 months, was extended for 3 more months, even though economic support for it had not been sustained.

Because of the children's chaotic day-to-day life experiences, the participatory action intervention approach had to be conceived as a "crisis intervention." As such, all of those involved had to be prepared for the challenge it posed to participants involved in the daily interactions. The clinical sessions were, in most cases, unique and valid in themselves, if only for the specific "here and now" (Bion, 1962, 1974, 1991, 1992, 1997; Fromm, 1993). The variety of stimuli, the overexcitement, and the emotional charge present just beneath the surface were manifested in the youngsters' ambivalent, aggressive, day-to-day communications and actions.

Providing supervision and support to therapists and instructors was crucial for working through the intense experiences brought up every day and understanding them outside of the explosive moment in which they took place. We therefore held regular supervision sessions—like those used in community sociopsychoanalytic work (Gojman de Millán, 1993)—every other week with the instructors and once a month with the therapists.

The work began with a 9-month period of therapeutic listening by the SEMSOAC clinicians, followed by the phase carried out mainly by the team members of the Center and the art instructors who conducted the various workshops (e.g., theater, circus arts, movie, music, art crafts, leather, clay) and established meaningful and sometimes steady relationships with the children. The art teachers were supervised by experienced psychoanalysts in regular group sessions[4] and in weekly board meetings.[5] Only after the initial period (in which analytic therapists and candidates participated) were we able to assess the teenage mothers using the AAI. The information from the AAI can be used to gain a deeper understanding of the children's life experiences and their difficulties in permitting steady relationships. Furthermore, the AAI exposes these children's constant fears, their unsolvable conflicts, and their insurmountable hope–dread of accomplishing what they desire most: to become close to others who are available to understand and help them. This knowledge was very useful to back up the orientation we gave to the instructors.

The day-to-day intervention with the youngsters, as expected, was an intense emotional challenge. Like professional clinicians in crisis interventions, instructors were faced with a tremendous amount of pain. The affective communication with the youngsters involved an unconscious emotional interchange through projective identification (Bion, 1992) with the hopelessness and distress of experiencing oneself as marginalized, even from the family institution, on which we so primordially rely.

Instructors, facilitators of artistic expression, became the repositories of the emotional containment established at the Center. They tended to become involved emotionally with the intense day-to-day affective demands of the youngsters. They experienced repeatedly the strength and violence of the manifestations and emotional expressions the children projected into them day after day.

Being able to use the AAI and what it revealed about the life histories of the interviewees (including the losses, traumas, and abuses they have suffered) and their day-to-day functioning helped us as clinicians to orient the instructors on how to understand the youngsters and their fear of becoming involved in a relationship not driven by violence, conflict, and destructiveness. This background knowledge facilitated our understanding of the critical interactions with the youngsters and clarified the instructors' "countertransference" positions (Devereux, 1967). This helped them to clarify their emotional responses, facilitating their intuitive acceptance and their following rational participation; this in turn helped the youngsters to stabilize themselves.

The Adult Attachment Interview

The young people in this project, who tended to be volatile, suicidal, violent, and addicted to drugs and alcohol, used to appear once at the Center, disappear for months, then reappear unexpectedly. Some of them who attended regularly for long periods and participated in the Center's activities, also quite frequently, just when they were about to complete a cycle, would abandon it completely, in keeping with their suicidal, self-destructive tendencies. There were only rare, if any, opportunities to gain a thorough idea of these children's problematic experiences or of the extent to which they could benefit from steady participation in the therapeutic opportunity the project provided for them.

SEMSOAC members who had been previously trained in attachment tools assessed the teenage mothers and their infants using the AAI[6] and the Strange Situation procedure, and filmed home observations (Ainsworth, Blehar, Waters, & Wall, 1978). The Interpretative Social Character Questionnaire was also administered to provide a view of the teenagers' shared experiences and character traits in their peculiar circumstances (Millán, 1993). We found the AAI to be an immensely resourceful tool.

The AAI offered us as clinicians not only an immediate and thorough view of the troubled life stories of these extremely traumatized teenage mothers but also, through its systematic method of analysis, the structure and dynamics of their present "states of mind" as clues to their unconscious mechanisms of defense. This knowledge significantly shaped our understanding and prognosis of their day-to-day evolution, their caregiving practices with their infants, and whether they might stay on to take advantage of the therapeutic opportunities offered to them (Gojman de Millán & Millán, 2006).

Assessment of the dyads by SEMSOAC members produced—as relational psychoanalysis nowadays clearly recognizes—an effect on the studied subjects, whose personal feelings and memories had been the focus of the intersubjective exchange. Center staff participants who collaborated in the project were also affected by their introduction to attachment tools.

A secondary product of the assessments was that all participants had a heightened awareness of the needs of these particular infants and teenage mothers. As a result, a special room for babies was established at the Center—and a "lullaby workshop" to complement the art workshops. This was designed by the music instructor, who became aware of the importance of facilitating intimate–affective sharing interchanges between the dyads. Some of the teenage mothers began to participate actively in the workshop and, as a result of their daily experience of putting the babies to sleep in the lullaby workshop, developed tender and affectionate interchanges with their babies. As we describe below, two of the mothers in particular became increasingly interested and participated actively in taking care of the babies in the special room for babies at the Center. It was also clear that they began to develop new, adaptive practices as an alternative to their long-established patterns for interacting with their infants.

An Experiential Account of the AAI and Its Contribution to the Subjective Therapeutic Process

The AAI approaches precisely the world of "primary experiences," the early formative experiences stored in the dynamic unconscious that are laid down prior to and in part determine the psychic structuring of the personality (M. Steele, personal communication, May 20, 2006). The interview produces a significant emotional interchange between the two participants. It challenges not only the interviewee but also the interviewer. Today, clinicians (Gojman de Millán, 1996, 2000; Lionells, Fiscalini, Mann, & Stern, 1995; Mitchel & Aron, 1999) are aware of these dual relational processes, as are researchers in the social sciences (Sanchez Diaz de Rivera & Almeida Acosta, 1991, 2005; Touraine, 2005).

In conducting and analyzing the interviews with girls who had been expelled or had run away from their homes at such young ages, one witnesses how much the mind does to achieve stability. Their AAIs also showed major similarities with those of nonrisk samples for whom the AAI was designed. Analyzing them through the regular classical system reveals repression and alteration of memories, and highlights the unnoticed inconsistencies of discourse and the fragmentation of communication that stem from traumatic experiences and allow contradictory states of mind to coexist. The interviews showed how much the brief, shared interpersonal encounter, if examined consistently, can contribute to our knowledge of the intimate processes and the impact of these primary experiences.

After the interviews, we realized that the AAI had fostered not only in the interviewers but also in the subjects and instructors (who became familiarized

with the AAI protocol) something rare in their lives: a personal recognition of
these youngsters' subjective past experiences. Talking about how the adults
around them responded to their specific circumstances—when they were ill,
when they hurt themselves, and so forth—and how they felt about it was a
unique way for these youngsters to focus on what had been happening to
them as children and to pay attention to their feelings. By noticing their children and realizing that they (both mothers and infants) had specific needs and
feelings, participants' interchanges focused awareness on the existence and
importance of subtle, tender, and personal feelings. These feelings were very
different from the usual, overt recognition of their own unsatisfied, insatiable
material needs and demands.

The teenagers' most frequently recognized demands have to do with their
insurmountable lack of material resources. On the one hand, these demands
are expressed openly as unabashed displays of envy, fostering unmanageable
rivalries between youngsters who have been able to "get something" and
those whose longing to do so fills them with nostalgia. Therapeutic intervention does, on the other hand, recognize and offer other alternatives, the non-
material sources of well-being that foster subjectivity. The act of conducting
the AAI, as well as other attachment assessments—filming Strange Situations
or home observations, or the Social Character Interpretative Questionnaire—
directs attention to this vital realm of subjectivity and intersubjectivity.
Focusing on early interactions, the attachment tools help us to observe carefully the primary tie with the mother or principal caregiver and to capture the
long-lasting transcendence of the quality of relations and intimacy, and the
strength of primary emotional ties.

Responding to the AAI is an emotionally intense experience. The interviewer gradually brings the speaker face-to-face with his or her most remote
past, with the emotional origins of the speaker's life. The challenge is twofold
(Hesse, 1999): on the one hand to access memories from the distant past—
tapping primary processes—and on the other to attend to questions of the
here and now, reflecting on the meaning of one's memories and the behavior
of primary attachment figures—tapping secondary processes (Mitchel, 2000).
The system for assessing the interview is fundamentally based on this interchange between past and present; this is what reveals the so-called "current
states of mind" (Main, Goldwyn, & Hesse, 2002). According to the system of
analysis, focusing on the way the experiences are transmitted and not just the
content reveals the emotional mechanisms used in the manipulation of attention, which are unnoticed by the speaker. They are evident in the interplay
between the two aspects of the task at hand: (1) the emotional experience and
the different ways of confronting it, and (2) the varying abilities of the speaker
to attend flexibly to both the present and the past (Main, 1997, 2000).

In describing childhood experiences, we reveal our type of mental organization, our present "state of mind," and what we repress, or fail to notice,
during the fleeting day-to-day communications about ordinary topics. These
can be detected through verbatim transcriptions of the interviews, which can

then be examined minutely. The AAI can achieve a remarkable, deeply penetrating discussion, through an exploration lasting no longer than 2 hours, between "two strangers" who have never met before.

The queries are direct and of increasing emotional intensity. The system for coding the transcript brings us into contact with deeply buried and often dark inner passions. This might in the dismissing (Ds) transcript include the need to shield oneself from whatever contradicts global mental conceptions that offer a superficial sense of security, or, in the preoccupied (E) transcript, to lose the current context of the interview and be absorbed in past experiences, or as is the case with unresolved (U) speakers, the fragmentation of one's own mind to allow the nonintegrated coexistence of contradicting, noncompatible elements. These are all examples of ways in which one can avoid any obligation to be ruled by, or subjected to, logical reasoning, except on the apparent surface.

The system used for analyzing the AAI is therefore a window in to the unconscious. It is a systematic examination of verbal expression during a current and ephemeral interchange that gives way to the richness of emotional experience about the needs, the "inferred" satisfied or unsatisfied requirements of early childhood. These early experiences with primary caregivers can mark later developmental evolution in the interchange with others, as has been documented in longitudinal studies (Grossman, Grossman, & Zimmermann, 1999; Sroufe, Carlson, Levy, & Egeland, 1999; Sroufe, Egeland, Carlson, & Collins, 2005).

Illustrative Cases

Dismissal and Idealization: An "Adaptive" Alternative for Living, without Disintegrating, in the Streets

Candida was 15 years old and going through her third pregnancy when she was administered the AAI. Coded through the classical procedure, she clearly came across as having a dismissing/idealizing (Ds1) transcript. She asserted that her mother was "caring," "understanding," "loving," and "supportive," because her mother had approved of her "having boyfriends" since she was 7 or 8 years old. In contrast, during that time, her father was seriously concerned about her dating and talking about boyfriends. Her mother was also described very positively by Candida for having been "accepting and understanding" of her "running away" with her companion at the age of 13.

In another part of the AAI, however, we learned that Candida's mother became extremely annoyed with her for not coming home one night from a party, and as a result, threw her out of the home with all of her belongings, because she (the mother) "did not like that kind of behavior." On that occasion, Candida had spent the night at a friend's house to avoid the risk of making the trip home in the middle of the night, since nobody was able to accompany her. One month later, she moved in with her companion. Her mother moved out of the family house soon after that and did not even tell Candida where she was going. Some time later, when they met again during a visit with her aunts at the family's house, Candida's mother scolded her angrily for "not having gone to visit" her.

Another event in which we were able to code the mother's negative "inferred behavior" toward Candida was her pressuring Candida to achieve during childhood. When Candida was 11 and seriously ill with a high fever, her mother gave her some medicine to lower the fever, then, after Candida had sweated a few hours, sent her out at night to collect money for the traditional Day of the Dead holiday, as is commonly done by children in Mexico's poorer neighborhoods, thus risking her health. Candida regarded this as a sign of the "loving–caring" attitude of her mother, because she provided "the medicine" and was really excited about the costume Candida was to wear. She did not take into account her own health or that the money she and other children collected would be used to meet basic survival necessities not being supplied to them by their impoverished parents.

Thus, Candida significantly "idealized" her mother throughout the interview, because she was not able to support the positive initial portrayal she gave of her experiences with her mother during childhood.

The most important contribution of the AAI in this case was that we were able to "detect" through the classical coding system how much the subject's "inferred experience with her mother" was not as positive as she openly asserted. The system highlights the inconsistencies in Candida's descriptions and reveals through them her "idealization" of childhood experiences with her mother. Candida maintained a positive view of these experiences, without any affective or emotional awareness of her own basic needs or feelings through these difficult and risk-laden experiences.

In complete keeping with her Ds state of mind, as indicated by the coding system, the only part of the interview transcript that denotes Candida placed some value on relationships was when she spoke about her wishes for her infant daughter at age 20. Candida responded that she hoped that her daughter would always have someone to love her and care about her, and that she would not be left alone. This gave the clinician a clue to the possibility that Candida might identify with her offspring in an abstract remote way, but not at present or in any factual sense.

We were able to confirm some of the AAI findings on Candida's "inferred experiences" with her mother through another assessment, the Social Character Interview (Fromm & Maccoby, 1996), in which Candida also clearly described the abandonment and neglect of her mother, the pressure to do household chores, and how Candida's mother punished her if she did not do them by not buying the clothes Candida needed. Candida was sent to live with her father's sisters from the age of 7 to 10 or 11, at which point she did, in fact, come back to live with her mother. Then Candida was sent away by her mother when she was 13, and had found temporary refuge. A month after this, Candida moved in with her companion, with whom she now, at the age of 15, had three children. The first was stillborn in the eighth month of pregnancy. Candida did not know the cause.

If we focus on Candida's behavior and evolution within the program at the Center, we see that she has taken advantage of the program's support for children and teenagers in terms of schooling, because she came back to study. It was especially difficult to enroll Candida, because she was rejected by both the institution that supports the "children"—because, in a way, she no longer was a child—and the one that supports adult schooling, which also posed difficulties because she was not exactly an adult either. The Center finally managed to admit her through the adults program, and Candida was very successful and persistent in pursuing her studies.

Very much in keeping with Candida's Ds state of mind, art instructors at the Center described her as particularly cold, resentful, distant, and impersonal. She asked them for the material things that were offered, and clearly showed that she was only interested in getting these things from them. She would never "smile or reciprocate their looks" by either looking into their eyes or acknowledging that she was being "seen" by them.

The instructors recalled that only when Candida was going through a temporary conflict did she begin to behave a bit differently, as if she were "trying to relate" to them in a more personal way. This was when Candida tried to separate from her companion, who was very openly humiliating her. Candida turned to her mother during this episode, and for a time she allowed Candida to stay with her. During that period, she would come to the Center from a long distance, looking much better but having left her infants all through the day rather than bringing them with her, despite the facilities offered to the teenage mothers for their babies. Soon after, however, she returned to live with her companion, an alcoholic who drank heavily, and again moved into his family home, well known by Center participants as a particularly ill-maintained, miserable, dirty place.

Despite what Candida said about her wishes for her baby girl, the infant was conspicuously avoidant–highly avoidant (A1), as coded by the Ainsworth Strange Situation, which is very consistent with Candida's AAI Ds1 state of mind. Also in keeping with what would be expected from her transcript, Candida clearly neglected her baby girl, as well as her second baby, delivered a few months after the AAI interview, leaving both very frequently with either her companion (even when he was drinking heavily) or her mother-in-law, who did not take care of or pay attention to the children.

After returning to live with her companion and starting a more personal communication with the instructors, Candida frequently mentioned, with some pride, that she "quietly tolerates everything" from him, and did not "complain about anything, as is proper," as she was always "advised by" her "mother, in order to live in peace."

When we shared the findings from Candida's AAI interview with her instructors, we were able to explain how her "dismissing state of mind" clearly pointed to her need persistently to ignore and avoid emotional relations and experiences, and how she unconsciously might be protecting herself from confronting her own painful experiences. The "idealization" of her experiences (with her mother) allowed Candida to live, rather than fall to pieces, in such extreme conditions. But it also prevented her from being sensitive and responsive to her infants in particular, and to other individuals in general. Thus, the instructors were able to understand Candida's generally consistent behavior, especially toward them.

The AAI scoring system begins by establishing "inferred childhood experiences" from the speaker's discourse during the interview, which is transcribed verbatim. Based on the consistency of all the events described throughout the assessment, the discourse is systematically analyzed so that it can later be compared with what the speaker does think, in general, about his or her past experiences and the effects they have had on his or her adult life. This may or may not be consistent with what is known throughout the interview process. As seen in her transcript, Candida's specific experiences are very different from her general, abstract view of her childhood. We think that being able to "infer" that these experiences are separate from what the subject believes about his or her childhood experiences, and learning systematically to weigh these conflicting beliefs, which define the "state of mind" in the system, can help us understand how they pervade later experiences and interpersonal relations. They are related to the most primary, early emotional experiences.

A Coherent Account of Extremely Traumatic Experiences Resulting in Depression

Zoila's transcript was classified as unresolved/disorganized (Ud), autonomous (F2), "somewhat dismissing or restricting of attachment." From the start, she described the extremely difficult experiences she went through after losing her father when she was 5, just 2 or 3 months after her mother and her father had separated because of chronic marital conflict. The mother took Zoila and her siblings to live with her parents, who provided them with organized, instrumental living (e.g., food, clothing and schooling), but no attention to their personal state or feelings. She clearly and specifically "remembers" loving experiences with her father, and how sad she felt when he went away with another woman and her daughter shortly before he died—of which Zoila was informed, as we will see, some time later.

Zoila then described having found refuge in an uncle who loved her dearly and became a father substitute. This uncle committed suicide, having virtually announced it to her when he came to say good-bye to her in bed one morning, as if he were going to work, as he usually did. This time, however, he told her to look for him in his room in an hour, telling her that if he did not answer, she should break the window to get in. Only 9 years old, Zoila woke up feeling that something was wrong. When she went to look for him with another uncle, they found that he had hanged himself. Zoila said she was unable to recover from that and had to be hospitalized for a year at the age of

11. This extreme behavioral reaction to the traumatic loss experience, and having fallen into drug consumption and lost all of her will to live, are the reasons Zoila's transcript was considered Ud (the only marker that can affect the classification of the transcript, based on past behavior), not for the loss *per se.*

When Zoila's father was alive, he provided her with an adequately loving experience, and it is a bit surprising how clear her early memories of him are, even though she was less than 5 years old. Her inferred experience with her mother in her AAI transcript appears highly contradictory, with marked differences between one part of Zoila's childhood experiences and another, after her psychiatric hospitalization. Early on, her relationship with her mother was very negative. Her mother left her with her maternal grandparents for 2 years, and was unloving and completely insensitive to her feelings about her father's absence. This insensitivity was so great that, very suddenly, when Zoila was 6, and was telling her mother how much she missed being able to give her father a present on Father's Day, her mother told her that she was "crazy," that her father had passed away and "did not exist any more." Zoila had in fact "not been informed" about her father's death until then, which reminds us of some of the episodes described by Bowlby (1979) on the processes of mourning and repression at early ages.

She clearly recalled how she felt and how unloving this was of her mother, how throughout that period she felt that her mother was the cause of all of her disgrace; while the interview was in progress, Zoila reflected on how she was not at all aware of what her mother might really have been going through on her part. Then when she was about 7, her mother began a relationship with a man who became her stepfather, and took Zoila back to live with her. In a somewhat idealized way, Zoila asserted that not until her uncle died and she had to be hospitalized, when she was around 11, did her mother really change toward her and begin to pay attention to her, taking care of her and supporting her. Zoila was then able to describe some specific loving experiences with her mother.

Zoila went to live with her companion when she was 12 years old. They spoke with her mother before leaving. He was one of the first youngsters who began attending the Center, and Zoila was at first reluctant to participate. After a while, she began to attend but did not speak a word for months. Gradually, she began to have friendly, smiling interchanges with the instructors and became very active in the "movie workshop," where the characters were made out of modeling clay. Lacking the material for the work she was doing, she asked for it and spoke to the instructors for the first time. After a while, very proud of having achieved her goal of making a movie, Zoila once asked the principal if she could be put in charge of the babies' room and was immediately accepted, because she obviously liked babies and was careful with them. The AAI assessment of her pointed to how appropriate this acceptance was. Zoila and her companion soon asked for a therapeutic couple intervention[7] that lasted only a few sessions, during which they both struggled to sustain their own complaints.

Zoila's companion became extremely violent in the Center for a time and had to be expelled permanently. When Zoila became responsible for the babies' room, it was obvious that his absence was a relief to her. He became jealous of her participation and he even began hitting some of the street children at the door, when they went out.

Zoila continued coming to the Center every day, got considerable help from other youngsters in taking care of the babies, and particularly got along with a boy (about 11 years old) who used to steal a lot. When he was confronted in a meeting with the instructors, Zoila, who had an openly warm and tender relationship with him, acknowledged that he was doing something he should not do; at the same time, she made it very clear that she nevertheless had warm and tender feelings toward him.

These congruent activities at the Center confirmed the coherent state of mind that we observed in Zoila's AAI, and that has given her such protection through her difficult experiences, despite her unresolved traumatic experiences of loss and her recurrent depressive episodes.

In discussing these aspects of her AAI assessment, the instructors at the Center commented—confirming to us her coherent state of mind—that when others would talk about expressing anger and hopelessness by hitting a pillow, Zoila would insist in the possibility of saying what was wrong and talking about her feelings. This was a resourceful contribution to the group meetings.

Moreover, even though it was clear that her companion was not welcome at the Center, when he was seriously hit by a car during the period he had been banned, Zoila brought him in, confident that he would be accepted, and both of them, together with their baby, were able to attend daily while he was recovering, and both received food from the program. It was obvious that Zoila refrained from eating during that time, placing his and the baby's needs before her own.

Zoila's companion resumed drug use intermittently, and she commented that she would like him to be able to stop in a more definitive way. She recalled that she was hospitalized several times for depression and drug use, and described, in the therapeutic sessions she attended, how difficult it was for her to resist a relapse. Avoiding the renewal of such painful psychiatric experiences was for her a sufficient incentive for such a lasting abstinence.

Zoila's AAI assessment allowed us to appreciate and understand the family history of this severely traumatized girl. Zoila went through the loss of her father at age 5, the suicide of her dearest uncle at age 9, was separated from her mother from age 5 to age 7, and was psychiatrically hospitalized for depression and drug consumption more than once before she was a teenager. At age 13, she gave birth to her first infant girl.

As a clinician, one comes to appreciate in cases like these how someone can overcome difficult experiences at such a young age, and how a 14-year-old teenage mother who lives in the toughest and most violent surroundings can so comprehensively tell her difficult story and relate to other children in a systematically caring and tender way. Perhaps in her earliest experiences, maybe even before language was established, there might have been a period of adequate care by a caregiver of whom Zoila has no memory that allowed her to become structured in a secure, autonomous way. Her fathers' caring and loving memories seem to have been transcendent.

Her secure–autonomous AAI transcript helps us understand how Zoila knows to look for help when she is most in need instead of running away, as do other teenage mothers we interviewed, and how she is able to participate appropriately in several of the activities and to raise a securely attached baby. Her baby girl's Strange Situation procedure reveals that the baby is in fact secure. The baby's attachment pattern, "secure with some elements of avoidance" (B2; Ainsworth et al., 1978; Main, 2000) does impressively correspond to Zoila's coherent narrative, her flexibility to attend to the context of the interview while bringing past memories to her mind (i.e., how and when she was asked about them). It is, in fact, an almost perfect fit (Main et al., 2002) with her Autonomous (F2) state of mind" classification—with some elements of idealization of her mother and, finally, some derogation with reference to her father's death. The F2 stance of her transcript seems to have protected her infant from the risk of being disorganized that is inherent in the unresolved quality of Zoila's transcript, a result that has also elsewhere (Schuengel, van IJzendoorn, Bakermans-Kranenburg, & Blom, 1997) been observed in cases that are secondarily autonomous in contrast to those who are insecure (Ds or preoccupied [E]).

The discourse she used while recounting her dramatic history during the queries on traumatic experiences is coherent and clear, indicating an impressive awareness of her own depressive feelings and her risk of resuming addiction. It shows Zoila's possibilities for self-development and resiliency, albeit shadowed by her unresolved loss experiences (Gojman de Millán & Millán, 2006).

Aggressive/Contradictory and Fragmented/Unresolved State of Mind Used to Cope with the Battles of the Street

Ursula was a very difficult case. This 17-year-old had gone through one of the most difficult childhood experiences a person can face, as we learned through her AAI interview. She mistreated her infant son from a very young age, in front of everyone at the Center, and it became very difficult to interview her: The AAI had to be suspended while the interviewer suggested someone from the Center be found to take care of the baby, because Ursula was beating him out of desperation.

Her transcript was rated as a cutoff from the source of fear of death of the child (Ds4), cannot classify (CC), fearfully preoccupied (E3), by traumatic events, angry/conflicted (E2), and passively preoccupied (E1), with very low coherence of transcript and coherence of mind, among the lowest possible in the system, between 1 and 2. Her narrative was marked by frequent passive expressions, and it was very difficult to follow what she intended to say.

Ursula did not really pay much attention to what was being asked in the interview queries. Throughout the transcript, even when it did not correspond to the question, she compulsively described how her aunt physically abused her, beating her repeatedly for no reason all through childhood. This started at the age of 4, when Ursula and her siblings were "rescued" by the aunt from her father, who had taken Ursula and her siblings to "sell them" in a distant town.

Ursula's mother had run away from her mercilessly abusive husband, leaving the children behind. Because Ursula regained contact with her mother when she was 15 years old, in different parts of the interview she alternated between a negative appraisal of her mother and positive, idealized expressions. She began by trying to give a positive initial portrayal of her mother, although it ultimately was not so positive, because of the qualification of some of her adjectives—"She loves us, in her own way," "She cared a lot about us," and "She loses her temper. There are times when I do not understand her"— but she was unable to support these statements. Ursula unconvincingly stated that her aunt would not let her go live with her mother, who was supposedly trying to have Ursula live with her, but the way Ursula contradicted herself throughout the transcript is not a believable account of her mother's real intentions.

Ursula's expressions seemed to channel mainly through a flood of anger toward her aunt. Since becoming an adolescent, from age 13 years on, her aunt began to take her regularly to a series of gynecologists "to check out" whether Ursula had had intercourse, because she thought Ursula was having sex with her husband (Ursula's uncle). Ursula's uncle was in fact the only caregiver around who seemed to have provided her with a mild inferred instrumental loving (a score of 2.5 in the system). The first doctor confirmed that Ursula was still a virgin, but the aunt persisted, taking her to one doctor after the other, all of whom arrived at the same conclusion. These images, recalled by Ursula intermittently, intruded into all of her descriptions of past experiences. Ursula thought that this—besides the beatings—was what made her feel the worst: "not worth anything at all," and "want to die." She tried to commit suicide once, and she fell heavily into drugs.

Her aunt and her mother were inferred to have been extremely rejecting (scores of 8 and 7, respectively), almost to the highest possible extent on the scale. The aunt, in fact, kept Ursula as a servant, pressuring her intensely to do multiple household chores. For this reason, her inferred pressure to achieve is also at the high end of obtainable scores on the scale.

As mentioned earlier, Ursula's openly abusive behavior toward her infant attracted the attention of instructors at the Center from the beginning. Ursula refused to give up her baby boy, even for a short while, while she took part in the workshops. The baby cried incessantly all day long while he was with her, exasperating everyone.

Only once, when she had to go with the other teenage mothers for a medical checkup, did Ursula agree to leave him (when he was 20 months old) at the Center, after having resisted at first, saying he would "hit all the other babies." As soon as she left, to the surprise of the instructors, who were ready to deal with a very difficult morning trying to calm him down, the baby became very peaceful, allowed himself to be comforted, was smiling, and even fell asleep. This was perfectly compatible with the disorganized baby's attachment pattern with Ursula, which we assessed in the Strange Situation.

Ursula scored very high on fear of loss of her infant through death in her AAI transcript, a dismissing category marker that together with her preoccupied signs classified her transcript as a CC, that is, a transcript that combines two or more essentially incompatible states of mind—defensive postures completely at odds with one another. This category is highly consistent with Ursula's general behavior toward her infant at the Center and with what we confirmed in filming the "home" observations, of feeding, changing diapers, and playing (Ainsworth et al., 1978), as we did with some other of these dyads at the Center. Although Ursula refused to relinquish her baby for even the briefest time, she did not pay attention to him. She would involve herself in anything else around, and in the films of her "feeding" the baby, she would look constantly at the ceiling and try to give the infant some food, but since he was constantly running around, Ursula ate his food, laughed when he fell down, and made funny expressions of embarrassment about him "not behaving properly." There was almost no eye contact between Ursula and the infant and only very occasional interactions. Ursula handed the baby a toy several times, but he did not take it; the baby handed her a toy, and she did not accept it. These observations clearly showed contradicting strategies, as does her AAI transcript: dismissing (Ds4) and heavily preoccupied with trauma (E3), anger (E2), and with some passivity (E1) (Minde & Hesse, 1996).

Ursula, now about to deliver her second child, said that the Center did help her a great deal to stop beating her baby and she did participate somewhat in the lullaby workshop, although she never became systematically involved with it.

When discussing with instructors at the Center the contradicting states of mind revealed in her AAI assessment, Ursula's behavior toward the Center made sense and shed some light on why she, along with other teenage mothers, disappear suddenly from the Center, precisely either when they are in serious trouble or are being beaten by their alcoholic companions, or when something especially good for them has been achieved. In Ursula's case, the Center had been able to register her to reenter high school, but as soon as this was possible, she vanished for a time.

Anorexia, Use of a Traumatically Unresolved and Idealized Combination to Avoid Becoming Violent-Aggressive

Ramona is 17 years old and has a 22-month-old infant. She ran away to live with her companion when she was 15 years old. Her companion was also a persistent visitor to the Center and to therapeutic sessions during the period they were provided. He seems to have benefited significantly from the experience.

Ramona's AAI transcript is a cannot classify (CC), Unresolved/disorganized (Ud), fearfully preoccupied by traumatic events (E3), preoccupied–angry conflicted (E2) and Passively preoccupied (E1), and dismissing–restricted in feeling (Ds3). There seems to be no single, predominant state of mind with respect to attachment. This classification is to be expected in high-risk populations and is very consistent with the self-destructive events in which Ramona has been involved on a daily basis, such as her anorexic episodes and heavy drug consumption.

Although Ramona began the interview saying her childhood experiences were "very happy," that her parents were very loving and all of the family was happy because they "used to buy Christmas trees and be together," she could not recall a single episode involving her mother to justify all the positive adjectives she used to describe her relation with her: "My mother was a very good woman," "Our relation with her was always a nice relationship," "She gave us care and love," and "She was understanding and respectful of me." The same was true for her positive characterization of her father: "a good relationship when I was very young."

The most striking characteristic of her transcript is the incoherence of mind (a score of 1, the lowest possible on the AAI scale): asserting contradictions throughout her descriptions, failing to respond relevantly to the interviewer's queries, and concentrating instead on the present anger-charged conflict with her mother and her cousin. Ramona's transcript was marked by phrases that were passive, vague, inchoate, going off on tangents of anger and worry, which is passive as well, failing to conclude sentences, and frequently confusing herself with her mother and her mother-in-law, so much so, that it was often difficult to follow the meaning of what she was saying. Once transcribed, this discourse is identified and scored in the AAI system as passive. When present in common language or in clinical sessions, such discourse can easily be considered as "slips of the tongue" or as unfinished free associations.

Ramona blamed herself for her parents' behavior toward her, and especially for the conflicts and frequent quarrels that prompted her to run away from home at the age of 15. She witnessed violence between her parents, but at the same time asserted that they did love each other dearly and had "a very nice relationship." She was at times aware of her reluctance to admit that her father used to beat her mother severely, but on other occasions she denied that it happened at all.

Fearful visual images about death and attending neighborhood funerals with her mother intrude on her interview responses out of context. These became associated later with a description of the loss of a stillborn niece, and of her godfather. When discussing the latter in the interview, Ramona demonstrated her nonresolution of this experience of loss, veering away from her description and speaking instead about episodes of violence and death, all permeated by her fear of dying and of losing her "husband" in a similar way.

We knew from the instructors that her attendance had been spotty. She would participate actively for a while, then disappear for a long time. We also knew that she went through periods of severe anorexia and seemed to use drugs frequently, although, significantly, in limited amounts, for a reasonably long period of time. The last time Ramona had returned after a prolonged absence, she was extremely thin. We were also told that her mother was well known as an outstandingly violent woman in general, and specifically toward her own husband, Ramona, Ramona's companion, and also her other offspring and their respective companions. The violence has been so great that Ramona had to stop coming to the Center after one such episode when she was severely beaten by her mother.

It was also evident at the Center that Ramona's mother openly favored one of her cousins—who was raised within the family—and with whom Ramona had had violent confrontations. Both Ramona and her cousin seem to be leaders on the street, and their companions belong to opposite gangs. From time to time, these gangs engaged in violent confrontations. It is difficult to ascertain, but not impossible to surmise, that the rivalry between the two cousins, fed by Ramona's mother, might play a key unconscious role in some of these violent street confrontations. Nevertheless, Ramona's participation normally indicated an attitude of passive resentment, calling our attention to the possible motivations for her anorexia.

We were able to confirm most of the difficulties manifested in her AAI transcript through her social character interview, in which she clearly manifested a passive–receptive character orientation (Fromm, 1947). Her thought process was concrete, with no subjective remarks, and it was not personal, which was particularly striking because it did not transmit any emotional resonance. Her only outbursts of anger in the interview occurred when she referred to her son as "a crybaby." Ramona made it clear that she could not understand him, and that he exasperated her. She seemed to feel passively hopeless, and mentioned dreaming about sitting in a park when someone came and took her baby away from her. Ramona felt and saw in her dream that nobody helped her get the child back, and she lost him, confirming once again—through her dream scenes—her hopeless passivity in the face of important events of her life. Her language throughout the interview was rife with clichés and ideological descriptions of things evidently intended to be proper responses about supposedly happy experiences of families and well-being. What is most striking about these statements is that they seem to have been taken straight from TV advertisements that market possessions that will bring "happiness." From this interview we learned that she spent a great deal of time watching TV soap operas, which mainly present the day-to-day experiences of others.

We were told that Ramona had recently shown great consistency and satisfaction in her participation at the Center, where her baby had a personal space. She seemed to be gradually learning to relate to her baby boy, while learning arts and crafts. She was especially involved in the leather workshop and relied on the teachers who seemed to have become a sort of supportive parental image for her. It seemed from these interactions that she enjoyed being taken care of and receiving food. She seemed to have found a new way of life, in which the Center had become the main axis, although her AAI transcript brings us back to the unpredictability of her further evolution.

Concluding Remarks

Clinical, nonclassical intervention projects with very difficult-to-engage or fast-deserting populations can benefit from the knowledge obtained through AAIs. A coherent account of this population's difficulties and states of mind can facilitate the complex interactive processes developed through the intervention and support the appropriate participation of the staff members who conduct them.

The continuous containment and supervision of the instructors and art teachers in their daily interactions with the youngsters—and with each other—through the 3½ years of therapeutic and developmental assistance and workshops supplied in a voluntary day Center for street children was sustained by social psychology–oriented psychoanalysts from the SEMSOAC, who conducted, transcribed, and assessed the AAIs of the attending teenage mothers (and assessed them and their infants on the Ainsworth Strange Situation, home observations, and the social character interviews).

The AAI transcripts served as an essential tool for obtaining background knowledge of the life histories of the teenage mothers, and the strikingly frequent unexpected (and unacceptable) developmental conditions they endure from extremely young ages. In an hour and a half or 2 hours, the AAI offers the professionals a thorough view of the girls' experiences that could not have been obtained in any other way. Systematic analyses of the transcripts also reveal the unconscious mechanisms that may lie beneath their ways of relating to others, to their infants, and to the therapists, instructors, and art teachers at the Center. The process of discovering through the AAI the "atypical" (for us) paths of development these children's lives have taken, and their ways of coping with "common" (for them) conditions contains diverse, penetrating moments.

Through the assessment experience itself, the AAI gives the interviewees an opportunity to focus, reflect, and elaborate on memories of the family lives from which they were separated so early.

They gave us, as mental health professionals, a glimpse into transgenerational family histories that are very seldom known. This knowledge can contribute significantly to preventive efforts. The "invisibility" of the street children's existence and their subjective experiences become a bit more "visible." It gives us insights into the defensive mechanisms that their minds use to adapt to such difficult conditions as they not infrequently resist the scarce but well-intended alternatives offered to them, which are often unsuccessful as a result.

Becoming systematically acquainted with what the AAI system calls "current states of mind" gives clinicians an opportunity to observe the unconscious mental mechanisms that separate the experiences and their effects into different and unconnected parts, and that cannot to be comprehended or connected by the interviewee's overall conscious intellectual effort. This is the basic purpose of "idealizing" parents or caregivers in general, and as we described earlier in two specific cases (Candida and Ramona), the reason that despite difficult and traumatic childhood experiences with their parents, the interviewee's global (unsupported) view, as expressed in the AAI, is positive—even very positive. The coldness and distancing they evidence in their interactions with the instructors at the Center reflect their defensive mechanisms. In these dismissing states, the mind seems to be able to defend itself by eliminating awareness of both these painful experiences of needing the caregiver and emotional vulnerability.

In contrast, a person with an autonomous or "coherent state of mind," according to the AAI system, is able to describe his or her childhood experiences in a coherent way, through memories that support their overall view of their parents or caregivers, whether through positive or negative experiences. The integrated mind allows the subject—even among extremely adverse conditions, as we have been seen—to attend flexibly to the interview questions and to his or her childhood experiences. In Zoila's case, this coherent integration first allowed clinicians to infer, and later was confirmed by the instructors, that Zoila was able to act coherently, continuing to participate when she achieved a goal of which she was proud, and looking for help when she was most in need, in spite of her somehow prevalent unresolved loss experience and her recurrent depressive state. This evolution of her participation at the Center clearly contrasts the recurrent behavior of fragmented, nonintegrated interviewees, who tenaciously hide their needs in times of crisis or run away precisely when most in need or when they are about to achieve a goal. They fall consistently—as we have seen—into the CC category and have nonintegrated interview transcripts (e.g., Ursula and Ramona).

The AAI, conducted and analyzed by clinicians specifically trained in the system, allows them to offer orientation in the form of informed supervision and containment of the instructors who participate in the daily interactions with the youngsters at the Center. The knowledge gained through the AAI provides for supervisors the background information on the psychic characteristics of the children, and helps the instructors and art teachers to establish and develop less ephemeral and longer-lasting relationships (to the extent possible) that ultimately can make the most difference in the children's lives.

To have firsthand contact with the origins of the traumatic and high-risk conditions of these human beings, who are otherwise seldom understood in their defensively confusing, violent, and provocative manifestations, and who disguise their underlying unconscious affective needs and mechanisms, is a first step into the daring consciousness of what both these youngsters and society have so much difficulty in recognizing: a first step in beginning to "know what you are not supposed to know" and, we hope, "to see what you are not supposed to see" (Bowlby, 1988).

The systematic development and careful assessment of the interviews fostered a coherent, empathic knowledge of the chaotic and irrational conditions that affect the development of the human mind and are characteristic of the "invisible children's" lives. It sensitized both clinicians and—through containment and supervision—staff members, so that they could balance out the weight of pure emotion that crops up when discussing trauma. It gave them an opportunity to integrate this information and consolidate their accounts into group interchanges to work through the difficulties of contact with such traumatized young human beings. It opened a path for both the professionals who conducted the interviews and the therapists to help the art teachers and instructors in the difficult work of sustaining close, empathic, contained, and meaningful interactions through the creative and intensely charged expressions of the youngsters.

The project, which was intended to facilitate the emotional and day-to-day lives of the youngsters who took part in it, allowed all of the participants involved to come into contact with our shared human nature: Coherently facing human pain brings us closer to being able to fully embrace and accept the meaning of the humanist phrase of de Unamuno (1982, p. 9), "Nothing human is alien to me."

Acknoledgments

The generous collaboration of Teresa Villarreal and of Verónica Espinosa as well as of the members of the Seminario de Socio Psicoanális A.C. (SEMSOAC) was crucial to the elaboration of this chapter. SEMSOAC is a group of professionals (psychologists, psychiatrists, psychoanalysts, anthropologists, sociologists and others) that has conducted multiple community participative action studies with the purpose of widening consciousness as a tool for fostering social change (see Gojman de Millán, 1991a, 1991b, 1992, 1993, 1997; Gojman de Millán, & Millán, 2000, 2004; Millán, 1992, 1993, 1996; Millán & Gojman, 1997; Reining et al., 1976). It is a member of the RENIECYT (the Mexican National Register of Scientific and Technological Institutions) and of the International Federation of Psychoanalytic Societies (IFPS).

Notes

1. The Center, one of eight established by a group of nongovernmental organizations that had the support of the federal agency INDESOL for supplying integral assistance to street children, is unique in its intention to stimulate children's and teenagers' creativity as a means to convey their emotional expression.
2. See Gojman de Millán & Millán (2004) for a thorough review of the study. It

involved the application and interpretation of 40 social character questionnaires adapted from the interviews originally proposed in 1930 by Erich Fromm (1984), and known as the "interpretive questionnaire" (Fromm & Maccoby, 1970/1996). These clinically oriented interviews are guided by major themes or questions that serve basically as a stimulus for establishing an in-depth dialogue with each individual studied. The social character questionnaire was developed by Fromm as a practical tool for studying the interrelations between emotional attitudes rooted in a person's character and the overall socioeconomic conditions under which he or she lives. The aim of the social character concept is to apply psychoanalytic categories to social investigation.

3. The analytic therapists were Esmeralda Arriaga, Patricia González, Angélica Rodarte, Lucina Montes, and José Bretón.
4. By didactic analyst Guadalupe Sanchez and supervisory analyst Angélica Rodarte.
5. By didactic and supervisory analyst Sonia Gojman de Millán.
6. AAIs were conducted by previously trained psychoanalysts and candidates: Patricia Gonzalez, Angélica Rodarte and Monica Maccise.
7. Supplied by a psychoanalyst and a candidate of the SEMSOAC.

References

Ainsworth, M. D., Blehar, M. C., Waters, E., & Wall, S. (1978). *Patterns of attachment*. Hillsdale, NJ: Erlbaum.
Artistas por la calle. (2005). *Nadie se dio cuenta nunca: Testimonios: Otras voces*. Mexico: Conaculta.
Bion, W. (1962). *Learning from experience*. London: Heineman Medical Books.
Bion, W. (1974). *Bion's Brazilian lectures*. Rio de Janeiro, Brazil: Imago.
Bion, W. (1991). *Seminarios de psicoanálisis: San Pablo, acerca del aquí y el ahora*. Mexico: Paidós.
Bion, W. (Ed.). (1992). *Seminarios clínicos y cuatro textos* [Clinical seminars and four texts]. Buenos Aires: Lugar.
Bion, W. (1997). *Aprendiendo de la experiencia: La experiencia emocional*. Barcelona: Paidós.
Bowlby, J. (1988). *A secure base: Clinical applications of attachment theory*. London: Routledge.
Devereux, G. (1967). *From anxiety to method in the behavioral sciences*. Paris: Mouton/Ecole Practique de Hautes Etudes.
de Unamuno, M. (1954). *The tragic sense of life*. London: Dover.
Fromm, E. (1947). *Man for himself: An inquiry into the psychology of ethics*. New York: Holt.
Fromm, E. (1984). *The working class in Weimar Germany: A psychological and sociological study* (W. Bonns, Ed., & B. Weinbergeer, Trans.). Cambridge, MA: Harvard University Press.
Fromm, E. (1993). *El arte de escuchar* [The art of listening]. Buenos Aires: Paidós.
Fromm, E., & Maccoby, M. (1996). *Social character in a Mexican village*. New Brunswick, NJ: Transaction. (Original published in 1970)
Gojman de Millán, S. (1991a). Los rasgos de carácter y el conicimiento de la pobreza: El proceso de intervencion sociopsicoanalitica. In *Cuadernos II. Seminario de Sociopsicoanálisis* (pp. 160–178). Mexico: IMPAC.

Gojman de Millán, S. (1991b). *Revaloración del Cuestionario Interpretativo en una Comunidad Minera después de Tres Años de Trabajo Comunitario* Diseño Experimental Pre y Post Aplicación a la Experiencia de Trabajo de Grupo. The Final Report to the National Council of Sciences and Technology (CONACYT). Mexico.

Gojman de Millán, S. (1992). A socio-psychoanalytic intervention process in a Mexican mining village. In *Science of Man: Yearbook of the International Erich Fromm Society* (pp. 47–56). Munster: Lit-Verlag.

Gojman de Millán, S. (1993). An overview of the Mexican project of sociopsychoanalytic participative research in a mining community. In *Cuadernos IV. Social character, its study: An experiential interchange. Seminario de Sociopsicoanálisis* (pp. 59–84). Mexico: IMPAC.

Gojman de Millán, S. (1996). The analyst as a person: Fromm's approach to psychoanalytic training and practice. In M. Cortina & M. Maccoby (Eds.), *A prophetic analyst, Erich Fromm's contribution to psychoanalysis* (pp. 235–238). Northvale, NJ: Aronson.

Gojman de Millán, S. (1997). A socioeconomic dimension of the therapeutic relationship. *International Forum of Psychoanalysis, 6,* 241–252.

Gojman de Millán, S. (2000, May). *Postmodern contextualism: Meaning and the theory of social character.* Paper presented at the 11th IFPS Forum, New York.

Gojman de Millán, S., & Millán, S. (2000). Attachment patterns and social character in a Nahuatl village: Socialization processes through social character interviews and videotaped attachment current methodology. *Fromm Forum, 5,* 38–42.

Gojman de Millán, S., & Millán, S. (2004). Identity in the asphalt jungle. *International Forum of Psychoanalysis, 13*(4), 254–263.

Gojman de Millán, S., & Millán, S. (2006, May). *Interpersonal developmental processes cases from an attachment research project.* Presented to the 14th IFPS Forum, Rome.

Grossmann, K., Grossmann, K., & Zimmermann, P. (1999). A wider view of attachment and exploration: Stability and change during the years of immaturity. In J. Cassidy & P. R. Shaver (Eds.), *Handbook of attachment: Theory, research, and clinical applications* (pp. 760–786). London: Guilford Press.

Hesse, E. (1999). The Adult Attachment Interview: Historical and current perspectives. In J. Cassidy & P. R. Shaver (Eds.), *Handbook of attachment: Theory, research, and clinical applications* (pp. 395–433). London: Guilford Press.

Lionells, M., Fiscalini, J., Mann, C., & Stern, D. B. (1995). *Handbook of interpersonal psychoanalysis.* Hillsdale, NJ: Analytic Press.

Main, M. (1997, June 26). Emmanuel Miller Address to British Association of Child Psychology and Psychiatry, London.

Main, M. (2000). The organized categories of infant, child and adult attachment: Flexible vs. inflexible attention under attachment-related stress. *Journal of the American Psychoanalytic Association, 48*(4), 105–109.

Main, M., Goldwyn, R., & Hesse, E. (2002). *Adult attachment scoring and classification system (Version 7.1).* Unpublished manuscript, University of California, Berkeley.

Millán, S. (1992). The Third World and social character. In *Science of Man, Yearbook of the International Erich Fromm Society* (pp. 57–68). Munster: Lit-Verlag.

Millán, S. (1993). Methodology for the evaluation of the interpretative questionnaire used during the sessions of the Mexican seminar of sociopsychoanalysis. In

Seminario de Sociopsicoanálisis Mexico (Ed.), *Cuadernos IV: Social character, its study an experiential interchange* (pp. 107–124). Mexico: IMPAC.

Millán, S. (1996). The social dimension of transference. In M. Cortina & M. Maccoby (Eds.), *A prophetic analyst, Erich Fromm's contribution to psychoanalysis* (pp. 325–340). Northvale, NJ: Aronson.

Millán, S., & Gojman, S. (1997, April). *The weekly clinical group supervision chaired by Erich Fromm.* Presented in Erich Fromm—Psychoanalyst and Supervisor, International Conference of the International Erich Fromm Society, Ascona, Switzerland.

Minde, K., & Hesse, E. (1996). The role of the Adult Attachment Interview in parent–infant psychotherapy: A case presentation. *Infant Mental Health Journal 17*, 115–126.

Mitchel, S. (2000). *Relationality from attachment to intersubjectivity.* Hillsdale, NJ: Analytic Press.

Mitchel, S., & Aron, L. (Eds.) (1999). *Relational psychoanalysis, the emergence of a tradition.* Hillsdale, NJ: Analytic Press.

Reining, P., Cámara, F., Chiñas, B., Fanale, R., Gojman de Millán, S., Lenkerd, B., et al. (1976). *Village women: Their changing lives and fertility.* Washington, DC: AAAS.

Sanchez Diaz de Rivera, M. E., & Almeida Acosta, E. (1991). La relacion humana simetrica: Fuente de accion y conocimiento. In Seminario de Sociopsicoanálisis Mexico (Ed.), *Cuadernos II* (pp. 30–44). Mexico: IMPAC.

Sanchez Diaz de Rivera, M. E., & Almeida Acosta, E. (2005). *Las Veredas de la Incertidumbre: Relaciones Interculturales y Supervivencia Digna.* Mexico: Lupus Magister.

Schuengel, C., van IJzendoorn, M. H., Bakermans-Kranenburg, M. J., & Blom, M. (1997). Unresolved loss, disorganized attachment, and frightening parental behavior: A pilot study. *Pedagogische Studien, 74*(5), 355–366.

Sroufe, A., Carlson, E., Levy, A. K., & Egeland, B. (1999). Implications of attachment theory for developmental psychopathology. *Development and Psychopathology, 11*(1), 1–14.

Sroufe, A., Egeland, B., Carlson, E., & Collins, A. (2005). *The development of the person: The Minnesota Study of risk and adaptation from birth to adulthood.* New York: Guilford Press.

Touraine, A. (2005). Prefacio. In M. Sanchez Diaz de Rivera & E Almeida Acosta (Eds.), *Las Veredas de la Incertidumbre: Relaciones Interculturales y Supervivencia Digna* (pp. 9–12). Mexico: Lupus Magister.

UNICEF. (2006). *The state of the world's children excluded and invisible.* Available online at *www.unicef.org*.

13

Adult Attachment
and Posttraumatic Stress Disorder in
Women with Histories of Childhood Abuse

K. CHASE STOVALL-McCLOUGH, MARYLENE CLOITRE,
and JOEL F. McCLOUGH

The Adult Attachment Interview (AAI; George, Kaplan, & Main, 1996) is a unique investigative tool designed to measure internal representations of attachment and has wide-ranging clinical applications. This chapter focuses on its use in a research sample of women with histories of prolonged childhood physical and/or sexual abuse that were recruited for participation in a treatment outcome study for abuse-related symptoms (Cloitre, Koenen, Cohen, & Han, 2002). In this chapter, we explore the relationship between attachment classifications and the clinical presentation and symptom picture of women in our sample, with a focus on the three primary attachment categories of secure, dismissing, and preoccupied. We then consider the relationship between unresolved trauma (as measured by the AAI) and clinical symptoms, with a particular focus on posttraumatic stress disorder (PTSD). Finally, based on our recent findings, we discuss the theoretical inferences that can be proposed regarding the maintenance of traumatized states of mind and their implications for treatment.

The AAI as a Measure of Emotion Regulation and Interpersonal Processes

Emotion Regulation

Internal working models of attachment, rooted in early experiences with care-givers, are thought to exert their influence later in life in at least two domains of functioning: emotion regulation and expectations regarding interpersonal reciprocity (Weinfeld, Sroufe, Egeland, & Carlson, 1999). Internal working models of attachment are thought to influence these two domains, because they are developed early in life during times of distress and in the company of caregivers. The patterns with which a caregiver responds to a child's distress gradually become part of the child's internalized strategies for managing his or her own affect and, consequently, influence the child's growing ability and willingness to reach out for help when in need. The caregiver who is able to reflect on a child's signals of distress as being real, legitimate, meaningful, and manageable most likely responds accordingly. As a result, the child is able to go to this parent with confidence during times of need. Through repeated experiences with a sensitive caregiver, the child learns to interpret accurately, label, legitimize, and effectively respond to his or her own internal states. Such a history of exchanges provides the building blocks of a secure internal work-ing model of attachment in adulthood.

For the child with a history of dismissing and rejecting primary care-givers, distress is not easily tolerated by the parent, and the child is made to feel that his or her distress is unreasonable, unwarranted and/or annoying. Such children may be pushed to feel better prematurely (i.e., to put on a brave front) and may be told that they are not distressed; rather, they are "just fine." Over time, repeated experiences such as these lead a child to develop a dis-torted sense of self-reliance and emotional fortitude, warding off and denying distressing experiences and their impact. Such a history would be consistent with a later dismissing attachment state of mind. On the other end of the con-tinuum would be the child whose caregiver responds in an overly emotional, exaggerated, or chaotic way to his or her distress. Such a child may experience the caregiver as unpredictable, helpless, or overwhelmed, and is likely to inter-nalize an exaggerated sense of his or her own distress. In the context of a care-giver who seems to "fall apart" in response to the child's distress, the child is likely to internalize a sense of his or her own distress as threatening and unmanageable. This may lead the child to overreact to internal cues and maxi-mize attention to distressing experiences, setting the stage for a preoccupied state of mind.

Interpersonal Processes

Internal working models of attachment also contain the implicit rules for how one "lives in relationships" (Slade, 1999, p. 585). The ability of the caregiver to understand a distressed child's mental state, and his or her readiness to respond in a sensitive manner sets the stage for the child's open willingness to trust others in times of need. These internal models are particularly active in attachment relationships with a clear hierarchical delineation between two individuals, in which one is perceived as "stronger and wiser" than the other (Bowlby, 1988). Bowlby originally highlighted the attachment nature of the patient–therapist relationship in adulthood, and several others have since noted the salient ability of the therapeutic context to elicit from the patient expectations and behaviors consistent with his or her history of attachment (Dozier, Cue, & Barnett, 1994; Farber, Lippert, & Nevas, 1995; Slade, 1999). Thus, compared to those with insecure attachment states of mind, an adult with a secure attachment state of mind is more likely to seek help *effectively* within a therapeutic context; that is, to seek help in a way that confirms his or her previous experience.

Attachment States of Mind in a Sample of Women with Histories of Severe Childhood Abuse

For the past 7 years we have conducted, scored, and analyzed AAI with women, ages 18–65, with histories of severe physical, sexual, and emotional abuse. The sample of almost 150 women was part of a larger randomized clinical trial exploring treatments for abuse-related PTSD (Cloitre et al., 2002). The women in the sample were self-selected in the following ways: (1) They identified themselves as having been abused by a caretaker before the age of 18; (2) they had trauma-related symptoms; and (3) they were interested in psychotherapy treatment to address these symptoms. The AAI was administered as part of the pretreatment and 3-month posttreatment evaluation package.

Secure, Dismissing, and Preoccupied Attachment States of Mind

In our sample so far, security of attachment has not been associated with abuse characteristics, such as the presence, duration, or severity of physical or sexual abuse (Stovall-McClough & Cloitre, 2006). However, security of attachment does appear to be associated with initial symptom levels and, more interestingly, the ability to use the evaluation process effectively to garner support and extended help. Below we provide examples of secure, dismissing, and preoccupied transcripts from this sample and discuss the associated strategies for seeking help.

Despite the number and nature of the attachment insults endured by this sample, approximately 50% ($n = 54$) have been rated as primarily or secondarily secure on the AAI thus far ($n = 108$). This percentage is less than the average (58–62%) found in normal populations, but higher than the average (13%) found in severe clinical samples (van IJzendoorn & Bakermans-

Kranenburg, 1996). These secure transcripts are characterized by an open access to positive and negative memories and emotions, straightforward and collaborative descriptions of abuse, and thoughtful comments regarding the effects of childhood experiences. In addition, despite having endured physical or sexual abuse by one or more caregivers, descriptions of caregivers remain contained and straightforward, with little exaggeration or defensive posturing. Below we offer an example of such a transcript.[1]

This interview was rated as secure (F4b: strong valuing of relationships, with some accompanying preoccupation). The woman's history includes the loss of her mother at young age and a subsequent move to live with her estranged father and stepmother in a different country. She underwent severe physical and emotional abuse at the hands of her stepmother and chronic sexual abuse by her live-in uncle. In the interview, she speaks about her stepmother in a way that conveys the severity of her maltreatment, without significant exaggeration or minimization. Her speech also conveys her open and curious psychological stance toward her experiences. Below she answers questions about her previous descriptions of her stepmother.

Q: You said "hate" to describe your stepmother. Do you have any early memories or incidents that make you say "hate"?

A: Well, I felt like, uh, the problems that happened to her had nothing to do with me. You know, maybe, you know, it was wrong of, I don't know, me being there. Maybe they should have never brought me up, you know, I thought about that. But that wasn't something that I could do anything about. And from the first day that I can think about it she never treated me like I was a child. Not even a stepchild that you care about. I was an outsider from day one. I mean, I got clothes and I was fed and everything, but when it came to emotion there was nothing, you know? I got to learn that from other people on the outside after I got to be a little bit older. But I never got a hug, I never got a kiss, I never got . . . things you say, like, "You did good," nothing like that from her, never. No matter how, how hard I tried to please it was never enough.

Q: How about, umm, you said you "wished she was dead." Can you describe an incident or memory that made you choose those words?

A: The hurting, just the way, you know. I know it's wrong for me to, to feel like that. I mean, she is a human being, but I felt like you shouldn't, you know, you don't treat children like that. That's how I felt. And then, when I told her what my uncle did to me, she threw me down the stairs. She told me he would never do something like that to me, because she said, "If he went to [Country] and brought you back to this country is because he was trying to help you, he would never do something like that." So that's why I say I wished she was dead, 'cause I really felt that way at the time.

Q: (Later in the interview) Umm, how would you say your experiences
with your parents have affected your personality as an adult?

A: Somebody looks at me, I'm like, I wonder what is wrong with me, you
know. I know the way I sound and people al- -, people always criti-
cize my accent. And it bothers me a lot. I don't like that. Uh, I guess
that's what I'm, you know, sort of insecure, I don't feel like I hate
some people, but I always feel like the things that happened to me, I
know there's people worst off than me, but I feel like the things that
happened to me shouldn'ta happened to me. I always say "Why
me?", but then I say "Well, why not me? Maybe I am stronger from
it." But I feel like it shouldn'ta happened as a child, no. A child cannot defend themselves, a child depends on an adult to take care of
them. But I still say sometimes "Why me?", you know. And then
sometimes I will, I will think, "Well, maybe if it was a different way,
maybe if my skin wasn't this (color), maybe my stepmother woulda
loved me a little bit more," you know, you know maybe she would
have cared for me. Or maybe, you know they wouldn't of called me
those things, that type of stuff, you know. So I'm very insecure about
what people think of me.

In these passages the woman's description of negative childhood experiences is
unqualified but contained, and even actively curious. She openly explores her
ambivalent feelings about her abusive caretakers. Despite her history, she continues to hold sacred the importance of actively loving a child and the knowledge that she deserved better treatment. Like many falling into the "earned"
secure category, however, she reveals some incoherency as she attempts to
understand her history. She struggles between the knowledge that she did not
deserve such treatment and the preoccupying idea that her skin color was (and
still is) to blame. Also interesting to note is her report that she learned how to
be cared for by others later in life.

The next most frequent AAI classification in this sample (excluding unresolved) is preoccupied, with approximately 38% ($n = 41$) falling into the
either the E1 (passively preoccupied, 19%), E2 (angrily preoccupied, 38%), or
E3 (fearfully preoccupied, 43%) classifications. The next excerpt is from a
woman physically abused by her mother and sexually abused by a neighbor.
She was classified as preoccupied (E2) on the AAI. Below she describes a series
of negative events in childhood in a way that reflects her ongoing resentment
of her caregivers and her need for the listener to agree with her perceptions.

Q: What about, do you have any memories of a time maybe when you
got hurt when you were little, like, scraping your knee of falling off a
bike or something like that?

A: When I was 8 years old I had two things happen—that—were very,

very serious. . . . I almost died twice that year. The first was, I was at a birthday party, and, they used to make those, those toys that you would . . . blow into and they'd unroll a little paper ball. Well, they had a little metal disc inside, uh, to make the sound. And, I held it to my mouth at a birthday party in a bowling alley—for one of my friends. And I went huh (*makes an inhaling sound*) and inhaled, and the disc came dislodged and was lodged in my throat, and I couldn't breathe. And I started . . . gasping, and clawing at the mother who was running the birthday party, but she was . . . a stupid woman, and she just thought I was throwing up. (*laughs slightly*) And she kindly ignored me. And here I was gasping for air and somehow God was with me and I was able to, it came flying out. So I almost died, and not much later than that I had developed, uh, a lump on one side of my face. But, actually, this goes a long way, you might be interested in this. This side of my jaw got big and puffy all of a sudden. And they thought I had mumps. And they ran X-rays and they didn't know what to do. And so they waited a few weeks, they figured it was probably mumps, it didn't go down. And so then they panicked, they thought it might be cancer, and they didn't tell me that. And they had me in the hospital and they . . . biopsied it, and they didn't see, I guess, any cancer cells, they were normal. And, um . . . so, they . . . decided just—everything was fine. And this is the part that might be interesting also, cause I just kept saying to them, "Don't call my parents."

Q: And why was that?

A: 'Cause I was taking care of them, they never took care of me. (*subject crying*) Never, and I knew it. And, I think the reason why my jaw grew, was the, the result of the trauma. It was a physiological reaction. To this day my jaw is very symmetrical, look at it. You don't see much asymmetry at all, if you see any, probably don't. And I think . . . that that's what happened, because I was so bottled up. Some people get stomach problems, some people get cancer. My jaw grew, you know, some part of my body was just crying out. (*heavy sigh*) I'm sure you've seen things like that.

Here the participant attempts to pull the listener in with an emotionally charged and oddly exaggerated account of two experiences in which she was portrays herself as helpless in the presence of incompetent or uncaring caretakers. In this particular passage, she communicates her underlying rage toward her caretakers with derogation and sarcasm rather than preoccupying anger. It is also important to glean from these passages the interpersonal dynamic that is created with the listener. The clinician is pulled by the subject to agree with hard-to-believe events and odd psychological explanations, or risk betraying, enraging, or otherwise reinjuring the client. In our experience, such tensions are a common part of the first clinical interactions with those classified as angrily preoccupied.

Finally, at the other end of the spectrum are the transcripts from women with dismissing states of mind, in which the emphasis is on self-reliance and personal strength derived from harsh early experiences. Our preliminary data indicate that only 12% (n = 108) of the sample falls into the dismissing categories (0.0% Ds1: idealizing; 21% Ds2: derogating; 79% Ds3: cognitively aware/emotionally restricted). This rate is substantially lower than the average 41% rate found across clinical samples, as well as the average 24% rate found across samples of nonclinical women (van IJzendoorn & Bakermans-Kranenburg, 1996). In the following case, a woman rated as dismissing (Ds3), raised by a severely mentally ill mother, was sexually and physically abused by her father. Here she talks about an incident in which her mother was suddenly psychiatrically hospitalized and remained in the hospital for 3 years. The woman, 9 years old at the time, was sent to live with her maternal grandmother. Below, the interviewer asks about the woman's emotional reaction to the sudden separation from the mother and placement with her grandmother.

Q: And so how did your grandmother respond to you at that time, and how did you respond to the separation?

A: She was very, well, first of all, my grandmother was a doer. She was raised in [Place], so she was around very . . . she was very socially and very politically, uh, savvy. So she knew agencies and how to get us help. We went, they, they tried to get us psychiatric . . . I already went through three psychiatric evaluations, 'cause I was very . . . I handled it very well, amazingly so. And, I just can't, like, I was fine for the whole thing. So when they, you know, my sister, we all got help, but they gave us the help in accordance to how much we needed it, and I think after the third visit they said, "She really doesn't have to come, she's fine." But my grandmother was a doer. So much to the point where I, it was actually a beneficial to us to be there, the three of us.

Q: (*Later in the interview*) How do you think all of these experiences with your parents have affected your adult personality?

A: Well, it made me a stronger person, whereas I have a younger sister that it didn't fare too well. She was very neglected at that specter [*sic*]. Uh . . . but uh, it just made me stronger. Now, that could have been either way. It could have been, I was stronger to begin with. I knew the warning signs and tried to keep out of harm's way.

Unlike the previous examples, this woman appears supremely proud of her own strength in the face of adversity, even going as far as to claim immunity from her mother's mental illness and subsequent hospitalization, abuse from her father, and neglect from her grandmother. She claims the maltreatment and other attachment-related traumas made her stronger. In these ways, her AAI exemplifies core features of the dismissing stance.

Clinical Symptoms, Initial Presentation, and Willingness to Engage

The 2-week evaluation process for this project involved several steps including an initial phone screen, institutional review board (IRB) consent, 6 hours of clinical evaluation over two visits, and a follow-up call for treatment recommendations. Although the evaluation was free of charge, and feedback and referrals were provided regardless of the outcome, participants were advised that they could not be guaranteed treatment by the research team. Thus, three factors—the emotional demands of the evaluation process, the time between the initial contact and the provision of services, and the lack of guaranteed treatment—made the evaluation process uniquely suited to evoke and illuminate patients' working models of attachment. To ensure that the process resulted in the most helpful and effective treatment recommendations, we implicitly relied on the ability of the participant to maintain a working, if not positive, alliance with the clinicians throughout the process. This required continuing patience, trust, and cooperation.

It was the experience of the clinical team that women with secure working models of attachment approached the evaluation process with the most cooperation and determination, and the least ambivalence. We can comment on this finding (see also the Afterword by Jacobvitz, this volume) both qualitatively and quantitatively. For instance, women with secure attachments tended to call during working hours, thus ensuring the availability of evaluators; made themselves easily available for appointments; generally appeared on time to appointments or called in advance to cancel or reschedule; and returned phone messages. Security of attachment also seemed to coincide with unique emotional experiences on the part of the clinicians. The histories generally evoked a strong sense of empathy and compassion in the clinician and even a desire to extend extra help. In other words, these individuals were generally well-liked by the evaluators and elicited nurturing reactions from them.

On the other hand, individuals initially presenting with interviews judged as insecure behaved in ways that were sometimes ineffective and/or alienating. Women with dismissing states of mind tended to be very compliant, even submissive, during the evaluation process, asking few questions and answering only the questions that were asked. They reported the fewest and least severe symptoms on almost all self-report measures. These evaluations were experienced by the clinicians as the "easiest," because these women tended to demand very little from the clinicians and staff. These individuals routinely completed the evaluation process quickly and were experienced by the staff as emotionally distant, even when talking about abusive experiences. In fact, in some cases, particularly when self-reported symptoms were minimal, the eval-uator was left wondering why the individual was coming in for treatment at all. Thus, although the staff responded in a professional and ethical manner, there was often a meta-awareness of what these clients "pulled for," with cli-nicians reporting that they felt less *emotionally* compelled to extend help. On the other extreme, individuals who were preoccupied regarding attachment tended to be less cooperative and, on rare occasions, even hostile during the evaluation process. These individuals tended to require more from clinicians in the form of extra phone calls and special arrangements. The evaluations generally took longer than the allotted time, with clinicians sometimes spend-ing 3–4 extra hours during the evaluation process. Not surprisingly, these evaluations were more likely to be described as "difficult" or "exhausting." These women also reported the most severe symptoms across all self-report measures. The emotional reactions of clinicians were mixed, with some of the participants coming across as hostile and suspicious, whereas others were experienced as overwhelming and chaotic.

In addition, detailed notes were recorded by our staff regarding cancella-tions, duration of time from initial contact to completion of the evaluation, disposition decisions, and eventual treatment compliance. Preliminary results revealed that secure and dismissing attachment was associated with an aver-age of 25 days from the initial phone call to the completion of the evaluation process, whereas preoccupied attachment was associated with an average of over 30 days. Also, the cancellation rate during the evaluation process was fairly low for secure (14.9%) and preoccupied individuals (9.7%), but higher for individuals rated as dismissing (28%), perhaps reflecting a reluctance to seek help. A similar picture emerged when we examined disposition decisions and follow-up. Although more individuals rated as dismissing were accepted into treatment (55% ruled in) compared to those rated as secure (44%) and preoccupied (42%), they were more likely to drop out of treatment once they had started (50% drop rate for dismissing vs. 18% for secure and 13% for preoccupied; $p < .05$).

Unresolved States of Mind in a Sample of Women with Histories of Childhood Abuse

The fourth attachment classification, unresolved regarding loss or trauma, provides yet another lens through which one can understand this traumatized population. Over half the sample (52.3%) has been judged to be unresolved regarding loss and/or abuse ($n = 57$), with 43% ($n = 47$) judged as unresolved regarding abuse. Whereas secure, dismissing, and preoccupied states of mind tell us about an individual's general stance regarding attachment and help to predict initial strategies for seeking treatment, the unresolved category tells us more specifically about an individual's emotion regulation and cognitive orga-nizational capacities during discussions of early abuse.

Nature of the Unresolved Scale

A classification of unresolved trauma is reserved for adults who are unable to speak coherently about experiences of attachment-related trauma, including physical and/or sexual abuse (Main & Hesse, 1990). Individuals who are classified as unresolved have had traumatic attachment-related experiences that remain emotionally raw and cognitively unintegrated. Unresolved transcripts are marked by sudden linguistic changes during discussions of abuse that reflect a momentary disorganization of mental state, in which the individual displays a lack of monitoring of discourse and/or reasoning. Main and Hesse (1992) have proposed that unresolved speech results from the unmonitored invasion of unassimilated or disorganized traumatic material into speech, which creates a momentary collapse in discourse strategy (Hesse, 1996). Examples of unresolved speech include inconsistencies regarding the time, place, age or other significant markers surrounding the event; use of unusual words to stand for the experience, as if unable to name it; interference of visual/sensory aspects of traumatic memories; unusual absorption into another state while telling of the traumatic event; feelings of being directly and personally causal; attempts to manipulate the mind; or oscillations between believing and not believing one was abused by a parent (Main, Goldwyn, & Hesse, 1984–1998). Evidence of such linguistic and/or mental disorganization, if repeated and left uncorrected by the speaker, earns the speaker an unresolved classification.

Psychological Mechanisms Underlying Unresolved States of Mind

Dissociative processes have been suggested as the mechanism underlying the lapses in discourse seen in unresolved transcripts (Hesse & Main, 1999; Liotti, 1995, 2004; Main & Hesse, 1992). Main and Hesse (1992) suggest that unresolved speech can be characterized as falling into three categories: (1) "efforts to dissociate memories from awareness"; (2) "current interference from partially dissociated memories"; and (3) "evidence of co-existing but incompatible and dissociated memories" (pp. 131–132). Liotti (1992, 2004) has proposed that both disorganized infant attachment and parental unresolved status are compatible with dissociative processes and has furthermore speculated that they are associated with vulnerability toward developing complex trauma-related dissociative disorders.

There is some limited empirical support for this link. In a nonclinical sample, Hesse and van IJzendoorn (1998) found that adults with unresolved loss scored higher on the Tellegen Absorption Scale compared to those who were not unresolved. In another study, West, Adam, Spreng, and Rose (2001) found unresolved loss in a clinical sample of adolescents to be correlated with dissociative-like symptoms, using a scale derived from the Youth Self-Report.

These data should be treated with some caution, however. Although absorption is a component of "normal" dissociative phenomena, it is not considered a clinical symptom and does not necessarily involve the degree of mental fragmentation and lapse in time–space orientation as is seen in clinically relevant dissociative phenomena. In fact, two studies have failed to support the link between clinical levels of dissociation (as measured by the well-validated Dissociation Experiences Scale) and maternal frightened–frightening behavior, the parental behavioral concomitant of unresolved attachment (Lyons-Ruth & Block, 1996; Schuengel, Bakermans-Kranenburg, & van IJzendoorn, 1999). Accordingly, although dissociative processes may indeed be present in adults with unresolved trauma or loss, more work is needed to understand the full range of clinical phenomena and potential cognitive mechanisms underlying this classification.

PTSD: Another Conceptual Model for Understanding Unresolved States of Mind

In the case of childhood abuse, cognitive models of PTSD offer a compelling framework for understanding the mental disorganization associated with unresolved states of mind (Fearon & Mansell, 2001; Lyons-Ruth & Block, 1996; Turton, Hughes, Fonagy, & Fainman, 2004). First, empirical evidence supports a strong link between early abuse and the presence of PTSD throughout development, even into adulthood, with several studies suggesting that PTSD is one of the most common diagnoses associated with childhood abuse (Briere, 1988; Browne & Finkelhor, 1986; Zlotnick et al., 1996). Second, cognitive models of PTSD share similarities with the current theoretical understanding of unresolved attachment (e.g., Brewin, Dalgleish, & Joseph, 1996; Elhers & Clark, 2000; Foa & Hearst-Ikeda, 1996; Horowitz, 1976). These cognitive models suggest that traumatic events are encoded and integrated into memory in a substantially different way than typical, everyday memories. Unlike other memories, the stimulus features of a traumatic event (sights, smells, sensations, sounds, pain, etc.) are tied closely to the response features experienced at the time of the traumatic event (fear, panic, hiding, freezing, dissociation, etc.). As such, a traumatized individual continues to experience the original fear-based response when confronted with reminders (i.e., reexperiencing). Experiences of intrusive recollection often lead to attempts to avoid the source of danger, whether the source is internal (thoughts, feelings, images) or external (people, places, things). Many of the characteristics of unresolved speech (e.g., psychological confusion, disorientation with respect to time–place, absorption, silences, sudden changes–invasions of trauma-related topics, and unsuccessful denial) are also phenomena consistent with reexperiencing and attempts to avoid reexperiencing as seen in PTSD.

Findings Regarding the Association between Unresolved Attachment and PTSD

In a study by Turton and colleagues (2004), the relationship between PTSD and unresolved loss was explored in a sample of pregnant mothers following the stillbirth of a previous child. The authors failed to find either a relationship between PTSD and unresolved loss or an association between maternal PTSD and disorganized attachment with the subsequent child. In another study of a nonclinical sample Holocaust survivors, Sagi-Schwartz, Koren-Karie, and Joels (2003) examined traumatic stress symptoms (although they were not DSM-IV derived symptoms) and unresolved loss on the AAI. The authors found that survivors had more PTSD-like symptoms, particularly avoidant symptoms, and scored higher on unresolved loss compared to controls. The authors did not look directly at the association between unresolved status and traumatic stress symptoms, however. So despite some theoretical interest in the potential role of PTSD in unresolved attachment (Fearon & Mansell, 2001), few studies have addressed the issue, with existing studies looking only at unresolved loss in nonclinical samples.

Findings from a Study of Childhood Abuse Survivors

For the past several years, we have turned our attention to the role of PTSD and unresolved attachment following experiences of childhood abuse. In an effort to extend previous work to clinical populations, we examined the distribution of attachment classifications in a sample of 60 treatment-seeking women with histories of abuse (Stovall-McClough & Cloitre, 2006). Special attention was paid to the associations between unresolved abuse, PTSD, and dissociation. This was an important group to study, because childhood abuse experiences are highly predictive of later PTSD (Briere, 1988; Browne & Finkelhor, 1986; Zlotnick et al., 1996). Among this sample of abuse survivors, we compared attachment representations among those who met DSM-IV criteria for PTSD (50%; $n = 30$) and those who did not. The inclusion of these two diagnostic groups allowed us to examine whether unresolved trauma on the AAI was uniquely associated with PTSD or whether it was a common feature among abuse survivors in general. Also, the inclusion of a relatively large sample of women meeting diagnostic criteria for PTSD allowed for a closer examination of the link between PTSD subscales and unresolved states of mind.

A breakdown of the four-way classifications revealed that over half the sample (57%) was classified as primarily unresolved regarding either abuse, loss, or both, and 45% of the women were classified as primarily unresolved regarding their early abuse. Furthermore, we found that unresolved childhood abuse strongly predicted the incidence of PTSD, as diagnosed by the well-validated Clinician-Administered PTSD Scale (Blake et al., 1995). Unresolved trauma was associated with a 7.5-fold increase in the likelihood of being diagnosed with abuse-related PTSD. Importantly, unresolved status contributed uniquely to the presence of PTSD; the primary or secondary classifications of secure, dismissing, and preoccupied attachment states of mind did not predict PTSD diagnosis. Interestingly, although women with PTSD in this sample reported more dissociative symptoms than women without PTSD in our sample, unresolved abuse was associated with only a marginally significant correlation with dissociative symptoms ($r = .27$, $p = .05$), as measured by the Trauma Symptom Checklist. In this sample, PTSD symptoms outperformed dissociative symptoms in predicting unresolved abuse status.

Finally, we examined the relationship between unresolved speech and PTSD subscale ratings (i.e., Reexperiencing, Avoidance, Arousal/Hypervigilance). We found unresolved abuse was most strongly associated with PTSD *avoidant* symptoms as compared to intrusive or arousal symptoms. These findings, although cross-sectional in nature, have led us to think more carefully about the impact of chronic avoidance of trauma-related information on unresolved attachment states of mind.

Chronic PTSD:
The Key to Understanding Unresolved States of Mind?

Chronic PTSD results when aspects of a traumatic experience remain unintegrated and fragmented in memory and continue to elicit fear and anxiety. Memory integration can be impeded by a number of factors. Foa and colleagues (Foa & Hearst-Ikeda, 1996; Foa & Kozak, 1986) suggested that ongoing disorganization of traumatic memories, including unintegrated perceptual–sensory aspects of a trauma, result from impediments to emotional processing. They argue that *avoidance* of traumatic cues and related internal states is particularly critical to maintaining the ongoing traumatized state. When a traumatic event and the associated emotions are kept "locked away," the result is often chronic struggles with PTSD symptoms, ongoing fragmentation of memory, and disruption of biological fear-based systems. In fact, with the exception of trauma severity, the strongest predictors of ongoing PTSD are avoidance and dissociative symptoms during the acute aftermath following a traumatic event (Bryant & Harvey, 1995).

In addition to placing one at risk for long-term PTSD, avoidance of trauma-related reminders (both internal and external) may also account for the appearance of unresolved speech years following a trauma, as in the case of childhood abuse. Fearon and Mansell (2001) suggested that cognitive avoidance explains the disruption in speech as it appears in the unresolved classification. Starting with the premise that attentional flexibility is critical to remaining coherent in the AAI (Hesse, 1996), Fearon and Mansell (2001) suggested that when aspects of a painful memory are triggered during the AAI, some individuals reflexively engage in "safety behaviors" that "take up time and processing resources" (p. 387). Safety behaviors include all of those responses aimed at *avoiding* the impact of a traumatic reminder, including effortful attempts to suppress thoughts, feelings, and memories. In our sample, such disruptions in attentional processes occur particularly in those women with abuse-related PTSD and appear to be responsible in part for their inability to monitor discourse closely during abuse-related discussions. In addition to unsuccessful attempts to avoid traumatic memories, some unresolved women also appear to be derailed by the emotions and associations triggered by discussions of abuse.

Below we provide some examples of unresolved speech from our sample that illustrate the breakdown in attentional processes that occur during discussions of abuse. From a PTSD perspective, these examples illustrate unsuccessful attempts to avoid trauma-related images, thoughts, and feelings, as well as evidence of flooding of emotions and reexperiencing phenomena. The first example is from a particularly avoidant participant who later dropped from treatment because, as she reported in a letter given to us later, she felt "too exposed." Note in particular the disorientation of speech, use of vague descriptors to stand for the abuse, and her struggles with memory as she speaks (italics added for emphasis).

> Q: What age are you thinking about when you think of those memories of him being "evil"?
>
> A: *Those things*, like, that was like when I was 12, you know, like 12, 13. But I mean, even before then, he was just, you know, he had a really short temper. You know, *that one*, that was just mean, but then when I got older *it* starts turning evil. You know, *it* changed, didn't stop there. Just twisted, or mind games. He did, like, *physical stuff*.
>
> Q: (Later, when speaking about physical abuse by father) And did your mom know about that?
>
> A: No, see, that's the thing, is that my mom didn't ever know any of it, 'cause, you know, of course he would threaten us if we said anything. *And then he always made sure that we were, our baths, and everything that we, you know, take our baths, make sure, before my mom ever came home.* So my mom was like clueless a long time.
>
> Q: (Now talking about sexual abuse by father) And was that a one-time incident or did it happen frequently?
>
> A: *I think it happened more than once but I don't remember, but I just remember it happening several times. And I would see him, and I think it happened before I even remembered. I don't know why I feel that way, I just think it did. 'Cause I felt, it was just, it was a memory, I didn't remember for a long time.*

Most notable in this passage is the patient's pervasive disoriented speech as she struggles to avoid naming the abuse and instead uses words or phrases to stand for the abuse in odd ways. Also important are her grammatically confusing sentences as she simultaneously proclaims and denounces her memory of the abuse.

In another example, a participant rated as unresolved appears to reexperience the original abusive scene as she recounts a story.

Q: Do you have a specific memory for nightmarish?

A: Uh and umm {3-second pause} one time I think—my sister and I use to share a bed and I was uncomfortable and I was in this cast and my face—I was uncomfortable so I don't think I was sleeping. I wasn't sleeping well and you know he just wanted us to shut up and go to sleep. . . . So, apparently I guess he went up to *come to bathroom which is just off* and he heard us talking and he came in and just started yelling. And *now it is dark* and he didn't- the light from the bathroom *it is on so we can see* his silhouette his form yelling and he, you know, he just said, you know, we were just talking. And he is like you are not suppose to talk so shut the "F" up and a bunch of expletives and uh {3-second pause} my sister was like 8, 8½. So, uh, he comes over *to bed*, he would always come to the bed and he smacks my sister. I was closest to the wall and she was at the end of the bed but I was taking up more room because of my arm and you know he, he, he came to smack me but then looked you know a forelonging look and saw that my arm was up like this so, he yanks my sister out of the bed by her bedclothes, by *her shirt up by her feet and she is hanging, see her hanging here. (It sounds like she is talking with her mouth full this entire time.) He goes down and smacks her on the side of her head and she falls. She lands and she is crying and she is like you know, "why did you do that. I didn't do anything, why did you do that?" And then she starts to scream, "oh my God, I am bleeding." I get up and she has blood coming out of her ear and he starts you know, "Shut up, it's late and you know and fucking if you had done what I asked you to do, you fucking bitches." And uh, you know, I stood up and I looking at my sister on the floor and there is blood* coming out of her ear and I just stood there and um— so anyway then he uh—he's like "Get the fuck up" to her and *she is, like, crying and—he is like,* "Shut the fuck up. I don't want the neighbors to hear your stupid shit" and he uh, then *he is like,* "Stop crying. Just shut up," and he kind of jerks her into the bathroom and is like, "Let me look at it!" and he just you know tells her to wash her ear out, gave her a cotton swab and said, you know, "Get the fuck back in that bed. I don't want to hear anything else," and that was the extent of it. So, you know {12-second pause} yeah.

In this example, the patient becomes so absorbed in the retelling of the event that she repeatedly uses the present tense, as if the event were happening again in front of her eyes. She also frequently slips into the voice of the abuser with little introduction. For this client, the trauma is only partially organized in her memory as a past event, with many parts of the event still capable of evoking the original overwhelming experience. As she tells this story, she also re-experiences aspects of the trauma, which in turn impedes her ability to monitor her speech. This is not an uncommon occurrence during the AAI in this sample, particularly for those who have not talked about the abuse for years.

In another example, the subject describes an initial dissociative reaction to sexual abuse. She claims the dissociative experience has been maintained over time through her apparent attempts to manipulate her mind and efforts at avoiding the memory and the topic.

> Q: (Asking more about the sexual abuse the subject has just reported) So you were, you were almost 13 you said, umm, you don't have to go into any more detail than you want, but could you just tell me briefly what the nature of it, what happened?
>
> A: . . . And, my sister and I was teasing him and trying to get his attention, and pulling his hair. I was acting like a little girl, I was pulling his hair, and like, "Nah, nah, nah," making faces at him and pinching him and poking him. And then he said, "I'll chase you," and then he said, "I'm gonna take your pants down. I'm gonna take your pants down and spank you." And, of course, I said, "Nah, nah, nah, nah." And he did, he took me down in the bedroom and he, he penetrated me. And—I had, when I saw blood after I thought I was getting my period. I didn't know about—I didn't know anything about sex. And I remember going in the bathroom and standing in the bathroom. *And I felt . . . like I was on a Ferris wheel when I was up in the air and I wasn't able to touch it. And I don't think I've touched the ground since. I'm just always floating around.* And I knew that something—irreparable—had happened and I had a feeling of dread. But, and *then I just repressed it all and I never told anybody.*

There are several aspects of this passage indicative of lack of resolution. The subject begins the story midsentence, without introduction, and shows further absorption by use of unexplained pronouns, referring to her abuser as "him." She describes her profound sense of depersonalization and derealization during the encounter, claiming these original feelings remain with her even today. In her efforts to avoid the memories of abuse, she had not spoken of them to anyone until this interview. As a result, when the topic is broached, the memory seems to evoke the original dissociative response, resulting in disrupted speech and a fragmented story.

Preliminary Treatment Outcome Findings

Following a trauma, most individuals undergo what is referred to as "extinction learning," wherein the person is exposed to trauma-related cues under safe conditions. Exposure to traumatic cues under safe conditions accomplishes two tasks: First, the loosening of the connection between traumatic cues and the initial fight–flight response (i.e., habituation), and second, the integration of the original traumatic memory into the larger store of autobiographical memories (i.e., placing the event in the past). Successful resolution of the trauma from this viewpoint is characterized by an ability to recall the original event with an attenuated emotional response, along with a secure sense that the event is over.

If chronic avoidance of trauma cues plays a role in the maintenance of both unresolved trauma and ongoing PTSD, then treatments designed specifically to address avoidance symptoms and promote the integration and organization of traumatic memories should result in a decrease in both unresolved trauma and PTSD. In a pilot study ($n = 18$) we investigated whether two PTSD treatments—one involving emotion regulation and interpersonal skills training, and the other involving prolonged imaginal exposure (Cloitre et al., 2002)—significantly affected rates of unresolved trauma and PTSD (Stovall-McClough & Cloitre, 2003). We were specifically interested in whether prolonged exposure techniques, which involve exposure to traumatic memories through repeated narrative storytelling (Foa & Kozak, 1986), were superior to emotion regulation skills training in reducing rates of unresolved attachment.

Results indicated that of the 13 women who were unresolved regarding abuse before treatment, 8 lost their unresolved status following treatment (62%). In addition, a loss in PTSD diagnosis following treatment was associated with a greater decrease in unresolved trauma scores. Most importantly, unresolved scores were significantly lower following imaginal exposure treatment compared to the skills training treatment. These findings suggest that a PTSD-informed approach to the treatment of individuals with unresolved abuse histories may be a fruitful direction for future research and clinical applications. Imaginal exposure in particular shows promise as a method for addressing the forms of mental disorganization that are associated with unresolved states of mind.

Conclusion: The AAI as an Important Clinical Tool in the Treatment of Childhood Abuse Survivors and Future Applications

The administration of the AAI as part of the initial evaluation in this randomized clinical trial has greatly facilitated the provision of effective treatment to this traumatized population in many ways. First, the interview elicited valuable information regarding early family and abuse history that could not otherwise have been gathered during the evaluation. This information was used to fill in gaps of knowledge, to identify inconsistencies, and to make better treatment decisions. Second, AAI classifications helped clinicians to be better prepared for treatment. Specifically, attachment states of mind informed clinicians' understanding of patients' strategies and deficits in emotional regulation and interpersonal relatedness. With this understanding, a clinician can more specifically tailor treatment to the needs of the individual. For instance, clinicians treating individuals initially judged as preoccupied might focus on methods for containing and managing affect, particularly in the service of meeting goals. Patients' initially judged as dismissing might focus with the clinician on the identification, labeling, and validation of negative emotional states. Finally, as reported earlier, preliminary data indicate that the AAI may provide clinicians with important information about who may be at greatest risk of dropping out of treatment. Although the treatment tested in our study has been associated with better retention rates compared to previous treatments with childhood abuse survivors (Cloitre et al., 2002), a significant proportion of individuals who have failed to complete this treatment were initially judged as dismissing.

The definitive link found between unresolved attachment states of mind and a diagnosis of PTSD in our sample is also of clinical importance. For clinicians in the PTSD and related trauma fields, unresolved classifications offer another valuable lens through which the traumatized individual may be understood. Unlike currently used measures of PTSD symptoms that rely on self-report, the AAI can uncover indices of ongoing traumatization to which the patient does not have conscious access. Fine-grained analyses of individual transcripts may also offer additional insights into areas of mental or emotional disorganization that may be targeted for treatment. Finally, with its unique ability to predict problematic parenting behavior (e.g., frightened–frightening) and disorganized attachment relationships with offspring, the unresolved classification of the AAI can call clinical attention to those individuals with PTSD who may need further assistance with their parenting skills.

The emphasis in the attachment literature thus far has been on the role of dissociation as the psychological mechanism underlying unresolved speech. Although our data do not refute a dissociation hypothesis, they do provide empirical support for the possibility of alternative cognitive process at work, especially PTSD reexperiencing and avoidance. For those who incorporate the AAI into their current clinical or research practice, the application of a PTSD framework to individuals with unresolved trauma opens up new possibilities for treatment. Based on our preliminary data, a clinician working with a traumatized individual characterized by unresolved states of mind may now consider whether current approaches to PTSD treatments might be an effective direction for treatment. Our data suggest that *in vivo* and imaginal exposure techniques carried out in a careful and sensitive treatment environment may be a promising treatment alternative for individuals with unresolved trauma.

Note

1. All excerpts from transcripts are provided only with the explicit permission of sub-jects. All identifying information, including some details of abuse, has been altered to protect confidentiality.

References

Blake, D. D., Weathers, F. W., Nagy, L. M., Kaloupek, D. G., Gusman, F. D., Charney, D. S., et al. (1995). The development of a clinician-administered PTSD scale. *Journal of Traumatic Stress, 8*, 75–90.

Bowlby, J. (1988). *A Secure base: Parent–child attachment and healthy human development.* New York: Basic Books.

Brewin, C. R., Dalgleish, T., & Joseph, S. (1996). A dual representation theory of post-traumatic stress disorder. *Psychological Review, 103*, 670–686.

Briere, J. (1988). The long-term clinical correlates of childhood sexual victimization. *Annals of the New York Academy of Sciences, 528*, 327–334.

Browne, A., & Finkelhor, D. (1986). Impact of child abuse: A review of the research. *Psychological Bulletin, 99*, 66–77.

Bryant, R. A., & Harvey, A. G. (1995). Avoidant coping style and post-traumatic stress following motor vehicle accidents. *Behaviour Research and Therapy, 33*, 631–635.

Cloitre, M., Koenen, K., Cohen, L., & Han, H. (2002). Skills training in affective and interpersonal regulation followed by exposure: A phase-based treatment for PTSD related to childhood abuse. *Journal of Consulting and Clinical Psychology, 70*, 1067–1074.

Dozier, M., Cue, K., & Barnett, L. (1994). Clinicians as care givers: The role of attachment organization in treatment. *Journal of Consulting and Clinical Psychology, 62*, 793–800.

Elhers, A., & Clark, D. (2000). A cognitive model of post traumatic stress disorder. *Behavioural Research and Therapy, 38*, 319–345.

Farber, B. A., Lippert, R., & Nevas, D. (1995). The therapist as attachment figure. *Psychotherapy, 32*, 204–212.

Fearon, R., & Mansell, W. (2001). Cognitive perspectives on unresolved loss: Insights from the study of PTSD. *Bulletin of the Menninger Clinic, 65*, 380–396.

Foa, E. B., & Hearst-Ikeda, D. (1996). Emotional dissociation in response to trauma: Aninformation-processing approach. In L. K. Michelson & W. J. Ray (Eds.), *Handbook of dissociation: Theoretical, empirical, and clinical perspectives* (pp. 207–224). New York: Plenum Press.

Foa, E. B., & Kozak, M. J. (1986). Emotional processing of fear: Exposure to corrective information. *Psychological Bulletin, 99*, 20–35.

George, C., Kaplan, N., & Main, M. (1996). *Attachment interview for adults.* Unpublished manuscript, University of California, Berkeley.

Hesse, E. (1996). Discourse, memory, and the Adult Attachment Interview: A note with emphasis on the emerging cannot classify category. *Infant Mental Health Journal, 17*, 4–11.

Hesse, E., & Main, M. M. (1999). Second-generation effects of unresolved trauma in nonmaltreating parents: Dissociated, frightened, and threatening parental behavior. *Psychoanalytic Inquiry 19*, 481–540.

Hesse, E., & van IJzendoorn, M. H. (1998). Parental loss of close family members and propensities towards absorption in offspring. *Developmental Science, 1*, 299–305.

Horowitz, M. J. (1976). *Stress response syndromes*. Oxford, UK: Aronson.

Liotti, G. (1992). Disorganized/disoriented attachment in the aetiology of the dissociative disorders. *Dissociation, 5*, 196–204.

Liotti, G. (1995). Disorganised/disorientated attachment in the psychotherapy of dissociative disorders. In S. Goldberg, R. Muir, & J. Kerr (Eds.), *Attachment theory: Social, developmental and clinical perspectives*. London: Analytic Press.

Liotti, G. (2004). Trauma, dissociation, and disorganized attachment: Three strands of a single braid. *Psychotherapy: Theory, Research, Practice, and Training, 41*, 472–486.

Lyons-Ruth, K., & Block, D. (1996). The disturbed caregiving system: Relations among childhood trauma, maternal caregiving, and infant affect and attachment. *Infant Mental Health Journal, 17*, 257–275.

Main, M., Goldwyn, R., & Hesse, E. (1984–1998). *Adult attachment classification system*. Unpublished manuscript, University of California, Berkeley.

Main, M., & Hesse, E. (1990). Adult lack of resolution of attachment-related trauma related to infant disorganized/disoriented behavior in the Ainsworth Strange Situation: Linking parental states of mind to infant behavior in a stressful situation. In M. Cumming (Ed.), *Attachment in the preschool years: Theory, research and intervention* (pp. 339–426). Chicago: University of Chicago Press.

Main, M., & Hesse, E. (1992). Disorganized/disoriented infant behavior in the Strange Situation, lapses in the monitoring of reasoning and discourse during the parent's adult attachment interview, and dissociative states. In M. Ammaniti & D. Stern (Eds.), *Attachment and psychoanalysis* (pp. 86–140). Rome: Gius, Laterza, & Figli.

Sagi-Schwartz, A., Koren-Karie, N., & Joels, T. (2003). Failed mourning in the Adult Attachment Interview: The case of Holocaust child survivors. *Attachment and Human Development, 5*, 398–408.

Schuengel, C., Bakermans-Kranenburg, M. J., & van IJzendoorn, M. H. (1999). Frightening maternal behavior linking unresolved loss and disorganized infant attachment. *Journal of Consulting and Clinical Psychology, 67*, 54–63.

Slade, A. (1999). Attachment theory and research: Implications for the theory and practice of individual psychotherapy with adults. In J. Cassidy & P. Shaver (Eds.), *Handbook of attachment: Theory, research, and clinical applications* (pp. 575–594). New York: Guilford Press.

Stovall-McClough, K. C., & Cloitre, M. (2003). Reorganization of traumatic childhood memories following exposure therapy [Special issue: Roots of mental illness in children]. *Annals of the New York Academy of Science, 1008*, 297–299.

Stovall-McClough, K. C., & Cloitre, M. (2006). Unresolved attachment, PTSD, and dissociation in women with childhood abuse histories. *Journal of Consulting and Clinical Psychology, 74*, 219–228.

Turton, P., Hughes, P., Fonagy, P., & Fainman, D. (2004). An investigation into the possible overlap between PTSD and unresolved responses following stillbirth: An absence of linkage with only unresolved status predicting infant disorganization. *Attachment and Human Development, 6,* 241–253.

van IJzendoorn, M. H., & Bakermans-Kranenburg, M. J. (1996). Attachment representations in mothers, fathers, adolescents, and clinical groups: A meta-analytic search for normative data. *Journal of Consulting and Clinical Psychology, 64,* 8–21.

Weinfeld, N., Sroufe, L. A., Egeland, B., & Carlson, E. A. (1999). The nature of individual differences in infant–caregiver attachment. In J. Cassidy & P. R. Shaver (Eds.), *Handbook of attachment: Theory, research, and clinical applications* (pp. 68–88). New York: Guilford Press.

West, M., Adam, K., Spreng, S., & Rose, S. (2001). Attachment disorganization and dissociative symptoms in clinically treated adolescents. *Canadian Journal of Psychiatry, 46,* 627–631.

Zlotnick, C., Zakriski, A. L., Shea, M., Costello, E., Begin, A., Perlstein, T., et al. (1996). The long-term sequelae of sexual abuse: Support for a complex posttraumatic stress disorder. *Journal of Traumatic Stress, 9,* 195–205.

14

AAIs in a High-Risk Sample

Stability and Relation to Functioning
from Adolescence to 39 Years

JUDITH A. CROWELL and STUART T. HAUSER

Attachment theory suggests that both early and ongoing secure base experiences lead to the development of mental representations (Ainsworth, 1985, 1991; Bowlby, 1969/1982; Bretherton, 1990; Bretherton & Munholland, 1999; Crowell, Treboux, Gao, et al., 2002; Crowell et al., 2001; Kaplan, 2003; Treboux, Crowell, & Waters, 2004; Waters, Hamilton, & Weinfield, 2000; Waters, Merrick, Treboux, Crowell, & Albersheim, 2000; Weiss, 1982). These representations are expected to be not only stable and influential in guiding behaviors but also open to significant change in light of experience, especially change in the caregiving environment. Studies of normative samples using the Adult Attachment Interview (AAI) provide empirical support for this hypothesis, with very high stability over months or even years (Crowell, Treboux, & Waters, 2002; Hesse, 1999). There is evidence that in such samples, secure patterns are especially stable, and change in attachment patterns is associated with significant life events (Crowell, Treboux, & Waters, 2002; Hamilton, 2000; Sagi et al., 1994; Waters, Hamilton, et al., 2000). Movement toward security appears to be associated with changes in the caregiving environment, such as positive relationships with intimate partners, education, and moving out of parents' homes. In this chapter, we examine the stability of attachment representations in a high-risk clinical sample, as well as the relations between AAI security status and social adjustment.

341

Stability of attachment patterns has been found to be generally lower in clinical or at-risk populations of children than in normative samples (Crowell & Feldman, 1988; Greenberg, 1999; van IJzendoorn & Bakermans-Kranenburg, 1996). This finding has been attributed to the occurrence of a greater number of significant life events or changes in the caregiving environment of at-risk or clinical samples. Clinical samples, both of children and adults, are characterized by high rates of insecure patterns (Greenberg, 1999; van IJzendoorn & Bakermans-Kranenburg, 1996) and a multitude of co-occurring risk factors, including low socioeconomic status (SES), less education, more impaired relationships, and ongoing illnesses, both mental and physical (e.g., Bardone, Moffitt, Caspi, Dickson, & Silva, 1996; Gotlib, Lewinson, & Seeley, 1998; Wohlfarth, van den Brink, Ormel, Kolter, & Oldehinkel, 1993). Given these circumstances, it seems that there would be reduced opportunity for movement toward security in clinical samples of adults compared with children, and indeed, there is the chance that such significant vulnerabilities might be associated with movement toward greater insecurity over time. However, there have been very few investigations of stability and change of attachment patterns in clinical samples in adult life, with the exception of one study by Diamond, Stovall-McClough, Clarkin, and Levy (2003) investigating stability–change in psychotherapy patients. In this chapter, we pursue several related questions about stability and change in attachment in at-risk samples through consideration of adults who, as adolescents, were hospitalized for serious psychiatric disorders.

Security Assessed with the AAI

The measure of representational security with the AAI coding system (Main, Goldwyn, & Hesse, 2002) is essentially equivalent to the coherence of the interview content (Fyffe, 1997), that is, one's ability to recount an organized, believable narrative when queried about attachment-relevant experiences, and a valuing of the influences of close relationships in one's personal development. The stance of a person with a secure representation in response to attachment-related questions at any point in time is cooperative, open, fresh, and balanced, reflecting both his or her own experience and perspective, and that of other important individuals. Insecurity is characterized by greater reluctance, or inflexibility, in attachment-related discourse, incoherence, less balanced responses, a lack of believability and relevance in response to attachment-relevant questions, limited or excessive information, and a more stereotypical manner of responding to questions.

Coherence does *not* imply any particular content of experience. Thus, an individual may describe either positive or negative experiences and/or feelings associated with experiences or attachment figures, and this content does not dictate their coherence/security. Rather, the *coordination* of the affective, cognitive, and behavioral elements of the discourse is equated with security within the interview. This coordination, or coherence, must be evident *within* sections of the interview, such that if the individual gives a broad assessment of an attachment figure as loving, then he or she must support this representation by describing specific past experiences with the person—in terms of remembered behaviors/actions, emotions, and thoughts. Coordination must also be evident *across* sections of the interview. For example, when an adult is asked to remember what happened when he or she was upset as a child, an adult speaker who previously provided the adjective "loving" to describe the relationship with his or her mother would be expected to provide a memory that includes turning to her, or receiving support from her, when upset as a child. Such an interview would likely be considered the product of a cohesive mind, or the narrative would be rated high for coherence of transcript and of mind because the individual has reflected convincingly on apparent contradictions.

Implications of Security for Adults

The coordination of cognition, emotion, and behavior that is reflected in the rating of AAI coherence/security has implications for adult social functioning in the domains of close relationships and management of stressful events. A number of studies show relations between AAI security and behaviors in peer and close relationships, both in parent–child and adult partnerships (Allen, Hauser, & Borman-Spurrell, 1996; Cohn, Cowan, Cowan, & Pearson, 1992; Cohn, Silver, Cowan, Cowan, & Pearson, 1992; Creasey, 2002; Crowell & Feldman, 1988; Crowell, Treboux, Gao, et al., 2002; Crowell et al., 2001; Das Eiden, Teti, & Corns, 1995; Furman, Simon, Shaffer, & Bouchey, 2002; Grossmann & Grossmann, 2003; Kobak, 1991; Main, Kaplan, & Cassidy, 1985; Otter-Henderson & Creasey, 2001; Paley, Cox, & Burchinal, 1999; Roisman, Madsen, Hennighausen, Sroufe, & Collins, 2001; Simpson, Rholes, Orina, & Grich, 2002; Treboux et al., 2004). An interaction between experiences of high stress and attachment security has also been demonstrated, such that individuals with insecure representations show worse functioning in intervals characterized by a high number of stressful life events compared to insecure individuals with few stressful events, or secure individuals experiencing a high number of stressful events (e.g., Dickstein, Seifer, & Albus, 2005; Treboux et al., 2004).

In contrast, relations between adult social functioning and attachment security in clinical or high-risk populations have been minimally investigated. Clearly, within these populations there are restricted ranges of attachment security alongside many other potential reasons for problems in relationships and impaired responsiveness to stress, including active mental illness that might influence specific and overall social functioning. Nevertheless, if attachment security, as an internal representational experience, is conceptualized as an integration or coordination of behavior, thought, and emotion regarding attachment, then we would predict that the "degree" of attachment security should *matter* for social functioning—even within predominantly insecure, high-risk individuals. Just such a link between attachment status and overall social adjustment has been found within the restricted range of a group of high-functioning women (Crowell et al., 1996). Associations between attachment status and other facets of social adjustment might be even more evident within a high-risk sample given that the attachment system functions as a major resource for managing stress, and this is a group in which stress tends to be high.

The Current Study

In the analyses presented here, based on high-risk men and women originally recruited as psychiatrically hospitalized adolescents, we examine two central questions:

1. What evidence is there for stability of attachment status across three assessment points over 13 years—from ages 26 to 39? Although most empirical research on stability and change of attachment patterns in high-risk samples suggests that members of these groups are characterized by instability, previous studies have examined children and adolescents. Based on our prior conceptual discussion, we expected the adults in our previous clinical sample to have predominantly insecure attachment classifications that would be relatively stable. We had a particular interest in whether the relatively few individuals with secure representations were stably secure, as is evident in normative samples (e.g., Crowell, Treboux, Gao, et al., 2002), or whether the vulnerability of these individuals in other domains of functioning might erode secure representations. We were also interested in men and women classified as unresolved, a pattern that is unstable in normative samples, unless there is ongoing trauma (Crowell, Treboux, & Waters, 2002). Given the high rates of traumatic life events in a high-risk sample, we hypothesized that this classification would be relatively stable.

2. What links might we find between attachment coherence and specific aspects of the individual's social functioning? We anticipated that attachment security would be associated with overall social adjustment and other domains of functioning, and that it would continue to be positively related to optimal social functioning over time; that is, individuals who were secure or showed "movement" toward security or greater coherence, would show higher, and even rising, levels of functioning, while those who were incoherent/insecure would not only show lower functioning but also might *decline* in their functioning over time, because co-occurring stresses and vulnerabilities would be less readily buffered.

In addition to examining these questions in the entire high-risk sample, we closely studied a group of nine previously hospitalized young adults who had been identified at age 26 as resilient, based on their high levels of functioning (e.g., attachment coherence, ego development, low criminality, low substance abuse, low psychiatric symptoms), and a contrast group of seven previously hospitalized adults whose ego development, close relationships, and other functioning dimensions were within the average range of all the former psychiatric patients (Hauser, Allen, & Golden, 2006). In this intensive substudy, the role of representational security in maintaining resilient status, as compared with other personal resources, was of particular interest.

Methods

Procedure

We have obtained data on individuals psychiatrically hospitalized in adolescence and comparison group participants at four times in their life course: across adolescence (ages 14–18 years); in young adulthood (average age = 25.9 years, SD = 1.1 years); approximately 7 years later, when the participants were in their early 30s (M = 33.9 years, SD = 1.8 years); and again 5 years later in midlife (M = 39.0 years, SD = 1.2 years). Data collected in all four waves were used in this study, and in the results that follow are referred to as the adolescent, age 26, age 34, and age 39 phases.

We obtained AAIs at the age 26, 34, and 39 waves of data collection. In addition, at each wave, the adults participated in at least one full day of data collection that included semistructured interviews and self-report measures. Most participants came directly to the laboratory (all individuals in the adolescent and young adult waves) and data collection was completed in a private setting. In later, adult waves of data collection, participants unable to travel to our laboratory were seen at an alternate, mutually agreed-upon private location—usually at an area college or university—and our research staff traveled to them. Every effort was made to make these locations comparable to the original lab setting. All participants signed informed consent and were reimbursed for participation in the study at each wave.

Our focus in this chapter is on the former psychiatric patients. At the age 26 data collection, all 70 of the former psychiatric patient participants were located and 65 were interviewed with the AAI. Twenty-six engaged in the AAI at the age 34 phase. (Although approximately 95% of those still living participated in other aspects of data collection, *only* participants who were in close relationships at the age 34 assessment were reinterviewed with the AAI at that time.) At the age 39 wave, 33 participants have been assessed to date, and 10 are scheduled or are in the process of being scheduled; 22 former participants have incomplete data in this wave: 5 participants have died; 12 have been lost or could not be accessed (i.e., in prison), and 5 refused participation in this phase completely and 1 refused to complete the AAI. With respect to AAI stability data, 44 of the 65 (68%) previously hospitalized men and women have participated in at least two AAIs to date.

High-Risk Sample

Our participants have been members of a longitudinal study for more than 25 years (Hauser, with Powers & Noam, 1991; Hauser et al., 2006). Seventy adolescents, an equal number of boys and girls, between the ages of 14 and 17 (M = 14.6 years) were recruited from a local private psychiatric hospital in the mid- to late 1970s. Recruitment criteria excluded individuals with diagnoses involving organic impairment, mental retardation, psychiatric symptoms associated with a medical illness, or psychosis. The adolescents were originally diagnosed based on criteria from the second edition of the *Diagnostic and Statistical Manual of Mental Disorders* (American Psychiatric Association, 1968). They were subsequently reclassified via chart review according to DSM-III-R (American Psychiatric Association, 1987) criteria. In this reclassification, 21% of the sample received a primary diagnosis of oppositional defiant disorder (ODD), 19% were classified as having conduct disorder (CD), 19% with a major depressive disorder (MDD), and 8% with other mood disorders. The remaining 33% included a variety of diagnoses, such as eating disorders, personality disorders, adjustment disorders, and substance abuse. Specific immediate reasons for hospitalization varied, but frequent among the precipitants were serious suicidal attempts or self-destructive behaviors, severe risks to health (e.g., eating disorders and substance abuse), and various disruptive and destructive behaviors. Although hospitalization in adolescence is the unifying factor in this sample, these individuals also report high rates of abuse and trauma, most often within their nuclear families. A more complete description of the original research design, sampling, measures, and findings from this study can be found in Allen and colleagues (1996) and Hauser and colleagues (1991, 2006).

Low-Risk Comparison Sample

Approximately the same number of boys and girls from a suburban public high school were recruited as a comparison group (n = 76). Adolescents from the community group did not differ significantly from those in the hospital group in terms of age, gender, ethnicity/race, birth order, number of siblings, or parents' marital status. Whereas both samples were predominantly upper and middle class, the hospitalized sample had a significantly lower SES (M = 2.7) than the community sample (M = 1.7; t = 1.32, p < .001).

Resilient and Contrast Groups

Two subsamples were derived from the former hospitalized group from a profile of assessments of these individuals in their young adult years to designate the at-risk individuals as resilient or contrast group members at age 26. (Detailed descriptions of the procedures for determining the young adult resilient and contrast groups are provided in Hauser et al. [2006].) These two subsets were identified using seven indices of functioning obtained at age 26 (ego development, attachment coherence, close friendships, close relationships, recent criminality, recent substance abuse, and global psychiatric symptoms). Nine of the 70 previously hospitalized individuals had scores on all of these measures that fell into the upper 50th percentile of the entire sample (comparison and former patient groups combined) at age 26, and these nine individuals were classified as *resilient*. Thus, this small group of high-risk young adults were functioning well in all domains at age 26, even with respect to original comparison group members. In addition, seven of the 70 formerly hospitalized young adults were designated as members of a *contrast* group, because all their functioning scores at age 26 fell between the 40th and 60th percentiles of the *former patient* group. Thus, these seven were not the most impaired participants, but rather those who were functioning in the mid-range for the high-risk group in all domains assessed.

AAI Assessment

The AAI (George, Kaplan, & Main, 1985) assesses adults' representations of attachment based on discussion of childhood relationships with their parents and the effects of those experiences on their development as adults and as parents, if relevant. In a semistructured interview format, the interviewer asks participants for adjectives describing childhood relationships with parents and illustrative incidents supporting those adjectives with regard to feelings of rejection and experiences of being upset, ill, and hurt; and separations, losses, and abuse. In addition, participants are asked about changes in their relationships with their parents since childhood, descriptions of their current relationships with their parents, and explanations regarding parents' behavior when the participant was a child. Finally, participants are asked about the effects of early childhood experiences on their adult personality.

Past childhood experiences with each parent are rated on 9-point scales for loving behavior, rejection, neglect, pressure to achieve, and involving/role reversing behavior in the coder's opinion (Main et al., 2002). Present state of mind regarding attachment is rated on a variety of scales, including coherence (e.g., believability, clarity, relevance to topic), idealization of parents, stated lack of recall, passivity of speech, metacognitive monitoring, derogation of attachment or attachment figures, current preoccupying anger toward parents, and lack of resolution of loss or trauma/abuse. An overall attachment classification is then generated, based on prototypical descriptions of the attachment classifications and guided by the coder's ratings of the subject's childhood experiences and present state of mind regarding childhood experiences. Although all the scales are important in guiding the coder's classification, a score equal to or above 5 on the coherence scale, reflecting a general ability to present an integrated, believable account of experiences and their meaning, is considered necessary for an individual to be classified as secure.

Participants were classified into one of three primary classifications (Main et al., 2002): *secure–autonomous* (F), *insecure–dismissing* (Ds), or Insecure–*preoccupied* (E) with respect to attachment. A transcript is assigned a "cannot classify" category (CC) if it contains strong elements not typically seen together in a transcript (e.g., high idealization of one parent and high active anger at the other). The CC designation is considered very insecure. In addition, a fifth classification of *unresolved* with respect to past abuse or loss (U) may be given in conjunction with one of the four best-fitting primary categories and is considered an insecure classification.

The interviews were audiotaped, transcribed, and scored from the transcriptions by Eric Hesse, Judith Crowell, and two other coders trained by Mary Main, Eric Hesse, and/or Judith Crowell: Eighty-three percent agreement ($k = .63$, $p \leq .01$) was achieved between Crowell and the other three coders using a five-way classification system—F, Ds, E, CC, and U—on 30% of the 123 interviews ($n = 37$). Crowell scored 80 of the interviews.

Assessments of Individual Functioning

Measures of social functioning were collected at each of the four waves of data collection. Given the longitudinal and developmental nature of the study, some of the measures varied over time, whereas others were given at each wave of the study. However, at each wave, measures assessed ego development, drug and alcohol use/abuse, social adjustment, relationship functioning, and self-reported symptoms of psychiatric disorders. In addition, a Wechsler Adult Intelligence Scale—Revised (WAIS-R) Vocabulary score was obtained at age 34 as a close proxy for a Full Scale IQ score.

The Loevinger Sentence Completion Task has been administered at each wave of the study. The assessment of *ego development* (Loevinger & Wessler, 1970; Loevinger, Wessler, & Redmore, 1970; Westenberg, Hauser, & Cohn, 2004) utilizes a 36-item sentence completion test and a theoretically derived scoring system. For this study, scores were obtained by summing each subject's 36-item scores to best approximate his or her typical level of ego development. There is much evidence for the reliability and validity of this instrument (Hauser, 1976; Hauser, Hennighausen, Billings, Schultz, & Allen, 2004; Loevinger, 1979, 1985). Interrater reliabilities within this data set (using intraclass correlations) have ranged from .70 to .92, and all coders have been kept blind to other data in the study.

Drug and alcohol use were measured with an instrument initially validated and normed in a longitudinal study of a national probability sample of adolescents (Elliott, Huizinga, & Menard, 1989). When obtained by sensitive interviewers who have established rapport with interviewees, such self-reports have been found to be reliable and to correlate significantly with reports obtained from independent observers and official records (Elliott et al., 1989;

Farrington, 1973). Soft drug use was measured as the total number of instances of use of soft drugs in the previous 6 months (e.g., alcohol and marijuana). Hard drug use was measured as the total number of instances of illicit use of each of five classes of hard drugs (e.g., heroin, cocaine, hallucinogens, amphetamines, and tranquilizers) within the same time frame. Because measures of drug use were highly skewed, logarithmic transformations were performed before analyses.

The *Social Adjustment Scale* (SAS; Weissman & Paykel, 1974), a semistructured interview that was administered when participants were 34 and 39 years old, was originally designed for use in an epidemiological study of depression in women. It yields six scores, assessing overall adjustment, as well as functioning, in five independent domains over the preceding 2 months: (1) work/management of finances, (2) social and leisure activities, (3) relationship with spouse (if applicable), (4) relationships with children (if applicable), and (5) relationships with extended family. Using individual response scores describing specific behaviors, the interviewer rates the interviewee using a 7-point scale for each domain. For the assigned global or overall adjustment score, the interviewer uses all the domain scores and the impression he or she has gained of global functioning (1 = *Excellent functioning in all areas*, 7 = *Marked or severe maladjustment in all areas*). The global score allows the interviewer to take into account information given by the participant that does not readily fit the domains addressed.

The global assessment score, which was used in the analyses below, is sensitive enough to assess therapeutic response and discriminates between subjects in psychiatric samples and those in the general population, as well as subjects with mild psychiatric disorders and those with severe disorders (Bothwell & Weissman, 1977; Mostow & Newberry, 1975; Weissman, Kasl, & Klerman, 1976; Weissman & Paykel, 1974).

The *Child and Adolescent Functional Assessment Scale* (CAFAS; Hodges, 1995), assessed adolescent functioning based on hospital records for the year prior to the hospitalization. It is similar to the SAS in the domains assessed. Functioning is rated as *Good* (0), *Mildly impaired* (10), *Moderately impaired* (20), or *Severely impaired* (30). Trained undergraduate raters demonstrated reliability with CAFAS training vignettes and with each other. Raters reviewed admission material, social work reports of developmental and family history, and discharge summaries. Rater's exact agreement was 77% (interrater reliability: $r = .57$, $p \leq .01$) (Best, Gerber, Schnitzer, & Song, 1997).

The *Wechsler Adult Intelligence Scale—Revised, Short Form: Vocabulary Subtest* (WAIS-R; Wechsler, 1981), a widely used and highly reliable measure of intellectual ability, was administered when participants were young adults (age 26). The Vocabulary subtest was used in this study. It contains 35 words arranged in order of increasing difficulty. Each word is presented orally and in writing, and the subject is asked to explain aloud its meaning. All examinees start with the fourth word, except those who seem to have poor verbal ability. Each word is scored 2, 1, or 0, and the subtest is discontinued after five consecutive fails. The Vocabulary subtest taps a variety of cognition-related factors, including learning ability, fund of information, and richness of ideas, memory, concept formation, and language development. The number of words known is correlated with the ability to learn and to accumulate information (Thorndike, Cunningham, Thorndike, & Hagen, 1991). The Vocabulary subtest is the best measure of g (general intelligence) in the scale (76% of its variance may be attributed to g). In addition, it is the most reliable subtest ($r = .96$) and has a high correlation with the Full Scale IQ ($r = .81$) (Feingold, 1983; Thorndike et al., 1991). All vocabulary subtests were audiotaped and scored by a trained clinical psychologist. Raw scores were converted into scale scores ranging from 5 to 17.

Relationship Measures

Participants completed the *Close Peer Relationship Interview* (Shultz, 1993), a semistructured interview designed to explore intimacy and autonomy in friendships and/or in romantic relationships. The young adults answered questions about their relationship with a current romantic partner and with a close friend, or with two close friends, if they did not have a current romantic relationship. The *Developmental Relationship Scales* (Shultz, 1993; Shultz & Selman, 1998) were constructed from the Close Peer Relationship Interview data by adapting previous developmental scales based on the interpersonal theory devised by Selman (1980; Selman & Shultz, 1990). The scales assess self-reported autonomy, and relatedness interactions and reflections about the two relationships.

Three scales were used in the analyses, with scores that ranged from low (0) to high (4), based on the participant's capacities to coordinate social perspectives. *Shared Experience* is defined as the relatively harmonious connection with another person through self-disclosure, doing things together, and spending time together. Low scores reflect limited emotional sharing while engaging in primarily practical or mundane activities. High scores reflect self-disclosure about personal and relationship issues, and a rich sharing of interests, activities, and values. *Interpersonal Negotiation* focuses on incidents and patterns of conflict resolution that the individual reports when describing actual interactions with the other person. Low scores indicate use of impulsive, egocentric strategies to get one's way (e.g., hitting or grabbing) or to avoid harm (e.g., hiding). High scores indicate more cooperative and collaborative strategies to resolve conflict, such as candid sharing and negotiation. The *Interpersonal Understanding* scale focuses on perspective taking. Low scores reflect limited or concrete perspective taking, whereas higher scores reflect greater awareness of different points of view.

Two trained coders scored each Close Peer Relationship Interview, then met together to reach a consensus on the codes. Interrater reliability was computed on the preconsensus scores ($\kappa = .47$ to $.67$). Consensus scores are used in the following analyses.

The *Dyadic Adjustment Scale* (DAS; Spanier, 1976), a 32-item measure of relationship satisfaction, was administered to individuals in close relationships at the age 34 and age 39 waves of data collection. The DAS correlates highly with other measures of marital/relationship satisfaction, and significantly discriminates between married and divorced spouses, with high internal consistency in the current study ($\alpha = .93$).

Symptoms

The *Hopkins Symptom Checklist-90—Revised* (SCL-90-R; Derogatis, 1983), a 4-point Likert-type scale, was used to provide an index of global psychological distress, based on a summation of ratings of 90 items describing symptoms commonly identified by psychiatric and medical patients.

The *Beck Depression Inventory–II* (BDI-II; Beck, Steer, & Brown, 1996) assesses depressive symptoms. It is a revision of the well-known BDI that corresponds to current DSM criteria for depression. It generates scores from 0 to 63, and differentiates between depression and anxiety. The BDI was administered at the age 39 assessment wave.

The *State–Trait Anxiety Inventory* (STAI), a valid, reliable, internally consistent assessment of state (20 items) and trait anxiety (20 items), was given at the age 39 wave (Barnes, Harp, & Jung, 1983; Knight, Waal-Manning, & Spears, 1983).

Data Reduction

Z-scores of coherence of transcript and the summary scores of the domains of functioning were calculated for the combined (clinical and comparison) samples to allow for comparison of the results using different assessment tools. Using the individual scores, an *index of social functioning was calculated as a composite of the scores from the six domains* assessed at each of the four waves of data collection (adolescence, age 26, age 34, and age 39). The six domains represent a variety of ways in which an individual's life can be understood as successful or at risk: Ego development, drug and alcohol use, self-reported symptoms, close relationship quality, and social adjustment. Thus, each individual received a composite or summary score of functioning at each wave, based on the sum of these domains, which allowed his or her comparison to the total sample (clinical and comparison groups combined), with a score of 0 representing a mean score for the total sample, a score above 0 indicating above average functioning, and below zero indicating below average function. In addition to this composite index, a single domain score was also examined: the global score of the social adjustment (SAS) obtained at ages 34 and 39. This score is a more focused indicator of functioning, because it assesses an individual's ability to engage effectively in key domains of life. Our analyses focused on the AAI coherence score, the composite score of functioning, and the global functioning score of the SAS.

Results

We examined stability of attachment security using both overall security (classified as secure or insecure based on major classification) and major classifications (secure [F], dismissing [Ds], preoccupied [E], and cannot classify [CC]). We also considered the stability of coherence of transcript and other scale scores. We separately examined the stability of the unresolved classifications. The intervals examined were ages 26–34, 34–39, and 26–39.

Attachment Stability in the High-Risk (Previously Hospitalized) Group

Sixty-five participants in the high-risk group received attachment classifications at age 26; 39 (60%) of them engaged in one (n = 26) or two subsequent AAIs (n = 13) at the time of these analyses. The distributions of the major classifications *at each wave* of data collection are shown in Table 14.1.

Stability of Major Classifications

Thirty-seven of the 44 (84%) individuals who had two or more AAIs were stable in their classifications across 13 years, with 2 participants classified as secure and 35 classified as insecure at each of their assessments. Fourteen (32%, 9 Ds, 2 F, 3 E) of these individuals had the same major classification at each assessment, while 23 (68%) of them were given different insecure classifications at the different waves. Nine of 17 (53%) individuals with interviews classified as dismissing continued to receive Ds classifications, whereas only 3 of 12 individuals (25%) classified as preoccupied were subsequently given E classifications. Interestingly, all of the individuals seen as CC at any point in time (n = 8) showed variation among insecure classifications.

Eight participants (16%) had unstable classifications insofar as they received both secure and insecure classifications over the 13 years. Four of them were originally classified as secure and subsequently were classified as

TABLE 14.1. Distributions of AAI Classifications at Ages 26, 34, and 39

	Secure	Dismissing	Preoccupied	Can't classify	Unresolved
Age 26 (n = 65)	9 (14%)	25 (39%)	21 (33%)	10 (15%)	27 (42%)
Age 34 (n = 26)	3 (12%)	18 (69%)	4 (15%)	1 (4%)	9 (35%)
Age 39 (n= 32)	4 (15%)	12 (44%)	6 (22%)	5 (19%)	13 (48%)

insecure (1 CC, 2 Ds, 1 E). Three who were originally classified as insecure (1 Ds, 2 E) were subsequently classified as secure. One participant was classified as E at both age 26 and 37, yet received a classification of secure at age 34.

Examination of the stability of secure versus insecure classifications revealed that 6 of the 44 participants were classified as secure at age 26, but only 2 were classified as secure subsequently (33%). Importantly three of the four individuals subsequently classified as insecure had provided interviews at age 26 that were coded unresolved. In other words, although they had many secure elements in their discourse, their discussion of loss and/or abusive experiences was disorganized and incoherent. In contrast, 38 of the 44 participants were classified as insecure at age 26, and 36 of the 38 (95%) were classified as insecure subsequently. Thus, not only are insecure patterns more prominent in the high-risk group but also the stability of the insecure classifications are also very high compared with the secure classification.

The kappa coefficient for secure versus insecure classifications from age 26 to age 34 was not significant. Kappa from age 26 to age 39 was significant ($\kappa = .51$, $p \leq .01$), and for four classifications (F, Ds, E, and U; $\kappa = .23$, $p \leq .05$). These coefficients were also significant from age 34 to age 39, secure versus insecure classifications ($\kappa = .63$, $p \leq .01$), and for four classifications ($\kappa = .43$, $p \leq .01$).

Stability of the Unresolved Classification

Overall, 24 of the 44 participants (54%) were stable with respect to their U–not U status. Of these, 9 were classified as U at all assessments (37.5%), and 15 (62.5%) were never classified as U. Twenty participants (44%) varied in their U classification over time. Of these, 9 participants (45%) who were not U at age 26 were given the classification at a subsequent assessment, and 11 (55%) who were classified as U at age 26 did not receive the classification subsequently. There were no significant kappa coefficients for U versus not U classifications.

Similar to normative samples (Crowell, Treboux, & Waters, 2002; van IJzendoorn & Bakermans-Kranenburg, 1996) in which the U classification is not stable (e.g., 46% U over 22 months compared with 91% not U), we also found that the U classification was *not stable*; that is, of participants who received a U classification at age 26, only 9 out of 24 (37%) remained classified as U. However, it is possible in this high-risk sample that there is more likelihood of being classified U subsequently; that is, of individuals classified as not U at age 26, only 15 out of 24 (62.5%) were classified not U in subsequent years.

Stability of Coherence Scores

Pearson correlations of coherence scores and other scales of the AAI were conducted across the waves of data collection. Coherence was generally sta-

TABLE 14.2. Stability Coefficients across Ages 26, 34, and 39

	Age 26 to 33 (n = 26)		Age 34 with 39 (n = 16)		Age 26 with 39 (n = 27)	
	r	p ≤	r	p ≤	r	p ≤
Coherence of Transcript	.27	ns	.55	.05	.57	.01
Experience Scales						
Loving—Mother	.31	ns	−.05	ns	.50	.01
Loving—Father	.38	.10	.63	.05	.67	.001
Rejecting—Mother	.29	ns	−.08	ns	.63	.01
Rejecting—Father	.40	ns	.25	ns	.36	ns
Involving—Mother	.83	.001	.70	.05	.87	.001
Involving—Father	−.15	ns	.72	.01	−.16	ns
Neglect—Mother	.08	ns	.35	ns	.38	ns
Neglect—Father	.61	.01	.45	ns	.31	ns
Pressure to Achieve Mother	.30	ns	1.00	.001	.47	.05
Pressure to Achieve Father	.42	.05	1.00	.001	.29	ns
State of Mind Scales						
Idealization—Mother	.37	.10	.62	.05	.54	.01
Idealization—Father	.19	ns	.34	ns	.30	ns
Anger—Mother	.53	.01	.48	.01	.48	.05
Anger—Father	.47	.05	.33	ns	.43	.05
Derogation—Mother	—	—	−.45	*ns*	.64	.01
Derogation—Father	—	—	.70	.05	.22	*ns*
Derogation of Attachment	.22	ns	.35	*ns*	.50	.01
Insistence on Lack of Recall	.59	.001	.62	.05	.56	.01
Fear of Loss	—	—	−.23	*ns*	—	—
Traumatic Memory Loss	−.18	*ns*	.17	*ns*	.41	.10
Metacognitive Monitoring	−.13	*ns*	.84	.01	.04	*ns*
Passivity of Thought	−.06	*ns*	.64	.05	−.10	*ns*
Unresolved for Loss	.52	.01	.05	*ns*	.08	*ns*
Unresolved for Trauma	.55	.10	.04	*ns*	−.13	*ns*

ble across the three waves of AAI data collection (see Table 14.2). Only two Experience scales were consistently stable: Father Loving and Mother Involving (see Table 14.2). Regarding state-of-mind scales, significant stability was found for Insistence on Idealization of Mother, Anger at Mother, and Lack of Recall. Other scales were correlated across specific segments of the study but not consistently. The least stable scales were Father Rejecting, Mother Neglecting, Idealization of Father, the Derogation scales, the Unresolved scales, Metacognitive Monitoring, and Traumatic Memory Loss.

Attachment Security and Functioning

As one means of understanding stability and change in attachment security, we examined the relations between AAI coherence and several assessments of functioning. We first examined the stability of the various domains of functioning using Pearson's correlations. Second, we assessed the relations between adolescent functioning *and* subsequent AAI coherence scores. Third, we examined the relations between AAI coherence and the various domains of functioning for each wave of data collection. Fourth, we examined the relations between the SAS social adjustment scores and the composite social functioning score described earlier at the different data collection waves. Last, we examined the subset of previously hospitalized young adults identified at age 26 as either resilient or contrast groups in greater detail and with respect to trajectories of AAI coherence and functioning domains from adolescence to midadult life. We considered this subset of our participants more intensively to explore aspects of change in coherence and functioning over time, and factors that seem to be associated with long-term resilient functioning.

Stability of Domains of Functioning

From adolescence to adulthood, ego development scores were generally very stable ($r = .68$ to $.82$), but symptom reports from adolescence to adulthood were not stable ($r = .02$ to $.11$). Within adulthood (26–39 years), global functioning ($r = .67$ for ages 34–39), soft drug use ($r = .46–79$), and hard drug use ($r = .26–.39$) were generally stable. Symptom reports in adult life were also stable from ages 26 to 39 ($r = .39$). In contrast, reports of relationship quality varied widely across the intervals in adulthood ($r = -.45–.60$).

Social Adjustment (SAS) and Composite Functioning Scores

We anticipated that these broad assessments of social functioning would be correlated, but not redundant, given that the SAS assesses functioning in the preceding 2 months based on information about managing finances, going to work, activities with friends and family, and so forth, and the composite score assesses resources for and hindrances to good functioning. A composite score was available for all four waves of data collection, and SAS scores for the ages 34 and 39 waves. SAS scores at age 34 were significantly correlated with the composite scores at age 34 [$r(54) = .59, p \le .01$]. SAS scores at age 39 were significantly correlated with composite scores at all waves: adolescence [$r(28) = .38, p \le .05$], age 26 [$r(28) = .53, p \le .01$], age 34 [$r(27) = .42, p \le .05$], and age 39 [$r(28) = .38, p \le .05$].

Adolescent Functioning and Subsequent Security

CAFAS scores (a low score represents the more optimal functioning) obtained in adolescence were correlated with AAI coherence at ages 26 [$r(65) = -.24, p \le .05$] and 34 [$r(26) = -.38, p \le .05$] but not at age 39 [$r(27) = .22, p = .12$], such that better adolescent functioning was associated with greater coherence in adulthood.

Attachment Security and Concurrent Adult Functioning

The relations between AAI coherence scores and individual domains of functioning were examined. AAI coherence was associated with concurrent ego development only at age 34 [$r(26) = .60, p \leq .001$]. Concurrent AAI coherence and day-to-day adjustment were not significantly correlated at age 34 but were at age 39 [$r(27) = -.36, p \leq .05$], such that higher coherence scores were associated with better functioning (1 = *Best functioning*, 7 = *Marked impairment*). Reports of relationship quality, symptoms, and soft and hard drug use were *not* associated with AAI coherence at any phase, nor was the composite functioning score.

Attachment Security and Adult Functioning over Time

We were especially interested relations between AAI coherence and social adjustment over time, because concurrent relations do not address the presumed enduring adaptive benefits associated with attachment security. Thus, we examined the correlation between highest AAI coherence score received by the participant at any phase and change in social adjustment. The Spearman *r* for the highest coherence score and a (age 39 to age 34) SAS Change score [$r(27) = -.50, p < .01$] indicated that the less coherent/secure the participant, the more likely there was to be a decline in overall functioning over the 5 year interval and, of course, the converse.

Examination of Cases: Attachment and Social Functioning in "Resilient" and "Contrast" Group Participants

The result just described led us to a more in-depth examination of selected cases, in which we explored how attachment security was associated with how individuals adapted (i.e., were or became resilient, or deteriorated). It also led to the creation of the individual "life" charts presented in Figures 14.1–14.5. We used the two groups of previously hospitalized individuals, who, at age 26, were identified as resilient or contrast group members as the subjects of this investigation. Our method for determining the composition of both groups was described earlier; however, it is important to note that with respect to the AAI, a coherence score greater than 3.7 placed an adult above the cutoff for resilience. Indeed, only two of the nine resilient men and women received a secure attachment status classification at age 26, and only three had coherence scores equal to or above 5, which, in most cases, would lead to a classification of secure. None of the seven members of the contrast group had been classified as secure.

The Resilient Young Adults

In the case of the nine adults who appeared resilient at age 26, we examined their functioning at ages 34 and 39. Five of them had remained at or above the mean of the overall group (high school and former patients) in terms of general functioning and social adjustment. Their original diagnoses were MDD (n = 2), ODD, CD, and obsessive–compulsive disorder (OCD). Interestingly, four of the five participants had received coherence scores equal to or greater than 5 for least one of their adult AAIs. Over time, they reported psychiatric symptoms hovering around the mean of the combined groups, but they describe a somewhat greater than average use of alcohol and soft drugs.

This continued resilient functioning is exemplified by Sandy (a fictitious name), illustrated in Figure 14.1. Sandy was originally hospitalized for a life-threatening suicide attempt, then diagnosed as having an MDD. She remained in the hospital for 6 weeks, a short time compared with most of the other former patients in residential treatment from 37 to 921 days, with an average 192.3 days. In both of her AAIs, Sandy (at ages 26 and 39) was classified as secure–autonomous. In a non-AAI interview at age 26, Sandy described concentrating on maintaining long-term connections with friends, a matter that was challenging for this young woman who had found friendships satisfying

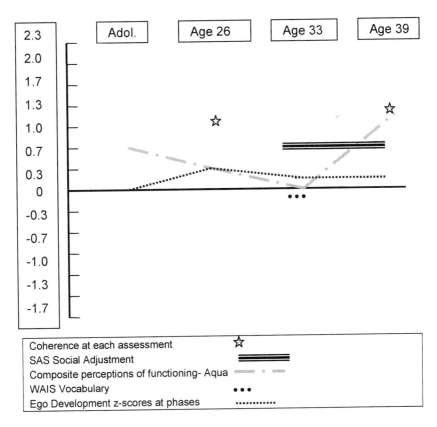

FIGURE 14.1. Sandy, a resilient group woman at age 26, was stable, secure, and had above average social functioning at ages 33 and 39.

but not consistently enduring. "It's not that I don't keep friends for long," she said, "but I've moved around. . . . I don't really keep in touch with people. I just kind of get caught up in my life" (Hauser et al., 2006, p. 196). Although she expressed this concern/observation as a young adult, it was interesting to find that she functioned well above the mean at ages 34 and 39, *especially* in her reports of relationships.

Figure 14.2 illustrates the trajectory of Donna, a woman originally diagnosed with CD. Donna, like Sandy, had a relatively short hospital stay. In her adult years, her attachment status changed from dismissing to secure between her age 26 and age 39 interviews. Despite her above average use of alcohol and/or soft drugs, we saw a rise in her functioning level paralleling her coherence scores.

In contrast to these participants, three of the nine resilient individuals showed a marked decline in social functioning after age 26. All three were

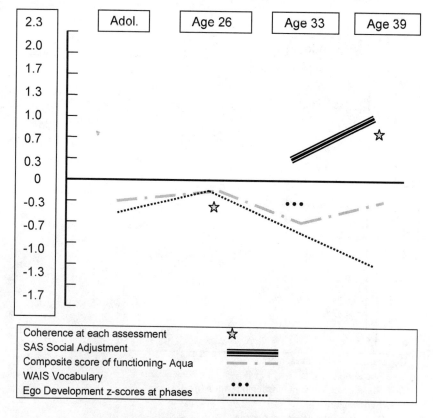

FIGURE 14.2. Donna, a resilient group woman at age 26, "became" secure and had above average social functioning at ages 33 and 39.

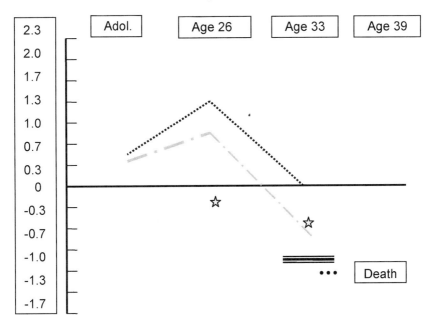

FIGURE 14.3. Eve, a resilient group woman at age 26, was stable, insecure, had markedly declining social functioning at age 33, and subsequently died.

classified as insecure on their AAIs. Eve exemplified this pattern. As can be seen in Figure 14.3, Eve's composite social functioning and ego development scores were above the overall sample mean during her adolescence and young adult years.

Figure 14.3 shows that Eve was classified as having a dismissing attachment status at ages 26 and 33. After marrying, working in a health service position, and having three young children, although only 26, she appeared to be gaining perspective on her adolescent hospitalization and family life. Although her original diagnosis was "hysterical," her greatest impairment appeared to have been heavy use of hard drugs compared with other study participants. By age 33 she had developed a chronic illness, and there was a precipitous decline in her functioning. Then, unexpectedly, she developed a severe and prolonged infection linked with an underlying illness and died.

The second of the three resilient individuals with precipitous declines, a woman named Rachel, was originally diagnosed as having bipolar disorder as an adolescent. In both her AAIs, at ages 26 and 39, she was classified as preoccupied. Rachel—as she had planned at age 16—had married, had a daughter, and then completed her own health professional training. At age 26, she was working in the kind of care setting she had envisioned, and was for the first time—from her perspective—experiencing *both* independence and closeness in the same relationship. "Independence is a new thing for me in this relationship because it's so close," she said. "It's something I'm afraid of, yet I strive for it. [Marie, her close friend] has it and I want it. . . . I go to school full time and she works 10 hours a day. That to me is independence right now" (Hauser et al., 2006, p. 155).

Rachel was clear that it was her own feelings and wishes that interfered with her independence. She told us of new insights about her major life concern, experiencing and sustaining satisfying close relationships: "I think that I'll have more friendships. I think that the trusting will start to come and I think I'll be better able to [let people be] themselves without becoming totally affected by what they say about me. Their impressions and feelings at any given moment won't really affect how I feel about myself" (Hauser et al., 2006, p. 156). Rachel then developed a life-threatening illness between ages 33 and 39. Following her illness, in her AAI at age 39, she no longer identified her problem as separating herself from others; indeed, she described a highly involving relationship with her adolescent daughter and was unable to recognize the parallels with her own early, involving attachment experiences with her mother.

The third young adult resilient group participant who showed a marked *decline* in functioning after age 26 was Pete. A young man whose original diagnosis was CD, Pete entered the hospital after provoking (his view) and continuing (also his view) many violent fights with peers and adults, triggering over 12 expulsions form public and private schools, all before his adolescent years. Pete remained associated with the hospital for 2 years, first as an inpatient, then as a day patient. Although he had successfully completed college and worked at a full-time position, and had stable friendships, Pete was first classified as U/Ds at 26 and the next time—at age 39—the number of contradictory strong elements in his description led the coder to assign a CC classification.

During his late 30s, Pete began treatment for a potentially lethal chronic infection. Two of Pete's friends had died from infections during the years before we saw him at age 39. Adding to his loss of friends and fears about his own mortality were conflicts with his father, who was now in a nursing home and had become fervently religious and even more disapproving of Pete's lifestyle. These were not new issues. But they were clearly emerging in new ways and with greater intensity for Pete in the years since he was 26 years old. We hypothesize that Pete's insecure–incoherent attachment representation and overall poor coping strategies provided little structure for comprehending and organizing these huge challenges; indeed, his attachment coherence paralleled his diminished social functioning, likely reflecting Pete's struggle with salient and preoccupying challenges to close relationships, separations, and bodily integrity.

Unfortunately, two of the nine individuals classified as resilient did not return after the age 26 assessment. One, classified as F at age 26, showed much academic and professional success in her later adolescent and young adult years. However, her adolescent diagnosis was MDD, and she died by suicide before the age 34 assessments. Another, Jimmy, refused the follow-up assessments at ages 34 and 39. His adolescent diagnosis was MDD and his young adult attachment classification was E.

The Contrast Group

Not surprisingly, the social functioning of men and women in the contrast group tended to be lower at ages 34 and 39 than that of the resilient group (e.g., age 39 SAS z-score mean of resilient group = .08, contrast group = −.67, one tailed t-test, p = .06; composite functioning z-score mean of resilient group = .34, contrast group = −.20, one-tailed t-test, p = .07). Despite this general trend, we found that two of the seven members of this contrast subgroup moved from below the mean at age 26 to rise above the mean for the entire sample along the lines of attachment and social functioning dimensions. Although both had received insecure classifications at age 26 (one preoccupied, the other cannot classify), they had higher coherence scores at subsequent assessments. The attachment pattern for one changed from preoccupied to secure, and the other's attachment pattern, although still insecure, became more organized.

Jeffrey, shown in Figure 14.4, illustrates how changes in attachment dimensions appeared to be associated with improved functioning levels. Jeffrey was admitted to the hospital as an adolescent following a serious and violent suicide attempt, with continued suicidal ideation thereafter. The attempt occurred in association with ongoing strife with his mother, in part over her unavailability to him in his prolonged grief about the untimely and sudden death of his somewhat distant father, to whom he nevertheless felt strongly connected. Jeffrey's diagnosis was MDD, and he had one of the longest hospital stays (576 days) of the entire adolescent hospitalized group, although this included his stay in a residential facility associated with the hospital. He was one of the highest functioning adolescents, based on our composite index, primarily because of his intelligence and ego development scores. He was an excellent student who sought to follow in his father's footsteps in the sciences.

The low point of Jeffrey's functioning was at age 26, at which time his AAI classification was E. Having completed college and graduate school, he was restless in relationships, unsure about his future, and filled with concerns about both his father's death and his mother's uneven presence in his life. When seen again at age 33, his social adjustment was clearly improving, and this was maintained at age 39. A powerful change had taken place in his life in his mid-20s and flourished in the succeeding years, when Jeffrey decided to become an artist, in contrast to pursuing the scientific career that he and his father had so highly valued and envisioned. At age 39, Jeffrey was assigned an

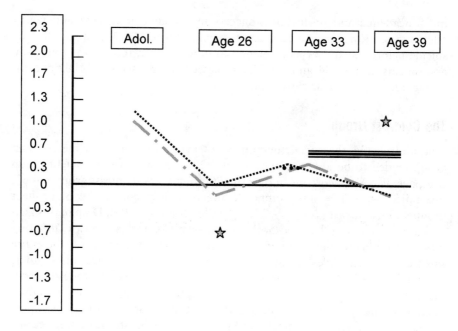

FIGURE 14.4. Jeffrey, a contrast group man at age 26, "became" secure and had above average social functioning at ages 33 and 39.

AAI classification of F. He had a dramatic shift in his coherence score primarily because he had come to understand and, to some extent, forgive his mother; at the same time, he clearly expressed how he managed their relatively limited relationship more satisfactorily for both of them.

Four of the seven contrast group participants remained below the mean in terms of their social functioning in adulthood. All were classified as insecure at all assessments, revealing well below average coherence scores. The adolescent diagnoses for three of these four contrast group adolescents were MDD, ODD, and, ODD morbid with attention-deficit/hyperactivity disorder (ADHD). The diagnosis for the fourth adolescent could not be determined with retrospective review. Only one of these former patients remained at the same level of "average" functioning at ages 34 and 39 as at age 26. The function of the other three deteriorated over time, and all three were highly symptomatic with respect to either psychiatric symptoms and/or soft drug use.

We can visualize this declining trajectory in Magda, who was diagnosed with ODD as an adolescent (see Figure 14.5). At the time of Magda's initial diagnosis, she was convinced her problems were caused by others. Extending from her adolescent anger and resentment toward adults, at age 26, Magda saw her difficulties with close adult relationships as being the fault of her partners, and she spoke with bitterness and intermittent incoherence about these

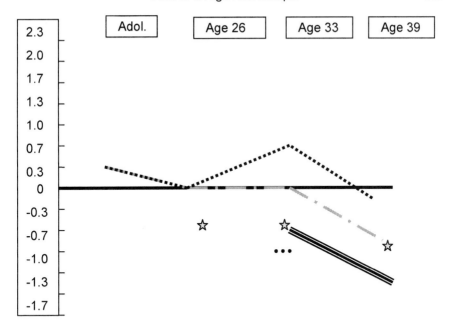

FIGURE 14.5. Magda, a contrast group woman at age 26, was stable, insecure, and had declining social functioning from ages 33 to 39.

problematic relationships (Hauser et al., 2006). As noted in the other cases, the parallel between AAI coherence and functioning level over time is notable.

Finally, one of the seven contrast group members did not return at ages 34 and 39. In adolescence he was diagnosed as having a CD, and he was given a CC attachment classification at age 26. He has up to now been lost to follow-up, unlike almost all other original participants, whose outcomes/whereabouts are known and with whom at least some contact has been maintained.

Discussion

Our study—*spanning more than 25 years of individual lives*—examined the stability of adult attachment status (including U and CC) and representational coherence in a sample of high-risk adults who had been psychiatrically hospitalized in adolescence, and many of whom also had significant trauma histories. Preceded by adolescent assessments, the measures we have reported cover over two decades, beginning with composites of functional strengths and weaknesses (e.g., ego development, symptoms, drug and alcohol use, relationship satisfaction) from the teenage years and encompassing three waves of subsequent data collection, including AAI data at ages 26, 34, and 39, and assessments of day-to-day functioning at ages 34 and 39. We examined associations between attachment security (representational coherence) and functioning level, and concluded our analyses, with more intensive consideration of these associations alongside individual life data over time for a subset of individuals identified at age 26 as either resilient or contrast group former patients (Hauser et al., 2006).

Overall, consistent with contemporary conceptualizations of resilience as being a transactional pattern, dependent on the interplay at any given time between individual strengths and contextual opportunities and challenges (Hauser et al., 2006; Luthar & Zelazo, 2003), resilience at age 26 did not guarantee continued high functioning, or even survival, over the next 13 years. Indeed, the outcomes of these individuals with psychiatric hospitalization in adolescence dramatically demonstrate how very much at risk these young people were and that adolescent diagnosis was not especially predictive. The risk is clearly illustrated, in that mortality was high; for example, two of the nine resilient group young adults (22%) died very young. Less than half of this group (44%) continued to function above the overall mean of the patient and nonpatient adolescents. Nonetheless, these later outcomes still differ from the contrast group of young adults. The majority (two-thirds) of these participants did not have positive outcomes, and one is missing despite our many search attempts.

Attachment Stability

We found high stability of attachment status in this sample, with 84% of participants remaining in the same attachment category (secure vs. insecure), especially the case for participants classified as insecure (95%). We saw some "movement" among the insecure classifications, particularly for those adults classified as CC and E. This is consistent with findings from normative samples (Crowell, Treboux, & Waters, 2002; van IJzendoorn & Bakermans-Kranenburg, 1996), but the reason for this difference with respect to those classified as CC and E is not entirely clear. Both classifications are driven, in many cases, on the interview questions eliciting active anger from the participant, which unlike idealization, may be more sensitive to interviewer style, to recent life events, and to specific topics in the relationships discussed. Despite the stability of the Anger at Mother scale, it is possible that a subset of individuals manifest "signs" of preoccupation only under some conditions (Crowell, Treboux, & Waters, 2002).

The low frequency of the F classification makes it somewhat difficult to speak to its stability in this high-risk sample. However, only one-third of the small number ($n = 6$) classified as secure at age 26 were subsequently classified as secure. But all those who "became insecure" could arguably have been considered insecure at age 26, because they were all given U/F classifications at that time. Both the low frequency of the F classification and its apparent low stability are in sharp contrast to findings for security in normative samples (e.g., Crowell, Treboux, & Waters, 2002). It is likely, given research with child clinical samples (e.g., Crowell & Feldman, 1988; Greenberg, 1999) and the experiences described by even our secure participants (e.g., Sandy, Donna, and Jeffrey), that very few of them experienced consistently secure relationships with their parents. Furthermore, the subsequent adversities (e.g., life-threatening illnesses, loss of close partners, and prolonged strain with parents) experienced by these participants may have undermined a marginally coherent representation.

Attachment Security and Social Functioning

The two methods of assessing functioning, composite score and social adjustment (SAS), were interestingly quite distinct, even though the global SAS score was included within the composite score. The SAS score tracks day-to-day functioning, unlike the composite score, which captures more macro-individual and contextual dimensions (e.g., drug use, symptoms, and ego development) and might enhance or interfere with the effectiveness with which an adolescent and adult can function in work, play, and love. These domains were also probably less sensitive to fluctuating or overall status, insofar as someone who never used hard drugs and/or abstained from alcohol and soft drug use would get a very positive z-score for those domains.

The relation over time between attachment security and day-to-day functional status is noteworthy. Five of the six (83%) men and women with coherence scores in the secure range were, in at least one assessment point, functioning above the entire sample mean (former patient and nonpatient combined) over an average of 13 years. None of the other individual domains assessed—including ego development, self-reported symptoms, drug use, relationship quality—were associated significantly with functional outcomes. Attachment status appears to predict both decline and rise in functioning over the 13-year span of assessment, such that the attachment-related coherence of individuals predicted subsequent functioning. We hypothesize that the ability to coordinate thoughts, feelings, and reported behaviors that is required to be classified as coherent–secure regarding attachment may also be a requirement of successful social adjustment/functioning in daily life. For example, adults who cannot recognize and adapt their behavior to modulate the impacts of an increasingly pervasive depression—less spontaneity, diminished or no hope/optimism, isolation from close relationships, irritability—may further compromise their experiences in his work, leisure, and family life. If strong unhappiness in a close relationship occurs alongside stifled behavior or cognitions about that relationship, then such unhappiness may erode functioning. However, if the feelings and thoughts associated with such symptoms or feelings are recognized and lead a person to seek help from various sources or to modify (for example) work expectations, then the impact of these symptoms is managed, and may not derail daily life. This coordination of thoughts, behaviors, and feelings would seem especially important as a buffering system for individuals who have experienced many adversities and stresses, including mental illness. Thus, the capacity reflected in representational attachment security (coherence) may be a marker of a person's ability to organize and coordinate stressful experiences in other realms of life.

Acknowledgments

This research was funded by National Institute of Mental Health (NIMH) Grant No. 2RO1MH 44934. We would like to express their appreciation to our participants whose continued involvement in the longitudinal study allowed us to conduct this investigation. We thank Joseph Allen, J. Heidi Gralinski-Bakker, Robert Waldinger, Anne Rifkin, Sarah Whitton, and our devoted project staff for their support. Special thanks are extended to Rebecca Billings for her valuable input and investment in performing many of the data analyses that support many of the ideas and conclusions of this chapter.

References

Ainsworth, M. D. S. (1985). Attachments across the life span. *Bulletin of the New York Academy of Medicine, 61*(9), 792–811.

Ainsworth, M. D. S. (1991). Attachments and other affectional bonds across the life cycle. In C. M. Parkes, J. Stevenson-Hinde, & P. Marris (Eds.), *Attachment across the life cycle* (pp. 33–51). London: Routledge.

Allen, J., Hauser, S., & Borman-Spurrell, E. (1996). Attachment theory as a framework for understanding sequelae of severe adolescent psychopathology: An eleven year follow-up study. *Journal of Consulting and Clinical Psychology, 64*(2), 254–263.

American Psychiatric Association. (1968). *Diagnostic and statistical manual of mental disorders* (2nd ed.). Washington, DC: Author.

American Psychiatric Association. (1987). *Diagnostic and statistical manual of mental disorders* (3rd ed., rev.). Washington, DC: Author.

Bardone, A. M., Moffitt, T. E., Caspi, A., Dickson, N., & Silva, P. A. (1996). Adult mental health and social outcomes of adolescent girls with depression and conduct disorder. *Development and Psychopathology, 8*, 811–829.

Barnes, L. L. B., Harp, D., & Jung, W. S. (1983). Reliability generalization of scores on the Spielberger State–Trait Anxiety Inventory. *Educational and Psychological Measurement, 43*, 729–734.

Beck, A. T., Steer, R. A., & Brown, G. K. (1996). *Manual for the Beck Depression Inventory-II*. San Antonio, TX: Psychological Corporation.

Best, K. M., Gerber, A., Schnitzer, E. K., & Song, G. K. (1997, April). *Rating adolescent "functional status" and adequate parenting among psychiatrically hospitalized adolescents and their parents*. Poster presented at biennial meeting of the Society for Research in Child Development, Washington, DC.

Bothwell, S., & Weissman, M. (1977). Social impairments four years after an acute depressive episode. *American Journal of Orthopsychiatry, 47*(2), 231–237.

Bowlby, J. (1982). *Attachment and loss: Vol. 1. Attachment*. New York: Basic Books. (Original work published 1969)

Bretherton, I. (1990). Open communication and internal working models: Their role in the development of attachment relationships. In R. A. Thompson (Ed.), *Nebraska Symposium on Motivation* (Vol. 36, pp. 59–113). Lincoln: University of Nebraska Press.

Bretherton, I., & Munholland, K. A. (1999). Internal working models in attachment relationships: A construct revisited. In J. Cassidy & P. R. Shaver (Eds.), *Handbook of attachment: Theory, research, and clinical applications* (pp. 89–111). New York: Guilford Press.

Cohn, D., Cowan, P. A., Cowan, C. P., & Pearson, J. (1992). Mothers' and fathers' working models of childhood attachment relationships, parenting styles, and child behavior. *Development and Psychopathology, 4,* 417–431.

Cohn, D., Silver, D., Cowan, P., Cowan, C., & Pearson, J. (1992). Working models of childhood attachment and couples' relationships. *Journal of Family Issues, 13*(4), 432–449.

Creasey, G. (2002). Associations between working models of attachment and conflict management behavior in romantic couples. *Journal of Counseling Psychology, 49,* 365–375.

Crowell, J. A., & Feldman, S. S. (1988). Mothers' internal models of relationships and children's behavioral and developmental status: A study of mother–child interaction. *Child Development, 59,* 1273–1285.

Crowell, J. A., Gao, Y., Lawrence-Savane, T., Abbott, G., Olmsted, M., & Lord, C. (2001, April). *When do attachment representations matter?: Relations among the AAI, CRI and behavior in the development of adult partnerships.* Paper presented at the biennial meeting of the Society for Research in Child Development, Minneapolis, MN.

Crowell, J. A., Treboux, D., Gao, Y., Fyffe, C., Pan, H., & Waters, E. (2002). Assessing secure base behavior In adulthood: Development of a measure, links to adult attachment representations, and relationships to couples' communication and reports of relationships. *Developmental Psychology, 38,* 679–693.

Crowell, J. A., Treboux, D., & Waters, E. (2002). Stability of attachment representations: The transition to marriage. *Developmental Psychology, 38,* 467–479.

Crowell, J. A., Waters, E., Treboux, D., O'Connor, E., Colon-Downs, C., Feider, O., et al. (1996). Discriminant validity of the Adult Attachment Interview. *Child Development, 67,* 2584–2599.

Das Eiden, R., Teti, D. M., & Corns, K. M. (1995). Maternal working models of attachment, marital adjustment, and the parent–child relationship. *Child Development, 66,* 1504–1518.

Derogatis, L. R. (1983). *Description and bibliography for the SCL-90-R and other instruments of the Psychopathology Rating Scale Series.* Unpublished manuscript, Johns Hopkins University School of Medicine, Baltimore.

Diamond, D., Stovall-McClough, C., Clarkin, J. F., & Levy, K. N. (2003). Patient–therapist attachment in the treatment of borderline personality disorder. *Bulletin of the Menninger Clinic, 67,* 227–259.

Dickstein, S., Seifer, R., & Albus, K. E. (2005, April). *Attachment patterns across multiple family relationships in adulthood: Associations with child outcomes.* Paper presented at the Society for Research in Child Development, Atlanta, GA.

Elliott, D. S., Huizinga, D., & Menard, S. (1989). *Multiple problem youth: Delinquency, substance use, and mental health problems.* New York: Springer-Verlag.

Farrington, D. (1973). Self-reports of deviant behavior: Predictive and stable? *Journal of Criminal Law, Criminology and Police Science, 61,* 99–110.

Feingold, A. (1983). The validity of the Information and Vocabulary subtests of the WAIS for predicting college achievement. *Educational and Psychological Measurement, 43,* 1127–1131.

Furman, W., Simon, V. A., Shaffer, L., & Bouchey, H. A. (2002). Adolescents' working models and styles for relationships with parents, friends, and romantic partners. *Child Development, 73,* 241–255.

Fyffe, C. (1997, April). *Empirical classification of adult attachment status: Predicting group membership.* Unpublished poster, presented at the biennial meeting of the Society for Research in Child Development.

George, C., Kaplan, N., & Main, M. (1985). The Adult Attachment Interview. Unpublished manuscript, University of California at Berkeley.

Gotlib, I. H., Lewinson, P. M., & Seeley, J. R. (1998). Consequences of depression during adolescence: Marital status and marital functioning in early adulthood. *Journal of Abnormal Psychology, 107,* 686–690.

Greenberg, M. T. (1999). Attachment and psychopathology in childhood. In J. Cassidy & P. R. Shaver (Eds.), *Handbook of attachment: Theory, research and clinical applications* (pp. 469–496). New York: Guilford Press.

Grossmann, K. E., & Grossmann, K. (2003, July). *Attachment, exploration and psychological security across 22 years: From mothers' and fathers' sensitivity and support to later attachment and partnership representations.* Paper presented at the ATICA: Attachment from Infancy and Childhood to Adulthood Conference, Regensberg, Germany.

Hamilton, C. E. (2000). Continuity and discontinuity of attachment from infancy through adolescence. *Child Development, 71,* 690–694.

Hauser, S., Allen, J., & Golden, E. (2006). *Out of the woods: Tales of resilient teens.* Cambridge, MA: Harvard University Press.

Hauser, S., with Powers, S., & Noam, G. (1991). *Adolescents and their families: Paths of ego development.* New York: Free Press.

Hauser, S. T. (1976). Loevinger's model and measure of ego development: A critical review. *Psychological Bulletin, 83,* 928–955.

Hennighausen, K., Hauser, S. T., Billings, R., Schultz, L. H., & Allen, J. P. (2004). Adolescent ego-development trajectories and young adult relationship outcomes. *Journal of Early Adolescence, 24,* 29–44.

Hesse, E. (1999). The Adult Attachment Interview: Historical and current perspectives. In J. Cassidy & P. R. Shaver (Eds.), *Handbook of attachment: Theory, research and clinical applications* (pp. 395–433). New York: Guilford Press.

Hodges, K. (1995). *Child and Adolescent Functional Assessment Scale.* Unpublished manuscript, University of Michigan, Ann Arbor.

Kaplan, N. (2003, April). *Attachment from infancy to young adulthood in the Bay Area Longitudinal Study: Predictions from early and middle childhood.* Paper presented at the Society for Research in Child Development, Tampa, FL.

Knight, R., Waal-Manning, H., & Spears, G. (1983). Some norms and reliability data for the State–Trait Anxiety Inventory and the Zung Self-Rating Depression Scale. *British Journal of Clinical Psychology, 22,* 245–249.

Kobak, R. R. (1991, April). *Attachment strategies in marital relationships.* Unpublished symposium paper presented at the biennial meeting of the Society for Research in Child Development, Seattle, Washington.

Loevinger, J. (1979). *Scientific ways in the study of ego development (Vol. XII)*. Worcester, MA: Clark University Press.

Loevinger, J. (1985). Revision of the Sentence Completion Test for Ego Development. *Journal of Personality and Social Psychology, 48*, 420–427.

Loevinger, J., & Wessler, R. (1970). *Measuring ego development: Vol. 1. Construction and use of a sentence completion task*. San Francisco: Jossey-Bass.

Loevinger, J., Wessler, R., & Redmore, C. (1970). *Measuring ego development: Vol. 2: Scoring manual for women and girls*. San Francisco: Jossey-Bass.

Luthar, S. S., & Zelazo, L. B. (2003). Research on resilience: An integrative review. In S. S. Luthar (Ed.), *Resilience and vulnerability: Adaptation in the context of childhood adversities* (pp. 510–549). New York: Cambridge University Press.

Main, M., Goldwyn, R., & Hesse, E. (2002). *Adult Attachment Rating and Classification Systems, Version 7.2*. Unpublished manuscript, University of California, Berkeley.

Main, M., Kaplan, N., & Cassidy, J. (1985). Security of infancy, childhood, and adulthood: A move to the level of representation. In I. Bretherton & E. Waters (Eds.), Growing points of attachment theory and research. *Monographs for the Society for Research in Child Development, 50*(Nos. 1–2, Serial No. 209), 66–106.

Mostow, E., & Newberry, P. (1975). Work role and depression in women: A comparison of workers and housewives in treatment. *American Journal of Orthopsychiatry, 45*(4), 538–548.

Otter-Henderson, K., & Creasey, G. (2001). *Frightened/frightening behaviors in romantic relationships—An attachment perspective*. Unpublished manuscript, University of Minnesota.

Paley, B., Cox, M., & Burchinal, M. R. (1999). Attachment and marital functioning, comparison of spouses with continuous-secure, earned secure, dismissing and preoccupied attachment. *Journal of Family Psychology, 13*, 580–597.

Roisman, G. I., Madsen, S. D., Hennighausen, K., Sroufe, L. A., & Collins, W. A. (2001). The coherence of dyadic behavior across parent–child and romantic relationships as mediated by the internalized representation of experience. *Attachment and Human Development, 3*, 156–172.

Sagi, A., van IJzendoorn, M., Scharf, M., Korne-Karje, N., Joels, T., & Mayseless, O. (1994). Stability and discriminant validity of the Adult Attachment Interview. *Developmental Psychology, 30*(5), 771–777.

Schultz, L. H. (1993). *Manual for scoring young adult close peer relationship interviews with the developmental relationship scales*. Unpublished manuscript, Harvard University.

Schultz, L. H., & Selman, R. L. (1998). Ego development and interpersonal development in young adulthood: A between-model comparison. In P. M. Westenberg, A. Blasi, & L. D. Cohn (Eds.), *Personality development: Theoretical, empirical, and clinical investigations of Loevinger's conception of ego development* (pp. 181–202). Hillsdale, NJ: Erlbaum.

Selman, R. L. (1980). The growth of interpersonal understanding: Developmental and clinical analyses. San Diego, CA: Academic Press.

Selman, R. L., & Schultz, L. H. (1990). *Making a friend in youth: Developmental theory and pair therapy*. Chicago: University of Chicago Press.

Simpson, J., Rholes, W. S., Orina, M. M., & Grich, J. (2002). Working models of attachment, support giving, and support seeking in a stressful situation. *Personality and Social Psychology Bulletin, 28*, 598–608.

Spanier, G. B. (1976). Measuring dyadic adjustment: New scales for assessing the quality of marriage and similar dyads. *Journal of Marriage and the Family, 38*, 15–28.

Thorndike, R. M., Cunningham, G. K., Thorndike, R. L., & Hagen, E. P. (1991). *Measurement and evaluation in psychology and education.* New York: MacMillan.

Treboux, D., Crowell, J. A., & Waters, E. (2004). When "new" meets "old": Configurations of adult attachment representations and their implications for marital functioning. *Developmental Psychology, 40*(2), 295–314.

van IJzendoorn, M., & Bakermans-Kranenburg, M. (1996). Attachment representations in mothers, fathers, adolescents, and clinical groups: A meta-analytic search for normative data. *Journal of Consulting and Clinical Psychology, 64*(1), 8–21.

Waters, E., Hamilton, C. E., & Weinfield, N. (2000). The stability of attachment security from infancy to adolescence and early adulthood: General introduction. *Child Development, 71*, 678–706.

Waters, E., Merrick, S., Treboux, D., Crowell, J., & Albersheim, L. (2000). Attachment security in infancy and early adulthood: A twenty-year longitudinal study. *Child Development, 71*, 684–689.

Wechsler, D. (1981). *Wechsler Adult Intelligence Scale—Revised (WAIS-R).* San Antonio, TX: Harcourt Assessment.

Weiss, R. (1982). Attachment in adult life. In C. M. Parkes & J. Stevenson-Hinde (Eds.), *The place of attachment in human behavior* (pp. 171–184). Englewood Cliffs, NJ: Prentice-Hall.

Weissman, M., Kasl, S., & Klerman, G. (1976). Follow-up of depressed women after maintenance treatment. *American Journal of Psychiatry, 133*(7), 757–760.

Weissman, M., & Paykel, E. (1974). *The depressed woman: A study of social relationships.* Chicago: University of Chicago Press.

Westenberg, P. M., Hauser, S., & Cohn, L. D. (2004). Sentence completion measurement of psychosocial maturity. In M. J. Hilsenroth & D. L. Segal (Eds.), *Comprehensive handbook of psychological assessment: Personality assessment* (Vol. 2, pp. 595–616). Hoboken, NJ: Wiley.

Wohlfarth, T. D., van den Brink, W., Ormel, J., Kolter, M. W. J., & Oldehinkel, T. J. (1993). The relationship between social dysfunctioning and psychopathology among primary care attenders. *British Journal of Psychiatry, 163*, 37–44.

15

Exploring the Mind
Behind Unresolved Attachment

Lessons from and for
Attachment-Based Interventions
with Infants and Their Traumatized Mothers

GREG MORAN, HEIDI NEUFELD BAILEY, KARIN GLEASON,
CAREY ANNE DEOLIVEIRA, and DAVID R. PEDERSON

Attachment theory and the rich body of research that it has stimulated have established that the initial attachment relationship between infant and caregiver is a critical basis for the child's successful social and emotional development (Rutter, 1997; Schore, 2001; Thompson, 1999). Understandably, then, a number of intervention programs aimed at enhancing early attachment relationships have emerged in recent years. Such programs have been designed for mother–infant dyads experiencing relationship difficulties or those known to be at risk for doing so. Given the theory's central hypothesis that maternal sensitivity is the primary determinant of the quality of the attachment relationship (Ainsworth, Blehar, Waters, & Wall, 1978), the majority of such interventions have aimed to increase the quality of maternal interaction (e.g., Juffer, Hoksbergen, Riksen-Walraven, & Kohnstamm, 1997; Riksen-Walraven, Meij, Hubbard, & Zevalkink, 1996; van den Boom, 1995). Others, however, have focused on not only enhancing maternal sensitivity directly but also modifying the mother's attachment-related cognitive representations (e.g., Bosquet & Egeland, 2001; Heinicke et al., 1999; Heinicke & Levine, Chapter

4, this volume; Lieberman, Weston, & Pawl, 1991; Toth, Rogosch, & Cicchetti, Chapter 6, this volume) that are seen as a critical determinant of the quality of the mother's interaction (Bretherton, 1991; Bretherton & Munholland, 1999; Main, Kaplan, & Cassidy, 1985) by many intervention programs.

A meta-analysis by Bakermans-Kranenburg, van IJzendoorn, and Juffer (2003) of reports of attachment-based interventions evaluated which of these approaches to intervention was more effective at enhancing maternal interaction and the attachment relationship. They came to the conclusion that those interventions featuring an intermediate number of sessions with a solely behavioral focus were more effective than more intensive programs that added support and therapy aimed at the mother's cognitive state. A more recently published meta-analysis of interventions directed at preventing disorganized attachment came to similar conclusions (Bakermans-Kranenburg, van IJzendoorn, & Juffer, 2005).

Although they are important summaries of research to date and guides for additional research, meta-analyses also have limitations, especially as bases for generalizations regarding the design of future interventions. In this case, although the meta-analysis by Bakermans-Kranenburg and colleagues (2003) included an examination of between-study variation in the populations involved in the intervention (e.g., single vs. multiple problems, clinical vs. community samples), its ability to examine within-sample sources of variation in outcome was limited, because such data were not systematically collected across studies.

Unresolved Trauma Moderated the Effectiveness of an Attachment-Based Intervention

Our intervention study (Moran, Pederson, & Krupka, 2005) fit clearly into Bakermans-Kranenburg and colleagues' (2003) "less is more" category: eight sessions when the child is between 6 and 12 months of age, focusing solely on altering maternal behavior. The program involved adolescent mothers, a population with an elevated prevalence of childhood physical and sexual abuse, and maladaptive parenting. Such factors likely contribute to a relatively high occurrence of mothers' dysfunctional interactions with their own infants that, in turn, are associated with the infants' nonsecure attachment relationships and developmental difficulties (Jaffee, Caspi, Moffitt, Belsky, & Silva, 2001). Previous research in our group had established that although adolescent mothers appear quite sensitive in interactions with their infants at 6 months, this sensitivity declines dramatically by the time the infants are 1 year of age (Moran et al., 2005). This population, therefore, is an important target for interventions aimed at enhancing mother–infant interaction and increasing the probability of a secure infant–mother attachment relationship.

Overall Efficacy of the Intervention

Clinically trained visitors performed eight home intervention sessions with 50 adolescent mothers and their 6- to 12-month-old infants; 50 other dyads served as a comparison group; all dyads were also observed in the home when the infants were 6, 12, and 24 months of age. The overall results of the study were consistent with Bakermans-Kranenburg and colleagues' (2003) conclusion that brief, behaviorally focused interventions improve the quality of the relationship between adolescent mothers and their infants: 57% of the mother–infant dyads receiving the intervention had secure attachment relationships when the infant was 12 months of age compared with only 38% of the comparison dyads. Moreover, those involved in the intervention sustained a higher quality of interaction: When infants were 24 months of age, 76% of the mothers in the intervention group displayed the same levels of sensitivity they had at 6 months, whereas this was true of only 54% of the comparison mothers.

Looking beyond the statistically significant success of the intervention, we were struck by the fact that the quality of the interactions of approximately 25% of mothers in the intervention group remained very dissimilar to those of mothers expected to develop and sustain a secure attachment relationship with their child. This anomalous result (Moran et al., 2005) was associated with a classification on the Adult Attachment Interview (AAI) of an unresolved/disoriented state of mind associated with childhood experiences of loss or abuse (Main, Goldwyn & Hesse, 2003; Main, Hesse, & Goldwyn, Chapter 2, this volume; Steele & Steele, Chapter 1, this volume). The unresolved/disoriented response to the AAI is indicated by a range of odd speech patterns when discussing a loss or trauma, including lapses in the monitoring of reason or belief—such as speaking about a dead loved one in the present tense, or not seeing that the death of the loved one is due to factors beyond one's control (instead, the belief "I caused the loss" is maintained). Such lapses in monitoring what is reasonable are also evident when, in the case of past abuse and trauma, an abusive figure (e.g., a stepfather) is not seen as the agent of the abusive act(s). In such instances, the speaker assumes unreasonable responsibility (e.g., "I was bad and deserved the abuse"). Also indicative of an unresolved/disoriented (U/d) stance in the AAI are lapses in the monitoring of speech, whereby an interviewee shows excessive attention to detail when recalling a past loss, perhaps identifying the year of the loss as occurring at different times, with no correction or clarification. Against this background, it is perhaps easy to see how attention and sensitivity to an infant's emotional needs are difficult to maintain for a mother who is unresolved. In our study, intervention group mothers classified as unresolved/disoriented or U/d showed the same patterns of decline in sensitivity from infant age 6 to 12 months and the same low levels of secure attachment at infant age 12 months as mothers who received no intervention. For these mothers, then, "less was not enough."

A brief, behavior-focused program of intervention failed to prevent the decline in the quality of the interactions that is such an impediment to the formation of a secure relationship. Clearly, unresolved mourning with regard to past loss or trauma, reliably identified in AAI responses, creates multiple problems for the mother, including difficulties with making use of standardized "brief" interventions, and pronounced social and emotional deficits in their children, beginning with disorganization during infancy (Hesse & Main, 2000).

This "less is not more" finding fits with data reported by Routh, Hill, Steele, Elliot, and Dewey (1995), who observed that mothers with U/d loss responses to the AAI were exceptional in that they did not benefit from a brief behavioral intervention for themselves and their school-age children with conduct disorder. Similar convergent evidence can be found in Steele, Hodges, Kaniuk, Hillman, and Henderson (2003), where AAI U/d status among adoptive parents of late-placed (previously maltreated children) was linked to more complicated adoptive outcomes. Taken together, these studies suggest that a pronounced need in mothers with unresolved grief demands more than a brief behavioral intervention to initiate and sustain positive change (for themselves and their children).

Unresolved Attachment and the Mother–Infant Relationship

Our finding that mothers classified as U/d generally were unable to benefit from an otherwise effective intervention program underscores the critical role played by the mother's organized state of mind regarding attachment in the development of a healthy and productive mother–infant relationship. A maternal U/d state of mind regarding attachment places the infant at risk for maladaptive development: Such dyads are more likely to develop disorganized attachment relationships, in which infants are unable to use consistently or effectively an organized strategy to deal with attachment-related stress and are at risk for behavior problems in later childhood (Lyons-Ruth & Jacobvitz, 1999; Main & Solomon, 1990; van IJzendoorn, Schuengel, & Bakermans-Kranenburg, 1999). Meta-analytic results indicate that parents classified as U/d develop disorganized relationships with their infants in 53% of cases (van IJzendoorn, 1995).

Explanations for the link between U/d and disorganized attachment have focused on the impact of unresolved trauma on maternal behavior. Essentially, these explanations suggest avenues through which infants experience an indirect, or second-generation, effect of trauma. Main and Hesse (1990) have argued that the same characteristics that predispose parents to unresolved lapses in the AAI substantially impair their interactions with their infants. They propose, for example, that traumatic memories intrude into a mother's awareness, producing contextually anomalous fearful or frightening expressions during interaction. The infant is thought to be particularly frightened and disoriented by such maternal expressions, because he or she perceives no connection between them and the interaction or the immediate environment (Main & Hesse, 1990). Unresolved/disoriented mothers have been found to display more fearful, frightening, and dissociative behaviors (Abrams, Rifkin, & Hesse, 2006; Jacobvitz, Leon, & Hazen, 2006; Schuengel, Bakermans-Kranenburg, & van IJzendoorn, 1999; see also the meta-analytic review by Madigan, Bakermans-Kranenburg, et al., 2006) and other atypical behaviors (Goldberg, Benoit, Blokland, & Madigan, 2003; Lyons-Ruth, Yellin, Melnick, & Atwood, 2005; Madigan, Moran, & Pederson, 2006). Evidence also has emerged that such atypical maternal behavior mediates the association between U/d attachment and the disorganized relationship (Madigan et al., 2006); however, the evidence falls far short of that necessary to understand fully the many causal links in the hypothetical chain of development.

Subsequent elaborations of Main and Hesse's (1990) original conceptualization have emphasized the potential for unresolved traumatic experiences to impact mother–infant interaction more broadly and pervasively. On the basis of their study of mothers with a profound disruption of the caregiving system, Solomon and George (1999) argued that disorganized attachment can arise from the chronic activation of the infant attachment system in dyads where the mother is unable to provide security and reduce fear. In a parallel fashion Lyons-Ruth, Bronfman, and Atwood (1999; Lyons-Ruth, Bronfman, & Parsons, 1999) have reasoned that maternal frightened or frightening interaction produces a breakdown of a child's attachment strategy only if it occurs chronically, and such chronic interactive disruptions can only take place if the mother has a characteristic inability both to monitor her interactive behavior and to calm and soothe a distressed infant (i.e., to repair the failed interaction) (Lyons-Ruth, Bronfman, & Atwood, 1999). These authors proposed that the mother's inability to monitor her interactive behavior and to respond to the child's resultant distress are products of the mother's own traumatic childhood experiences that she has been unable to resolve and integrate (Lyons-Ruth, Bronfman, & Atwood, 1999; Lyons-Ruth, Bronfman, & Parsons, 1999).

Exploring the Unresolved Mind: Sequelae of Unresolved Complex Trauma

To a greater or lesser degree, these theories implicate maternal childhood trauma and pervasive, substantially disrupted parenting in the development of U/d adult attachment. This link, in turn, suggests that, at least within at-risk populations, the roots of the psychosocial–emotional difficulties faced by such mothers lie in their experience of psychological symptoms more generally associated with chronic or complex trauma. Chronic childhood maltreatment is a frequently cited example of complex trauma, commonly defined as severe and/or chronic trauma with a cumulative psychological impact (Briere, 2002; Courtois, 2004; Herman, 1992; Roth, Newman, Pelcovitz, van der Kolk, & Mandel, 1997). Over half of our sample of adolescent mothers reported a history of childhood trauma (emotional, physical, or sexual abuse) on the AAI, and 38% were classified as U/d (Moran et al., 2005). These high rates of childhood abuse and U/d attachment provided an opportunity to investigate the disruptive effects of childhood trauma, and in particular, unresolved trauma, on the attachment relationship.

To date, there has been little empirical investigation of the mental processes of mothers with a history of complex trauma who display U/d states of mind: Few such investigations previously have been possible because the majority of research on the U/d classification has been conducted with low-risk samples, in which a history of childhood abuse is less common. The remainder of this chapter describes the two lines of research by our group that provide preliminary evidence of the complex mental processes underpinning U/d states of mind and their pernicious influence on parenting. This research was intended to enhance our understanding of the U/d state of mind that is such an impediment to effective mother–infant interactions and to the success of interventions to establish the requisite maternal sensitivity to form an organized attachment relationship. We view this and related research as foundational to the development of alternative programs of intervention for mothers with unresolved trauma. Our rationale for the two lines of research was as follows:

1. Attachment theory holds that the U/d state of mind is associated with trauma-related symptoms such as reexperiencing and dissociation (Fearon & Mansell, 2001; Main & Hesse, 1990; Main & Morgan, 1996). Recent explanations of the cognitive processes leading to unresolved/disoriented lapses on the AAI, however, have made reference to a wider range of more pervasive interpersonal and regulatory difficulties that are typically seen as the outcome of complex trauma (Bailey, 2003; Bailey, Moran, Pederson, & Bento, 2007; DeOliveira, Bailey, Moran, & Pederson, 2004; Lyons-Ruth, 2003; Lyons-Ruth & Block, 1996; Lyons-Ruth, Yellin, Melnick, & Atwood, 2003). A primary objective of the first line of inquiry in this study, then, was to determine whether mothers classified as U/d report these more pervasive difficulties.

2. An inability to regulate emotions is another common manifestation of complex trauma with clear implications for the mother–infant relationship (DeOliveira et al., 2004; Lyons-Ruth, Bronfman, & Atwood, 1999; Lyons-Ruth, Bronfman, & Parsons, 1999; Solomon & George, 1999). As described more comprehensively in DeOliveira and colleagues (2004), mothers who have failed to resolve or integrate childhood abuse are likely to have difficulty perceiving their children's emotions accurately and responding to them in an open and flexible manner. These maternal skills are critical to the infant's acquisition of dyadic and self-regulatory strategies. Thus, our second line of research focused on assessing mothers' emotion regulatory processes.

Unresolved Attachment and Chronic Trauma-Related Symptoms

The high frequency of childhood abuse histories among adolescent mothers in our intervention study led us to wonder whether they, and in particular, those with a U/d state of mind associated with childhood trauma were experiencing chronic trauma-related symptoms that have been associated with a history of childhood maltreatment. The terms "complex posttraumatic stress disorder (PTSD)" and "disorders of extreme stress, not otherwise specified" refer to a constellation of pervasive and chronic symptoms associated with the experience of complex trauma such as childhood abuse. Symptoms include extreme affect, and difficulties regulating this affect; disturbance in self-perception and the perception of others; and impaired interpersonal relationships (Briere, 2002; Courtois, 2004; Herman, 1992; Neumann, Houskamp, Pollock, & Briere, 1996; Roth et al., 1997; van der Kolk, 1996).

Accounts of the cognitive processes underlying a U/d state of mind have recently been broadened to encompass the complex trauma-related reactions displayed by some following chronic childhood maltreatment (Bailey, 2003; DeOliveira et al., 2004; Lyons-Ruth, 2003; Lyons-Ruth & Block, 1996; Lyons-Ruth et al., 2003). It has been suggested that chronic early abuse impairs the ability to integrate trauma-related information, thus increasing the likelihood of U/d attachment in adulthood (Bailey, 2003; DeOliveira et al., 2004; Liotti, 1999a, 1999b; Lyons-Ruth, Bronfman, & Parsons, 1999; Lyons-Ruth et al., 2003; Main & Hesse, 1990). This proposal stems from the idea that children exposed to maltreatment or otherwise inadequate caregiving cope with their circumstances through use of dissociative and avoidant strategies (Fischer et al., 1997; Fonagy, Target, & Gergely, 2000; Kernberg, 1975; Landecker, 1992; Terr, 1991). They avoid reflecting on interpersonal experiences in an open, flexible manner because it would lead to anxiety-provoking conclusions (Fonagy et al., 2000); however, this benefit comes at the cost of preventing the processing and mental integration of these and subsequent critical experiences (Fonagy et al., 2000; van der Kolk, 1996), leading to a fragile, restricted state of mind concerning attachment. Main and colleagues (Hesse & Main, 2000; Main & Hesse, 1990; 1992; Main & Morgan, 1996) have argued that such dissociative processes are the source of some of the observed lapses in reasoning that are diagnostic of U/d attachment: In one prototypical example, while a speaker was conveying a traumatic memory, a second, unintegrated and usually unconscious memory appeared to intrude, producing "a dramatic alteration in the speaker's mental state" (Hesse & Main, 2000, p. 1113).

In a parallel fashion, an overreliance on dissociative processes is also seen as the source of chronic and pervasive trauma-related symptoms: A failure to reflect on interpersonal experiences, thus integrating information pertaining to the self and significant others, is thought to lead to fragmented representations of the self and others (Fischer et al., 1997; Fonagy et al., 1995; Ogawa,

Sroufe, Weinfield, Carlson, & Egeland, 1997; van der Kolk, 1996). These inconsistent and fragmented representations are believed to give rise to fluctuating perceptions of significant others (e.g., alternating between representations of others as "all good" or "all bad") and in turn to difficulty maintaining close relationships over time, a problem commonly reported by those with chronic trauma-related symptomatology. Theory and research suggest that recurrent traumatic family interactions during childhood foster the development of negative representations of the self and others (Lyons-Ruth et al., 2005; Roth et al., 1997). Symptoms associated with complex trauma also include extreme emotions, and difficulty regulating these emotions. It has been proposed that these symptoms result from the experience of intense negative affect in childhood coupled with inadequate assistance from parents in regulating these strong emotions (Briere, 2002).

Research with clinical populations points to a probable association between such chronic trauma symptoms and U/d attachment: The constellation of complex PTSD symptoms resembles those characteristic of borderline personality disorder (BPD; American Psychiatric Association, 1994; Courtois, 2004), and U/d attachment is observed disproportionately among persons with BPD (Fonagy et al., 1995, 1997; Patrick, Hobson, Castle, & Howard, 1994). To our knowledge, however, our study was the first to investigate empirically the link between U/d attachment and chronic trauma-related symptoms in a nonclinical sample.

At the same time that we focused on the possible role of this broader range of symptoms associated with chronic trauma, we also probed for the presence of symptoms more traditionally associated with PTSD, including reexperiencing, avoidance, and dissociation. The first two of these symptoms has been the focus of several influential theoretical accounts of the link between trauma-related processes and U/d attachment (Fearon & Mansell, 2001; Main & Hesse, 1990). Evidence for an association between traditional PTSD symptoms and U/d status has been mixed. In a recent study of female childhood abuse survivors, U/d status was significantly associated with concurrent PTSD diagnosis and avoidance symptoms (Stovall-McClough & Cloitre, 2006); however, women meeting criteria for BPD, a diagnosis expected to have a high comorbidity with PTSD within this population, were excluded from the study. Other research with mothers with a history of stillbirths found no concurrent association between unresolved loss and PTSD (Turton, Hughes, Fonagy, & Fainman, 2004).

Subjective dissociative experiences are common among trauma survivors, often occurring with traditional and complex forms of posttraumatic stress reactions (Bremner, Vermetten, Southwick, Krystal, & Charney, 1998; Gershuny & Thayer, 1999; Roth et al., 1997). Derealization (a feeling of detachment from the physical world) and depersonalization (a feeling of detachment from oneself) may result from the use of cognitive dissociative processes, similar to those discussed previously, that serve to segregate unwanted information from awareness. Higher levels of dissociative symptoms have been reported by individuals classified as U/d (Schuengel et al., 1999; West, Adam, Spreng, & Rose, 2001).

Observed Links between AAI Unresolved Status and Chronic Trauma Symptoms 4 Years Later

Trauma-related symptoms were assessed when children were 4 years of age, approximately 2–3 years following the intervention study that prompted this follow-up research (see Bailey, 2003). Sixty-two mothers completed the Trauma Symptom Inventory (TSI; Briere, Elliott, Harris, & Cotman, 1995) and the Borderline Features scale of the Personality Assessment Inventory (PAI; Morey, 1991). These measures assessed a broad array of trauma-related symptoms, including the reexperiencing and avoidance symptoms characteristic of PTSD, and also symptoms associated with complex trauma-related sequelae: dissociative symptoms, self-harm, affective instability, identity problems, and negative relationships.

We found that mothers who had been classified as U/d when their children were 6 months of age had significantly higher total scores on the Borderline Features scale measuring chronic trauma-related symptoms. In particular, U/d mothers reported substantially and significantly greater relationship problems, including a history of intense, ambivalent, and unstable relationships, and concerns about being abandoned. They also reported significantly higher levels of identity confusion on the TSI, indicating a conscious awareness of a relatively incoherent sense of self (e.g., they reported feeling unsure who they really were, confused about what they thought or believed, and/or had difficulty distinguishing their own feelings from those of other people). In addition, they were significantly less consistent in their responses on the TSI. Inconsistent responses to items on a self-report instrument can be viewed as a behavioral indication of identity confusion that, unlike an explicit self-report of impaired self-understanding, has the advantage of not being dependent on conscious awareness (Bailey, 2003). Finally, a significantly greater endorsement of dissociative symptoms by the U group (e.g., feeling like they were watching themselves from far away, or that they were in a dream) indicated that subjective dissociative experiences, including depersonalization and derealization, were more common. Descriptive statistics for the U/d and not-U/d groups are listed in Table 15.1 together with F values and associated effect sizes.

We also tested directly whether chronic trauma symptoms were related to an inability to maintain or improve sensitivity as a result of the intervention. Mothers who did not benefit from the intervention reported significantly higher scores on the Borderline Features scale of the PAI [$t(24) = 2.43$, $p < .05$], and on two of its subscales: Identity Problems [$t(24) = 3.63$, $p < .01$] and Negative Relationships [$t(24) = 2.39$, $p < .05$].

Although U/d mothers displayed significantly higher levels of chronic trauma-related symptoms, they were not distinguished by the hallmark

TABLE 15.1. Trauma Symptom Scales by Unresolved/Disoriented Status

	U/d (n = 23) M(SD)	Not U/d (n = 39) M(SD)	F(1, 60)	Partial η²
TSI scales				
Intrusive Experiences	6.35 (5.33)	4.90 (4.14)	1.43	0.02
Defensive Avoidance	7.43 (4.88)	6.13 (5.50)	0.89	0.02
Dissociation	7.22 (7.29)	4.41 (3.22)	4.38*	0.07
Impaired Self-Reference	6.70 (4.70)	3.87 (3.34)	7.60**	0.11
Inconsistent Response	5.09 (1.98)	3.39 (2.35)	8.32**	0.12
PAI-BOR subscales				
Self-Harm	10.85 (2.72)	9.59 (2.55)	3.09†	0.05
Affective Instability	12.35 (3.01)	10.97 (3.35)	2.38	0.04
Identity Problems	13.20 (3.52)	11.97 (2.85)	2.08	0.04
Negative Relationships	15.90 (3.06)	12.03 (2.85)	22.24**	0.29

Note. TSI, Trauma Symptom Inventory; PAI-BOR, Personality Assessment Inventory, Borderline Features scale. Three mothers classified as unresolved did not complete the PAI-BOR; therefore, results for these scales are based on n = 20 U/d and n = 39 not-U/d mothers; 1, 57 df for univariate F-tests.
*p < .05; **p < .01; †p < .10.

symptoms of PTSD: reexperiencing and avoidance. Because complex reactions to early trauma are more persistent over time, it is possible that the 4-year delay between the assessment of U/d attachment and trauma symptoms may have contributed to our finding of elevated levels of complex, but not traditional, PTSD symptoms among U/d mothers. Regardless, these findings lend empirical support to the hypothesized link between chronic trauma-related symptoms and U/d attachment, particularly in high-risk populations in which childhood abuse is prevalent, and the related suggestion that these more pervasive symptoms may be the source of the negative impact of unresolved maternal attachment on mother–infant interaction and attachment relationships.

The endorsement of chronic trauma symptoms by mothers classified as U/d and the association of such symptoms with a failure to benefit from intervention suggest a number of substantial barriers to sensitive, responsive parenting that carry negative implications for the developing mother–infant relationship. Beyond the subjective distress that may accompany identity confusion, an inconsistent sense of self is associated with behavioral inconsistency (Wilkinson-Ryan & Westen, 2000); infants might find inconsistent and contradictory maternal responses confusing and unpredictable. Identity confusion could also hinder the ability to set consistent routines and work consistently toward goals (Wilkinson-Ryan & Westen, 2000).

Clearly, U/d mothers' highly elevated reports of relationship problems warrant further investigation: We need to understand better the interpersonal processes contributing to perceived relationship difficulties and the extent to which these problems extend to the mother–infant relationship. In our study, mothers who reported chronic trauma symptoms were significantly more likely to have displayed an emotionally distant interactive style and less likely to have behaved in an accepting, sensitive manner in home interactions observed 3 years earlier, when their infants were 1 year of age (Bailey, Moran, & Forbes, 2003). Furthermore, their infants were significantly more likely to have displayed profiles of interaction that were unharmonious and withdrawn. Such patterns of maternal and infant behavior were associated with disorganization in this sample (Bailey et al., 2007).

Unresolved AAI Status, Complex Trauma Symptoms, and Disorganized Mother–Infant Attachment

Measures of chronic trauma symptoms were collected at the 4-year assessment visit (62 dyads). The association of maternal U/d status with mother–infant disorganized attachment found for the full sample was no longer significant in this smaller subsample (Pearson's $\chi^2 = 2.10$, $p < .15$), making it impossible to test directly whether these trauma symptoms mediated this association. Overall, disorganized attachment was not related to maternal reports of trauma symptoms. However, among mothers classified as U/d with respect to loss or abuse, disorganized mother–infant relationships were associated with maternal reports of greater complex trauma symptoms. A multivariate analysis of variance (MANOVA) with U/d and disorganized attachment as independent variables revealed significant overall effects for U/d status [Pillais' $F(7, 47) = 2.65$, $p < .05$], reflecting the pattern of associations with chronic trauma symptoms previously described. The analysis also revealed a significant interaction between U/d and disorganized attachment [Pillais' $F(7, 47) = 2.27$, $p < .05$]. The interaction effect was specific to reports of identity concerns as measured on the Borderline Features scale of the PAI: Mothers classified as U/d who had developed disorganized relationships with their infants displayed the highest prevalence of identity concerns [$F(1, 53) = 6.76$, $p < .05$; partial $\eta^2 = 0.11$; see Figure 15.1].

Along the lines of the significant result shown in Figure 15.1, similar trends were found for reports of identity concerns on the TSI and maternal self-reports of negative relationships on the Borderline Features scale of the PAI. Although these findings are exploratory, they suggest that chronic, pervasive symptoms associated with the experience of complex trauma may be implicated in the development of a subset of disorganized attachment relationships.

Therapists typically find it challenging to work with individuals with pervasive interpersonal and self-regulatory problems. Their relative inability to develop a trusting therapeutic relationship, to follow through on plans, and to integrate experiences cognitively contribute to their slower progress in therapy and risk for premature termination (van der Kolk, 1996). It is not surprising,

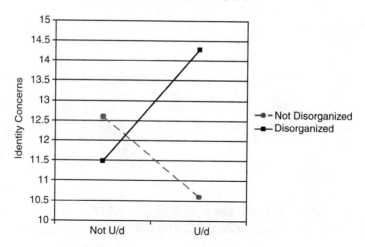

FIGURE 15.1. Average scores on the Identity Concerns subscale of the Personality Assessment Inventory, Borderline Features scale of unresolved/disoriented mothers in disorganized and not disorganized relationships with their infants.

therefore, that mothers classified as U/d in our intervention study, who endorsed a number of chronic, pervasive trauma symptoms, failed to benefit from the eight behaviorally focused intervention sessions. Our results suggest that future interventions with high-risk mother–infant dyads must address these more basic self-regulatory and interpersonal deficits, and provide the necessary support for relatively lower functioning mothers to improve their parenting skills. A more detailed description of such interventions is provided in our summary section.

This examination of trauma-related symptoms provides important empirical support for theoretical accounts of the relation between U/d attachment and trauma symptoms. Furthermore, the positive findings call attention to the importance of routinely assessing chronic trauma symptoms in intervention work with populations with a high frequency of childhood abuse. A significant limitation to this research, however, was its reliance on self-report. This limitation was especially problematic considering that cognitive dissociative processes would almost by definition limit self-awareness and the ability to report symptoms accurately.

Emotion Regulatory Processes: Perception of Infant Emotions and Perceived Ability to Regulate Infant's and One's Own Emotions

In this second and final series of analyses, we investigated the impact of maternal unresolved trauma on an aspect of interpersonal functioning—emotional processing and regulation—directly applicable to parenting. This is a particu-

larly relevant area of exploration, because disturbances in emotional understanding and regulation are hallmark indicators of complex PTSD and associated characterological difficulties (Briere, 2002; van der Kolk & Fisler, 1994).
As mentioned previously, a reported history of early chronic trauma has been
associated with severe disruptions in the ability to regulate negative emotions
such as fear and anger (Herman, Perry, & van der Kolk, 1989; Zanarini,
Dubo, Lewis, & Williams, 1997), as well as disturbances in self-perception
and perception of others (van der Kolk & Fisler, 1994). Adult survivors of
chronic abuse typically were raised within a dysfunctional and dysregulated
emotional socialization environment: Such a history of maladaptive emotion
socialization may substantially limit the development of a mother's understanding of emotions in the self and others (DeOliveira et al., 2004; Fonagy,
Gergely, Jurist, & Target, 2002) and significantly impair her ability to be emotionally available to her own child (Koren-Karie, Oppenheim, & Getzler-
Yosef, 2004).

It has been suggested that different attachment representations are linked
directly to specific conscious or unconscious strategies for responding to emotions, strategies that in turn serve to preserve that representation (Cassidy,
1994; Haft & Slade, 1989). Empirical studies of physiological and interpersonal responses to emotions in the self and in others have lent broad support
to these assertions (Adam, Gunnar, & Tanaka, 2004; Dozier & Kobak, 1992;
Kobak & Sceery, 1988). This functionalist interpretation implies that some
degree of agency or "strategy" underlies an individual's responses to emotions. A related but distinct hypothesis is that insecure, and particularly unre-
solved/disoriented, individuals may have enduring *deficits* in their affective
repertoire dating back to limitations in the emotional socialization and affect
mirroring environment of their own early infancy (DeOliveira et al., 2004;
Fonagy et al., 2002). Rather than being voluntary, the unresolved/disoriented
mother's response to her infant's emotions may be largely automatic and outside of her conscious control.

There is some evidence, albeit limited, that mothers with distinct organized attachment representations respond differently to their children's' emotional cues, with autonomous mothers generally being more open and responsive to a range of emotions (DeOliveira et al., 2004; Haft & Slade, 1989;
Zeanah et al., 1993). There is a dearth of research linking U/d representations
and specific patterns of emotional responding. In fact, there has been little
research in general on the impact of childhood trauma on caregiving, and
much of this has relied on self-report measures of behavior and attitudes (but
see Burkett, 1991; Lyons-Ruth & Block, 1996). The existing work suggests
that a maternal history of sexual abuse is associated with decreased involvement, role reversal, and self-reported difficulties, with parenting stress, anxiety, and confidence in the parenting role (Alexander, Teti, & Anderson, 2000;
Burkett, 1991; Cole, Woolger, Power, & Smith, 1992; DiLillo & Damashek,
2003; Lyons-Ruth & Block, 1996; Ruscio, 2001). A history of physical abuse

has been linked to increased hostile–intrusive behavior (Lyons-Ruth & Block, 1996) and more self-reported punitive practices (Banyard, Williams, & Siegel, 2003).

None of these studies has looked specifically at the impact of maternal childhood trauma and/or U/d states of mind on emotional understanding, awareness, and responsiveness. In these analyses, therefore, we explored the impact of U/d status on the automatic processing of emotions and on a mother's understanding and regulation of emotions in herself and her toddler. Observations were performed on 89 of the dyads in our larger study, when the children were 24 months old.

Examination of Emotional Awareness: The IFEEL Pictures Task

We used the IFEEL Pictures task created by Emde, Osofsky, and Butterfield (1993) to evaluate mothers' automatic responses to emotional stimuli when their infants were 24 months of age. Data were available from 89 of the original 100 mothers from the Moran and colleagues (2005) intervention study (46 intervention, 43 control). Participants were shown 30 color photographs of infants expressing spontaneous emotion and were asked to describe in one word the feeling depicted in each photograph; these descriptions were then assigned to one of 12 categories (Emde et al., 1993). Central to the theme of this report was our expectation that mothers with a history of trauma would have difficulty separating their own and others' emotions and/or would project their own internal representations onto ambiguous stimuli; that is, ambiguous images could provoke established expectancies of emotional responses of others based on childhood traumatic experiences (e.g., as hurtful/rejecting; see Magai, 1999, and discussion in preceding section).

We tested the a priori hypothesis that mothers with U/d representations ($n = 28$) would differ from mothers who were not U/d ($n = 61$) in their responses to the IFEEL Pictures, using the Mann–Whitney nonparametric rank-sum test (due to the presence of very negatively skewed distributions). The z-statistic associated with this test was significant for the emotions content, surprise, passive, and shame/guilt. Specifically, we found that U mothers had significantly fewer responses that fit into the content category and significantly more responses that fit into the surprise, passive, and shame/guilt categories (all p's < .05). Surprise and shame perceptions are also more prevalent among mothers at risk for maltreatment (Butterfield, 1993). Furthermore, Osofsky and Culp (1993) found that mothers with fewer responses that fit in the content category were more likely to have had incestuous experiences, and were more at risk for difficulties accepting their pregnancy and for having a poor relationship with the baby's father. Interestingly, the category Passive, chosen relatively often by U/d mothers in this study, included responses such as "dazed," "bored," "tired," "stoned," and "spaced out," all potentially reflecting a projected dissociative affective state.

We further compared each participant to the reference sample provided by Emde and his colleagues (1993) to investigate whether there was a higher prevalence of "atypical" responses among U/d mothers. We defined an "atypical response" as the use of an emotion category with prevalence of less than 5% for that picture in the reference sample. U/d mothers were significantly more likely than autonomous mothers to have low frequency (atypical) responses to the stimuli ($p < .01$, see Table 15.2).

Maternal Affective Mindset: The Meta-Emotion Interview

We chose the Meta-Emotion Interview (MEI; Gottman, Katz, & Hooven, 1997; Katz & Gottman, 1986) as a tool for examining how mothers with U/d attachment representations differed from other mothers in reported thoughts and feelings about their own emotions and the emotions emerging in their toddlers. The MEI provides parents with the opportunity to describe their philosophies, attitudes, and strategies pertaining to their own experiences of internalizing (fear, sadness) and externalizing (anger) emotions, and on those emerging in their children.

See Table 15.2 for a summary of the results. As reported elsewhere (DeOliveira et al., 2004), we found that unresolved mothers reported significantly more difficulty regulating their emotions than did autonomous mothers. They tended to describe these emotions as overwhelming, out of their

TABLE 15.2. A Comparision of AAI Classifications on Measures of Emotional Awareness and Socialization

Measure	Dismissing $M(SD)$	Autonomous $M(SD)$	Unresolved $M(SD)$	F statistic
IFEEL—Low frequency responses	4.65 (2.51)	3.73 (2.46)	5.97 (2.43)	5.74**
Meta-Emotion Interview (MEI)				
Regulation of Own Emotion	+0.152 (2.52)	+0.869 (1.39)[+]	−8.69 (2.32)[+]	4.14*
Response to Child's Fear	−1.03 (2.86)[+]	+1.44 (1.55)[+]	+0.005 (2.54)	6.70**
Response to Child's Anger	+0.04 (1.73)	+1.02 (1.51)[+]	−0.80 (1.77)[+]	7.35**
Response to Child's Sadness	−0.29 (2.60)[a]	+1.24 (1.54)[b+]	−0.76 (2.23)[+]	5.52**
CES-D	15.09 (10.71)[a]	8.65 (4.97)[b+]	18.23 (9.93)[a+]	7.90**
Emotional Availability Scales (Spider task)	4.08 (0.60)	4.40 (0.54)[a]	3.83 (0.91)[b]	4.39*

Note. MEI scales reported here represent aggregations of standardized subscales. Means in the same row with different superscripts differ significantly at $p < .05$ with Tukey's post hoc statistic. Means in the same row with the superscript + differ significantly at $p < .01$.
*$p < .05$; **$p < .01$.

control, and potentially dangerous. We also found that U/d mothers were significantly more likely to report clinical levels of depressive symptoms on the Center for Epidemiologic Study Depression Scale (CES-D; Radloff, 1977), congruent with past research indicating that U/d individuals are more highly represented in samples of individuals with significant affective disturbances. When talking about their toddlers' emotions, these mothers described lower levels of responsiveness to their children's anger and sadness. There was a similar sense of these emotions as being overwhelming. For example, when asked about her experiences of her child's anger, one U/d mother said, " . . . umm, uncontrollable, like I feel like I, I, I've, I have no control over her sometimes when she's angry. Um, helpless, helpless, like I mean she's angry a lot of the time." Despite the fact that U/d mothers were not coded as being less responsive to their children's *fear* in the MEI, objective observation of their behavior in a anxiety-evoking laboratory paradigm indicated that they might indeed have difficulty responding to this emotion. In this laboratory episode, the Interesting But Scary paradigm designed to evoke mild anxiety in the toddlers, a remote-control spider figure was driven into the observation room where the children were playing with their mothers following a Separation–Reunion paradigm. Eighty-six of the 89 mothers participated in this task (33 dismissing, 25 autonomous, 28 unresolved/disoriented). The episode was coded using Osofsky's Emotional Availability Scales (Osofsky, Cup, Eberhart-Wright, & Hann, 1990). The overall analysis of variance (ANOVA) comparing dismissing, autonomous, and U/d AAI classifications was significant ($p < .05$). Post hoc tests revealed that U/d mothers were coded as being significantly less emotionally available to their children than autonomous mothers in this potentially anxiety-evoking situation ($p = .01$; see Table 15.2).

Summary

In summary, we found that mothers with a U/d classification had distinctive and often atypical attributional responses in the face of ambiguous infant emotional stimuli. U/d mothers also described their own emotions as more overwhelming and dysregulated. When asked about their thoughts and feelings about their toddlers' emotions, U/d mothers were rated as demonstrating less responsiveness toward their children's anger and sadness. Moreover, in our independent laboratory paradigm, U/d mothers were rated as being less emotionally available to their children in a potentially fear- or anxiety-evoking situation.

These results raise provocative questions regarding the extent to which these aberrant patterns of perceiving and processing emotions may lead mothers with trauma and/or U/d representations to respond to their infants' emotions in a maladaptive manner. Our preliminary observations of such mothers' lack of responsiveness in an affect-laden situation are consistent with the impact of an atypical affective mindset, as revealed in the MEI, and with the impact of automatic, perhaps unconscious, aberrant affect perceptions revealed by maternal responses to the IFEEL Pictures stimuli. Clearly, further research is required to understand these dynamics; nonetheless, the results raise some important empirical and clinical issues. It would seem likely, for example, that interventions aimed at improving maternal emotional availability should ideally focus on both the "conscious" affective scripts and attributional processes, as well as the more automatic/implicit response to internal and external emotional cues. To the extent that emotional awareness and responsiveness is occurring at both automatic and unconscious levels, interventions designed to modify behaviors over which the mother has little functional control will be limited in their effectiveness.

Explorations of the Unresolved Mind: Summary and Implications for Intervention

The research presented in this chapter was prompted by our finding that mothers with a U/d state of mind regarding attachment, as coded in the AAI, were unlikely to benefit from a behaviorally focused intervention that was largely effective with mothers who were not U/d. We subsequently argued that both the maladaptive style of interaction of these mothers and their resistance to otherwise effective interventions could be understood as the reflection or consequence of the cognitive and emotional processes that arise from a childhood history of pervasively disrupted parenting and trauma. A series of investigations with a sample of adolescent mothers produced results that dovetail in support of this suggestion. First, consistent with the theoretical models of Main and Hesse (1990) and Lyons-Ruth (Lyons-Ruth, Bronfman, & Atwood, 1999; Lyons-Ruth, Bronfman, & Parsons, 1999; Lyons-Ruth et al., 2003, 2005) mothers with U/d attachment representations were more likely to report psychological symptoms characteristic of complex trauma reactions, reflecting these mothers' significant challenges with emotion regulation and interpersonal relatedness. We also found that adolescent mothers with a U/d state of mind regarding attachment displayed deficits in emotional awareness, regulation, and responsiveness. Moreover, these attributional and emotional deficits appeared to operate at both the conscious and unconscious levels.

These results qualify rather than contradict the general "less is more" conclusion of Bakermans-Kranenburg and colleagues' (2003) meta-analysis, which suggested that shorter-term, interaction-focused interventions were more effective than prolonged programs that included efforts to modify representations and offer broad support to mothers. This pattern held true for samples of mothers with multiple risk factors, including young, low-income mothers such as those in our study: Such factors were not found to moderate significantly the effectiveness of the intervention. This meta-analysis did not, however, examine the impact of U/d attachment on the effectiveness of such interventions. Although a history of childhood trauma was prevalent among the adolescent mothers in our sample, U/d attachment on the AAI was a better predictor of a failure to benefit from intervention than was experiencing such abuse. It appears then that the U/d state itself, and the associated maladaptive cognitive and emotional processes revealed by the investigations described here, lie at the heart of the challenges to assisting these mothers and their infants. It is especially important that we meet this challenge, because the U/d maternal state of mind is both theoretically and empirically linked to the development of the disorganized attachment relationship. Disorganization, in turn, has been shown to be associated with significantly maladaptive outcomes in later childhood and adolescence (see meta-analysis by van IJzendoorn et al., 1999).

In understanding the ineffectiveness of standard behaviorally focused interventions with mothers with unresolved trauma (i.e., why "less is not enough" for these mothers), it is important to consider the multiple effects that early and chronic trauma have on an individual's memory, attributional structures, and emotional processes. Trauma is often encoded through nonverbal, implicit, and sensory modalities, including deeply suppressed cognitive structures (Briere, 2002; van der Kolk, 2001). This powerful imprint of early trauma would be largely inaccessible and out of the conscious control of the mothers. To make matters worse, the implicit memories, along with the associated intense negative affects, sensory experiences, and powerful but primitive defensive processes (e.g., dissociation), are often triggered by interpersonal stimuli (Briere, 2002) and, in the case of these young mothers, may be triggered by features of the mother–infant relationship. Frightened, intrusive, rejecting, and otherwise dysfunctional maternal behavior may, in fact, be a reflection of this traumatic reenactment within the relationship, but it may be almost as inexplicable to the mother as it is to the infant. The results of our study are congruent with the hypothesis that mothers with unresolved trauma show implicit and explicit emotional and attributional deficits that could well be the basis for the interactive behavior that Main and Hesse (1990) have suggested frightens or startles their infants, as well as being linked to the broader helpless–hostile stance within the relationship (Lyons-Ruth, Bronfman, & Atwood, 1999; Lyons-Ruth, Bronfman, & Parsons, 1999).

This leaves the empirical and clinical question: Is it better to "work through" or "work around" the trauma to best assist these vulnerable dyads? "Working through" would involve directly addressing the impact of the early trauma and relational disruptions on the mother's internal working model of attachment and consequent relationship with her child, with the ultimate goal of changing internal working models of relationships. Some theorists argue that targeting mothers' internal working models takes precedence when intervening in the mother–infant relationship (Berlin, 2005). However, there are some significant practical impediments to using what is generally a longer-term, more intensive approach to mother–infant therapy when working with mothers with fragile self-identities and severe sensitivity to abandonment and perceived rejection, possibly accompanied by potentially dangerous tension reduction and self-soothing behaviors (e.g., alcohol/drug use, self-harm behaviors, sexual "acting out"; Briere, 2002). Generally, even "brief" psychodynamic interventions with individuals with personality disorders take significant time to be effective (Hoglend, 2003). Moreover, the process of "working through" transference and defensive processes may be accompanied by regression and temporary worsening of symptoms, thus possibly producing null or negative intervention effects and increasing the infant's vulnerability, at least in the short term. Indeed, Bakermans-Kranenburg et al. (2003) observed that some of the more comprehensive interventions they reviewed actually produced iatrogenic effects.

The attachment relationship develops quickly during a small window of time, and interactions with the mother are critical determinants of the nature and quality of the development process. Thus, even interventions that may ultimately be beneficial to the mother may be too prolonged or intense to avoid detrimental effects on the infant and the relationship. Representation-oriented or trauma-focused work with mothers with unstable personality structures and unresolved trauma must be planned with these concerns in mind. At this time, however, these concerns are hypothetical and speculative, and the question of whether this work can be effective in the short term with mothers who are unresolved with respect to trauma remains to be empirically determined.

Benoit (personal communication, March 2006) has suggested one approach that could be effective in circumventing the challenge of using trauma-focused therapy with mothers shortly after the birth of their child, thus potentially disrupting even further the critical development of the first year of life. She is investigating the use of trauma-focused cognitive-behavioral therapy (Cohen, Mannarino, Berliner, & Deblinger, 2000) during pregnancy. Although this approach is promising, it would of course be limited to populations in which risk can be determined and intervention accepted prior to birth.

In light of these issues, another option is to "work around" the trauma, not addressing the trauma directly within the mother–infant intervention, but focusing on the effect of these early disruptions on the attachment relationship. In an innovative example of one such approach, Benoit has focused on the direct reduction of those frightening/frightened (FR) behaviors that are hypothesized to be so disorganizing (Main & Hesse, 1990) through modified interaction guidance (Benoit, Madigan, Lecce, Shea, & Goldberg, 2001; Madigan, Hawkins, Goldberg, & Benoit, in press). This approach contrasts with most interaction-focused interventions where the entire emphasis is on modeling and increasing the likelihood of sensitive responsiveness. Instead, Benoit and her colleagues (2001) focus directly and explicitly on reducing the atypical, potentially disruptive actions of the mother, in addition to reinforcing positive, sensitive parenting behavior. This approach is not inconsistent with the parent–infant work described elsewhere in this volume (see Baradon & Steele, Chapter 8, and Jones, Chapter 7).

Such targeted interaction guidance has shown promise in enhancing maternal interaction in multiple-risk samples (Benoit et al., 2001; Madigan et al., in press) but the concern remains that such change may be short-lived. Lyons-Ruth and colleagues contend that these isolated atypical maternal actions occur in a broader context of disrupted parenting. Such parenting features a failure to alleviate the child's fear in times of attachment-related stress and to repair negative mother–infant interactions (Lyons-Ruth, Bronfman, & Atwood, 1999; Lyons-Ruth, Bronfman, & Parsons, 1999), and involves pervasive, substantially disrupted patterns of interaction (Lyons-Ruth & Spielman, 2004; Lyons-Ruth et al., 2005). No existing theoretical model would suggest that changing specific behaviors is likely to alter substantially the representational and attributional difficulties or implicit affective memories and responses underlying these atypical behavior patterns. Failure to address these issues directly may result in symptom substitution at new developmental stages, when changing dynamics within the mother–child relationship reactivate suppressed cognitive structures and related sensory and affective processes (Briere, 2002).

An alternative approach that also "works around" the trauma might be to *acknowledge* the impact of the trauma on the mother–infant relationship without targeting the trauma itself within the context of the mother–infant therapy. Initial stages of therapy would include education (and acknowledgment/support) around the impact of trauma on maternal emotion regulation and responses in interpersonal relationships, including the attachment relationship. For example, some attachment-based therapies such as the Circle of Security intervention (Marvin, Cooper, Hoffman, & Powell, 2002) and the Attachment and Biobehavioral Catch-up intervention (Dozier, 2003; Dozier & the Infant Caregiver Lab, 2002) assist parents in reflecting on how past experiences trigger defensive processes that materialize within the mother–child relationship, so that they can use this insight to change their responses. The proposed intervention would include a specific focus on (and normalization of) the implicit and explicit relational dynamics associated with a history of complex (unresolved) trauma.

Although it may be initially difficult to extinguish the "FR behaviors" (particularly those that are automatic and out of conscious awareness), mothers may be coached to recognize the cues from the infant and from their own affective experiences that there has been a significant rupture in the interaction, possibly related to emotional or cognitive intrusions from the past, and then to *repair* the interaction through empathy, nurturing, and responsiveness. The lack of repairing of disrupted interactions might arguably be what is most damaging in the relationship between U/d mothers and disorganized infants (Gianino & Tronick, 1988; Lyons-Ruth, Bronfman, & Atwood, 1999; Lyons-Ruth, Bronfman, & Parsons, 1999; Lyons-Ruth et al., 2005).

In addition, approaches might be borrowed from established trauma therapies to develop mindfulness, interpersonal skills, and emotion regulatory strategies. These techniques could then be integrated with specific relationship-specific coaching around empathy, emotional responsiveness, and reflective functioning, as outlined in the Marvin and colleagues (2002) and

Dozier and colleagues (2002) interventions. Structured treatments of the interpersonal and self-regulatory sequelae of complex trauma include cognitive-behavioral therapy (e.g., Levitt & Cloitre, 2005; Meichenbaum, 1999), dialectical behavior therapy (DBT; Linehan, 1993), self-trauma therapy (Briere, 2002), and other phase-oriented treatment, including progressive exposure (e.g., eye movement desensitization and reprocessing) and sensory processing (e.g., van der Kolk, 2001). DBT is a four-stage treatment approach that initially focuses on stabilization, decreasing life-threatening and therapy interfering behaviors, and increasing coping skills (e.g., behavioral skills, mindfulness, emotion regulation, and distress tolerance). Only when progress is made in these areas does the focus move to processing traumatic experiences, followed by increasing interpersonal and life skills, and finally self-validation and self-respect (Linehan, 1993). Although at this time we caution against proceeding to the final stages, which involve "working through" the trauma, the work around stabilization and coping that takes place in the earlier stages of DBT might well be combined with an attachment-based intervention, such as mother–infant interaction guidance, to target both the self-regulatory and interactional correlates of U/d attachment status.

The "working through" and "working around" approaches—targeting internal representations and interactional behaviors—are not necessarily mutually exclusive; that is, intervention that focuses on improving the quality of the mother–child relationship by increasing awareness, empathic responding, and sensitivity or targeting atypical maternal behavior may at the same time facilitate the development of a more coherent and flexible internal working model of relationships. Moreover, increasing maternal coping skills and self-efficacy can also improve both the mother–child relationship and representational models of relationships. In a randomized preventative intervention trial aimed at infants and maltreating mothers, Cicchetti, Rogosch, and Toth (2006) found that *both* infant–parent psychotherapy *and* a psychoeducational parenting intervention were effective at increasing attachment security and reducing disorganization in these high-risk dyads. More research is called for in the form of well-designed intervention studies to address these issues specific to mothers classified as U/d with regard to attachment. What is clear from this discussion is that further knowledge of precise cognitive and affective process difficulties, such as those revealed in the research outlined here, provides a framework for the design of interventions with mothers who are not able to benefit from traditional programs of support.

References

Abrams, K., Rifkin, A., & Hesse, E. (2006). Examining the role of parental frightened/frightening subtypes in predicting disorganized attachment within a brief observation procedure. *Development and Psychopathology, 18,* 345–361.

Adam, E. K., Gunnar, M. R., & Tanaka, A. (2004). Adult attachment, parent emotion, and observed parenting behavior: Mediator and moderator models. *Child Development*, 75(1), 110–122.

Ainsworth, M. S., Blehar, M. C., Waters, E., & Wall, S. (1978). *Patterns of attachment: A psychological study of the Strange Situation.* Oxford, UK: Erlbaum.

Alexander, P. C., Teti, L., & Anderson, C. L. (2000). Childhood sexual abuse history and role reversal in parenting. *Child Abuse and Neglect*, 24(6), 829–838.

American Psychiatric Association. (1994). *Diagnostic and statistical manual of mental disorders* (4th ed.). Washington, DC: Author.

Bailey, H. N. (2003). *Associations between childhood abuse history, unresolved attachment, and trauma symptoms in a high-risk sample of adolescent mothers.* Unpublished doctoral dissertation, University of Western Ontario, London, Ontario, Canada.

Bailey, H. N., Moran, G., & Forbes, L. (2003, April). *Adolescent mothers: Trauma symptoms, unresolved attachment, and maladaptive parent–child interactions.* Presented at the Society for Research in Child Development Conference, Tampa, FL.

Bailey, H. N., Moran, G., Pederson, D. R., & Bento, S. (2007). Associations between childhood abuse history, trauma symptoms, and unresolved attachment in an at-risk sample of adolescent mothers. *Development and Psychopathology*, 19, 313–343.

Bakermans-Kranenburg, M. J., van IJzendoorn, M. H., & Juffer, F. (2003). Less is more: Meta-analyses of sensitivity and attachment interventions in early childhood. *Psychological Bulletin*, 129(2), 195–215.

Bakermans-Kranenburg, M. J., van IJzendoorn, M. H., & Juffer, F. (2005) Disorganized infant attachment and preventative interventions: A review and meta-analysis. *Infant Mental Health Journal*, 26(3), 191–216.

Banyard, V. L., Williams, L. M., & Siegel, J. A. (2003). The impact of complex trauma and depression on parenting: An exploration of mediating risk and protective factors. *Child Maltreatment: Journal of the American Professional Society on the Abuse of Children*, 8(4), 334–349.

Benoit, D., Madigan, S., Lecce, S., Shea, B., & Goldberg, S. (2001). Atypical maternal behavior toward feeding-disordered infants before and after intervention. *Infant Mental Health Journal*, 22(6), 611–626.

Berlin, L. J. (2005). Interventions to enhance early attachments: The state of the field today. In L. J. Berlin, Y. Ziv, L. Amaya-Jackson, & M. T. Greenberg (Eds.), *Enhancing early attachments: Theory, research, intervention, and policy* (pp. 3–33). New York: Guilford Press.

Bosquet, M., & Egeland, B. (2001). Associations among maternal depressive symptomatology, state of mind and parent and child behaviors: Implications for attachment-based interventions. *Attachment and Human Development*, 3(2), 173–199.

Bremner, J. D., Vermetten, E., Southwick, S. M., Krystal, J. H., & Charney, D. S. (Eds.). (1998). Trauma, memory, and dissociation: An integrative formulation. In J. D. Bremner & C. Marmar (Eds.), *Trauma, memory, and dissociation* (pp. 365–403). Washington, DC: American Psychiatric Association.

Bretherton, I. (Ed.). (1991). *Pouring new wine into old bottles: The social self as internal working model.* Hillsdale, NJ: Erlbaum.

Bretherton, I., & Munholland, K. A. (1999). Internal working models in attachment relationships: A construct revisited. In J. Cassidy & P. R. Shaver (Eds.), *Hand-*

book of attachment: Theory, research, and clinical applications (pp. 89–111). New York: Guilford Press.

Briere, J. (2002). *Treating adult survivors of severe childhood abuse and neglect: Further development of an integrative model.* Thousand Oaks, CA: Sage.

Briere, J., Elliott, D. M., Harris, K., & Cotman, A. (1995). Trauma Symptom Inventory: Psychometrics and association with childhood and adult victimization in clinical samples. *Journal of Interpersonal Violence, 10*(4), 387–401.

Burkett, L. P. (1991). Parenting behaviors of women who were sexually abused as children in their families of origin. *Family Process, 30*(4), 421–434.

Butterfield, P. M. (Ed.). (1993). *Responses to IFEEL pictures in mothers at risk for child maltreatment.* Madison, CT: International Universities Press.

Cassidy, J. (1994). Emotion regulation: Influences of attachment relationships. *Monographs of the Society for Research in Child Development, 59*(2–3), 228–249.

Cicchetti, D., Rogosch, F. A., & Toth, S. L. (2006). Fostering secure attachment in infants in maltreating families through preventative interventions. *Development and Psychopathology, 18*, 623–649.

Cohen, J. A., Mannarino, A. P., Berliner, L., & Deblinger, E. (2000). Trauma-focused cognitive behavioral therapy for children and adolescents: An empirical update. *Journal of Interpersonal Violence, 15*(11), 1202–1223.

Cole, P. M., Woolger, C., Power, T. G., & Smith, K. D. (1992). Parenting difficulties among adult survivors of father–daughter incest. *Child Abuse and Neglect, 16*, 239–249.

Courtois, C. A. (2004). Complex trauma, complex reactions: Assessment and treatment [Special issue]. *Psychotherapy: Theory, Research, Practice and Training, 41*(4), 412–425.

DeOliveira, C. A., Bailey, H. N., Moran, G., & Pederson, D. R. (2004). Emotion socialization as a framework for understanding the development of disorganized attachment. *Social Development, 13*(3), 437–467.

DiLillo, D., & Damashek, A. (2003). Parenting characteristics of women reporting a history of childhood sexual abuse. *Child Maltreatment: Journal of the American Professional Society on the Abuse of Children, 8*(4), 319–333.

Dozier, M. (2003). Attachment-based treatment for vulnerable children. *Attachment and Human Development, 5*(3), 253–257.

Dozier, M., & the Infant Caregiver Lab. (2002). *The attachment and biobehavioral catch-up intervention: A training manual for foster parents.* Unpublished document, University of Delaware, Newark.

Dozier, M., & Kobak, R. R. (1992). Psychophysiology in attachment interviews: Converging evidence for deactivating strategies. *Child Development, 63*(6), 1473–1480.

Emde, R. N., Osofsky, J. D., & Butterfield, P. M. (1993). *The IFEEL Pictures: A new instrument for interpreting emotions.* Madison, CT: International Universities Press.

Fearon, R. M. P., & Mansell, W. (2001). Cognitive perspectives on unresolved loss: Insights from the study of PTSD [Special issue]. *Bulletin of the Menninger Clinic, 65*(3), 380–396.

Fischer, K. W., Ayoub, C., Singh, I., Noam, G., Maraganore, A., & Raya, P. (1997). Psychopathology as adaptive development along distinctive pathways. *Development and Psychopathology, 9*(4), 729–748.

Fonagy, P., Gergely, G., Jurist, E. L., & Target, M. (2002). *Affect regulation, mentalization, and the development of the self*. New York: Other Press.

Fonagy, P., Steele, M., Steele, H., Leigh, T., Kennedy, R., & Mattoon, G., et al. (Eds.). (1995). *Attachment, the reflective self, and borderline states: The predictive specificity of the adult attachment interview and pathological emotional development*. Hillsdale, NJ: Analytic Press.

Fonagy, P., Target, M., & Gergely, G. (2000). Attachment and borderline personality disorder: A theory and some evidence [Special issue]. *Psychiatric Clinics of North America*, 23(1), 103–122.

Fonagy, P., Target, M., Steele, M., Steele, H., Leigh, T., Levinson, A., et al. (1997). Morality, disruptive behavior, borderline personality disorder, crime and their relationship to security of attachment. In L. Atkinson & K. J. Zucker (Eds.), *Attachment and psychopathology*. New York: Guilford Press.

Gershuny, B. S., & Thayer, J. F. (1999). Relations among psychological trauma, dissociative phenomena, and trauma-related distress: A review and integration. *Clinical Psychology Review*, 19(5), 631–657.

Gianino, A., & Tronick, E. Z. (Eds.). (1988). *The mutual regulation model: The infant's self and interactive regulation and coping and defensive capacities*. Hillsdale, NJ: Erlbaum.

Goldberg, S., Benoit, D., Blokland, K., & Madigan, S. (2003). Atypical maternal behavior, maternal representations, and infant disorganized attachment. *Development and Psychopathology*, 15(2), 239–257.

Gottman, J. M., Katz, L. F., & Hooven, C. (1997). *Meta-emotion: How families communicate emotionally*. Hillsdale, NJ: Erlbaum.

Haft, W. L., & Slade, A. (1989). Affect attunement and maternal attachment: A pilot study [Special issue]. *Infant Mental Health Journal*, 10(3), 157–172.

Heinicke, C. M., Fineman, N. R., Ruth, G., Recchia, S. L., Guthrie, D., & Rodning, C. (1999). Relationship-based intervention with at-risk mothers: Outcome in the first year of life. *Infant Mental Health Journal*, 20(4), 349–374.

Herman, J. L. (1992). Complex PTSD: A syndrome in survivors of prolonged and repeated trauma. *Journal of Traumatic Stress*, 5(3), 377–391.

Herman, J. L., Perry, C., & van der Kolk, B. A. (1989). Childhood trauma in borderline personality disorder. *American Journal of Psychiatry*, 146, 490–494.

Hesse, E., & Main, M. (2000). Disorganized infant, child, and adult attachment: Collapse in behavioral and attentional strategies. *Journal of the American Psychoanalytic Association*, 48(4), 1097–1127.

Hoglend, P. (2003). Long-term effects of brief dynamic psychotherapy. *Psychotherapy Research*, 13(3), 271–292.

Jacobvitz, D., Leon, K., & Hazen. N. (2006). Does expectant mothers' unresolved trauma predict frightening maternal behavior?: Risk and protective factors. *Development and Psychopathology*, 18, 363–379.

Jaffee, S., Caspi, A., Moffitt, T. E., Belsky, J., & Silva, P. (2001). Why are children born to teen mothers at risk for adverse outcomes in young adulthood?: Results from a 20-yr longitudinal study. *Development and Psychopathology*, 13(2), 377–397.

Juffer, F., Hoksbergen, R. A. C., Riksen-Walraven, J. M., & Kohnstamm, G. A. (1997). Early intervention in adoptive families: Supporting maternal sensitive responsiveness, infant–mother attachment, and infant competence. *Journal of Child Psychology and Psychiatry*, 38(8), 1039–1050.

Katz, L. F., & Gottman, J. M. (1986). *The meta-emotion interview.* Unpublished manual, University of Washington, Seattle, WA.

Kernberg, O. (1975). *Borderline conditions and pathological narcissism.* New York: Aronson.

Kobak, R. R., & Sceery, A. (1988). Attachment in late adolescence: Working models, affect regulation, and representations of self and others. *Child Development, 59*(1), 135–146.

Koren-Karie, N., Oppenheim, D., & Getzler-Yosef, R. (2004). Mothers who were severely abused during childhood and their children talk about emotions: Co-construction of narratives in light of maternal trauma [Special issue]. *Infant Mental Health Journal, 25*(4), 300–317.

Landecker, H. (1992). The role of childhood sexual trauma in the etiology of borderline personality disorder: Considerations for diagnosis and treatment. *Psychotherapy: Theory, Research, Practice and Training, 29*(2), 234–242.

Levitt, J. T., & Cloitre, M. (2005). A clinician's guide to STAIR/MPE: Treatment for PTSD related to childhood abuse. *Cognitive and Behavioral Practice, 12*(1), 40–52.

Lieberman, A. F., Weston, D. R., & Pawl, J. H. (1991). Preventive intervention and outcome with anxiously attached dyads. *Child Development, 62*(1), 199–209.

Linehan, M. M. (1993). *Cognitive-behavioral treatment of borderline personality disorder.* New York: Guilford Press.

Liotti, G. (1999a). Disorganization of attachment as a model for understanding dissociative psychopathology. In J. Solomon & C. C. George (Eds.), *Attachment disorganization.* New York: Guilford Press.

Liotti, G. (1999b). Understanding the dissociative processes: The contribution of attachment theory [Special issue]. *Psychoanalytic Inquiry, 19*(5), 757–783.

Lyons-Ruth, K. (2003). Dissociation and the parent–infant dialogue: A longitudinal perspective from attachment research. *Journal of the American Psychoanalytic Association, 51*(3), 883–911.

Lyons-Ruth, K., & Block, D. (1996). The disturbed caregiving system: Relations among childhood trauma, maternal caregiving, and infant affect and attachment [Special issue]. *Infant Mental Health Journal, 17*(3), 257–275.

Lyons-Ruth, K., Bronfman, E., & Atwood, G. (1999). A relational diathesis model of hostile–helpless states of mind: Expressions in mother–infant interaction. In J. Solomon & C. C. George (Eds.), *Attachment disorganization.* New York: Guilford Press.

Lyons-Ruth, K., Bronfman, E., & Parsons, E. (1999). Maternal frightened, frightening, or atypical behavior and disorganized infant attachment patterns. *Monographs of the Society for Research in Child Development, 64*(3), 67–96.

Lyons-Ruth, K., & Jacobvitz, D. (1999). Attachment disorganization: Unresolved loss, relational violence, and lapses in behavioral and attentional strategies. In J. Cassidy & P. R. Shaver (Eds.), *Handbook of attachment: Theory, research, and clinical applications* (pp. 520–554). New York: Guilford Press.

Lyons-Ruth, K., & Spielman, E. (2004). Disorganized infant attachment strategies and helpless–fearful profiles of parenting: Integrating attachment research with clinical intervention [Special issue]. *Infant Mental Health Journal, 25*(4), 318–335.

Lyons-Ruth, K., Yellin, C., Melnick, S., & Atwood, G. (2003). Childhood experiences of trauma and loss have different relations to maternal unresolved and hostile–

helpless states of mind on the AAI. *Attachment and Human Development*, 5(4), 330–352.

Lyons-Ruth, K., Yellin, C., Melnick, S., & Atwood, G. (2005). Expanding the concept of unresolved mental states: Hostile/helpless states of mind on the adult attachment interview are associated with disrupted mother–infant communication and infant disorganization. *Development and Psychopathology*, 17(1), 1–23.

Madigan, S., Bakermans-Kranenburg, M. J., van IJzendoorn, M. H., Moran, G., Pederson, D. R., & Benoit, D. (2006). Unresolved states of mind, anomalous parental behavior, and disorganized attachment: A review and meta-analysis. *Attachment and Human Development*, 8(2), 89–111.

Madigan, S., Hawkins, E., Goldberg, S., & Benoit, D. (2006). Reduction of disrupted caregiver behavior using modified interaction guidance. *Infant Mental Health Journal*, 27(5), 509–527.

Madigan, S., Moran, G., & Pederson, D. R. (2006). Unresolved states of mind, disorganized attachment relationships, and disrupted interactions of adolescent mothers and their infants. *Developmental Psychology*, 42(2), 293–304.

Magai, C. (1999). Affect, imagery, and attachment: Working models of interpersonal affect and the socialization of emotion. In J. Cassidy & P. R. Shaver (Eds.), *Handbook of attachment: Theory, research, and clinical applications* (pp. 787–802). New York: Guilford Press.

Main, M., Goldwyn, R., & Hesse, E. (2003). *Adult attachment scoring and classification system*. Unpublished manuscript, University of California, Berkeley.

Main, M., & Hesse, E. (1990). Parents' unresolved traumatic experiences are related to infant disorganized attachment status: Is frightened and/or frightening parental behavior the linking mechanism? In M. T. Greenberg, D. Cicchetti, & E. M. Cummings (Eds.), *Attachment in the preschool years: Theory, research, and intervention* (pp. 161–182). Chicago: University of Chicago Press.

Main, M., Kaplan, N., & Cassidy, J. (1985). Security in infancy, childhood, and adulthood: A move to the level of representation. *Monographs of the Society for Research in Child Development*, 50(1–2), 66–104.

Main, M., & Morgan, H. (1996). *Disorganization and disorientation in infant Strange Situation behavior: Phenotypic resemblance to dissociative states*. New York: Plenum Press.

Main, M., & Solomon, J. (Eds.). (1990). *Procedures for identifying infants as disorganized/disoriented during the Ainsworth Strange Situation*. Chicago: University of Chicago Press.

Marvin, R., Cooper, G., Hoffman, K., & Powell, B. (2002). The Circle of Security Project: Attachment-based intervention with caregiver–pre-school child dyads. *Attachment and Human Development*, 4(1), 107–124.

Meichenbaum, D. (1999). Treatment of patients with posttraumatic stress disorder: A constructive-narrative approach [Behandlung von patienten mit posttraumatischen belastungsstörungen: Ein konstruktiv-narrativer ansatz]. *Verhaltenstherapie*, 9(4), 186–189.

Moran, G., Pederson, D. R., & Krupka, A. (2005). Maternal unresolved attachment status impedes the effectiveness of interventions with adolescent mothers. *Infant Mental Health Journal*, 26(3), 231–249.

Morey, L. C. (1991). *The Personality Assessment Inventory: Professional manual*. Odessa, FL: Psychological Assessment Resources.

Neumann, D. A., Houskamp, B. M., Pollock, V. E., & Briere, J. (1996). The long-term sequelae of childhood sexual abuse in women: A meta-analytic review. *Child Maltreatment, 1*(1), 6–16.

Ogawa, J. R., Sroufe, L. A., Weinfield, N. S., Carlson, E. A., & Egeland, B. (1997). Development and the fragmented self: Longitudinal study of dissociative symptomatology in a nonclinical sample. *Development and Psychopathology, 9*(4), 855–879.

Osofsky, J. D., & Culp, A. M. (Eds.). (1993). *Perceptions of infant emotions in adolescent mothers.* Madison, CT: International Universities Press.

Osofsky, J. D., Culp, A. M., Eberhart-Wright, A., & Hann, D. M. (1990). *Emotional Availability Observation Scales.* Unpublished manuscript, Louisiana State University Medical Center, New Orleans.

Patrick, M., Hobson, R. P., Castle, D., & Howard, R. (1994). Personality disorder and the mental representation of early social experience. *Development and Psychopathology, 6*(2), 375–388.

Radloff, L. S. (1977). The CES-D scale: A self-report depression scale for research in the general population. *Applied Psychological Measurement, 1*(3), 385–401.

Riksen-Walraven, J. M., Meij, J. T., Hubbard, F. O., & Zevalkink, J. (1996). Intervention in lower-class Surinam–Dutch families: Effects on mothers and infants. *International Journal of Behavioral Development, 19*(4), 739–756.

Roth, S., Newman, E., Pelcovitz, D., van der Kolk, B., & Mandel, F. S. (1997). Complex PTSD in victims exposed to sexual and physical abuse: Results from the DSM-IV Field Trial for Posttraumatic Stress Disorder. *Journal of Traumatic Stress, 10*(4), 539–555.

Routh, C. P., Hill, J. W., Steele, H., Elliott, C. E., & Dewey, M. E. (1995). Maternal attachment status, psychosocial stressors and problem behaviour: Follow-up after parent training courses for conduct disorder. *Journal of Child Psychology and Psychiatry, 36*(7), 1179–1198.

Ruscio, A. M. (2001). Predicting the child-rearing practices of mothers sexually abused in childhood. *Child Abuse and Neglect, 25*, 369–387.

Rutter, M. (1997). Clinical implications of attachment concept: Retrospect and prospect. In L. Atkinson & K. J. Zucker (Eds.), *Attachment and psychopathology* (pp. 17–46). New York: Guilford Press.

Schore, A. N. (2001). Effects of a secure attachment relationship on right brain development, affect regulation, and infant mental health. *Infant Mental Health Journal, 22*, 7–66.

Schuengel, C., Bakermans-Kranenburg, M. J., & van IJzendoorn, M. H. (1999). Frightening maternal behavior linking unresolved loss and disorganized infant attachment. *Journal of Consulting and Clinical Psychology, 67*(1), 54–63.

Solomon, J., & George, C. C. (1999). The place of disorganization in attachment theory: Linking classic observations with contemporary findings. In J. Solomon & C. C. George (Eds.), *Attachment disorganization.* New York: Guilford Press.

Steele, M., Hodges, J., Kaniuk, J., Hillman, S., & Henderson, K. (2003). Attachment representations and adoption: Associations between maternal states of mind and emotion narratives in previously maltreated children. *Journal of Child Psychotherapy, 29*(2), 187–205.

Stovall-McClough, K. C., & Cloitre, M. (2006). Unresolved attachment, PTSD, and dissociation in women with childhood abuse histories. *Journal of Consulting and Clinical Psychology, 74*, 219–228.

Terr, L. C. (1991). Childhood traumas: An outline and overview. *American Journal of Psychiatry, 148*(1), 10–20.

Thompson, R. A. (1999). Early attachment and later development. In J. Cassidy & P. R. Shaver (Eds.), *Handbook of attachment: Theory, research, and clinical applications* (pp. 265–286). New York: Guilford Press.

Turton, P., Hughes, P., Fonagy, P., & Fainman, D. (2004). An investigation into the possible overlap between PTSD and unresolved responses following stillbirth: An absence of linkage with only unresolved status predicting infant disorganization. *Attachment and Human Development, 6*, 241–253.

van den Boom, D. C. (1995). Do first-year intervention effects endure?: Follow-up during toddlerhood of a sample of Dutch irritable infants. *Child Development, 66*(6), 1798–1816.

van der Kolk, B. A. (1996). The complexity of adaptation to trauma: Self-regulation, stimulus discrimination, and characterological development. In B. A. van der Kolk, A. C. McFarlane, & L. Weisaeth (Eds.), *Traumatic stress: The effects of overwhelming experience on mind, body, and society* (pp. 129–154). New York: Guilford Press.

van der Kolk, B. A. (2001). The psychobiology and psychopharmacology of PTSD [Special issue]. *Human Psychopharmacology: Clinical and Experimental, 16*(Suppl. 1), S49–S64.

van der Kolk, B. A., & Fisler, R. E. (1994). Childhood abuse and neglect and loss of self-regulation. *Bulletin of the Menninger Clinic, 58*(2), 145–168.

van IJzendoorn, M. (1995). Adult attachment representations, parental responsiveness, and infant attachment: A meta-analysis on the predictive validity of the Adult Attachment Interview. *Psychological Bulletin, 117*(3), 387–403.

van IJzendoorn, M. H., Schuengel, C., & Bakermans-Kranenburg, M. J. (1999). Disorganized attachment in early childhood: Meta-analysis of precursors, concomitants, and sequelae. *Development and Psychopathology, 11*(2), 225–249.

West, M., Adam, K., Spreng, S., & Rose, S. (2001). Attachment disorganization and dissociative symptoms in clinically treated adolescents. *Canadian Journal of Psychiatry, 46*(7), 627–631.

Wilkinson-Ryan, T., & Westen, D. (2000). Identity disturbance in borderline personality disorder: An empirical investigation. *American Journal of Psychiatry, 157*(4), 528–541.

Zanarini, M. C., Dubo, E. D., Lewis, R. E., & Williams, A. A. (1997). Childhood factors associated with the development of borderline personality disorder. In M. C. Zanarini (Ed.), *Role of sexual abuse in the etiology of borderline personality disorder*. Washington, DC: American Psychiatric Association.

Zeanah, C. H., Benoit, D., Barton, M., Regan, C., Hirshberg, L. M., & Lipsitt, L. P. (1993). Representations of attachment in mothers and their one-year-old infants. *Journal of the American Academy of Child and Adolescent Psychiatry, 32*(2), 278–286.

16

Hostile–Helpless States of Mind in the AAI

A Proposed Additional AAI Category with Implications for Identifying Disorganized Infant Attachment in High-Risk Samples

SHARON MELNICK, BRENT FINGER, SYDNEY HANS,
MATTHEW PATRICK, and KARLEN LYONS-RUTH

This chapter reports on the early stages of development, validation, and application of an approach potentially capable of identifying an additional Adult Attachment Interview (AAI) category, and a potential indicator of mental states of disorganization such as unresolved (U) and cannot classify (CC). Our work toward developing this new category is intended, then, to identify another clinically significant "disorganized" (D) state of mind in the AAI. The proposed additional "disorganized" category extends the description of incoherence in states of mind to features of the transcript as a whole that are thought to index identifications with hostile or helpless childhood attachment figures that appear unintegrated in the mind of the speaker. The new hostile–helpless (HH) coding system does not duplicate or supplant the original AAI coding system for organized, U, and CC states of mind. It may be especially useful for capturing features of states of mind that are pervasively unintegrated with respect to evaluations of attachment figures, and that may not be captured during discussions of loss or trauma, or via the "contrasting insecure states of mind" originally used to identify the CC category.

Whereas a lack of integration characterizes all insecure strategies to some extent, the failures of integration described here are pervasive, and the coding focuses on unintegrated features of the representation of the attachment relationship itself, as may appear in more clinically disturbed samples, rather than discourse around experiences of loss or trauma per se. Studies to date indicate that this approach to identifying HH relational representations may add to our ability to predict intergenerational transmission of disorganized attachment from parent to child, as reviewed below. We begin with an account of the currently established links to infant disorganization, define the contribution we believe the HH system can make, and discuss the possible adult correlates of the disorganized–controlling strategies that appear in early and middle childhood, and were first noted and linked to infant disorganization by Main and Cassidy (1988). We summarize the HH system and three independent studies that have provided initial indications of the potential validity of this addition to the existing approach to scoring the AAI (Main, Goldwyn & Hesse, 2003; Main, Hesse, & Goldwyn, Chapter 2, this volume).

Disorganized attachment in infancy has been linked repeatedly to parental lapses of reasoning or discourse when discussing experiences of loss or abuse in the AAI (van IJzendoorn, Schuengel, & Bakermans-Kranenburg, 1999). Main and Hesse (1990) proposed that it is the parent's failure mentally to integrate losses or traumatic experiences that lead to such lapses in his or her AAI. This is termed an "unresolved" state of mind and, together with a "cannot classify" category developed by Hesse (1996; see also Main et al., 2003), is one of the two adult representational measures of a D state of mind with respect to attachment. Within the AAI classification system, the coding of lapses in reasoning or discourse in relation to experiences of either loss or other traumatic experience results in the U classification.

Until recently (see, e.g., Behrens, Hesse, & Main, in press) the U and CC categories of the AAI were placed together in a single, collapsed category termed U/CC. Despite links between the adult U/CC and infant D classifications (van IJzendoorn et al., 1999), in a meta-analysis of nine attachment studies, a weaker relationship has been observed between the U and D classifications than between autonomous or dismissing (Ds) adult categories of organized attachment and their infant counterparts (van IJzendoorn, 1995). Specifically, in this 1995 analysis, an average of only 53% of disorganized infants had a parent classified U/CC, although van IJzendoorn also reported that the degree of U/CC parent to D infant match was greatly increased when coders had had more training in the D system. On average, then, this leaves 47% of D infants unaccounted for by parental U states of mind. Thus, there appears to be a great deal of variance in infant disorganization that remains to be accounted for by factors other than parental U/CC states of mind.

A key methodological issue that may weaken the prediction from the U category to infant D is that coding for U status depends on the reporting of a specific loss or abuse experience. If no loss or abuse experience is reported by the participant, then adult state of mind cannot be coded U. In addition, in a departure from the practice established for other states of mind, only aspects of the interview that can be tied to the participant's state of mind regarding the loss or abuse experience are relevant to the coding of a U state of mind. A parent's discourse about traumatic events per se may constitute too narrow a window for indexing the range of attachment-related representational distortions seen among adults with more difficult childhood experiences and, possibly, clinical disturbances.

In one approach to this dilemma, Hesse (1996) has developed criteria for designating an AAI as CC if both a Ds and a preoccupied strategy are evident in different parts of the interview (i.e., in discussing mother vs. father or present vs. past). This additional classification provides one method for indexing a lack of integration over the entire AAI protocol, and in the most recent version of the AAI scoring and classification system (Main et al., 2003), experienced coders are encouraged to utilize the CC category even in the absence of directly conflicting (e.g., Ds and preoccupied) states of mind. Thus, when the coder has sufficient practice, simple low coherence running throughout the text in the absence of elevated scores on the AAI scales identified with particular insecure states of mind can now shift an interview to the CC category. This most recent extension of the CC category, utilized in a Swedish sample, was shown to be common in adolescents with obsessive–compulsive disorder (Ivarsson, Chapter 9, this volume), as well as noted to be predictive of D–controlling/CC 6-year reunion behavior in a Japanese low-risk sample (Behrens et al., in press).

Our approach to this dilemma was to think about the adult counterparts of earlier controlling attachment stances in childhood and adolescence. Developmental work has shown that by age 3–5 years, many previously D infants adapt their attachment behaviors into either a controlling–punitive attachment pattern (hostile or humiliating behavior toward parent) or a controlling–caregiving pattern (helping, protecting, worrying about the parent) (Main & Cassidy, 1988; Main, Kaplan, & Cassidy, 1985; National Institute of Child Health and Human Development [NICHD] Early Child Care Research Network, 2001; Wartner, Grossmann, Fremmer-Bombik, & Suess, 1994). These controlling adaptations are thought to serve the function of maintaining the attention and involvement of an otherwise emotionally distanced caregiver and have also been associated with the development of psychopathology (Lyons-Ruth & Jacobvitz, 1999; Main & Cassidy, 1988). Tying developmental histories of disorganized attachment to later adult states of mind through forms of child and adolescent controlling behavior could provide an important explanatory mechanism for continuity in adaptation among D infants over time, whether or not later abuse or loss occurs (Hennighausen & Lyons-Ruth, 2006; Lyons-Ruth, Yellin, Melnick, & Atwood, 2005).

The chapter is organized as follows: First we review the clinical and theoretical frameworks that provided key theoretical constructs for the development of the concept of HH states of mind; next, we describe the HH coding system, including points of convergence and divergence with the existing Main and colleagues (2003) system; third, we report on the first three studies that have partially validated the HH construct in relation to infant disorganization and more severe psychopathology; and, finally, we outline clinical implications of the system.

Hostile–Helpless States of Mind: Conceptual Framework

Main, Hesse, and Goldwyn (2003) and Main and Solomon (1990) have described contradictory and unintegrated behavioral and mental processes as a core phenomenon of D attachment relationships. Extreme forms of segregated mental systems have also been described in the psychoanalytic and trauma literatures under the labels of "splitting" and "dissociation." Although the psychoanalytic literature emphasizes disruptions in early caregiving, whereas trauma research examines traumatic events occurring throughout the life course, both describe pervasively unintegrated states of mind in adulthood. Evidences suggests that individuals who encounter traumatic events in the context of a disruptive caregiving environment may be at greatest risk for developing these disturbances (Putnam, 1989; Zanarini, 1997). However, an even more specific hypothesis put forward by Liotti (1992) was that disorganized infants who encounter trauma later in life are at increased risk for dissociation. This has received empirical support from two studies (Carlson, 1998; Ogawa, Sroufe, Weinfeld, Carlson, & Egeland, 1997).

Melanie Klein (1946) is credited with introducing the concept of splitting of positive and negative mental representations. However, Klein, and also Margaret Mahler (1971), viewed splitting as the primary form of *normal* mental representation of experience in infancy and early childhood, thereby drawing an analogy between the mental representational processes of normal infants and those of personality disordered adults. This formulation is now discredited as an account of normal development, but it has merit as an account of development proceeding along a severe psychopathological course, as we and others have argued elsewhere (Lyons-Ruth, 1991; Steele & Steele, 1998).

Bowlby drew on aspects of both the Klein and Mahler formulations but recast them in claiming that children's repeated transactions with caregivers lead to the construction of increasingly sophisticated representations or "internal working models" of themselves and their caretakers that serve to guide behavior under a variety of circumstances. In his view, when a parent displays sensitivity and concern for the child's emotional needs, the child is more likely to construct a working model of the self as worthy of care and the parent as valuable and caring, and to integrate negative and positive characteristics of self and other into singular working models (Bowlby, 1973, 1980).

Conversely, children of more insensitive caregivers come to represent their attachment figures as unreliable, rejecting, or cruel and are more likely to develop a corresponding internal working model of themselves as shameful and unworthy of care (Bowlby, 1980). Following earlier psychoanalytic theory, Bowlby theorized that if these negative perceptions persist, the child would seek protection from painful affective consequences via suppression or isolation from awareness, so that they were no longer part of the child's active (conscious) working model of the attachment relationship. Bowlby argued that it would lead to the existence of two or more incompatible working models of an attachment figure, and two or more irreconcilable models of the self

(Bowlby, 1980). Such incompatible models of self and other hinder a coherent sense of self, and prevent an accurate and integrated appraisal of intimate relationships. Bowlby viewed such segregated systems as characterizing all insecure models.

Bowlby's general account of the segregation of intolerably painful experiences is consistent with more recent work of trauma researchers who have subsequently documented elevated rates of dissociation and borderline personality disorder among abuse victims. This literature also regards dissociation as a defensive process leading to a segregation of trauma-related affects and self-schemas (Horowitz, 1986; Kluft, 1991). Several trauma researchers, including Terr (1991), Herman (1992), and van der Kolk and Fisler (1994), suggest that the more discrete biological symptoms of alternating numbing and flooding characteristic of acute posttraumatic stress disorder are likely to stem from a single overwhelming event, whereas the more severe and pervasive characterological pathologies involving splitting and severe dissociation are likely to occur in the context of repeated, early, and prolonged interpersonal trauma. The HH coding system was developed in an effort to capture these clinical phenomena that have been proposed to be relevant to disturbances in early attachment, traumatic experiences, and severe psychopathology.

Hostile–Helpless States of Mind on the AAI

The HH coding system comprises a number of indicators that culminate in an overall scaled score from 1 to 9 for the level of HH state of mind. The level of HH state of mind is meant to reflect the overall lack of integration between more extreme forms of positive and negative evaluations in the individual's consideration of childhood experiences. Protocols achieving a scaled score of 5 or higher are classified as reflecting an HH state of mind.

HH states of mind express themselves in the AAI as globally devaluing and explicitly contradictory emotional evaluations of caregivers and self. In HH discourse, one or more caregivers are described in all-encompassing globally devalued terms (either as malevolent or as abdicating the parental role), yet opposing evaluations of the same caregiver(s) are made at different points in the transcript without metacognitive comment. Typically, the individual continues to avow or to demonstrate identification with an attachment figure who elsewhere in the transcript is represented in globally negative terms (e.g., "My mother was horrible/I'm just like my mother"). The global nature of the person's continued representation of the other is seen as an indication that the person has not sufficiently integrated various thoughts and feelings to a point where self or other can be seen as multidimensional, with both positive and negative attributes. Other forms of contradiction and disavowal of vulnerability over the transcript are also taken into account (e.g., "I don't miss my father/I'm so mad at my mother for making him leave"). At a conceptual level, these aspects of the transcript are taken as evidence that the person has not engaged adequately in reflection to bring these contradictions or disavowals to a conscious level, so that the intense feelings associated with each set of contents remain segregated.

Within the overall category, two general subtypes, a more hostile prototype and a more helpless prototype, are noted on the AAI. The "hostile" subtype refers to the subgroup of subjects who tends to represent attachment figures in malevolent terms, and who provides evidence of a continued identification with a hostile or punitive attachment figure. Theoretically, we view a hostile adult stance as a likely outgrowth of a controlling–punitive stance in childhood (Cassidy, Marvin, & the MacArthur Working Group, 1991; Main & Cassidy, 1988). Individuals in this group may describe themselves as currently very close to, in daily contact with, or dependent upon attachment figures toward whom they also expresses hostility or global devaluation in other portions of the interview. The "helpless" subtype refers to a subgroup of subjects whose states of mind may be pervasively fearful or passive, and who may be identified with, and often caretaking of, a parent globally devalued as helpless or as abdicating of a parental role. These two extremes of an HH state of mind are described separately, because the protocols can look quite different. We have reasoned elsewhere that both hostile and helpless profiles may represent alternate expressions of a single dyadic HH model of relationship (Lyons-Ruth, Bronfman, & Atwood, 1999). However, a "mixed" subtype may be quite common in some samples.

Most individuals in the hostile group are quite explicit about many of their negative childhood attachment experiences, while omitting a full discussion of the painful feelings or consequences of these experiences [e.g., when asked, "Did you ever feel rejected?," answers, "Yeah, all the time (*laughs*)"]. Consequently, they may convey an attitude of being "tough" or resilient in the face of those experiences, as suggested by their matter-of-fact or even darkly humorous presentations of painful events. Therefore, their omission of vulnerable affects often lacks the conventional Ds strategies of an insistence upon a lack of memory or of idealization of parent figures. Some discourse will fulfill criteria for classification in the Ds2 (dismissing/derogating of attachment) category described by Main and colleagues (2003). However, the Main and colleagues scales for derogation describe "cool" derogation, that is, a dismissal of the other as not important enough to warrant an emotional response. Much of the derogation indicative of a predominantly hostile state of mind, however, has a much "hotter" feel, in that the language may elicit emotion in the listener and reveals strong emotion in the speaker, even though the speaker may deny any personal impact or current feeling about the person.

Characteristically, the subject also does not appear to be struggling actively with angry feelings as would a preoccupied (E) speaker. The engaged quality of involving anger is typically absent as are the qualities of speech characteristic of a preoccupied/angry (E2) protocol as described in the Main and colleagues (2003) coding system. Rather, the subject tends to be more devaluing or intermittently hostile than involved in continuing anger. This combination of frank relating of negative experiences, "hot" devaluation, minimization of vulnerability, and a concise narrative would provide a poor fit to either of these existing insecure AAI categories. Further work is needed to assess whether it will fit with recent changes in the CC criteria (Main et al., 2003; see also Main et al., Chapter 2, this volume).

Predominantly helpless states of mind are characterized by references to fear, global descriptions of the caregiver as helpless, and by identification with a helpless caregiver. Theoretically, we view this stance as a likely outgrowth of a controlling–caregiving adaptation in childhood (Cassidy et al., 1991; Main & Cassidy, 1988). Many such speakers also display indications of identifying with a helpless caregiver toward whom they have attempted to adopt a vigilant and protective caregiving role in childhood. They may give indications of helping, worrying, protecting, or fighting in defense of a parent. This caregiving stance may have been exhibited in childhood only or may have continued into present-day adult relationships with attachment figures. Since the attachment figures in our protocols appeared abdicating of a parental role rather than actively involving of the child, these individuals were often not given very high scores for probable experience of an involving role reversing relationship with the parent in childhood in the Main and colleagues (2003) system.

In some cases, the need to understand, protect, and organize the caregiver in childhood may have led to precocious development of the ability to reflect on others' mental states (Steele, 2004). Such reflectiveness in the subject can complicate the differentiation between a helpless-fearful stance and some autonomous subtypes in the Main and colleagues (2003) system, particularly those in which difficult childhood experiences are described. Helpless–fearful speakers are more likely to have identified with the hurtful aspects of their attachment experiences by internalizing blame, justifying their parents' behaviors, or rationalizing their own caregiving stances, leading them to question repeatedly without resolution why things happened as they did. Thus, their transcripts are marked by a global self-representation as especially bad or unworthy and also by active efforts not to blame or feel angry with caregivers whom they experienced as helpless. Anger is inhibited, expressed indirectly, or dissociated, often emerging in punitive, angry, or devaluing assertions that are not integrated with the more predominant caregiving attitude, particularly as the individual is beginning to question aspects of the parent's behavior (e.g., "I talk to her about everything. . . . I don't trust her").

Alternatively, a helpless stance may be characterized less by an active controlling–caregiving orientation and more by a helpless, overwhelmed, fearful stance in relation to a malevolently described caregiver. The individual may demonstrate considerable mental involvement with the malevolent figure (as described in vivid fearful imagery and intrusions of the past into the present), but nevertheless evidence considerable denial of vulnerability. The reader has the impression that the speaker has been repeatedly placed in situations as a child in which he or she helplessly suffered at the hands of a cruel, neglecting, or rejecting parent, which left the child overwhelmed and unable to find a consistent coping response to these relational experiences. We speculate that theoretically this form of a helpless stance may be related to the inability to organize a controlling stance in childhood, and to the persistence of contradictory and disorganized forms of response to the parent, as first identified by Main and Cassidy (1988). Consistent with this speculation, recent data suggest that by school entry, about one-third of disorganized infants have failed to organize a controlling strategy (Moss, Nicole, Dubois-Comtois, Mazzarello, & Berthiaume, 2006).

There is also some similarity to descriptions of the insecure–passively preoccupied (E1) subgroup of the Main and colleagues (2003) system in the lack of autonomy of voice seen among helpless–fearful individuals. However, our classification criteria focus on the speaker's stance toward a parent's abdication of the parental role, and not on specific indices of passive speech. In the research to date, many speakers classified in the helpless–fearful subgroup do not achieve sufficient ratings on passive speech to justify an E classification within the Main and colleagues coding system. Our classification also has some points in common with Main and colleagues' description of subgroup E3, "overwhelmed by trauma," but differs in not requiring the presence of traumatic experience per se. Instead, fearful affects may be referred to around a variety of experiences, many of which are not traumatic. The HH coding system also includes 10 individual frequency codes that partially anchor the qualitative rating and guide the final HH classification (see Appendix 16.1 for descriptions of these codes and examples).

Hostile–Helpless States of Mind, Infant Disorganization, and Maternal Trauma and Psychopathology

The HH coding system has now been applied to the AAIs of three high-risk research samples, all of which were also coded with the Main and colleagues (2003) system. The first study evaluated the association between maternal AAIs collected at child age 7 and infant Strange Situation behavior at both 12 and 18 months among a high social risk sample. The HH classification was significantly associated with D infant attachment at 18 months, at which age two-thirds of D infants were classified D–insecure, whereas U status on the AAI was not. However, in the 12-month Strange Situations, where most disorganized infants were D–secure, our findings were reversed, in that U status on the AAI was associated with disorganized attachment, as has traditionally been expected, whereas the HH classification was not. With respect to the relation between state of mind and infant D attachment, then, U status was a stronger correlate of predominately disorganized–secure classifications at 12 months, whereas HH was a stronger predictor of predominately D–insecure classifications at 18 months. HH was also found to be related to maternal trauma history and disrupted mother–infant affective communication in this study. In the second, Chicago study the relation between HH classification and infant disorganization, and substance abuse was evaluated. In the third study, the classification was partially validated in discriminating between borderline and dysthymic psychopathology among psychiatric outpatients. In both high-risk studies with infant attachment data, the HH classification in two out of three assessments accounted for variance in infant attachment not accounted for by the U classification. Both studies had high ratios of infant disorganized–insecure classification. Therefore, in the context of high-risk samples, the U classification in the Boston study appeared particularly discriminative of D–secure infant classification at 12 months, whereas the HH classification was stronger in discriminating D–insecure infants at older ages in the context of high-risk samples. This deserves much further study, because Ainsworth and Eichberg (1991) found U to be similarly predictive of both D–secure and D–insecure infants.

Study 1: Hostile–Helpless States of Mind, Infant Disorganized Attachment, and Disrupted Mother–Infant Communication in a High-Risk Sample

Four hypotheses guided the initial study of HH states of mind and infant attachment disorganization. First, it was expected that the HH coding system would overlap with the current CC and fearfully preoccupied by traumatic events (E3) categories of the Main and Goldwyn (1998) coding system and provide additional specifications for those states of mind. Second, maternal HH states of mind were predicted to account for variance in D infant behavior not associated with the U classification. Third, HH states of mind were predicted to relate to disruptions in maternal affective communication with the infant, as coded by the Atypical Maternal Behavior Instrument for Assessment and Classification (AMBIANCE) instrument (Lyons-Ruth, Bronfman, & Parsons, 1999), and the extent of these disruptions was expected to mediate any relation between maternal state of mind and infant attachment disorganization. Fourth, HH states of mind were expected to be associated with the severity of trauma in the mother's childhood.

HH states of mind were assessed among 45 socioeconomically stressed mothers with high rates of childhood trauma who were administered the AAI when their children were age 7 (Lyons-Ruth et al., 2005). Of the 45 families, 18 were low-income families referred to infant home visiting services by health or social service agency staff because of concerns about the quality of the parent–infant relationship, and 27 were demographically matched families from the community, with no history of child maltreatment or psychiatric hospitalization. The sample was largely European American, with 27% Latino and African American participation. Strange Situation assessments had been collected at infant age 18 months (see Lyons-Ruth, Connell, Grunebaum, & Botein, 1990). AAIs were concurrently and independently coded in separate labs using both the Main and colleagues (2003) coding system and the coding system for HH states of mind. Strange Situation videotapes were also coded for disrupted maternal communication with the infant using the AMBIANCE coding system (Lyons-Ruth, Bronfman, & Parsons, 1999), which comprises a scaled score (1–7) and a dichotomous classification for extent of disrupted communication, including five domains: Affective Communication Errors, Role Confusion, Negative–Intrusive Behavior, Disorientation, and Withdrawal (for a more extended description, see Lyons-Ruth, Bronfman, & Parsons, 1999). Validity and stability meta-analytic data are available in Madigan and colleagues (2006), both for coding in the Strange Situation and in independent lab assessments.

Descriptively, using the Main and Goldwyn (1998) system, 58% of AAI's were classified in organized categories: 29% as U, and 13% considered CC. Using the HH coding system, 51% of the mothers were classified as displaying a HH state of mind. First, contrary to the first hypothesis, the aspects of discourse that indexed an HH state of mind did not overlap substantially with criteria for classification as U, CC, or E3. The individual frequency codes that contribute to the HH coding system were also unrelated to these classifications. Therefore, rather than elaborating on the current criteria for existing AAI classifications, the HH codes appear to delineate additional trauma-related aspects of contradictory or pervasively unintegrated states of mind not captured by current classification criteria. In addition, it was notable that none of the protocols classified HH were classified Ds by Main and Goldwyn criteria, despite such indicators of denial of vulnerability as "laughter at pain." These protocols were not coded as Ds because of the low or inconsistent levels of idealization displayed in the devaluations of caregivers and the frankness with which negative experiences were discussed. They were also not primarily coded as E, because the negative evaluations were usually not presented in the context of angry, entangled speech patterns but as closed judgments in the context of a concise or even constricted discourse structure. Rather, HH transcripts were cross-classified in all categories of the Main and colleagues (2003) system (see Table 16.2), meaning that high indices of HH were similarly probable for speakers otherwise classified as F, Ds, E, U, or CC.

Second, some features of mother's HH states of mind on the AAI were significantly related to the extent of D attachment behaviors displayed by the infant. Table 16.1 displays the associations between maternal states of mind on the AAI and extent of infant D attachment behavior at 18 months (as noted earlier, HH did not relate to disorganized attachment at infant age 12 months).

Table 16.1 shows that specific codes for global devaluation of caregivers, laughter at pain, and ruptured attachments were correlated significantly with the infant's disorganization. Identification with a hostile caregiver and references to fearful affect were also marginally significant. Finally, and again at 18 months but not 12 months, an HH state of mind explained a significant portion of the variance in infant disorganization not accounted for by U and CC

TABLE 16.1. Magnitude of Association between Maternal States of Mind on the AAI and Extent of Infant Disorganized Attachment Behavior

Hostile–Helpless AAI codes	Lyons-Ruth et al. (2005)[a]	Finger (2006)
Overall state of mind codes		
Level of HH state of mind	.35*	.41***
HH classification	.35*	.34***
Indicator codes		
Identification with a hostile caregiver	.29[x]	.17*
Global devaluation of caregiver	.31*	.16*
Sense of self as bad	.27[x]	.08
Recurrent references to fearful affect	.28[x]	.07
Recurrent laughter at pain	.36*	−.08
Ruptured attachments in adulthood	.43**	.15*
Identification with a helpless caregiver	—	.16*
Global representation of helpless caregiver	—	.16*
References to punitive behavior in childhood	—	.00
References to caregiving behavior in childhood	—	−.01
Main and Hesse (1998) codes		
Classification as unresolved (cannot classify)	.05	−.07
Classification as unresolved or cannot classify	−.10	.03

Note. [a]From Lyons-Ruth et al. (2005). Pearson correlations are shown, except for HH and U or CC classifications, where point biserial correlation is shown.
[x]$p < .10$; *$p < .05$; **$p < .01$.

status on the AAI in a regression analysis [$F(1, 39) = 5.74$, $p = .02$, $\beta = .36$]. Among mothers of D–insecure 18-month-olds, in particular, only 23% were classified U or CC, whereas 75% were classified HH.

Third, maternal HH states were also related to maternal disrupted affective communication with the infant, which we rated using the AMBIANCE coding system ($r = .39$, $p = .03$). Maternal disrupted communication, in turn, partially mediated the relation between maternal HH states of mind and infant D attachment behavior.

Finally, HH states of mind were strongly related to severity of trauma in mother's childhood (Lyons-Ruth, Yellin, Melnick, & Atwood, 2003). However, mother's childhood experiences of trauma had no direct relation to infant D in the next generation. Instead, severity of maternal trauma in childhood was related to HH state of mind, and HH state of mind, in turn, was a significant predictor of infant D. Unexpectedly, mother's childhood experiences of separation, divorce, parental death or out-of home care showed trends toward a negative relation to HH states of mind. Further work with the HH system will be needed to clarify this finding, but based on inspection of the data, one interpretation is that parental absence "makes the heart grow fonder," so that loss acts to suppress devaluation of the lost parent.

In summary, rather than elaborating on current criteria for existing AAI classifications, the HH codes appear to delineate additional ways in which a contradictory or pervasively unintegrated state of mind can be manifested on the AAI. The HH system would appear to combine elements of the existing rare classifications (Ds2, E3) into more elaborated and theoretically grounded profiles associated with the intergenerational transmission of disorganization. As is evident, this work exists within, and is an extension of, the Main and colleagues (2003) theoretical framework regarding integrated and unintegrated states of mind. However, this research begins to outline a proposed model of intergenerational transmission of D attachment based on the coherence of mental representations of attachment relationships themselves, rather than on the coherence of discourse and reasoning related to loss or trauma. It was also notable that the HH classification was not specific to any single AAI group, with as many as 56% of interviews judged autonomous–secure also being coded HH (see Table 16.2, below).

Study 2: Hostile–Helpless States of Mind and Relations to Infant Disorganization and Maternal Drug Use

In the second study (Finger, 2006), 149 low-income African American mothers and their 12- to 18-month-old infants were studied to examine the maternal correlates of infant attachment among drug-dependent mothers. The sample included a group of 62 women receiving methadone treatment for heroin dependence and a community nontreatment comparison group of 87 women. Videotaped Strange Situations were coded by the study's author, who has been certified reliable in the coding of A (avoidant), B (secure), C (ambivalent), and D (disorganized) attachment categories through training at the University of Minnesota. In addition, tapes identified as being especially difficult were sent

TABLE 16.2. Hostile–Helpless (HH) Distribution by Main, Goldwyn, and Hesse Classification System

Main, Goldwyn, and Hesse (2003) classification	Proportion classified HH			
	Lyons-Ruth et al. (2005)	Finger (2006)	Lyons-Ruth et al. (2007)	Total
n	45	149	23	
Autonomous	.56 (18)	.21 (19)	1.00 (2)	.41 (39)
Dismissing	0 (3)	.39 (49)	.60 (5)	.39 (57)
Preoccupied	.80 (5)[a]	.71 (14)[b]	.50 (6)[c]	.61 (25)
Unresolved	.77 (13)	.51 (67)	1.00 (10)	.60 (90)
Cannot classify	.50 (6)			.50 (6)

Note. Cell n's in parenthesis give total number in each Main, Goldwyn, and Hesse (2003) classification by study.
[a]No preoccupied subjects were subclassified E3 (fearfully preoccupied).
[b]Three of the six preoccupied subjects subclassified E3 were also classified HH.
[c]Two of two preoccupied subjects subclassified E3 were also classified HH.

to an expert coder at the University of Minnesota for further review. The coder was blind to all identifying information.

AAIs were collected at infant age 12–18 months and coded by the author who has been certified reliable in the coding of the four category (U, Ds, F, and E) Main and Goldwyn (1996) AAI classification system. A second coder, also reliable in the four-category system, evaluated a subset of 27 randomly selected interviews to establish reliability with the first coder. Twelve of these interviews were selected from the methadone group and 15 from the control group. Both coders were blind to all identifying information. AAIs were assigned random ID codes to prevent the first coder, who coded the Strange Situation, from recognizing the participant case numbers for the respective mother–infant Strange Situation assessment. Intercoder agreement was 74% for the autonomous versus nonautonomous distinction; 67% for the Ds, F, and E distinctions; and 81% for the U versus not U classification. The final distribution of AAI codes revealed that 33% of the sample was classified Ds, 13% F, 9% E, and 45% U.

After completing this first round of coding with the Main and Goldwyn (1996) system, the first coder achieved reliability in the HH coding system and recoded all AAIs according to the HH system. Forty-five percent of the sample received an HH classification, including 39% of Ds mothers, 21% of F mothers, 71% of E mothers, and 51% of U mothers (see Table 16.2). Mothers in the methadone group were significantly more likely to be classified HH (56%) than were mothers in the control group (37%) (χ^2 (1) = 5.66, p = .020).

As with the original validation study at 18 months, an HH state of mind was associated with D infant status, whereas U status on the AAI was not, as depicted in Table 16.1. Although this finding is at odds with existing meta-analytic data indicating a robust association between the U and D categories (van IJzendoorn, 1995), the study did replicate significant associations between the AAI Ds and Strange Situation avoidant categories (χ^2 (1) = 7.29, p = .006), as well as the AAI F and Strange Situation secure categories (χ^2 (1) = 5.74, p = .013). As is the case with several other high-risk samples, however, the AAI E classification was not significantly predictive of the strange situation resistant category (van IJzendoorn, 1995). Furthermore, from the current Chicago study, 74% of mothers of D infants were classified as HH, compared with only 35% of the remaining 111 mothers (χ^2 (1) = 17.00, p = .000). The finding was significant for the methadone group, in which 82% of D infants had mothers classified HH (χ^2 (1) = 8.93, p = .003), as well as the control group, in which 63% had mothers classified HH (χ^2 (1) = 5.58, p = .018).

Further analysis of infant disorganization indicated that 71% (27) of D infants in this sample received a secondary insecure classification. HH states of mind were particularly prevalent among mothers of D–insecure infants, 81% of whom were classified HH, but not significantly related to the smaller subset of mothers with D infants receiving a secondary secure classification, 55% of whom were classified HH. As with the original HH validation study, this finding suggests that HH coding may be particularly useful for identifying

states of mind common to mothers of D infants who also display avoidant or
resistant attachment strategies.

Since existing meta-analytic data are clear that there is a robust association between the U and D categories over most samples (van IJzendoorn,
1995), these findings may indicate that there are particular high-risk and clinical populations for whom the U category needs to be augmented by additional
indicators such as CC and HH.

Study 3: A Controlled Study of Hostile–Helpless States of Mind in Relation to Borderline and Dysthymic Disorders

In collaboration with Hobson and Patrick, we further proposed that HH
states of mind might be particularly relevant to the delineation of attachment
representations of patients with borderline personality disorder (BPD; Lyons-
Ruth, Melnick, Patrick, & Hobson, 2007). Participants were adult women, 12
with BPD and 11 with dysthymia, on an outpatient psychotherapy waiting list
of a major teaching hospital. Diagnostic assessments were made from extensive psychiatric case notes employing DSM-III-R checklists (the groups were
constituted before DSM-IV had appeared), and were performed without reference to patients' early childhood experiences or relationships with their parents. All patients with BPD met at least 7 of the 8 DSM-III-R diagnostic
criteria for BPD, and patients in the dysthymic group exhibited none of the
eight DSM-III-R BPD characteristics and fulfilled DSM-III-R criteria for
dysthymia.

In an earlier study of this sample, the two groups were strongly distinguished utilizing the standard AAI coding system (Patrick, Hobson, Castle, &
Maughan, 1994). All 12 patients with BPD, but only four patients with
dysthymia, were classified as E (Fisher's exact test, two-tailed, $p = .001$).
Moreover, 10 of the 12 patients with BPD were classified into one particular
(very rare) AAI subcategory, fearfully preoccupied (E3), meaning that for
women with BPD, as opposed to women with dysthymia, descriptions
of frightening events repeatedly and inappropriately intruded into queries
regarding topics unrelated to traumatic experiences. Finally, although the
overall rates of experiences of trauma and loss as defined by the AAI manual
did not differ between the groups, among those who did have such experiences, discrimination between the groups was especially strong. Thus, all nine
of the women with BPD who reported loss or trauma were classified as U,
compared to only two women with dysthymia reporting loss or trauma
(Fisher's exact test, two-tailed, $p = .0007$).

In addition to these previous findings, according to blind ratings of AAI
transcripts, 100% of the BPD group in this study was rated over the threshold
for an HH state of mind, whereas this was the case for 55% of the dysthymia
group (Fisher's exact test, $p = .01$, $\phi = .55$). Therefore in contrast to the earlier
study (Patrick et al., 1994) of this same sample using the traditional AAI cod-

ing system (Main et al., 2003), HH states of mind were not specifically associated with a single diagnosis but were especially prevalent among women with pervasive personality disorder characteristics. Also, when specific indicators were examined, women with BPD were more likely than women with dysthymia to portray caregivers in globally devalued terms ($\eta = .66, p < .001$). Women with BPD were also marginally more likely to give evidence of identification with a globally devalued caregiver, with 58% of women with BPD conveying a sense of being like the devalued caregiver, compared to 18% of women with dysthymia (Fisher's exact test, $p = .09, \phi = .41$). Finally, a significantly greater number of participants with BPD (75% compared to 27% in the dysthymia group; Fisher's exact test, $p = .04, \phi = .48$) conveyed that in childhood they had engaged in punitive or caregiving forms of controlling behaviors toward parents (Main & Cassidy, 1988), stances that we have reasoned elsewhere may represent childhood precursors of adult hostile and helpless states of mind, respectively (Lyons-Ruth, Yellin, et al., 2005). In summary, HH states of mind were not associated with a single diagnosis, but were characteristic of all the women with a BPD diagnosis, and half of the women with a diagnosis for depression.

It was also notable that women with BPD who were classified as E3 using the Main and Goldwyn (1966) classifications were significantly more likely than other women to describe caregiving behavior toward the parent in childhood, yet in their present discourse also make devaluing comments about the same caregiver. Such unreflected-upon contradictions in orientation toward attachment figures illustrate the central contradictory aspects of the HH state of mind.

These results add credence to the view that borderline psychopathology is associated with pervasively unintegrated ways of representing attachment relationships, as well as unresolved experiences of loss or trauma. The findings also implicate a developmental account that includes earlier attempts to control the attention of important caregivers by punishing and/or providing care for adult attachment figures, as first reported by Main and Cassidy (1988). This study provides evidence, then, that there is an important relation between the psychiatrically defined disorder of self-experience, mood, and relationship that constitutes BPD and the quality of the disordered individuals' HH mental representations of attachment figures, in addition to their U and E3 states of mind in relation to traumatic experiences.

Clinical Implications of a Hostile–Helpless State of Mind
Hostile–Helpless State of Mind and Parent–Child Relations

If a parent has not experienced comfort in relation to his or her own fear or shame-evoking experiences, we would expect that parent to lack an inner dialogue through which to integrate and contain the activation of intense reexperiencing of his or her own early vulnerability in the presence of the infant's pain, distress, fear, anger, or perceived rejection. This may place parents in jeopardy of becoming flooded by intense affects that they cannot regulate or act on adaptively, leading to the display of hostile (e.g., suppressing children's emotions, yelling) or helpless (dissociating, withdrawing) responses to their children.

Drawing on our conceptualization of the HH construct, and particularly a parent's propensity for globalized and devaluing representations of attachment figures, the parent may see the child in idealized "all good" or devalued "all bad" terms, neither of which enables the parent to represent adequately the complex individual subjectivity of the child. This is consistent with George and Solomon's (1996) finding that parents of controlling 6-year-olds tend to view their children as disproportionately powerful, often feeling helpless to influence the child.

HH states of mind have also been related to observed parental behaviors, as coded on the AMBIANCE scales (Lyons-Ruth, Yellin, et al., 2005). Furthermore, in previous work, sexually abused mothers were shown to be more likely to manage their negative affects by withdrawing from interaction with the infant, whereas mothers who had been physically abused engaged in hostile–intrusive forms of interaction (Lyons-Ruth & Block, 1996).

Developmentally, results of the research collaboration with Hobson (Lyons-Ruth et al., 2007) suggested that HH states of mind among patients with BPD were accompanied by references to punitive or caregiving stances toward the parent in childhood. If such punitive, caregiving, or mixed punitive–caregiving attachment strategies were sustained into adulthood, they might result in the intense, conflictual, and often coercive patterns of relatedness observed among both patients with BPD and those with substance abuse. Prospective longitudinal research is needed to examine directly this hypothesis regarding the continuity between childhood controlling adaptations and adult HH states of mind.

Clinically, we found that parents who have developed such HH adaptations to past experiences can benefit from becoming aware of why they may have adopted these adaptations. In particular, parents can come to understand and appreciate that an HH adaptation may have developed as one of the few routes available for both involving parents in their care and protecting themselves from reexperiencing the fear and emotional abandonment thought to be associated with infant disorganization (Main & Cassidy, 1988). A more compassionate view of one's own attachment needs and empathy for the difficulty of one's own past attachment experiences is an essential foundation for having empathy for a child's similar needs. From the point of view of the patient–therapist relationship, an explicit understanding of controlling attachment strategies may help to prevent rupture of the therapeutic alliance when punitive, helpless, or caregiving adaptations are repeated in the clinical relationship.

Convergence with Models of Psychopathology

The AAI has been proposed as an assessment tool for identifying relevant areas of treatment, as well as an outcome measure for evaluating the effectiveness of various methods of clinical intervention (Diamond et al., 1999; see also Diamond, Yeomans, Clarkin, Levy, & Kernberg, Chapter 11, and Ammaniti, Dazzi, & Muscetta, Chapter 10, this volume). The HH system adds to descriptions of unusual features that make transcripts from clinical samples especially difficult to classify. Our findings suggest that HH relational models may be particularly relevant to clinical work involving individuals with BPD and substance abuse. Classen, Pain, Field, and Woods (2006) propose that current diagnostic criteria for BPD leave us incapable of distinguishing between borderline features resulting from disorganized parent–child attachment relationships and those resulting from trauma exposure. They speculate that early disorganized attachments relate to the tendency actively to pursue intense interpersonal relationships, as well as mentally to compartmentalize loving and devalued representations of attachment figures, leading to unstable relationships and affective instability. In contrast, victims of later abuse, who may have maintained organized attachment relationships in childhood, may be more likely to utilize dissociation as a consistent defense, to maintain an emotionally numbed presentation, and to withdraw from close relationships. Persons with the dual disadvantage of disorganized attachment strategies, and early and prolonged trauma may present the most severe pathology, involving a mix of unresolved trauma and unintegrated representations of attachment figures themselves. The HH coding system may prove particularly well suited to exploring these distinctions.

In previous research on trauma, the symptomatic impact of traumatic events has largely been considered outside the context of the attachment relationships that buffer or augment the fear-arousing potential of the event itself. However, recent prospective longitudinal studies from infancy indicate that chronic impairment in caregiver responsiveness may be more central to the etiology of dissociative symptoms than abusive events per se (Lyons-Ruth, Dutra, Schuder, & Bianchi, 2006; Ogawa et al., 1997). Other longitudinal work has shown that both maternal disrupted affective communication with the infant and later abuse experiences make independent and additive contributions to borderline traits in young adulthood (Lyons-Ruth, Holmes, & Hennighausen, 2005). Further work is needed to differentiate empirically the effects of abusive events per se from the effects of ongoing caregiver hostility, withdrawal, role reversal, or helplessness to protect (see also Bradley, Jenei, & Westen, 2005).

Findings also indicate that the HH state of mind may be particularly evident among women seeking treatment for substance abuse. Previous research has demonstrated strikingly high rates of relational trauma among this population (Chandy, Blum, & Resnick, 1996; Malinosky-Rummell & Hansen,

1993; Simpson & Miller, 2002; Woodhouse, 1992), suggesting that many individuals with trauma histories may be drawn to use substances to dampen trauma-related affect (Khantzian, 1985, 1997). Schindler and colleagues (2005) further suggest that users' dependence on substances may indicate that they lack other strategies for regulating unwanted emotions. Substance-using patients displaying an HH state of mind would likely benefit from treatment that enhances their ability to tolerate and integrate attachment and trauma-related memories and emotions to limit their dependence on illicit substances.

We suggest that the lack of a relational context to integrate intense emotions safely leads to an enduring emotional coping style from childhood, in which one distances from one's own vulnerability and painful affects, while maintaining hypervigilant attention to the parent's states. Such a psychological adaptation may lead to severe character pathology, such as borderline personality disorder and hard drug abuse. The HH approach to looking at AAIs may help to identify these clinical problems and facilitate interventions to prevent them. The HH coding system adds an additional relational dimension to the existing AAI coding system for unresolved trauma. As a proposed additional category for the AAI, the HH system may extend the power of the AAI to capture states of mind associated with more serious forms of relational psychopathology.

It remains for future researchers to explore more fully the links between the original AAI classification system (Main et al., 2003) and the HH system in high-risk or clinical samples, so that the relevance of HH to understanding trauma specifically, or attachment difficulties more generally, may be better appreciated. This is called for because the HH ratings in these high-risk samples were not associated with a particular classification in the standard AAI coding system. In HH ratings across the three studies reported in this chapter, 41% of secure–autonomous interviews were also found to be HH, as were 39% of Ds interviews, 61% of E interviews, 60% of U interviews, and 50% of CC interviews. In addition, the data thus far suggest that HH states of mind may be most predictive of infant D–insecure attachment behavior, which is also more prevalent among high-risk samples. Given the demonstrated strength of the standard coding system for the AAI, the HH descriptors presented and validated here are not intended to substitute for the primary coding system, but to add to our understanding of the relational organizations that may accompany or augment other indicators of unintegrated states of mind on the AAI. Furthermore, as concerns the relative power of HH as opposed to U–loss/trauma in the AAI system, there remains the HH failure at 12 months (as opposed to the mother's U classification) to identify D babies in the Boston study (Lyons-Ruth, Yellin, Melnick, & Atwood, 2003). Along these lines are the findings that the original AAI ratings of E3 and U differentiated between BPD and depression in the Patrick and colleagues study (1994), somewhat more dramatically than the HH ratings. Future work utilizing the original coding system alongside the HH scoring of AAIs may examine more fully the proposed longitudinal connection between infant–mother disorganization of attachment, controlling patterns of behavior in middle childhood, and trauma-related pathology in adolescence and adulthood.

References

Ainsworth, M. D. S., & Eichberg, C. (1991). Effects of infant–mother attachment of mother's unresolved loss of an attachment figure, or other traumatic experience. In C. M. Parkes, J. S. Hinde, & P. Marris (Eds.), *Attachment across the life cycle* (pp. 160–183). London: Routledge.

Behrens, K. Y., Hesse, E., & Main, M. (in press). Mothers' attachment status as determined by the Adult Attachment Interview predicts their 6-year-olds' reunion responses: A study conducted in Japan. *Developmental Psychology.*

Bowlby, J. (1973). *Attachment and loss: Vol. 2. Separation.* New York: Basic Books.

Bowlby, J. (1980). *Attachment and loss: Vol. 3. Loss, sadness and depression.* New York: Basic Books.

Bradley, R., Jenei, J., & Westen, D. (2005). Etiology of borderline personality disorder: Disentangling the contributions of intercorrelated antecedents. *Journal of Nervous and Mental Disease, 193*(1), 24–31.

Cassidy, J., Marvin, R. S., & the MacArthur Working Group on Attachment. (1991). *Attachment organization in preschool children: Coding guidelines* (3rd ed.). Unpublished manuscript.

Chandy, J. M., Blum, R. W., & Resnick, M. D. (1996). Female adolescent with a history of sexual abuse. *Journal of Interpersonal Violence, 11,* 503–518.

Classen, C. C., Pain, C., Field, N. P., & Woods, P. (2006). Posttraumatic personality disorder: A reformulation of complex posttraumatic stress disorder and borderline personality disorder. *Psychiatric Clinics of North America, 29,* 87–112.

Diamond, D., Clarkin, J., Levine, H., Levy, K., Foelsch, P., & Yeomans, F. (1999). Borderline conditions and attachment: A preliminary report. *Psychoanalytic Inquiry, 19*(5), 831–884.

Finger, B. (2006). *Exploring the intergenerational transmission of attachment disorganization.* Unpublished doctoral dissertation, University of Chicago, Chicago.

George, C., & Solomon, J. (1996). Representational models of relationships: Links between caregiving and attachment. *Infant Mental Health Journal, 17*(3), 198–216.

Hennighausen, K., & Lyons-Ruth, K. (2005). Disorganization of behavioral and attentional strategies toward primary attachment figures: From biologic to dialogic processes. In S. Carter, L. Ahnert, K. Grossmann, S. Hrdy, M. Lamb, S. Porges, & N. Sachser (Eds.), *Attachment and bonding: A new synthesis* (Dahlem Workshop Report No. 92, pp. 269–301). Cambridge, MA: MIT Press.

Herman, J. L. (1992). *Trauma and recovery.* New York: Basic Books.

Hesse, E. (1996). Discourse, memory, and the Adult Attachment Interview: A note with emphasis on the emerging Cannot Classify category. *Infant Mental Health Journal, 17,* 4–11.

Horowitz, M. J. (1986). *Stress response syndromes.* Northvale, NJ: Aronson.

Khantzian, E. J. (1985). The self-medication hypothesis of addictive disorders: Focus on heroin and cocaine dependence. *American Journal of Psychiatry, 142,* 1259–1264.

Khantzian, E. J. (1997). The self-medication hypothesis of substance use disorders: A reconsideration and recent applications. *Harvard Review of Psychiatry, 4,* 231–244.

Klein, M. (1946). Notes on some schizoid mechanisms. *International Journal of Psychoanalysis, 27,* 99–110.

Kluft, R. (1991). Multiple personality. In A. Tansman & S. Goldfinger (Eds.), *Review of psychiatry* (Vol. 10, pp.161–188). Washington, DC: American Psychiatric Press.

Liotti, G. (1992). Disorganized/disoriented attachment in the etiology of the dissociative disorders. *Dissociation, 5*(4), 196–204.

Lyons-Ruth K. (1991). Rapprochement or approchement: Mahler's theory reconsidered from the vantage point of recent research on early attachment relationships. *Psychoanalytic Psychology, 8,* 1–23.

Lyons-Ruth, K., & Block, D. (1996). The disturbed caregiving system: Relations among childhood trauma, maternal caregiving, and infant affect and attachment. *Infant Mental Health Journal, 17*(3), 257–275.

Lyons-Ruth, K., Bronfman, E., & Atwood, G. (1999). A relational diathesis model of hostile–helpless states of mind: Expressions in mother–infant interaction. In J. Solomon & C. C. George (Eds.), *Attachment disorganization* (pp. 33–70). New York: Guilford Press.

Lyons-Ruth, K., Bronfman, E., & Parsons, E. (1999). Maternal frightened, frightening, or atypical behavior and disorganized infant attachment patterns. In J. Vondra & D. Barnett (Eds.), Atypical patterns of infant attachment: Theory, research, and current directions. *Monographs of the Society for Research in Child Development, 64*(3, Serial No. 258).

Lyons-Ruth, K., Connell, D., Grunebaum, H., & Botein, S. (1990). Infants at social risk: Maternal depression and family support services as mediators of infant development and security of attachment. *Child Development, 61,* 85–98.

Lyons-Ruth, K., Dutra, L., Schuder, M., & Bianchi, I. (2006). From infant attachment disorganization to adult dissociation: Relational adaptations or traumatic experiences? *Psychiatric Clinics of North America, 29,* 63–86.

Lyons-Ruth, K., Holmes, B., & Hennighausen, K. (2005, April). *Prospective longitudinal predictors of borderline and conduct symptoms in late adolescence: The early caregiving context.* Paper presented as part of a symposium entitled Borderline Psychopathology and Early Caregiving: Concurrent and Longitudinal Relations (P. Hobson & K. Lyons-Ruth, Co-Chairs) at the biennial meeting of the Society for Research in Child Development, Atlanta, GA.

Lyons-Ruth, K., & Jacobvitz, D. (1999). Attachment disorganization: Unresolved loss, relational violence, and lapses in behavioral and attentional strategies. In J. Cassidy & P. R. Shaver (Eds.), *Handbook of attachment: Theory, research, and clinical applications* (pp. 520–554). New York: Guilford Press.

Lyons-Ruth, K., Melnick, S., Patrick, M., & Hobson, R. P. (2007). A controlled study of hostile–helpless states of mind among borderline and dysthymic women. *Attachment and Human Development, 9*(1), 1–16.

Lyons-Ruth, K., Yellin, C., Melnick, S., & Atwood, G. (2003). Childhood experiences of trauma and loss have different relations to maternal unresolved and hostile-helpless states of mind on the AAI. *Attachment and Human Development, 5,* 330–352.

Lyons-Ruth, K., Yellin, C, Melnick, S., & Atwood, G. (2005). Expanding the concept of unresolved mental states: Hostile/helpless states of mind on the Adult Attachment Interview are associated with disrupted mother–infant communication and infant disorganization. *Development and Psychopathology, 17,* 1–23.

Madigan, S., Bakermans-Kranenburg, M., van IJzendoorn, M., Moran, G., Pederson, D., & Benoit, D. (2006). Unresolved states of mind, anomalous parental behavior, and disorganized attachment: A review and meta-analysis of a transmission gap. *Attachment and Human Development, 8,* 89–111.

Mahler, M. (1971). A study of the separation–individuation process and its possible application to borderline phenomena in the psychoanalytic situation. *Psychoanalytic Study of the Child, 26,* 403–424.

Main, M., & Cassidy, J. (1988). Categories of response to reunion with the parent at age 6: Predicted from infant attachment classifications and stable over a 1-month period. *Developmental Psychology, 24,* 415–426.

Main, M., & Goldwyn, R. (1998). *Adult Attachment Scoring and Classification System, Version 6.3.* Unpublished manuscript, University of California, Berkeley.

Main, M., Goldwyn, R., & Hesse, E. (2003). *Adult Attachment Scoring and Classification System.* Unpublished manuscript, University of California, Berkeley, Department of Psychology, Berkeley.

Main, M., & Hesse, E. (1990). Parents' unresolved traumatic experiences are related to infant disorganized attachment status: Is frightened and/or frightening parental behavior the linking mechanism? In M. T. Greenberg, D. Cicchetti, & E. M. Cummings (Eds.), *Attachment in the preschool years: Theory, research and intervention* (pp. 161–184). Chicago: University of Chicago Press.

Main, M., Kaplan, N., & Cassidy, J. (1985). Security in infancy, childhood and adulthood: A move to the level of representation. In I. Bretherton & E. Waters (Eds.), Growing points of attachment theory and research. *Monographs of the Society for Research in Child Development, 50*(1–2, Serial No. 209), 66–104.

Main, M., & Solomon, J. (1990). Procedures for identifying infants as disorganized/disoriented during the Ainsworth Strange Situation. In M. T. Greenberg, D. Cicchetti, & E. M. Cummings (Eds.), *Attachment in the preschool years: Theory, research and intervention* (pp. 121–160). Chicago: University of Chicago Press.

Malinosky-Rummell, R., & Hansen, D. J. (1993). Long-term consequences of childhood physical abuse. *Psychological Bulletin, 114,* 68–79.

Moss, E, S., Nicole, C. C., Dubois-Comtois, K., Mazzarello, T., & Berthiaume, C. (2006). Attachment and behavior problems in middle childhood as reported by adult and child informants. *Development and Psychopathology, 18*(2), 425–444.

NICHD Early Child Care Research Network. (2001). Nonmaternal care and family factors in early development: An overview of the NICHD Study of Early Child Care. *Journal of Applied Developmental Psychology, 22,* 457–492.

Ogawa, J. R., Sroufe, L. A., Weinfield, N. S., Carlson, E. A., & Egeland, B. (1997). Development and the fragmented self: Longitudinal study of dissociative symptomatology in a nonclinical sample. *Development and Psychopathology, 9,* 855–879.

Patrick, M., Hobson, R. P., Castle, P., Howard, R., & Maughan, B. (1994). Personality disorder and mental representation of early social experience. *Development and Psychopathology, 6,* 375–388.

Putnam, F. W. (1989). *Diagnosis and treatment of multiple personality disorders.* New York: Guilford Press.

Schindler, A., Thomasius, R., Sack, P. M., Gemeinhardt, B., Kustner, U., & Eckert, J. (2005). Attachment and substance use disorders: A review of the literature and a study in drug dependent adolescents. *Attachment and Human Development, 7*(3), 207–228.

Simpson, T. L., & Miller, W. R. (2002). Concomitance between childhood sexual and physical abuse and substance use problems: A review. *Clinical Psychology Review, 22,* 27–77.

Steele, H. (2004). The social matrix reloaded: An attachment perspective on Carpendale & Lewis. *Behavioral and Brain Sciences, 27*(1), 124–125.

Steele, H., & Steele, M. (1998). Invited debate: Attachment and psychoanalysis: Time for a reunion. *Social Development, 7,* 92–119.

Terr, L. C. (1991). Childhood traumas: An outline and overview. *American Journal of Psychiatry, 148*(1), 10–20.

van der Kolk, B., & Fisler, R. (1994). Childhood abuse and neglect and loss of self-regulation. *Bulletin of the Menninger Clinic, 58,* 145–168.

van IJzendoorn, M. H. (1995). Adult attachment representations, parental responsiveness, and infant attachment: A meta-analysis on the predictive validity of the Adult Attachment Interview. *Psychological Bulletin, 117,* 387–403.

van IJzendoorn, M. H., Feldbrugge, J., Derks, F., & de Ruiter, C. (1997). Attachment representations of personality-disordered criminal offenders. *American Journal of Orthopsychiatry, 67,* 449–459.

van IJzendoorn, M. H., Schuengel, C., & Bakermans-Kranenburg, M. J. (1999). Disorganized attachment in early childhood: Meta-analysis of precursors, concomitants, and sequelae. *Development and Psychopathology, 11,* 225–249.

Wartner, U. G., Grossmann, K., Fremmer-Bombik, E., & Suess, G. (1994). Attachment patterns at age six in south Germany: Predictability from infancy and implications for preschool behavior. *Child Development, 65,* 1014–1027.

Woodhouse, L. D. (1992). Women with jagged edges: Voices from a culture of substance abuse. *Qualitative Health Research, 2*(3), 262–281.

Zanarini, M. C. (1997). Evolving perspectives on the etiology of borderline personality disorder. In *Role of sexual abuse in the etiology of borderline personality disorder* (pp. 1–14). Washington, DC: American Psychiatric Association.

APPENDIX 16.1. The HH Frequency Codes and Examples

Note that there is no simple algorithm that relates frequency of these indicators to a particular level of HH state of mind.

1. "Global devaluation of a caregiver" is scored whenever the participant's language suggests that globally negative representations of caregivers were held in the past and that these representations continue to be active in the present (i.e., have not been mitigated or distanced) in adulthood. Examples include references such as "she was a witch," "horrible," or "I hated him." As previously noted, this "all-bad" language could also be described as "hot" devaluation in comparison to the "cool" derogation described by Main, Hesse, and Goldwyn (2003) as a hallmark of the DS2 Dismissing subcategory. However, "cool" derogation is also coded here when indicative of a globally negative representation.

Examples:

"I even feel contempt. I don't hate them any more. I used to hate them. I used to daydream what I'd do to them, how I'd kill them, but she is not worth it."

"Inept. Inept in being anything, being a so-called father, being a husband, probably even being a person."

2. "Global representation of a caregiver as helpless or abdicating of parental role." This code is the equivalent of a "global devaluation" code, except that the caregiver is represented as helpless, pervasively anxious, frightened, or abdicating of a parental role through inadequacy (rather than as hostile or angry). It indicates that the individual has been negatively affected by the parent's helplessness such that his or her global representation endures (e.g., "I think my mother was frightened most of the time") and interferes with integration of emotional evaluations of the parent.

Examples:

"I mean, there is partly a kind of hysteria involved in that when she can't cope, she takes to bed. And she actually took to bed for 2 years."

"Not emotional help. You can never depend on her for emotional help. She's a basket case for the way it is emotionally."

3. "Identification with a hostile caregiver" is scored whenever a globally negative evaluation of a caregiver is stated, yet the reader notes that the participant also identifies with and appears to value or accept similarities between the negatively evaluated attachment figure and the self. In some cases the parent's negative qualities are emphasized throughout the interview and the identification with the parent is repeated in unrecognized form in the present (e.g., participant's parent was criticized as extremely anxious and overprotective, and participant justifies her overly restrictive actions toward her own child). In other cases the parent's negative qualities are emphasized, but the participant's similarity or closeness to the parent is also emphasized (e.g., "She was my enemy/We're very close.") This form of contradiction differs from the immediate evaluative oscillation that Main and colleagues (2003) identify as a preoccupied discourse feature, in that these contradictions need not occur between comments presented within a single passage, but typically occur between passages located within separate portions of the interview.

Examples are reprinted with permission from Lyons-Ruth et al. (2007). Identification with a hostile or helpless caregiver is usually coded not for a single passage but for the combination of global devaluation and evidence of identification over the entire interview.

Examples:

" . . . and I used to shout at them in the same way that people I felt threatened by used to tell me off, like school teachers and things, and my mother. I use the same tone and say the same sort of things."

" . . . it's very seldom that I get angry, which is the same as my father, but when I do get angry, I fly off the handle, I just go totally AWOL type uurrgh, which again is exactly the same as my father, because my father never expresses his anger to start with. He never says 'You're making me cross.' He lets it go and go and go and go, until you've made him so furious that he has, he loses control and that's exactly the same as I've got now."

4. "Identification with a helpless caregiver." This code is the equivalent of "identification with a hostile figure," except that the individual describes a primary caregiver as helpless or abdicating of the caregiving role in some way, and also describes him- or herself as acting similarly to or having a lot in common with or being "very close to" that caregiver.

Examples:

"I feel worried and guilty about him, you know, fearful as well, because I just didn't have the equipment to bring up children and I brought those two up."

"I have put distance between us um . . . so in some sense we are very close but, um . . . it is almost like I have to be a professional with her."

5. "Recurrent references to fearful affect" is coded whenever the participant makes a reference to his or her own experiences of fearful affect states in the interview. Fearful references can pertain to a variety of unrelated and/or not particularly threatening circumstances. High frequency suggests a continued pervasively fearful state of mind.

Examples:

" . . . so there was a feeling around all the time that something dreadful was going to happen at any minute."

" . . . I, kind of, am terrified of what is round the next corner really."

6. "Sense of self as bad" refers to an internalized global sense of "badness" or "blameworthiness" in which the participant feels guilty, responsible, deserving of disrespectful treatment, or undeserving of positive attention. By noting the continuation of this attitude into adulthood, this code is thought to index an ongoing need to preserve a positive view of caregivers by continuing to blame the self, as well as a lack of autonomy in making sense of childhood events.

Examples:

" . . . it was my fault that she was sick and so, when she got sick and got old I felt it was my fault, you know, it was all my fault that she was just getting old, you know."

" . . . it always made me feel like a bit of an outsider, the troublemaker of thefamily."

7. "Laughter at pain" is coded whenever laughter follows anecdotes about psychological or physical distress. Laughter at pain is understood as a defensive use of laughter to dismiss the impact of childhood experiences of vulnerability.

Examples:

" . . . then I was 9 when I took my first overdose." [You were 9 when you took an overdose?] (*Subject laughs.*)

" . . . you know, I could have put in a cardboard substitute for myself and nobody would really have noticed." (*Subject laughs.*)

8. "Ruptured attachments" is coded when a participant refers to no longer having contact with one or more members of his or her nuclear family through a deliberate decision to terminate contact. Ruptured attachment relationships have been theoretically tied to global and unintegrated "all good–all bad" representations in the clinical literature.

Examples:

"I went through quite a long period um . . . a few years, about 4 years, 5 years ago having no contact whatsoever with my parents."

"I mean, I don' t speak to him now. I don't want to have anything to do with him at all."

9. "References to controlling–punitive behaviors toward parent in childhood." Controlling–punitive behavior in childhood is coded when the subject spontaneously reports instances of his or her own behavior toward the parent in childhood that are dominating, humiliating, or intended to be hurtful. Examples include tantruming to get something from the parent, "fighting a lot" with a parent, or deliberate attempts to hurt or be punitive toward a parent.

Examples:

"I used to say some hateful things to her . . . and taunt her . . . [What would you say?] That she deserved what he was doing to her."

"I would push them to a certain point. . . . They'd start to break . . . because I was very, like, insolent and cheeky and demanding."

10. "References to Controlling–Caregiving Stance Toward Parent in Childhood." This code is analogous to the references to controlling–punitive stance in childhood, except that reference to caregiving stance in childhood is coded when the interviewee spontaneously makes direct statements indicating equality of roles between child and parent, of child helping parent, protecting parent, worrying about parent, displaying vigilance regarding the parent's needs, fighting in defense of parent, or in other ways displaying a parental attitude toward the parent.

Examples:

" . . . I think the only way I could experience closeness was to take care of her. Get her tea when she came in from doing this work and go out with her and help her."

" . . . I was aware that I was, kind of, responsible for her and I used to . . . if I was at school I used to be worrying was she alright."

V

The AAI, Foster Care, and Adoptive Placements

17

Forecasting Outcomes
in Previously Maltreated Children
The Use of the AAI in a Longitudinal Adoption Study

MIRIAM STEELE, JILL HODGES, JEANNE KANIUK,
HOWARD STEELE, SAUL HILLMAN, and KAY ASQUITH

It is hard enough to predict the weather. That you can predict child
outcomes from knowing the parent's state of mind about attachment
is truly remarkable!
— JOHN BOWLBY (personal communication, May 24, 1989)

When he shared this remark, John Bowlby was speaking about the emergence
of the Adult Attachment Interview (AAI) as a powerful tool for forecasting
infant–parent patterns of attachment (Main, Kaplan, & Cassidy, 1985). Years
later we applied the AAI to the question of how best to forecast child outcomes when they are most uncertain, that of adoption concerning a school-
age child with a history of maltreatment. This chapter details our findings on
use of the AAI in this context.

Although adopted children are already overrepresented in mental health
and special needs services (Miller et al., 2000; van IJzendoorn & Juffer, 2006),
evidence suggests that adopted children who have been maltreated within
their families of origin experience even greater difficulties. However, compelling data indicate that, especially in the long term, the majority of adoptees
show favorable adjustment. Although this has mainly been documented in the
case of infancy adoptions, overall, adoption has often been described as the

most radical and powerful intervention we have to alter the course of the lives of traumatized children (O'Connor & Zeanah, 2003; van IJzendoorn & Juffer, 2006). Adoption provides in a child's world the chance for change from repeatedly making and breaking of affectional bonds to experiencing benign and, we hope, enduring permanent caregiving arrangements. This chapter highlights how the AAI may significantly forecast these possibilities when administered to adoptive parents of late-placed (older) children with a history of maltreatment.

van IJzendoorn and Juffer (2006) summarize data in their meta-analytic study of adoption research, which highlights the impact of early compared to late adoptions. They found a significant difference in catch-up between early- (before age 12 months) and late-adopted (after age 12 months) children. Once adopted, the early-adopted children managed to catch up almost completely with nonadopted children in terms of attachment security, whereas the late-adopted children lagged substantially behind their peers.

However, what happens if not only the age of the child but also the state(s) of mind of the new caregiver(s) are taken into account? In one of the first studies to look at the connection between foster care mothers' attachment state of mind as assessed with the AAI and infant attachment as assessed by the Strange Situation, Dozier, Chase-Stovall, Albus, and Bates (2001) found a remarkable association. When placed with foster mothers who were secure–autonomous in response to the AAI, infants—most of whom suffered early neglect and some of whom suffered abusive parenting—demonstrated more secure attachment to their new foster mothers than infants placed with insecure foster mothers. There was a 72% match between the foster mother's state of mind and child attachment. Only 21% of secure–autonomous foster mothers had children with disorganized attachment, compared with 62.5% of nonautonomous (i.e., insecure) foster mothers. The children were all between 3 and 20 months of age at time of placement; interestingly, variations in child age at placement were not associated with infant security status. Based on these findings, the authors proposed that foster children may organize their attachment around the availability of their foster parents. An interesting feature of this work highlighted some children's tendency to "miscue" their caregivers, that is, behaving in a way that indicates they are not in need of nurturance or attention when actually they could use some. The secure foster parent is the one who can skillfully "override" this signal and provide sensitive caregiving despite the message that none is sought. It is understood that histories of interactions characterized by neglect or nonoptimal care can give rise to the development of this particular defensive strategy (Cooper, Hoffman, Powell, & Marvin, 2005; Dozier, Higley, Albus, & Nutter, 2002). The caregiver who is sensitive to this behavior is gently able to look beyond what may otherwise be felt as pushing away or rejection, and not respond with retaliatory rejection, or as described by Dozier, "a response in kind" (Dozier et al., 2002). We have described similar clinical phenomena in intervention work with older children (Steele et al., 2007) as part of what goes into the recovery process as their new caregivers seem able to absorb these and any other potentially hurtful behaviors and respond with "attachment-facilitating behavior," whereby caregivers let the children know—perhaps for the first time in their lives—that it is safe to seek out proximity and contact. As the children learn through repeated interactions that there is now someone available and responsive to them, they begin to show proximity-seeking and contact-maintaining behavior when distressed, and correspondingly discover new energies for exploration of their environment. Our wish to chart these possible changes empirically led to our investigation into how the development of attachment relationships proceed when maltreated school-age children undergo adoptive placement.

The Attachment Representations and Adoption Outcome Study

This study, a collaborative effort between experts in social work, child maltreatment, attachment research, and clinical work, was initiated by Jeanne Kaniuk, head of the Coram Family Adoption Service, with Miriam Steele (from the Anna Freud Centre at the time the study was initiated) and Jill Hodges of Great Ormond Street Hospital. One of the unique features of the Coram Family Adoption Service is its specialty in finding permanent families for "hard to place" children, that is, those that have endured repeated maltreatment, neglect, and emotional, often physical, and sometimes sexual abuse. They are further deemed "hard to place" because they are older, making the prospect of finding suitable families even more challenging. The focus of our study was to observe potential change across many dimensions, beginning with not only the assessment attachment representations in both parents and children but also features of the child's cognitive development, behavioral strengths, and difficulties when first placed, then 2 years later. Importantly the study included a comparison group of maltreated children who were adopted in the first 12 months of their lives and were matched to the current age of the late-placed group. Although this group shared the common feature of having been adopted, the children had very different experiences than the older adopted children in terms of the length of time in adverse situations. The study was unique in its attempt not only to investigate possible correlates between the *nonbiologically*-related parents' attachment states of mind in terms of both their own childhood experience but also its focus on the attachment representations of the previously maltreated children as expressed in the repeated assessment of attachment story stem completion narratives. A further important and unique feature of the study was the inclusion of fathers, so often left out of developmental and social work research, who undoubtedly have a critical role to play in the development of their children.

The potential for capturing aspects of the children's attachment representations as they may change over time was a central focus of the study. To do this we used the Story Stem Assessment Profile (SSAP; Hodges, Steele, Hillman, & Henderson, 2003), one of a number of available approaches using doll play and attachment story completions found to be reliable and valid means for accessing the inner world of the child (see Emde, Wolf, & Oppenheim, 2003). In predicting a possible overlap between the adoptive parents' responses to the AAI and their newly placed children's responses to a range of attachment story completion tasks, we were drawing on the conceptual understanding that these two tasks shared some similar features. As well, previous research has shown meaningful and statistically significant overlap between AAIs of mothers and story completions of their genetically linked—and raised from birth—children (Gloger-Tippelt, Gomille, Koenig, & Vetter, 2002; Steele et al., 2003). Both the AAI and attachment story completion tasks are interview techniques in which the respondent's audio-recorded narrative (the story stems are also video-recorded) is the focus of close scrutiny by trained raters, so that we are able to assess thoughts and feelings expressed by the participants in their "own voices." To a marked degree, albeit of course in very different ways, both tasks demand that the listener consider what he or she might do (or in the case of the AAI, might have done) when faced with emotionally challenging situations that are part of everyday childhood experience, including emotional upset, physical hurt, separation from parents, parental discipline, and rejection/exclusion. Furthermore, specific prompts in both tasks invite the respondents to express how they think a parent ought to behave in response to children's misdemeanors. Finally, both interview methods tax speakers' capacities for providing an emotionally balanced and coherent story that may be seen to represent a resolution to frequently occurring dilemmas in routine family life.

In an early study that originated in findings of strong and significant overlaps between parents' AAIs and infant–parent attachment (Steele, Steele, & Fonagy, 1996), we found that when we compared AAIs from these primiparous biologically related mothers and their children's narrative story completions at age 5, mothers whose AAIs were judged secure–autonomous had children whose narratives also demonstrated aspects of security and autonomy (Steele et al., 2003). Thus, children with secure–autonomous mothers differed from the remaining children in that they provided story completions that depicted routine, nonthreatening, and readily expectable events that might happen in everyday family life, with caregivers providing help in the face of distress and firmly but fairly setting limits. In contrast, when parents' attachment narratives were observed to be strikingly lacking in coherence and correspondingly insecure (dismissing or preoccupied and/or unresolved), we observed elevated levels of reference to attachment figures who were inconsistent, ineffective, or overly (physically) punitive in setting limits. We also found that when limit setting was absent from children's story completions, depictions of sadness, anger, confusion, and aggression were more likely to be present.

Similar relations between maternal AAIs and children's' story completions have been observed in two other studies of low-risk samples, one British (Goldwyn, Stanley, Smith, & Green, 2000) and one German (Gloger-Tippelt et al., 2002). Emotion narratives have also been collected from maltreated children, and researchers working with these children note that the trauma they have experienced is amply represented in the emotionally dysregulated and negative story completions they provide (e.g., Toth, Cicchetti, MacFie, & Emde, 1997; Warren, 2003). However, the latter studies of emotion narratives in maltreated children did not include AAIs with the parents. Thus, the work reported here is the first to compare adoptive parents' AAIs and their children's emotion narratives in a sample of older adopted and previously maltreated children.

To date we have reported on several different aspects of this study. We have found, for example, interesting associations between the adoptive mothers' AAI classifications and their newly placed maltreated adoptive children *within* 3 months of the placement. We compared the salient themes of children who were placed with mothers whose AAIs were independently classified as secure or insecure (either dismissing or preoccupied or unresolved/disorganized). We found that those children placed with insecure mothers had significantly more of each of the following themes in their story stem completion narratives than did the children of secure mothers: catastrophic fantasies, child aggression, adult aggression, throwing out or throwing away (of a character or prop), bizarre or atypical content, child injured or dead, adult injured or dead, and adult actively rejects child (Steele et al., 2003).

When we turned these variables into a composite, internally consistent score for "aggression," further links to the maternal AAIs were observed (Steele et al., 2003). Themes of aggression, 3 months into the adoptive placement, correlated significantly with a number of the 9-point interval scales indexing the speaker's "state of mind" concerning attachment (Main, Goldwyn, & Hesse, 2003) such as *insistence on the inability to recall* one's childhood, a signal feature of the insecure–dismissing interview pattern. Similarly, children's high scores on the aggression theme correlated positively with mothers' *derogation* of their own fathers and correlated *negatively* with the hallmarks of an autonomous–secure interview pattern (i.e., ratings of *coherence of mind and coherence of transcript*).

Looking at which themes were most prevalent in the children's story completions (early in the placement) if they were placed with mothers whose AAIs were classified as unresolved with regard to loss/trauma, we observed a number of significant differences, in that they scored highest (in comparison to children placed with nonunresolved mothers) on the following themes: parent appearing child-like, adult aggression, throwing out or throwing away (a child, adult, animal figures, conveying a "rubbishing" of characters). They also scored significantly lower on the themes of realistic mastery and sibling or peer helps (Steele et al., 2003).

These findings suggest that unresolved mourning in a parent, or an insecure (dismissing or preoccupied) state of mind, may exacerbate the emotional worries of a recently adopted child, and confirm and extend the pioneering work linking unresolved mourning to infant disorganization (Main & Hesse, 1990). Adoptive mothers with unresolved prior loss or trauma, or other pronounced attachment insecurities, appeared less able to help a newly placed, maltreated child use or develop an organized strategy to deal with the kinds of conflict depicted in the story stem prompts. A most compelling feature of these results was that we were able to observe differences in the children within a very short period of time after being introduced to their adoptive parents, that is, within 3 months (Steele et al., 2003). These results confirm the Dozier and colleagues (2001) findings in a much younger group of children, but with almost equally rapid results.

Change in the children's story stem themes across the first 2 years of the adoptive placement in this late-adopted group has been reported (e.g., Hodges, Steele, Hillman, Henderson, & Kaniuk, 2005). First, in relation to the nonmaltreated comparison group of adopted children who were the same age as the maltreated children when assessed, we found differences in their story stem assessment narratives that fit with differences in their experiences. For example, the previously maltreated group showed more avoidance and more disorganized themes as a strategy to resolve the dilemmas in the stories, and this difference remained even at 2-year follow-up. However, despite continuing to have higher levels of the more negative indicators of avoidance and disorganization in comparison to the nonmaltreated group, overall they showed decreased negative indicators compared to those in assessments when they were first placed (Hodges et al., 2005). Second, all the children in the previously maltreated group showed increases in their "secure" themes. This hugely important finding highlights the success of the adoption intervention in this high-risk sample. It also highlights an important aspect concerning the nature of mental representations, with interesting implications for therapeutic intervention, because it focuses on potential trajectories for change and adaptation; that is, it seems much easier to accommodate and take on positive representations than to "extinguish" negative representations, as indicated by the persistence of avoidance and disorganized themes. This has obvious and important implications for clinical work with both children and adults. As Hodges and colleagues (2005) explain:

> Children develop new and more positive sets of mental representation in competition with the existing negative representations rather than the new replacing the old. The old expectations and perceptions remain as vulnerabilities in that they can easily be triggered by events and interactions that seem to confirm their validity. It is all too easy for adoptive parents inadvertently to provide such triggers; they may have no idea of the way in which the children, on the basis of their abuse history, construe a particular interaction. The job of adoptive parents is one of active disconfirmation of the negative models that the children have brought

with them and the building up of competing models that eventually, if all goes well, may become the predominant ones. (p. 115)

In the results presented in this chapter, we ask whether the state of mind of the adopters, *both the mothers and the fathers*, at time of placement may be shown to relate to the state of mind of the children *2 years after* having been placed into the adoptive home. If longer-term links to parents' state of mind concerning attachment can be found, we wondered, might we not gain a fuller understanding of how not only positive secure emotional themes may increase (as we have seen to be the case for all children), but also how negative insecure themes may decrease? Additionally, we report on the extent to which the AAIs of these adoptive parents resemble the distribution in the general population (van IJzendoorn & Bakermans-Kranenburg, 1996, Chapter 3, this volume).

Methods

Sample

The main sample comprised 58 "late-placed" children between the ages of 4 and 8 years (M = 5.5 years, SD = 1.4 years). These 58 children were adopted by 41 mothers, 25 of whom adopted one child, 15 of whom adopted sibling pairs, and 1 who adopted a trio of siblings. Five of the adopters were single. The mean age of the mothers was 40 years (SD = 6); mean age of the fathers was 43 (SD = 7).

The sample of children comprised 43% boys, and 85% were Anglo-European. The children had all suffered serious adversity, including neglect, physical abuse, and sexual abuse. A global tally for type and severity of abusive experiences yielded an index with a range from 2–5, with a mean of 3.2 (SD = 0.7), indicating that all children had experienced at least two or more of the following types of abuse (physical, sexual, severe neglect). The number of caregivers they had experienced ranged from 2 to 18 different placements (M = 5.2, SD = 2.8).

Measures

Adult Attachment Interview

The AAI was administered to 40 of the 41 adoptive mothers and 34 of the 36 adoptive fathers. By the time of the 2-year follow-up, two adoptive placements had broken down (in both cases the parent(s) were insecure; one was also unresolved). This left us with AAIs available from 32 couples whose 47 children provided attachment story completions. The interview is described in detail (Hesse, 1999; Main, Hesse, & Goldwyn, Chapter 2, this volume) and the protocol followed in the work reported here adhered fully to the established procedure. The 74 interviews were audio-recorded and transcribed verbatim for later study by a trained, experienced, and reliable rater (M. Steele). Twenty of these transcripts (from 8 fathers and 12 mothers) were independently rated (by H. Steele), and there was 100% two-way agreement (insecure vs. secure) with the primary rater. High three-way (90%) and four-way (100%) agreement was also achieved. In two cases (10%) of this reliability set, where there was agreement that the interviews were unresolved with respect to loss, conferencing was required to agree the best-fitting insecure alternative (dismissing or preoccupied). Also considered was a cannot classify (CC) designation (see Main et al., Chapter 2, this volume), which was conceived, in part, for these rare cases that combine both dismissing and preoccupied themes. In the results below these two interviews are included in the insecure category.

For the results reported, we computed four types of parent AAI data according to 47 children who had parents with AAI profiles showing that (1) neither parent was secure ($n = 7$), (2) only the father was secure ($n = 6$), (3) only the mother was secure ($n = 17$), and (4) both parents were secure ($n = 17$). We further reduced the AAI classification data into two groups: children whose parents' AAI data suggested that neither parent was secure ($n = 7$), and those that indicated one or both parents were secure ($n = 40$).

Story Stem Assessment Profile

The SSAP comprises in part five story stems originally devised by Jill Hodges for use in clinical and research settings, with an original, clinically based coding system (Hodges et al., 2003). In three of these five stories human doll figures are used, and in two stories, animal figures. Eight additional stems from the MacArthur Story Stem Battery (MSSB; Bretherton & Oppenheim, 2003) are included in the protocol, for a total of 13 story stems. The stems are always administered in the same order and are designed for children between the ages of 4 and 8 years. The interviews with the children are video- and audio-recorded, and are not only transcribed in terms of the verbal narrative but also contain a record of what the child portrayed in nonverbal actions. Transcripts in this study were then rated according to the manual (Hodges et al., 2003), with each of the child's 13 stories rated for the presence of 30 themes. These themes broadly cover the following areas: adult and child representations, aggressive manifestations, indicators of avoidance, aspects of positive adaptation, and indicators of disorganization.

For our present purposes we rely on two distinct aggregate and internally consistent scales, based on 15 discrete coding categories applied to the children's story completions at 2-year follow-up: one concerning "disorganized" themes and the other capturing a range of clearly "insecure," aggressive themes, including both extreme aggression and avoidance.

The internally consistent aggregate scale ($\alpha = .72$) indicating "disorganization" was based on the following six coding categories: (1) *catastrophic fantasy*; (2) *bizarre/atypical material*; (3) *bad-to-good shift* (shifts between a figure being represented as bad or frightening, alternating in an unexplained way with portrayals of the same figure being "good" or from going from good to bad); (4) *extreme aggression*; (5) *magic omnipotence*; and (6) *child appearing parent-like or role reversal.*

The "insecure" composite, which at the 2-year follow-up was found to have excellent internal consistency (α = .78) was based on the following nine codes: *child endangered, child injured/dead, adult unaware, adult actively rejects, adult injured/dead, excessive compliance, extreme aggression, neutralization*, and *throwing away.*

To permit cross-tabulations of two-way AAI data (neither parent secure vs. one or both parents secure) and the children's attachment narratives, we recoded the composite scores for children's disorganization and insecurity into three equal groups, creating low-, medium-, and high-scoring groups for insecurity and disorganization. We then relied on these in computing the results presented below.

Results

Results are organized into three sections. The first section considers the distribution of observed AAI classifications. The second section concerns the crosstabulation of parent AAI groups (neither parent secure vs. one or both parents secure) and children's low versus high scores for insecurity and disorganization derived from their story completion responses 2 years into follow-up. We also consider here what interval scale scores derived from the AAIs were most informative relative to parent membership in the neither parent secure versus one or more parents secure groups. The third and final section concerns qualitative data, in terms of excerpts from parents' AAIs and children's story completions, to illustrate the quantitative findings.

Distribution of the AAIs from the Adoptive Mothers and Fathers

The AAIs obtained from the 40 adoptive mothers yielded a four-way distribution of 27 (68%) autonomous–secure, five (12%) insecure–dismissing, zero (0%) insecure–preoccupied, and eight (20%) unresolved concerning past loss or trauma. The eight interviews judged unresolved were alternatively categorized as dismissing in four cases, preoccupied (E1, passively preoccupied) in two cases, and autonomous–secure in two cases. Regarding the AAIs obtained from the 34 adoptive fathers, the four-way distribution revealed 18 (53%) autonomous–secure, 12 (35%) insecure–dismissing, two (6%) insecure–preoccupied (E1), and two (6%) unresolved. The two unresolved interviews were alternatively categorized in one case as dismissing and in the other as preoccupied. For the purposes of computing the results below, we collapsed insecure interviews into one group (dismissing or preoccupied) for comparison with the autonomous–secure group.

Links between Parents' AAIs and Children's Stories

Combining maternal and paternal AAI classifications for the 47 children in two-parent families who completed the 2-year follow-up yielded the following distribution: 5 families in which neither parent was secure (7 children adopted); 5 families in which only the father was secure (6 children adopted); 12 families in which only the mother was secure (17 children adopted); and 10 families in which both parents were secure (17 children adopted).

We then correlated the children's low-, medium-, and high-scoring groups for insecurity and disorganization in the SSAP with parents' AAIs, that is, neither parent secure versus one or more parents secure. Children's insecurity correlated significantly with the parental AAI variable (Spearman's $r = -.29$, $p < .05$, two-tailed), such that the presence of one or more secure parents in the children's lives made insecure themes in the children's stories significantly *less likely*. Similarly, and more significantly, children's disorganization correlated negatively with parental security (Spearman's $r = -.36$, $p < .01$, two-tailed), such that parental insecurity was strongly linked to elevated levels of disorganization in their adopted children. In other words, when neither parent's AAI was secure at the time of adoptive placement, at 2-year follow-up, 86% of their children scored in the highest group for disorganization.

Qualitative Results: Illustrative Examples from Parents' AAIs and Children's Story Completions

This section of our results presents verbatim excerpts from the AAIs of adoptive mothers and fathers, obtained prior to the placement of the children. This section also includes verbatim excerpts from the attachment story completion responses of the children, from the 2-year follow-up. The material presented below follows two families: one—called here the Smith family—in which both parents' AAIs were judged autonomous–secure *and* in which low levels of insecurity and high levels of security were evident in their child's story completions at the 2-year follow-up; and the other—here called the Drew family—in which both parents' AAIs were classified as insecure *and* in which their child's story completions indicated high levels of disorganization and insecurity 2 years into the adoptive placement.

Both Parents' AAIs Classified Autonomous–Secure: The Case of the Smith Family

Mrs. Smith's childhood experiences with her parents, as revealed in her AAI, were rather complicated and provided her with neither any consistent feeling of a safe haven or a secure base. Fortunately for her, these vital attachment experiences were delivered by her paternal grandmother. Mrs. Smith provided a compelling example of what is known as an "earned" secure interview, because her mother was neglectful and emotionally abusive, but Mrs. Smith was able to draw on these experiences in a balanced and thoughtful way. During the AAI she was asked, "Which parent were you closest to in childhood?" Mrs. Smith responded:

> "Didn't have a parent I was close to. It was my grandmother . . . I actually, I actually felt like an orphan, which was mad, because I actually had four parents, right, I sort of, mother, father, stepmother, stepfather, and I actually did not have anybody but this grandmother who knew every single, tiny thing that happened in my life. I mean she really was my soul mate she would sort of listen to all the details I shared about my life at school, with friends and with other people in the family. She was so absorbent it was unbelievable; in fact I've got all my listening skills from her, totally and it was partly she had the time to do that in that she only she had only one son so I was like a sort of daughter to her and, umm, I've never, ever come across somebody like her, and she really took it all in as well because she would remember it and when I would say something later she would tie it all to the other things I said, so umm, an extraordinary listener."

Despite having reason to look down upon or derogate her parents, Mrs. Smith does not do this. Instead her mind is attuned to all the good lessons she learned from her grandmother. Later in the interview, when asked about the loss in her adult life of this grandmother, Mrs. Smith demonstrates her understanding of this important loss; in fact, she highlights something crucial to the pathway toward resolution (i.e., being convinced that the dead loved one is, in fact, dead and gone). Consider how Mrs. Smith responds to the following question from the AAI concerning the loss of her grandmother:

> INTERVIEWER: What were the circumstances surrounding the death of your grandmother? (*Mrs. Smith began by describing a long illness, during which time she visited her grandmother frequently, until eventually she "slipped away."*)
>
> MRS. SMITH: So, it was terribly peaceful, I mean, it couldn't have been more calm.
>
> INTERVIEWER: And you went to her funeral?
>
> MRS. SMITH: Yeah. And I saw, in fact that was the only body I have ever seen, you know, visited, and that really helped actually, because it made it quite clear that person was definitely gone.

Toward the end of the interview, Mrs. Smith contemplates the following questions, tapping into her hopes for the future and for her adopted child:

> INTERVIEWER: If you can think, looking forward in 20 years' time, what three wishes would you have for your children?

MRS. SMITH: The main thing is for him to be happy all throughout his childhood with us, you know. I want him to be happy and to look back, and to say that he has been happy is more important than academic achievements, or jobs or anything else. I really want a lot of sort of sunshine in his life. So that's overriding everything. Next thing, umm, gosh, 20 years time, so he'll be in his mid-20s, umm, to be doing something that he feels is fulfilling. . . . And I suppose, thirdly, that he is rounded enough and not scarred enough, of course, he is coming to us very damaged and will carry that inside at some level, but umm, that he is able to enter into and enjoy decent relationships of his own making . . . that he is able to, to carry through a relationship rather than have lots of things that block it . . . that he will have had enough of a normal loving life to be able to, to share.

INTERVIEWER: And what would you like your children to take away as adults from having been parented by you and your husband?

MRS. SMITH: That is a lovely question actually, umm, just things like warmth and love really, I can't be specific, but umm, a feeling utterly relaxed and that he could do anything, say anything, and it would not all effect how we felt about him. I mean, he could say that he has robbed a bank or something, and we'd be very concerned but we'd help him face the consequences—but hopefully through being honest with us and sharing, I'd hope that he make the kinds of choices that don't often lead to sad or painful consequences. Yeah, I would love him to take away a feeling that he could share anything at all with Mr. Smith and me.

Mr. Smith, in his own preplacement AAI, shows why fathers in this "one or more parents secure" group had significantly higher "coherence of mind" scores, and "reflective functioning" scores than their insecure counterparts. Here he talks about the effect that losses (of his parents) might have on his parenting. He is balanced, open, valuing of attachment and resolved.

INTERVIEWER: Do you think the losses have had an effect or are likely to have an effect and you and how you bring up these prospective children?

MR. SMITH: Well, I shall talk openly about death with him, which my parents hardly ever did to me, to talk about the possibility. One doesn't want to go on about it, but death is a part of life and everybody has to face it in the end and if you got children you got to face the fact that your parents are going to die. And, I shall not hold back in talking about it, but I won't go on and on about it and bore him to tears with it. But certainly shall not hold back about it.

Mr. Smith, in his AAI, shows insight into how he might feel being separated from the child he is about to have placed with him:

MR. SMITH: Well, you mentioned separating. I see what you mean, umm, I don't think I have thought about it at all. I am still imagining the situation of coming together with him and getting to know him and establishing a bond. How on earth, well, I have not reached the stage of imagining how I would be separating from him. Well, I think, if I had established a bond with him and I have established a sort of bond that he has come to rely on me and see me as a father figure, umm, well obviously he will miss me. The real question, what's my reaction going to be? Umm, depends on what the circumstance are, if it was just the question of him going away on holiday for a week, I don't think I would have a problem. But the problem, the thing about children, particularly disturbed children, is they are, quite sure you realize it, they are quite often far more reliant on the parental figures than the average child is. Eventually the children have got to go off and grow up and be on their own. And I think that that process starts pretty early. I mean, I don't mean you chuck a 4-year-old out the front door, but you sort of prepare them for the idea that they are separate people and their parents are separate people, and that you have this wonderful bond, in the end, you do move physically apart.

Mr. Smith then echoes the sentiment and belief of Mrs. Smith in emphasizing the value they will place on truthfulness or honesty.

INTERVIEWER: Is there any one particular thing you have learned from your own childhood experience, from your own upbringing?

MR. SMITH: Yes, I think you should always be honest with children. Don't mean you have to tell them everything all at once. I mean if they ask where babies come from you don't give them an hour lecture on biology. But you always tell them the truth.

John was 6 years old when he was placed with the Smiths. He had been in six previous homes prior to joining the Smiths. In terms of the 5-point tally of abusive experiences, John scored 4, at the 70th percentile for the sample. He was placed with a sibling. We present John's response to the "bike story" stem that sets up a scene in which the protagonist boy asks his mother if he and his friend can ride their bikes. Mom agrees but says, "Be careful," and the stem continues with the protagonist falling and getting hurt. Here is what John provided when he was 8 years old, after having lived for 2 years with the Smiths. The representation of a protective, caring mother is evident in his story completion.

INTERVIEWER: Can you show me and tell me what happens now?

CHILD: The boy fell over.

INTERVIEWER: The boy fell over. So what happens?

CHILD: Uhm, he calls, he calls his mum, and she says, "The boys have been knocked over."

INTERVIEWER: Then Dave goes and tells George's mum. And what happens?

CHILD: She picks him up, and they go to a hospital.

INTERVIEWER: She picks him up and goes to a hospital.

CHILD: Where's the hospital?

INTERVIEWER: You make it up. You show me where it might . . .

CHILD: Here!

INTERVIEWER: Right. So, he takes him to hospital, and what happens?

CHILD: Uhm, he goes onto . . . the couch and laid down, to check what's wrong with him.

INTERVIEWER: They go and see what might be wrong with him.

CHILD: Yeah.

INTERVIEWER: I see. What happens?

CHILD: Uhm, that's the end!

INTERVIEWER: That's the end?

CHILD: Yeah.

INTERVIEWER: Nothing else happened?

CHILD: No.

INTERVIEWER: Okay. Is he OK after that?

CHILD: Yeah!

Both Parents Classified as Insecure: The Drew Family

The following excerpt is from a mother's AAI classified as insecure–dismissing (Ds1, the subcategory of dismissing in which both high idealization and insistence on lack of an ability to recall are identified). The father's interview was also classified as insecure–dismissing (Ds3, the subcategory of dismissing in which scores on the above variables may be lower, and some recounting of negative experiences or feelings may be offered and then withdrawn). The child's story stems over the period of 2 years since he was placed indicate little change in the negative themes he expressed when first placed.

The mother's narrative responses to the AAI reveal how her view of her father is high in idealization, and the attitude she conveys toward the mother in the interview is somewhat derogatory, but with good reason, because the picture she presents is of a mother who derogated her. Also, she reveals that the "help" that was on offer at home as she was growing up was occasional help (from father) with schoolwork, but emotional help, in the sense of a parent being available as a safe haven, was not apparent. We pick up the AAI with the mother as she elaborates on why she remembers her father as having been helpful.

> INTERVIEWER: The third adjective you gave was "helping" so if you can think of a time, remembering an incident, that could illustrate what made you think of that word.
>
> MRS. DREW: Yeah. Umm, I can't remember now. Umm, he, umm—of the things that I was allowed to do being a girl and Dad would always help me if he could. So he would, umm, always help me if I had problems with schoolwork like math, which was not, I was never very good at, er, and he would sit and he would help me with that. So sort of saying that he, you know I wasn't allowed to do certain things, but the things that I was allowed to do . . . then he would always, he would always be there to help, you know, he would help me so, umm, whereas perhaps my mum would be less, umm, of the two my mum's a lot more intelligent and sharp than my dad, so I think perhaps he, he would recognize, umm, someone who needed help in something that he could do, whereas my mum used to say "Don't you want to be able to do it? What's the matter with you? Are you stupid or what?" Umm, Dad would sort of say "Oh well, you do this, you do that" and he, he'd sit and he would help me and then, you know, sort of . . .

Later in the same interview, Mrs. Drew is asked to contemplate what it felt like to be distressed as a child.

> INTERVIEWER: When you were upset as a child, what would you do?
>
> MRS. DREW: Umm—if I was upset, umm, I would probably do my best to avoid letting anyone know I was upset [hmm hmm] in case it was seen as, umm, as, umm, a sign of weakness.

And further into the interview, Mrs. Drew is asked one of the questions that in our view demands "reflective functioning"; that is, the subject is asked to evaluate her attachment experiences by putting herself in her parent's shoes and to think about the thoughts, feelings, and intentions that may help to explain her parents' behavior.

> INTERVIEWER: Why do you think your parents behaved as they did during your childhood?
>
> MRS. DREW: {3-second pause} Why? Because that's the way that every-body else behaved. You kn-, I wouldn't, I mean I, I, probably it was, the way that my parents behaved was no different from the way that other people of my age's, where I lived, parents behaved. Umm, they,

er, it was probably the way that their parents brought them up and they just passed that on, umm, so they, you know, their, their behavior . . . and just sort imposed that on their children.

In terms of reflective functioning, this would score at the low end of the 10-point scale, because Mrs. Drew shows little interest in exploring the specific lessons that her parents may have learned from her grandparents. She stays at the level of banal generalizations about the norms of "other people of (her) age."

Mr. Drew's AAI, akin to the one provided by his wife, also revealed an insular dismissing emotional stance, but he was able (cognitively) to recall challenging family circumstances in his family of origin. This is typical of the Ds3, insecure–dismissing AAI pattern, in which the speaker reveals some childhood difficulties but without displaying or describing accompanying emotions. We join his interview as he is asked to think of memories that illustrate the adjective phrase "determined for the kids to do well" in respect of his childhood relationship to his mother.

> INTERVIEWER: OK. In terms of your mother being "very determined for the kids to do well" do any specific memories or incidents come to mind which reflect that?
>
> MR. DREW: Long hours going through school books umm, reading, writing skills, this sort of stuff, a lot less time spent on playing. I can't remember playing at all with me mother or me mum or anything like that. She just wasn't that sort of person. Umm, you played with your brothers and sisters.

When Mr. Drew is asked to describe his childhood relationship with his father, the only term he provides is "quite remote," and he is asked to provide a supporting memory.

> INTERVIEWER: Can you think of sort of a specific memory from your early childhood?
>
> MR. DREW: {Subject exhales.} Very early childhood, umm, the only memories I've had of my very early child-, childhood with my dad is when I've done something wrong. {Subject gives wry laugh.} That's basically when he's, he's around to give the old sort of like turn-off.

Further into his AAI, Mr. Drew is asked to consider what it felt like to be distressed as a child, and then ill as a child:

> INTERVIEWER: When you were upset as a child, what would you do?
>
> MR. DREW: Probably bottle it up I should think. Yeah, still do now I suppose. {Subject laughs.}

INTERVIEWER: How did you react when you were ill?

MR. DREW: I'd just be in bed. {*Subject laughs.*} I think on that, umm, I'd probably be after tea and sympathy. Umm, the only other real illness that I had—I suppose was, umm, I used to get asthma quite a bit as a kid, umm, and it used to frighten the life out of my parents and teachers and stuff like that until you, you get used to, get used to it. Umm, but that was only, you know, alright, I had an asthma attack and a couple of hours later I'd be over it so you know again you just, I can't really think of any other long ter-, well it wasn't any real long-term illness or anything, lots of it just coughs and colds. Apart from that I was fairly healthy.

Toward the end of the AAI, Mr. Drew is asked one of the interview questions that arguably demands that he show the extent to which he can be reflective and thoughtfully examine the consequences of his upbringing.

INTERVIEWER: In general, how do you think your overall experiences in your childhood have affected your adult personality?

MR. DREW: Umm . . . I definitely have the organizational trace of my mum. Umm, I tend to, er, be too tidy apparently. Er, well it depends, you know, I try not to go to extremes. Er, Jenny's [Mrs. Drew] probably a bit the other way, umm, so we have a little bit of fun and banter about that. Umm, so I've definitely got that. Umm, I'm definitely not very keen on physical violence against kids. I can see how kids have, are brought up and what the, one thing I really hate is things like grazing (i.e., eating snacks throughout the day instead of regular meals), er, and no fixed meal times, no this that and the other and I, I think kids lose a lot out with the order and the discipline that you would have had earlier on. Er, on the other hand, I probably would be, although I'm not very touchy-feely and I'd probably not. I still don't show emotions very well and I should probably do that a bit more.

This response from Mr. Drew shows a glimpse of understanding about how his emotionally restricted childhood has left him, well, emotionally restricted, but it would seem that the function of his speech is to distance himself from emotional concerns and focus instead on tidiness, eating behavior, and a statement about his opposition to violence against children (uncontroversial and impersonal). This passage would attract low scores on both coherence and reflective functioning. Overall, the AAI provided by Mr. Drew indicates an attachment state of mind that was classified as insecure–dismissing of the "restricted in feeling" subclass. This subject does point out some of the lack of closeness with his parents, but he does not dwell on thinking about the implications this may have had. When speaking about his illness as a child, there seems to be a strong wish to be regarded as strong because he was able to get over asthma attacks quickly, as if it were no big deal. We do catch a glimpse of a possibility, or perhaps our hope, that for his own sake and perhaps that of his newly placed adoptive child, he would begin to move toward a more valuing of attachment stance as he says, "I should probably do that [show emotions] a bit more."

Two years into his placement, we see the following narrative examples from 7½-year-old Donald Drew's story completions. Donald had been in six previous homes prior to being placed with the Drews. He was placed with a sibling. In terms of the 5-point tally of abusive experiences, Donald scored a 3, at the 40th percentile for the sample. In this first example, the interviewer sets out a scene in which a little boy (designated by Donald to be Sam) has made a drawing at school that he thinks is very good and is then shown going home with it. When asked to show and tell the interviewer what happens next, Donald does as follows (note that Donald involves a brother doll he calls Bill, who is at home when Sam returns with his picture from school):

INTERVIEWER: Can you show and tell me what happens now?

CHILD: And then dad goes . . . Bill goes to answer the door. And then Sam comes and says Mum, Dad, Mum, look at my picture, look, look . . . Will you please get out of the telly?
Mum, I am not inside the telly.
But get out of the way.
But look at my picture.
Oh that's good.

INTERVIEWER: Mummy says that's good.

CHILD: Yeah . . . and then Bill says what about me? What about me?

INTERVIEWER: Then he says show me . . . Wha: What is Bill doing?

CHILD: Jumps up and falls on Sam.

INTERVIEWER: Falls on Sam.

CHILD: Then Sam starts hurting Bill. Stamping on him.

INTERVIEWER: Why is he doing that?

CHILD: Don't like him.

INTERVIEWER: I see, what happens then?

CHILD: The next day, he went back to school and the teacher said, "why did you take your picture home?" He said I thought it was good. I go home . . .

INTERVIEWER: So he went back home.

CHILD: Ding dong. Bill goes to the door and just stands there. [repeated by interviewer]
He doesn't answer the door. [repeated by interviewer]

INTERVIEWER: So what does Sam do?

CHILD: Gets a big hammer and smashes the door open.

INTERVIEWER: What does he do?

CHILD: (Shows doll landing on mother and father dolls on the sofa.)

INTERVIEWER: So he lands on mommy and daddy on sofa?

CHILD: Yeah.

INTERVIEWER: What happens then?

CHILD: And then Bill comes to see what is happening?

INTERVIEWER: So Sam is underneath the sofa now. What is Bill doing?

CHILD: Then he falls out and then the sofa falls on Bill. And no one knows and everyone is saying, "Where is Bill?" But no one knows he is under the sofa.

INTERVIEWER: Why is he under the sofa?

CHILD: 'Cause this happens, the sofa went in the air and landed on him.

INTERVIEWER: So what happens to him?

CHILD: Killed him.

INTERVIEWER: Is that the end of that story?

CHILD: Yes.

INTERVIEWER: In this story, did Mummy and Daddy say anything about the picture Sam did?

CHILD: Dad said that's good.

We see in this story many themes reflecting insecurity and disorganization, including intense sibling rivalry leading to injury and death of a child; bizarre- or atypical-type sequences with a sofa flying through the air and landing on people, which all happen because a child brought home a picture from school about which the child feels "good and proud." It is so interesting that the level of aggression is elicited by a story depicting a positive event, which brings up questions about how a sense of pride in achievement and confidence in attach- ment figures can come to be established when severe adversity, including diverse forms of chronicled abuse, and sudden changes in caregiving have typ- ified the first 5 years of life—and when the new adoptive home is run by par- ents with documented insecurities of their own.

Discussion

The first thing to note is the distribution of parents' AAIs collected prior to the adoptive placement. On the one hand, there is the impressive result that, compared to the general population meta-analysis (n = 889 nonclinical mothers) of van IJzendoorn and Bakermans-Kranenburg (Chapter 3, this volume), in which 20% were dismissing, 55% were observed to be secure–autonomous, 10% were insecure–preoccupied, and 15% were unresolved in four-way groupings, the highly skilled social workers selected more secure–autonomous mothers (68%), and no mothers with insecure–preoccupied states of mind (0%). However, there was also a sizable minority, on the model of the general population, of adoptive mothers whose interviews were classified insecure–dismissing or unresolved. Additionally, the interviews from the adoptive fathers show comparable levels of the secure–autonomous group to that observed in the general population of nonclinical fathers (van IJzendoorn & Bakermans-Kranenburg, 1996), but somewhat higher levels (35%) of insecure–dismissing states of mind, more than twice the level observed (15%) in the general population of nonclinical fathers. It would appear that the social workers' focus veered toward greater sensitivity to the applicant mothers. This is important because, as we discuss, at least in this first study, having a secure–autonomous mother *or* father appears equally predictive of a better outcome in terms of the adoptive child's attachment representations. Because we know that there is a world-wide acute shortage of appropriate foster and adoptive parents willing to accept a school-age child with a history of maltreatment, special attention could be paid to the attachment states of mind of interested fathers— especially because these men could make all the difference and their potential might be too easily overlooked. For an attachment-informed model of how the interest of adoptive fathers and adoptive mothers can be cultivated and supported, there are now a variety of valuable resources (see Bick & Dozier, Chapter 18, this volume; Steele et al., 2007).

We turn next to our findings regarding insecurity and disorganization in the attachment narratives from the adopted children after 2 years in the adoptive home. Our previous (Hodges et al., 2005) report that negative themes in the adopted children's stories decline over time can now be qualified. For some children, it would appear that the themes of insecurity and disorganization in their attachment narratives remained high or escalated over time, that is, in those children who had *both* of their parents' AAIs judged insecure prior to the adoptive placement. On the other hand, insecure and disorganized themes did decline for other children, the vast majority of whom who were placed with one or more adoptive parents whose AAIs were classified secure–autonomous. In other words, the current findings support and extend the results reported in Steele and colleagues (2003), that being placed with a secure–autonomous (as opposed to insecure–dismissing or –preoccupied or unresolved) adoptive mother led to significantly lower levels of insecurity within 3 months of placement. Here we have shown that this pattern continues to hold after 2 years in the adoptive home, and this positive outlook is evident if *either* parent's AAI was secure–autonomous at placement. Below we examine how we might understand this link between parents' AAI responses and their children's attachment story completions, collected 2 years after placement in the adoptive home.

How is it that parental attachment states of mind are transmitted in these unique situations when the child has endured significant and prolonged adversity before beginning the new relationship? First, we are mindful that for all children in the study, the adoption involved dramatic changes in their caregiving environments, with permanence over 2 years being a radical and welcome arrangement. And in this respect it is noteworthy that for the full sample of late-adopted children there was steady and increasing evidence of more secure narrative themes across the three time periods of observation covering the first 2 years in the adoptive home (Hodges et al., 2005). That for some of the sample this was accompanied by a significant decline in insecure and disorganized themes suggests that the permanence of the new adoptive home penetrated, and changed, more deeply the inner world of the adopted child. Daniel Stern has recently written on how subjective experiences must reflect actual lived experiences to achieve change:

> The basic assumption is that change is based on lived experience. In and of itself, verbally understanding, explaining or narrating something is not sufficient to bring about change. There must also be an actual experience, a subjectively lived happening. An event must be *lived* with feelings and actions taking place in real time, in the real world, with real people, in a moment of presentness. (Stern, 2004, p. xiii, original emphasis)

We think this description is especially pertinent to imagining how the experiences in children's daily lives impacted their attachment representations, so that secure themes were likely to increase over time. These ideas bring us back to some of Bowlby's early writings on how the actual experience of the child in interaction with the caregiver is of crucial importance. Relative to the traumatic histories of the adopted children in our study, Bowlby had sobering thoughts on the influence of early experiences on later development:

> Once a sequence of behaviour has become organized, it tends to persist and does so even if it has developed on non-functional lines and even in the absence of the external stimuli and/ or the internal conditions on which it first depended. The precise form that any particular piece of behaviour takes and the sequence within which it is first organized are thus of the greatest consequence for its future. (1973, p. 201)

This perspective raises questions about the extent to which current positive "lived experience" (Stern, 2004) may overwrite, transmute, or otherwise change early harsh experiences. Clues as to how such comprehensive change may happen come from the children in our study who showed not only a rise in secure themes (Hodges et al., 2005), but also a decline in disorganized and insecure themes (Steele et al., 2003). These fortunate children, the vast majority of the current sample, had been living in a new adoptive home for more than 2 years with one or both parents whose AAIs at placement were categorized autonomous–secure. Given what we know about the strong stability of AAI security over time (see Crowell, Treboux, & Waters, 2002), we can assume that the autonomy and security observed in one or both parents at placement remained and spread across other family members, including the newest family member with a harsh past. How did this security spread? We speculate that it did so because the secure adoptive parent was open to the entire range of emotions shown by the adopted child, both positive *and* negative. This we know to be a defining feature of parents who facilitate a secure attachment in the children: They not only support and enjoy their children's exploration and play, forming a secure base, but they are also attuned to signs of distress, concern, or protest from their infants, thus creating a safe haven. The probable characteristics of the ongoing, day-to-day interactions that typify children and their autonomous–secure, as opposed to insecure (dismissing, preoccupied, unresolved) mothers may be conceived of in the following way. Of central importance, commonly seen in mothers of securely attached children, is the spontaneous and balanced readiness to respond to and discuss negative emotions openly (Grossmann, Grossmann, & Schwan, 1986; Laible & Thompson, 1998; Steele, Steele, Croft, & Fonagy, 1999). Truthfulness in conversations that include but are not overburdened by negative emotion may indeed be the core feature of secure–autonomous relationships (see Cassidy, 2001). This perspective would seem to be one that is shared by Mr. and Mrs. Smith, who both emphasized, in their AAIs (cited earlier in the Results section), the value they place on truthfulness. It is not difficult to take delight in the joy of young children; the challenge is to take notice of their distress and respond without becoming overwhelmed by, or derogating of, their negative emotional displays.

Trying to delineate how parental representations lead to qualities of interacting with their older adopted child, which in turn lead the child to form attachment representations with more secure and less insecure and disorganized themes, has been the focus of a recent chapter based on close observations of parent–child interactions in the context of adoption (Steele et al., 2007). That work highlighted the value of adoptive parents addressing their children by name, referencing shared personal experiences, and being able to "override any inclination they feel to ignore or reprimand the child, and instead see the child's behavior as a wish to be included" (Steele et al., 2007, p. 80). By contrast, other adoptive parents in that work, whom we here speculate to have had insecure AAIs, showed a troubling, adverse cyclical pattern of parent–child interaction, including parents and children exchanging negative facial expressions and insensitive touch in the context of sparse impersonal conversation.

We finish this chapter by summarizing two main findings from our study of attachment representations in previously maltreated children and their adoptive parents, and pointing to practical implications.

1. In comparison to nonclinical samples, the AAIs from the adoptive mothers revealed greater than expected levels of secure–autonomous states of mind, whereas the interviews from the fathers revealed greater than expected levels of insecure–dismissing states of mind.
2. In terms of the attachment narratives collected from the adopted children 2 years into placement, security had increased significantly for all the children (compared to early in the adoptive placement), but insecurity and disorganization *were significantly lower* in those children placed with parents in which a secure–autonomous state of mind prevailed in at least one parent's AAI.

We conclude that the AAI may be a useful way of both forecasting positive outcomes for children with complicated traumatic histories and identifying adoptive parents toward whom therapeutic and social support services may be most prudently directed. Furthermore, our findings point to the spreading effect of attachment security: Given a couple taking the brave step of providing a permanent home for a child who has known only disruption and a lack of permanency, the attachment security likely to be sufficient for the child if, at placement, *only one* member of the couple (mother or father) is secure–autonomous.

Acknowledgment

We are grateful for the generous support of the Sainsbury Family trusts (the Tedworth Charitable Trust and the Glass-House Trust).

References

Bowlby, J. (1973). *Attachment and loss: Vol. 1. Attachment.* New York: Basic Books.
Bretherton, I., & Oppenheim, D. (2003). The MacArthur Story Stem Battery: Development, administration, reliability, validity, and reflections about meaning. In R. Emde, D. Wolf, & D. Oppenheim (Eds.), *Revealing the inner worlds of young children: The MacArthur Story Stem Battery and parent–child narratives* (pp. 55–80). New York: Oxford University Press.
Cassidy, J. (2001). Truth, lies, and intimacy: An attachment perspective. *Attachment and Human Development, 3,* 121–155.
Cooper, G., Hoffman, K., Powell, B., & Marvin, R. (2005). The Circle of Security intevention: Differential diagnosis and differential treatment. In L. J. Berlin, Y. Ziv, L. Amaya-Jackson, & M. T. Greenberg (Eds.), *Enhancing early attachments: Theory, research, intervention, and policy* (pp. 127–151). New York: Guilford Press.
Crowell, J. A., Treboux, D., & Waters, E. (2002). Stability of attachment representations: The transition to marriage. *Developmental Psychology, 38,* 467–479.
Dozier, M., Chase-Stovall, K., Albus, K., & Bates, B. (2001). Attachment for infants in

foster care: The role of caregiver state of mind. *Child Development, 72*(5), 1467–1477.

Dozier, M., Higley, E., Albus, K., & Nutter, A. (2002). Intervening with foster infants' caregivers: Targeting three critical needs. *Infant Mental Health Journal, 23*, 541–554.

Emde, R., Wolf, D., & Oppenheim, D. (Eds.). (2003). *Revealing the inner worlds of young children: The MacArthur Story Stem Battery and parent–child narratives.* New York: Oxford University Press.

Gloger-Tippelt, G., Gomille, B., Kooenig, L., & Vetter, J. (2002). Attachment representations in 6-year olds: Related longitudinally to the quality of attachment in infancy and mother's attachment representations. *Attachment and Human Development, 4*(3), 318–399.

Goldwyn, R., Stanley, C., Smith, V., & Green, J. (2000). The Manchester Child Attachment Story Task: Relationship with parental AAI, SAT, and child behaviour. *Attachment and Human Development, 2*(1), 71–84.

Grossmann, K. E., Grossmann, K., & Schwan, A. (1986). Capturing the wider view of attachment: A reanalysis of Ainsworth's Strange Situation. In C. E. Izard & P. B. Read (Eds.), *Measuring emotion in infants and children* (Vol. 2, pp. 124–171). New York: Cambridge University Press.

Hesse, E. (1999). The Adult Attachment Interview: Historical and current perspectives. In J. Cassidy & P. R. Shaver (Eds.), *Handbook of attachment: Theory, research, and clinical applications* (pp. 395–433). New York: Guilford Press.

Hodges, J., Steele, M., Hillman, S., & Henderson, K. (2003). Mental representations and defences in severely maltreated children: A story stem battery and rating system for clinical assessment and research applications. In R. Emde, D. Wolf, C. Zahn-Waxler, & D. Oppenheim (Eds.), *Narrative processes and the transition from infancy to early childhood* (pp. 240–267). New York: Oxford University Press.

Hodges, J., Steele, M., Hillman, S., Henderson, K., & Kaniuk, J. (2005). Change and continuity in mental representations of attachment after adoption. In D. Brodzinsky & J. Palacios (Eds.), *Psychological issues in adoption* (pp. 93–116). Westport, CT: Praeger.

Laible, D. J., & Thompson, R. A. (1998). Attachment and emotional understanding in preschool children. *Developmental Psychology, 34*, 1038–1045.

Main, M., Goldwyn, R., & Hesse, E. (2003). *Adult Attachment Classification System, Version 7.2.* Unpublished manuscript, University of California at Berkeley.

Main, M., & Hesse, E. (1990). Parents' unresolved traumatic experiences are related to infant disorganised attachment status: Is frightened and/or frightening parental behaviour the linking mechanism? In M. T. Greenberg, D. Cicchetti, & E. M. Cummings (Eds.), *Attachment in the preschool years: Theory, research and intervention* (pp. 161–182). Chicago: University of Chicago Press.

Miller, B., Fam, X., Grotevant, H., Christensen, M., Coyl, D., & Van Dulmen, M. (2000). Adopted adolescents' overrepresentation in mental health counseling: Adoptees' problem or parents' lower threshold for referral? *Journal of the American Academy of Child and Adolescent Psychiatry, 39*, 1504–1511.

O'Connor, T., & Zeanah, C. (2003). Attachment disorders: Assessment strategies and treatment approaches. *Attachment and Human Development, 5*, 223–244.

Steele, H., Steele, M., Croft, C., & Fonagy, P. (1999). Infant–mother attachment at one-year predicts children's understanding of mixed-emotions at six years. *Social Development*, 8, 161–178.

Steele, H., Steele, M., & Fonagy, P. (1996). Associations among attachment classifications of mothers, fathers, and their infants: Evidence for a relationship-specific perspective. *Child Development*, 67, 541–555.

Steele, M., Hodges, J., Kaniuk, J., Steele, H., D'Agostino, D., Blom, I., et al. (2007). Intervening with maltreated children and their adoptive families: Identifying attachment-facilitative behaviors. In D. Oppenheim & D. F. Goldsmith (Eds.), *Attachment theory in clinical work with children* (pp. 58–89). New York: Guilford Press.

Steele, M., Steele, H., Woolgar, M., Yabsley, S., Johnson, D., Fonagy, P., et al. (2003). Children's emotion narratives reflect their parents' dreams. In R. Emde, D. Wolf, C. Zahn-Waxler, & D. Oppenheim (Eds.), *Narrative processes and the transition from infancy to early childhood*. New York: Oxford University Press.

Stern, D. (2004). *The present moment in psychotherapy and everyday life*. New York: Norton.

Toth, S. L., Cicchetti, D., MacFie, J., & Emde, R. N. (1997). Representations of self and others in the narratives of neglected, physically abused, and sexually abused preschoolers. *Developmental Psychopathology*, 9, 781–796.

van IJzendoorn, M., & Bakermans-Kranenburg, M. J. (1996). Attachment representations in mothers, fathers, adolescents, and clinical groups: A meta-analytic search for normative data. *Journal of Consulting and Clinical Psychology*, 64, 8–21.

van IJzendoorn, M., & Juffer, F. (2006). The Emmanuel Miller Memorial Lecture 2006: Adoption as intervention: Meta-analytic evidence for massive catch up and plasticity in physical, socioemotional and cognitive development. *Journal of Child Psychology and Psychiatry*, 47, 1228–1245.

Warren, S. (2003). Narratives in risk and clinical populations. In R. Emde, D. Wolf, & D. Oppenheim (Eds.), *Revealing the inner worlds of young children: The MacArthur Story Stem Battery and parent–child narratives* (pp. 222–239). New York: Oxford University Press.

18

Helping Foster Parents Change

The Role of Parental State of Mind

JOHANNA BICK and MARY DOZIER

The Adult Attachment Interview (AAI; George, Kaplan, & Main, 1996) is a rich clinical and research instrument. In a matter of 60–90 minutes, it is possible with this instrument to uncover characteristic ways that the individual approaches attachment-relevant memories, thoughts, and feelings. The AAI reveals the individual's "state of mind with regard to attachment" (Main, Goldwyn, & Hesse, 2003). In our work, we have developed an intervention program to help foster parents provide nurturing, sensitive care to their children. The task for parent trainers is very different depending on parents' state of mind. The AAI is integral to what we do in terms of tailoring a manualized treatment procedure, and in the predictions we make regarding treatment use and effectiveness. In this chapter, we describe the use of the AAI in this work.

Our intervention targets several key needs for babies in foster care. With regard to each of these issues, parental state of mind is important, because it helps us to identify how to help parents alter their views of parenting, as well as to appraise how open parents are to the possibility of change. We have found that babies who enter foster care are especially in need of nurturing care (Dozier, Stovall, Albus, & Bates, 2001). Two different things may get in the way of their receiving nurturing care. First, the babies themselves may fail to elicit nurturance (Stovall & Dozier, 2000; Stovall-McClough & Dozier, 2004). We have found that many infants in foster care are avoidant or resistant when distressed, making the foster parents' job difficult. Reinterpreting behavioral signals appears easier for parents with autonomous states of mind than for parents who are not autonomous. Second, foster parents' state of mind with regard to attachment may directly interfere with their provision of nurturing care. Our training emphasizes the importance of providing nurturing care when babies are distressed, even when caregivers are not comfortable providing it. Third, foster children are often dysregulated at behavioral and biobehavioral levels; caregivers need to provide a responsive, controllable environment, so that children's regulatory capabilities are developed. Following the child's lead flies in the face of some parents' view of appropriate parenting, and this is often linked with parental state of mind. The intervention we have developed is called the Attachment and Biobehavioral Catch-up intervention. We describe the components of this intervention in more detail and discuss how parental state of mind affects the delivery of the intervention and the use of training with regard to each component.

To this point, we have delivered parent training in the context of a randomized clinical trial to a sample of 200 foster parents. Foster parents are randomly assigned to receive the Attachment and Biobehavioral Catch-up intervention or a control intervention of the same duration and frequency. The control intervention was modified from a program originally designed to enhance children's cognitive and linguistic capabilities (Ramey, McGinness, Cross, Collier, & Barrie-Blackley, 1982; Ramey, Yeates, & Short, 1984). We call our modification of this control intervention developmental education for families. We administer the AAI prior to beginning both of the manualized trainings. Six parent trainers conduct the Attachment and Biobehavioral Catch-up intervention program. The parent trainer assigned to administer the Attachment and Biobehavioral Catch-up intervention to a certain foster parent and infant always conducts the that parent's AAI, because this session marks the beginning of the clinical relationship.

Preliminary results provide support for the efficacy of the Attachment and Biobehavioral Catch-up intervention. Children whose foster parents have received the Attachment and Biobehavioral Catch-up intervention show fewer behavior problems compared with children whose foster parents have received the Developmental Education for Families intervention program (Dozier, Peloso, et al., in press). Foster children who participated in the Attachment and Biobehavioral Catch-up intervention showed lower cortisol values across the day when compared with foster children assigned to the control treatment. Additionally, caregivers who received the Attachment and Biobehavioral Catch-up intervention reported that their children showed less avoidance when distressed than did caregivers who received the control intervention (Dozier, Brohawn, Lindhiem, Perkins, & Peloso, in press).

Attachment State of Mind

Bowlby (1969/1982) suggested that individuals develop mental representations or "internal working models" on the basis of early relationship experiences. Internal working models are hypothesized to be carried forward in the context of stable, consistent care and to shape the formation of future inter-personal relationships. Internal working models are thought to serve as a tem-plate for parent–child relationships, as well as romantic relationships (Hazan & Shaver, 1987), friendships, and treatment relationships (Bowlby, 1988; Dozier, 1990; Dozier, Cue, & Barnett, 1994; Korfmacher, Adam, Ogawa, & Egeland, 1997).

The AAI was developed by Mary Main and colleagues (George et al., 1996) to assess an adults' internal working model of relationships, or their state of mind with regard to attachment. Attachment state of mind is assessed by examining the adult's memories, thoughts, and feelings about attachment experiences and attachment figures. Individuals who are coherent in their ver-bal conceptualization and discussion of attachment-related experiences are said to be "autonomous" with regard to attachment. This is seen in high scores on interview discourse coherence and metacognitive abilities. Such indi-viduals present a consistent and reflective presentation of their early child-hood experiences. These adults are likely to have babies with secure attach-ments to them, that is, babies who show attachment needs directly and are soothed effectively by them (van IJzendoorn, 1995). Links from parent state of mind to parent behavior to child attachment have not demonstrated that parent behavior mediates (or accounts for) the association between state of mind and attachment (Madigan, Moran, & Pederson, 2006; van IJzendoorn, 1995). Nonetheless, it seems likely, for example, that adults who are comfort-able reflecting upon both negative and positive attachment-related events are able to respond effectively to their child's distress.

Individuals who dismiss or devalue attachment-related experiences are classified as having a "dismissing" state of mind with regard to attachment. Often, the interviews of dismissing adults suggest that early experiences have remained largely unexplored or pushed away from current attention. This is seen in elevated scores on scales measuring the extent to which early attach-ment representations are idealized or derogated. These adults most often have babies with avoidant attachments to them, that is, babies that turn away from them when distressed. Presumably, these adults' discomfort with their own attachment issues leads them to minimize children's show of attachment needs.

Individuals who are identified as having a "preoccupied" state of mind with regard to attachment have difficulty staying on topic when questions about their childhood experiences are raised during the AAI. These individu-als present an unclear, incoherent picture of their early experiences. This is associated with high scores on scales measuring discourse passivity and involving anger, and low scores on discourse coherence. These adults most often have babies with resistant attachments, that is, babies that fuss and resist the parent when distressed. Presumably, these adults' own issues inter-fere with their being consistently responsive to their babies.

Mothers who are classified as "unresolved" show a breakdown in rea-soning or discourse when discussing loss or trauma during the AAI. For example, an unresolved state of mind may be seen in the mother losing track of time while discussing a traumatic event, or showing a lapse in reasoning while discussing difficult traumatic experiences. These adults most often have babies with "disorganized" attachments, that is, babies who show a lack of an organized strategy or a breakdown in strategy when distressed. Presumably, when unresolved about loss or abuse, the parent is vulnerable to behaving in ways that are frightening to the child (Schuengel, 1997; Schuengel, Bakermans-Kranenburg, & van IJzendoorn, 1999), leading the child to become disorganized when distressed.

State of Mind and Foster Caregiver Treatment Use

Given that attachment state of mind reflects an individual's approach to his or her own attachment issues, it is not surprising that state of mind is associated with how an individual reacts to, and uses, treatment. We found in earlier work in our lab that state of mind was related to how open and receptive people with serious psychiatric disorders were to receiving help from their case managers (Dozier, 1990). More specifically, greater autonomy was associated with better use of treatment. Relative to those who were less dismissing, people who were more dismissing were more rejecting of treatment and disclosed less to treatment providers.

Consistent with these findings, Korfmacher and colleagues (1997) found that state of mind was important among high-risk mothers who were offered intervention services. A mother's state of mind was associated with her participation in treatment, and the type of intervention she received. More specifically, mothers with autonomous states of mind showed higher levels of commitment to treatment than did mothers with dismissing states of mind. Compared with unresolved mothers, autonomous mothers showed higher levels of participation, fewer treatment roadblocks, and more positive relationships with the treatment facilitator and other participants in a group setting.

In the Attachment and Biobehavioral Catch-up intervention, descriptive analyses of foster parents who took part in the program revealed that 54% of the parents were coded as secure–autonomous, 22% were classified as dismissing, and 24% were classified as having an unresolved state of mind. Only one foster parent was classified as preoccupied. Importantly, this caregiver was also classified as unresolved (Dozier et al., 2001). Observation of intervention sessions, as well as the parent–trainer report of the foster parent and the sessions, reveals that foster caregivers with autonomous states of mind participate in the intervention program openly, collaboratively, and nondefensively, and demonstrate a high level of cooperation toward the tasks of the intervention. In many ways, the manner in which an autonomous caregiver approaches the intervention sessions reflects the mother's discussion of her early experiences in the AAI. In the intervention sessions, as in the AAI, high levels of, metacognitive monitoring, coherency, and openness to discuss potentially painful or sensitive topics without minimizing the experiencing or becoming enmeshed, characterize the mother's approach to the treatment. In line with previous examinations of the role of state of mind in treatment use (see Afterword by Jacobvitz, Chapter 15 by Moran et al., and Chapter 5 by Teti et al., this volume), autonomous foster caregivers appear open to suggestions about parenting, are also generally receptive to the clinician's guidance, and are reflective about the ways their own childhood experiences affect current parenting practices toward the infants in their care.

The training is more challenging for mothers with dismissing states of mind than for those with autonomous states of mind. Consistent with the Korfmacher and colleagues (1997) findings, dismissing caregivers involved in the Attachment and Biobehavioral Catch-up intervention tend to show greater levels of discomfort and defensiveness than other parents when discussing attachment-related issues (Dozier & Sepulveda, 2004). Dismissing caregivers often idealize the care they received from their parents, making it difficult to explore these issues as they relate to the care they provide to their children. In addition, such a caregiver often resists discussing the child's need for nurturance and emphasizes that the child for whom she cares is spoiled. Parent trainers are required to work harder to reduce resistance of dismissing parents compared to other parents when discussing relationship difficulties. Previous work has indicated that foster children with dismissing caregivers are at increased risk for developing disorganized (rather than avoidant) attachments (Dozier et al., 2001). Thus, it appears especially important that dismissing parents provide nurturing parenting, even though it may not "come naturally" to them.

Although few foster mothers in the Infant–Caregiver Project have been classified as having a preoccupied state of mind with regard to attachment, preoccupied caregivers face unique challenges throughout the intervention sessions. Previous work involving preoccupied caregivers has revealed that they appear comfortable turning to the treatment provider for help but subsequently have difficulty maintaining focus on the treatment tasks (Dozier, 1990; Dozier & Tyrrell, 1997). Preoccupied caregivers involved in the Attachment and Biobehavioral Catch-up intervention tend to become caught up or enmeshed in topics introduced during the intervention sessions. This parallels preoccupied caregivers' frequent high scores on passivity of discourse, and involving anger when discussing a primary caregiver. Parent trainers working with preoccupied caregivers are required to redirect the focus of the intervention to the child's needs for consistent, nurturing care.

Caregivers who are classified as unresolved with regard to loss or trauma tend to face distinct hurdles throughout the treatment process (see Moran et al., Chapter 15, this volume). In that unresolved caregivers remain disorganized with regard to a past loss or trauma, some of the intervention tasks are especially challenging for them. Parent trainers help parents to consider how their own attachment-related experiences affect their responses to the children in their care. Furthermore, issues of having been frightened as a child are addressed very specifically. These are difficult issues for unresolved parents, but they are key to caring for children who have experienced their own traumas. Consistent with the findings of Korfmacher and colleagues (1997), parents who are unresolved have difficulty developing trusting relationships with therapists and committing to the treatment program. Additionally, unresolved caregivers struggle with sessions that focus on behaving in nonthreatening ways toward their children.

Given the association between state of mind and approach toward treatment (Dozier, 1990; Dozier & Tyrrell, 1997; Korfmacher et al., 1997), the consideration of attachment state of mind when working with foster mothers and infants throughout the Attachment and Biobehavioral Catch-up intervention program is critical. Appreciation of the parent's state of mind can provide the clinician with expectations of challenges that are likely to affect the course of treatment. Such expectations allow the clinician to work most effectively by tailoring the treatment to the caregiver's individual needs. In the following sections we discuss how parent trainers deliver each of the three components of the intervention to foster parents, while keeping in mind the parents' state of mind with regard to attachment.

Intervention for Foster Caregivers and Infants

The Attachment and Biobehavioral Catch-up intervention incorporates findings from previous research highlighting three critical issues of foster mothers and infants. Infants who experience disruptions in care often behave in ways that fail to elicit nurturance from their caregivers (Stovall & Dozier, 2000; Stovall-McClough & Dozier, 2004). The first component of the intervention helps foster caregivers learn to reinterpret their infants' signals when foster infants display alienating behaviors. In particular, caregivers are helped to see that the children in their care need nurturance, even if it is not apparent.

Children placed in foster care are especially at risk for developing disorganized attachments. In particular, if not placed with autonomous caregivers, these children develop disorganized attachments at high rates (Dozier et al., 2001). The second component of the intervention emphasizes the importance of providing a nurturing and caring environment, even when it does not come naturally to the parent. Parent trainers work closely with foster parents to help them override their own issues that may interfere with providing nurturing care.

Infants depend on their caregivers to help them regulate their emotions and physiology, until they are gradually able to take over self-soothing capabilities on their own. The experiences of disruptions in care and/or maltreatment leave children at risk for physiological, behavioral, and emotional dysregulation. This dysregulation has been observed among human and nonhuman infants who have been separated from parents (Dozier et al., 2006; Levine & Stanton, 1990). The third intervention component targets dysregulation by helping the parent learn to follow the child's lead (Barnard & Morisset, 1995), to touch and hold the child (Field, Hernandez-Reif, Diego, Schanberg, & Kuhn, 2005; Field et al., 2004), and to allow the expression of negative emotion. Focusing on these critical needs is expected to help infants in foster care develop adequate self-regulatory capabilities.

These intervention components are introduced through 10 sessions in the parents' homes. Caregivers' state of mind affect their responses to the intervention content. Whereas autonomous caregivers are generally open to the intervention content and grasp the concepts easily, parent trainers spend more time helping nonautonomous caregivers to "override" their natural behaviors.

In many sessions foster parents have an opportunity to practice the intervention topic. For example, foster parents are videotaped while they follow their children's lead or as they provide nurturance following a brief separation. Parent trainers reinforce their positive behaviors during the interactions and while the parent trainers and foster parents review the videotaped interaction. At the completion of the session, parent trainers encourage parents to employ the new technique over the next week, even if it does not come naturally, and to record their experiences in doing so. The first portion of the next session is always devoted to a discussion about the previous week. Through this process, parent trainers help foster parents to be cognizant of their initial reactions and beliefs that may prevent them from providing nurturance or from following the child's lead. Foster parents are helped to respond in ways that override these automatic responses and allow for sensitive and nurturing care.

Caregiver State of Mind and the First Component (Providing Nurturance When It Is Not Elicited)

When babies are placed into foster care after about 1 year of age, they tend to behave in ways that may suggest to their caregivers that they do not need them (Stovall & Dozier, 2000; Stovall-McClough & Dozier, 2004). In particular, foster infants tend to behave in avoidant or resistant ways when distressed. In response to the infants' alienating behavior during times of distress, foster mothers tend to behave "in kind" to the avoidant or resistant behaviors (Stovall-McClough & Dozier, 2004). When babies behave in avoidant ways, foster mothers tend to ignore them. When babies behave in resistant ways, foster mothers tend to respond in fussy, irritable ways themselves. These transactional effects are seen among foster parent–child dyads regardless of caregiver state of mind. Given that caregiver nurturance is critical to the children's ability to develop an organized attachment, children's failure to elicit nurturance in the early months of placement is problematic.

The first component of the targeted treatment focuses on teaching caregivers to reinterpret infants' alienating behaviors. Parent trainers help foster parents see that the infants in their care need them, even though their behaviors suggest otherwise. In this sense, caregivers are taught to respond therapeutically to their infants' alienating behaviors. Emphasis is placed on foster infants' need for nurturance, especially in times of distress, regardless of what infants appear to be communicating overtly. Foster caregivers are first taught to recognize their children's alienating behaviors, such as pushing the caregiver away or turning away when upset, and to think of the impact that these behaviors have on the care they are inclined to give. Caregivers are then helped to learn to reinterpret the infants' behaviors, to see that their children *do* need them. Abilities to understand, recognize, and reinterpret alienating behaviors allow caregivers to provide nurturance even when their infants fail to elicit it.

One of the ways this is handled in an intervention session is through the review of a diary record of episodes when the child appeared distressed over the past week (completed as homework between sessions). Both the child's behavior and the caregiver's response to the distress are discussed. In the discussion, the parent trainer highlights the child's secure, avoidant, or resistant behavior, while illustrating how the caregiver responded in each circumstance. Indications that the child needs the caregiver are highlighted, as are any signs of nurturance provided by the caregiver. In this session, it is critical that the caregiver is helped to see that the child values her and/or to see her own strengths in responding in a nurturing fashion. In instances when the infant has displayed avoidant or resistant behaviors, the parent's trainer emphasizes how powerful the infant's behavior is in eliciting complementary responses. The parent is helped to see how difficult, but how critical, it is to behave in nurturing ways even when they are not always elicited by the infant.

For caregivers with autonomous states of mind, the two sessions introducing this issue are typically uncomplicated. Caregivers often have an "aha" experience, and easily recognize that they were being put off by their children's behaviors. They often spontaneously generate examples of times when this has occurred in the past. In the second session, autonomous foster mothers often report having changed their behavior as the result of the intervention, which is consistent with the parent trainer's impressions.

In general, the first intervention component is not especially threatening, even for dismissing foster parents. Because it is *about the child*, dismissing parents do not feel as challenged as they do when the focus is more on their own issues. Nonetheless, the message of the first two sessions is to provide nurturance even when babies do not indicate that they need it—something that is at odds with the parenting philosophy of most dismissing parents. Dismissing parents often indicate that they are doing exactly what we are suggesting (whatever it might be), and that they do not have any problems in parenting. It is essential that parent trainers gently challenge such parents to consider times when they felt pushed away, or when they found it difficult to be available to the child. This takes persistence and confidence on the part of the parent trainer. Just as it is easy for the foster parent to "buy" the child's presentation that he or she does not need the parent, it is easy for the parent trainer to "buy" the foster parent's presentation that she is doing just what she needs to do for the infant. Therapeutic work involves not buying the parent's presentation, though, but in a nonthreatening manner challenging her to change.

Foster caregivers with a preoccupied state of mind with regard to attachment also have difficulty focusing on the needs of the child and reinterpreting the child's alienating behavior. Preoccupied caregivers' tendencies to become enmeshed in attachment experiences make it difficult for them to maintain sufficient focus on the infant so that they can reinterpret the infant's alienating behaviors. The parent trainer is required to work closely with the preoccupied caregiver to maintain focus on the infant's underlying need for nurturance.

Caregiver State of Mind and the Second Component (Providing Nurturance When It Does Not Come Naturally)

The second component of the intervention focuses on caregivers' issues that interfere with nurturing their foster infants during times of distress. Whereas the first component emphasizes the role of infants' behaviors in failing to elicit nurturance, the second component explores the importance of the caregivers' contributions. In addressing this component, an emphasis is placed on helping caregivers recognize what goes through their heads when their children seek reassurance from them. They are helped to think about their own attachment experiences that may affect their reactions to their children during times of distress. Finally, parents are helped to consider overriding their previously automatic thoughts and feelings, so that they can provide nurturance.

For autonomous parents, the issues raised in these sessions may be sensitive and even challenging but nonetheless compatible with their usual approach to the world. It is with dismissing parents that the sessions are particularly difficult and at odds with parents' characteristic approach to the world. Given that parent trainers have conducted the AAIs themselves, they enter these sessions with a sense of the issues that are likely to arise. The most likely response, and quite consistent with many dismissing parents' states of mind, is the insistence that the parents' own caregivers were very responsive and available, and that there just are *not* any issues that affect caregiving currently. We attempt to handle this in a paradoxical way. We point out that everyone has times during parenting that are difficult, and that acknowledging such issues represents a personal strength. Thus, we attempt to turn what would be perceived as a weakness (acknowledging a difficult issue in caregiving) into a strength. This handling of the issue is clearly not magical: What is required on the part of the parent trainer is sensitivity and persistence. It is a "chipping away" process in which we ask parents to open up very gradually (though within several sessions) to explore things that have been largely unexplored.

The intent is not to change parents' states of mind. Rather, the intent is to make parents sensitive to "voices from their past," so that these thoughts and resulting actions are no longer automatic. Once parents become aware of their previously automatic thoughts (e.g., "You'll spoil that child if you pick him up"), they can choose to behave in a way that is consistent or inconsistent with the "voice." Thus, we try to get parents to become aware of automatic thoughts, and to *override* these thoughts.

During the sessions, parent trainers and caregivers discuss instances when it may be difficult to provide nurturance to the infants in their care. The activities in this session encourage foster caregivers to recognize their feelings in the moment, when their infants need them, yet respond sensitively to their infants regardless of their natural inclinations. Parent trainers help parents understand the need to override their automatic responses and respond sensitively to their children's needs.

Parent trainers talk with dismissing caregivers about the challenge of responding sensitively to their infants, when they themselves may not have received nurturance as young children. Caregivers are helped to see how their own histories affect how they react to their children's distress. For example, when hearing her baby cry, previous experiences may lead a dismissing mother to think, "Don't be a baby. You're not hurt, you just want attention." She then says to herself, "Wait, that's just the voice from my past. Of course he's hurt and he needs me." She then can pick her baby up and soothe him. Again, the primary goal of the intervention is not to change the initial reaction of caregivers, but to help them override this first reaction and provide nurturance.

Caregivers with preoccupied states of mind with regard to attachment tend to be more comfortable than dismissing caregivers with exploring how past attachment-related experiences may affect their current behaviors. However, preoccupied caregivers differ from autonomous caregivers in that the examination of past experiences may become the primary focus of the session. Foster caregivers with preoccupied states of mind therefore have difficulty consistently focusing on and responding immediately to their children's needs. Throughout the sessions, they are helped to see how their own needs may supercede their children's at times, making it difficult for them to respond in nurturing ways. Thus, although the first inclination they may have when their children need them is "Not right now, I'm busy," they are helped to see that children who have experienced adversity need sensitive care promptly, whenever possible. This allows them to override their automatic responses to take care of their own needs rather than their children's.

Caregiver State of Mind and the Third Component (Providing a Responsive Environment)

The third intervention component helps caregivers provide a responsive and predictable environment that enhances children's regulatory capabilities. Infants in foster care often show physiological dysregulation, even when they may appear to have adjusted to their new environment (Dozier et al., 2006). This phase of the intervention helps caregivers provide a controllable, responsive interpersonal environment for their infants. This is accomplished primarily through teaching foster parents to follow their children's lead in interactions, to behave in ways that are nonthreatening to their children, and to hold and to touch their children.

As with the first and second components, caregivers' response patterns vary according to state of mind. Consistent with responses to the first and second components, caregivers with autonomous states of mind tend to express a higher level of comfort and ease with these tasks than do nonautonomous caregivers. Parent trainers are required to anticipate obstacles that prevent dismissing, preoccupied, or unresolved caregivers from grasping and utilizing knowledge gained from these sessions. Given dismissing caregivers' tendencies to show more discomfort with attachment-related activities (Dozier, 1990), they often struggle with the concept of following the child's lead. Because dismissing mothers prefer some interpersonal distance, they are likely to adopt a teaching style when interacting with their children (Korfmacher et al., 1997). Therefore, parent trainers need to help dismissing caregivers understand the importance of following their children's lead during the interaction, because it helps create a controllable interpersonal environment for their children. Given preoccupied foster mothers' difficulty focusing on the needs of their children, parent trainers are required to help them stay tuned to their children's actions and follow their children's lead during play, without losing focus.

Unresolved caregivers also struggle with this component of the intervention. Foster parents with unresolved states of mind often find that some aspects of the third component (following the child's lead in play or providing physical comfort) are not especially challenging. However, sessions devoted to reducing frightening behavior toward their infants often prove to be difficult. An unresolved state of mind with regard to past trauma or loss has been associated with exhibiting behavior that is frightening to children (Schuengel, 1997; Schuengel et al., 1999) and that increases risk for infants in foster care to develop disorganized attachment classifications. Parent trainers spend time helping unresolved foster parents respond to children in a way that is predictable, even if their natural tendency is to play too roughly or to interact in a way that is threatening or scary.

Varied Experience of Caregivers in the Intervention

The role of the client–therapist relationship in treatment has long been emphasized as a primary determinant of treatment success (e.g., Beutler, Clarkin, Crago, & Bergen, 1991). In the Attachment and Biobehavioral Catch-up intervention, the relationship between the parent trainer and the foster mother is an important aspect of the treatment process. In that one intervention goal is to help caregivers openly consider how they are parenting their children, trust is critical for acceptance and use of the intervention concepts. Autonomous caregivers are typically more accepting of the parent trainer and intervention initially than are nonautonomous parents. Conversely, nonautonomous parents require more time to develop trusting relationships than do autonomous parents. Whereas the length of time to establish a trusting relationship varies, the relationship between parent trainer and foster parent is of utmost importance for robust treatment effects (Horvath & Luborsky, 1993). Bowlby (1988) suggested that there is little hope for the therapeutic process if the patient (here, the foster mother) does not regard the therapist (here, the parent trainer) as a secure base.

Nonautonomous caregivers are expected to respond to the parent trainer in ways that may be somewhat alienating or counterproductive. For example, a dismissing caregiver may tend to show more resistance than other caregivers during the initial phases of the treatment and have difficulty accepting the parent trainer's suggestions. Preoccupied caregivers may behave in ways that fluctuate between needing reassurance from the parent trainer and displaying annoyance with the treatment components or ideas.

The task for the parent trainer is to respond in a way that not only facilitates a trusting relationship but also helps the caregiver make fundamental changes. Strategies to accomplish this in the Attachment and Biobehavioral Catch-up intervention vary. Frequently, this task is accomplished by responding in a manner that does not endorse, but gently challenges the strategies of the caregiver. For example, the parent trainer needs to be mindful of the foster parent's usual approaches to relationships so as to gently encourage change. The naturally elicited reaction to a dismissing caregiver is to "buy" the parent's presentation that she does not have any issues with caregiving. However, this will not lead to change. Therefore, the parent trainer's task is gently to challenge the parent to change her usual way of parenting. While striving to respond in this gently challenging way, parent trainers accentuate and support positive attributes. Emphasizing strengths in the caregiver's relationship with the child, remaining empathic about the difficulties in parenting children who are difficult to soothe, and acknowledging the foster parent's struggles with her own issues contribute to a trusting relationship. Although change in the caregiver's behaviors may not be apparent immediately, behavioral change and acceptance of the intervention often occur as the level of trust for the parent trainer increases.

To maximize the potential for change, the three intervention components are introduced sequentially. Components covering less sensitive subject matter are introduced first. The more sensitive components that require greater trust between the parent trainer and foster parent are introduced in later sessions. The first component, providing nurturance even when it is not elicited, is provided in Sessions 1 and 2. This is the least threatening material for most caregivers. The second component, behaving in nurturing ways even when nurturance does not come naturally to the caregiver, is provided in Sessions 6, 7, and 8. When we first developed the intervention, we planned to introduce this component immediately after the first component. We found, however, that the parent trainer needed to develop a stronger relationship and greater trust with the parent before issues in the second component were introduced. The third component, providing a responsive, interpersonal world, is provided in Sessions 3, 4, and 5 (all which concern following the child's lead and reducing frightening behaviors), and Sessions 9 and 10 (holding and touching the child, and responding to the child's negative emotions).

Just as autonomous and nonautonomous caregivers grow to accept the program and trust the parent trainer at different rates, change is expected to occur at different points in the intervention program for autonomous and nonautonomous foster parents. Because the intervention topics often take time to "sink in" for some foster parents, reinforcement of the intervention topics is not isolated to the session in which specific topics are explicitly covered. For example, during a session that focuses on following the child's lead, if the child bumps his head but resists the parent when she attempts to console him, the parent trainer may comment on the parent's willingness to provide help even when it is not elicited. This technique helps to remind foster parents of intervention principles and to practice the previously introduced concepts.

If an intervention component is not fully understood and used by the caregiver at the time it is introduced, it is not considered a setback to treatment progress. For example, a dismissing mother may struggle with the need to provide nurturance to her child early on (the first component). However, the importance of nurturance may become clearer when the parent trainer and foster parent discuss aspects of the foster parent's past experiences that have made it difficult to provide nurturance (the second component).

Case Examples

Ms. F

Ms. F is an example of a foster mother with an autonomous state of mind (F3, prototypically secure–autonomous). At the time of intervention, she was a 50-year-old mother with two grown biological children. She had fostered several children before beginning our intervention. She began participating in our intervention with her 18-month-old foster daughter Amber, who had been living with her for 2 months. At the start of our program, she expressed concerns about Amber, particularly regarding her shyness and inhibition, and made it clear that Amber's needs were her priority. When working with the parent trainer, Ms. F remained very open and reflective toward the intervention topics. During discussions, Ms. F readily provided personal examples when asked. She openly acknowledged that, even though she always tried to make sure Amber was OK if hurt, it was harder to do so when Amber got hurt after doing something she was not supposed to do, because Amber's behavior was frustrating to Ms. F. She also revealed that it was difficult to find times to follow her child's lead throughout the day because of her busy household.

Throughout the sessions, Ms. F became aware of how important it was to provide nurturance when Amber needed her, regardless of the situation, and began to attend more closely to those times. Additionally, with help from the parent trainer, Ms. F found ways she could follow Amber's lead during the day (e.g., during mealtime and bath time) rather than direct these activities to save time. In general, Ms. F remained open to feedback and made a conscious effort to use what was covered in the intervention between sessions.

In the AAI, Ms. F was classified as autonomous. She talked openly about difficult experiences of being left with a grandmother for the summer, and her father's premature death. She was able to consider very clearly how important her mother's availability was to her own parenting. This openness and coherence was reflected in her response to the demands of the intervention as well. She was very willing to think about how her experiences as a child influenced her approach to her foster child. This allowed her to think through issues regarding being emotionally available to her child and to put these ideas into practice readily.

Ms. D

Ms. D is an example of a foster mother with a dismissing state of mind (Ds3, restricted in feeling). At the time of the intervention, she was a 45-year-old, single mother with one foster child, Jason, who was 20 months old. When first interacting with the parent trainer, Ms. D was polite and accommodating. In the intervention sessions, Ms. D initially appeared interested in the sessions. However, after the first few sessions, she adopted a more defensive and closed stance. For example, Ms. D began canceling appointments, stating that she did not have time for the sessions, and that the material presented was not going to help her child. She claimed that although there were behavioral problems she wanted to target with her child, their resolution was unrelated to her relationship with her child. For example, Jason often cried and threw things, and Ms. D responded by putting him in his playpen until he calmed down. Her approach to treatment and her willingness to work on her relationship with Jason changed over the course of the intervention sessions, though. Over time, the parent trainer helped Ms. D recognize that the behavior problems of concern were connected with times when Jason was trying to get her attention when he needed her. Ms. D began to understand the importance of reading Jason's signals. Furthermore, she began to become aware that the way she had been parented as a child affected her ability to be available for Jason. As Ms. D began to be more emotionally available to Jason, she was able to see a change in his behavior. He became better able to signal to her that he was upset; for example, when he needed her, he came over to her with raised arms rather than becoming angry and throwing toys.

In the AAI, Ms. D was classified as dismissing. Throughout the interview, Ms. D described her parents as loving and caring, but she could not provide many specific examples to corroborate these descriptions. In the interview, she stated that she knew they loved her, because they unfailingly provided her with everything that she needed when growing up. She also commented that when she was upset about something, she dealt with it on her own, because she did not have the kind of relationship with her parents that allowed her to talk about things that upset her. By gently challenging and maintaining a stable, trusting relationship with the caregiver, the parent trainer was able to help Ms. D to become more open to the intervention content. Ms. D not only began to read Jason's cues but she also recognized her own difficulties in responding to him.

Ms. E

Ms. E is an example of a foster mother with a preoccupied state of mind with regard to attachment (E1, passive). Ms. E was a mother of a 4-year-old biological child and a 9-month-old foster child, Melissa. At the start of the intervention, Ms. E expressed enthusiasm for participating in the Attachment and Biobehavioral Catch-up intervention. However, when discussing how to read her child's signals, she had difficulty keeping the focus of the session on Melissa; she often talked at length about concerns regarding her marital relationship and her older son's problems in preschool. While acknowledging that these matters were stressful and needed attention, the parent trainer tried continually to bring the focus of the intervention session back to the foster child. Between sessions, Ms. E had difficulty completing the homework assignments that documented times where she responded to her child with nurturance. She provided one or two examples of responding sensitively when Melissa was upset over the previous week, but asserted that it was not possible to be responsive consistently due to other things going on in her life. Throughout the sessions, the parent trainer helped Ms. E to recognize the importance of prioritizing Melissa's signals and responding with nurturance, even when her life became very hectic. By the end of the sessions, Ms. E learned that by consistently responding to Melissa even when it was difficult for her, Melissa would be able to signal more clearly the times when she needed her.

In the AAI, Ms. E was classified as preoccupied and presented a mixed picture of her conceptualization of her childhood experiences with her parents. She talked about her mother in very positive ways at first, then vacillated between intense anger and positive feelings. She often lost track of what she was saying and wandered off topic. Throughout the intervention sessions, she exhibited the same tendency to become enmeshed in other aspects of her life that made it hard for her to respond to her foster child in a consistent fashion. During sessions, Ms. E had to be redirected to the focus of the session, as was the case on the AAI. With the help of the parent trainer, Ms. E began to realize that her own neediness got in the way of responding sensitively to Melissa on a regular basis. Once she realized this, she was increasingly able to pull herself back to focus on her child rather than herself.

Ms. U

Ms. U is an example of a foster mother with an unresolved state of mind with regard to attachment. Ms. U, a 42-year-old single mother, lived alone with two biological children and a 12-month-old foster child, Xavier. During the AAI, Ms. U disclosed that she was taken away from her biological parents at the age of 7 and placed in foster care, because she was being physically abused by her stepfather. She said that this experience continued very much to affect her, and that she still felt great anger toward her stepfather and mother. She admitted that a main goal in taking in a foster child was to help other children who might have experienced similar conditions to those she had experienced.

Throughout the sessions, the parent trainer observed that Ms. U at times felt overwhelmed when caring for her children. Even though she stated that she generally felt in control, she admitted that at times, when "it gets to be too much," she yelled at them and threatened to give them a beating, but that she did not intend actually to hurt her children. When this behavior occurred during one of the intervention sessions, the parent trainer observed that the behavior markedly scared the child. The parent trainer also noticed that there were times where Ms. U played a tickling or wrestling game with the child. As the game became rough, the child laughed but appeared overwhelmed at the same time. The parent trainer helped the foster parent to understand how confusing and unsettling it can feel for children when the adult they trust is also frightening to them. After grasping this concept, the parent trainer and Ms. U worked together to identify situations in which the frightening behavior was likely to arise. Ms. U strove to be mindful of her initial impulses to "fly off the handle" in these situations, and instead tried to calm herself down and respond in a more productive, sensitive fashion. Ms. U also learned the value of recognizing more subtle cues that indicate whether a child is having fun or feeling overwhelmed.

Ms. U was classified as unresolved based on the presentation of her past experiences of abuse by her stepfather during the AAI. As a result, the parent trainer was able to anticipate how Ms. U's traumatic experiences affected her current parenting of her children. Ms. U was aware of how powerful her frightening behavior was to her children. What changed through the intervention was that she became empathic with her children, realizing how horrible it was for them to be frightened of her. She gradually learned to control her behavior most of the time. When she failed to control her behavior, she was often able to realize what she was doing, to stop herself, and to reassure her children.

Conclusion

State of mind with regard to attachment is a primary consideration in our Attachment and Biobehavioral Catch-up intervention for foster mothers and infants for both clinical and research purposes. In terms of research, it enables us to assess the impact of a treatment intervention (Attachment and Bio-behavioral Catch-up) and control intervention (Developmental Education for Families) on caregivers with differing states of mind. From a clinical perspective, state of mind with regard to attachment is central to how foster mothers care for their infants and respond to the intervention. Foster parents' conceptualizations of their own attachment experiences carry over to their relationships with their infants and with treatment providers. We expect that an understanding of a foster mother's state of mind is a key to helping her provide nurturing, responsive care. First, the AAI is a necessary step in establishing rapport with the client. Second, and more important, the AAI gives the parent trainer a sense of the foster parent's characteristic approach to dealing with attachment issues. The way the foster parent regards the parent trainer, and the intervention more generally, is very much affected by the parent's state of mind (Dozier, 1990; Korfmacher et al., 1997). With an appreciation of the foster parent's state of mind, the parent trainer can anticipate difficult issues, both in sessions and between sessions, for this parent. Such knowledge increases the probability of helping foster parents change and provide better environments for their foster infants.

References

Barnard, K. E., & Morisset, C. E. (1995). Preventive health and developmental care for children: Relationships as a primary factor in service delivery with at risk populations. In H. E. Fitzgerald, B. M. Lester, & B. Zuckerman (Eds.), *Children of poverty; research, health and policy issues* (pp. 167–195). New York: Garland.

Beutler, L. E., Clarkin, J. F., Crago, M., & Bergen, J. (1991). Client–therapist matching. In C. R. Snyder & D. R. Forsyth (Eds.), *Handbook of social and clinical psychology: The health perspective* (pp. 699–716). New York: Pergamon.

Bowlby, J. (1982). *Attachment and loss: Vol. 1. Attachment.* New York: Basic Books. (Original work published 1969)

Bowlby, J. (1988). *A secure base: Clinical applications of attachment theory.* London: Routledge.

Dozier, M. (1990). Attachment organization and treatment use for adults with serious psychopathological disorders. *Development and Psychopathology, 2,* 47–60.

Dozier, M., Brohawn, D., Lindhiem, O., Perkins, E., & Peloso, E. (in press). Effects of a foster parent training program on young children's attachment behaviors: Preliminary evidence from a randomized clinical trial. *Child and Adolescent Social Work Journal.*

Dozier, M., Cue, K., & Barnett, L. (1994). Clinicians as caregivers: Role of attachment organization in treatment. *Journal of Consulting and Clinical Psychology, 62,* 793–800.

Dozier, M., Manni, M., Gordon, K., Peloso, E., Gunnar, M., Stovall-McClough, K. C., et al. (2006). Foster children's diurnal production of cortisol: An exploratory study. *Child Maltreatment, 11,* 189–197.

Dozier, M., Peloso, E., Lindhiem, O., Gordon, M. K., Manni, M., Sepulveda, S., et al.

(in press). Preliminary evidence from a randomized clinical trial: Intervention effects on foster children's behavioral and biological regulation. *Journal of Social Issues.*

Dozier, M., & Sepulveda, S. (2004). Foster mother state of mind and treatment use: Different challenges for different people. *Infant Mental Health Journal, 25,* 368–378.

Dozier, M., Stovall, K. C., Albus, K., & Bates, B. (2001). Attachment for infants in foster care: The role of caregiver state of mind. *Child Development, 72,* 1467–1477.

Dozier, M., & Tyrrell, C. (1997). The role of attachment in therapeutic relationships. In J. A. Simpson & W. S. Rholes (Eds.), *Attachment theory and close relationships* (pp. 221–248). New York: Guilford Press.

Field, T., Hernadez-Reif, M., Diego, M., Feijo, L., Vera, Y., & Gil, K. (2004). Massage therapy by parents improves early growth and development. *Infant Behavior and Development, 27,* 435–442.

Field, T., Hernandez-Reif, M., Diego, M., Schanberg, S., & Kuhn, C. (2005). Cortisol decreases and serotonin and dopamine increase following massage therapy. *International Journal of Neuroscience, 115,* 1397–1413.

George, C., Kaplan, N., & Main, M. (1996). *Attachment Interview for Adults* (3rd ed.). Unpublished manuscript, University of California, Berkeley.

Hazan, C., & Shaver, P. (1987). Romantic love conceptualized as an attachment process. *Journal of Personality and Social Psychology, 52,* 511–524.

Horvath, A. O., & Luborsky, L. (1993). The role of therapeutic alliance in psychotherapy. *Journal of Consulting and Clinical Psychology, 61,* 561–573.

Korfmacher, J., Adam, E., Ogawa, J., & Egeland, B. (1997). Adult attachment: Implications for the therapeutic process in a home visitation intervention. *Applied Developmental Science, 1,* 43–52.

Levine, S., & Stanton, M. E. (1990). The hormonal consequences of mother–infant contact. In K. Barnard & T. B. Brazelton (Eds.), *Touch: The foundation of experience* (pp. 165–194). Madison, CT: International Universities Press.

Madigan, S., Moran, G., & Pederson, D. R. (2006). Unresolved states of mind, disorganized attachment relationships, and disrupted interactions of adolescent mothers and their infants. *Developmental Psychology, 42,* 293–304.

Main, M., Goldwyn, R., & Hesse, E. (2003). *Adult attachment scoring and classification system.* Unpublished document, University of California, Berkeley.

Ramey, C., McGinness, G., Cross, M., Collier, A., & Barrie-Blackley, S. (1982). The Abecedarian approach to social competence: Cognitive and linguistic intervention for disadvantages preschoolers. In K. Borman (Ed.), *The social life of children in a changing society* (pp. 145–174). Hillsdale, NJ: Erlbaum.

Ramey, C. T., Yeates, K. O., & Short, E. J. (1984). The plasticity of intellectual development: Insights from preventive intervention. *Child Development, 55,* 1913–1925.

Schuengel, C. (1997). Unresolved loss, disorganized attachment, and frightening parental behavior: A pilot-study [Onverwerkt verlies, gedesorganiseerde gehechtheid en beangstigend opvoedersgedrag: Een vooronderzoek]. *Pedagogische Studiën, 74,* 355–366.

Schuengel, C., Bakermans-Kranenburg, M., & van IJzendoorn, M. (1999). Frightening maternal behavior linking unresolved loss and disorganized infant attachment. *Journal of Consulting and Clinical Psychology, 67,* 54–63.

Stovall, K. C., & Dozier, M. (2000). The development of attachment in new relationships: Single subject analyses for 10 foster infants. *Development and Psychopathology, 12,* 133–156.

Stovall-McClough, K. C., & Dozier, M. (2004). Forming attachments in foster care: Infant attachment behaviors in the first two months of placement. *Development and Psychopathology, 16,* 253–271.

van IJzendoorn, M. H. (1995). Adult attachment representations, parental responsiveness, and infant attachment: A meta-analysis on the predictive validity of the Adult Attachment Interview. *Psychological Bulletin, 117,* 387–403.

Afterword

Reflections on Clinical Applications of the Adult Attachment Interview

DEBORAH JACOBVITZ

The Adult Attachment Interview (AAI) protocol, developed in the early 1980s (George, Kaplan, & Main, 1984, 1985, 1998), was initially used chiefly with low-risk populations. However, as clinicians began using the AAI with individuals experiencing emotional or mental disturbances (see van IJzendoorn & Bakermans-Kranenburg, Chapter 3, this volume), the instructions for administration were extended to include more specific guidelines by interviewers studying clinical populations (George et al., 1998). The guidelines for interviewing, and practice in interviewing, are now extensive (George et al., 1998, pp. 19–38) and—under supervision of trained coders—can be utilized by individuals who have not yet been trained in the accompanying system of interview analysis (Main, Goldwyn, & Hesse, 2002; see also Main & Goldwyn, 1984). In short, even in the absence of training in its analysis, the interview protocol in itself is now ready for (supervised) use by clinicians, and as this book has demonstrated, the AAI has been a valuable tool in clinical practice.

The detailed system for coding the AAI developed by Main and colleagues (2002) has allowed researchers and clinicians to quantify adults' current state of mind with respect to attachment experiences during childhood. As most readers are already aware, as administered to parents, the AAI has now made it possible not only to "predict" (or "retrodict") an infant's Strange Situation behavior with a parent from that parent's discourse or conversational pattern during the AAI, but also to predict parental treatment of the offspring (for a comprehensive review, see Hesse, 1999). Since the mid-1990s, however, researchers have also begun to uncover relationships between an adult's state of mind on the AAI and psychiatric diagnoses. First, adults classified as unresolved with respect to loss and trauma are generally overrepresented among clinically diagnosed patients (van IJzendoorn & Bakermans-Kranenburg, Chapter 3, this volume; Riggs & Jacobvitz, 2002). However, unresolved trauma, as well as the "fearfully preoccupied" subclassification (E3) of the Preoccupied group has most specifically been associated with borderline dissociative disorders and symptoms (e.g., Adam, Sheldon-Keller, & West, 1996; Fonagy et al., 1995; Patrick, Hobson, Castle, Howard, & Maughan, 1994; see IJzendoorn and Bakermans-Kranenburg, Chapter 3, this volume, for an overview).

This landmark book demonstrates how the AAI can be used with clinical populations undergoing therapy and with parents participating in attachment-based interventions. I begin by discussing the stability of attachment over time, highlighting studies that identify life events or experiences that can precipitate change in an adult's state of mind. Here I also discuss programs being implemented during critical life transition periods that may provide unique opportunities for change, enhancing the effectiveness of an intervention. I then discuss the relations between the AAI and the overall aims of psychotherapy, and propose that interventions may be termed successful not only when they succeed in moving adults from insecure into fully secure states of mind (as seen in Levy et al., 2006), but also by simply moving from a disorganized (unresolved [U] or cannot classify [CC]) to an organized classification but still insecure (dismissing [Ds] or preoccupied [E]) states of mind. Next, I discuss articles that use the AAI to anticipate who can benefit from therapy. Finally, I describe the remarkable ways that the authors in this book have used the interview itself as a clinical tool.

Stability of Attachment

Security of attachment in infancy is based on an infant's repeated interactions with the caregiver. Whereas infants whose caregivers accurately perceive and respond immediately and appropriately to their distress over the first year of life are more often classified as secure, those whose caregivers have been consistently emotionally unavailable or interfering are insecure, either anxious–avoidant or anxious–resistant (Ainsworth, Blehar, Waters, & Wall, 1978). Children internalize this early relationship, forming an "internal working model" of the self, others, and relationships (Bowlby, 1980). Once developed, the essential characteristics of the internal working model are resistant to change. Thus, some argue that insensitive caregiving in childhood can have adverse effects on a person for a lifetime. The idea that the internal working model tends to persist over time is supported by impressive longitudinal studies demonstrating that (no doubt primitive internal working models of) security with the mother during infancy predict exploration in toddlerhood (Main, 1973, 1981; Matas, Arend, & Sroufe, 1978), emotion regulation during the preschool years (Sroufe, 1983), and the coherence of that person's life narrative at ages 19–22 (Hamilton, 2000; Main, Hesse & Kaplan, 2005; Waters, Merrick, Treboux, Crowell, & Albersheim, 2000) and age 26 (Sroufe, Egeland, Carlson, & Collins, 2005).

Yet early caregiving experiences do not fully forecast a person's life course. When Crowell and Hauser (Chapter 14, this volume) examined the extent to which negative life events precipitate transformations in an adult's state of mind, they found that between age 26 and either age 34 or age 39, nine (20%) of the 44 adults in their study of persons psychiatrically hospitalized during adolescence shifted from being organized–insecure, either Ds or E, to unresolved status. Crowell and Hauser noted that an increase in stressful life events challenges the attachment system, making it even harder for insecure people to cope.

Over the same time period, some previously hospitalized adults, however, moved in a more positive direction. Eleven (25%) of the 44 adults shifted from an unresolved to an organized (Ds, E, or secure [F]) attachment classification (Crowell & Hauser, Chapter 14, this volume). Exploring why this shift occurred could provide valuable insights to guide intervention. One possibility is that there are periods when a person is more open to change. Critical life transitions when new relationships are formed, such as dating, marrying, and having children, provide opportunities to reevaluate early attachment relationships.

A strength of the Heinicke and Levine (Chapter 4, this volume) intervention program is that it took place during the transition to first-time parenthood, when mothers might be more motivated to change. The program began before birth and ended when the offspring was 2 years of age. Arguably the most comprehensive intervention program undertaken, it emphasized helping mothers build a trusting relationship with a home visitor, who went to the mother's home every week during the first year and every other week during the second. The home visitor provided mothers with support and guidance in responding sensitively to their own children. Weekly mother–infant group sessions also provided women with support from their peers. Finally, the program empowered mothers to seek help from home visitors when needed to advocate on their behalf on issues related to child care, work, health care delivery, preschool, or other social systems. The program was strikingly successful shown by Heinicke and Levine (Chapter 4, this volume; see also Heinicke, Fineman, Ponce, & Guthrie, 2001), because child security at 2 years was strongly associated with both the mother's prebirth status on the AAI and the extent of her involvement in the work of intervention.

Other critical life transitions provide unique opportunities to intervene. Data from the Minnesota longitudinal study suggest impressive stability in the organized states of mind as assessed by the AAI between ages 19 and 26. The overall 3×3 chi-square was 14.27 ($p = .006$; Sampson, 2004). However, the percentage of adults classified as dismissing somewhat declined over time, with 57.2% classified as dismissing at age 19 and 38% at age 26. Changes in the caregiving environment and, specifically, leaving home, may provide some adolescents and young adults the opportunity to evaluate more freely the quality of their relationship with their parents.

Optimal Outcomes of Therapeutic Intervention

To evaluate whether an intervention is successful, it is important to clarify the overall aim of the therapeutic program. Helping adults move toward greater security is clearly desirable but, as I noted at the outset, may not be the only marker of important and beneficial change. Ammaniti, Dazzi, and Muscetta (Chapter 10, this volume) described remarkable shifts from disorganized to organized mental states. Specifically, they describe the case of Marco, who was initially diagnosed as obsessive–compulsive, displayed dissociative symptoms, and was classified as unresolved/disorganized (Ud), with a secondary cannot classify (CC) placement. The CC placement was due to the fact that Marco was both overwhelmed by fear, warranting placement in the preoccupied (E3) category, and showed dismissing strategies (Ds1).

After 2 years of intensive psychotherapy, two to four sessions weekly, Marco moved from an extremely disorganized state (i.e., with both U and CC classifications) to an organized–insecure state of mind. Thus, following therapy, Marco was no longer unresolved and was able to maintain a consistent discourse strategy throughout the interview—a preoccupied state of mind (E1/E3). On the surface, it may seem disappointing that Marco did not become secure (F), but a realistic and important goal of therapeutic intervention may be to help clients form consistent narratives that provide them at least some strategy, albeit an insecure one, to defend against the disorganizing and disorienting effects of early trauma.

Moran, Bailey, Gleason, DeOliveira, and Pederson (Chapter 15, this volume) question whether all interventions aimed at improving the infant–caregiver relationship should focus on altering an adult's attachment status. If there is a short window of time, such as a critical period when the infant–caregiver relationship forms, then longer-term therapy focused on changing the organization of affect, cognition, and behavior may not be reasonable. In these cases, it may be imperative to focus on parenting behaviors, helping the parent to recognize and repair miscues and ruptures in communication with their infant. Steele and Steele (2008) eloquently describe how parents classified as insecure with respect to attachment frequently have an impoverished ability to reflect on themselves and their early negative relationship experiences that leaves them at risk for frequent ruptures in communication between themselves and their babies that are *not* repaired. The AAI might be used to identify and to help adults at risk *work around* rather than *work through* their problems.

Bakermans-Kranenburg, van IJzendoorn, and Juffer's (2003) meta-analysis of the effectiveness of interventions aimed at enhancing maternal sensitivity and infant attachment security indicate that shorter-term interventions may be useful. More specifically, they concluded that interventions implementing an intermediate number of sessions with a behavioral focus were more effective than more intensive programs that involve more in-depth psychotherapy.

The effectiveness of therapy for increasing attachment security, however, may stem not only from its intensiveness but also from finding the right kind of therapy for a particular disorder. For example, Levy and colleagues (2006) compared the effectiveness of three types of therapeutic interventions for borderline patients: (1) transference-focused psychotherapy (TFP), which involves modification of representations of self and others as they are enacted during treatment; (2) dialectical behavior therapy (DBT), a cognitive-behavioral treatment, which includes both individual therapy whereby patients track their daily behaviors and group skills training; and (3) psychodynamic supportive therapy (PST), which is psychoanalytically oriented therapy aimed at fostering the patient's identification with the reflective capacities of the therapist. All of these treatments were intensive, with sessions lasting from 45 minutes to 2.5 hours and taking place either once or twice a week over the course of a year. Yet not all of these intensive interventions worked. Only participation in TFP for 12 months resulted in significant increases in narrative coherence on the AAI. Furthermore, following TFP (but not DBT or PST) there were significant changes in attachment patterns: A higher percentage of patients were classified as securely attached.

Moreover, most studies of the effectiveness of attachment-based interventions rely on assessments of functioning during the initial and final stages of the intervention. Studies following patients for several years after they have participated in treatment may help to determine whether the longer-term approaches of Ammaniti and colleagues (Chapter 10, this volume), Baradon and Steele (Chapter 8, this volume), Heinicke and Levine (Chapter 4, this volume), and Jones (Chapter 7, this volume) are more lasting.

Who Benefits from Intervention?

The AAI can also be used to anticipate an individual's capacity to make use of an intervention. It is perhaps unsurprising, then, that mothers with both primary (F)—and in some studies, secondary (U/F)—secure–autonomous states of mind appear to be the best candidates for intervention with high-risk children. It is remarkable, however, that an organized secure state of mind forecasts good child outcomes in both foster parents caring for previously maltreated infants (Bick & Dozier, Chapter 18, this volume), and in adoptive parents of older (ages 3–8 years) previously maltreated children (Steele et al., Chapter 17, this volume). Moreover, Steele and colleagues found that as long as one parent was autonomous–secure, the outcome 2 years into the adoption was significantly more favorable in terms of *less* disorganization and *less* insecurity in the children's attachment story completions.

It is important to understand *why* secure–autonomous adults benefit more from intervention programs than do adults classified as insecure. The parenting interventions described in this book typically involve reflecting on one's own life, establishing a trusting relationship between the therapist/home visitor and parent, and becoming a more sensitive and responsive caregiver. The secure–autonomous mothers described in this volume were more strongly committed to participating in intervention programs specifically designed for those with premature children (Teti et al., Chapter 5, this volume) or foster children (Bick & Dozier, Chapter 18, this volume), and were also more receptive than insecure mothers to a home visiting intervention program (as had previously been found by Korfmacher, Adam, Ogawa, & Egeland, 1997). Across all attachment categories, Heinicke and Levine (Chapter 4, this volume) found that the capacity for relating to the home visitor, which was most marked in U/F mothers, significantly predicted parents' capacity to form a positive relationship with their children and their children's positive social-emotional development.

Adults classified as U with respect to loss and trauma, and especially those who are classified as alternately insecure in their state of mind (i.e., U/E and U/Ds or U/CC) appear to be the least likely to benefit from intervention (Heinicke & Levine, Chapter 4, this volume; Moran et al., Chapter 15, this volume; Teti et al., Chapter 5, this volume). One reason for this finding is that adults classified as U with respect to loss and trauma have more chronic trauma-related symptoms. U status has been associated with more severe physical and sexual abuse, as well as other frightening experiences, for example, witnessing one's mother undergo a psychotic break or having parents who repeatedly threaten abandonment (Jacobvitz, Hazen, & Leon, 2006). Early experiences of abuse also have been linked to posttraumatic stress disorder (PTSD; Stovall-McClough, Cloitre, & McClough, Chapter 13, this volume), and chronic and recurrent abuse can lead to inconsistent and fragmented representations (Hesse & Main, 2006; Moran et al., Chapter 15, this volume; Melnick, Finger, Hans, Patrick, & Lyons-Ruth, Chapter 16, this volume; for a more detailed review, see also Lyons-Ruth & Jacobvitz, in press). This could result in perceiving others as all good or all bad (splitting or disintegration); dissociative symptoms, whether or not in normal range (Hesse & van IJzendoorn, 1998); identity confusion (Hesse & Main, 2006; Moran et al., Chapter 15, this volume); and relationship violence (Holtzworth-Munroe, Stuart, & Hutchinson, 1997). Dissociative tendencies, identity confusion, and greater relationship problems may, of course, make benefiting from therapeutic intervention more difficult.

Because the parenting of some of these deeply troubled adults improved as a result of participating in a therapeutic intervention, it is vital to evaluate the effectiveness of interventions for different subgroups of unresolved adults. Adults classified as U may also be assigned either an F or insecure secondary attachment classification. Specifically, it is possible that losing track of the discourse context or showing a lapse in reasoning during discussions of loss or abuse warrants placement into an unresolved category can co-occur with recounting ones' life in a coherent and clear way and valuing the importance of attachment during the rest of the interview. When this occurs, the adult is considered unresolved with respect to trauma but is also given a secondary secure classification. As briefly noted earlier, Heinicke and Levine (Chapter 4, this volume) found that adults classified as U with a secure secondary classification were more involved in therapy, and a mother's involvement in therapy was related to an increased likelihood that she and her infant would form a secure attachment.

Data from our longitudinal study following 250 adults (125 couples) over the transition to first-time parenthood are consistent with the findings reported by Heinicke and Levine. Women classified as U more often sought therapy than those who were not U. Specifically, 11 (69%) of the 16 U women assigned a secondary secure classification and 10 (77%) of the 13 unresolved women given a secondary insecure classification had undergone psychotherapy during their lives compared with 28 (49%) of 57 women classified as F and 11 (31%) of 35 women classified as insecure but not U (χ^2 = 10.86, p = .013, n = 121). However, U women assigned a secondary secure classification had spent significantly *more time* in therapy ($\bar{x}$ = 38 months) than those considered U with a secondary insecure classification ($\bar{x}$ = 8 months). Interestingly, women classified as F spent an average of 17 months in therapy whereas those classified as insecure (either Ds, E, or CC but not U) spent, on average, only 6 months in therapy.

Data from our project also indicate that adults classified as F on the AAI more often participated in couple therapy than those classified as insecure (Riggs, Jacobvitz, & Hazen, 2002). Specifically, 27 (37%) of the 65 women classified as F had undergone couple therapy with their current partner compared with 0 (0%) of the 17 women classified as Ds, 2 (22%) of the 9 women classified as E, and 7 (24%) or the 29 women in the U group (χ^2 = 10.62, p = .013). Similar results were obtained when U women were placed in their best-fitting category. Women classified as F spent more time in couple therapy than did those placed in the Ds or E groups (3 × 2 χ^2 = 6.62, p = .049). Similarly, a significantly higher percentage of men classified as F participated in couple therapy with their current partner than did those classified as Ds or E (3 × 2 χ^2 = 6.84, p = .048).

Another issue raised in this book is whether adults classified as Ds or E have the capacity to make use of intervention. The authors diverge on this point. Specifically, Baradon and Steele (Chapter 8, this volume) suggest that undergoing the AAI might be more useful for adults who are preoccupied with their past than for those classified as Ds. This idea is consistent with Crowell and Hauser's (Chapter 14, this volume) finding that E adults were more likely than Ds adults to change classification. However, E adults most often became Ds, not secure–autonomous. Administering the AAI before and after treatment, Bick and Dozier (Chapter 18, this volume) found that adults classified as Ds prior to participating in their intervention program showed improved caregiving quality.

Discrepancies across chapters likely stem from differences in the components of the interventions, as well as characteristics of the therapist or practitioner implementing the intervention. The success of an intervention may be related to the extent to which it challenges an adult's working model of attachment. Bick and Dozier (Chapter 18, this volume) described how their intervention program focuses on challenging adults' overall attachment classification. Therapeutic interventions also can be tailored individually on the basis of scores on the specific AAI scales that contribute to a person's overall state of mind. Most Ds adults insist that they cannot remember the past and idealize their parents: They describe their parents as extremely loving, yet do not provide convincing illustrations. For these clients or parents, empathic listening may increase their awareness of the abuse and/or neglect during childhood.

Adults classified as E, on the other hand, are more likely than others to heighten their attachment system in response to even mild threat. These adults appear more anxious and fearful: During the AAI they go on and on and on, taking more than their conversational turn and often losing track of what the listener, or interviewer, had in fact asked. Yet there are differences among preoccupied adults warranting placement in different preoccupied subgroups (Main et al., 2002). Whereas some adults classified as E become angrily involved in recounting each of the ways their parent wronged them and their parents' shortcomings other adults classified as E primarily have trouble focusing on the interview question and aimlessly wander to other topics. For persons who become angrily involved in blaming their parents, empathic listening may actually heighten their anger toward their parent, and the corresponding level of anxiety may make change less likely. These adults may need help regulating their anxiety, so that they can calm themselves when distressed. It may also be important to help them take their parents' point of view and forgive the parents for their wrongdoings. Adults who tend to lose track of the discourse context and aimlessly wander to other topics may need help focusing on early painful relationship experiences, so that they can work through them. Main and colleagues (2002) suggested that adults' abilities to take a balanced view of their relationship with their parents during childhood, blaming neither themselves nor their parents to excess, is one of the hallmarks of attachment security.

Attachment State of Mind in the Therapist and Client

Diamond, Yeomans, Clarkin, Levy, and Kernberg (Chapter 11, this volume) suggest that during therapy, the therapist's own representational model of attachment, or expectations regarding the nature of infant–caregiver interactions, are mobilized along with that of the patient. If this is the case, then it is important for therapists to discover their own states of mind with respect to attachment prior to treating patients. Slade (1999) eloquently described the feelings evoked in the therapist when interacting with patients who are primarily Ds or E. Because the Ds stance involves pushing feelings away, therapists interacting with these clients are likely to feel "intrusive, melodramatic, helpless, ridiculous and excluded"; on the other hand, the preoccupied pattern involves feeling confused and overwhelmed by emotion, along with a strong resistance to collaborating with the therapist, and interacting with these clients is likely to make the therapist feel "swamped, confused, angry and helpless" (p. 588).

A fruitful avenue for future research is to understand further the ways that therapists' representational models of attachment interact with those of their clients. In the context of a trusting relationship, as noted earlier, Bick and Dozier (Chapter 18, this volume) suggested that it may be important for the therapist to challenge the internal working models of their clients. A therapist may be more likely to challenge clients' working models of attachment effectively when they differ from that of the therapist. This was illustrated in Dozier, Cue, and Barnett's (1994) study, in which most of the caseworkers delivering therapy to patients with schizophrenia were classified as either secure–autonomous or E on the AAI; a few case workers were dismissing of attachment. Although therapists classified as secure–autonomous (vs. E) responded more effectively to their clients, regardless of clients' attachment classification, it was particularly detrimental to pair an E client with an E therapist.

Effect of the AAI on the Therapeutic Relationship

John Bowlby (1975) suggested that the central role of the therapist is to "provide the patient with a temporary attachment figure" (p. 291). Diamond and colleagues (Chapter 11, this volume) highlighted the important connection between the therapist and patient. Similar to parent–infant attachment, the therapeutic relationship is thought to involve attachment-seeking behaviors (e.g., seeking proximity, crying, calling) on the part of the client that evoke the caregiving behavior (e.g., protecting and soothing) from the therapist.

Administering the AAI is in itself likely to affect the therapeutic relationship. Jones (Chapter 7, this volume) elegantly described how the AAI evoked emotion and vulnerability in clients, who otherwise seemed very tough and uncaring. Practitioners and therapists who use this instrument may be able to understand their patients differently and feel more empathic; thus increasing their motivation to help them (Gojman de Millán & Millán, Chapter 12, this volume). For example, Jones mentioned that she was able to move from a tendency toward sadomasochistic exchanges to more mutually collaborative interchanges as she began to understand her patient differently.

Moreover, the AAI can help therapists identify adults, other than an abusive parent, in clients' lives who served as subsidiary attachment figures and provided more adequate care for them. If the therapist can align with a positive alternative figure rather than an abusive parent, then the client is likely to have a more positive transference. Successful treatment plans may involve helping an adult client draw on a model or internal representation of a more caring adult, and thereby allow him or her to enter into more trusting and satisfying relationships.

Recent findings from our longitudinal study suggest that a relationship with a subsidiary attachment figure anytime during one's life promotes secure–autonomous states of mind during adulthood (Saunders, Jacobvitz, Zaccagnino, Riggs, & Hazen, under review). The AAI was used to assess women who were in their last trimester of pregnancy with their first child. Among women who recalled having unloving relationship with *both* parents during childhood, those who received higher levels of emotional support from a subsidiary attachment figure were more often classified as secure–autonomous on the AAI, and their infants were classified as secure, as assessed by the Strange Situation. These relations were significant even after researchers controlled for depressed mood. Interestingly, subsidiary attachment figures, whose emotional support was related to research participants' ability to achieve a secure state of mind on the AAI despite having had negative childhood experiences with their parents, were people unrelated to their family members, such as teachers, neighbors and therapists.

Timing of AAI Administration

One question, then, is at what point in treatment should the AAI be administered? Should the therapist conduct the AAI at intake or wait until later in therapy? Many of the authors in this volume used the AAI early in treatment, because it provided therapists with a guide for listening to their patients (Ammaniti et al., Chapter 10; Gojman de Millán & Millán, Chapter 12; Heinicke & Levine, Chapter 4). For example Baradon and Steele (Chapter 8) remarked that administering the AAI early in treatment enabled their client Alice to bring her own relational trauma into the discourse, allowing them to identify and focus on issues that were especially relevant for Alice.

Others suggest that it might be beneficial to wait a few months before administering the AAI, or to have someone other than the therapist administer it (Steele & Steele, Chapter 1, this volume). Some therapists do not want to know their patients' secrets about, say, sexual abuse, until the patients themselves elect to reveal them. And the patient who does not elect to disclose or does not know how to discuss difficult early experiences might be left feeling guilty or that he or she was dishonest.

Metacognitive Monitoring and Reflective Function

As several writers in this volume have suggested (Ammaniti et al., Chapter 10; Baradon & Steele, Chapter 8; Diamond et al., Chapter 11; Jones, Chapter 7), experiencing the AAI itself may effect at least a temporary change in the patient's state of mind with respect to attachment (an impression that, of course, has yet to be tested). By answering a set of structured questions about the relationship with one's parents during childhood, an adult has the opportunity to monitor his or her own remarks. Main views an adult's ability to "step back and consider (one's own) cognitive process as objects of thought and reflection" (1991, p. 134) as *metacognitive monitoring*. Metacognitive monitoring is at the core of a coherent narrative. Placing parents or clients in the role of observer allows them to reflect more fully on their early relationships with their own parents and may, as part of a larger treatment plan, alter representational models of attachment (Ammaniti et al., Chapter 10; Baradon & Steele, Chapter 8; Toth, Rogosch, & Cicchetti, Chapter 6, this volume).

Fonagy and his colleagues (Fonagy, Steele, Moran, Steele, & Higgitt, 1991; Fonagy et al., 1995) extended Main's work by suggesting that coherence and metacognitive monitoring signal an ability to reflect upon one's own and others' internal affective experience in complex ways. The term *reflective function* refers to the capacity to mentalize or to understand ones' own and others' behavior in terms of mental states such as intentions and feelings (Slade, 2005). Experiencing the AAI itself could help patients to develop reflective functioning: If they can reflect on their own, their parent's, and their child's inner experiences, then they can also reflect on their own parenting behavior and take responsibility for abusing or neglecting their own children (Ammaniti et al., Chapter 10, and Jones, Chapter 7, this volume). Jones describes how her client, in the course of recounting the effects of his relationship with his father on his adult personality, realizes for the first time, that by repeatedly whipping his children, he might have damaged his own son.

Drawing on ideas about metacognitive monitoring, we (Jacobvitz, Booher, & Hazen, 2001) created an observational assessment of metacognitive monitoring in the context of marital interactions. Husbands and wives were independently administered the AAI in a laboratory setting and were observed 2 weeks later participating in a series of interactions tasks at home. Each member of the dyad was coded on a 7-point Self-Reflection–Flexibility scale. This measure tapped a person's capacity to take in and reflect upon feedback received from his or her partner during conflictual exchanges, such that he or she could shift mental state (as demonstrated by the attitudes and emotions expressed). Husbands and wives classified as F (vs. Ds or E) on the AAI scored significantly higher on Self-Reflection–Flexibility.

Furthermore, scores on Self-Reflection–Flexibility distinguished between secure women who had an unloving relationship with both parents during childhood (based on scores less than or equal to 3.0 on *both* the Mother and

Father Loving scales on the AAI) and secure women who had memories of loving experiences with one or both parents (continuous-secure group). Women in the earned-secure group scored significantly higher on the Self-Reflection–Flexibility scale than did women in the continuous-secure or insecure groups. Moreover, women in the earned-secure group reported spending significantly *more time* in psychotherapy during their lifetime than those placed in the continuous-secure or insecure categories.

Concluding Remarks

In conclusion, the rich array of studies and clinical interventions described in this book attest to the value of using the AAI in clinical practice. The discovery of a way to elucidate and indeed to quantify adults' states of mind, as provided by the AAI with respect to attachment, can be used to design successful intervention programs aimed at fostering secure infant–caregiver attachment relationships, particularly with adults at risk for difficulties with caregiving and in the context of children with special needs. Researchers and clinicians alike have also demonstrated that the AAI itself can be used to effect change in adults participating in psychotherapy as well as in the therapeutic relationship.

A promising area for future study is to understand better the developmental origins, correlates, and outcomes for adults placed in the CC group (Hesse, 1996, in press; Minde & Hesse, 1996). These adults have difficulty settling on a consistent strategy for describing their relationship with their parents during childhood and show a mix of secure–autonomous, Ds, and/or E strategies. Thus, these transcripts are considered unclassifiable not because of errors in transcription or administration of the AAI, but because these individuals show a global breakdown in finding a strategy to describe the relationship with their parents during childhood (Hesse, 1996). Among adolescents hospitalized for psychiatric disorders, those placed in the CC group were more likely to have engaged in criminal activity (Allen, Hauser, & Borman-Spurrell, 1996). Moreover, the CC category was found to be overrepresented in a study of drug-addicted, homeless, female adolescents (Taylor-Seehafer, Jacobvitz, & Steiker, 2008).

Main and Hesse (personal communication, 2007) have begun to expand the CC category. They suggest that adults who score very low on coherence throughout the interview and do not score high on any of the dimensions related to an organized–insecure state of mind (Ds or E) may be considered CC, just like persons classified as CC based on a mixture of opposing strategies on the AAI. Like CC-opposing strategy parents, CC-low coherence parents are expected to have disorganized and/or unclassifiable offspring, as has recently been illustrated in a longitudinal study in Japan (Behrens, Hesse, & Main, 2008).

Further research is needed to understand why some women show a *global* collapse in strategies across the entire interview (CC), whereas others display a *brief* collapse during discussions of loss and trauma (U adults). One explanation that we have begun to explore is that adults' who display a *global* collapse in strategies had a parent who contributed to a mixed or confused mental representation of his or her relationship with their other parent during childhood. For example, one participant in our study (placed in the CC group) had memories of seeking and gaining comfort from her father when she was upset, yet her mother recounted all the ways her father had wronged her (e.g., telling her "Your father was so drunk he never even made it to the hospital when you were born"). It is interesting to note that the parents of CC adults, like the mother of this participant, often made negative comments about the other parent's behavior or intentions that the child did not directly experience, thus making the claim harder to verify.

We suspect that if one parent harbors intense anger toward his or her spouse, he or she is more likely to interfere with the children's representation of their own relationship with that parent. To examine this idea, 2 weeks after we administered the AAI, we interviewed mothers in our study again using the AAI questions, but substituting the phrase "your parents' marriage" for "your relationship with your mother" or "your relationship with your father" (Jacobvitz, 1992). Women in the CC group (vs. those who were not CC) recalled significantly higher levels of conflict in their parents' marriage during childhood (Jacobvitz, Umemrua, Mock, & Hazen, 2008).

Finally, most of the clinical interventions to date have focused on helping mothers respond with greater sensitivity to their children. The Steele and colleagues (Chapter 17, this volume) intervention program with adoptive fathers highlights the value of paying more attention to fathers. The authors note that it would be a mistake to overlook the potential of interested fathers to make a huge difference in their children's lives. This and so many other novel and important observations have arisen on account of the AAI being applied in diverse clinical contexts, where—to paraphrase the conclusion offered by Gojman de Millán & Millán—the nature of our shared humanity has been richly illuminated.

References

Adam, K. S., Sheldon-Keller, A. E., & West, M. (1996). Attachment organization and history of suicidal behavior in clinical adolescents. *Journal of Consulting and Clinical Psychology, 64*, 264–272.

Ainsworth, M. D. S., Blehar, M. C., Waters, E., & Wall, S. (1978). *Patterns of attachment: A psychological study of the Strange Situation.* NJ: Erlbaum.

Allen, J., Hauser, S., & Borman-Spurrell, E. (1996). Attachment theory as a framework for understanding sequelae of severe adolescent psychopathology: An eleven year follow-up study. *Journal of Consulting and Clinical Psychology, 64*, 254–263.

Bakermans-Kranenburg, M. J., van IJzendoorn, M. H., & Juffer, F. (2003). Less is more: Meta-analyses of sensitivity and attachment interventions in early childhood. *Psychological Bulletin, 129*, 195–215.

Behrens, K. Y., Hesse, E., & Main, M. (2008). Mothers' attachment status as determined by the Adult Attachment Interview predicts their 6-year-olds' reunion responses: A study conducted in Japan. *Developmental Psychology, 43*, 1553–1567.

Bowlby, J. (1975). Attachment theory, separation anxiety and mourning. In D. A. Hamburg & K. H. Brodie (Eds.), *American handbook of psychiatry* (2nd ed., pp. 292–309). New York: Basic Books.

Bowlby, J. (1980). *Attachment and loss: Loss, sadness, and depression* (Vol. 3). New York: Basic Books.

Dozier, M., Cue, K., & Barnett, L. (1994). Clinicians as caregivers: Role of attachment organization in treatment. *Journal of Consulting and Clinical Psychology, 62*, 793–800.

Fonagy, P., Steele, M., Moran, G., Steele, H., & Higgitt, A. (1991). The capacity for understanding mental states; the reflective self in parent and child and its significance for security of attachment. *Infant Mental Health Journal, 13*, 200–217.

Fonagy, P., Steele, M., Steele, H., Leigh, T., Kennedy, R., Mattoon, G., et al. (1995). Attachment, the reflective self, and borderline states: The predictive specificity of the Adult Attachment Interview and pathological emotional development. In S. Goldberg, R. Muir, & J. Kerr (Eds.), *Attachment theory: Social, developmental and clinical perspectives*. Jersey City, NJ: Analytic Press.

George, C., Kaplan, N., & Main, M. (1984, 1985, 1996). *The Adult Attachment Interview*. Unpublished protocol, University of California, Berkeley.

Hamilton, C. E. (2000). Continuity and discontinuity of attachment from infancy through adolescence. *Child Development, 71*, 690–694.

Heinicke, C. M., Fineman, N. R., Ponce, V. A., & Guthrie, D. (2001). Relationship based intervention with at-risk mothers: Outcome in the second year of life. *Infant Mental Health Journal, 22*, 431–462.

Hesse, E. (1996). Discourse, memory and the Adult Attachment Interview: A note with emphasis on the emerging cannot classify category. *Infant Mental Health Journal, 17*, 4–11.

Hesse, E. (1999). The Adult Attachment Interview: Historical and current perspective. In J. Cassidy & P. R. Shaver (Eds.), *Handbook of attachment: Theory, research, and clinical applications* (pp. 395–433). New York: Guilford Press.

Hesse, E. (in press). The Adult Attachment Interview: Current perspectives. In J. Cassidy & P. R. Shaver (Eds.), *Handbook of attachment: Theory, research, and clinical applications* (2nd ed.). New York: Guilford Press.

Hesse, E., & Main, M. (2006). Frightened, threatening, and dissociative parental behavior in low-risk samples: Description, discussion, and interpretations. *Development and Psychopathology, 18*, 309–343.

Hesse, E., & van IJzendoorn, M. (1998). Propensities towards absorption are related to lapses in the monitoring of reasoning or discourse during the Adult Attachment Interview: A preliminary investigation. *Attachment and Psychopathology, 1*, 299–305.

Holtzworth-Munroe, A., Stuart, G. L., & Hutchinson, G. (1997). Violent versus nonviolent husbands: Differences in attachment patterns, dependency, and jealousy. *Journal of Family Psychology, 11*, 313–331.

Jacobvitz, D. (1992). *The Grandparent Marriage Interview*. Unpublished manuscript, University of Texas at Austin.

Jacobvitz, D., Booher, C., & Hazen, N. (2001, February). *Communication within the dyad: An attachment-theoretical perspective.* Paper presented at the meeting of the Society of Social and Personality Psychologists, San Antonio, TX.

Jacobvitz, D., Hazen, N., & Leon, K. (2006). Does expectant mothers' unresolved trauma predict frightening/frightened maternal behavior?: Risk and protective factors. *Development and Psychopathology, 18,* 363–379.

Jacobvitz, D., Umemrua, T., Mock, L., & Hazen, N. (2008). *Relations among adults' representation of early family relationships, coherence on the Adult Attachment Interview, and placement into the cannot classify group.* Unpublished manuscript, University of Texas, Austin.

Korfmacher, J., Adam, E., Ogawa, J., & Egeland, B. (1997). Adult attachment: Implications for the therapeutic process in a home visitation intervention. *Applied Developmental Science, 1,* 43–52.

Levy, K. N., Kelly, K. M., Meehan, K. B., Reynoso, J. S., Clarkin, J. F., Lenzenweger, M. F., et al. (2006). Change in attachment and reflective function in the treatment of borderline personality disorder with transference focused psychotherapy. *Journal of Consulting and Clinical Psychology, 74,* 1027–1040.

Lyons-Ruth, K., & Jacobvitz, D. (in press). Attachment disorganization: Unresolved loss, relational violence, and lapses in behavioral and attentional strategies. In J. Cassidy & P. R. Shaver (Eds.), *Handbook of attachment: Theory, research, and clinical applications* (2nd ed.). New York: Guilford Press.

Main, M. (1973). *Exploration, play, and cognitive functioning as related to child–mother attachment.* Unpublished doctoral dissertation, Johns Hopkins University, Baltimore.

Main, M. (1981). Avoidance in the service of proximity: A working paper. In K. Immelmann, G. W. Barlow, L. Petrinovich, & M. B. Main (Eds.), *Behavioral development: The Bielefeld Interdisciplinary Project* (pp. 651–693). New York: Cambridge University Press.

Main, M. (1991). Metacognitive knowledge, metacognitive monitoring and singular (coherent) vs. multiple (incoherent) model of attachment: Findings and direction for future research. In C. M. Parkes, J. Stevenson-Hinde, & P. Marris (Eds.), *Attachment across the life cycle* (pp. 127–159). London: Routledge Press.

Main, M., & Goldwyn, R. (1984). *Adult Attachment Scoring and Classification System.* Unpublished manuscript, University of California, Berkeley.

Main, M., Goldwyn, R., & Hesse, E. (2003). *Adult Attachment Scoring and Classification System.* Unpublished manuscript, University of California, Berkeley.

Main, M., Hesse, E., & Kaplan, N. (2005). Predictability of attachment behavior and representational processes at 1, 6, and 19 years of age: The Berkeley Longitudinal Study. In K. E. Grossmann, K. Grossmann, & E. Waters (Eds.), *Attachment from infancy to adulthood: The major longitudinal studies.* New York: Guilford Press.

Matas, L., Arend, R., & Sroufe, L. A. (1978). Continuity of adaptation in the second year: The relationship between quality of attachment and later competence. *Child Development, 49,* 547–556.

Minde, K., & Hesse, E. (1996). The role of the Adult Attachment Interview in parent–infant psychotherapy: A case presentation. *Infant Mental Health Journal, 17,* 115–126.

Patrick, M., Hobson, P., Castle, D., Howard, R., & Maughan, B. (1994). Personality disorder and the mental representation of early social experience. *Development and Psychopathology, 6,* 375–388.

Riggs, S., Jacobvitz, D., & Hazen, N. (2002). Internal working models of attachment and previous therapy-seeking behavior among middle-class expectant couples. *Psychotherapy: Theory and Research, 39,* 283–296.

Riggs, S. A., & Jacobvitz, D. (2002). Expectant parents' representations of early attachment relationships: Associations with mental health and family history. *Journal of Consulting and Clinical Psychology, 70,* 195–204.

Sampson, M. (2004). *Continuity and change in patterns of attachment between infancy, adolescence, and early adulthood in a high risk sample.* Unpublished doctoral dissertation, University of Minnesota, Minneapolis.

Saunders, R. C., Jacobvitz, D. B., Zaccagnino, M., Riggs, S., & Hazen, N. (under review). Pathways to earned-security: The role of subsidiary attachment figures.

Slade, A. (1999). Attachment theory and research: Implications for theory and practice of individual psychotherapy. In J. Cassidy & P. R. Shaver (Eds.), *Handbook of attachment: Theory, research, and clinical applications* (pp. 575–594). New York: Guilford Press.

Slade, A. (2005). Parental reflective functioning: An introduction. *Attachment and Human Development, 7,* 269–281.

Sroufe, L. A. (1983). Infant–caregiver attachment and patterns of adaptation in preschool: The roots of maladaptation and competence. *Minnesota Symposium in Child Psychology, 16,* 41–83.

Sroufe, L. A., Egeland, B., Carlson, E., & Collins, W. A. (2005). *The development of the person: The Minnesota Study of risk and adaptation from birth to adulthood.* New York: Guilford Press.

Steele, H., & Steele, M. (2008). On the origins of reflective functioning. In F. Busch (Ed.), *Mentalization: Theoretical considerations, research findings, and clinical implications* (pp. 133–156). New York: Analytic Press

Taylor-Seehafer, M. A, Jacobvitz, D., & Steiker, L. H. (2008). Patterns of attachment organization, social connectedness, and substance use in a sample of older homeless adolescents: Preliminary findings. *Family and Community Health, 31,* 81–88.

Waters, E., Merrick, S., Treboux, D., Crowell, J., & Albersheim, L. (2000). Attachment security in infancy and early adulthood: A twenty-year longitudinal study. *Child Development, 71,* 684–689.

Index

Page numbers followed by *f* indicate figure, *t* indicate table